PASTMASTERS

*the text of this book is printed
on 100% recycled paper*

Pastmasters

SOME ESSAYS ON AMERICAN HISTORIANS

EDITED BY MARCUS CUNLIFFE
AND ROBIN W. WINKS

HARPER TORCHBOOKS

HARPER & ROW, PUBLISHERS
NEW YORK, EVANSTON,
AND LONDON

First HARPER TORCHBOOK edition published 1975.

STANDARD BOOK NUMBER: 06–131746–2

Contents

Introduction

There are various ways of approaching historiography, each of them potentially unsatisfactory. One way, when the field is as broad as the history of the United States—the theme of our volume—is to define sundry "schools" and "movements" and to allot historians to these. Such categories are useful, and there is no doubt that historiographical emphases shift from generation to generation, or even from decade to decade. To base one's approach on interpretations instead of on personalities, on collective trends rather than on individual historians, is to achieve an attractive semblance of tidiness. The difficulty lies in establishing firm, true categories, and in fitting actual scholars into them.

Schools and movements, for scholars no less than creative writers, are sometimes retrospective inventions, imposed upon figures who in their own day may have had little or no sense of such shared identity. Once created, categories tend to assume a tyrannical character. Or they may be so vague as to be almost meaningless—a charge that could be brought against J. S. Bassett, who in 1917 dubbed certain scholars "The Middle Group of American Historians." In the middle of what? Another drawback to tidy categories is that they ignore the special, personal quality of each particular historian. Not only does he think for and speak for himself; also, his working life may well extend over as much as half a century. Historians, like other men, are apt to modulate from one viewpoint to another, to change their minds, and so apparently to contradict themselves. Having assigned them to a definite "school," the historiographer is on occasion embarrassed at, and unable to cope with, the seeming defection to another "school" of his intransigent subjects.

A further problem is that of sheer quantity. In the late 1960's there are some five thousand professional historians in American colleges and universities, and possibly another three hundred in Canada, Britain, and other countries, whose primary interest is the history of the United States. A quite high proportion of these have published respectable work in the field. Score upon score of them deserve a mention, if not more, in a general survey of American historiography.[1] At least fifty could be deemed worthy of extended treatment. Even by 1900 or 1910, when the guild was far smaller, there was a fairly numerous company of competent Americanists. To fasten upon a limited number of historians is therefore on the face of it to risk injustice to others of equal eminence. But where and how to distinguish between them? It is arguable that review-articles are the proper place for multiple enumeration. A historiographical volume which seeks to be genuinely inclusive quickly and intractably turns into bibliography, allowing room for no more than brief and necessarily superficial assessments.[2]

Difficulties of this nature, considerable enough in the case of deceased historians, are greater still with those who are living. The more important a scholar, the more likely he is to have stirred up controversy. Almost by definition he is a troublemaker, a person who challenges received interpretations—to the delight of certain of his peers, and to the discomfort of others. Objectivity in analyzing his work is thus probably an unattainable goal and, moreover, perhaps not to be encouraged, except by those who prefer dull politeness to lively discussion. It might appear a mistake to have a historian dealt with by someone who endorses his views, or who is at least a close acquaintance. If we were to lean too much toward courtesy and good fellowship, we could end up with a sort of reciprocal *Festschrift*—a mutual admiration society like that said to exist between the English savants Bishop William Stubbs and Edward A. Freeman (who succeeded Stubbs as the occupant of Oxford's chair of modern history in 1884). They were a prolific pair, given—it was alleged—to extravagant praise of one another's books:

> Ladling butter from alternate tubs
> Stubbs butters Freeman, Freeman butters Stubbs.

On the other hand, it could be a worse mistake to have a scholar dissected by some implacable opponent, whether of an older or a younger generation than himself. "My desire is . . . that mine adversary had written a book. . . ." In academic life the very root of the trouble is that one's adversary *has* written a book, has become an adversary in so doing; and the standard retaliation is to write something back at him. How are we to draw the fine line that separates argument from disputation, criticism from denigration?

Still, no task is without difficulties. The writing of historiography is merely difficult, not impossible. In a book of different scope from ours John Higham and his associates, Leonard Krieger and Felix Gilbert,[3] have managed to cram an extraordinary amount of comment and information into one volume, though sometimes at the expense of clarity or completeness. Our solutions have, we believe, a logic and value of their own. Our compromises between various approaches are, we hope, workable.

We have confined ourselves to essays on Americans who are historians of the United States. We have in the process excluded non-Americans and, more significant, American historians whose primary interest happened not to be the history of the United States. This meant eliminating a distinguished company of scholars, past and present. Among the former, for example, would be figures of the caliber of John William Draper (*History of the Intellectual Development of Europe*, 1863; *History of the Conflict Between Religion and Science*, 1875), Henry Charles Lea (the historian of the Inquisition), and Henry Osborn Taylor (*The Medieval Mind*, 1911). But our primary desire is to show some of the ways by which American scholars have attempted to account to themselves for their own social environment.

Among deceased Americanists, as with living scholars, we made no attempt to be comprehensive. As our subtitle indicates, *Pastmasters* consists of *some* essays, not all the essays that we think desirable. The student who seeks information on, say, Richard Hildreth, John B. McMaster, Hermann von Holst, or Edward Channing will have to look elsewhere: for example, to the historiographical works of H. Hale Bellot or Michael Kraus, or Harvey Wish, or to the *Marcus W. Jernegan Essays in American Historiography* (Chicago, 1937), edited by William T. Hutchinson.[4] We restricted ourselves to a few figures: Francis Parkman, Henry Adams, Frederick Jackson Turner, Charles

A. Beard, Vernon L. Parrington, Perry Miller—all of undeniable stature and influence, active within the past hundred years. The list of historians could of course easily be augmented. Carl L. Becker and Arthur M. Schlesinger, Sr., for example, would be obvious candidates if these essays were to stretch to a second volume.

What is a "historian," within our terms? The title offers a clue. In the *Shorter Oxford Dictionary* the word "pastmaster" is defined as:

1. One who has filled the office of "master" in a guild, civic company, freemasons' lodge, etc.
2. A thorough master (of a subject).

Apart from our (we trust) forgivable pun, we have in the main conceived of the historian, at least for the present day, as a professional scholar, filling the office of a professoriate in a history department of a college or university. If the rule had been rigidly applied, however, this would in fact have excluded the late Perry Miller, who was a member of the English Department at Harvard University. It would not have made much sense to employ such a yardstick for previous decades. Vernon L. Parrington was likewise a professor of English; much of Charles A. Beard's work was done after he severed his connection with Columbia University; and while Henry Adams and Francis Parkman had Harvard ties, neither could be regarded as an academic historian in the modern sense of the expression. Indeed, Parkman's Harvard chair was not in history but in horticulture.

Our rule is only a rule of thumb, and it implies no bias against "amateurs." Some of the most brilliant writing on American themes comes from men (Edmund Wilson and Lewis Mumford are instances) who have not burdened themselves with Ph.D.s, permanent appointments, or other badges of professionalism. Nor were we prejudiced in favor of history as the study merely of "past politics" (the dictum proposed by Freeman and emblazoned on the walls of the history seminar in the newly founded Johns Hopkins University of the late nineteenth century). History departments of the late 1960's are broad enough to encompass almost every aspect of the past. But it is a matter of common observation that during the twentieth century the vast majority of publishing historians have been involved in institutions of higher learning, and that in this respect they have been professionals rather than amateurs.[5] In limiting ourselves to a group of *representative* historians we were obliged to limit the catchment area of possible figures around whom to build essays. So, with reluctance, we narrowed our gaze and agreed not to take into account certain luminaries from related fields such as the history of law, or of literature or of art. If we had been compiling another sort of survey, we might well have made room for essays on scholars of this type: Charles Warren, for example, Constance Rourke, F. O. Matthiessen, or Van Wyck Brooks.

Among living historians we present no more than a handful. We do so with no invidious pretense that they alone are the "best." A second volume could readily be made up of essays on equally excellent historians who by chance are not featured in this selection. Our belief is only that the historians who are treated here were all clearly worth a place, on the grounds of weight, influence, and representativeness. In other words, they have a weight of authorship behind them, meaning an *oeuvre* of substance and influence and, of course, of high quality. For this reason they are a group of middle-aged or older scholars. History is something that takes place; the writing of it is something that takes time. There are plenty of gifted younger American historians. Some have already produced books which may become classics. Our concern, though, was with established reputations, for this is what the word "influence," in part, connotes. The historians appraised in *Pastmasters* are people who, either as teachers and inspirers of research or through the effect of their interpretations, or both, have had a noticeable impact on the very shape of American historical scholarship. One mark of an influential scholar is that his students find themselves, long years afterward, gossiping about the man as well as his ideas, not always with affection or agreement but nevertheless with a curious attachment. They may admire him, they may ridicule him, but they cannot ever quite dismiss him from their thoughts. Sometimes, indeed, they are impelled to exaggerate, to heighten the lineaments of a former professor who was in actuality a person of no real idiosyncrasy.

The historian should want to know the truth about his professional past as much as he wishes to explore the past of some group or subject matter distant from him. This is so obviously true as hardly to require saying, and yet historians as a group have been reluctant to engage in public controversy with each other. Although all historians know that in order to assess the weight, validity, and peculiar contribution of any given book, one must know something about its author, the circumstances under which it was written, and the intended audience, not all historians are willing to admit that the ongoing work of men upon the crest of their own waves should be submitted to the kind of scrutiny applied to a figure more distant in time. We believe that extensive, critical, yet cordial discussion of the work of scholars now in their prime is essential to the discipline itself, as well as for those who participate in such discussions. Why, for example, do certain types of personalities gravitate toward history? Or does a lifetime devoted to the discipline tend to produce similar characteristics in men once utterly dissimilar? Or, in fact, are the implications in either of these questions correct? Historians cannot be separated from their work, after all, and to discuss historiography means that we must discuss personalities, whether given the added color of idiosyncrasies recollected in tranquillity or not.

Our third criterion, representativeness, means that we have sought out historians who could be taken to stand for different and prominent lines of historiographical development. Each is important in his own right, as an individual force; and each exemplifies a special area or realm of historical inquiry upon which his stamp is indelible. Indeed, the area may have been virtually of his own creation.

So, although several able scholars might have served the purpose, Perry Miller was singled out both to illustrate the vigorous growth of the realm of intellectual history in general and to show the subtlety and resource with which he and a number of colleagues have recaptured the complex world of Puritan New England. In a related realm, Richard Hofstadter reveals the value of bringing to bear the methods of the historian of ideas, and of the psychologist and sociologist, upon more recent political and social episodes of the nation's past. Samuel Flagg Bemis stands as a sturdy representative of the exacting study of American foreign policy—a field which acquired an ever greater significance as the nation's responsibilities widened during the twentieth century into what is nowadays called "global" history.

David Potter is a dual exemplar. He is a scrupulous investigator of what still remains a central question of American history, perhaps *the* central question of the nineteenth century: what brought about the

Civil War? He is also, in company with other scholars, fascinated by
the problem of national character, and the ways in which the concept
may be refined. C. Vann Woodward shares this interest and is
acknowledged as one of the outstanding expounders of the history of
the South. The peculiar progress of this section—possibly the sole
genuinely distinct section in the United States—is still and with
justification a theme of major interest, and its history raises important
questions about the validity of "regional studies." Oscar Handlin,
while he has other claims to our attention, may be regarded as a
spokesman for the field of social history, and more especially as an
explorer of the role of the immigrant in American life. Daniel J.
Boorstin shares with Handlin the wish (and the imaginative ability)
to unite the many strands of national history in some vivid synthesis.
Both are healthily aware of the inherent tendency of professionalism
to slide into pedantry. They lift the reader's vision beyond the gray
expanse of *Monographia Deserta*; they display the impulse toward
what the French describe—with no pejorative intent—as *haute vulgarisation:* namely, high-level, readable interpretation. In addition,
Boorstin sustains into our day a determination which has animated
the work of at least some men in every generation of American
historians. It involves a continuing search, which must proceed from
a deep underlying need, for those elements in the nation's story
which are truly "American"—which map its emotional no less than
its geographical distance from the Old World. Finally, the career of
Arthur M. Schlesinger, Jr., helps to focus on another crucial problem
that intrigues every student of the past who is anxious not to retreat
into antiquarianism. His progress, reminiscent of that of the ardent
Jacksonian George Bancroft, raises these questions: What is the duty
of the historian to his own day? How far ought he to engage himself
in the political struggles of here and now? Does such a man jeop-
ardize his own scholarly detachment? May he on the contrary gain in
understanding, through firsthand knowledge of the centers of power?

The reader already familiar with the work of these historians will
recognize another element that binds them. Each has attempted,
some explicitly and others only by implication, an overview of the
American experience. Each has sought to find a prominent, even
fundamental, factor which would help explain to Americans why
they are as they are, in historical terms. Turner found his explanation
in the significance of the frontier in American history; Potter and

Woodward have had occasion to emphasize abundance and free security, respectively, while others discussed here have dwelt upon some other central aspect of the American character. In this sense each has attempted a sweeping interpretation of the whole fabric of the American experience. This is not to say that other historians have failed to make such attempts, and with equal success, for there are many who have contemplated the problem of national character. Indeed, several of these historians are discussed within the essays, for each author has been asked to use the figure upon whom he has concentrated to illumine an entire spectrum of historical inquiry.

The editors owe a further explanation to the reader, as to the principles on which the writers of the essays in *Pastmasters* were chosen. An explanation, not an apology: our contributors are all quite expertly qualified to tackle their assignments. Some critics may wonder, though, why we have not turned to the newly emergent figures of the historical wing of the New Left, who report their dissatisfaction with the controlling assumptions of American historiography. One answer is that some of their objections are in fact summarized—for example, in the essay on Richard Hofstadter by Arthur M. Schlesinger, Jr. Another answer, which perhaps amounts to the same thing, is that the New Left has not as yet arrived at a distinct, coherent position.[6]

There is, though, one somewhat novel side to the list of contributors. Five of the thirteen are British. The reason is not, or at any rate not primarily, that one of the editors is himself an Englishman. Our aim rather was to go outside the United States, where appropriate, for the sake of an extra element of distance, impartiality, independence. American history, hitherto the province in Britain of a handful of exceptional scholars whose *doyen* is Sir Denis Brogan, has in the last twenty years spread rapidly through the universities of the United Kingdom. Several British Americanists have published reputable monographs and general histories. Our hope was that the British essayists might convey, together with the essential close knowledge of their material, a certain freshness of approach—the result of gazing upon the United States across three thousand miles of ocean. Whether such wise innocence has been achieved the English coeditor of *Pastmasters* feels unable to say. The American coeditor feels the same reticence as to the contributions in his domain. We are content to leave the ultimate judgment to the reader.[7]

> Marcus Cunliffe
> *University of Sussex*
>
> Robin W. Winks
> *Yale University*

May, 1969
Brighton and New Haven

PASTMASTERS

Francis Parkman

WILLIAM R. TAYLOR

1)

READING yesterday's historians can be very interesting, but it is not easy. Indeed, it is probably for this reason that it is not often done, or in any event, not done very well.[1] Since these historians seldom any longer speak with authority about the particular past they are attempting to recover, they tend to be overlooked by those who are investigating either the age in which they lived or about which they wrote. This tendency to dismiss historical writings of another time has led us to neglect especially the narrative historians of the nineteenth century—Prescott and Parkman in America and Macaulay in England—whose diligence and literary skill are often praised but who, at least by historians, are more often patronized than read.

There is, I think, a way of approaching such writing which gives it an immediate and striking relevance and makes its usefulness to those who would understand the thinking of any historical time fully as great as the scientific writings, also in a sense outmoded, which historians of science are beginning to explore to our immense enlightenment. What the historian ultimately seeks in any age or time—what he means or, in any event, should mean by "understanding" the past—is its "feel," the impalpable yet characteristic stamp which sets it off from the life of other times and places. To reach this kind of understanding he must, like other sensitive readers, possess imagination and be willing to use it: he is finally in quest of nothing less than a sense of the past, a past which, while cut off from his own time by all the barriers that confine us to the culture in which we live, probes questions and concerns that persist in engaging our interest.

In such a quest there are no maps, no secure guidelines; but the works of previous historians are among the best of these, since they have spoken to their own times, if they have been successful, with a subtlety and assurance which can only come from their having caught within their prose, probably unconsciously, the preconceptions, expectations, and anxieties of the society in which they lived and for which they wrote. In building a past for another age they have helped to illuminate their own social and intellectual world, and, in doing so, their writings have become a valuable part of our past and of the past of every succeeding age. They are, in a sense, the intellectual ruins that each age inherits from the last. Only partially intelligible in and of themselves, they remain to confound us if we do not exercise our imagination upon them.

The writings of great historians, then, never lose their significance, even when they may be shown to have mistaken or misjudged the society they are exploring and analyzing. This is so not simply because they reveal the values of their own time, but also because great history is always in some sense ironic. It is always, that is to say, concerned with the plight of men attempting in the light of what they know to understand the historical forces which are playing over their lives and shaping their destinies, men unknowingly caught up in the myths, expectations, and comforting illusions with which every age protectively surrounds itself. Such understanding as historical actors have, as we should be the first to know, is always partial and uncertain, like our own, and it is for this reason that historical narrative speaks to us with such immediacy. In history of this kind and in the plight of the historians who wrote it, if we are honest and alert, we can scarcely avoid seeing ourselves, since for all our advances in historical technique, our use of quantification and our tables and charts, we confront the future with great uncertainty.

Francis Parkman, more than any other historian of the nineteenth century—except possibly Henry Adams—has succeeded in retaining this kind of enduring interest, yet the reasons for his success remain obscure and unexplained, and certainly he deserves to be better known than he now is—and for different reasons. Recent attention which Parkman has received seems to owe more to personal rather than to historical achievement. A few years back a biography, his journals, and his letters were all in print but only one volume of his history.[2] He is known principally as the author of *The Oregon Trail*, his earliest and most autobiographical book. This is less surprising than it seems, however, since in a sense Parkman made a drama out of his own life: the mysterious ailments which beset him—his partial blindness and his curious nervous debilities—and his ingenious and courageous efforts to circumvent them have made him one of the best-publicized but least-known figures in American intellectual life. He remains in large measure a figure of paradox, celebrated less for what he did than for his capacity, against overwhelming odds, to do it.

In Parkman, we have to reckon with historical *opera* of a kind no longer characteristic of professional historians. His vast multivolumed history, *France and England in North America*, a project conceived while he was still a young man, required his whole life to complete. At the time of his death in 1893 he was still at work revising and reshaping it. Thus, in a sense, the work in Parkman was coterminous with the life. His first and best-known book, *The Oregon Trail*, appeared in 1849. He had published in 1851 his *Conspiracy of Pontiac*, which was to become, after its revision in 1870, a kind of postlude to his history, since the events of it pertained to a slightly later period. Nonetheless, it set the theme for the history itself in its dwelling upon the Indian and the American forest at the moment when both seemed clearly doomed. Beginning in 1865 the volumes of the history saw publication one by one at fairly regular intervals. *Pioneers of France in the New World* appeared that year. *The Jesuits in North America* appeared two years later, in 1867. The first version of his account of the explorer La Salle, *The Discovery of the Great West*, came out in 1869. A revised *Pontiac* appeared in 1870, and *The Old Regime in Canada* in 1874. Finally came the three works which carried the conflict between France and England to the siege of Quebec in 1759: *Count Frontenac and New France Under Louis XIV*, 1877; *Montcalm and Wolfe*, 1884, and *A Half-Century of Conflict*, 1892. In addition to the history itself Parkman wrote a number of short stories, numerous articles on topical events, a novel, and an authoritative book on the cultivation of roses. This is not to include what might be termed his "working writings": his logs, journals, bibliographic letters, book reviews, speeches, and professional ephemera. While Parkman intended that each volume of his history should have a kind of free-standing autonomy, it is evident from the scope and interconnectedness of his writings that nothing less than a review of his historical production in its totality will give us a sense of his achievement.[3]

Nothing about his writing, at first glance, seems to speak to us directly. On the surface, at least, his histories possess most of the limitations which are said to explain the present neglect of his almost equally popular contemporaries, George Bancroft, W. H. Prescott, and J. L. Motley, all of whom made great sums of money from the sale of their books. He accepted, with only minor qualification, the nineteenth-century belief in progress, especially the progress of Protestant, Anglo-Saxon civilization, which he saw as predestined to overrun the world. In other ways, too, his social views are strikingly inconsistent with the articulate liberalism of some of his more vocal admirers, like the late Bernard De Voto. He was an outspoken racist who looked upon the Indian and the Negro as inherently and irretrievably inferior, and his contempt for the Catholic nations of Europe was only barely concealed beneath the veneer of romanticism with which he provided them, and by an indomitable spirit of fair play which led him to look for virtues where he most expected to find faults. In other matters he discusses he was anything but objective, and his judgments were frequently inhumane. His initial portrayal of the English removal of French Acadians from Nova Scotia, an event which has been sentimentalized by Longfellow's *Evangeline*, is a notorious instance of his strong pro-English bias. He felt that political democracy had debauched American society, sapped its vitality, and converted us into a nation of money-grabbers, and he was a fanatic opponent of extending suffrage to women.

Until comparatively recently, to be sure, he has escaped the kind of detailed criticism by other American historians which had long before condemned his colleagues to dusty shelves, but now even this kind of criticism has begun to appear: historians who have tracked him through the sources he used are beginning to make their findings public. Almost every kind of historical fallibility has been ascribed to Parkman. In his *France and England in North America*, the work of a lifetime, he describes the conflict between French Canada and the English Colonies from the period of settlement until the Peace of Paris in 1763; yet contemporary critics have rightly pointed out that Parkman was more concerned with telling a story than with understanding the underlying reasons for the chain of events which took

Montcalm and Wolfe in 1759 to the memorable battle, described by Parkman, on the Plains of Abraham below Quebec.[4]

Parkman shows scarcely any understanding of the economy of New France, and he takes the feudal terminology of its social system at face value, whereas recent studies of colonial feudalism reveal that the attempt to impose a hierarchical social system on the society of the Canadian frontier met with little more success than similar attempts elsewhere in North America. Only opportunity and the promise of social mobility proved capable of luring settlers, and modification followed modification until the end result would have been almost unrecognizable to Frenchmen familiar, say, with only the seigneurial system of metropolitan France. Students of ethnology, furthermore, have shown that Parkman, despite long and detailed descriptions of Indian life, had little knowledge of the Iroquois, their system of government, or the rationale for their wars on the French and on other Indian nations, wars which he almost invariably ascribed to their wolfish proclivities.[5]

Most important of all, not only did he persist in organizing many of his books around the lives of individuals, but he appears to have chosen his heroes a little at random, more for the dramatic possibilities he saw in their lives than for their historical significance. In his desire to find progressive forces at work among the French, he both exaggerated and distorted the dubious role of Count Frontenac, governor of Canada during the period of La Salle's discoveries, and he passed over other explorers of much greater importance, as for example D'Iberville, the founder of Louisiana, in order to devote a key volume of his history almost entirely to La Salle, whose objective accomplishment was minor. To cap it all, he tried to obscure the fact that La Salle during the period of his explorations seems to have suffered from a grave mental infirmity and was almost paranoid by the end of his life.[6]

If all these criticisms are true—and they appear to be—what now remains of the fabric he wove? Parkman, of course, had been bitterly criticized by a few Catholic historians in Canada from the moment his books were published. Now, three-quarters of a century after his death, American historians have turned upon him. What justification remains for continuing to read him? Clearly we do—and shall—continue to read Parkman, but why? I suppose it is safe to assume that one can learn from another historian only by determining what it is that *he* is investigating and what in fact concerns *him*. It scarcely matters that his questions are not ours, and it would be ahistorical to insist that they should be. Obviously, we today turn to his past with different questions, but we can discover something of importance if we can learn what drove Parkman to write as he did.

At least part of the explanation for the character and thematic content of Parkman's historical work lies in his close ties to the city of Boston, where he was born in 1821 and lived with only occasional exits until his death in 1893.[7] On both the Parkman and Hall sides of his family he was descended from a long line of New England clergymen stretching back to the Cottons on his mother's side. The Parkmans had a clerical history not quite so distinguished that included a great-grandfather, who had been ironically dubbed "the first bishop of Westborough" for his magisterial style, and Parkman's father, a Unitarian of the cool, rational persuasion characteristic of early nineteenth-century Boston. Parkman's paternal grandfather, Samuel Parkman, had broken from the family tradition and acquired a great fortune during the eighteenth century as a merchant trader. Through intermarriage the Parkmans formed part of that network of similar families, like the Holmeses, Brookses, and Shaws, that made up Boston's social and intellectual elite. Their graceful Federal style row houses and mansions were scattered along the narrow, winding streets of Beacon Hill between Boston Common and Scollay Square. Their children attended local academies and Harvard College, intermarried, and settled into houses built by parents or grandparents. Increasingly as the nineteenth century progressed some members of these families lost touch with the social and economic realities that were reshaping other parts of America.[8] Increasingly, too, the children born to these families sensed the closeness of the Boston air and recoiled in one way or another from the hermetic provinciality of their upbringing. They revolted against the narrow choice of careers: the ministry, law, or business. In the course of doing so, certain of them produced an intellectual culture of some distinction. It was this group that the elder Holmes, father of the justice, called "Brahmins." They formed a coterie within the larger elite whose life style and values they in varying degrees continued to share and represent, even in places far removed from Boston. Even in Boston, the Brahmin caste was continually enriched by adopted Bostonians from Longfellow to Howells and the Brothers James whose life and work reflected a broadening range of intellectual endeavor.

It was to this group that Parkman belonged during the whole of his life. In fact, he reflected some of the problems it confronted in a peculiarly acute way, since unlike his younger contemporaries Oliver Wendell Holmes and Henry Adams, he never moved away; yet he felt the confining nature of Boston, one suspects, fully as much as any contemporary. Nothing about the externals of his life suggests the slightest deviance. In his education, his marriage, his associations, and the manner in which he lived Parkman conformed to what was expected of a man of his birth and condition. He attended Harvard College, belonged to the right clubs, married a proper Boston girl, studied law, traveled to Europe on Boston's version of the grand tour, lived on Beacon Hill, participated in the social and intellectual life of the Saturday Club and St. Botolph's, wrote peevishly Mugwump letters to the *Boston Advertiser*, and became successively an Overseer and Fellow of the Corporation of Harvard College. At the time of his death in 1893 he still owned his father's house at 50 Chestnut Street in the heart of Beacon Hill.

There were features of Parkman's life, his illnesses most of all, that set him off from his family and friends, but these peculiarities of temperament were quite within the limits of Boston eccentricity and neurasthenia. The Parkman family had, in fact, produced its share of eccentrics, black sheep, invalids, and outright defectors. One of his father's brothers was notorious for the curious dress he adopted as he walked the streets of Boston's poorer sections collecting his rent in person. Another brother, "Naughter Sam," the family called him, divorced his wife and went to live in Paris, one gathers as something of a rake. A cousin and childhood playmate, Coolidge Shaw, was converted to Catholicism by the Jesuits in Rome. Parkman himself appears to have been tempted by Catholicism and wrote with fascination about a brief stay at a Passionist monastery in Rome. He also fell in love with a young woman from Keene, New Hampshire during a summer holiday and must have considered the possibility of marrying outside the fold. Parkman's own deviance, however, was of a more characteristically Bostonian and internal nature. It took the form of a sense of vocation or calling of a classical Puritan kind that possessed him while he was still a student at Harvard.

His descriptions in later life of the steps through which he moved as he groped his way toward the writing of his history have the ring of a seventeenth-century Puritan recounting his progress toward conversion. A five-year period living in nearby Medford in the house of his maternal grandparents provided Parkman as a young schoolboy with his first glimpses of wilderness. The nearby Middlesex Falls, as they are now called, were then as now a rocky, forested area teeming with floral and animal life. From the frequency of his later mention of these years, it seems clear that his wandering and climbing in this first sampling of primeval nature made a lasting impression on him. It also had the effect of stimulating his interest in Indian artifacts. An interest in natural history and geology rapidly extended itself to an interest in ethnology and the archeology of the departed French civilization that had once made an assault on the American wilderness. From this time on he had, as he put it, "injuns on the brain," and he sought every opportunity to extend his knowledge of the wilderness areas and the vestiges of French occupation, New England, and New York. During his first two college summers, he explored the White Mountains, the area around Lake George and the ruins of Fort William Henry, and the routes of French *couriers de bois* in wild river valleys in the region of the Connecticut Lakes, exhausting his traveling companions and himself in his ambitious and tireless efforts to taste every kind of physical hardship. By the time of his sophomore year at Harvard he had already formulated a plan to write a history of the Seven Years' War, parts of which had taken place in the region he had been exploring.

It was this project that seems to have preoccupied, indeed possessed, him during the next twenty years. "My favorite backwoods," he later recalled, "were always on my mind. Before the end of the sophomore year my various schemes had crystallized into a plan of writing the story of what was then known as the 'Old French War' . . . [a plan] later enlarged to include the whole conflict between France and England; in other words, the history of the American forest."[9] Behind this mounting drive, one suspects, lay the blunted imagination and intellectual blandness of Unitarian Boston, which Parkman saw as a society living on inherited wealth and inherited ideas, a kind of opaque screen interposed between himself and raw experience. The development of his anticlericalism paralleled the growth of his historical interests and his fascination with the primeval. What he sought in each instance was the concrete, the specific, and the untreated past—experience, in other words, that was not secondhand. In this respect, as in others, his quest was not altogether different from that of his great contemporaries, Emerson and Thoreau. "My theme fascinated me," the same reminiscence continues, "and I was haunted by wilderness images day and night. . . . While not exaggerating the importance of my subject, I felt it had a life of its own, to me irresistibly attractive."[10] What he sought to do, as he said again and again, was to revivify and expand New England's sense of a past and to portray the society of Puritans and American colonials from a fresh perspective that was at once less parochial and less complacent. A similar drive to cast a longer and more colorful shadow behind New England seems to have motivated Parkman's Boston contemporaries, George Ticknor, William Hickling Prescott, and John Lothrop Motley in their efforts to delineate the qualities of Spanish civilization and to show its place in the discovery of the new world and in the rise of republicanism in Europe. The brash, swashbuckling and passionate character of Spain in the age of Conquest fascinated them in much the same way that France fascinated Parkman and provided him with a counter-image of the Anglo-Saxon civilization of Old and New England. From the outset, however, Parkman adopted a more radical and skeptical stance than the others. Existing histories dissolved into baseless generalities and he increasingly sought the concrete and the particular. Whenever possible, he combed the landscape himself and fingered the artifacts and paced off the battlements of French ruins. He sought, in so far as this was then possible, to experience firsthand the kinds of physical hardship encountered by French explorers, to taste the sense of discovery, and to familiarize himself with Indian life in all its phases. Where he was forced to rely upon the experience of others, as in the assessment of the character of his major historical figures, he chose narratives, memoirs, and other documentary forms closest to firsthand observation and even these sources he scrutinized with a doubting, critical eye that would have done honor to contemporary Unitarian Biblical scholars, like the father of h friend, Charles Eliot Norton. It was, in fact, a search for some spoiled examples of Indian life that took him on his famous ; along the Oregon Trail in 1846. This exhausting and endle taking, together with the strain of similar and earlier trave' have been responsible for his total collapse that fall sustained surrender to the congeries of illnesses that l "the Enemy," a sort of satanic presence out of hi Lost that returned periodically to torment him

It is interesting to note that Parkman's history appears to have been commenced just after his recovery from the severe nervous collapse which followed the death of his wife in 1858. It seems clear, as several psychiatrists have recently suggested, that Parkman had suffered from some kind of neurotic ailment, at least from the time of his return from Oregon in 1848 and probably since young manhood. Recurrent attacks of nervous disability, accompanied by physical disorders of one type or another, occurred throughout his life, but they appear to have been most severe in the period between 1848 and the close of the Civil War. The exact diagnosis of his problem varies a good deal from authority to authority and is scarcely to the point. The medical specialists whom Parkman himself consulted in America and Europe were, as a matter of fact, no more successful in getting at the source of his difficulty, and one doctor told him frankly that he might expect to go mad any day. A Paris physician, Dr. Brown-Séquard, who had treated Charles Sumner after his beating in the Senate, could offer him no prospect of recovery; others prescribed hot baths, water cures, and other fashionable remedies of the day.[11]

He himself, it would appear, was his own best diagnostician, and he seems to have sensed, at least by the early sixties, that he suffered from what we would call a compulsion neurosis that drove him mercilessly until his "health" collapsed and he was forced to remain idle for a time. In a long autobiographical letter written—for posterity—in 1864, he gave a graphic description of his symptoms. In speaking of the period of the forties when he first became conscious of having a problem, he noted, almost clinically, his progressive lack of control as he drove himself unslackingly to his historical project:

Labor became a passion, and rest intolerable. . . . The stimulus rapidly increased. Despite of judgment and of will, his mind turned constantly towards remote objects of pursuit and strained vehemently to attain them. The condition was that of a rider whose horse runs headlong, with the bit between his teeth, or of a locomotive, built of indifferent material, under a head of steam too great for its strength, hissing at a score of crevices, yet rushing on with accelerating speed to the inevitable smash.[12]

This kind of compulsive activity was followed by an attack of "the enemy": "a wild whirl possessed his brain, joined by a universal turmoil of the nervous system."[13] His response to this paralyzing ture, as soon as its severities had become attenuated, was "counterattack": work, work, all the work and activity he could force himself to perform. Thus, in a way, he retained the illusion of control, never suspecting that though compulsion was his problem and "the Enemy," as he persisted in calling it, it was what, in fact, saved him from a total collapse and, conceivably, madness.

Howard Doughty, in his sensitive study of Parkman's writings, suggests that his illnesses, whatever their origin, acted as a presiding genius that operated to take him from an active life in his mid-twenties and confront him with a heroic situation that would, in his own terms, chasten and purify the life of ease and comfort into which he had been born. They thus provided him with an honorable exit from its most confining parochialism. Certainly, it is clear that a literary life would have been difficult to manage for one in Parkman's circumstances and that he himself was at least ambivalent about it. "I . . . conceived literary ambitions," he later recalled, "and, at the same time, began to despise a literary life."[14] While he craved a life of action, drove himself mercilessly and was prone to wild and exciting seizures of the imagination that would have projected him through his intended work in a few brief years, his illness acted to temper and restrain his impetuosity and to delay the fulfillment of his dream of young manhood until his literary powers and ripening historical judgment were adequate to the task. What might have been a succession of romantic and colorfully written episodes from the American past became, under the successive onsets of "the Enemy," a triumphant assertion of the human will and, in its final qualities, an American "Remembrance of Things Past," a sensitive and circumspect estimate of the tragic denouement of French power in the new world and its replacement by another already possessed of the earmarks of doom. To achieve what he finally achieved Parkman needed more than his experience of the wilderness and his ability to render the wilderness environment in its hard and exacting if poetic factuality. He also needed to assess the ineptitude of policies and the fallibility of judgments. If his illness provided a discipline, like the Catholic order he for a time thought of joining, it was also his school of statecraft from which he derived his principal insights into human character and its bearing on the achievements and on the councils of men.

The Civil War and Parkman's response to it were clearly formative events in the ripening of his political opinions. It was during the years between Sumter and Appomattox that Parkman appears to have rounded out his conceptual scheme and fixed upon an explanation for the dissolution of French power. The war seems also to have heightened his apprehensiveness concerning the viability of the English civilization that replaced France and moved Parkman to an almost cranky posture concerning the shortcomings of the American heirs of this civilization. An extensive period of disability unhappily, as I have suggested, coincided with the Civil War, and Parkman, much to his distress, was forced to sit out the fighting and content himself with writing "letters to the editor," a dismal consolation for a man who saw in struggle of all kinds, and especially in warfare, salvation for himself, for his class, and for the country as a whole.[15]

Between the outbreak of the Civil War and 1869, the year in which he published his first edition of *The Discovery of the Great West,* Parkman wrote something like a dozen long open letters to the Boston *Daily Advertiser* and an article for *The Nation,* all of which were concerned with the debility of the genteel classes or the weaknesses of American culture generally. Before the publication of his final version in 1879 he had taken up many of the same questions in yet another article entitled "The Failure of Universal Suffrage," for the still-influential *North American Review,* which until 1876 had been edited by Henry Adams. He had also explored these matters in personal letters. What concerned him throughout this period was the apparent inability of the United States to produce a class of political and military leaders and to place men of superior talent in a position where they could employ their talents effectively for the national good. This point is emphasized in the titles he gave to his newspaper manifestoes: "The Nation's Ordeal," "Where Are Our Leaders?" "Why Our Army Is Not the Best in the World," "The Weak Side of Our Armies," "The Chiefs of the Nation," "Aristocrats vs. Democrats," and "Our Best Class and the National Politics."

Through the whole period of the war Parkman, in these years himself an almost totally helpless invalid, poured into these letters to the public the passionate convictions which he would have preferred to discharge in battle; he exhibits the intense frustration of a man who, in a time of national emergency, was left, as he wrote to a friend in 1864, impotently "holding the pen with a hand that should have grasped the sword."[16] A day spent at an army encampment at Readville in 1862 had left him with a bad case of the glooms, and he complained to his cousin-in-law and confidante, Mary Dwight Parkman, of the effect made upon him by seeing "the banners I was not to follow,—the men I was not to lead, the fine fellows of whom I could not be one. I thought I had known what deprivation is, but I had not. It was the lamentation of the moth, in despair, because, being burned already, he cannot fly into the candle."[17]

These letters, coming as they do on the eve of Parkman's main historical work, make extraordinarily interesting reading. Even the language of his historical writing is anticipated in his talk of America's delinquencies and his call for men characterized by a sense of "honor," "traits of high and finished manhood," "chivalric courage," and the like. Political crises evoke comparison with threatening storms, and the future is "black with disaster." At the same time, it is important to note, he was opening his heart to Mary Parkman concerning his failure to win the hand of Ida Agassiz, a daughter of Louis Agassiz, Harvard's famous zoologist and anti-Darwinian, who persisted in looking upon him as a friend rather than as a suitor—mostly, it appears, because he never revealed his true feelings to her. She soon, to Parkman's chagrin, married a wounded war hero and close friend of his, Henry Lee Higginson.

New England culture, as Parkman during these same months assessed it, was that of a civilization without effective intellectual leadership, and grown soft through its exclusive pursuit of commercial interests. The lower orders of society had become victim to the Yankee ethos. Wealth and the exclusion from positions of responsibility were turning the Brahmins into a class of effeminate dilettantes or, at best, recluses. In an irate article entitled "To the Lingerers," he called on the "worthless young imbeciles" and "wastrels" of "Beacon Street" to volunteer for service. Too much money, too much prosperity and individual opportunity, he declared, had eroded the qualities of character which had typified the Adamses, Otises, Putnams, and other Revolutionary heroes, and had brought a set of opportunistic demagogues to the fore—the very "scum" of American society, "rail-splitters" from the West and vulgar Irish war bosses in the East.[18] As he wrote a few months after the disastrous defeat at Bull Run:

The individual is rare and the nation never yet seen which the smiles of
fortune could not weaken or pervert. Our own unmatched prosperity has
wrought its inevitable work. We are a *parvenu* nation with the faults and
follies of a *parvenu*.[19]

Parkman's fanatical commitment to the necessity of good breeding
and the careful cultivation of an elite is never more apparent than in
his little-known work *The Book of Roses*, a study of horticulture
which he published in 1866. This book led to his only Harvard
teaching appointment—in a field, ironically, far removed from history. It contains what can only be called a Brahmin theory of rose
gardening, and gives still further evidence of his growing interest in
evolutionary science. Much of what he has to say is highly technical
and reflects the considerable interest in horticulture which he apparently formed during the long years of convalescence when he spent
his days puttering around the garden of his summer house on Jamaica
Pond. At certain points, however, the metaphorical tenor of his discussion of rose breeding is obvious. "Like all things living, in the
world of mind or of matter," he notes, for example,

the rose is beautified, enlarged, and strengthened by a course of judicious
and persevering culture, continued through successive generations. The
art of horticulture is no leveller. Its triumphs are achieved by rigid systems of selection and rejection, founded always on the broad basis of intrinsic worth. The good cultivator propagates no plants but the best. He
carefully chooses those marked by conspicuous merit; protects them from
the pollen of inferior sorts; intermarries them, perhaps, with other varieties of equal vigor and beauty; saves their seed, and raises from it another
generation. From the new plants thus obtained he again chooses the best,
and repeats with them the same process. Thus the rose and other plants
are brought slowly to their perfect development. It is vain to look for
much improvement by merely cultivating one individual. Culture alone
will not make a single rose double, or a dull rose brilliant. We cultivate
the parent, and look for our reward in the offspring.[20]

Parkman, in other words, was no advocate of natural selection. One
sees in this passage many of the arguments which would soon be
employed in behalf of immigration restriction; but it was one thing to
experiment with roses and quite another to control the evolution of
society. Parkman, of course, sensed this and gave considerable attention to the vexing set of problems which social evolution presented.
He came to believe that aristocracies, like individuals, were strength-

ened and invigorated by war, which became in his thinking the grim selector of those of "martial spirit" who were most fit to rule. Only careful intermarriage and continual wars could keep such a ruling class in trim.

For a time in the early sixties Parkman appears to have believed that the Civil War was a good and beneficial thing, since conflict was of the essence of vigorous national life and the North might through adversity experience the need to assume a more "martial stamp." "Already, like a keen fresh breeze," he wrote in 1861, "the war has stirred our clogged and humid atmosphere."[21] This early optimism, however, was of short duration, and he was soon forced to recognize that, win or lose, the delinquencies of New England culture would not be remedied by this or any other war. "Our best culture," he wrote a year later, "has become in great part, nerveless and emasculate. . . . The country has need of all its manhood."[22] On the very day of the Union victory at Gettysburg, July 4, 1863, his pessimism reached its highest pitch. To call for a Northern aristocracy was a futile gesture, he concluded: "Who are the best? They are gone; their race is died out . . . they have withered and dwindled away."[23]

The trouble with Boston's "Brahmin caste," as he persisted in calling it, was the diminishing incentives which America provided for high achievement. To these men of established wealth, money was scarcely an object and their social position could hardly be improved. "It lacks a career," he concluded despondently.[24] The Brahmin caste had thus been drawn away from the active arena of political and military life and forced to find expression in the quiet but unchallenging backwaters of the professions, scholarship, and art. It had become inert, squeamish, and somewhat effeminate. The real vitality of Northern culture resided in those who were propelled upward by the shock waves of economic and political opportunism. Mind and muscle in the North were thus almost entirely dissociated; Northern culture had in his imagination assumed the ominous shape of the now-extinct prehistoric dinosaur. "If we may be forgiven the metaphor," he wrote in 1865, "our civilization is at present a creature with a small and feeble head, a large muscular and active body, and a tail growing at such a rate that it threatens to become unmanageable and shake the balance of the vital powers."[25] The war itself, meanwhile, had assumed most of the characteristics he was to find in the conflict between New France and New England. The struggle which had been going on between South and North, he wrote a week or so after the victory at Gettysburg, was one between "Oligarchy and Democracy, the strong head and the strong body":

A head full of fire, a body ill-jointed, starved, attenuated, is matched against a muscular colossus, a Titan in energy and force—full of blood, full of courage, prompt for fight, and confident of victory.[26]

❖

With the long period of preparation at an end and "the Enemy" at least temporarily at bay, Parkman was able to commence the writing of his history. While it is not accurate to think of him as having recovered, since arthritis, rheumatism, and the old spinning of the brain were to recur periodically until his death, Parkman's health gradually improved after his return to Europe in 1859, and during the next twenty years he was able to devote the greater part of his energies to the task of composing the succession of volumes that appeared during this period. Meanwhile, once the emotional storms of his marriage had subsided, his life assumed a pattern of relative stability. During the winters he lived with his mother and sisters in Boston. Summers were spent writing and gardening at a house on Jamaica Pond that he had acquired shortly after his marriage. He grew especially close to his sister Lizzie, and after the death of Mary, another Parkman invalid, in 1866, and the death of his mother in 1871, Lizzie devoted herself to her brother and, except for his occasional travels, was his constant companion, confidante, and nurse until his death. During these years Parkman made almost annual trips of a few weeks to Canada, and on four occasions made somewhat more ambitious European excursions, but by the sixties his own most active period of discovery was at an end, and he traveled afterward on specific business, to see old friends and to shore up his uncertainty on matters of detail. This was also the period of his most active social existence. He took his responsibilities on the governing boards of Harvard seriously, for a brief period he held a professorship of horticulture at Harvard's Bussey Institute, and he regularly exhibited the horticultural specimens that were the products of his leisure hours. Despite this gradual expansion of his life, however, he managed to spend all the time his system would permit in his third-floor study at 50 Chestnut Street, where all but the earliest volumes of his history were composed.

Some of the qualities of the narratives that began to make their appearance in 1865 derive from the state of historical scholarship and the conception of historical writings on the eve of a revolution that was to transform the character of historical work and to give rise to the modern professional historian with his accoutrements of seminars, monographs, graduate schools, and institutional associations. Although the American Historical Association was founded in 1885 and Henry Adams, whom Parkman knew, was conducting a historical seminar at Harvard in the seventies, Parkman was almost totally untouched by these developments. Parkman's own work belongs to the phase of historical development that might properly be called "The Age of Recovery." It was a period of enormous archival achievement in which some of the great historical collections were initiated, libraries were founded, and documents of all kinds bearing on the American past were collected, edited, translated, and published. It was a period of discovery, as well as recovery, in which the artifacts and records of the colonial past and the American Revolution were reclaimed from obscurity and made available for future scholars. Although older historians like George Bancroft, whose account of the colonial period began appearing in the 1830's, were responsible for completing part of this enormous task by calling attention to the sheer variety of sources available and by quoting such documents wholesale in their histories, the bulk of the work was done by men who were principally archivists and editors. Foremost among these was a former Unitarian minister, Jared Sparks, who had accepted the McLean chair of American history at Harvard in 1839 and who had edited the diplomatic correspondence of the Revolution and collected and edited the writings of Franklin and Washington in the years before Parkman began to write. Sparks's achievement has been dimmed by the discovery that he shamelessly bowdlerized Washington's writings to make them accord with popular idolatry of Washington, but Sparks was clearly a major force in stimulating scholarship in American history and in gaining it a place in the curriculum of American colleges. The twenty-five volumes of his *Library of American Biography*, which he sponsored and edited, were the first systematic attempt to put together a historical portrait gallery of important American political figures. It was, suitably, Sparks to whom Parkman first wrote for information during his sophomore year at Harvard when he was about to commence work on his *Pontiac*. More immediately relevant to Parkman's project was the work of Lyman C. Draper, who founded the Wisconsin Historical Society and made it the home of the largest nineteenth-century collection of Western Americana. Without the previous and thorough scourings of Draper through the west and the massive collections of documents that were published by his society, the work of Parkman would have been set back at least twenty years. He was perhaps Parkman's most frequent correspondent in the years during which Parkman was planning his history. There were at least three other collectors and editors whose work was essential to Parkman. Edmund B. O'Callahan, a Canadian émigré and the state historian of New York, who had published nine volumes of his *Documents Relative to the Colonial History of New York* by 1861, was another correspondent and consultant whose work and advice was invaluable to Parkman. So was John G. Shea, who left the Jesuit novitiate as a young man and published two volumes describing Western discovery and the work of Catholic missionaries during the 1850's. It was the twenty-six volumes of Jesuit *Relations*, edited by Shea, consisting in the whole corpus of Jesuit writing about the New World, that was Parkman's single most important source. The third figure was a Frenchman, Pierre Margry, librarian and collector at the Archive de la Marine et Colonies in Paris who ruthlessly and almost singlehandedly hoarded together every conceivable document bearing on the French colonization of North America. He proved at times an intractable and ungenerous spirit, even for Parkman, whose tact and diplomacy in unlocking sources possessed by others excelled those of most contemporaries. Once Parkman had succeeded in getting a congressional grant of $10,000 to underwrite the publication of six volumes of Margry's collections, he proved more generous and is finally to be enlisted among Parkman's friends.

This list, incomplete as it is, is sufficient to suggest the falsity of a portrayal of Parkman as a lonely tyro. Virtuoso he was, as I think it will become clear, but it is necessary to recognize that it was others who wrote the notes for his music, so to speak, and that in his work he was dependent upon associations at least as important as those of historians today, although these associations antedate the organization of history as a profession. His genius lay in his assiduity and in the skepticism with which he worked with materials gathered by others, in the critical posture which he assumed toward his own times and, most of all, in his imaginative powers, in his capacity to shape the design of a vast swath of the North American past and to relay it with the concreteness and excitement of his own discovery. The timing of this vast redaction of historical materials was such that Parkman could come to it while it was still largely terra incognita to other Americans, while the sheen of freshness was still upon it. He developed the capacity to render, as Henry James would say, his own experience as a traveler and reader and to translate the reflections of Jesuit missionaries and French voyageurs into terms of meaning for his own time. To do so, he sought aid from every conceivable source, including the infant science of Indian ethnology, which was making its first stirrings in the fifties with the work of Henry Rowe Schoolcraft and Lewis Henry Morgan. It was Schoolcraft who determined Parkman to take his Oregon trip in 1846, and he depended heavily on Morgan's work on the Iroquois in the writing of *The Jesuits*, though he disagreed with many of Morgan's conclusions—to the detriment of his history, it might be added. Nonetheless, Parkman's standing among ethnologists was such that he was offered the presidency of the American Ethnological Society when it was founded in 1878.[27]

Despite the long interval that separated conception from final completion, the seven works that make up his *France and England in North America* have a remarkable coherence. Taken together they span a period of slightly over two centuries, from the first broaching of the North American continent in the fifteenth century to the defeat of Montcalm's army outside Quebec in 1759. Throughout the whole of it, he retained a fidelity to the dramatis personae of historical forces he had introduced in the preface of his opening volume: French intellect, English muscle, human will (a quality without nationality but in these volumes principally exemplified by the French), and the forest itself. Like the American South and the North, to whom Parkman had given the same contrasting qualities, the two nationalities that competed for the American continent were in Parkman's eyes handicapped by limitations of an ominous kind. The great intellectual thrust that mapped and laid bare the extent of the continent was supplied by the French, yet the French proved incapable of peopling what they themselves had discovered. Thus, France stood for a magnificent act of mind that was tragically flawed at its very outset. England, on the other hand, extended the long hand of middle-class materialism to the New World. Her energizing force was supplied by political liberty, religious reform, assiduity, and commercial opportunism. If her colonial effort was devoid of the intellectual distinction and colorful pageantry of the French, England was riding a crest wave of history that predestined success. Thus, the qualities of mind and will that characterized Parkman's French heroes were balanced against the powerful but mediocre qualities of mind that carried English imperialism to its ascendancy. New France, as Parkman put it, "was all head," while New England was "a body without a head."[28] The great virtue for Parkman of examining the contest for the American continent lay in the clarity with which these opposing powers were limned against the wilderness setting, where they stood out like toy armies on a sand table. There the waning of the Middle Ages was enacted before one's eyes, as political absolutism, feudalism, and Rome slowly sank into the Canadian tundra. The fall of France thus spelled out a lesson of broader application, since "out of her fall grew revolutions whose influence is felt through every nation of the civilized world."[29]

Such was Parkman's plot, outlined in bold abstractions, and to a surprising degree he adhered to its general outlines. Recurrently throughout the histories Parkman introduces his four characters, like leitmotifs. France, of course, occupies the center of the stage through most of the story. It is French explorers, missionaries, soldiers, and governors who range the continent, consolidate their power, organize Indian allies, war against the English, and quarrel among themselves. The small New England settlement along the eastern littoral is referred to in the opening volumes principally to keep Parkman's contrast alive and as an ominous indicator of things to come, like distant thunder. The character of the forest or wilderness is kept before the reader at every moment. It is a virgin continent that stretches before the explorers with its enormous potential, and it is the forest, too, that acts as an ensnarement and obstruction in the face of every effort to conquer it. Only the indomitable will incarnate in Parkman's principal protagonists makes the abortive French effort to subdue the wilderness feasible at all. At the close of the story both French and English are behaving true to character, as Lord Amherst stolidly cuts his way through the forest and his wily and adaptable French adversary attempts to elude an English force that moves against him like an armored division. The brilliance of Wolfe's assault upon Quebec, Parkman leaves no doubt, might have proved insubstantial had it not been for the English fleet that soon assembled in the St. Lawrence below. It is by sheer numbers and by logistical superiority that England finally triumphs.[30]

We do not need, however, to read Parkman's histories with great care in order to see that despite his faithfulness to his original conception, his emphasis was of a slightly different kind. At least in practice he did not give equal attention to each phase of his epic conflict. First of all, of the three empires that are introduced into his plot, it is, as we have seen, France that preoccupies him through most of the narrative. Parkman, in fact, initially thought of entitling his history simply *France in North America*. England is introduced as a foil in the closing volumes. The United States, of course, appears only embryonically and by inference, although Parkman appended an obiter dictum to *Montcalm and Wolfe*, in which he solemnly warned that "it now remains for [the United States] to prove, if she can, that the rule of the masses is consistent with the highest growth of the individual; that democracy can give the world a civilization as mature and pregnant, ideas as energetic and vitalizing, and types of manhood as lofty and strong, as any of the systems which it boasts to supplant."[31] The very language of Parkman's adjuration, moreover, betrays his most obvious concern, as well as revealing the source of his principal anxieties. It is the response of human intellect and will to challenge that clearly interests him most. In this sense, the whole cycle of French power is merely a stage on which Parkman ahistorically parades his own version of the *comédie humaine*.

Parkman's version of the course of empire consists in three fairly distinct stages: an age of discovery and exploration recounted in *The Pioneers, The Jesuits,* and his *La Salle*; an age in which French power is at its zenith, described in *The Old Regime* and *Frontenac*; and a period of dissolution and final defeat that is retailed in *A Half-Century of Conflict* and *Montcalm and Wolfe*. Theoretically, each of these stages should have evoked equal attention from him, yet it is clear from even a cursory reading that Parkman has little interest in describing the slow workings of the dry rot that is lodged within New France after the two governorships of Count Frontenac. *A Half-Century of Conflict*, which spans the gap between Frontenac and the French defeat at Quebec, would have been a crucial volume in delineating the dissolution of French power, yet it was the last thing

Parkman wrote and it becomes a catchall for a succession of disconnected episodes without central theme. One can see why Parkman himself thought of *Montcalm and Wolfe* as his greatest tour de force, since the events he describes have a built-in dramatic unity and clear symbolism that beautifully fitted his initial conception and provided him with a narrative climax, which through its development of the character of the French general Montcalm possessed the overtones of tragedy. Yet, despite its dramatic suspense, the events recounted at the end of the history are somehow external to the history that Parkman had written. The climactic battle on the Plains of Abraham is fought by professional armies employing the tactics of European warfare, and the victory is clinched by the arrival of the British navy. It takes place away from the forest which had figured so importantly in earlier volumes and which had transformed the nature of warfare for Englishman and Frenchman alike. It also takes place without the complicating fact of Indian allies or enemies.[32] The personification of Roman absolutism in the Jesuit hierarchy has disappeared from the scene, although Parkman leaves no doubt that Catholicism will persist as an abiding force in Canadian life long after the French armies have left.

Perhaps most important of all, the significant divisions within New France itself have disappeared from consideration. Parkman's contention in *The Old Regime* and *Frontenac*, which outline the structure of government and the forces at play within it, was that the forest had acted as a dialectic upon the thinking of those who experienced it. An important—and for Parkman crucial—conflict thus developed between the policies concocted in metropolitan France and those conceived in the wilderness by men who had grown to know it. As Howard Doughty has suggested, Parkman comes close to anticipating Turner's "frontier hypothesis" over a decade before Turner's own important pronouncement.[33] Louis XIV, through his representatives in Canada, made known his wish to centralize the government of the colony and to confine the fur trade to Montreal. He saw no reason why New France should not be governed as any other French province, and he accordingly called for an abandonment of French trading forts and canceled the licenses of merchant-traders like La Salle. Arrayed against the "Bourbon System," as Parkman calls it, is the thinking of Frontenac, who is portrayed as a man familiar with the realities of forest warfare and forest commerce.

His innovating temper has led him to institute a network of forts, governed by his subordinates, between the Gulf of Mexico and the St. Lawrence. These forts were intended as "strategic hamlets," as I suppose we should call them, and as guarantees to the security and trade of the continent. It is the natural system of Frontenac that prevails, Parkman tells us, since the policy of the monarchy was unworkable. Thus, Frontenac becomes for Parkman the principal architect of policies that were rooted in the New World rather than Europe. As such he becomes a proponent of modernization and a transitional figure between the medieval past, with which his dress and love of ceremony ally him, and the dawning age of liberty.

It is in the broaching of the modern world that Parkman finds his principal imaginative excitement, especially at those moments when progressive forces ironically appear on the scene in the armorial garb of French soldiers or in the clerical robes of the Roman hierarchy. Except for the unusual governorships of Count Frontenac, there was little about the administration of the colony or of its Catholic hierarchy that evoked Parkman's interest. There was even less to concern him about the circumstances of their inevitable decline. It is probably for this reason that the innovating institutional history contained in *The Old Regime* and *Frontenac* seems so dogged, since Parkman was clearly creating a context in which he could place the energizing and progressive figure of Frontenac. Paradoxically, Parkman immersed himself most completely in the first stage of his cycle, the age of exploration and discovery. At the beginning of this period the whole of the American continent was in a condition of historical fecundity, as Parkman's description of landfalls along the eastern seaboard continually reminds us. Thus, when Champlain's ship sailed into the St. Lawrence, Parkman characteristically remarks that "he was the Aeneas of a destined people, and in the womb [of his ship] lay the embryo life of Canada."[34] It is science that informs the spirit of Parkman's principal protagonists, including Frontenac. The quest for knowledge, when combined with the hard practical wisdom of the forest, explains in large part the triumphant achievements of Champlain, La Salle, and a half-dozen others whose explorations are recounted in the first three volumes of the history. Champlain is portrayed as a child of the Renaissance, a map maker and geographer, who was distinguished most of all for "the light that he threw on the dark places of American geography." He was less obsessive than La

Salle and more disinterested, but he clearly can be ranked among those men, like Frontenac and La Salle, who transcend their own time.[35]

❖

If Parkman composed a single work which can be considered to epitomize what he had to say as a historian, it is his account of La Salle's exploration of the Mississippi in the third volume of his trilogy of exploration. La Salle's character and motivation, the momentous obstacles he was forced to overcome, and the pervasive irony of the narrative provide a microcosm of the whole history. Parkman's difficulties in implanting his own vision upon the materials with which he worked tell us more than anything else he wrote about the quirks and oddities of his procedures as a historian.

The study of La Salle is principally concentrated in the decade of the 1680's, and chronologically parallels his *Frontenac*, although Parkman, in order to give a thread of continuity to his over-all work, introduces occasional flashbacks that permit him to pick up the themes of earlier volumes.

The very directness with which he seems to proceed toward its climax—La Salle's discovery of the mouth of the Mississippi in April, 1682—is illusory, since the organization of the book is almost perversely complex. This particular voyage of discovery occupies a mere twenty pages in a book of well over three hundred pages. There are three long chapters at the beginning, four in the middle, and two at the end in which La Salle himself does not appear and is scarcely discussed. The denouement which takes La Salle through his disastrous attempt to place a motley colony of French settlers on the lower Mississippi to his murder on the Texas prairie in 1687 is almost as long as the whole previous narrative of La Salle's activities. The revised narrative, in other words, even with the additional materials on La Salle, which Parkman added in 1878, is far from a triumphant account of one man's successful attempt to probe the geographical unknown. Rather, it is a harrowing depiction, with many of the qualities of a recurrent nightmare, of the resistance, the obstacles, and the frustrations that attend an ambitious and visionary endeavor, and of the illusory and transient nature of success itself.

Parkman had studied his Gibbon to good effect: no one, certainly not La Salle himself, escapes the pervasive irony with which he views the hopes, dreams, and simple faith of all those involved. Writing from his perspective in the Protestant post-Darwinian United States of the 1870's, Parkman reduces to a Lilliputian scale the factional squabbles and conspiracies of La Salle and his political enemies, Jesuit and seigneur, France and England, over possession of the rich Mississippi Valley. It is perfectly clear from the outset that no man's hopes can be fulfilled, neither the peaceful and prosperous agricultural paradise—the "feudal domain"—envisioned by La Salle nor the "new Paraguay" with its regulated Catholic society of French peasants and pious natives which the Jesuit order aimed to establish. He never lets his readers forget that every vestige of French culture, except for a few Acadians and Creoles speaking in strange dialects, is predestined to disappear and give place to the culture and society of Parkman's contemporary America.

The narrative contains constant reminders that this is the case. La Salle passes by the present sites of Peoria and St. Louis, and the intractable wilderness through which he forces his way is "in our own day," Parkman observes, "strangely transformed—yellow in harvest time with ripened wheat, and dotted with the roofs of a hardy and valiant yeomanry."[36] In a footnote of several pages he also shows how, by a fascinating piece of detective work, he located the site of the Great Illinois Town near the contemporary town of Utica, Illinois. It is also evident that Parkman does not think of all these changes as for the good. Civilization was first of all an encroachment on a virgin wilderness that still in La Salle's time retained its primal beauty. He speaks of the prairie as a "boundless pasture of the buffalo and the deer," animals doomed to disappear along with much of the other wildlife the explorers encounter.[37] The monumental "Starved Rock" which plays such a central role in the narrative is now daubed with an advertisement of a brand of pills. The Falls of St. Anthony which Hennepin discovered is now the site of two modern cities of questionable beauty. "Beside the falls," Parkman contemptuously interjects in a note,

stands a city, which, by an ingenious combination of the Greek and Sioux languages, has received the name of Minneapolis, or City of the Waters, and which, in 1867, contained ten thousand inhabitants, two national banks, and an opera-house; while its rival city of St. Anthony, immediately opposite, boasted a gigantic water-cure and a State university. In short, the great natural beauty of the place is utterly spoiled.[38]

Progress, though to Parkman inexorable, has not in every instance brought improvement, and the struggle for survival—between man and the wilderness and between Frenchman and English colonial—which is Parkman's subject throughout his histories has brought losses as well as gains. The losses, furthermore, are irretrievable, and some of the gains—the vigorous commercial life of the United States, for example—he considers of questionable value, as his slighting mention of banks, water cures, and patent medicines suggests. At the time Parkman was working on these early volumes, moreover, the nation was engaged in a Civil War which Parkman deemed strikingly similar to the one he was busy recording, and in his *La Salle* there are passing references to this struggle. As La Salle pushes toward his destination down the Mississippi, he passes the sites "since become historical, of Vicksburg and Grand Gulf."[39]

The most triumphant moments in La Salle's career are rendered ironically and underscore the impermanence of French imperial dominion and La Salle's personal achievement. When La Salle assembles his followers at the mouth of the Mississippi, erects a column in honor of "Louis Le Grand," and in grandiloquent language claims most of the Trans-allegheny West in his name, Parkman conceded it was "a stupendous accession"—"on parchment"; made, he quickly adds, "by virtue of a feeble human voice, inaudible at half a mile."[40]

Throughout the narrative the human beings who move across the landscape are dwarfed by the very size of the continent and beset by forces they can neither understand nor control. At every turn Parkman emphasizes the smallness and ineffectiveness of human agency and the gigantism of nature itself. When a party of explorers in an early chapter embark on a tributary of the Wisconsin and start south, Parkman, with what become characteristic stylistic devices, renders the helplessness of their plight in the face of a personified and grandly indifferent nature:

The river twisted among lakes and marshes choked with wild rice; and, but for their guides, they could scarcely have followed the perplexed and narrow channel. It brought them at last to the portage, where, after carrying their canoes a mile and a half over the prairie and through the marsh, they launched them on the Wisconsin, bade farewell to the waters that flowed to the St. Lawrence, and committed themselves to the current that was to bear them they knew not whither—perhaps to the Gulf of Mexico, perhaps to the South Sea or the Gulf of California. They glided calmly down the tranquil stream, by islands choked with trees and matted with entangling grape-vines; by forests, groves, and prairies, the parks and pleasure-grounds of a prodigal nature; by thickets and marshes and broad bare sand-bars; under the shadowing trees, between whose tops looked down from afar the bold brow of some woody bluff.[41]

Many things about this passage are typical of Parkman's language whenever man encounters the wilderness, especially the idea of nature as an obstructive, constricting force. Rivers "twist" and are often compared to snakes; the underbrush is "choked" and channels or paths are "perplexed." The wilderness is an entanglement, its snares and the potential threat it offers to those who penetrate it are usually stated or implied. Exploring parties are nearly always described with passive verbs, or the activity is attributed to nature itself. It is the river which twists and brings the party to the portage, and the explorers "commit" themselves to the Wisconsin and are borne by it "they knew not whither." The diminutive scale of the men is expressed both by the way in which nature is personified and by the perspective from which, at the end of the passage, they are viewed. The fact that the forests and prairies are described as "the parks and pleasure-grounds of a prodigal nature" implies not only the gigantism of nature but also seems to suggest that Parkman conceives of nature as a glorious spendthrift, a kind of deity-king as indifferent to his subjects as the *Roi Soleil* in whose name and for whose glory they labor. Finally, the visual imagery forces us to see the exploring party from an increasing height, as the eye is carried up from the "shadowing trees" to the "bold brow" of the bluffs which "looked down" upon them.

The vision of nature which is expressed in this and other passages is very different from that of earlier American writers like Cooper, for example, who were inclined to look upon nature as a benign and salubrious force, a source of intuitive truth or, at the very least, a recourse for those who sought out the picturesque. The pantheistic suggestion that God is immanent in the wilderness is nowhere to be found in Parkman's writing, where nature is mute—or to quote Parkman, "a voiceless solitude"—and man is solitary. There are passages, to be sure, where nature seems to smile and peace and plenty prevail, but these are almost invariably a signal for trouble, for nature when it is not indifferent and aloof is portrayed as vicissitudinous, even treacherous, like the savages who inhabit it. Nowhere does it provide reliable comfort or solace. The sunny, calm waters of Lake Huron, over which La Salle makes his way, are suddenly whipped by a violent storm; the junction of the Missouri with the gentle current of the upper Mississippi sends a canoe careening wildly:

A torrent of yellow mud rushed furiously athwart the calm blue current of the Mississippi; boiling and surging, and sweeping in its course logs, branches, and uprooted trees. They had reached the mouth of the Missouri, where that savage river, descending from its mad career through a vast unknown of barbarism, poured its turbid floods into the bosom of its gentler sister.[42]

The introduction at this early point of the ideas of savagery and madness into the personification of nature prepares the way for much that is to come: it brings to the description of nature a set of terms fundamental to Parkman's portrayal of *human* nature, also regarded by him as uncontrollable, treacherous, and essentially unfathomable. Those who look to God, like the priests, in expectation that He will intervene in man's affairs, or who think of themselves as in a position to exercise some control over nature or the Indian, are always viewed ironically. Parkman's language betrays his contempt for such superstitious pretensions, whether of Jesuit or Indian. During the storm on Lake Huron, for example, when La Salle's ship, the *Griffin*, seems about to capsize or be swamped, Parkman observes that those on board "clamored to the saints":

St. Anthony of Padua was promised a chapel in his honor, if he would save them from their jeopardy; while in the same breath La Salle and the friars declared him patron of their great enterprise. The saint heard their prayers. The obedient winds were tamed. . . .[43]

The belief held by the Jesuits that they had Christianized the Indians is handled in much the same way. When Father Allouez goes among the Foxes of Green Bay and induces them to discard their tribal deities and worship the cross, Parkman interjects: "Nay, he succeeded so well, that when he showed them his crucifix they would throw tobacco on it as an offering."[44] When a little later Allouez tells them the story of the cross and Constantine, they go off to battle with crosses daubed on their shields and return victorious and converted.

"Thus it is," writes Dablon, who chronicles the incident, "that our holy faith is established among these people; and we have good hope that we shall soon carry it to the famous river called the Mississippi, and perhaps even to the South Seas."[45]

The only kind of religious faith which wins his admiration is the burning internal faith of the early Jesuit missionaries who "lived with the self-abnegation of saints and died with the devotion of martyrs," and even they seem admirable only because of what, as civilized men, they were able to endure.

The natural setting in which Parkman places his La Salle is one without any rational order and bereft of its gods, where chaotic and unpredictable forces are constantly at work. Indian nature is scarcely distinguishable from physical nature and is delineated in similar terms. Storm metaphors appear to be Parkman's favorite device for describing the onset of an Indian attack. When the Iroquois prepare for war "a storm is gathering," and their attack is compared to lightning. No reasons are assigned to the Iroquois for their assault on the Great Illinois Town; their behavior is as unaccountable and unpredictable as the weather. They are just as often compared to beasts of prey: "A hyena warfare," Parkman comments, "had been waged against the dead. . . . The threatened blow had fallen, and the wolfish hordes of the five cantons had fleshed their rabid fangs in a new victim."[46] Having said this, Parkman, apparently feeling that his language might seem hyberbolic, gives further supporting evidence concerning the savage nature of Indian warfare in a long footnote.

All human motivation is finally caught up in the essential irrationality of a savage nature. The white man, as Parkman sees him, is not so much corrupted by the wilderness as revealed to be what he basically is. Deep unconscious cravings and brutal aggressions, long held in check, are unleashed. Men kill one another almost on a whim. Others shed the thin veneer of civilization and go native. The lure of unbridled Indian life and the easy accessibility of Indian women, Parkman implies, simply unveil human nature's essential characteristics: a brutal selfishness propelled by wild and uncontrollable passions. The terminology of savagery and civilization become interchangeable. The Iroquois are referred to as "forest Machiavels," and the attempted poisoning of La Salle in the wilderness is compared in a footnote to a contemporary incident in Paris which arose out of intrigues at court.[47] Finally, in a touch of characteristic irony, Parkman has the civilized European pin the label of savagery on himself. After La Salle has witnessed the depredations of the Iroquios upon the Illinois, he journeys on to find the ship he had left half-built destroyed by those to whom he had entrusted its completion. Scrawled on a plank are the words *"Nous sommes tous sauvages"* followed by the Christian date.[48] Very little plausibility is given to any man's actions, except for those few men who are "mere merchants," as Parkman calls them, and are therefore in the wilderness simply to enrich themselves or, in the case of the Jesuits, to aggrandize their order. All the rest act mostly from essentially irrational motives or at least inscrutable ones, even La Salle. "The wilderness," Parkman comments on the occasion of La Salle's murder, "is a rude touchstone, which often reveals traits that would have lain buried and unsuspected in civilized life."[49]

The journey which La Salle is described as taking is a voyage of exploration in two senses. It is a probing of the geographical unknown in which, as Parkman puts it, "the mystery of this vast New World was more and more unveiled." It is also a journey into the human mind, an exploration of human nature: strange monstrous features turn up at each bend of the river. Horribly painted Indian idols which assure the priests that the Devil is abroad, rocks that look like the battlements of ruined châteaux, a huge catfish which perceptibly jolts a canoe and startles its occupants, an ugly spadefish, the man-devouring alligator (which the Frenchmen are astonished to learn is hatched from an egg), the mammoth desert rattlesnake and the Texas horned toad all appear successively, as do an astonishing procession of Indian tribes with their varying rituals and customs, each, it appears, a little stranger and more eccentric than the one before. In this sense Parkman was writing his own vicarious *Voyage of the Beagle*, duly recording the impression made by each novelty of American nature as it is first confronted by civilized man. But finally, and I think much more significantly, the journey for Parkman became one in which he was probing the inner recesses of human behavior, the motives which drive men to act as they do. Cannibalism and sexual perversions as practiced by the Indians, though mentioned, are too horrifying to receive detailed consideration, though the more commonplace vices of theft, lying, treachery, and murder are discussed at length. Even vanity and plagiarism receive rather extended consideration in the long account of Father Hennepin's real and imagined journeys. While he actually did discover the Falls of St. Anthony on the upper Mississippi, in a later edition of his travels, published after La Salle's death, he fraudulently claims to have been the first to follow the river to its mouth, thus robbing La Salle of his principal claim to renown.

At this point, and at certain others, the history takes on the characteristics of a detective story as Parkman, like Poe's M. Dupin, proceeds by deduction to unravel the motives which could have led Hennepin to make such an insupportable claim and to show that the trip which he insisted he had made could not have been completed in the time which his original narrative allowed for. He then goes on to discount the apparent accuracy of Hennepin's narrative by showing with unmistakable certainty that he had lifted his description, sometimes word for word, from a journal kept by a Récollet missionary who had accompanied La Salle. In a disordered and irrational world held in check by only a few human qualities, veracity to Parkman became an almost fanatical ideal, and his indictment of Hennepin's behavior on this occasion is at least equal in its severity to his treatment of much more serious crimes. "The records of literary piracy," he concluded, "may be searched in vain for an act of depredation more recklessly impudent."[50] The fact that Parkman employs here in reference to the pseudo-explorer Hennepin terms such as "piracy" and "depredation" which he ordinarily reserved for acts of outrage committed by the Indians only further emphasizes the thin line which in his mind divided civilized from savage behavior, and raises still again the persistent problem of what drives men in a given set of circumstances to singular acts of depravity or, in the case of La Salle and a few others, heroism.

Certainly the most serious questions posed by Parkman's documentary sources were those concerning the motive or motives which impelled La Salle to his initial success and to his ultimate ruin, which enabled him—or *compelled* him, for this proved to be the real question—to endure years of hardship in the hostile wilderness of Canada and the Mississippi Valley, to force his way again and again across frozen prairies and wind-blown lakes in the face of opposition from Canadian authorities, treacherous intervention by the Jesuits and the Iroquois, and natural disasters of a kind which would have paralyzed ordinary men. Or so, at least, Parkman conceived of La Salle's situation and of his accomplishments.

A curious air of uncertainty and ambiguity surrounds Parkman's discussion of La Salle's motivation from the outset of the narrative. It seems apparent that nothing in the story fascinated or troubled him more. He returns to the problem again and again, sometimes simply repeating in different words what he has said before, sometimes contradicting himself and, in several instances, obviously evading the implications of evidence which he himself cites. From time to time Parkman is forced to concede that La Salle acted out of a desire to enrich himself, out of a driving personal ambition for renown and for power, out of opportunism of the most ruthless kind; and to intimate toward the end of the narrative that he may have acted out of the compulsions of a sick and deluded mind which left him no peace and prohibited him from sparing either himself or those whom he forced to follow him on and on and on across the wastes of southern Texas toward the "fatal river," as Parkman calls it, which La Salle was destined to trace to its mouth and in the hapless pursuit of which he finally perished. Nonetheless, despite these occasional concessions—and, in the light of the evidence, Parkman could scarcely have evaded them—his emphasis was of a different kind.

A number of things about La Salle's character are given unusual stress, often on the slenderest evidence—a feature in his history which it is not possible to dismiss lightly in view of Parkman's fanatical desire for accuracy, his tireless efforts to tie down the exact location of every physical feature, every singular rock formation, tributary, and fortified encampment which La Salle or his contemporaries encountered or inhabited. The qualities of La Salle's character upon which Parkman most insists are his gentility, his veracity, his disinterested patriotism, his self-control, and his essential modernity. A number of other qualities are implied by, or associated with, these underlying traits: will power, inexhaustible energy, and the capacity to concentrate them on the attainment of a single lofty objective. It is this last capacity which makes La Salle the outstanding exemplar of the most pre-eminently masculine trait in Parkman's human lexicon—"constitutional hardihood"—a subtle blend of manly fortitude, intellect, and gentility. There is no mistaking Parkman's eagerness to establish a close association between good breeding, cultivation, and courageous endurance and achievement. "The pioneer of western pioneers," Parkman comments of La Salle, "was no rude son of toil, but a man of thought, trained amid arts and letters." He then in a footnote goes on to quote a Rocky Mountain trapper who once told him that

"a gentleman of the right sort will stand hardship better than anyone else." The history of Arctic and African travel [Parkman continues], and military records of all time, are a standing evidence that a trained and developed mind is not the enemy, but the active and powerful ally, of constitutional hardihood. The culture that enervates instead of strengthening is always a false or a partial one.[51]

Without the possession of constitutional hardihood, Parkman makes clear, La Salle's heroic achievement and endurance would have been impossible.[52] A certain number of words and phrases which designate this quality reappear like Homeric epithets throughout the narrative: "inexorable," "indomitable," "ironhearted," "unbending," "inconquerable," "self-contained," "impenetrable," "adamant," "impregnable," "inscrutable," and many others which denote La Salle's almost total detachment from, independence of, and imperviousness to all and everything which surrounds him.

La Salle is thus portrayed as having transcended his natural environment, as having elevated himself above the materialism, opportunism, superstitions, vices, and temptations—in other words, the sense of values—which characterize most of those who move through the forests of French Canada. While it is this quality of transcendence which gives him, as Parkman interprets his character, the "vision" necessary to achieve his purpose, the very remoteness which it implies from the feelings and needs of others is, ironically, what defeats him and leads to his "assassination," as Parkman calls it, or, really, his murder—which is what it amounts to. La Salle's heroic qualities were thus, in the end, self-defeating, and his purpose was frustrated by the great river itself, which is described with many of the same epithets—by uncomprehending followers and subordinates and by the wavering purpose of an indifferent monarch, who finally turns his attention to other matters and leaves the pitiful little settlement on Matagorda Bay to its fate. This, in brief, is the tragic portrayal of La Salle that Parkman forces upon the evidence he collected and reviewed with such painstaking care. How well does it fit, and what kind of proof is offered to demonstrate that La Salle possessed those traits which are attributed to him?

Certainly it is fair to say at the outset that these heroic qualities are supported more casually and circumstantially than any other assertions in the book. La Salle's gentility hangs by a thread. Some of his distant relatives, Parkman notes, were in the service of the crown, and his father and uncle, though merchants, lived "more like nobles than like burghers."[53] In a footnote he goes on to add that La Salle, like François Marie Arouet, known as Voltaire, took the name from the family "estate," although he neglects to mention that this was a common practice everywhere in Europe, even among those with only small holdings. Thorstein Veblen's father, a poor Norwegian immigrant, had done the same thing. La Salle's social position is further supported by Parkman's repeated and literal application to him of such terms as "seigneur" and "feudal lord" and "domain." Parkman, moreover, considerably improved the literary qualities—and, in fact, the literacy—of La Salle's letters in the translations he made of them from French documentary sources.

The case for La Salle's modernity is scarcely stronger. He is introduced as one who "showed an inclination for the exact sciences,"[54] whatever that might have meant in Rouen of the early seventeenth century. When a large comet blazes across the sky in 1680, La Salle, Parkman observed, "coolly notes down the phenomenon, not as a portentous messenger of war and woe, but rather as an object of scientific curiosity."[55] In doing so, he contends in a footnote, La Salle exhibited his freedom from the superstitious terror which the same comet evoked from Increase Mather in New England. He is called a "hero of modern practical enterprise" early in the book and, in the summary of his character that occurs after his murder, Parkman observes that he "belonged not to the age of the knight-errant and the saint, but to the modern world of practical study and practical action."[56]

Questions concerning La Salle's disinterested patriotism, his sanity —and hence his self-control—and, even, his veracity are raised by a number of incidents which Parkman discusses in detail. If we are to take La Salle at his word, a more quixotic venture could scarcely have been imagined than that of landing a small party of Frenchmen at the mouth of the Mississippi, herding the intractable and feuding Indian tribes from the upper valley to the Rio Grande—a fantastic proposal in view of La Salle's extensive experience of Indian life— and capturing the Spanish silver mines in Mexico, yet this is precisely what La Salle does propose in one memorial to Louis XIV. This memorial and several other documents which Parkman cites raise both the question of La Salle's disinterestedness and that of his veracity. The case for his veracity rests mostly on the dubious evidence of a memoir written about him at the time he returned to Paris in 1678 by a person obviously bent on promoting La Salle's standing at court. Although Parkman concedes that the memoir exhibits "intensely partisan feeling," he nonetheless cites it at length on the subject of La Salle's truthfulness: "He distinguishes perfectly," Parkman quotes the memoir as saying, "between that which he knows with certainty and that which he knows with a mingling of doubt."[57] In the case of the two memorials to the king, prepared during a second visit to Paris in 1683, there seems little question, as a recent article has shown, that La Salle was involved in a political intrigue of some kind. The passionate enemies which he had in Canada and in France are further evidence of his involvement with factional politics to a degree that Parkman, although he makes much of La Salle's many enemies, never admits. In this instance, Parkman goes to extraordinary lengths to discount the evidence of La Salle's desire to exploit the war with Spain in the interest of advancing his own position and winning greater support for his colonizing scheme. Although he concedes that La Salle had acted somewhat disingenuously—"he thought he needed a more glittering lure to attract the eyes of Louis and Seignelay"[58]—the explanation which he preferred was of another, quite surprising, kind.

Rather than yield to the obvious and agree that La Salle had acted opportunistically and somewhat dishonestly, Parkman quite suddenly interested himself in the charge commonly made by La Salle's enemies that he was insane, or at least suffered from a mental infirmity of some kind. All through the narrative, Parkman had

turned such charges back upon La Salle's accusers with contempt and
impugned their motives for making them. Now he was willing to
admit that La Salle had proposed a "madcap" scheme and that "his
head was turned," but this was only for the moment.[59] Mostly,
when he considered La Salle's personality, he preferred to deal in
terms which were vague and ambiguous and, finally, much more
applicable to Parkman himself than to La Salle. He calls him "shy,"
"retiring," "reserved," and "haughty" and refers to his "shadowed
nature" and his "solitary disposition."[60] In a long chapter entitled
"La Salle Painted by Himself," inserted in the 1879 edition and
based on letters which Parkman discovered in the Margry documents,
Parkman makes much of La Salle's brief confession of natural "timidity" that kept him from associating freely with his men, and of his
protestation that he found it difficult to write letters or to converse
with men more sophisticated than himself. Since this particular letter
was written not to a personal friend—to whom a shy man might be
expected to reveal such things—but rather in answer to criticisms
from a distrustful and disgruntled creditor, there is some suggestion
that La Salle here, too, might have acted a bit disingenuously, and
was certainly acting defensively. Nonetheless, Parkman rushes on to
portray La Salle as he, Parkman, must have conceived of himself. He
was characterized by "shyness; a morbid fear of committing himself;
an incapacity to express, and much more to simulate feeling—a trait
sometimes seen in those with whom feeling is most deep."[61] This
was the quality which induced him to leave France and spend his life
alone in the wilderness, and propelled him to turn his attention from
commerce and material pursuits, and devote himself to a principled
life of honor, achievement, and lofty and grandiose projects for the
good of France. Despite the impression he gave to others, Parkman
concluded, La Salle's was "a nature at war with itself," and the effect
of this silent, internal "strife"—which Parkman concedes was an
"infirmity"—was "to concentrate and intensify the force within." His
final madness is allowed for, but not really acknowledged by Parkman's theory that La Salle's "lonely and shadowed nature needed
the mellowing sunshine of success."[62]

Parkman's willingness in his portrayal of La Salle to ride roughshod
over his own evidence and his tortuous efforts to absolve La Salle of
any taint of opportunism or mercantile concern—to clear him, in
other words, of the charge that he was what he appears to have been

in fact, a Canadian parvenu, a man on the make—obviously calls for an explanation, especially in the case of a historian so scrupulously accurate and cautious in other matters. There is no mistaking the heroic role for which Parkman intended him. In the claims that are made for him following his death, La Salle is compared to the King of Israel, Coriolanus, paladin, crusader, and pilgrim, and in the last paragraph of the book he is referred to as a representative specimen of "a grand type of incarnate energy and will."[63] For Parkman this kind of assertion was clearly a matter of more than passing interest, since the recovery for his own time of a concept of heroism, of masculine yet genteel fortitude, was for him, as for many of his contemporaries, an undertaking of the most pressing urgency. In other words, he was advocating the virtues of the "strenuous life" with the same kind of zeal that was soon to prompt other members of the genteel classes in the East, as for example Theodore Roosevelt, to write about masculine exploit in much the same way. This sense of urgency, which he strongly felt and to which he repeatedly gave expression in letters to the press, especially when combined with the needs put forward by his personal problems, goes a long way toward explaining why it was he found the figure of La Salle so "arresting."

A reimmersion in Parkman's *La Salle*—or, for that matter, in any of the succession of narratives that make up the history—is apt to leave the contemporary reader, if he is a historian, with an odd mixture of feelings. Parkman wrote at an innocent stage in the development of historical art, before history became freighted with the responsibilities of social science and before it became entirely distinct from imaginative literature. Not only did Parkman adhere to a conception of history as story; he also conceived of his larger task as the interweaving of countless stories of individuals and groups whose corporate biographies comprised the experience of the society. Abstract generalizations are rare in Parkman, and for the most part confined to his prefaces. Even generalizations about large bodies of people are sparse. Parkman seems most comfortable with groups no more numerous than might be handled in a single novel. His method, too, is novelistic. He tends to offer a telling anecdote where one would expect to be provided with a historical analysis—and to the same purpose. The points he seems most anxious to make are essentially dramatic and moral rather than sociological. The resources of the human spirit in the face of adversity evoke his most lyrical writing, for the same reason that expressions of achievement and satisfaction by his historical figures provoke his wryest instances of irony. Parkman seemed to think of himself as living in a time when all heroes were dead or about to pass forever from the scene. In this sense, for all his obsession with concreteness and veracity, he appears to have undertaken a task no less amorphous than depicting the decline and fall of the human Will.

Henry Adams

J. C. LEVENSON

2)

HENRY ADAMS once tried lightly to explain how it felt to be the heir of Presidents and the inheritor of a pew in the granite church of Quincy, Massachusetts. Since few Americans are aware of hereditary pew holding, much less of President grandfathers, explanation was in order—and misunderstanding was to be expected. Adams' anecdote was to become an essential datum in the popular interpretation of his literary and historical work:

> The Irish gardener once said to the child: "You'll be thinkin' you'll be President too!" The casualty of the remark made so strong an impression on his mind that he never forgot it. He could not remember ever to have thought on the subject; to him, that there should be a doubt of his being President was a new idea. What had been would continue to be. He doubted neither about Presidents nor about Churches, and no one suggested at that time a doubt whether a system of society which had lasted since Adam would outlast one Adams more.[1]

Since *The Education of Henry Adams* became a posthumous best seller almost at the same time as Brooks Adams published *The Degradation of the Democratic Dogma* (Brooks's tendentious title and dark introduction set the tone for his collection of Henry's late, and often gloomy, speculations on historical development), it was easy to simplify the complex artist by reference to the cranky theorizer. The shortest way through a difficult book was to suppose that the gardener's words traumatized Henry Adams, prefigured a life of frustration at not becoming President of the United States, and led to final sublimation in an apocalyptic vision of cosmic disaster. By this view, the spoiled child of the republic became father to the man, and Adams' argument that anarchic twentieth-century society would have the power and might have the stupidity to blow up the world could be put off as the outrageous fantasy of a decadent and a sorehead. Nowadays, when the spoiled-child interpretation is more easily caricatured than believed in, the task remains to find some better way of connecting Adams' individual experience with his intellectual achievement. In a sense, we must reinterpret the incident in the garden which brought him the awful knowledge of historical change. What impressed Adams himself in the incident was not a shock of personal disappointment. Rather, he emphasized the way a child can expose what an adult might conceal, principally the assumption that the world is likely to go on as it is now or, even better, as it used to be. Standing for naïve blindness to the real changes of history, the child of the anecdote represents the vague attitudes of people in general. More specifically, the child—with his President grandfather and family pew—represents an immediately felt relation to church and state. The controlled multiplicity of the figure is evidence of rational skill rather than off-guard confession on the part of Henry Adams, but like any good symbol it says more than may have been consciously intended: the encounter with the Irish gardener announces that for Adams the age of politics is over. This theme runs through almost all of Henry Adams' mature work until the *Education*; and even in the *Education*, the passing of the age of statesmanship, ideally set in the eighteenth century, is his recurrent subject.

But Adams' response to this subject was by no means a matter of misery and lamentation. In the most grand-scale projection of the theme, in his *History*, he seemed to argue that the successful establishment of a democratic republic made politics obsolete; in the American democracy men behaved patriotically by giving up an archaic concern for public affairs and turning their energies to their individual tasks. Adams' own practice in accordance with this teaching was singularly successful, enough so that he may be said to have eluded the spell that was cast on him in the Quincy garden. That he attained the presidency of the American Historical Association is worth taking seriously as something more than an ironic fall: for once, an Adams, though he might repel popularity and avoid honors, could not prevent official recognition of what he did for his country. Moreover, the subjective importance of his work was as great as its objective value: of the many characters which he showed the world, that of professional historian was perhaps the closest to the center of his being. The point may be argued from his own usage in the *Education,* where his epithet for himself was "the historian," but there is no need to settle for his own testimony when the externally verifiable facts of his biography are so persuasive. Until he became a historian, Adams lacked a calling. Given the custom of the country whereby men define themselves by the work they do, not even the heir of Presidents was exempt from the popular pragmatism. To be without a calling was, to some degree, to lack an identity. The story of Henry Adams' education is his learning to give up the expectation of a career in government and, after the loss of childhood security and hereditary self-conception, his making an identity of his own by becoming "the historian."

Adams shifted his ambition from politics to history by a very gradual process. At Harvard, he was elected Class Orator for 1858, but he took the success to be literary rather than political. He did not for that reason think of a literary career, for he then conceived of literature as the product either of Sketch-Book sensibility or of Concord uplift, and his practical temperament rejected both. On the other hand, he did not follow the family pattern of going on at once to study law and prepare himself for an eventual career in public service. He chose the more roundabout course of going first to study the civil law in Berlin. There, instead of perfecting his scholarly preparation, he found himself to be less serious than he expected— and less gifted in the German tongue. Though he worked at the language, it was a case of German for German's sake: there was no visible progress in the law. As an innocent abroad, he learned that behind the appearance of a great university were such realities as stuffy halls, mumbled lectures, and the opportunity for a graduate student to drift at pleasure for as long as the money kept coming from home. When the money stopped coming, he returned to read law in Boston. But he soon dropped one family tradition in order to follow another, giving up law in order to serve as his father's confidential secretary, first in Washington and then for seven years in London. There the wavering toward and away from politics continued. As the son of the Civil War Minister to Great Britain, he was an apprentice diplomat; as an anonymous correspondent for the Boston *Courier* and the *New York Times*, he was a semiprofessional maker of public opinion; as an avid student of history and political theory, he was training himself to be the philosophical statesman of the future. On the other hand, he was given to speculation on the mysteries of his own consciousness and of the cosmos, he suffered and triumphed with the vicissitudes of clubland society as well as the Union cause, and his meeting the poet Algernon Charles Swinburne impressed him even more than his meeting John Stuart Mill. Although politics was the end in view for the young Henry Adams, it was not the only end.

Back in Washington, after the Grant administration made it shockingly clear that it had no openings for junior statesmen, he stayed on as a political journalist, and his staying may be regarded equally as his sticking with politics in an unofficial role or as his orderly retreat from youthful hopes to alternative possibilities. The same ambiguity persisted when he accepted an assistant professorship of history at Harvard in 1870: part of the attraction of the post was that along with it he undertook the editorship of the *North American Review*, and his Cambridge obligations did not keep him from continuing as an organizer of an Independent movement that tried to exert leverage on both political parties. There was no irrevocable commitment involved with his move to Harvard. His family, in their urging him to accept the position, evidently thought it was time for him to exchange public for private ambitions, but he himself came to that view slowly and not so much by deliberation as by the commitment which comes with effort and experience. Nevertheless, by the time he returned to Washington in 1877, the change had come. Although playing politics remained his avocation, understanding American political history was his certain work. And in his enthusiasm for the task, he assumed the characteristic which, in his *History*, he would someday argue to be quintessentially American: having given up an archaic concern for political power, he performed the highest patriotic duty by turning his energy to individual ends. By returning to Washington *as a scholar*, he was helping to make it into a great capital:

One of these days this will be a very great city if nothing happens to it. Even now it is a beautiful one, and its situation is superb. As I belong to the class of people who have great faith in this country and who believe that in another century it will be saying in its turn the last word of civilisation, I enjoy the expectation of the coming day, and try to imagine that I am myself, with my fellow *gelehrte* here, the first faint rays of that great light which is to dazzle and set the world on fire hereafter. Our duties are perhaps only those of twinkling, and many people here, like little Alice, wonder what we're at. But twinkle for twinkle, I prefer our kind to that of the small politician.[2]

Unlike Prescott, Parkman, and Bancroft, Henry Adams was a professor before he was a historian. In this respect, he belonged to the new generation that was fixing norms for academic professionalism in America. But the lines between generations, especially in his case, were blurred. He went to Harvard as an amateur and, after his seven years' labor there, he resigned in order to pursue history as an independent man of letters. Moreover, he tended to classify himself intellectually as well as socially with the older group of gentleman scholars. Like his distinguished elders, he made his own collection of original documents on which to base his work. Financially able to conduct research on both sides of the Atlantic, he made good use of his social position to win access to archives in Paris and Madrid—and Washington, too—which had never before been opened to historians. Wherever he worked, he left busy scribes behind him to gather his harvest, quite in the grand style of the independent scholar. But there were other kinds of research, beyond anyone's private means, which suggest some of the differences that the new organization of historical study made. A simple instance occurred when Adams, happily independent and working at his summer residence in Beverly Farms, exercised the privilege of a sometime faculty member and arranged with the Harvard library for shipment upon shipment of old newspaper files. Just as great institutional libraries now stood in contrast to even the best individual collections, so also the mass of historical information began to exceed the resourcefulness of the individual researcher. Adams' reading in depth in the period of his *History* was a different kind of study from the exhaustive search of archives: going through state papers, one assumes a fixed limit to the possibly relevant primary sources, whereas the materials of social history are virtually inexhaustible. In practice the questions of the researcher limit the data he takes in, but the old idea of scholarly authority makes the researcher constantly try to extend his powers of absorption and intelligent discrimination. The shift from political to more broadly social history implies professionalization in two respects, the pooling of resources in great libraries and the constantly increasing number of mutually dependent researchers who try to keep up with the materials. In addition, these technical changes accompany and perhaps encourage a shift of scholarly interest from the premodern era with its limited surviving evidences to the modern, post-1789 period, for which there are superabundant materials. In all these respects, Henry Adams was a representative scholar. His liberation from politics, in his professional as in his personal life, was gradual and incomplete, to be sure, but he had a deep underlying awareness of the changes that were required of his profession by the modern world. He wrote to this effect in a letter to Parkman:

The more I write, the more confident I feel that before long a new school of history will rise which will leave us antiquated. Democracy is the only subject for history. I am satisfied that the purely mechanical development of the human mind in society must appear in a great democracy so clearly, for want of disturbing elements, that in another generation psychology, physiology, and history will join in proving man to have as fixed and necessary development as that of a tree; and almost as unconscious.[3]

Apart from the rather dated notions of social science which so often catch the eye in this letter, it is well worth noting the plain central statement that names democracy as one more reason why political history is to be supplanted by social. Ironically, Adams' gloomy prognosis for political history was based on a political premise—namely, the Jeffersonian and in general the American assumption that stateless society was the ideal liberal and democratic order. Along with professionalism and modernism, a sense that democracy was—and ought to be—the main direction of the age affected Adams' historical practice and set him apart from the old school.

Political history was hard to escape. As a mode of historical writing, it preceded the making of the professional academic discipline with professional standards. It originated in a classical concern for statecraft, whereby history served to instruct a ruling prince or a governing class. But the classical conditions of statecraft changed: the highly rationalized eighteenth-century balance of power, which seemed to

Gibbon the greatest European achievement since the Pax Romana, depended on the coexistence of modern nation-states; with no central force for order, it blew apart under the pressure of revolution. In 1815 much was restored, but the Metternich concord of nations, which replaced the abstract symmetry of pre-Revolutionary Europe, only half-concealed the new forces. In this nineteenth-century environment, a generation of historians arose who were more concerned for the nation than for the state; in the general revival of medieval studies which then took place, they sought national origins rather than political wisdom. In the United States, however, the Middle Ages were not so visible as in Europe, not so tangibly present in the daily experience of the nation, and so the historian's situation was less hospitable to nationalism. By a survival of eighteenth-century cosmopolitanism and a stretch of the visual imagination, Americans could include in their own premodern history the age of the conquistadors or the general rise of Protestant liberalism; but the cultural distance between Prescott's and Motley's subjects and their audience meant that their histories, picturesque, dramatic, and scholarly as they were, did not compel the deepest involvement. For premodern history, Bancroft and Parkman found the more effective American subject by turning to the colonial period. Bancroft, arguing from impressive research to a few simple generalizations, set the scheme of patriotic liberalism for generations of textbook writers and, indirectly at least, stimulated wave after wave of scholarly revisionism. Bancroft survives mainly as an influence; Parkman survives in his own right for having fashioned a history of great and complex meaning out of virtually definitive knowledge of his subject. That he saw America as an integral part of European civilization established a breadth of view which made it easier for Adams to set his *History* in its international context. Yet Parkman's most characteristic accomplishments in defining his subject differ so much from Adams' at so many points of correspondence that the older historian seems to have been an ironic model for the younger. Parkman was remarkably nonpartisan in treating the major conflict of his story, since his love of so-called medieval qualities of manhood made him see an almost chivalric contest between France and England, with little point to the choosing of sides, even though patriotic liberalism gave the slight emotional odds to England. Parkman, as he rendered the leading figures of his story, wrote from a sense of epic greatness and a conviction that he could supply numerous examples from a heroic age, now utterly past. Parkman, at his most original in discovering the relation of his subject to his own time, made the great American forest his peculiar symbol of value, evoking a love for untouched nature and a regret that the "progress" of organized society should displace it. By contrast, Henry Adams was to make progress his subject and ignore unimproved nature except as a logistical problem. He was at one with Parkman in focusing on the development of national institutions and the problem of political and military hegemony over the North American continent, but he was to be antiheroic in tone and would direct his analysis toward the future, not the lost past.

Romantic history, like earlier history, was political; realistic history was even more so. The organization of academic scholarship, the textual criticism of documentary evidence, and the élan of finding that earlier histories did not stand up before a search for the way things really happened gave the intellectual advantage to realism. His youthful sojourn in Berlin spoke well of Henry Adams' historical instincts: he had found the very center of the new movement. Even though he had got only a vague conditioning rather than a real training there, the rigorous young professor of Anglo-Saxon law stood for German rather than, say, British standards and methods. He read widely in the German authorities and studied Old English charters in the German critical fashion; he established a graduate seminar along German lines and, from its program of research, produced the first Harvard Ph.D.s in history; with his best students as fellow contributors, he published in 1876 *Essays in Anglo-Saxon Law*, an early monument of collaborative scholarship. The progression of his interests also followed the pattern of the new academic orthodoxy. He started as a medievalist, moved on to American Colonial history, and completed the move from medieval to early modern to modern history by setting up a course on the history of the United States from 1789 to 1840. Whether the rigor of his studies ought to be ascribed to German academicism or simply to the New England background, the energy and intellectual forcefulness were certainly his own. He made his teaching of medieval institutions less remote by getting his students to regard it as a special training in Anglo-American law. In the Colonial period, he made himself expert enough to stand as authoritative critic of Bancroft's volumes as they came to hand; eventually, old Mr. Bancroft himself was using Adams as a private critic of his draft text. In the national period, he got into the controversial questions of American particularism and Federalist separatism: he not only reviewed his student Henry Cabot Lodge's *Life of George Cabot*, but also rebutted it with overwhelming evidence in his 1877 volume, *Documents Relating to New England Federalism, 1800–1815*. The realistic history which Adams produced as an academic scholar was legalistic, exacting, and of interest principally to the historical profession. Above all, it was as thoroughly political as history had ever been. At his most modern, in his pragmatic view that his history courses might serve to educate future lawyers, he was also closest to the most traditional motive of historical study, namely, the education of a governing class. The particular pride he took in Lodge—historian, lawyer, and active politician already showing the signs of future leadership—was not simply that of a nineteenth-century academician; the friendship between teacher and student was classical and New Englandly, also.

The immediate effect of professionalization was to make history more rather than less political: the watchword of the day became Edward A. Freeman's "History is past politics, politics is present history." Adams, who conducted his researches in that faith, was part of an academic vanguard. He became, as he ironically boasted, the modern authority on "sac and soc." He had traced that verbal formula to the point where its two terms stood for intelligibly different feudal rights, and yet he was uneasy at the pedantic nature of his achievement. He lacked a legal theory like that of his friend and colleague Oliver Wendell Holmes, Jr., for whom the disclosure of historical origins was a step toward making the law more pliable to current historical needs. But politics served Adams, as legal philosophy served Holmes, to provide a context of meaning. His studies took on life when, writing about Anglo-Saxon courts, he showed how judicial history might be seen as past politics. He seemed to project his own concern with Jeffersonian America back to the England of Alfred the Great: as he told the story, the chance for a national, secular judicial system in a strong, free nation-state was lost because Alfred failed to establish institutional means for prolonging the national power beyond his own reign. Later in his career, Adams would suggest a similar argument against Jefferson's failure to consolidate gains that depended at first on his influence as a popular leader. Anglo-Saxon England provided him with an occasion for

defining the responsibilities of statesmen and measuring the cost of
what they left undone. His political concerns, local and recent as they
were in origin, helped him to form a comprehensive and focussed
view of his subject; yet his faithful labor at the intricacies of legal
history helped him to establish his subject as something other than
the projection of a merely topical interest. Between the two aspects
of his medieval study, its topicality and its remoteness, he attained
intellectual liberation and professional authority: he learned to know
a world not his own. He had respect enough for the facts to let that
world stand in its own right, and at the same time he had personal
interest enough to make it imaginatively his. To paraphrase his own
comment on the use of learning languages, a second history doubles a
man. Whatever the limitations of political history, within those
limitations Adams mastered a field of learning that did not merely
broaden his view of his own society, but gave him a new perspective
altogether.

In his Harvard years, Adams made little effort to get beyond the
history of past politics. As a teacher of medieval history, he read
Ruskin and prepared lectures on Gothic architecture, but such excursions were few. When he had trained a successor to take over his
medieval courses, he himself turned to American Colonial history, a
field where he was apparently content to ask traditional questions.
One reason he could so easily settle for narrow limits was that cultural recognition scarcely required a conscious effort; ancestral ties
and tangible monuments provided all the topicality he needed.
When he noted, for example, that New England had produced men
who were intolerant even for their age, to reconstruct that age and
the local frame of mind did not require a great leap of historical
imagination. When Lodge succeeded him as the instructor of American Colonial history and produced his *Short History of the English
Colonies in America,* he dedicated the book to Adams; the acknowl-
edgment of debt implied a common, and traditional, definition of the
subject. Moreover, the close connection of Lodge's *Cabot* and
Adams' *Documents* indicates that the presentness of their grandfathers' political battles was a lively part of the two men's historical
interest. Indeed, Adams' last official act in his professorship was to
propose that Lodge also have a course in American history after 1789
so that, as he wrote to President Eliot, the rival views might serve "to
stimulate both instructors and students, and to counteract . . . the

inert atmosphere which now pervades the college." Having been as
aggressive as possible in presenting his proposal as a practical device
for teaching, he went on to suggest that it was also a device for
applied libertarianism: "His views being federalist and conservative,
have as good a right to expression in the college as mine which tend
to democracy and radicalism."[4] Within the limits of political history,
Adams had arrived at a conception of his discipline that was extremely modern in its relativism. Implying that, along with the
scientific establishment of the data, the values of the inquirer had
much to do with what the past seemed really to be like, Adams was
already transcending the assumptions of old-fashioned realism. In his
conception of historical knowledge, he responded to a philosophical
revolution that was in its earliest stage, even though, in his idea of
what facts a historian is concerned to deal with, his commitment to
politics appeared to be fixed.

Since, as Adams early observed, values condition any inquiry into
the past, it is important to note that he declared himself to be a
democrat and a radical. His affirmation deserves to be taken at face
value even though it is hard to fill out the meaning of the terms.
Since he did not always share the sentiments and ideas by which
American democrats or radicals are conventionally classified, his
statement of belief is often ignored or dismissed as insincere. He
never idolized those who labor in the earth or in the shop, he only
respected them as men. He never cherished a dream of the barri-
cades, for to him the revolutionary impulse (which he too sometimes
felt) was essentially anarchic. He seriously thought that in this
country democracy had once and for all taken possession of the
national government and that secession movements, after 1798, were
right-wing revolutions, antidemocratic and antilibertarian in nature.
These democratic and unionist convictions were the widely shared
convictions of his generation, a generation that fought to preserve the
national government in the trial of civil war. But as the historical
interpretation of the Civil War has undergone successive revisions
since then, the sense of democratic nationalism has become harder
and harder for later generations to recover. Without such a recovery,
however, we can understand neither Adams nor his age.

The great beliefs that carry nations through wars do not lead
quickly and clearly to practical programs for reorganizing society in
the aftermath of wars. So with Adams, his great beliefs came in the

postwar period to appear very much like the politics of respectability. Democracy, the Union, and the moral law came down in practice to a few rather prosaic articles of belief. Hard money, for example, once the common-sense economics of agrarian and popular movements, was in the post–Civil War years the policy of the financially conservative upper middle class. Although Populist-influenced students tend to view hard money as antiagrarian in intent, Republican bankers were following a path that Jacksonian planters had been over before them: they hoped that reason and morals and the "free" operation of the economy would bring under control the enormous industrial expansion which their policies were also abetting. Postwar capitalists, if they were to be judged by their official reasoning, were not very different from prewar planters. In both cases, the ideal of regulation—*without regulators*—bespoke a faith in the so-called normal market and an assumption that if only men would behave morally, which was to say naturally, they would have the best of all possible economies. Other parts of the early Adams program have become dated less than his fiscal policy but still, understandably, lacked wide appeal in his time. On the question of civil-servce reform, it is self-evident that the merit system would be less popular than the earlier shibboleth of rotation in office. Even though the administrative branch might claim to be much less corrupt than the legislative, still it was clear that the bureaucracy had to be rationalized, if only for the sake of getting a moderate efficiency. But the moralism of the reformers implied that one need only cure the symptoms of corruption in order to restore a normal, righteous order. The reform effort assumed an ideal republic under the Constitution, once attained, recoverable now, potentially stable if not absolutely unchanging, and it reasoned as if individual moral defect was the only cause of social change. Adams, by the 1890's, would radically change his political ideas to take other social forces into account, but in the 1870's and 1880's, when he was at work on his *History*, he was only beginning to find his way around the traditional American assumptions and his intellectual findings were not immediately converted into political terms. Yet he did support criticism of the classical economic case for limiting wages; and writing to a friend in England, he advised that raising wages and subdividing capital were a social and political necessity: "Your working-men, as a class, are still too poor."[5] But when he wrote thus, he seemed not to realize the implication of his own advice, namely, that in an industrial age equality is not providentially given—as it had been, evidently, in the American past—but has to be achieved by rational political effort. But even though he had not thought through all the implications, his instinct of statecraft stood him in good stead. His conception of political possibility, lively enough when he thought of British politics, logically contradicted the ideal of the unregulated market and kept him from ever accepting outright the norms of the Manchester economists. There was justice in his later claim that "he had never in his life taken politics for a pursuit of economy," and if, for a time, he accepted the passing of statecraft, he did not do so for the sake of an abstract market ideal. Rather, the position he took in his middle years was that in America the end of positive government had done what Jefferson said it would, namely, make possible the rise of a great democratic society. The social, not the economic, effects of negative government reconciled him to the facts of American political history.

The Jeffersonian faith that the less governed the better, although it was a dubious guide to political justice in the 1870's and 1880's, served Adams very well as an interpretive principle for early nineteenth-century history. It was possible, in other words, for the historian to function without first having solved all the current problems of the political theorist or the social scientist. Nevertheless, Adams' or any other historian's sense of his own age is crucial to his work; it balances his having a second past and keeps him a historian rather than an antiquarian. The response to one's own time may be in large part unstated. A reservoir of conviction is in fact better than a set of pat answers, since ideological neatness may keep a historian from learning anything that he cannot account for a priori. Sure solutions to present problems can be very well dispensed with, but a clear sense of the problems themselves cannot, for it is the urgent pressure of unsolved problems that leads to the search for a relevant past.

In this respect, Adams was fortunate that his professorship entailed his being editor of the North American Review. Thanks to his extraordinary energy, he managed, along with his regimen of study and research, to give the North American a last great period before the age of quarterlies finally waned. He not only knew but also helped elicit the best thought of his countrymen on the leading issues of the day; and in the interplay of editor and writers, some of his leading historical ideas took shape. The occasion of the national centennial in 1876 led him to his largest undertaking in contemporary history, for he decided to present a survey by experts of the nation's progress in science, political and economic thought, religion, law, and education. This survey of 1876 supplied him with questions that he would later put into his own surveys of 1800 and 1815 that begin and end his *History:* he could discern the trends of so short a span as fifteen years only because he looked forward to the present as well as looking back to a more distant past. And the findings of Simon Newcomb, William Graham Sumner, Daniel C. Gilman, and the rest concerning America's first century are interestingly close to Adams' findings about the American democracy's first decade and a half. Their collective report found that politics had decayed and was beset by corruption, but in the other fields a special kind of progress could be noted. Adams, if not his contributors, could see that the changes closely followed the pattern which Tocqueville had described a generation before. The higher arts and more theoretical areas of knowledge—science, theology, political economy—required the kind of sustained, disinterested, and costly effort that might be looked for in aristocratic societies; in America, they tended to fall into neglect. On the other hand, except in politics there were compensatory advances in the direction of practicality, mildness, and short-run benefit: technology rather than science, general morality rather than theological distinction, universal schooling not matched by progress in higher education. The experts who took part in Adams' survey were more effective, perhaps, when they criticized than when they praised, but the kinds of progress which they recorded were evidence of the rise of a great democracy.

Before the centennial year was over, Adams used the *North American* as the platform for both his farewell to politics and his profession of faith. In his caustic essay "The Independents in the Canvass," he scored off both parties and the reformers as well, denouncing corruption and ritual promises of mended ways, on the one side, and on the other, naïveté and ineffectuality. But his more important contribution to the October, 1876, number was a review of von Holst's *Constitutional and Political History of the United States.* Moving to the international scale restored his breadth of view: while closeness to politics at home could engender disgust, criticism from abroad roused his national feeling. Since the outside critic in this instance represented the highest Germanic scholarship, Adams' professional mettle was challenged along with his patriotic self-esteem. So the occasion prompted him to discover more than he might otherwise have done of the implications of his own beliefs. He found that, with all due respect for von Holst's strictness and learning, he had to suggest that there were limits to the intellectual usefulness of legalism and moralism and the demand for perfect logical consistency in men or institutions. Distinguishing between the judgments of a German professor and "those of a politician who is forced to act within the limitations of the possible," he disclosed a political flexibility in his own mind that was at odds with the moral rigidity of the would-be reformer. He advocated logical rigor as strongly as ever, but in putting his own professional judgments up against those of the foremost institutional historian in the field, he spoke up for the other kinds of perception which had to be practiced along with "microscopic analysis." The intangibles of national feeling and general forces had to be taken into account, he argued, and the fallacy of applying perfectionist criteria had to be understood. Against what he took to be the antidemocratic tenor of von Holst's argument, he counterattacked sharply:

One of the most bitter charges brought by Dr. v. Holst against the American political system is that it destroyed the idea of representation, and degraded representatives into mere mouth-pieces of their immediate constituents. And now he takes the broad ground that self-government is impossible because a majority of the legislature, influenced thereto by a few strong-willed men, did what he is violent against them for not habitually doing, that is, adopted a measure [the war declaration of 1812] without waiting for a mandate from their constituents. . . . From internal evidence it seems probable that the sentiment is intended solely for a German audience, and that its aim is to demonstrate that Prince v. Bismarck is essentially as good a representative of self-government as Washington and Madison.[6]

Adams expanded on what von Holst left out—the establishment of the Constitution and the emergence of the nation—until he recognized that he was writing a kind of "centennial oration" of his own.[7] The warm rhetoric of his review and the hammering ironies of his essay on the Independents defined the range of pride and indignation that he carried with him from his life as politician, editor, and professor to his labors as an historian during the next span of his life. Characteristically, his hammer was more noticed than his bellows: his

publishers did not like the anti-Republican remarks in "The Independents in the Canvass," and Adams felt obliged to resign from the
North American. He was evidently as glad to leave the editorship as
to give up trying to rally the now-dispersed reformers, and he was also
ready to quit Boston and Harvard, where he found too little genuine
intellectual friction to strike the sparks of originality. He expressed
his exasperation with the placidity of his academic life somewhat
more fully than he did his gravitation to Washington for its politics
and society and the professional ambition which he scarcely formulated even to himself. But with the chance to edit the Gallatin papers
and write the biography of Jefferson's great Secretary of the Treasury,
he made the break from teaching and moved back to the national
capital. He went this time as a committed historian, more detached
from politics and yet more deeply concerned with political questions
than he had ever been.

The *Life of Albert Gallatin*, with its three accompanying volumes
of his papers, was of a scope and detail beyond anything Adams had
touched before. The subject freed the biographer equally from the
academicism of Anglo-Saxon law and the provincialism of New England Federalist controversy. Gallatin's career in Congress, in the
Treasury, and in diplomatic service, based as it was on careful mastery
of the public business, led Adams into the exhaustive study of legislative, administrative, and diplomatic processes; and permitted him
to develop the kind of historical authority which can only be built
upon such study. Nothing less than presidential papers could have
been more important for leading the historian into the intricacies of
Jeffersonian democracy and early nineteenth-century American history; and before coming to them, it was worth while for Adams to
have the view from one step away and to formulate his main questions independently of the central figures whom he would examine
later. Gallatin's only limitation as a subject was his exemplary virtue,
which revived for Henry Adams some of the perfectionist longings
which he had exorcised in his review of von Holst. Gallatin proved to
be the one statesman of the era whose greatness never diminished
under scrutiny, the only one whom he admired without reservation
even when he knew all there was to know about him. His own
forebears John and John Quincy Adams came in for their share of his
stern judgments, but Gallatin consistently provided an ideal standard

of political behavior. Evidently the highest rational standards were attainable in this one instance, anyway, but so much the worse for that. The moral of the story, as Adams privately summed it up for Lodge, seemed to be the vanity of party politics. The ex-politician wrote to his highly political student: "The inevitable isolation and disillusionment of a really strong mind—one that combines force with elevation—is to me the romance and tragedy of statesmanship."[8] At the very moment when the historian's grasp of his subject was first opening out to its full scale, he was also the biographer who narrowed his focus to the individual and saw with unique clarity the fine shadowed lines of missed aims, lost zeal, and gathering weariness.

The tragic theme which Adams imputed to his biography of Gallatin is important if only because it contrasts with the rising action of his History, in which the emergence of American democracy sets an affirmative tone and the shortcomings of statesmen are treated satirically rather than pathetically. In part the difference is accounted for by the nature of the two works: in a biography, what a man seeks and fails to attain is lost with the finality of individual life; in a history, groups of men who do their work partially and are thrust aside are succeeded by others who do the same. Men are mortal, but politicians as a class go on forever. Beyond that, the idea of an emergent nation coming into its first youth is the very opposite of pathetic. The conception of social progress that Adams had in his History excluded a conception of tragedy such as he tried to build into his Gallatin, and conversely, the interpretation of events which lent itself to Adams' tragic view of the Gallatin had to be revised before he could write the History. This difference of argument arose, I would further argue, because Adams felt too close to Gallatin to perceive political meanings other than those which came out of the actual party conflicts. The political problem is set forth in his summary of where Republican controversialists of 1800 stood on the ultimate political issue: "The interests of the United States were too serious to be put to the hazard of war; government must be ruled by principles; to which the Federalists answered that government must be ruled by circumstances."[9] In the event, war was the great externally imposed limitation on Jeffersonian hopes and ideals, but this formulation from the Gallatin was too patly dualistic to cover all the elements of the case as Adams himself presented them. For he had previously said that, in the contest of principles, the very real battle

of the 1790's had been won by those who wished the new nation to
be ruled by the people themselves and had been lost by those who
were blind to the power of that principle in the public forum. And by
the end of the biography, Adams could observe that the democratic
ideal had won so complete a victory that "there was no longer any
essential disagreement among the people in regard to political dogmas."[10] In this fundamental respect, then, Adams ignored the
triumph of principle over circumstance in order to get to another
aspect of that ambiguously worded conflict in which the result was
just the reverse. With slightly altered emphasis, Adams could suggest
that the model society which the Jeffersonians sought to create was a
utopian illusion: "Mr. Gallatin, his eyes fixed on the country of his
adoption, and loathing the violence, the extravagance, and the corruption of Europe, clung with what in a less calm mind would seem
passionate vehemence to the ideal he had formed of a great and pure
society in the New World, which was to offer to the human race the
first example of man in his best condition, free from all the evils which
infected Europe, and intent only on his own improvement."[11] The
hope for a New World to contrast with the Old was generous,
humane, and in tune with the people's actual feelings, but the
keeping of peace—good in itself and necessary to popular economic
development—was not simply a matter of choosing goals and wishing
hard. Peace-keeping was also a practical problem. The means which
the Jeffersonians counted on, economic sanctions and diplomatic
manipulation of the balance of nations, were inadequate to the task,
for neither Napoleon nor Canning calculated national interest on the
basis of short-term trade advantages, and in any case trade—or even
peace—with the United States did not weigh decisively in the councils of the great powers. The belief that the world would follow
reason and interest and leave the United States in peace proved
untenable, and the Republicans had then to deal with the circumstances of international embroilment and actual war. Gallatin saw
that leadership had passed from the Treasury, where the chief
planning of domestic policy had been done, and in such a time, when
he could serve his country best in diplomacy, he was only too happy
to take on a new role. As the chief negotiator of the Treaty of Ghent,
he proved himself once more to be the main reliance of the Republican administration. After the war was over, however, he stayed in the
diplomatic service rather than re-enter the political arena: "Riper,
wiser, and infinitely more experienced than in 1800, Gallatin had still

lost qualities which, to a politician, were more important than either experience, wisdom, or maturity. He had outgrown the convictions which had made his strength. . . ."[12] What Gallatin had lost was the key to political success, "that sublime confidence in human nature which had given to Mr. Jefferson and his party their single irresistible claim to popular devotion."[13]

The *Gallatin* is a work of enduring scholarly value because Adams analyzed the governmental process so precisely and showed in such detail the impact of democratic policy and of foreign complications on American institutions in their formative years; but his interpretive confusions proved that it was not so easy for the historian to shift from microscopic to general views. Circumstance turned out to be stronger than principle, he argued, but he had not yet comprehended his own demonstration that principle was one of the circumstances which affected political events. He attributed to Gallatin more world-weariness and loss of conviction than the documentary evidence supported, thus disclosing his own perplexity about the relation of belief to action. He seemed unbelievably antirational in declaring Gallatin's mind to have been strongest when least experienced, unless he was deviously saying simply that men's energies decline as they get older. He also suggested, more believably, that Gallatin's improving mind had little to do with his deteriorating political position; when the Secretary of the Treasury, beset by faction, stepped aside as a political leader, Adams commented: "There are moments in politics when great results can be reached only by small men,—a maxim which, however paradoxical, may easily be verified. Especially in a democracy the people are apt to become impatient of rule, and will at times obstinately refuse to move at the call of a leader, when, if left to themselves, they will blunder through all obstacles, blindly enough, it is true, but effectually."[14] The unstated assumption that the nation could do what its government could not do would come to the surface in the argument of the *History,* but even in this early form it ambiguously suggested both an affirmation of national spirit and an admission of collective blindness. The ideas which Adams tried out on his material seemed often to lead to contradiction, and yet they had one thing in common. In one way or another, they all expressed a disenchantment with politics which he would have to learn to qualify before he could make his mastery of political history complete.

Democracy, the novel which Adams wrote for recreation while completing work on the *Gallatin*, confirms this sense of where Adams stood at the end of the 1870's. Behind its bright ironies and lively incidents, there is disenchantment—and a touch of pathos. The heroine, Madeleine Lee, widowed, lonely and restless, goes to Washington to see power at close range and is almost beguiled into marriage with the impressive but corrupt Senator Ratcliffe. When she discovers that she has almost, for motives she is shrewd enough to question, condoned what she judges to be morally insupportable, her revulsion makes her flee. She can conceive no middle ground between perfectionism and total corruption. Her recoil is, as Henry Aiken has suggested, that of the middle class abandoning politics to the politicians; and despite the presence in the novel of a historian who preaches faith in democracy as the ground for putting up with the defects of American government, there is room to question whether Adams saw his heroine's moral shock in historical perspective. In *Democracy* even more than in the *Gallatin*, there is an antipolitical sentiment that exceeds the rational implication of the materials presented. Adams could not yet claim the breadth of moral perspective which he had commended in the von Holst review.

Adams' departure for Europe in the spring of 1879 conveniently marks a new stage of his career. He had seen the *Gallatin* volumes through the press and sent the manuscript of his novel to Henry Holt for anonymous publication. Of these works, the former established Adams' unique scholarly authority in his field, and the latter gave proof that he had imaginative energy to spare. Manifestly, he was ready for a greater undertaking than anything he had yet done; and as he set about his search of European archives, he now mentioned a professional purpose that he had never before stated. To James Russell Lowell, who helped him get access to state papers in Madrid, he wrote: "I want to tell the whole truth, in regard to England, France, and Spain, in a 'History of the United States from 1801 to 1815,' which I have been for years collecting material for."[15] In thus announcing his long-nourished project, he was right to connect Europe with "the whole truth" as he conceived it. Simply in personal terms, his national consciousness came to complete expression only when challenged from abroad. He needed to respond to von Holst as well as to his fellow Independents, as it were: concerned with American affairs by themselves, he was always the stern analyst; when international comparisons were in question, he showed a warmer side. As a descendant of John Yankee, he had a natural affinity for the old American theme of the transatlantic contrast. But professionally even more than temperamentally, he needed to deal with Europe in order to get the whole truth. The enlargement of significant context was crucial: he arrived by his own path at Ranke's view that nation-states, while they might be the units of historical consideration, could be considered only as interrelated parts of general history. And on the scale of the general historian, he once more proved his authority. The transcripts he had made in 1879, now in the Library of Congress, have been so complete a resource for his successors in the field, that only in the last decade has research begun to frame questions which expand the range of scholarly relevance and lead to the gathering in of new evidence. In theoretical and technical as well as more or less unconscious ways, Adams' researches in Europe indicate the emergence of a master.

It was after conducting his exhaustive search of state papers and political documents that Adams began systematically to read through old newspapers and to study the various sources of social and cultural history. Whatever his convictions about the future of historical writing, he himself worked to transcend political history, not abandon it. With his intellectual powers asserting their control over more and more material, he thought about the Jeffersonian era in a different way. The passing of an age of politics, so that the time was out of joint for the Gallatin of his portrait (and for the heroine of his novel), no longer seemed a matter of pathos. The change Adams described was easier to accept when thought of as part of a larger movement, and the pattern as he now conceived it brought him once more to a view like that of Ranke. The great German historian believed that the beginning of the nineteenth century separated an epoch of dynastic conflict, in which the foreign policy of the leading states was the basic subject for historical study, and a modern age in which nations turned inward and fixed their primary energies on material growth, the development of science, constitutionalism, and popular struggles for power. In Adams' version, this shift in subject matter implied a necessary change in historiography, a new form of social history to go with the new content. Even more important, he gave a special American slant to the pattern, so that the theoretic contrast between the Old Regime and the modern era was reinforced by the spatial and cultural polarity of Europe and America.

While these general ideas were giving shape to the *History*, the minor works that came from Adams' hand, while not so clever or arresting as *Democracy*, showed his greater sureness of purpose. His broadly satirical biography of John Randolph (1882) hit its target so hard that the echoes of the impact can still be heard. His candor in paying off an old family score is almost disarming, as if the book were an exercise in raillery; but a tone of bitterness comes in when the story turns to what Adams regarded as the unnatural marriage of the states'-rights philosophy to the slavery interest. When, as on slavery, he could see an issue clear, Adams showed no inclination to be politically uncommitted. On the other hand, his second novel, *Esther*, published pseudonymously in 1884, showed that he could represent a world bigger than that which was bounded by politics and political disillusionment. The conflicts of science and religion, reason and emotion, which he built into his plot, bespoke an awareness of tragic losses and withal, a sense of how the spirit may accommodate to the nature of things. He himself had to accommodate, the next year, to the calamity of his wife's suicide, by which, as he said, half his life seemed cut away. For bearing that loss, one of his resources was the professional discipline he had cultivated so long and well. Though the élan had gone out of his life, he continued for almost five more years in the work he had begun, and despite his belief that his writing must show the ebb of spirit which he dated from that moment, he sustained his conception to the end. In 1889 he brought out the first two of his nine volumes; by the summer of 1890 he had seen to the last details of maps, indexes, and revision; before the last volumes were published in 1891, he had fled to the South Seas and begun the long struggle with the problem of who he was when he ceased to be a historian.

Composing his *History* at the height of his powers, Adams framed the conception he would hold to: he viewed his subject as fundamentally a rising action. In his mind, the emergence of the American nation was one and the same story as the taking shape of American democratic society. He argued, in effect, that before 1800, when there had been an active political culture, there had been neither an American nation nor an unquestionably established democracy. The other side of his argument was that after 1815 there was a nation and a democracy in America, but very little of politics in the old sense.

Between those dates occurred the passing of the reign of politics, of which he would be the chronicler. Since he wrote primarily as a political historian, the negative side of his ironic subject is what first meets the eye, not the rise of democratic nationality but the fall of statecraft. But the reader's difficulty, if it exists, is with form and not with content. Certainly Adams did not delimit the period of his narrative in order to be gloomy. On the contrary, had he extended his survey but a few years longer, he would have had to include the debate over the Missouri Compromise, that "firebell in the night" which startled a tranquil nation with its signal of disaster; but Adams regarded the Civil War as the *other* great story of nineteenth-century America, a story which he left to his friend John Hay, the biographer of Lincoln. Although the *History* contains evidence enough of Adams' antipathy to slavery and racism, there were few occasions when he needed to do more than touch upon those tragic themes. Irony, not tragedy, set the tone of his account. The decline of politics and the rise of democracy would have been a pessimistic subject from an eighteenth-century Tie-Wig point of view, but Adams was far from being a Federalist. He referred to eighteenth-century norms for satirical effect, but they were not the only political standards by which he invited his readers to judge the action. On the other hand, his affirmation of democratic nationality was for the most part indirect. Following his brother Charles' advice to "suppress the patriotic glow,"[16] he understated his favorable judgments and let the facts, subtly ordered, speak for themselves. But the principal irony, beyond his satire and his indirection, is at his own expense: anxious to write the history of a nation, he was trained—in what he thought was an outworn convention—to write the history of a state. His originality lay in accepting his limitations and thereby making the most of his talents. In his magnificent introductory chapters, he pointed the way to his successors as he used new methods and new materials, but in his main narrative, he narrowed his subject to the fate of politics during an era of emergent nationality.

How could social history turn into politics? Adams was able to modulate from one form to the other because he redefined the key term. Distinguishing between politics in the sense of statecraft and the political character which is deducible from the underlying economic and social institutions of a country, he gave his first attention to the more fundamental. At the very beginning of his work, he presented the economic and social conditions of 1800 and the irreducible question of physical survival. That the American people could hold together a continental nation despite enormous natural obstacles was, he argued, truly in doubt. There were no known means of maintaining communications, much less a social organization, over such distances. The accumulated experience of civilized man offered little help with this problem of space, and where the great powers of the Old World had made almost no progress, the Americans gave no sign that they would be capable of a new departure. Compared with the nation-empires of France and Britain, they certainly had no advantages in the power they could bring to the task. Yet a difference in "political arrangement" seemed to the Americans themselves to be revolutionary in its potential effect, and if the people thought so, then the social historian would be justified in exploring the idea. Adams instinctively adopted the principle of taking point of view into account, and he thereby established a basis for writing political history: if politics occupied the minds of the people, then political history was in this case popular intellectual history.

The popular point of view was by no means the only criterion for including data. Adams felt obliged to record both what people believed they were doing and what in fact they accomplished through their political effort; a discrepancy between intention and event might prove an irony at the expense of the people or their government or both. But such a discrepancy suggested that there were causes which shaped events but escaped the consciousness of the time, unknown forces beyond anyone's control that could affect the course of things in essential ways. The social and economic force which Adams had in mind this early was technology, but he was still very far from conceiving it as the occult mechanism which he later symbolized in the Dynamo. His symbols in the *History* were the steamboat, first of all, the factory elevator, the pivot gun, and the tall-masted sloop; and these were the symbols not of occult power but of human art. Moreover, the popular sense of democracy as a social force was confirmed paradoxically. Adams listed the spiritual successors of Benjamin Franklin—Eli Whitney, Oliver Evans, Robert Fulton, and others—and he made it clear that while the ordinary people seemed unaware of change, it was from their ranks that the agents of change came: "All these men were the outcome of typical American society, and all their inventions transmuted the democratic instinct into a practical and tangible shape. Who would undertake to say that there was a limit to the fecundity of this teeming source?"[17] Economic equality and social freedom were, for Adams, the essential characteristics of the American democracy as it confronted the physical challenge of mastering a continent. That the people should have thought of political, rather than economic and social, arrangement as accounting for their strength would prove wrong if the term referred to statecraft. For the ultimate historical test of physical survival, however, the historian confirmed the popular belief that democracy, in the sense of equality and freedom, made the difference between defeat and triumph.

Adams' own complex attitudes are woven into the fabric of the *History*. He managed at once to express the convictions of an American democrat and to study the limitations of American political democracy, and his personal commitment did not temper his rigor. But the author's views must be distinguished from those of his characters. Jefferson's opponents, useful because they registered his every inconsistency or ineptitude in the strong clear language of interested observers, do not speak for the historian himself. Their pungent criticism, right by the canons of logic and strict morality, was often wrong in a broader sense, for the trouble with Federalist opinion in general and New England judgments in particular was a tendency toward doctrinaire rigidity. Those so-called practical men understood the world's experience too well to believe that it could change. Refusing to share Jefferson's "illusions" about the nature of man and the possibilities of society, they also could not see that Jefferson spoke for the beliefs and hopes of most of his countrymen. Given the blindness of contemporary observers, the historian had to make explicit his own insight. He concluded his magnificent introductory survey of the social and intellectual scene in 1800 with a chapter on "American Ideals," which is crucial for all that follows. The chapter shows his imaginative penetration of the substance of things hoped for by the Jeffersonians, and it further shows his commitment to the proposition that beliefs can affect the course of events. Insofar as he argued that what was in men's minds could make a difference in their destiny, he freed himself as never before from the imputation of simple materialistic determinism. His historical practice was thus committed to an articulate and self-conscious version of the faith that had motivated the American democrat of

1800. Writing of that hypothetical representative man, Adams declared that "his dream was his whole existence" and that his enemies, instead of sneering at the hard money-getting American of their caricature for his materialism, should have noticed that, even on his sordid side, he was, rather, the "victim of illusion":[18]

The men who denounced him admitted that they left him in his forest-swamp quaking with fever, but clinging in the delirium of death to the illusions of his dazzled brain. No class of men could be required to support their convictions with a steadier faith, or pay more devotedly with their persons for the mistakes of their judgment. Whether imagination or greed led them to describe more than actually existed, they still saw no more than any inventor or discoverer must have seen in order to give him the energy of success.[19]

In his own version of the "will to believe," Adams linked the ordinary citizen and his American dream with the "visionary" inventor who reversed the meaning of practicality by seeing more in his world than experience-so-far could attest. Indeed, he went on to suggest that Emerson in his field, Robert Fulton in his, and Jefferson in the area of politics all represented the same visionary aspect of the national character. If "down to the close of the eighteenth century no change had occurred in the world which warranted practical men in assuming that great changes were to come,"[20] then the energizing faith of the Americans proved to be a historical fact of the greatest importance.

The American faith of 1800 was to be tried by the political experiment: could ordinary men, left in peace to pursue their own interests, make a free nation out of the virtually unorganized, geographically overextended, technically unequipped republic? Freedom, for the Jeffersonians who were assuming office, virtually came down to the one great objective of leaving men alone. In domestic politics, this meant the removal of those vested powers and artificial restraints by which government had inhibited the enterprise of private individuals. In reducing the activity of government, however, they neglected to cut its legal powers, and most notably, given their professed fear of monarchism, they did nothing to limit the executive authority which a President might exercise. In foreign policy, Jeffersonianism meant a single-minded pursuit of peace. The peace policy extended the principle of negative freedom, being left alone, to the international scene, but it was especially cherished because of its implications for domestic policy: a military and naval establishment would be a costly burden and an artificial class interest imposed on the free development of society. Through the intricate chronicle of the many activities of the Jefferson and Madison administrations, Adams traced the working out of this American experiment. He took careful account of the centrifugal pressures of American society and of the actual danger from the clashing imperial forces of the Napoleonic era, and he showed how often the Jeffersonians defied logic, experience, and common sense in their sanguine hopes for national security without governmental effort. His ironical argument seemed to be that, despite multiplied errors of judgment and act, the confidence was justified by the event. But even though the experiment was on the whole a success, the lesson was ambiguous. Adams bore witness to the historic efficacy of the Jeffersonian faith, but he offered little encouragement for anyone to expect future survival on a basis of faith alone.

The Jeffersonian intent could be summed up in a sentence: "Congress and the Executive appeared disposed to act as a machine for recording events, without guiding and controlling them."[21] But the first important action of the *History* pointed in just the opposite direction. The Louisiana Purchase, in Adams' view, had an importance for American history comparable only to that of the Declaration and the Constitution. In seizing the opportunity to buy Louisiana from France, Jefferson acted on the assumed existence of sovereign powers, and he implicitly gave up the idea of restricting government to the expressly delegated powers of the Constitution. Not only constitutionally, but geographically and socially too, his act put an end to any real hope of establishing a limited federal state on the model he had set forth in the 1790's. By 1803, barely two years after his coming to office, the experiment in minimal government and social decentralization was over, logically speaking. Moreover, Jefferson and Gallatin seemed to perceive the direction society might then take, for as soon as cost cutting and tax cutting had the effect of bringing increased revenues to the Treasury, they proposed to expand governmental activity. Not that they reverted, in their swing back to positive government, to a policy of military and naval build-up: they proposed national sponsorship of economic and educational improvements, namely, a national road and canal system and a national university. The proposals of 1806 and 1808 were never realized, because of legislative and popular indifference as well as increasingly complicated foreign relations; that is, in an interpretation of the event that Adams had revised since writing the *Gallatin,* the trouble lay not only with the harsh circumstances of world affairs, but also with the persistence of outworn ideas among Jefferson's fellow democrats in Congress and out. The nation generally remained firm in the ideology of 1800, even though Jefferson proved that a politician could have more important qualities than consistency, such as the capacity to learn and grow.

But the circumstances which outran plans and foresight did not always offer an opportunity for growth, and Jefferson did not consistently grow. His early success led him into circumstances which were far more equivocal. When American expansionism turned toward Florida, Spain would not sell. Claiming that West Florida had been included in the Louisiana Purchase, the Americans argued a fictitious point that could only be made good by armed intervention. Intending to bluff but not to fight, they found themselves embroiled in the diplomatic conflicts of Europe, where negotiations were habitually backed by force. While Jefferson spoke of "the effect which the strong language toward Spain was meant to produce in the Tuileries,"[22] Talleyrand spoke of the attention he expected the American government to give to "the events of the last campaign."[23] The contrast was heightened by the crossing rhythms of the narrative: while Jefferson moved with incredible slowness to put down the Burr conspiracy, Napoleon disposed the armies of France with speed that was equally remarkable and, between his overpowering campaigns against Prussia and Austria, found time to issue the Berlin Decree and assert absolute control over foreign commerce with Europe. Jefferson also had to deal with British blockades and impressment of seamen off American ships, and Orders in Council which virtually asserted absolute control over foreign commerce at sea. On the domestic front, meanwhile, the breakup of his congressional support into Old Republicans (defenders of the states'-rights principles of 1798) and New left him without legislative managers—and often without legislative support—for his administration. The historical challenge, it thus turned out, was not whether he could enact his vision of positive government, but whether he could "save the country from faction at home and violence abroad."[24]

The problem of survival had been recast as a problem in politics, but Adams invited the reader to consider whether politics was of prime importance. Although the state was threatened with collapse or destruction, society in every other respect seemed healthy. Apparently the people might succeed where their political leaders failed. Engrossed as they were with their daily tasks, they moved unconsciously toward the great goal of converting American society into something new: in Ranke's terms, the historical phases shifted from the primacy of foreign policy to material development; in Herbert Spencer's sociology, man was advancing at last from the military to the industrial stage of civilization; in Adams' own language, the practice of statesmanship was becoming less important than the evolution of democracy. The Burr conspiracy, in his view, was defeated by the same public indifference that caused the Jeffersonian program of internal improvements to languish and expire. Moreover, nonpolitical history, like political history, could be something more than a negative force. The experiments of Fulton, followed step by step, marked the approaching time when the Western territories would be brought within reach of the coastal settlements, and the problem of holding the vast country together would be solved. Also, the strength that internal development would draw from the steamboat might prove to be the nation's best ultimate defense. The difference between social history and political was pointed up by Adams, as he juxtaposed the humiliating *Chesapeake-Leopard* encounter and Fulton's first public demonstration with the *Clermont*. The *Chesapeake*, forced to strike its colors under fire and yield four seamen to the British boarding party, took the center of public attention, but the historian suggested that had the *Clermont* been noticed and its significance appreciated, the public might well have ignored the British attack. It was ironic that men sought political solutions to political problems, but the spell of the past still held men's minds.

But Adams' comment—"The reign of politics showed no sign of ending"[25]—had another meaning, whether he fully intended it or not. He went on writing political history not only to be ironic or because he was the prisoner of his professional technique. Rather, he recognized that long-range prospects and underlying causes do not free men or nations from the necessity of dealing with an immediate challenge. He was never so beguiled by the idea of social evolution as to think that eventual progress would make up for actual catastrophe. Napoleon and Canning might be scornfully regarded as medieval and barbarous, but so long as Americans must live in the same world with them, the historian must assert the primacy of foreign policy. Perhaps the most remarkable thing about the *History* is that it is a study of middle-class pacifism and American isolationism written at just that time when the peace of Europe seemed most assuredly to be organized as economic competition and when the internal development of the United States seemed most remote from foreign entanglements. Looking back to the Napoleonic era from the 1880's, Adams learned from historical study to ask disturbing questions before actual events forced them on more complacent minds.

Jeffersonian foreign policy was founded on the same basic premise as domestic, namely, that letting people or nations pursue their own concerns in peace is not only the most desirable but also the most efficacious course. The United States asked nothing except to be let alone, and if other governments were not enlightened enough to do so, then the natural operation of the free market could be counted on to bring them into line. The waste and destructiveness of war were avoidable when the means of peaceable coercion were at hand for the control of possible aggressors. In a sentence which Adams thought important enough to quote twice over, Jefferson declared: "Our commerce is so valuable to them, that they will be glad to purchase it, when the only price we ask is to do us justice."[26] When, by 1807, both England and France made it impossible to hope that foreign commerce could be protected by the automatic operation of interest, the embargo transformed the policy of negative government into its opposite. Collectors of customs, governors, and court officials could not enforce the law without troops and vessels actually patrolling the coastwise trade and the avenues to Canada. States' rights and decentralized government were contradicted more directly than in the matter of the Louisiana Purchase, and this time the ideal of statelessness was contradicted on a consistent, daily basis. Measuring the costs of peaceable coercion as against war, Adams found that "personal liberties and rights of property were more directly curtailed in the United States by embargo than in Great Britain by centuries of almost continuous foreign war."[27] The constitutional cost was matched by an economic one which could be figured with respect to government revenue and the reversal of capital expansion, but Adams regarded the moral cost as greater still:

If war made men brutal, at least it made them strong; it called out the qualities best fitted to survive in the struggle for existence. To risk life for one's country was no mean act even when done for selfish motives; and to die that others might more happily live was the highest act of self-sacrifice to be reached by man. War, with all its horrors, could purify as well as debase; it dealt with high motives and vast interests; taught courage, discipline, and stern sense of duty. Jefferson must have asked himself in vain what lessons of heroism or duty were taught by his system of peaceable coercion, which turned every citizen into an enemy of the laws,—preaching the fear of war and of self-sacrifice, making many smugglers and traitors, but not a single hero.[28]

Finally, there were the political costs: at home, each major sectional interest was alienated from Jefferson's administration, and abroad the United States lost the chance to stand at the head of the popular movement which even then was beginning to rise against Napoleonic tyranny. Though Adams conceded that the mild pressure of economic sanctions might work if applied much longer than military force, he did not sympathize with Jefferson's reluctance to see the embargo lifted. Believing that the "experiment" in peaceable coercion had been worth trying, he also believed that it had failed.[29]

The meaning of the failure was war. American pacifism and isolation proved untenable, and the American people must no longer shun "the common burdens of humanity" or hope to evade "laws of Nature."[30] But nothing could hurry the event: the Madison administration seemed to drift toward collapse, and only the arrival of a new generation in Congress restored energy to government. When war finally came, Adams treated Madison's hope that it would create a strong national spirit to back the government as a parody of Hamilton's militaristic philosophy. But only a parody. Given the mediocrity of political leadership, Adams once more argued that the people took over the functions of saving the state: "Not so much the glories as the disgraces of the war roused public sympathy; not so much the love of victory as the ignominy of defeat, and the grinding necessity of supporting government at any cost of private judgment. . . . The slow conviction that come what would the nation must be preserved, brought one man after another into support of the war, until the Federalists found their feet in quicksand. The 'crisis' produced the opposite effect to that which Burke's philosophy predicted."[31] Tracing the conduct of the war in detail, the historian did have victories as well as defeats to relate, but the one general triumph he claimed was that of the people rising to the ultimate challenge. Under analysis, that triumph was due to such national traits as adaptability and quickness, that is, capacity for organizing and deploying their force as needed and speed in mastering the technology of war, whether with such old weapons as artillery and ships of the line or such new inventions as the pivot gun and the fast schooner. The demonstration of national character through military history is, as I have argued elsewhere, one of Adams' great technical feats; but he did not stop with social history even when he found such a device for presenting it. The people triumphed also by producing the men who were needed, such generals as Jacob Brown and Andrew Jackson, such diplomats as William Pinkney and Albert Gallatin. In generalship and diplomacy he found the last irreducible areas of statecraft, in which the individual still counted. At the very moment when he was clinching his argument that national character, primarily formed by social democracy and an industrial bent, accounted for national survival, he also asserted the older belief that the individual handling of power made a real difference in how events came out.

Adams was not contradicting himself. Rather, he was finding the point at which historians, like politicians, must accommodate their principles to circumstance. Just as events tended to outrun ideologies, historical evidence tended to outrun historical preconceptions. Hence Adams' contrast between the lawyer's argument and the historian's: "The lawyer is required to give facts the mould of a theory; the historian need only state facts in their sequence."[32] In his rigorous commitment to describing how things really happened, he disproved a good many theories, both Federalist and Republican, and left few standing without need of qualification. His own conception that social forces were the determinants of social events he found qualified by the "element of individuality," which he regarded as the "free-will dogma" of historians.[33] It was only a modest qualification, to be sure, for what he mostly showed was how limited was the freedom of action which a diplomat might have. But given the pressure of long-term causes, the momentum of past actions, and the tangle of recent negotiations, there was always room for a new departure. When President Madison was ready for a more positive stand, Pinkney in London brought issues to a head by exerting his initiative within the narrow limits set by his instructions from Washington and the situation at hand. When the nation urgently needed peace, Gallatin at Ghent gradually assumed leadership of the American delegation, harmonizing sectional claims and dissuading his colleagues from untenable demands until the Americans and the British could agree on terms of armistice. It was an inconclusive treaty, but "in referring all their disputes to be settled by time, the final negotiator, whose decision they could safely trust,"[34] the American mission returned the major issues from the political arenas of war and diplomacy to the impersonal working out of social evolution. The interest of the negotiation lay in the fact that the more precisely Adams defined the restrictions that bound his diplomatic figures, the more surely he demonstrated the power to act which remained to them within the art of the possible. As he had commented on a William James proof of free will, it seemed "a very microscopic quantity": "Although your gift to the church seems to me a pretty darned mean one, I admire very much your manner of giving it, which magnifies the crumb into at least forty loaves and fishes."[35] He too magnified the crumb and thereby made the free-will element of the *History* the center of interest. And the interest was not simply metaphysical. His major underlying thesis took a political form: when men do not exert their conscious wills, they are not left alone but caught in the natural drift toward violence; in a world where war is the historic condition which societies have had to undergo, peace does not come with wishing but has to be made. This is the work of "practical politics." It lacks the grandeur or assurance of the old-style moral statesmanship, "being commonly an affair of compromise and relative truth," but it is "a human attempt to modify the severity of Nature's processes."[36]

Adams considered that, once the Treaty of Ghent was signed, America was free to direct its full energies inward to the development of the continent. The historian's mind turned inward, too, and he concluded as rapidly as he could with a survey of the economic, intellectual, and social situation of 1815 and the direction which the evolution of American society had seemed to take. For him, the nature of American democracy and its survival were settled, the last phase of dramatic—that is, dramatizable—history had passed, and the future belonged to demography and econometrics as far ahead as he could see. Though he still had questions to raise about a nation that had taken shape as intelligent and quick, mild and peaceable, he tried to convey a sense of evolutionary fixity in his closing chapters. But the facts which he had so strenuously labored to set in order did not fit the mold of a theory. Even as he turned his back on political history, he taught more lessons about its possible usefulness than he himself altogether fathomed.

More than ten years' sustained concentration on the *History* left Adams exhausted, and his own personal disaster left him cut off from much of the active life he once had relished. As he went into virtual retirement, his professional activity was reduced to the scale of gesture. His presidential message to the American Historical Association in 1894 (not delivered in person, but sent as a letter from Mexico) and his article on "Count Edward de Crillon" for the first issue of the *American Historical Review* in 1895 suggested between them that his generalizing and his empirical faculties had somehow shrunk apart. Thinking that the profession had been too long regarded as safe and harmless, he spoke up for the "four out of five serious students of history" who had felt the ambition to reduce their subject to the working out of scientific laws, and he ambiguously encouraged the young to move into a realm of ideas where their work would be at once dangerous and responsible.[37] On the other hand, in offering a minor correction of the *History,* he expressed concern that "at the most moderate estimate the historian can hardly expect that four out of five of his statements of fact shall be exact."[38] He managed to affirm both meanings of scientific history—interchangeable generalization and factual accuracy—and at the same time to cast doubt on the attainability of either.

But the silence to which he then pledged himself was not to last. He had ahead of him the remarkable second career that produced *Mont-Saint-Michel and Chartres* (1904) and the *Education* (1907), books that made history his very personal subject. In these works, history *as it had been felt* meant as it had been felt by him, and yet each depended on the author's impressions being founded on a prior professional mastery of his subject. The *Chartres* could make its unique contribution to medieval cultural history only because Adams had previously learned with such pains the way in which illusion may be a social force: "Illusion for illusion, courteous love, in Thibaut's hands, or in the hands of Dante and Petrarch, was as substantial as any other convention;—the balance of trade, the rights of man, or the Athanasian Creed."[39] And the late R. P. Blackmur read a political moral in Adams' treatment of the medieval church; the catholicity with which the church accommodated those forms of devotion that seemed to exceed the bounds of orthodox theology thus appeared as "The Harmony of True Liberalism." The *Education* also, though its form must be described as something quite other than history, deals with historical subject matter and develops motifs from Adams' earlier work.[40] Inviting "active-minded young men" to attend to the problem of how to control power, the book suggests that neither teacher nor student will turn out to be a "Gargantua-Napoleon-Bismarck."[41] Yet there is a new urgency in the relation between the two. As the autobiographical protagonist of the narrative assumes the identity of the "historian," he moves upon an international scene that is radically changed from the placid 1880's: in time of peace he had insisted on mankind's common destiny of having to deal with war; now acutely conscious that man had entered a century of total war and potential global catastrophe, he sought the clue to running order through chaos. As a historian, his duty was to set his own experience in order even though, in the nature of things, his Dynamic Theory was more useful as a model of inventiveness than as a mold to contain the whirl of facts and forces. As a teacher, his duty was to teach the intelligent mind how to react, and his hope was that the effort of the historian would be matched, in political man, by the effort to make peace.

Frederick Jackson Turner

HOWARD R. LAMAR

3)

ANYONE WHO KNEW Frederick Jackson Turner found it impossible to dislike him. By all accounts he was the most honorable, approachable, and charming of men. His warm manner and vibrant voice conveyed the idea that teaching was a great pleasure and historical research was an exciting voyage of discovery. Open-minded, humorous, and full of flashing insights, he inspired and released students as much as he trained them. Turner demonstrated the importance of being eager, Ulrich B. Phillips recalled.[1] This characteristic, combined with a photographic sensitivity to everything he saw, experienced, or read, made him seem a charismatic, uninhibited scholar-historian.

Yet Frederick Jackson Turner's reputation as a "great interpreter" of American history is not based on his scholarly breadth and range, but squarely on the fame of his "frontier hypothesis," which he delineated in a paper read before the American Historical Association in 1893. Entitling his address "The Significance of the Frontier in American History," he told his fellow historians that American democracy and the American character were products of a wilderness or frontier experience operating in conjunction with "the existence of an area of free land, its continuous recession, and the advance of American settlement westward" over a period of some two hundred years.[2]

On this single occasion Turner suggested that American democracy was native-born; he introduced the environmental and economic element of "free land" as a major determinant in American history;

he defined the American character as innovative and ruggedly individualistic; and he made the "frontier" or "West" a causal factor which either affected or determined most of the major events and national legislation in American history. He went on to modify the traditional meaning of the word "frontier" as a national border to mean a sparsely populated region which was undeveloped, and he suggested that with the disappearance of such a frontier in America in 1890 the country had come to a major turning point in its history.

Today the frontier thesis, with its stress on environmental determinism, is no longer considered an adequate or an accurate explanation of the American past, and for more than forty years scholars have labored to reject, modify, correct, or delimit the concept. To dismiss Turner because of the inadequacies of his thesis, however, is to miss the point. The frontier theory proved to be so provocative and influential, and Turner himself performed such a variety of roles as a major historian between 1893 and his death in 1932, it is impossible to treat historical writing during that time without making him a central figure in the discussion.

Charles A. Beard, who was certainly no advocate of the Turner thesis, saw him as a founding father of the profession. "It was Mr. Turner who led in putting history on a scientific plane. Besides this, he is a scholar of fine talents and unwearying industry. His stamp is deep and indelible on historical writing in America."[3]

That stamp has been identified on an amazing number of things. He has been called a pioneer social historian and the father of a "multiple hypothesis" theory of history, and, to Richard T. Ely, he was a good economist. Even Beard praised him for restoring "economic facts to historical writing in America." Howard Odum called Turner a "master" of social science in 1927, and the latest generation of social scientists and quantifiers have renewed the accolade, for they feel he used methods and approaches in studying voting behavior that resembled their own. Merle Curti, one of Turner's last students, asserts that Turner anticipated the ideas and methods James Harvey Robinson advocated in his *The New History* by some twenty years.[4]

In the last twelve years of his life Turner formulated a theory concerning the role of sections in American history, which still shapes the framework of most college history courses that treat the coming of the Civil War.

The list of credits does not stop there. Critics have argued that

New Dealers were so depressed by Turner's relating democracy and economic well-being to the existence of free land and by the fact that free land had gone that they turned in desperation to collectivism and projects like the WPA in an effort to create a substitute "safety valve." The frontier thesis became, in short, an idée-force which determined national policy.[5] Certainly the almost worshipful praise of Turner and his teachings since his death suggests that a "cult" has been formed by his followers.

It is not my purpose here to review once again the pros and cons of the Turner frontier hypothesis, for several superb critiques and historiographical essays are easily available for students who wish to know its history.[6] Rather one should turn to his concept of history, to what he was trying to do as a "great interpreter," and note the degree of success or failure of his efforts. And finally I wish to assess Turner's findings in the light of my own studies of certain specific American frontiers.

To a singular degree Turner's essay "The Significance of the Frontier in American History" was the product of a highly personal search for meaning in history. One suspects he was a great teacher partly because he managed to communicate an exciting sense of significant discovery and understanding over and above an intelligent rendering of the facts. "I sometimes wonder if after all I have not been simply, rather blindly, trying to explain America to myself instead of writing history," he confided to Carl L. Becker. And then he added, "No, there is no science of history."[7]

Turner's statement was revealing in many ways. Clearly his approach to the past was empirical, relativistic, and pragmatic. In an essay, "The Significance of History," written in 1891, he said that each generation had to reinterpret the past to fit its own needs.[8] Things palpable, real, and present overwhelmed Turner so that he always saw history in terms of current events. Somewhat like Tennyson's *Ulysses*, which Turner was fond of quoting, he felt that he, too, was the product of all that he had seen. Turner was, then, a student of his own society and, perhaps more than would be the case with other historians, we must look at the environmental, emotional, and intellectual elements that went into Turner's make-up.

Turner was born on November 14, 1861, in Portage, Wisconsin, where his father, Andrew Jackson Turner, ran the local newspaper.

Portage had recently gone through the frontier stage, and the sensitive young Turner could still see evidences of the Indian and fur-trapping days around him. During his youth the rougher farmlands were passing from the hands of small squatters and subsistence farmers into the possession of commercial farmers and recently arrived German immigrants. Portage itself was a miniature melting pot, for one-third of its population was foreign-born.[9]

Andrew Turner appears to have been an observant, firm, historically minded man whom "Fritz"—the family nickname for young Turner—greatly admired. Turner senior was a booster who praised Portage's accomplishments. Turner dedicated his *Rise of the New West* to Andrew and wrote as well: "The midwestern country editor was a leader of his people, not just a patent-insides recorder of social functions but a vigorous and independent thinker and writer." The description fitted the father, for he had abandoned the Democracy to join the party of Union before the outbreak of the Civil War and had become prominent in Republican state politics. Andrew also dabbled in political history and late in life published articles in which he claimed that Portage and not Ripon was the true birthplace of the Republican party. It is instructive to find in his account that a cousin, one Aaron Turner, was praised for being a party founder.[10]

Although Turner was to become a Democrat later in life, the Republican party was not just a party in Turner's youth, it was Wisconsin's party. It had saved the Union in 1861 and was still engaged in the reconstruction of the South during most of his boyhood. Turner himself never forgot this, nor did he ever fail to mention in his essays that national leaders like Harrison, Lincoln, Grant, Sherman, Garfield, and Chase had sprung from the soil of the Old Northwest. Both father and son felt they were part and parcel of "real America."

Writers have made much of Turner's formative years in Portage. He later told Constance Lindsay Skinner that they had shaped his ideas about the frontier, and it is true that Turner responded to the wilderness with an enthusiasm similar to Parkman's. His happiest moments came when he was hiking, canoeing, fishing, or enjoying a pipe and good talk with companions around a campfire. Still it would probably be more accurate to say he was equally affected by the atmosphere of a progress-oriented, middle-class, Midwestern town in which his family's own New England–New York cultural tradition was being reinforced by the presence of a rising "genteel tradition." Since Turner believed societies evolved in similar ways, Portage was "every town"; Portage and Wisconsin were America, and, given the proper analysis, their history might be the history of people everywhere.[11]

Meanwhile for the first time in a hundred other Midwestern communities talented young men and women had the chance to go to college and professional schools. The more original and imaginative ones absorbed what was taught with an incalculable zest and, fascinated by the horizons of a wider intellectual world, they flowered as writers, leaders, and scholars. During Turner's youth, William Dean Howells had already become a kind of regional hero, and scores of would-be writers and critics were heeding his advice to be introspective about their own experiences. The products in Turner's own generation and in fields that interested him were impressive: James Harvey Robinson and Lester Frank Ward hailed from Illinois; Charles A. Beard and John R. Commons were from Indiana; and Carl L. Becker was from Iowa. In Turner's own state Thorstein Veblen, Robert M. LaFollette, and Charles Richard Van Hise came out of a pioneer rural environment to achieve national prominence.[12] To ignore Turner in this social context is to miss part of the meaning of his frontier essay.

This dual awareness of one's own section and expanding horizons was not confined to future scholars. Throughout Turner's youth Wisconsin, Illinois, Minnesota, and Iowa had been centers of Granger, Greenback, and Farmers' Alliance movements. Protesting what Lee Benson has called the great economic depression brought on by a world communications revolution, they, too, were claiming to be the backbone of the nation, and they protested the economic hardship caused by high railroad charges, depressed grain prices, and scarce credit. This group had also produced its publicists, who ranged in variety from Henry George to Ignatius Donnelly. Some fifteen years before Turner stated his free-land thesis, George had said virtually the same thing in *Progress and Poverty*.[13] Young Turner grew up in an area that took pride in burgeoning physical and cultural accomplishments, possessed a keen sense of patriotic purpose, and had a vivid awareness of economic dislocation.

Turner entered the University of Wisconsin in 1880 just as it, too, was beginning to flourish. President John Bascom instilled in both

Turner and Robert M. LaFollette the idea that a university should serve the state, so much so that some writers feel Bascom laid the foundations for the "Wisconsin idea" during these years.[14] In this healthy atmosphere of growth and change Turner encountered a remarkable teacher in William Francis Allen, a medievalist who, as one authority has put it, was a true renaissance man in his range of learning and talents. Although he was trained at Jena by Arnold Hereen and was an institutional historian, Allen taught the history of the origins of institutions as a history of society. From Allen's superb lecture notes one can surmise that Turner absorbed a flowing sense of the origins and evolution of man from primitive society onward to the immediate present. Allen discussed everything: the evolution of families into tribes, the growth of parliaments, ancient history, and the evolution of law and religion.[15] He taught, and Turner learned, in an age fascinated by Darwin, Spencer, and their proponents, and it seems reasonable to believe Allen made Turner a social evolutionist in outlook. Allen also wrote about community life, and one of his essays, "The Place of the Northwest in American History," may have laid the basis for Turner's interest in the frontier.[16]

Later Turner stated that Allen had taught him everything he had learned. One can certainly see the impact of Allen's teaching when we find young Turner writing in his "Commonplace Book": "Investigate land holding peasantry about Madison . . . just as one would the remains of ancient land systems."[17] When land seemed to transform peasant Germans into nonpeasant Americans, it was but a step to make "free land" a causal factor in American history.

After Turner graduated from Wisconsin in 1884 he spent a year working as a reporter, but a career of journalism proved unattractive and he returned to the University to take up graduate work. Once more guided by Allen, he became familiar with the Lyman C. Draper Collection in the Wisconsin State Historical Society and befriended its vigorous young director, Reuben Gold Thwaites. Although Turner's training had been in medieval and ancient history, he wrote a master's essay on the character and influence of the fur trade in Wisconsin in which he predictably used an institutional and an evolutionary approach.[18]

From the beginning it was apparent that a university career awaited the handsome, intelligent, sensitive young man from Portage. After a first appointment as an instructor in English and Rhetoric in

1885, he went into history. Turner was then persuaded by his wiser mentors to go to The Johns Hopkins University to get his doctorate, although at the time he seems to have thought further training was unnecessary.

The story of Turner's hostile reactions to the institutional and "germ theory" approaches to history then in vogue at Johns Hopkins has been greatly exaggerated. Turner later told William E. Dodd he had resented Herbert Baxter Adams' statement that American history had been "mined out" so that one had to study the European origins of American institutions instead.[19] It is true that Turner was in fundamental disagreement with Adams on this point, and he spent his whole life proving Adams to be wrong. Still Turner learned much at the university during his brief stay there (1888–1889). Here was the first major German-style graduate school in America, and both its teachers and its students were bright, aggressive, self-conscious system- and discipline-building young men. Four of Turner's teachers, Adams, Albion W. Small, Richard T. Ely, and Woodrow Wilson, were founding fathers in the modern American disciplines of history, sociology, economics, and political science respectively.[20]

Turner was to echo his teachers and the Hopkins interdisciplinary approach for the rest of his life. Ely introduced him to John Stuart Mill and the Manchesterians with the result that Turner has been called a Manchesterian in outlook.[21] Ely later taught Turner how to use maps and handle statistics. Turner himself insisted that he was a student of society more in the sociological sense than in the historical sense.

The ideas he shared with his young teacher, Woodrow Wilson, were many. Out of their conversations came Turner's conviction that New England and the South, by having taken extreme positions on slavery, states' rights, and abolition before the Civil War, had read themselves out of the mainstream of American history. The next deduction was obvious: the Middle West had remained at the center. Forty years later, Frederick Logan Paxson, Turner's ardent admirer and successor at Wisconsin, was to echo this view when he exclaimed that the South went wrong and ruined the American story while the East went wrong by going industrial and Anglophile. But, said he, "the West stayed West."[22]

Having cleared the way for a Midwestern interpretation of American history, Turner and Wilson also laid the foundations for a sectional approach, which had overtones of a regional "status revolution" concept as well. Turner further concluded that slavery was an incidental rather than a fundamental issue in American history. Slavery to him had been greatly overstressed by abolitionists and such didactic historians as Hermann von Holst.[23]

Rather early in his career Turner had eliminated a great deal from the forefront of American history: the European origins, New England and the South in the late nineteenth century, slavery and the Negro, moral interpretations, the great-man approach, and Edward A. Freeman's dictum that history was "past politics." While Turner's outlook seems narrow and provincial on the surface, he made amends for the excisions by saying he was interested "in the interrelations of economics, politics, sociology, culture in general, with the geographic factor, in explaining the United States of today."[24] Claiming to be a social historian he looked for change in the mass of the people, he spoke of types, and he sought meaning in voting behavior and regional history rather than in the acts of government. Turner's attempts to be objective, his disdain for the moral issues involved in the coming of the Civil War, his later questioning of the inevitability of that war, and his emphasis on process seem to place him in the ranks of the social scientists and to make him an early "revisionist" historian as well.

Still Turner did not really repudiate the germ theory or the institutional approach. He simply moved the germinal stages to the American continent and liberalized his use of the word "institution"—as he did with all words. One can see echoes of the German folkmoot in the Watauga Association and compare the German "wandering of the peoples" with the mobility of the American frontiersman. In short Turner borrowed everywhere—he was a glutton for data, said Phillips—and tried to synthesize and select in order to find theme and meaning.

But what was to be the value of history and the purpose of meaning beyond intelligent understanding? Turner found a partial answer in President Bascom's belief that the university must serve the state and educate the citizen. This same view could be found at Johns Hopkins, where at least a half dozen of its graduates had written articles on state extension work. Adams himself was interested in the service role of the state university. Although cast in often abstract and portentous terms, there was a "we can make a better

world" spirit at Hopkins which resembled the later reform sentiment
of Progressivism. Burleigh T. Wilkins has observed that John W.
Burgess at Columbia, building on Germanic ideas, was also using
history to preach civic responsibility and national self-consciousness.[25]
If Turner experts are going to argue that he was overwhelmed by a
communications revolution, a "closed space" theory, and Achille
Loria, it seems equally plausible to argue that he must have been
affected by the social philosophies espoused by his fellow historians
and, indeed, by a large part of the entire academic community during
his formative student years.

That Turner was not yet a rebel may be seen in his dissertation,
The Character and Influence of the Indian Trade in Wisconsin
(1891), which was an obvious outgrowth of his master's essay on the
fur trade.[26] In it he spoke of the trading post as an "influential
institution" which broke the "cake of custom" (Walter Bagehot's
phrase) by juxtaposing a primitive and an advanced society. After
paying obeisance to his Hopkins teachers by tracing the patterns of
ancient trade routes in the Mediterranean, he passed on to the
Wisconsin experience. Local history continued to be a microcosm of
all history, while the trader as a type was to become the first protagonist in the evolving story of all primitive regions. Another part of
the frontier essay had now been articulated.

Once back at Wisconsin Turner threw himself into his work with
the vigor of a crusader. When Allen died in 1889 Turner succeeded
him as the head of the Department of History. He reorganized
courses, popularized the seminar method, taught extension work, and
wrote idealistically about the public-service function of the educator
and the state university. Turner became a full professor at thirty-one
and a professor of American history at thirty-two. During these years
Turner supported President Thomas C. Chamberlin's program to
make Wisconsin a famous graduate center, something Chamberlin
succeeded in doing in the field of geology, for he was America's
leading glaciologist.[27] Both men also agreed on a "multiple hypothesis" approach to the past and felt, therefore, that interdisciplinary
schools were needed. When Richard T. Ely wrote Turner in 1892
that he wanted to leave Johns Hopkins, Chamberlin made Ely the
director of an impressive new School of Economics, Political Science,
and History. He then made Turner an associate editor of the *Bulletin,* which the School began to publish.

These were Turner's most productive years. As a department head he persuaded Charles Homer Haskins to fill the medieval chair at Wisconsin, appointed Carl Russell Fish to teach New England history, and got Ulrich B. Phillips to accept the post in Southern history. His own talent as a graduate teacher was reflected in the doctoral thesis of his student Orin G. Libby on *The Geographical Distribution of the Vote of the Thirteen States on the Federal Constitution, 1787–8*.[28] Turner felt that Libby's findings were so important he offered to let Libby give a paper in place of himself at the 1893 meeting in Chicago![29] Many years later Charles A. Beard acknowledged that Libby's work had laid the foundation for his own study, *An Economic Interpretation of the Constitution*.

Meanwhile Turner was in process of developing a social and economic history course which appears to have begun as a history of the Old Northwest. When B. A. Hinsdale's *The Old Northwest* was published in 1888, Turner produced an outline for such a course. After he reviewed the first two volumes of Theodore Roosevelt's *Winning of the West* (1889) for the *Dial*, the course expanded to include part of the Old Southwest. Turner was also conscious of the Far West, for Herbert Baxter Adams had paraded the writings of his former students in front of the seminarians almost daily, always with the idea of inspiring the new crop of students to imitate their predecessors. Turner had read Charles H. Shinn's *Mining Camps: A Study in American Frontier Government* (1885), and he must have known of Josiah Royce's *California* (1886), which bore the interesting subtitle: "A Study of American Character." Both men had been students of Adams'. Turner also referred to H. H. Bancroft's *Popular Tribunals* in his frontier essay, and while Bancroft was not an Adams student, all three men told a similar story of the evolution of California society from chaotic gold-rush conditions to that of an orderly democracy. Each praised the orderly instincts of the miners and noted their Anglo-Saxon genius for self-government.[30]

Naturally a social evolutionist was interested in the impact of physical environment. Chamberlin's presence kept alive his interest in geography and geology, and Turner's good friend Charles Richard Van Hise had already published a monograph of Wisconsin geology.[31] Turner was also affected by reading Francis A. Walker's *Statistical Atlas of the United States Based on the Results of the Ninth Census, 1870* (1874), in which the author defined a frontier

both as a moving area and as one with a sparse population. Still
another study, by Henry Gannett and Fletcher W. Hewes, *Scribner's Statistical Atlas of the United States*, which analyzed the
census of 1880, not only used Walker's concept of a sequential
set of frontiers, but also listed the order in which the pioneers
came as being hunter, trapper, herdsman, farmer, and manufac-
turer.[32] These readings took on meaning and context as Turner exchanged ideas with Ely about the man-land ratio and the use of
maps and statistics in history. A kind of climax to his studies must
have come when he read in the *Eleventh Census Report* (1892)
that the frontier line in the American West had virtually disappeared.

As scores of critics have noted, Turner moved logically from these
considerations to the land exhaustion theme which was being played
up in popular and learned jounals all over the Western world. The
air was blue with talk about the end of rural life, Henry George's
"unearned increment" and the single tax, the Alliance movement, a
world agricultural depression, and the like. C. Wood Davis was
writing many articles on the meaning of the end of cheap land in the
Country Gentleman magazine.[33]

These "closed space" ideas, as James C. Malin has called them, not
only shaped Turner's thinking, they were also reinforced by his
reading of Achille Loria, an Italian land economist who posed the
attractive theory that the political freedom of a country bore a real
relation to land ownership. Small holdings and/or free simple ownership were, for example, the equivalent of political liberty. Loria used
Italian, English, and American history to bear out his premise, and
he went on to argue that since society had evolved everywhere in
similar ways, America had the key to the historical enigma which
Europe had sought for in vain, for "the land which has no history
reveals luminously the course of universal history."[34]

All these ideas made a great deal of sense to Turner as he operated
in the environmentally and sociologically oriented curriculum of Wisconsin.[35] By using these ideas and by building on Lord Bryce's
remark in the *American Commonwealth* that the West was the most
American part of the United States, Turner was ready to talk about
the end of the frontier and the role of free land in American history.
What he gave to the work of others and to the voluminous materials

he had amassed was a theme, insight, causal explanation, and, above all, a seemingly full explanation of the parlous state of his own times.

The main points of Turner's *The Significance of the Frontier in American History* are so well known it is not necessary to review the thesis in detail here. Let us turn instead to the implications of the essay, for it was the implications rather than what he said in cold print that made Turner a pastmaster.

After reviewing American history rather generally, Turner maintained, as we have noted, that the greatest influence in shaping American democracy and society had been the frontier and free land. He defined the frontier in a peculiarly American way. Drawing on Walker, Gannett, and Hewes, and the *Census Report of 1890*, he declared it was not a border between two countries but a belt of free unoccupied land where under six people per square mile lived. This belt might be a hundred miles in depth; it could also be a moving belt which after three hundred years had finally crossed the country. At times it was a solid, slow-moving ribbon; at others it jumped about, as the frontier did in the case of the gold rush to California and the "Great Migration" to Oregon.

The definition of the American frontier concept was flexible in other ways. It could be a specific place, an evolving phase or "process" of settlement in any place, an arrested set of conditions in which the economy and society remained in a formative or a "primitive" state. It might be, as Turner later maintained, an attitude or a "state of mind." Later it even became the equivalent of a set of American ideals for Turner. Since he also employed the words "West" and "frontier" interchangeably, critics and defenders alike have been maddened by the vagueness of the terms. Yet the ever-changing meaning of the concept was characteristic of the man. All his insights, however valid and profound, were imprecise, evanescent, and sometimes contradictory. Still Turner had created a new meaning for frontier—a meaning that for all its faults permitted historians to describe the process of westward expansion more easily.[36]

Turner next argued that the experience of living on the frontier was so overwhelming in its first stages, so demanding of an individual—and especially European man—that in conquering the frontier the frontier conquered him. To oversimplify the example, the European came to America, walked into the forest, cast off his old

habits and customs in order to survive, became simple, even as La
Salle's savages, adjusted to the new life, and walked out an American.
Since this process affected everyone on the frontier, all pioneers had
something in common. The reduction to more or less equal economic
and social status created, in turn, ideal psychological and physical
conditions for the rise of social and political democracy.

According to Turner this "return to the native" did not occur on
the Atlantic coast which, said he, remained European in character.
Rather it took place in the interior—in the backwoods of New
England, in the Shenandoah Valley, in frontier Kentucky and Tennessee, and in the Ohio Valley and the Old Northwest. There the
remoteness of Europe and common problems involving the survival
of families, land acquisition, formal government, and the Indian
menace forced the pioneers to be self-sufficient, self-governing, and
innovative. Here Turner used some of the ideas and heroic descriptions of frontier life that Roosevelt had portrayed in his vigorous
Winning of the West.

The process, said Turner, was both repetitive and cumulative, for
as the frontier moved farther West, sons of the first pioneers became
even more independent and asocial than their fathers. As more
frontier "Wests" went through the process, those with a pioneering
experience or heritage came to outnumber those who lacked it.
Eventually by sheer size of region and number of population the
frontiersmen forced the East to consider their needs and accept their
more democratic way of life. He intimated that this came to pass in
the 1820's when the West, led by Henry Clay and Andrew Jackson,
had come into national prominence. This belief that the Western tail
eventually wagged the Eastern dog was central to Turner's argument,
although the oversimplification of causal factors seems most apparent
here. But again the argument was characteristic of Turner: environment created the type, the type expressed itself by statistical and
democratic majority, and change was recorded through voting patterns and mass attitudes.

Turner then described a series of sequential frontiers and noted
how on each the pioneer evolved from his primitive "white savage"
stage into that of the herdsman-rancher, the prospecting miner, the
squatter, the pioneer farmer, and, finally, the commercial farmer.
When all was conquered and safe, the urban pioneer and the city
and industry appeared on the ex-frontier.

In simpler fashion J. Hector St. John de Crèvecoeur, Francis A. Walker, Hewes and Gannett, and many travelers had already chronicled Turner's frontier stages. John C. Calhoun, E. L. Godkin, and a dozen Europeans, including Hegel and Alexis de Tocqueville, had also commented on the impact of vacant lands on the American character.[37] Turner went further, however, to say that the frontier process created a composite nationality and that its self-sufficiency decreased dependence on England and the rest of Europe in such a way as to make the American Revolution and the rise of a laissez-faire economy inevitable. The demands of the various Wests shaped significant national legislation concerning internal improvements, the tariff, land policy, and the purchase of Louisiana. This legislation forced, in turn, a broad interpretation of the Constitution. To Turner self-sufficiency in the frontiersman resulted in a weak government, a hostility to taxes, a spoils attitude, rotation in office, and because of the inevitable debtor status found in a new area (hardly a definition of self-sufficiency), a fondness for paper money. In one sweep Turner seemed to explain Shays's Rebellion, Jeffersonian and Jacksonian democracy, Greenbackism, the Grangers, and Free Silver.

Turner then claimed that the frontier produced in the individual traits of coarseness, shrewdness, inquisitiveness, innovation, a practical turn of mind, restless energy and optimism about the future, and, of course, egalitarianism. These qualities allowed him to move about freely and to expand and conquer new areas. In a sentence Turner now seemed to explain American mobility and the workings of Manifest Destiny, and to rationalize both the imperialist urge of the 1890's and the social Darwinist views of the time.

One of the most important points in Turner's essay was that man's interaction with different soils and climates had spawned different sectional economies and societies, a form of differentiation of species which led to conflict, crises, and Civil War. Here Turner ruled out the "hand of God" and a conspiracy theory of the Civil War. While his was an economic explanation of sorts, it was not Marxian. Indeed, Turner spent his life trying to exclude a "class conflict" explanation of American history from his thinking. Instead Turner tried to give the nation a scientific, environmental explanation which laid the guilt on sections rather than on citizens. Turner's ability to talk in evolutionary terms without being precisely Darwinian or Spencerian, and to be deterministic without being Marxian, was not just vagueness; it demonstrated his fundamental urge to include a little of everything and to reconcile all views. As we shall see this urge to find consensus later became a dominating theme in his life.

Free land was absolutely basic to Turner's whole thesis. Land had lured the pioneer westward and made him economically independent; it gave him rights and responsibility; endowed him with the stable middle-class attitudes of a property owner, and made government seem less necessary. Using Loria's ideas, the concept of the Jeffersonian yeoman, and the Populists' praise of the dirt farmer, Turner equated American freedom with the absence of feudal land laws and institutional forms. Here he most clearly rebelled against his Hopkins teachers by saying that American history was distinctive because of an *absence* of those very institutions his mentors had said were so important. When one looks at the frontier hypothesis in retrospect this was perhaps his most valuable insight, for free land did play a vital role in the way the country was settled, in shaping its society, in affecting its economy, and as a psychological symbol of abundance and security.

Turner ended his essay on a nostalgic, even pessimistic note. He observed that before 1890, when hard times and depression came, the unemployed could go West and start again on a plot of free land. This "safety valve" idea was an old one, but Turner dramatized it anew by suggesting that free land had drawn off revolutionary elements from the settled areas so the nation could have a peaceable development. The point seemed to have special relevance in the 1890's, when in one decade there occurred the Panic of 1893, the Homestead and Pullman strikes, and the appearance of a supercorporation in the form of United States Steel. Since Turner approved of the imperialist urge to take overseas colonies, it is likely that he saw new possessions as another kind of safety valve.[38]

When one remembers that Turner used Hans Droysen's remark that history was the "self-consciousness of humanity" about its past, it is clear that he had done what he had always wanted to do: make American history meaningful by using it to explain the present. But Turner had done more than that. With great sensitivity he had captured the nostalgia for a simpler America—a remarkably persistent national syndrome—that the Populists were just then erecting into an ideology. As Joseph Schafer remarked with unintended wit: the essay was "the second greatest 'farewell address' " in American history. He gave America a nationalistic interpretation of its growth just as it was emerging as a world power. Theodore Roosevelt shrewdly guessed Turner's many purposes when he wrote, "I think you have struck some first class ideas and have put into definite shape a good deal of thought which has been floating about loosely."[39]

Turner's own nostalgia was for an older and fairly definable set of frontiers which lay between the Shenandoah Valley and the Mississippi River and existed in time between 1700 and 1850. Later he expressed the view that the "West" of the Great Plains had been a dependent and social frontier rather than an independent and individualistic one. The Mountain West and the Pacific coast frontiers were too new to have much effect, he thought, and besides, they were controlled by railroad monopolies and Eastern interests. But once again we must speak of what the words "West" and "frontier" came to mean rather than what they meant in 1893, for Turner's language, then and now, was general enough to seem to apply to all Wests. As John W. Caughey has noted, at some time or another virtually every region and community in America went through a frontier or Western phase.[40] Turner's greatest practical achievement may well be that he made every community feel it had contributed to the shaping of American democracy, for the thesis brilliantly related the average man and his past to national history and the national character. Although Turner never wrote about Oklahoma, E. E. Dale declared that Turner's writing seemed to explain Dale's own experience on the Southwestern frontier.[41]

The connecting of grass roots and national history had its practical results. Turner attracted students from the whole country and they went back to teach the history of the West and of their own "West" in every part of the Union. Later he boasted that half the Western history courses being taught in American colleges were being offered by his former students.

Turner invoked still other images of frontier and West that had an emotional value for the Easterner. Theodore Roosevelt had captured the spirit and vigor he wanted Americans to have in an earlier West, that of the Shenandoah Valley and frontier Kentucky. At the same time he lived in a contemporary West when he ranched in the Dakotas during the 1880's. Roosevelt also combined Francis Parkman's love of the wilderness and the outdoor life—a kind of romantic primitivism—with a desire to preserve both American resources and an older Western America by advocating conservation. Owen Wister, the bored Philadelphia gentleman lawyer, had developed such a love for the ranching West of Wyoming that he declared in 1891, "I want to be the hand that once and for all chronicled and laid bare the virtues of this extraordinary phase of social progress." Wister's *The Virginian* still rides today.

Frederic Remington, savagely antagonistic to the conformist ways of Eastern business, was putting the West of cowboy and soldier on canvas and in bronze.[42] And though Turner had dismissed the rougher "Wild West" almost cursorily in his essay, others related Buffalo Bill, Erastus Beadle's dime novels, and the whole fantasy world of the Western pulp novel to the thesis. By providing the theory and language to give all these local, sectional, patriotic, and subconscious feelings meaning, Turner had portrayed an American past which the average citizen found recognizable and attractive. It would be many years before anyone asked whether the concept described a real or a mythic American past.

Turner appears not to have realized at first what he had begun, but the favorable reception of his paper led him to test, enlarge and defend its major points in a number of ways. By 1895 his "History of the West" had expanded to embrace the whole trans-Mississippi West. In that same year he published his "Western State Making in the Revolutionary Period," in which he suggested that the new states of Kentucky and Tennessee were products of a democratizing frontier experience, although the study itself was not really a defense of the frontier hypothesis. Under his guidance, and partly because he worked so well with Wisconsin's new president, George Kendall Adams (1892–1901), the department had expanded into a distinguished "School of History" by 1900 and offered splendid graduate training.[43]

Meanwhile Turner had moved onto the national scene. He became an active reviewer for the *American Historical Review*, he edited documents pertaining to foreign affairs during the American Revolution, and he wrote an impressive article pointing out the gaps in American historiography.[44] By 1900 he was a member of the inner circle of historians who ran the American Historical Association.

The American public came to know Turner when he published an article for the *Atlantic Monthly* in September, 1896, just as the Bryan-

McKinley campaign was in full swing. Entitling it "The Problem of the West," he described the region as a "form of society" whose social conditions had resulted from the "transforming influences of free land." "The history of our political institutions, our democracy," he declared, "is not a history of imitation, of simple borrowing, it is a history of the evolution and adaptation of organs in response to changed environment, a history of the origins of new political species."[45]

Turner's real purpose, however, was to explain Midwestern Populism to a hostile East. Couching his argument in scientific and historical terms, he played the role of honest broker. Conveniently expanding the borders of the Middle West on this occasion to take in Iowa, Kansas, Nebraska, and the Dakotas, Turner struck up what was to become a familiar refrain. It was this West which had developed laissez-faire attitudes and had produced Lincoln and most of the nation's leaders since 1860. Now, in the chaotic industrial society that was emerging in the 1890's—the nation seemed "like a witches' kettle," he exclaimed—the Old Northwest could once again bring harmony by providing the "original social ideals" which had guided the nation in the past.[46]

In a postelection article for the *Atlantic Monthly* in 1897 Turner once again claimed that the Middle West was the "keystone of the American commonwealth," the population and manufacturing center of the nation, and the home of six out of seven presidents since 1860. To prove his point Turner gave a brilliant summary of the population origins of the eight Northwestern states. Using methods that anticipated scientific voter analysis by some fifty years, he delineated the social origins of each state and took into consideration religious factors, ethnic origins, soil conditions, and social customs. The article indicated what Turner could do with scientific research methods if he so chose and does establish some claim to his title of "master social scientist."[47]

Still the message was the same. The Middle West was "real America"; its vote in the presidential election of 1896 had been typical rather than radical; Populism reflected the older American ideals. And with the Old Northwest serving as mediator a way could be found to unify the nation and set it on the right course.

Turner's pleas dramatically revealed the sense of "status revolution" that had now enveloped his own region. Still his purpose was not defiance but reconciliation, and the more one reads Turner the more apparent it is that he hated any form of conflict. It seems significant that in his earlier writings Henry Clay became Turner's heroic symbol of the West. Clay's portrait is the only illustration which graces his *Rise of the New West*. Later Clay evolved into a symbol of commercial and agrarian America being reconciled in the American System, although Andrew Jackson soon outdistanced Clay as his most frequent example of a representative American frontier leader. Naturally Lincoln remained the supreme figure in the frontier pantheon, but since Turner's writing concerned the pre–Civil War period, the Great Emancipator was never treated in detail.

The reconciliation theme was repeated again in two articles written in 1901 and in 1903.[48] By this time the Middle West had become a "Heartland" (to borrow the vocabulary of the geopolitician Halford J. Mackinder), for it included—conveniently for Turner's argument this time—the capitalism of Pittsburgh on the East and the Populism of the prairies on the West. Turner published more articles on the frontier between 1903 and 1920, but more precise definitions and new insights were singularly absent. The language became more rhetorical and flamboyant as he increasingly stressed the pioneer's national vision, his spirit, and his ideals. By the beginning of the First World War both the frontier and the pioneer had become abstractions.[49]

Turner's last serious effort to illustrate the role of the frontier in American history in any large way came in his book *The Rise of the New West, 1819–1829* (1906), which Albert Bushnell Hart persuaded him to write for the American Nation Series.[50] Its title aptly explains the dominant theme, for it traces the coming of Jackson and the new Western states to national power and the resulting democratization of government and society in the United States.

The Rise of the New West was a fresh breeze in American historical writing. Turner exhibited a modern, crisp, factual style and flashing, epitomizing phrases which suggest that he could have been a good descriptive historian. The necessity of writing about the whole of America and its national problems forced Turner to see the period in terms of sections, and the book is constructed around this approach. Still the over-all effect is disappointing, for Turner suffered agonies with the organization and parts of it become a mere compendium of facts. His individuals tend to be stereotypes: Clay and Jackson were the West, John Quincy Adams was New England, and, all too often, John Randolph, crabby and schizophrenic, was the South. At times the role of the West seemed literally thrust into an otherwise standard narrative.

Something had happened to Turner which ruined his zest for writing and his search for new ideas. After 1900 he seemed unable to write much, and for the rest of his life he failed to meet publishers' deadlines. Hart had to push Turner to the point of acute embarrassment to get him to complete *The Rise of the New West*.[51] At least one Turner scholar has suggested that the death of two of his children in 1899 left him so dispirited he never recaptured his old pace. He wrote Carl L. Becker later that year that "I have not done anything, and have not the heart for anything."[52] Ten years later he told a friend apologetically that his "craft" went tramping about to so many ports of call he could not settle to write. He also said, somewhat unconvincingly, that after age thirty a man has no new ideas.

One could argue equally well, however, that Turner was too busy being the master teacher. "Turner is a dear fellow," said Edward Channing after Turner went to Harvard, "but he has no idea of the value of time. He has never written any big books." E. E. Dale remembered Turner as the most approachable man in the world.[53] And certainly Turner's concern for Becker, when the latter was just beginning his career, suggests something of the doting father in Turner.[54] Turner did crave the companionship of students, but there is little evidence that he spent much time preparing for classes. Becker has given us an unforgettable account of the master puffing into class armed with maps and piles of index cards, from which he put together a lecture. The manner was warm and intimate and he had a vibrant voice and twinkling eyes. Nevertheless these qualities did not hide the fact that he was no orator. Often there was a painful silence as he shuffled the cards to find his reference. Except for brilliant beginning and ending lectures in which he talked about the thesis and American character, he tended to be factual and detailed in his presentation and undergraduates found these lectures boring and disappointing.[55]

In graduate seminars Turner was flexible, charming, open-minded, and wonderfully informed but also seldom organized. One student recalled that in a seminar devoted to the Van Buren administration the class spent the whole term getting the Little Magician elected. Still, in private conference Turner could provide the kind of flashing insight and inspirational enthusiasm—Phillips' the importance of be-ing eager—that left them awe-struck. By constantly dissipating the formality that often hinders a free flow of ideas between teacher and student, he liberated their minds. He delighted in this role and once confessed to Becker that he always wanted to be a "radiator" and not an "educator."[56] He also paid strict attention to student manuscripts and writing style and did not hesitate to criticize while giving gentle encouragement.

When one looks at Turner's students there is every evidence that he trained them well in a wide variety of fields. If he dissipated his energies on them, he realized himself in their works. Libby and Becker worked in the Revolutionary and early national periods. Ben-jamin Hibbard and Wendell H. Stephenson worked on land policy. Constance Lindsay Skinner, Thomas P. Abernethy, and Avery Craven went into Southern history. Joseph Schafer, Edmond Meany, and Frederick Merk carved out fields in Western history, while E. E. Dale concentrated on Indians and the story of the cattleman. Louise P. Kellogg and others wrote about the fur trade, and Homer C. Hockett concentrated on national political history. Merle Curti became an outstanding scholar, indeed a founder, of the new field of American intellectual history.[57] Some of Turner's students were more literal-minded and aggressive about the frontier thesis than others, but there is no evidence that Turner ever forced them to think his way.

The picture of a much-loved "Mr. Chips" realizing himself in his students is considerably belied by Turner's role in academic affairs. He was a shrewd judge of character, and as an outgoing, vigorous organizer he was soon a power at the University of Wisconsin. When Richard Ely went to Madison in 1892, Turner publicized the ap-pointment in the local papers as if it were a great coup for the university. After President Adams decided to retire in 1901, Turner campaigned successfully to make his close friend C. R. Van Hise president. His colleagues dubbed him "Kingmaker" for his efforts. He then became one of Van Hise's closest advisers, and when the new president became involved in LaFollette's crusade to reform Wisconsin politics and government, Turner occasionally felt the wrath of conservative legislators who believed that LaFollette, Van Hise, and Turner were working together.[58]

Turner also cultivated and enjoyed the members of his profession all over the country, so that it came as no surprise to those who knew him that he was elected president of the American Historical Association in 1910 or that his students presented him with a *Festschrift* when he was only forty-nine. That same year Turner, after turning down offers from Stanford and Chicago, accepted his professorship at Harvard, where he taught until his retirement in 1924. As a major member of the historical establishment he influenced colleagues, shaped programs, and gave advice. When a group of younger historians rebelled at this "establishment" in 1916 and particularly at the refusal of the *American Historical Review* to discuss controversial issues or Marxist ideas, Turner was greatly upset and felt, perhaps correctly so, that he had been personally attacked.[59]

Richard Ely has said that by 1906 Turner bore the marks of his struggles with the university and the Wisconsin legislature on his sensitive face, struggles which helped persuade him to retreat to the calmer confines of Harvard. If he thought that life at Cambridge would lead to new ideas and publications, he was soon to be disappointed. His publishing career virtually ended with his presidential address in 1910. Calling it "Social Forces in America History," he tried to explain the factors of change which had been transforming American life since 1893. After its appearance and the publication of the Edward Channing, Hart, and Turner *Guide to the Study and Reading of American History* in 1912, his name disappears from the index of the *American Historical Review* for years at a time.[60]

Whether it was personal grief, devotion to teaching, university administration, or sensitivity to criticism which accounts for Turner's lack of ideas after 1900, it is certain that he was sorely troubled by the problems of his own day. In his presidential address in 1910, he exclaimed that a revolution had taken place between 1893 and 1903. He felt he was witnessing the birth of a new America. It was now a country torn by capital and labor, overrun by the "new immigration," haunted by the specter of socialism, confronted by trusts and labor unrest, and uncertain as to the place of government, the individual, and traditional democratic beliefs in the new era.

Like a sensitive barometer he began to reflect the change in his essays. The "unchecked development of the individual," which was a product of frontier democracy, had combined with the corporate form to produce great danger, he admitted. "Time has revealed that these two ideals," the squatter ideal and the democratic ideal, "had elements of mutual hostility and thus contained the seeds of its dissolution." He began to describe his beloved Jacksonian democracy in negative terms, of which later scholars such as Richard Hofstadter, Lee Benson, and Bray Hammond might approve. "Pioneer society," he concluded, "was not sufficiently sophisticated enough to work out to its logical result the conception of the self-made man."[61]

The new immigration troubled him so much that Pittsburgh, once described as the pride and gateway of Midwestern capitalism, now became a "social tragedy," where Huns, Bulgars, and Poles lived. On another occasion he referred to the "dull-brained" Italian immigrants crowding Eastern cities and wondered how America could keep from having to adjust its unique democracy to a European type. Turner now saw the full deterministic implications of his statement that the absence of free land meant the end of an older democracy. Naturally his views were used as a powerful argument by John Fiske and other members of the Immigration Restriction League.[62]

Turner was especially haunted by the prospect of class warfare. Although he began an essay in which he tried to predict what a labor-dominated America would be like, he was unable to finish it.[63] It was now Turner's role to follow rather than lead, for he felt that Progressivism was trying to find substitutes for free land that would continue to safeguard democracy. Naturally he supported LaFollette's and Van Hise's efforts to realize the "Wisconsin Idea" in his home state. He read with keen interest Van Hise's book on conservation as well as his *Concentration and Control: A Solution to the Trust Problem of the United States* (1912), which sought to reconcile labor-capital conflicts. Later he wrote that he was delighted by "insurgency."[64] He also echoed the Progressive views of Herbert Croly and Theodore Roosevelt, although he followed with more sympathy the ideas and the political career of his friend and former teacher Woodrow Wilson.

The borrowing of ideas had its amusing side. In 1912 Wilson used Turner's frontier thesis to describe the ideal conditions which had allowed the little self-made man to rise in this country. Two years later Turner agreed with Wilson that the answer to American woes lay in leadership, democratic ideals, and a return to laissez-faire conditions through government regulation. It is not often that a historian personally knows and admires three presidential aspirants simultaneously, in this case Roosevelt, LaFollette, and Wilson. That very fact, dramatized by Turner's occasional visits to the White House during the Roosevelt and Wilson administrations, must have made the writing of history seem very dull.

Meanwhile Turner urged that in the search for answers Progressives not forget the frontier heritage. Employing his history as the "self-consciousness of humanity" thesis, Turner related frontier ideals to the Progressive's faith in, and definition of, democracy. In similar fashion he connected the preservation of frontier ideals with the fight to save the world for democracy when the United States declared war against Germany in 1917. He supported the war and Wilson's administration with all his energy.

The events of the First World War and the fight over American membership in the League of Nations developed in Turner a belief that yet another historical watershed had occurred in American life. The reluctance of LaFollette and the Middle West to support the war effort left him somewhat disenchanted with his old homeland. All sections, it seemed, could be sectional. He wrote Wilson that a knowledge of the history of American sectional attitudes and demands might throw light on the patterns of national rivalries in Europe.[65]

After American entry into the League had been defeated, Turner brought out an essay in which he suggested that the United States with its sections was a potential league of nations. Congress was where the nations negotiated treaties of agreement. The Farm Bloc had been formed in the Middle West, the solid South backed cotton and Democracy, Chicago was fighting with New York over the proposed St. Lawrence Waterway, the scientific concept of regionalism was becoming popular, and Turner's Harvard colleague, Josiah Royce, had published an essay on provinces and provincialism as a part of his crusade against standardization.[66]

The old pattern was familiar. Once again Turner was trying to synthesize and give meaning to past and present while delivering a message: we must learn to compromise; sections were good but must not become autonomous. Turner's own disillusionment with the World War and its causes led him to suggest that the Civil War had been an unnecessary conflict, a theme which his student Avery O. Craven, among others, was to pursue in developing a major new school of historical revisionism.

Turner himself continued to elaborate his own theory of sections which had been an integral if sometimes contradictory part of the frontier thesis and all his work since the 1890's. Although other scholars were also developing sectional and regional approaches to American history, Turner's important essay, "The Significance of the Section in American History," published in 1925, expressed the idea most succinctly. After Turner's death his good friends Max Farrand and Avery O. Craven published this and other essays in *The Significance of Sections in American History*. The volume received the Pulitzer Prize for History in 1932.[67]

Turner's discussion of sections was not merely historically oriented, and it was far more than a modified form of states'-rights ideas. It bore some relation to Howard Odum's studies of American regions, to Walter Prescott Webb's later approach to the Great Plains, and to scientific regional planning. By implication Turner was reiterating two favorite older themes: first that if we study the forces which shape our lives we can achieve national consensus; second, that a sectional explanation of conflict can serve as a substitute for a Marxist theory of history.

Since the social, ethnic, political, economic, and environmental factors making for sectionalism were endless in number, Turner's willingness to collect and order masses of data suggest how deeply he was committed to the older concept of "total" or "social" history espoused by James Harvey Robinson (who hoped that a full knowledge of the past could be used to better the lot of mankind) as well as to the kind of social history which Charles A. Beard, Arthur Schlesinger, Sr., and Dixon Ryan Fox were beginning to write. Turner's own interest in social evolution and process, his in-depth studies of regions, his interdisciplinary training, and his concern for the operation of forces and masses, rather than of individuals, should lead historians to reconsider the role Turner's approach and ideas played in the writing of American social history between 1920 and 1940. Certainly Arthur Schlesinger's *Paths to the Present* and Schlesinger's and Fox's *History of American Life* volumes accept and elaborate Turnerian themes and assumptions about American nationality and culture. Turner's concepts also anticipated some of the approaches used in the behavioral sciences today, and he is a respectable collateral, if not direct, ancestor of today's quantifying historians.

While Turner's enthusiasm for research never waned, his energy was running out. After he retired from Harvard in 1924 he returned to his beloved Madison, but ill health forced him to seek the sun. When Max Farrand offered him a senior research post at the Huntington Library in California, Turner accepted and moved to Pasadena. By this time Turner's view of the world was rather pessimistic. He disliked the conformity of postwar America and he deplored the "obese" conditions of the 1920's. Beard's critical review of his collected essays, *The Frontier in American History*, hurt him deeply, and left him anxious to counter with an essay on the significance of the city, but he never did so.

Once in California Turner noted that Herbert Bolton had overstressed the Spanish frontier period and urged, instead, that a "business research institution framed on modern lines" be set up to study modern California, its powerful cities, and the western hinterlands.[68] Turner himself returned to sectional studies and was working on a volume, *The United States, 1830–1850*, when he died in 1931 at the age of seventy-one. His former student, Avery O. Craven, edited the manuscript and the book was awarded the Pulitzer Prize, Turner's second, when it was published in 1935.[69]

The United States, 1830–1850 is an impressive study of the workings of sections, a fascinating compendium of statistics, detailed information, and shrewd insights. The volume exhibits Turner's ability to use voting maps, but there are no new methods in evidence and it contains no new seminal ideas. Since it is an unfinished work it is unfair to judge him by it. While this final volume glows with an abiding faith in democracy and reveals the extraordinary amounts of factual information Turner had at his command, it seems conclusive that Turner expressed his best ideas to and through his students, whose works are cited throughout the book.

By now Turner's major ideas, his methods, his view of history, his role as a professional historian, and his impact on American historical writing and American thought should be clear. The question remains: what happened to the frontier thesis after his death?

The muted criticisms that first appeared during the 1920's—when Charles A. Beard noted that the frontier could not explain slavery, the growth of the city, the industrializing process, and the rise of labor—turned into a full-scale attack in the 1930's. Benjamin F. Wright found that, contrary to Turner, democracy was a European and East-coast concept that found congenial soil in the West but was not indigenous to the region. He also demonstrated that pioneers were not inventive but imitative when they formed their local governments and that the pioneer phase usually lasted such a short time in most frontier areas that it seldom forced men to throw off their past and assume a new personality. Other critics pointed out that the West did not control the East, and Louis B. Wright concluded that whatever the impact of the frontier, American civilization remained essentially British in origin and nature.[70] George Wilson Pierson, in a masterful study of the frontier thesis and the way historians had used it, found that Turner had overstressed the freehold phase, had standardized what was really a varied pioneer experience, and had ignored the existence of other types of settlers in the westward movement. The whole thesis, concluded Pierson, was "a hazy and shifting concept, riddled with internal contradictions, overlaid with sectional bias, and saturated with nationalistic emotion."[71] More recently Earl S. Pomeroy noted in a general reappraisal of the whole pioneering process that "inheritance, continuity, and conservatism" explained American development far better than the frontier thesis.[72]

Most critics were content to concentrate on aspects of the thesis rather than go after the whole concept. The economic historians found the "safety valve" corollary particularly unacceptable. People did not move in depression periods, they said, and those that did were not laborers but farmers. Fred A. Shannon found, however, that for every farmer who moved to the frontier twenty moved to the city.[73] James C. Malin maintained that Turner was so overwhelmed by a "closed space idea" that he confined his theme of "mobility" to mean horizontal or geographic mobility and ignored economic mobility. In similar fashion David M. Potter commented that Turner saw land as "abundance" but failed to see that technology and industry also produced "abundance."[74]

The endless criticisms all pointed to the fact that Turner had posed his thesis before the facts were in. He was so much a part of the warp and woof of American thought, however, that neither he nor the frontier concept could be dismissed. Even if the claim is overstated, the evidence seems overwhelming that just as Turner in 1893 saw the closing of the frontier as an apocalyptic turning point in American history, writers, intellectuals, and politicians—whether left, liberal, or conservative—used the absence of a frontier to explain the severity of the Depression and the apparent decay of capitalism, and to justify the new government controls and economic experimentation. As Steven Kesselman has observed, the New Dealers eventually employed the Turnerian idea that the past was irrelevant to develop an antihistorical attitude which would allow them to deal with the present and the future in a practical, *ad hoc* way.[75]

In 1961, exactly thirty years after Turner's death, incoming President John F. Kennedy reversed the older concept of the frontier as irrelevant past. He declared that an international "New Frontier" existed for Americans in the realizable future. This refurbishing and use of a word which has patriotic and almost mystically reverent meaning for all Americans had an appreciable psychological effect on the entire country.

Long before the word "frontier" took on an international and millennial meaning, however, scholars were busy using the frontier thesis in other ways. Many a budding historian cut his eye teeth on Turner by discussing him in a critical article. The thesis became a point of departure or reference in the same way that Weber's "Protestant Ethic" or Beard's "economic interpretation" have come to be used. While many of Turner's students exhibited less flexibility than the master, they continued to turn out excellent factual books in all areas of American history. College courses on the American West remained and still remain in the curriculum and hundreds of thousands of students continue to debate, for academic purposes, the validity of the frontier thesis. Although the older chronological divisions of American history and traditional concepts like "Jacksonian Democracy" popularized by Henry Adams, Channing, Turner, Beard, and others have come under heavy fire by contemporary historians, most general American history courses still reflect the outlines laid down by Turner and the other masters.

Sometime before Turner's own death a kind of Turner-frontier-pioneer cult also grew up. It drew its support from professional historians, antiquarians, Westerners with an anti-Eastern bias, patriotic groups, and local communities seeking to preserve their "wild Western" past. In Madison itself Turner's former student, Joseph Schafer, turned the *Wisconsin Magazine of History* into a vehicle dedicated to honoring the memory of Turner.

In recent years social and intellectual historians have found the Turner thesis a fascinating device to use in getting at past American culture and thought. It has proved valuable in studies of primitivism, romanticism, and nature in American life. While holding the frontier concept at arm's length and heartily criticizing it, these historians have prolonged its fame by making it a part of the American heritage.

The result has been impressive. Arthur Ekirch suggested, for example, that free land made us progress-oriented; Roy Harvey Pearce concluded that the lure of free land made us anti-Indian. Henry Nash Smith felt that the existence of a "virgin land" has preserved an American fascination for the primitive, while John William Ward found that the Jacksonians felt that the good life was a balance between civilization and savagery. Charles L. Sanford observed that the United States so believes in a cult of nature that it keeps alive Turner's ideas. Arthur K. Moore, while launching a savage attack on Turner in his *The Frontier Mind*, observed that Americans had a need for a legendary primitive past and noted that the frontier met that need.[76] In the eyes of these writers Turner becomes an honest if unconscious portrayer of basic American beliefs and folk myths while at the same time providing a vocabulary for a higher criticism of himself and his ideas. What historian could ask for more than to become a part of the rhetoric used in debating the nature of American civilization? The debate goes on in more somber form today as all Americans query whether or not a fascination for guns and violence is not one of the darker heritages of the frontier.

Turner did not quite intend it this way, but by being a reflector of turn-of-the-century national and regional values, he emerges as an important historic figure in his own right. This symbolic role rather than that of straight historian lays the real basis for his claim to be a master of the past. "There was something of the poet and much of the philosopher about Turner," said Avery O. Craven admiringly. His was, Becker recalled, "a fresh and original mind that goes on its way, careless of the proprieties, inquiring into everybody's business, hobnobbing with cartographers, economists, sociologists, geographists, census compilers [and] editors of *Who's Who*."[77]

One may ask finally, how does Turner's thesis look to the student of Western or frontier history today? Assuming that most scholars have rejected the claim that the frontier concept explains American history, and assuming that the detailed criticisms are more or less valid, what is there left to discuss? Some twenty years of teaching a course on the role of the West in the development of the United

States have left this writer with some firm ideas about Turner's contributions and limitations.

Let us start with what Turner left out. By beginning American history in the middle and late stages of the colonial period he played down the English and European heritage, skipped the coastal frontier, and reduced the importance of the early Puritan and Virginia experiences. His bias against Europe blinded him to the German-American cultural heritage which by 1890 was powerful, old, and respectable. It seems safe to say he did not glimpse that marvelous construct, the Puritan mind, or appreciate that congregationalism contained the seeds of democracy. Turner was proud of his New England heritage and he frequently discussed religion but he never got inside their content and meaning. He wrote intelligently about social process and evolution but not about the socializing process or about society. Thus New England remained—until fairly late in his life—a series of stereotypes: the Puritan, the minister, schoolmistress to the nation, provincial and abolitionist. Even his excellent "The First Official Frontier of the Massachusetts Bay" (1914) discusses outward forms only and abstracts the frontier experience from the social context.[78]

Similarly he ignored the unbelievable adjustment that Englishmen and Europeans had to make on the coastal frontiers—as forested, hostile, and challenging as any Daniel Boone ever encountered. It was these groups who created a society which by 1700 knew how to cope with American environment, and had given government, concepts of liberty, land system, religion, and most social institutions an American cast. By 1750 Americans had as many theories about what to do with the frontier as mercantilist and imperial planners did in London and Paris.

Turner's implied explanation of these omissions was that neither New England nor Virginia was a melting-pot area, while Pennsylvania and the Middle Colonies were. When we consider Turner's first frontier, or "Old West," we do find him on firmer ground.[79] It was an area of sparse population with little or no government in evidence. The conditions were primitive, an Indian menace existed, land was available, though not always free, and everything was in a state of rapid change. In such conditions frontier leaders like John Sevier and Daniel Boone did emerge; voluntary associations such as Watauga did spring up and democratically train people in the practical experiences of self-government. It is also clear that a segment of the population of eighteenth- and early nineteenth-century America adapted to a wilderness life and "rejected Athens" in order to live by the lessons of nature. But the mechanism by which all settlers were reduced to a composite nationality is never made clear. Turner never faced the question of how many people went through all or even one of his pioneer stages. He also ignored the presence of renters, townspeople, speculators like Judge Richard Henderson, professional men, and government policies. The persistence of a Virginia style of landed aristocracy in Kentucky also implied that the impact of the leveling experience had been a limited one.[80] As the history of the post-frontier Old Southwest became increasingly difficult to fit into the thesis, Turner tended to talk about the Old Northwest and the upper central and prairie states, where some of his settlement patterns and pioneer democratic attitudes did exist.[81]

In discussing the frontier's impact, though, Turner was trapped in a dilemma of causation. The environment determined the man, but the man was a rugged individualist who could do anything, which meant overcoming his environment and ending frontier conditions. He encountered still more problems in explaining pioneer beliefs. The pioneer man, said he, was primarily economic and materialistic in his views. Yet Turner felt that the great American heritage consisted of pioneer ideals which he described as democratic, national-minded, large in scope, future- and progress-oriented, and patriotic. Again the evidence simply will not support such generalizations.

Turner encountered still a third dilemma in the fact that the frontier was supposed to be nationalistic. This meant ignoring the inevitable qualities of separatism and localism which have characterized all American frontiers. Moreover, the nationalist concept conflicted with Turner's later idea that it was a nation of sections. This forced him to say that one of the sections was "real America" while the others were not.

While Turner's particular definition of the frontier was a creative contribution, it made him ignore the older concept of a frontier as a border between two countries. Yet the Ohio and Mississippi Valleys, up to the War of 1812, were areas of international intrigue for contending great powers. Spain and the United States made the future states of Alabama, Mississippi, and Florida a no man's land for many years. Britain's interest in the Old Northwest produced conflict there from 1783 to 1814. Andrew Jackson grew up on a frontier where

Spanish and British intrigues were as real a threat as the Indians, and his fame as a leader came largely in a war with the British. Turnerians have criticized Parkman for writing about the American wilderness without conceiving of the frontier's impact. The fact is that Parkman saw this international stage of the frontier in correct perspective and stressed the importance of powerful governments and strong leaders rather than the acts of ordinary pioneer individuals.

Let us turn now to a frontier region which Turner occasionally included in his Middle Western frontier. In 1947 I undertook a study of Dakota Territory during its settlement and politically formative years (1861–1889).[82] Since my main interest was in political history, it became necessary to ask the question: Did free land and frontier conditions here produce democracy on the Upper Missouri? Was it a place where economic rugged individualism, political liberalism, and innovation flourished? Was it more American in its society than older parts of the nation?

While the fur trader on the Missouri had broken "the cake of custom" there between 1807 and 1855 and was followed by small settlers, it appears that in large part nonfrontiersmen determined the pattern of settlement, society, and government in Dakota. Settlement in southeastern Dakota, for example, was promoted by Minnesota and Iowa townsite companies who had well-thought-out plans to seize both the choice land areas and the local and territorial governments. Backed by entrepreneur-politicians in the neighboring states, they used companies, group endeavor, legal devices, congressional lobbies, and speculative techniques of a sophisticated sort to gain control of this new frontier. They also had an evolutionary system of exploitation in mind by which every stage of the frontier would pay them a profit. In so doing they operated within the framework of the traditional system of territorial government and party organization, and exhibited the usual American political values. They had, in short, a working theory for the development of a frontier region just as John Jacob Astor had a working theory about the exploitation of the fur resources of the West. Much of the political strife occurring in the formative years in Dakota Territory was not so much democracy in action as it was the politics of "great expectations." Here Turner was right in saying the pioneer was materialistic in his views. But land to these pioneers meant towns, quick wealth, and control. Such men and such systems were not to be overcome by environment.

If the politician-entrepreneur preceded the pioneer farmer, what was the lot of the latter? They encountered in Dakota some remarkably harsh conditions in the form of snow, drought, fire, insect plagues, and Indian attacks, which, once experienced, were unforgettable. The fact is they adjusted to the physical conditions but retained most of their older characteristics.[83] Many, like the Russian-German and the Scandinavian immigrants, settled in groups and never gave up the idea that they could re-establish, in some modified form, their previous way of life.

From the very beginning both the entrepreneur-politician and the farmer sought aid in developing their region. They solicited subsidies from Washington in the form of Indian contracts, military posts, wagon roads, land surveys, federal political patronage, and railroad grants. Frances Wright had observed many years before that the Western states "brought up under the eye of the federal government" were naturally nationalistic. In Dakota the efforts to get help were so successful that the territorial government became an economic-development agency of sorts. This pattern, far from being unique to the Dakotas, characterized the development of most of the Western territories after 1860. To write a history of a frontier without including the role of the federal or local government is to eliminate a central theme in the history of the exploration, settlement, and development of the American West.[84]

The railroad did not come to the Dakotas until fourteen years after the region was settled, but its citizens had "railroad fever"—just as the settlers of the Old Northwest had had "canal fever"—from the moment they arrived. As Turner himself observed, they sought not self-sufficiency or isolation but commerce and communication with the rest of the country. In their first railroad building scheme they employed the somewhat dubious methods used by the Union Pacific, even to the parallel of creating a local equivalent of the Crédit Mobilier. These were imitative methods, not innovative ones.

Eventually the territory became a place in which Minnesota and Eastern capital was invested to such a degree that absentee owners soon acquired most of the railroads and partial control of the economy. After the great bonanza wheat farming boom began in the 1880's, the region became so dependent on the railroad and railroad charges and abuses became so notorious that local leaders demanded reform, and sought the end of territorial status and economic colonialism. This rebellion may have sounded radical—and some of the

Dakota ideas were radical—but by and large it was the age-old plea for "home rule" stated in the familiar language of liberty and democracy which had been voiced in various parts of the country since the American Revolution. At various times it took the clear form of states' rights and popular sovereignty, at others it took the form of Populism, but all of the pleas were just as much a set of old beliefs in a new context as they were a set of radical ideas.

The irony of the Dakota crusade for economic freedom and home rule—which got swept up into the Populist movement—was that the most eloquent defender of self-government and self-determination in South Dakota was Dr. Joseph Ward, a minister and college president educated at Andover. Its most radical defender of states' rights and popular sovereignty was Hugh Campbell, a former carpetbag politician from Louisiana, and its most statesman-like conservator of public lands was General W. H. H. Beadle, a New Yorker. As Earl S. Pomeroy has observed, "The colonial chafed against his colonial status but in a traditional way. Institutions and values changed less than geography, individual fortunes and techniques."[85] The fact was that while opportunity (the safety valve?) always existed on the Dakota frontier, the chance for self-government, economic balance, and a functioning local democracy came at the end rather than at the beginning of the frontier period.

Before the Dakota experience is called typical, it should be subjected to a comparison with the territorial experiences of other parts of the West. In a study of the New Mexican frontier for the years 1846–1912, I found that although the Spanish-Americans lived under frontier conditions for some two hundred years, their society was recognizably Spanish and it was certainly not democratic.[86] Here heritage and environmental conditions had determined otherwise. When the Americans conquered New Mexico in 1846, two cultural frontiers in the European sense met. Still the Spanish-Americans resisted democratic institutions until the incoming Anglo-Americans were able—with the help of the federal government—to establish traditional American democratic government there.

By the time Americans arrived in New Mexico most free lands had been disposed of in the form of private land grants. Turner could argue with some justice that the absence of a free-land system explained the absence of democracy. But Americans soon acquired these lands—as they did those in California—and applied exploitative and speculative techniques used on other frontiers. The presence of harsh frontier conditions or even of another culture did not stop the Americanizing process that was imposed by Americans and the American government.

In Utah Territory the Church of the Latter Day Saints, itself a child of the New York frontier, imposed its predetermined beliefs on one of the most uninviting physiographic regions in North America. The society they created there was communal and theocratic rather than individualistic or democratic, until federal action in the form of an antipolygamy crusade forced the territory to adopt standard American political and social customs.[87]

By now it must be obvious that these frontiers went through different experiences partly because of the past heritage and traditional beliefs of their settlers. We can see, too, that the frontier went through an international stage, a national development stage, and a maturing but usually sectional stage. In all of these, neighboring settled areas and the federal government had a powerful impact on the evolving frontier. Finally we must conclude that talented men, brilliant entrepreneurs, total societies in miniature, commercial, social, and religious companies and sects, and politicians all came to the frontier with clear-cut plans to shape it to their wills. In the course of time they and the settlers leveled mountains, erased distances, created newer Americas, and bent nature to the will of man. The significant thing about the American frontier, it seems, was that it did not overcome us, we overcame it.

Still American expansion westward differed in some respects from that of expanding societies elsewhere. Without Turner's frontier thesis and his insistence on this difference, American scholarship would be less rich. He "bound the subject matter of western historians for them as no one had ever done it before," Earl Pomeroy observed recently.

While his theory of sections is also of lasting and fundamental importance in explaining American history, his greatest contribution was his appreciation of the part free land played in the thoughts, plans, and economy of eighteenth- and nineteenth-century Americans. "The land," writes John W. Caughey, "was a very strong conditioning factor in practically every activity that was carried on." Samuel Phillips Huntington, in noting the lack of institutional innovation in American politics, concluded that the United States is a new society with an old polity and he attributes American ability to get along with more of the medieval and Tudor English constitution than the English did to the presence of free land.[88] While it has been left to others to spell out the many implications of free land, it was Turner who first saw its seminal relation to the nature of American history.

As a sensitive man whose career coincided with the "take-off" period in American historical scholarship, Turner reflected and popularized newer methods of research, theorized, and taught while trying to preserve what he thought were unique democratic ideals born of a particular frontier at a particular time. At times he seems a propagandist, at others a mere historicist, and on occasion, Whitmanesque. A man who touches the historian, the social scientist, the intellectual, the antiquarian, the mass subconscious mind, and the average citizen, man and boy, may not have been a great historian in the orthodox sense, but he was something of an intuitive genius. Somewhat like Thomas Jefferson he felt he had the "sense of America"; and just as Jefferson can be called democracy's spokesman, Turner deserves the title "democracy's historian." Until the words "frontier," "free land," and "democracy" disappear from the American historians' vocabulary, the name of Turner remains secure.

Charles A. Beard

FORREST MCDONALD

4)

THE DEGREE of a historian's "influence and immortality," Charles Austin Beard said in 1933, "will depend upon the length and correctness of his forecast" about the movement of history in the future— "upon the verdict of history yet to come."[1] In the short run, at least, he was wrong, dead wrong, and more will be said about that in due course; but perhaps more than any other historian before or since, Beard had earned the right to talk to his fellows about influence and immortality. In his lifetime (1874–1948) he authored or coauthored forty-nine volumes, comprising 21,059 pages, in the field of history and its problems, not to mention another twenty-eight volumes in political science and related matters and a host of articles on both historical and current subjects. One measure of his influence is that, by 1952, some 11,352,163 copies of his books in history had been sold. Another is that four of his books—*An Economic Interpretation of the Constitution* (1913), *The Economic Origins of Jeffersonian Democracy* (1915), and his two volumes on Franklin Roosevelt's foreign policy (1946, 1948)—"excited more controversy and more denunciation than any other history of the half century." Still another is that his interpretations of the three most significant political events of America's first century as a nation—the making of the Constitution, the origins of the party system, and the Civil War and Reconstruction—came into almost universal acceptance, as did his interpretations of a large number of lesser events. Yet another is that his monumental *Rise of American Civilization* (1927), written in

collaboration with his wife, is still regarded as one of the most successful large-scale syntheses of American history ever attempted.[2]

So large was his output, indeed, and so vast his influence, that it
may be that any effort to analyze his work is, as he said of all written
history, a matter of choosing topics and arbitrarily delimiting their
borders—"cutting off connections with the universal." I do not,
however, believe so. There is a unity and a more or less logical progression about all his work, first to last. This essay will attempt to
describe and illustrate this unity and progression, to appraise Beard's
craftsmanship as a historian, and to evaluate his long-range effect
upon the study of history.

At the outset, a word may be offered about the pedigree of Beard's
views about the past. He did not originate the theory of the economic
interpretation of history, with which his work is so closely identified,
nor did he contribute much in the way of refinement of that body of
theory. Rather, he was the first great practitioner of economic interpretation, standing to the earlier theorists much as a business entre-
preneur stands to a technological innovator. But there was this
difference: Beard was exposed to the great theoretical works after,
and not before, he arrived at his conviction that visible political
events are but the superficial manifestations of the "real economic
forces" that underlie, condition, and cause them.[3]

"People ask me," Beard once said, "why I emphasize economic
questions so much. They should have been present in the family
parlor, when my father and his friends gathered to discuss public
affairs." Beard's father had been a successful farmer, land speculator,
building contractor, and small-town bank president; in Beard's words,
he was a "copper-riveted, rock-ribbed, Mark Hanna, true-blue Republican." More revealingly, Beard said that "My father was named
William Henry Harrison Beard, and you will understand better some
of the differences in the approach of Frederick Jackson Turner and
myself if I add that his father was named Andrew Jackson Turner."[4]

What Beard meant by this was that he grew up in the Whig
tradition and the underlying Federalist tradition—that he learned
early, and never forgot, to share the cynical view of man and the
idealistic view of the United States that had been held by Hamilton,
Marshall, Biddle, Webster, Clay. Cardinal to this tradition was the
proposition that private rights to property are morally anterior to

government, and that all people, whatever their protestations, so believe and so behave. To be sure, the public good (by which was meant the national interest and, in turn, national progress) must be served, but it could be served only by recognizing that men are moved primarily by their love of power and desire for property, and by erecting governmental institutions on the foundation of that recognition. American governmental institutions were so erected; and therefore, when seeking to understand what government was doing in America, one should look not to the public record but to the underlying affected property interests.

To Beard these notions were not merely abstract ideas, but "givens," built-in assumptions about the nature of things. In considerable measure his formal education constituted a search for a book-learned theory that would rationalize what he thus already knew. His teacher as an undergraduate at DePauw, Colonel James R. Weaver, introduced him to the works of John Ruskin, Karl Marx, and other theorists of the industrial revolution, and Beard thoroughly re-read Marx at least twice in later life. Ruskin appealed to Beard a great deal, for in Ruskin there seemed to be a solution to the evils of industrialization (which Beard had seen and been shocked by, first in the stockyards district of Chicago and later, as a graduate student at Oxford, in the "black country" of England's industrial towns); but Ruskin was too narrow to satisfy Beard's intellectual needs, his "search for a theory of causation." Marx was far broader, and Marx helped Beard clarify his thinking about economic classes; but in the end Beard largely rejected Marx, too, for Beard was seeking "an open-ended system of causal analysis," and what Marx had to offer was only a "closed system of utopian prophecy."[5]

In and around Columbia University, where he took a Ph.D. degree and began to teach in 1904, Beard found and learned from kindred souls. Among these was the economist E. R. A. Seligman, whose work *The Economic Interpretation of History*, along with the works of J. Allen Smith and the socialist Algie Simons, supplied much of the immediate inspiration for Beard's first significant book. Others included the historians James Harvey Robinson and Harry Elmer Barnes and the philosopher John Dewey, who together with Beard and a handful of others formed for many years a loosely knit collection of pragmatists, reformers, and leaders in the "revolt against formalism," the awakening of scholarly concern with social and economic forces rather than institutional forms. Equally important, a number of historians around the country shared Beard's dissatisfaction with the prevailing school of "barren political history," as written and taught, in the spirit of the German scholar Leopold von Ranke, by the "scientific historians" at Johns Hopkins and Harvard. The most significant of these fresh thinkers, from Beard's point of view, were Frederick Jackson Turner and his students, especially Carl Becker and Orin G. Libby.[6]

All these influenced and helped shape Beard's thinking, but none satisfied him in his quest: it was not until he "discovered" James Madison that Beard found a theory of political behavior that would accommodate what he had learned in his father's parlor. It has been charged, sometimes persuasively, that Beard distorted or misread Madison's celebrated theory of factions, as enunciated in *The Federalist* number 10; but true or not the charge is beside the point. What matters is that, as he read the tenth Federalist, Beard saw in it an interpretive system that seemed at once flexible, pluralistic, and in accordance with Beard's own understanding of the "realities" of politics.[7]

Beard read the tenth Federalist as follows. First was Madison's definition of a faction: "a number of citizens, whether amounting to a majority or minority of the whole, who are united and actuated by some common impulse of passion, or of interest, adverse to the rights of other citizens, or to the permanent and aggregate interests of the community." Then, after remarking on mankind's strong "propensity to fall into mutual animosities," Madison suggests that men will in fact invent "frivolous and fanciful" distinctions, such as speculative points of religious or political theory, as bases of division if no real bases exist. "But," Madison emphasizes, "the most common and durable source of factions has been the various and unequal distribution of property. Those who hold and those who are without property have ever formed distinct interests in society. Those who are creditors, and those who are debtors, fall under a like discrimination. A landed interest, a manufacturing interest, a mercantile interest, a moneyed interest, with many lesser interests, grow up of necessity in civilized nations, and divide them into different classes, actuated by different sentiments and views. The regulation of these various and interfering interests forms the principal task of modern legislation, and involves the spirit of party and faction in the necessary and ordinary operations of the government."[8]

In his first great work, his *Economic Interpretation of the Consti-*

tution, Beard said explicitly that "the inquiry which follows is based upon the political science of James Madison," and the entire tenor of the book, especially when it is read with its sequel and companion volume on the origins of the party system, rules out the possibility that Beard was merely using a revered Founding Father as protective coloration for unpopular ideas. In his own later theoretical work, *The Economic Basis of Politics* (1922), Beard wrote that Madison's theory constituted "the grand conclusion" about political behavior; and all Beard's writings during his great creative period as a historian, 1913 to 1933, show him to have been a consistent Madisonian, as he understood Madison.[9]

As indicated, Beard was responsible for controversial interpretations of four major events of American history—the making of the Constitution, the emergence of the party system, the Civil War, and the coming of the Second World War. The last is different from the first three. Because it was so inconsistent with what most of his longtime friends and admirers wanted to believe, they generally rejected it and regarded it as some kind of aberration from Beard's earlier work. I believe and shall attempt to demonstrate that it was not a sudden departure but the logical outcome of Beard's entire career; but in any event it was different, if only because it never gained wide acceptance, and it will be treated later. For now, we may summarize briefly each of the other three major interpretations and appraise each in the light of subsequent scholarly research.

Beard's first great work was *An Economic Interpretation of the Constitution of the United States*. The central points in this work were as follows. "Large and important groups of economic interests were adversely affected by the system of government under the Articles of Confederation [adopted in 1781], namely, those of public securities, shipping and manufacturing, money at interest; in short, capital as opposed to land." After failing to safeguard their property rights against state legislative attacks and promote their special interests, "particularly those of the public creditors," through the existing legal channels, these groups brought about a convention in the hope of obtaining "the adoption of a revolutionary programme." In other words, the movement for the Constitution originated with and was pushed through by "a small and active group of men immediately interested through their personal possessions in the outcome of their labors. . . . The propertyless masses were . . . excluded at the outset from participation (through representatives) in the work of framing the Constitution. The members of the Philadelphia Convention which drafted the Constitution were, with a few exceptions, immediately, directly, and personally interested in, and derived economic advantage from, the establishment of the new system." "As a group of doctrinaires, like the Frankfort assembly of 1848, they would have failed miserably; but as practical men they were able to build the new government upon the only foundations which could be stable: fundamental economic interests."[10]

In essence, then, the Constitution was "an economic document drawn with superb skill by men whose property interests were immediately at stake; and as such it appealed directly and unerringly to identical interests in the country at large." It was based upon "the concept that the fundamental private rights of property are anterior to government and morally beyond the reach of popular majorities."

The system "consisted of two fundamental parts—one positive, the other negative." The positive part comprised four great powers conferred on the new government: "taxation, war, commercial control, and disposition of western lands." This meant for the manufacturers a protective tariff; for trade and shipping groups, tariffs and other legislation against foreign shipping; for money interests, the prevention of "renewed attempts of 'desperate debtors' like Shays"; and for public creditors, ample revenues for the payment of their claims. The negative portion placed restrictions on the states: "Two small clauses embody the chief demands of personalty against agrarianism: the emission of paper money is prohibited and the states are forbidden to impair the obligation of contract."

In the contest over ratification, Beard concluded, only about a fourth of the adult males were eligible—or interested enough—to vote on the question, and the Constitution was ratified by no more than a sixth of the adult males. In five states it was "questionable whether a majority of the voters participating . . . actually approved the ratification." "The leaders who supported the Constitution in the ratifying conventions represented the same economic groups as the members of the Philadelphia Convention; and in a large number of instances they were also directly and personally interested in the outcome of their efforts." Of the voters on ratification, those favoring the Constitution were "centred particularly in the regions in which mercantile, manufacturing, security, and personalty interests generally had their greatest strength." The holders of public securities "formed a very considerable dynamic element, if not the preponderating element, in bringing about the adoption of the new system." The opposition, on the other hand, came primarily from the agricultural regions and from the areas in which debtors had been formulating paper-money and other depreciatory schemes. In short, "the line of cleavage for and against the Constitution was between substantial personalty interests on the one hand and the small farming and debtor interests on the other."

If we extract from this tightly and skillfully woven system of ideas those parts which are essentially nonconjectural—those that are susceptible of a reasonable measure of validation or invalidation as historical facts, and upon which the interpretive superstructure is erected—three propositions come into clear focus:

1. The Constitution was essentially "an economic document" drawn by a consolidated economic group "whose interests knew no state boundaries and were truly national in their scope."

2. "In the ratification, it became manifest that the line of cleavage for and against the Constitution was between substantial personalty interests on the one hand and the small farming and debtor interests on the other."

3. "Inasmuch as so many leaders in the movement for ratification were large [public] security holders, and inasmuch as securities constituted such a large proportion of personalty, this economic interest must have formed a very considerable dynamic element, if not the preponderating element, in bringing about the adoption of the new system. . . . Some holders of public securities are found among the opponents of the Constitution, but they are not numerous."

Though Beard's work was greeted with a great deal of denunciation from the time it was published in 1913, it came into widespread acceptance in the 1920's and thereafter, and it was almost 1950 before any substantial portion of it was subjected to systematic scholarly research and analysis. Since that time six historians have thoroughly checked out all or parts of it: Philip A. Crowl, Richard P. McCormick, William C. Pool, Robert E. Thomas, Robert E. Brown, and myself. The first four, after extensive and careful research, mainly in sources that had not been used by Beard, reported that Beard's conclusions in regard to the states of Maryland, New Jersey, North Carolina, and Virginia were far wide of the mark. Professor Brown's work was an internal analysis of the logic, assumptions, and methodology of Beard's book; and though it has been criticized, with some justice, for its intemperateness of tone, it is nonetheless devastating. My own work was an effort to compile economic biographies of the 1,805 men directly involved in the writing and ratification of the Constitution, and otherwise to fill in the details and do the research that Beard did not do. My conclusions may be summarized briefly.[11]

From a thorough re-examination of the Philadelphia Convention, it appears that fully a fourth of the delegates had voted in their state legislatures for paper-money and/or other debtor-relief laws—the very kinds of laws which, according to Beard, the delegates had convened to prevent. Another fourth of the delegates had important economic interests that were directly and immediately affected in an adverse way by the Constitution they helped write. The most common and by far most important property holdings of the delegates were not, as Beard asserted, mercantile, manufacturing, and public security investments, but agricultural property. Finally, it is abundantly evident that the delegates, once inside the Convention, behaved as anything but a consolidated economic group, there being virtually no correlation between their economic interests and their votes on issues in general or on key economic issues.

As to the proposition that the line of cleavage in the contest over ratification was "between substantial personalty interests on the one hand and the small farming and debtor interests on the other," the following conclusions result from a detailed state-by-state analysis. In three states (Delaware, New Jersey, and Georgia) the vote of the ratifying conventions was unanimous, a fact that Beard explained by suggesting that ratification was pushed through by personalty interest groups before agrarian and paper-money groups could organize their forces. Actually it turns out that agrarian interests dominated all three conventions, and that in each convention there were approximately equal numbers of delegates who had voted earlier for and against paper money. In two states (Virginia and North Carolina) the great majority of the delegates on both sides of the question were farmers. Here Beard suggested that ratification represented the victory of wealthy planters, especially those rich in personalty other than slaves, over small slaveless farmers and debtors; in fact, it turns out that in both states wealthy planters (those having and those not having other personalty) were approximately evenly divided on the issue of ratification, that in North Carolina small farmers and debtors were also more or less equally divided, and that in Virginia most of the small farmers and debtors favored ratification. In four states (Connecticut, Maryland, South Carolina, and New Hampshire) agrarian interests dominated the ratifying conventions, but large minorities of delegates had personalty interests. Beard opined that the contests in these states were between commercial and other personalty groups (Federalists) and farmers and advocates of paper money (anti-Federalists). It turns out, however, that in each of these states a majority of the men of personalty interests favored ratification, but that similar majorities of the farmers also favored ratification; in one of the states there had been little demand for paper money, in another a large majority of the advocates of paper money also advocated ratification, and in the other two supporters of paper money were almost equally divided on the question of ratification. Finally, in four states (Massachusetts, Pennsylvania, New York, and Rhode Island) men having personalty interests were in a majority in the ratifying conventions. For Massachusetts Beard's description of the contest was fairly accurate, but in each of the others substantial majorities (ranging from two-thirds to three-fourths) of the farmers and friends of paper money supported ratification, and men of substantial personalty interests were more or less evenly divided on the question—indeed, when there was any appreciable difference more of them opposed than favored the Constitution.

As to the third proposition, that holders of public securities were "a very considerable dynamic element, if not the preponderating element, in bringing about the adoption of the new system," a similar set of conclusions emerges from detailed research and analysis. In the three states which voted unanimously for ratification, only extremely small fractions of the delegates held securities, and the same is true of two of the states in which the contests were close. In the remaining eight states there were considerable numbers of security holders in the ratifying conventions: in three of these the advocates and opponents of the Constitution included approximately the same percentages of security holders, in two states considerably larger percentages of the friends of ratification held securities, and in three states considerably larger percentages of the foes of ratification held securities.

On all counts, then, Beard's interpretation of the making of the Constitution has proved to be incompatible with what is now known about the event, and the thesis has been all but abandoned. One historian has suggested that it might be possible to resurrect the thesis by thoroughly recasting it and devising for it a new set of categories, a new logic, and a new method of proof; but only one other historian has taken up the suggestion and attempted to put it into practice.[12] This is not by any means to imply that efforts to describe the making of the Constitution in "hard" or "realistic" or "tough-minded" terms have been dropped, but it is to say that Beard's particular economic interpretation of the event has been discarded by most professional American historians.[13]

Beard's second major work, his *Economic Origins of Jeffersonian Democracy*, was never the subject of anything like the controversy that attended the first. The major points of this work, in addition to a reiteration of the thesis advanced in the book on the Constitution, were these: Contrary to prevailing belief, as expressed in the works of J. S. Bassett and Orin G. Libby, the alignments that had been formed on the question of ratifying the Constitution (1787–88) continued, by and large, to prevail during the Federalist Era (1789–1800). Federalist policies, particularly the financial measures of Alexander Hamilton, were designed in behalf of the same personalty interest groups which had pushed through the Constitution, they were passed through Congress largely through the efforts of men who directly profited by them, and they were contrary to the interests of farmers and landed groups in general. For the last reason a goodly number of wealthy Southern planters who had supported the Constitution soon crossed over to the ranks of the anti-Federalists—who, under the leadership of Jefferson, were coming to be known as Republicans. By 1794 the Federalists had aroused such opposition among agrarian interests that their program was seriously jeopardized —a jeopardy that was intensified by widespread opposition to the Federalist Administration because of its refusal to support Revolutionary France. The Jay Treaty, 1794, was an effort by the Federalists to bolster up their program; its effects were to support the Hamiltonian system, favor northern commercial and other personalty interests, and incidentally further alienate Southern planters. During John Adams' administration (1797–1801) the alignments between "capitalists and agrarians" hardened, as was clearly recognized by the spokesmen for each side (principally Hamilton and Adams for the.

one and Jefferson and John Taylor of Caroline for the other). By 1800 the nation's small farmers, united and directed under the leadership of aristocratic planters, supported by urban working classes, and pursuing their economic interests as diligently as the personalty groups had been pursuing theirs, finally succeeded in gaining control of the national government.[14]

As a whole, this work met less opposition and gained quicker acceptance than the work on the Constitution, and it has never been subjected to such thorough analysis. Recent work in the history of the period, however, has been sufficient to suggest that it is as unsatisfactory as the work on the Constitution. The first premise, that there was an essential continuity of parties from 1787–88 onward, has been almost completely demolished by the works of Joseph Charles, Noble Cunningham, and William Chambers on the development of the party system and the works of Stephen Kurtz and Manning Dauer on the presidency of John Adams. Paul Goodman's work on Massachusetts, which in Beard's analysis was one of the three most important states, demonstrates not only that there was no continuity of "party" there, but that Beard had the entire story pretty thoroughly garbled; and Kenneth Rossman's biography of Governor Thomas Mifflin has similar effects on Beard's analysis of Pennsylvania. Alfred Young's long, thorough, and careful work on New York contradicts Beard's thesis in almost every important particular while remaining a "tough-minded" work in its own right. Young found (1) that the mechanics and other lower classes in New York City, whom Beard assumed were anti-Federalists in 1788 and Republicans throughout the 1790's, were in fact predominantly Federalist in 1788, tended to drift toward Republicanism in 1793–94, split and saw many of their numbers move back toward Federalism during the French crisis of 1797–98, and were thoroughly divided in 1800; (2) that the city merchants, whom Beard assumed were overwhelmingly Federalist in 1788 and continued to be so through 1800, were strongly Federalist in 1788 but split in 1792 into a Hamiltonian wing and a Republican wing headed by the powerful Livingston clan, and continued to be divided throughout the decade; and (3) that the Republicans, far from being a continuous and relatively cohesive agrarian party from 1788 onward, were a shifting coalition of three major factions whose leadership, like that of the Federalists, was made up of merchants, large landholders, speculators, lawyers, and office-holders. Finally, these several works, taken together, demonstrate that there was not one Federalist "party" but two (which have come to be designated as High Federalists and Low Federalists), and that the person principally responsible for molding the Republican Party (after long, persistent, and before 1800 only intermittently successful efforts) was not Thomas Jefferson but James Madison.[15]

Beard's third major thesis, that concerning the Civil War and Reconstruction, was not the subject of a special monograph, but was developed in several of his works, most fully in *The Rise of American Civilization*. This thesis was that the Civil War, the "Second American Revolution," was a "social cataclysm in which the capitalists, laborers, and farmers of the North and West drove from power in the national government the planting aristocracy of the South. Viewed under the light of universal history, the fighting was a fleeting incident; the social revolution was the essential portentous outcome." The conflict was a powerful stimulus to economic growth, for the Northern victory,

while destroying the economic foundation of the slave-owning aristocracy, assured the triumph of business enterprise. As if to add irony to defeat, the very war which the planters precipitated in an effort to avoid their doom augmented the fortunes of the capitalist class from whose jurisdiction they had tried to escape. . . . Northern leaders in banking and industry reaped profits far greater than they had ever yet gathered during four years of peace. When the long military struggle came to an end they had accumulated huge masses of capital and were ready to march resolutely forward to the conquest of the continent.

Then, acting through a servile Republican Party, these newly rich Northern businessmen rammed through Congress a program of tariff protection, sound money, subsidies to railroads, government-financed river and harbor improvements, an immigration act that gave capitalists a supply of labor "analogous to the indentured servitude of colonial times," and other measures that ensured the triumph of capitalism.[16]

Like Beard's other theses, his interpretation of the Civil War gained wide acceptance for a generation and more, only to be seriously questioned, if not totally undermined, by recent research—again, it should be emphasized, in great quantities of sources that were not available to Beard when he wrote. A few of the recent efforts may be cited. Thomas Cochran has demonstrated, beyond challenge, that the short-term effect of the Civil War was not to stimulate industrial and other economic growth, but in fact to retard such growth; and he has argued persuasively (though on this point he has been challenged) that the war had similar long-range effects—that it delayed for almost a generation America's industrial and financial development, which was "rapidly maturing" before being interrupted by war.[17] Stanley Coben, in a brilliant article, has demonstrated that the protective tariff, far from representing the triumph of united capitalists,

split northeastern businessmen more than any other issue. So fierce was business competition in this era, and so eager were the antagonists to use every possible means of winning an advantage, that almost all important tariff schedules became battle-grounds between industries, as well as between firms within the same industry. The copper, iron, linseed, and woolen textile industries, for example, were bitterly divided on crucial tariff schedules. The most significant split, however, was between certain high protectionist Pennsylvania interests on one side and influential low-tariff groups in New England and New York on the other.

The New England low-tariff groups included some of the woolen textile producers and most of the cotton textile manufacturers, who wanted low tariffs as a means both of ensuring cheap raw materials and of discouraging the growth of domestic competition.

New York merchants, shippers, and those who financed their activities opposed tariffs which might restrict imports, while the railroad financiers protested that under the proposed tariff of 1866 the Erie and the New York Central systems alone would have to pay out annually about two million dollars by way of protection.[18]

By far the most powerful of the re-examinations of part of Beard's "Second American Revolution" thesis is the work of Irwin Unger on the politics of public finance from the war to the resumption of specie payments in 1879. So thorough and so subtle is Unger's book that an extremely long treatise would be required to do justice to it, but a few of its more relevant observations may be cited. Rather than there being a single new-rich industrialist (hard-money) group opposing an agrarian (soft-money) group, Unger writes, there were

at least three well-defined soft money currents in the early postwar years. One of these, identified politically with western and Pennsylvania Republicans, drew its support from promotional business elements. This was the very group which recent historiography has pictured as the controlling postwar elite. Yet through 1870 their program of free banking had been frustrated by the resistance of Agrarians [!] and more conservative business elements. A second soft money force was compounded largely of political elements—Jeffersonian Agrarianism, Democratic opportunism, and Copperhead thirst for revenge. . . . A third current, which drew from the same ideological reservoir as the postwar greenback Democracy, was utopian and reformist in nature and expressed the frustrations and aspirations of labor and the extremist humanitarian reformers in the uncongenial postwar era.

As to the hard-money men,

On the whole they were a socially superior breed, representing an older elite of eastern merchants, commercial bankers, textile manufacturers, professional men, gentlemen reformers, and respectable literati. By all the teachings of recent history they should have been as extinct in this era of spoilsmen and industrial primitives as perukes and small clothes; at the very most they might have been expected to survive as a frail, disorganized remnant. But although they were politically weaker than in the days when a gentleman sat in the President's mansion, they were to prove capable still, through the potent moral and intellectual force of puritan New England, of confounding the massed power of the new leaders of Industrial America.[19]

It is clear, then, that each of Beard's major interpretations, once almost universally accepted, has been consigned to the scrap heap of obsolete ideas—or at least, at the moment, seems well on its way toward becoming so consigned. This is not to suggest, however, that his influence is no longer with us. We must, as Unger put it,

remember that he was a courageous pioneer who destroyed in a succession of powerful blows the stifling pieties of nineteenth-century historiography. Our debt to him is profound. If we are able to see farther it is only because, like the Moderns of the old quarrel of Ancients and Moderns, we stand on the shoulders of giants.[20]

It is tempting to account for the waxing and waning of Beard's influence in terms of his own relativist philosophy of history—that is, to suggest that his interpretations came into wide acceptance because they suited the needs and aspirations of the progressive milieu in which he wrote, and that they began to be rejected as a result of the conservative reaction that came during the McCarthy and Eisenhower years. Such an explanation, however, is far from satisfactory.[21]

On the one hand, Beard's influence rested on something considerably more substantial than the shifting hopes and prejudices of his contemporaries. After all, his work was roundly denounced during the progressive era, gained wide acceptance in the anything-but-progressive climate of the 1920's, and went virtually unchallenged during the Great Depression, the New Deal, World War II, and the Truman years.[22] Rather, Beard's interpretations gained favor because they were brilliant, bold, provocative, and simple: because they made the whole sweep of American history intelligible and, at the same time, opened up broad vistas for fruitful study of every aspect of that history.

Similarly, the ultimate rejection of most of Beard's work arose from things far more tangible than a mere conservative political climate, if indeed the American political climate since 1952 can be so described. Rather, Beard's interpretations were undone by a tremendous explosion in the quantity of reliable factual knowledge about the American past, by three or four weaknesses inherent in his methodology that were revealed as a result of this change, and by a tragic flaw in the character of the man himself.

The reasons for the "factual explosion" of the last decade and a half are scarcely a mystery: the means for gathering data have been revolutionized. There are far more workers in the field, for there has been a vast expansion in the number of trained historians. Emphasis on research as the key to professional advancement has increased incentive, the fashionability of liberal leave policies has provided opportunity, and the abundance of foundation and university grants has supplied the wherewithal. And sources are far easier to find, to gain access to, and to use. Such agencies as state archives and historical societies, the Library of Congress, the National Archives, and a host of special libraries have collected vast quantities of materials, catalogued them, and otherwise rendered their study more convenient. Travel to the repositories is easy and cheap—and often unnecessary, for microfilm and other duplicating techniques, as well as interlibrary loans and the publication of manuscript collections, have made much of the material available to scholars in their own libraries in any part of the country. As a consequence of these developments, the sheer quantity of what is known by specialists in every period of American national history has increased five, ten, twenty times, and more. For Beard's interpretations—based as they were on a relative paucity of data—to have survived this factual onslaught would have been little short of miraculous.[23]

Of the weaknesses in Beard's historical methodology, among the first to be revealed by the new information was the inadequacy of his Madisonian model.[24] In its day, Beard's adaptation of Madison's concept of interest groups in politics was a great breakthrough: it was dynamic and pluralistic and open-ended, and far more refined, flexible, and realistic than either the sterile scientism of the academic establishment or the Manichaean class struggle of the Marxists. In the light of what is now known, however, the Beard-Madison system appears to be far too gross to describe any open society beyond the most primitive.[25]

For example, in his *Economic Interpretation of the Constitution*, Beard laid the foundations for his "main line of division" in the contest over ratification by analyzing the major interest groups existing in the United States in the 1780's. In one major category, that of "substantial personalty interests," he delineated five major interest groups: the moneyed interest (private creditors), holders of government bonds and other paper (public creditors), merchants and shippers (whom he classified as one), manufacturers, and speculators in western lands. In his other major category, that of real property interests, Beard distinguished three groups: the Southern plantation masters, the Hudson Valley manor lords, and the small farmers all over the nation. In practice he divided the planters and manor lords into two groups each, those who had and those who did not have sizable investments in personalty as well as land. He described the small farmers as "a remarkably homogeneous class" and identified them as "the debtor class"; but in practice he divided them into two groups also, those living on navigable rivers or near the coast and "therefore commercial" and those living in more remote areas and therefore less commercial—a concept he borrowed from Orin G. Libby. Finally, Beard delineated one more group, the artisans and mechanics of the towns, though he tended to lump these with the small farmers in the "debtor class." In all, then, Beard constructed a profile of American society and the American economy that consisted of eight to twelve interest groups, divided into two broad categories. One broad category, as he saw it, was affected favorably by the making of the Constitution and strongly favored its ratification; the other was unfavorably affected and furnished the overwhelming majority of the opposition to ratification.[26]

At a glance that analysis of the economy may seem quite sophisticated; doubtless Madison would have so regarded it. Modern research, however, has made it clear that Beard's schema is much too simple to describe what he attempted to describe. Furthermore—and this is of equal importance—it is questionable whether any imaginable system of interest groups or classes would have been adequate for Beard's purposes. If I may quote again from the findings of my own research:[27]

There were in the United States in 1787 at least twenty basic occupational groups having distinctly different economic characteristics and needs, and there were six basic forms of capital in addition to capital incidental to occupational activity. Most of the occupational groups and all the forms of capital may be divided into two to seventy-five subdivisions [not counting the differences arising from the fact that interest groups operated in the framework of thirteen different political jurisdictions]. Of the grand total of major economic interest groups and forms of investment, about 30 per cent were affected by the Constitution directly and immediately in a favorable way, and about 15 per cent were directly and immediately affected in an unfavorable way. The remaining 55 per cent were either not directly affected at all or were affected in indefinite, indecisive, or unpredictable ways.

Among the more important groups that were affected favorably there were numerous conflicts. The interests of manufacturers were opposed to those of importing merchants and of land speculators. The interests of public security holders were divided: the interests of those favorably affected by ratification coincided with those of manufacturers but conflicted with those of land speculators and purchasers of confiscated property. The interests of wheat merchants and wheat farmers also conflicted with those of many land speculators, and so on.

It is therefore not even theoretically possible to devise a single set of alignments on the issue of ratification that would explain the contest as one in which economic self-interest was the principal motivating force.

If the Madison-Beard system is too gross for interpreting a major political event in the United States in 1787–88, it seems axiomatic that it would prove even less adequate for later events, for by and large American society grew more complex as time went by. The recent works on the 1790's, cited earlier, indicate that this was true regarding Beard's interpretation of the origins of the party system, and the work on the Civil War and Reconstruction done by Unger, Coben, and others abundantly demonstrates that Beard's analysis of the interest groups involved in this later period was likewise too simplistic to be meaningful.

A second weakness implicit in Beard's interpretive method was that it required far more detailed knowledge than anyone could reasonably be expected to have, even by the standards of the times. Studies of isolated events by his method had little value, and Beard, recognizing this, attempted to canvass the whole range of American national history and modern European history in the bargain. But, though the breadth of Beard's knowledge of history became awesome, the depth remained rather less so. Indeed, he seems to have had little interest in or patience for uncovering minutiae, and the uninformed speculation about larger things that ensued from his ignorance of details is sometimes positively embarrassing.

Scores of illustrations could be offered, but one substantial example should suffice.[28] One of the most sensational features of Beard's book on the Constitution was the implication that the Founding Fathers had written the document, at least in part, as a means of lining their own pockets, particularly through speculations in public securities. Justice Oliver Wendell Holmes, a man not easily perturbed and in fact an admirer of Beard and his work, epitomized the distress over this "belittling innuendo." Protesting, in a much-quoted letter, that "high-mindedness is not impossible to man," Holmes said that he preferred to believe that the framers "wanted to make a nation and invested [bet] on the belief that they would make one, not that they wanted a powerful government because they had invested."[29]

Now, to anyone who will read, with detachment, the *Economic Interpretation* and his related works, Beard's profound respect for the framers is palpably obvious; but the way he anticipated (and later engaged in) the argument over the matter was both curious and typical of his method. "It is here assumed," he said, "that when a member of the Convention appears upon the funding books of the new government he was a public creditor at the time of the Convention. Of course, it is possible that some of the members who are recorded as security holders possessed no paper when they went to Philadelphia, but purchased it afterward for speculation. But it is hardly to be supposed that many of them would sink to the level of mere speculators." And in his sequel volume Beard reiterated that sentiment: "Respect for the framers of the Constitution should impel us," he said, to assume that the framers did not purchase their securities after the government was established, when their influence "would have helped determine the value of their holdings."[30]

The argument, however, took place in a vacuum, and could have been easily resolved. Had Beard really wanted to know when and how the members of the Philadelphia Convention acquired their securities, he need not have assumed anything: he need only have looked. In almost every instance, in the very records from which Beard learned that the framers were security holders it is clearly indicated whether the person funding the securities was the original holder— that is, whether the person funding them acquired them for money lent or goods or services supplied during the war, or got them from some other person who had originally come to the need of Congress or the state governments. Justice Holmes' ignorance in the matter is excusable. Beard's is less so; and yet, given Beard's broad approach to history such ignorance or oversight of important details must inevitably abound in his work—and it does.[31]

A third weakness in Beard's approach is closely related to the second: in his impatience he overreacted to the "barren" political and institutional studies of the scientific school of historians, sometimes to his own detriment. To be sure, Herbert Baxter Adams, the leading American founder of that school, was somewhat naïve in his faith that historical knowledge would one day be absolute and reducible to scientific laws; but at least he had the wisdom to recognize that veritable mountains of data must be gathered before any reasonably reliable interpretation of the past, scientific or otherwise, could be made. Accordingly, Adams believed, his and perhaps several future generations of historians should devote their efforts to laying the factual foundations for later scholars, for "at the very beginning of all conquest of the unknown lies the fact, established and classified to the fullest extent possible at the moment." But Beard—along with Turner, Becker, Robinson, Barnes, and the other New Historians— could not wait; he wanted to understand and explain before finding out just what it was he was explaining. As one critic put it, Beard emulated the medieval alchemist who sought to transmute base elements into gold, before learning how to handle simpler things.[32]

In choosing this course Beard and the others performed an immense disservice to historical scholarship. The next generation of historians, following their lead, dissipated a large part of its energies in filling in the details of the broad outlines sketched by the master interpreters—whether the outlines could actually accommodate the details or not. Of those who did not do this, many occupied themselves in an equally fruitless pursuit, arguing over and refining subtle points in the master interpretations. In short, in their revolt against the extravagances of scientific history Beard and the New Historians all but abolished from historical study a priceless approach to research and analysis, the inductive method.[33]

Beard's overreaction against the study of institutional and political forms also had a direct and detrimental effect upon his own work. That is, it sometimes led him to forget that the institutional structure of politics can determine not only *how* things can happen in government but often, indeed, *what* things can happen as well—and what is more, as many of Beard's fellow progressives recognized, even as economic forces can move political events political forms can govern economic development. These are particularly important facts in dealing with American history, for in the United States power has always been scattered vertically along the various levels of the federal system, horizontally among the various branches of each government, and both ways inside the machinery of political party organizations. Historically the businessman seeking governmental favors, the lobbyist working for special-interest groups, the political fixer—all those behind-the-scenes powers who fascinated Beard so much—have succeeded pretty much in proportion as they knew just who and where, in the complex and cumbersome American governmental system, the locus of particular powers was at particular times. The same knowledge is indispensible to anyone who would interpret American history in "hard-boiled" or "tough-minded" terms. Beard knew all this, of course, and he was particularly sensitive to it in his analysis of the coming of the Civil War; but such was his aversion to institutional forms that in regard to other matters he often overlooked it.

For example, in analyzing the election of 1800 in his *Economic Origins of Jeffersonian Democracy*, Beard was acutely conscious of the fact that most presidential electors were then chosen not by popular vote but by the state legislatures. The fact, indeed, posed quite a methodological problem for him, for he was interested in discovering whether (or showing that) the principal voter support for

Jefferson came from the masses of farmers and planters—and voter analysis without voters is obviously impossible. At least he did not, on this occasion, entirely ignore the problem imposed by the way things worked politically, though it could be argued that the ingenious method he devised for circumventing it amounted to the same thing. (What he did was analyze the socioeconomic basis of the popular vote for electors in three of the four states where voters chose them directly, analyze the vote for legislators in two states, analyze the vote in one more state by projecting the party vote for governor as a reflection of sentiments on the presidency, and largely ignore the other states, including four which were overwhelmingly populated by small farmers but cast all their electoral votes for Adams.)[34]

But on a later occasion, in dealing with this same election in a more general fashion in *The Rise of American Civilization*, he ignored the problem and related problems completely, with the result that he made at least four broad statements that were both wrong and in contradiction to his earlier account: He said (1) that the election was up to the voters; (2) that the news of the election of Jefferson was known in the autumn of 1800; (3) that the Federalists controlled a majority of the state delegations in the House of Representatives, which decided the election after it turned out that Burr had received the same number of electoral votes as Jefferson; and (4) that as a result Hamilton was able to swing the election in favor of Jefferson.[35]

The last weakness in Beard's approach to history—the personal attribute that lends a tragic continuity to his entire life's work—is more delicate and more involved. Superficially the attribute seems innocuous enough: it was that, in his *Economic Interpretation of the Constitution* and in most of his other writings as well, Beard wrote primarily not as a historian but as a teacher. Great though his renowned opposition to waste and injustice may have been, greater yet was his hostility to the closed mind, to the narrow, the self-righteous, or the bigoted view.[36] Opening up the closed mind and forcing it to think is the greatest possible role of a teacher, and this, I believe, Beard regarded as his most important function in life.

But let us look at some obvious things about the teaching function and the function of historian—how they are connected and how they differ—so that, in looking closely at how Beard carried his teaching methods into his writings, we can better appreciate some of the perils of so doing. Let us recall, first, that until the latter part of the nineteenth century history was not a formal academic discipline; it was only very late in the century that it came to be widely taught in American colleges. Thus Beard, Turner, the scientific historians connected with Johns Hopkins, and the others of that generation were essentially the first generation of American historians with whom the profession of college teacher was combined in the same person with the professional historian, and thus the first for whom it was possible to confuse and intermix the two functions.

Most historians who teach in colleges know that the rules of the two games are different. In the first place, most of us realize that what we teach in the classroom is not and cannot be an account of "history as it actually happened." As for myself, in a semester, after holidays, quizzes, and other such things are allowed for, I have opportunity to deliver about thirty-eight lectures in a given course, and I can expect my students to read roughly fifteen books or the equivalent. Were I teaching a course on the summer of 1787, it might be possible to really teach some history within those limits. As things are, my lecture course in the fall is a course covering twenty years of American history and, in the spring, is one covering seventy years of American history. At that I am more fortunate than some of my colleagues (and probably most members of the profession), who have to cover several countries and a hundred, five hundred, even a thousand years and more in those thirty-eight hour-long lectures. Under such circumstances, it is absurd to deceive ourselves into believing that we can convey any real knowledge of what has happened in the human past. At worst, we must resort to generalizations so general as to be meaningless and to statements so oversimplified as to be distortions of what we know to have been the case. At best, we can do what Beard did, use the study of the human past as a device for stimulating, provoking, or forcing our students to think. In either event, what we teach is not history and we know it—or we should know it.

And even at best we find it valid, useful, and necessary to resort to various devices in the classroom which would not be tolerable in our writings. We oversimplify; we exaggerate; we depend upon secondary sources of questionable reliability; we attempt to stimulate our students by stating as fact theories we have not verified and have no intention of even investigating; when we have intelligent and well-informed students, we even challenge them occasionally by advancing as fact statements which we know to be false. In the classroom, I repeat, these are perfectly legitimate devices.

But when the class is over such devices must be left behind, and that is not always easy; indeed, the teacher-historian's most dangerous and insidious occupational peril is the tendency to confuse and intermix the function and methods of the teacher with those of the historian. When the confusion is inadvertent, it corrupts; when it is deliberate, it corrupts absolutely.

The relevance of all this to Charles A. Beard can be appreciated by recalling his career as a college professor. Though he retired from regular teaching in 1917—after a celebrated dispute over academic freedom—enough recollections of his methods in the classroom have been preserved to afford a revealing portrait. Apparently one of his favorite techniques was one that most good teachers use at least occasionally: playing the devil's advocate. He would come into class, exuding a contagious enthusiasm from every pore, and in an exciting and convincing way describe and interpret some major historical event or another. As often as not, some of the "facts" he used in delivering his account might be pure fabrication, and more often than not, he would delete certain salients, lift others from context, and generally select and order his data so as to lend credence to his interpretation for the day. And though he might come in the next day and deliberately present a diametrically opposed interpretation, in just as convincing a fashion, he would never admit it to his students. If his students challenged him he was delighted, and the student who could effectively demolish one of his interpretations endeared himself to Beard forever. But it was a part of the technique, as Beard used it, to defend the interpretation when it was challenged, no matter how spurious Beard knew it to be, and to defend it with consummate intellectual dexterity. If his account went unchallenged, or was not effectively challenged, Beard might or might not bother to correct it.[37]

I believe that in his heart Beard never left the classroom; instead, through his writings, he extended its boundaries a thousandfold. He was not a great historian, if he was really a historian at all—though in later life he came to desire, passionately, to be remembered as a great historian. But all along he *was* a great teacher, in the highest and most noble possible sense: his aim was to provoke thought, to jar people out of their clichés, to force them, by the brilliance of his own arguments and by deliberate sophistry, to look at things in a fresh way.

This was precisely what Beard set out to do, and precisely what he said he hoped to do, in writing the *Economic Interpretation of the Constitution.* "These pages," he said in the first two lines of his preface, "are designed to suggest new lines of historical research." He published the book, he said, "in the hope that a few of this generation of historical scholars may be encouraged to turn away from barren 'political' history to a study of the real economic forces which condition great movements in politics"—in short, to look at the subject in a fresh way.[38]

The excessive veneration with which most Americans viewed the Constitution and the Founding Fathers was, to Beard, objectionable not principally as a barrier to social justice (as many progressives were asserting in 1913), but as a barrier to open-minded study and understanding of the subject. To make possible a break from the narrow view, Beard set out to humanize the Founding Fathers: to demonstrate that they were not demigods, but real people who had lived in a real world, not in a vacuum. In a sense, at least, the kind of interpretation he chose as a vehicle for his task was of secondary importance. In 1916, in fact, after pointing out to his students in class that "one effective propaganda method is the method of emphasis and exaggeration," he said that in his book he had given "exclusive emphasis" to the economic approach, "not because I believed that it was the only correct one, but because it was an important (perhaps the most important) and a neglected one." It is conceivable that had Beard grown up in a different time and place—had he heard, say, Freud instead of hard-nosed politics being discussed in his father's parlor—he might, to have accomplished his purpose, very well have written a treatise on the sex lives of the Founding Fathers, rather than on their economic lives.[39]

In putting the book together, Beard was clearly more concerned with making a challenging, convincing, and provocative case than he was with being accurate. The book has two or three hundred minor factual inaccuracies that I know of, but that is not the point. What is instructive to note is the many instances in which Beard stated as fact something which he had every opportunity to know was not fact. In these instances—even after one allows for the possibility that some errors may be attributable to overeager graduate students to whom he may have assigned parts of the research—Beard's errors are such that one is forced to conclude that he was either incredibly careless, which I cannot believe, or blind stupid, which he was not, or deliberately stacking the cards.

A few examples may be cited. In describing the economic interests of Daniel of St. Thomas Jenifer, a delegate from Maryland to the Philadelphia Convention, Beard wrote that Jenifer himself held no public securities, but that his son, Daniel Jenifer, Jr., had several thousand dollars' worth of them; and on that basis Beard, in his summaries, classified Jenifer as being among the large security holders in the convention. But Beard knew, it was scarcely possible for him not to have known, that Jenifer had no children—at least no legitimate ones—for in both of the sources Beard used to gather data on Jenifer, it is expressly stated that Jenifer was a bachelor. Indeed, Beard quoted directly from William Pierce's five-sentence sketch of Jenifer, and two of those five sentences are comments on Jenifer's bachelorhood. In the case of Gunning Bedford, Jr., a delegate from Delaware, the source Beard used goes to great pains to explain that there were two Gunning Bedfords in Delaware, that the delegate was a man of modest means, and that the other Gunning Bedford, not the delegate, later became governor, under whose administration the Bank of Delaware was created. Yet with that as his only source of information, Beard calmly asserted that the delegate Gunning Bedford later became governor, under whose administration the Bank of Delaware was created. This in fact was a bit of double sophistry; for in another part of his book Beard used a documentary source that makes it clear that the governorship of Delaware was merely a figurehead position, carrying with it no influence over legislation whatever. Again, in numerous instances—for example, regarding delegates Nicholas Gilman, William Samuel Johnson, Charles Pinckney, and others—Beard stated that delegates owned securities at the time of the convention, or at least funded securities under the Act of 1790, whereas the sources he cited clearly record that the securities were acquired five to ten years later.[40]

The list of such instances in which Beard's sources do not say what he told us they say, or even contradict what Beard told us, could go on and on. Equally interesting is another sophistic device, that of making a statement which is literally true but which, because something is left out, suggests something quite untrue. In describing the security holdings of William Few, for example, Beard says that this delegate from Georgia funded a certificate of 1779 having a "nominal" value of $2,170. This is perfectly true. But in context the implication is that "nominal" value means par or face value, that Few was the owner of $2,170 worth of securities. What Beard left out is that the certificate had, much earlier, been scaled down to a par value of $114.80—a fact which, given the way the account books are set up, it was all but impossible for Beard not to have noticed. The market value of Few's holding, incidentally, his cash investment in it, was about $15. In describing the holdings of Thomas Fitzsimons, Beard did the same kind of thing, using the same volume of the records of the Loan of 1790. Again, Few furnishes another example of the same technique. Beard wrote that Few "was connected with the Georgia Union Company, which was involved in the Yazoo land deals" in the early 1790's, and the implication is that it was by such shady ventures that Few was ultimately able to accumulate a sizable fortune. It is perfectly true, as Beard indicated, that Few was "involved in" the infamous Yazoo frauds: his involvement consisted of instigating the investigation that resulted in a nullification of the fraudulent grants, and Beard's source of information makes that clear.[41]

And so on. In none of these instances, considered separately, does the minor misstatement of the facts seem particularly important, but their cumulative effect is enormous. For example, these and similar devices result in almost doubling Beard's list of large security holders in the Philadelphia Convention. In the book as a whole the distorting effect is tremendous.

Whether, in this instance, Beard's adaptation of his classroom methods for use in a book was justifiable, I am not prepared to judge. In doing what he did here, Beard did historical scholarship an invaluable service, for even more than his students, the historical profession needed to be jarred out of its inertia, its conservatism, its rut.[42] Quite possibly no less spectacular a teaching job could have accomplished the task.

But incalculable are the moral perils inherent in such an undertaking. The teacher's role is to open up the mind and set it in motion. The historian's role is to serve as custodian of man's memory of himself. He who takes it upon him, as teacher or for whatever reason, to present history-as-thought which is consciously at variance with history-as-past-actuality thereby decides what it is *desirable* for man to remember. This is the most presumptuous decision imaginable; it is nothing less than a decision to play God. In the short run, it is merely folly; in the long run, it inevitably corrupts the man who would do it.

In the short run, Beard's work merely accomplished the opposite of what he set out to accomplish. Such was the powerful persuasiveness of the thesis, as Beard wove it, that despite his warning, his readers took it at face value, rather than as a challenge, as he intended it. Thus the Founding Fathers, instead of being humanized, became more institutionalized than ever before. Transformed from demigods into economic men, they re-emerged in a new set of artificial, institutional trappings that would be palatable to the skeptical twentieth century, as their earlier image would not. To be sure, this was not Beard's fault, but that of his fellows and followers. He handed them a light, and he can scarcely be denounced for their remaining in darkness.[43]

But once having elected to write, as fact, statements which he had every reason to know were not fact, Beard had made an irreversible move. The road to corrupt use of his methods was a long one, but the first step had been taken.

He took the next step four years later. Some readers may remember the work of the Creel Committee—the Committee on Public Information, the official American propaganda agency during World War I. Fewer, I daresay, will remember the history subcommittee of the Creel Committee, for this is a chapter in American historiography of which historians are not particularly proud and which has all but disappeared from the accounts of the war. This subcommittee, following the pattern set by the history branch of Wellington House, the British counterpart of the Committee on Public Information, wrote and disseminated tons of history, distorted history, and open lies called history, for purposes of war propaganda. And not only did the subcommittee distribute its pamphlets and books in fantastic quantities—literally millions—but it also invaded the high schools, indoctrinating history teachers, removing textbooks it considered objectionable, and ordering certain passages clipped from others.[44]

The propaganda had many aspects, but in general the idea was to depict the Germans as barbarians, militaristic but second-rate in actual warfare, and to show that Anglo-American relations had always been friendly and that American relations with Germany had always been bad. Thus, for example, would the Apsley House historians bestow all the credit for the victory at Waterloo upon the Duke of Wellington and ignore the vital part played by the Prussians under Blücher. The Creel Committee historians could hardly expunge the American Revolution, but they could revise it considerably. Thus General von Steuben disappeared, and the Revolution itself was changed into a struggle not between Britain and America but between American colonists over who should rule at home, a struggle that became a war only because George III, a mad German king of England, hired German mercenaries to whip the Americans into line.

But what the propaganda line was is not so important as the fact that a large number of American historians forsook their responsibility to scholarship, and their avowed dedication to seek and tell the truth, no matter how painful or unpopular, and lent their energy, their talents, and their prestige to a deliberate distortion of history. I do not intend to pass judgment on these men for what they did; I could not even if I wished, for the details of individual responsibility are, as yet, too little known. But it is a fact that as a group, from which any could secede if he objected to what was being done, they put something else—in this instance, what they sincerely regarded as the national interest—ahead of their feeling of obligation to tell the truth as they saw it.

The reader will recognize the names of many of these historians. Guy Stanton Ford, then dean at the University of Minnesota, later president of his institution and of the American Historical Association, headed the subcommittee; among his fellow workers were Andrew C. McLaughlin, Evarts B. Greene, J. Franklin Jameson, Frederick L. Paxson, William E. Dodd, Dana C. Munro, Frederick Jackson Turner, Carl Becker, and Charles A. Beard.[45] The full extent of Beard's direct participation I do not know; I only know that he was active, that he contributed to the propaganda *War Cyclopedia*, and wrote a text for the armed forces in which, among other things, he developed the idea that during the Revolution the Americans and British were really friendly all along, and equally interested in casting off the tyranny of George III, which "facts" brought about the war.[46]

That Beard worked and wrote for an organization whose sole function was the production and dissemination of war propaganda is extremely interesting in view of the antiwar books he wrote during the 1930's and 1940's. It is more interesting, however, as another step in his career: in his writings he had now selectively emphasized and exaggerated—which is to say, consciously distorted—not as a means of opening minds but as means of closing them, as a means of influencing the present course of history.

After the war Beard returned to teaching through books, and also became an international figure for his advisory work in governmental reform, particularly in the area of city planning and management. In the next decade his principal historical writings were textbooks, and in the decade of the 1930's he increasingly wrote tracts, articles, and books on current political subjects. I do not intend to trace here the downhill evolution in the quality of his works as he moved from historian to teacher to writer of texts to propagandist, except to say this—and it can be abundantly documented: that as his prestige and political activity increased he apparently felt increasingly free to use his old classroom methods, and to write history not as he understood it to have happened, but as he thought it desirable that people should believe it happened.[47]

He gave his rationale for doing so in his presidential address before the American Historical Association in 1933, a paper which he called "Written History as an Act of Faith."

Any written history [he reasoned] involves the selection of a topic and an arbitrary delimitation of its borders—cutting off connections with the universal. Within the borders arbitrarily established, there is a selection and organization of facts by the process of thought. This selection and organization—a single act—will be controlled by the historian's frame of reference, composed of things deemed necessary and of things deemed desirable. . . . Whatever its nature the frame is inexorably there, in the mind. And in the frame only three broad conceptions of all history as actuality are possible. History is chaos and every attempt to interpret it otherwise is an illusion. History moves around in a kind of cycle. History moves in a line, straight or spiral, and in some direction. The historian may seek to escape these issues by silence or by a confession of avoidance or he may face them boldly, aware of the intellectual and moral perils inherent in any decision—in his act of faith.

It was in this connection that Beard said that a historian's immortality "will depend upon the length and correctness of his forecast" about the way history moved and would move in the future. His own guess, his own view of things desirable and probable, he said, was that the world was moving in the direction of a collectivist democracy.[48]

There emerge at this point two fundamental aspects of Beard's psyche as a man, as a teacher, as a historian; or, if one balks at the word "psyche," substitute Beard's philosophy of history and his concept of the teacher-historian-citizen. One was the conviction that the historian should perform what had, in fact, been the universal function of historians among the ancients and the primitives, namely to preserve and adapt myths about the past to suit the changing needs of changing times; that, indeed, the historian could do no other, for the pursuit of pure truth was chimerical. The other was the belief that the great and immortal historian was the one who, in Cushing Strout's paraphrase, "wove the warp of the future into the weft of the past by an act of prophetic discernment, proving his power by the accuracy of his prediction."[49]

These things came together, and Beard's career as a historian came to its tragic final climax, in his last major historical work—his vitriolic, heavily documented, two-volume indictment of Franklin Roosevelt's foreign policy, published in 1946 and 1948. That work was an effort to prove that Roosevelt led the United States into war in 1941 by deliberately provoking an attack by the Japanese, all the while hypocritically reassuring the American people that he was seeking neutrality and peace. To make his case Beard employed complete sophistry, with reckless abandon intermixing facts and fancy and twisted logic. The performance alienated virtually all of Beard's followers and admirers, who found it inexplicable that Beard, who had warmly supported the New Deal, should suddenly turn upon the president and, in a palpably fraudulent manner, hurl wild and malicious charges at him.[50]

But this was not, I submit, a sudden aberration on Beard's part; it was the logical outcome of his having decided that he could play at being God. Cushing Strout, in a brilliant analysis, has traced the process by which Beard came to write the final chapter. When the Depression came and as the New Deal began, Beard was not dismayed but hopeful: he believed that through technology and rational government planning, this was for America "the dawn, not the dusk, of the gods." But then two things happened. One was that the Nye Committee (1934) and the revisionist historians who worked with the committee's findings (1934–39) convinced Beard that America's entry into World War I had, after all, been more the doing of munitions makers and industrialists and international bankers than it had been a function of American idealism. The other was that, as the clouds of war began to gather again over Europe and Asia, Beard began to be possessed by the reflection that the Jeffersonians, the Jacksonians, and the Wilsonians had all suffered their reform programs to be diverted and compromised and ultimately destroyed by war, and possessed also by the fear that Roosevelt would follow the same course. By February of 1935 Beard was ready with an ominous prognostication: "The Pacific war awaits."[51]

Thereafter, as Strout points out, "Beard's historical writing became an increasingly tendentious and sardonically phrased plea for a policy of continentalism." He cast off the mantle of the disinterested scholar and testified in the House of Representatives against building up the navy and in the Senate against the Lend Lease program, and advised such prominent isolationists as Charles A. Lindbergh. "With what a sense of outraged sanity must Beard have watched history move not toward his predicted and cherished goal of a last outpost of collectivist democracy, where men reaped the harvests of an abundant civilization, blessed by technological triumph, but instead toward American intervention in a vast war. It could not be. . . ." Beard's concern with the "realities" underlying appearances had always leaned him toward a conspiratorial view of events, and now he decided that

some perverse influence must have deflected the proper course of history. Beard's act of faith was a bold toss of the dice; the stakes were too high for him to lose gracefully. Someone must have rigged the game. There had, therefore, to be some villainous dark soul who had arrogantly upset the best laid plans of thinking men. In his indictment of Roosevelt all the various threads of Beard's historical philosophy came together with as impressive an appearance of inexorability as could be found in his own accounts of the remorseless sweep of historical forces.[52]

I close with a word addressed to the professional historian rather than to the general reader. There is in Beard's career a lesson for all of us. There is little likelihood that many of us will ever deliberately falsify in our writings. The danger is great, however, that we may falsify inadvertently, and the greatest danger is not that our work will be corrupted by our political biases, but by intermixing and confusing our roles as teacher with our roles as historian. If doing so could corrupt a man of the superior gift, massive intellect, and high moral purpose of Charles A. Beard, it can certainly corrupt you and me. Let the teacher-historian beware.

Vernon Louis Parrington

RALPH H. GABRIEL

5)

THE CONVERSATION in publishing circles in New York in the 1920's drifted frequently to the astonishing rise of a new firm established in 1919 by two young men from Henry Holt. Their names were Alfred Harcourt and Donald C. Brace. In that order they assumed the roles of editor and business manager. In 1920 they swept the market with *Main Street* and followed this success with other Sinclair Lewis titles which became household words. At the same time the enterprising Harcourt brought Carl Sandburg into his company of authors.

Some time in the early part of the twenties Van Wyck Brooks served for a period as literary adviser to Harcourt, Brace and Company. He told Alfred Harcourt one day about a manuscript he recently had read for two other publishers. It interested him. To each house Brooks had sent a recommendation that it be published. The work dealt with American thought in the Colonial period and had been written by an unknown, a Vernon L. Parrington of the University of Washington. Both houses had turned it down—too limited in scope to sell enough copies to make it a justifiable commercial venture. The story intrigued Harcourt, an editor on the prowl for books. He wrote to Parrington asking him to send on what he had written. The man from the Coast complied and added an outline of two more proposed volumes. But Parrington's letter said more. "He had, however," Alfred Harcourt wrote later, "stopped work on the project, because the rejection of the first volume on the Colonial period had discouraged him, and he didn't want to take it up again unless someone would publish the first book."

When he read the manuscript, Harcourt agreed both with the judgment of Brooks and with that of the houses which had rejected it. But the outline of the proposed second volume seemed to promise a wider readership and textbook sales. Harcourt decided to gamble. "I wrote Parrington," he said, "that if he would finish the second volume, we would agree to publish them both. This was even more encouraging than he had hoped, and he completed it promptly."[1] The two volumes appeared in 1927 with the title, *Main Currents in American Thought*. It won the Pulitzer Prize.

Harcourt's tale of a discouraged Parrington quitting work on the writing of a book that was to being him immediate fame raises questions about the author. The project had not been recently undertaken. From a note which Parrington sent to Cambridge on the occasion of the Twenty-fifth Reunion of his Harvard Class of 1893, he seems to have begun the work in 1913. The twice-rejected manuscript represented, ignoring a few short pieces, the first fruits of more than a decade of labor. The abandonment of the work because of disappointment suggests an emotional temperament. The emotional quality of the published work is unmistakable.

It was no accident that in the chatter of the campuses in the 1930's the name of the author practically supplanted the title of the book. *Main Currents* is to an uncommon degree a personal statement. Parrington presented his characters as people whom he liked or disliked, sometimes even as heroes or villains. Of John Cotton, who stepped into the beginning of his story, he wrote: "An apologist— and whoever has felt the charm of John Cotton's personality easily becomes an apologist—will perhaps find some grounds of excuse for his later conduct."[2] Parrington found the grounds "in the roots of his environment." When the man from the West came to Cotton Mather who brought New England's first Puritan century to an end he went all out. "What a crooked and diseased mind lay back of those eyes that were forever spying out occasions to magnify self. He grovels in proud self-abasement. He distorts the most obvious reality. . . . His egoism blots out charity and even the divine mercy."[3] It was refreshing for a generation which had been nourished on histories of American letters straight out of the genteel tradition to stumble on a scholar who was willing not only to speak his own mind but also to speak for the Lord.

As he read the literature of the South in ante-bellum days Parring-

ton came upon a story of injustice—doubly poignant because it
involved a man of the people. The Society of Charleston snubbed
their fellow townsman, William Gilmore Simms. A man of humble
birth and an irregular education became the writer of tales of the
back country as vigorous as the frontier itself. Parrington resented the
slights suffered by a man of letters whose writings added luster to the
town at the hands of its social Establishment. "After all these years,"
wrote the Western democrat, "one may cherish a grudge against the
amiable little city for its shabby treatment of Gilmore Simms."
Parrington went on to tell the sad story of an "ardent Southerner
loyal to all the Carolinian totems and taboos" overcome and defeated
by his environment. After the death of his wife Simms married a
widow possessed of a plantation and thus won admission to a sort of
anteroom of the club. He turned to the writing of society romance.
But the very ardor of his identification palsied his hand. His ro-
mances were trash. Parrington mourned the decline of an artist. He
agreed with Simms' friend Paul Hayne, who wrote after the author's
death: "Simms' genius *never had fair play!*"

Parrington found in Thomas Jefferson the hero for his story. He
did not give as much space to the discussion of Jefferson as to other
men who have made American history. But a Jeffersonian spirit
pervades the book. "To all who profess faith in the democratic
ideal," said Parrington,

Jefferson is a perennial inspiration. A free soul, he loved freedom enough
to deny it to none; an idealist, he believed that the welfare of the whole,
and not the prosperity of any group, is the single end of government.
. . . Among the greater thinkers of the constitutional period Jefferson
remains by far the most vital and suggestive, the one to whom later
generations may turn most hopefully.[4]

This personal manner of writing—these expressions of enthusiasms,
of hostilities, of regrets—gave verve to the book. One can begin to
understand that a man of such intensity of feeling might have been
bowled over when his manuscript came back twice from New York
with polite notes that it was interesting but that not enough people
would buy it to make it publishable. One wonders if this frank and
emotional personal quality of the writing which Van Wyck Brooks
was called upon to judge was not one of the reasons why he could
not forget the manuscript he had seen twice turned down. Parrington's prose made *Main Currents* a contribution to letters.

Such a book, in its turn, could not fail to arouse enthusiasm, hostility, and regrets. Charles A. Beard led the cheers when it first appeared. The historian of New Milford, Connecticut, wrote in the *Nation* on May 18, 1927: "In carrying out this project he (Parrington) has written a truly significant book; according to signs on every hand, a work that promises to be epoch-making, sending exhilarating gusts through the deadly miasma of academic criticism." The immediate and continued success of the book, particularly as a text for courses in American literature, demonstrated that there were many who agreed with the Beard appraisal.

But *Main Currents* evoked hostile appraisals as personal and forthright as those of Parrington himself. Stark Young said a word in 1937. He spoke against the background of experience as a one-time professor of literature, a dramatic critic for the *New Republic*, a poet, a playwright, and a novelist. As one of the Fugitives he, following Jefferson, had been an agrarian. He turned to Parrington's account of Simms. "Snappy," said Young,

facile, glib, sounds sharp and searching, but it won't hold water. . . . Sometimes I think what a terrible thing it is to be articulate, or at least to have a rush of words that seem to express your very mystery. Take Parrington's sentences implying that if Simms had been more intellectual he would have gained detachment from the present and immediate, been capable of aloofness and hence capable to criticism of Charleston society —analysing, comparing, and judging not being possible to a nature so ardent! How plausible it all sounds! But it is only half truths. If you want to say that if Simms had had more intellect, he might better have *penetrated* the principles, bases, and so forth of the society he believed in, that would have made sense. As for the notion that ardor blocks analysis, comparison, and judgment, we could scarcely say that Simms was more ardent than Dante, for example, or St. Augustine. . . . As for standing apart, detached, what about Tolstoy and Dostoievsky?[5]

Young concluded: ". . . a lively and aggressive patchwork of half-baked theories." Young, however, wrote only a dissent to a majority opinion in that decade when "Parrington" was the standard text in American literature courses and found its way into some history courses.

Parrington's life experiences provide some clues to his temperament and to his animosities and enthusiasms. James L. Colwell has liquidated the old and plausible myth that the author of *Main Currents* was an angry young man of the Populist persuasion.[6]

Parrington's father was a young lawyer in Illinois when the crisis of the 1860's drew him into the Civil War. He served as an officer with the Fourth Colored Infantry, received a wound at the second attack on Petersburg and was mustered out in 1866, a brevetted lieutenant colonel. In 1877 the Colonel moved his family, which now included Vernon Louis (born in 1871), to Lyon County, Kansas, and made his home on the land. The elder Parrington prospered, becoming possessed, in addition to the home farm, of three others together with some town real estate. Active in Republican politics, he won election as judge of probate in 1884. He then moved to Emporia, the county seat, and sent Vernon to the preparatory department and then to Emporia College itself. In these years memories of his service with the Fourth Colored Regiment and possession of a comfortable office and property conditioned the post-bellum Republicanism of Parrington senior. He was one of those substantial citizens who helped to establish that rock-ribbed tradition which, still robust fifty years later, enabled Kansas to give Alf Landon to the Republican Party. The boy, Vernon, inevitably absorbed the political outlook of his family. Only when he became adult did he look at the national political and economic scene with new eyes.

The Presbyterian College of Emporia confirmed young Vernon Parrington in an orthodox religious faith. Though his abilities on the baseball diamond brought him to the attention of his classmates, his undergraduate triumph seems to have been an oration entitled "God in History" delivered to a hushed audience. The speaker saw progress through history as a working out of divine purpose. He looked to a future where progress would continue. Two certitudes—biblical orthodoxy and the inevitability of progress—provided the underpinning of the thought of the young Kansas collegian at the beginning of the final decade of the nineteenth century.

At Harvard, where he got his degree in 1893, some reading of Henry Drummond and Herbert Spencer brought evolution into his world view. Religious convictions acquired in Emporia began to fade. Perhaps they had never been tenaciously held. As an adolescent his interest turned toward art. In Emporia College he painted well enough to attract the attention of his classmates. When he was sixteen, he decided that he would seek a career in painting. At Harvard his aesthetic interests continued but came to focus in the study of literature.

After graduation he came back to his Kansas alma mater to teach English and French and to publish poems in the college periodical. William Allen White has left a picture of Emporia in 1897 which illuminates, though faintly, the milieu in which the young instructor in literature moved. In that year White returned to Emporia from an exciting trip to New York City, where he had met some of the great and the near great of the East. When he went home to Emporia, he reminisced later, he

strolled into the corner bookstore where Vernon Parrington and Will Griffith, a painter who had studied in Paris and later was to have his own fame on the Pacific Coast, and John Van Shaick, the young English professor at the College of Emporia, John Madden, who had once run as a Populist candidate for Congress, and maybe Vernon Kellogg—if he was home that year—were loafing. . . . For years that corner in the book-store there in Commercial Street was a hangout for the young fellows around town, young fellows too proud for pool, too wicked for prayer meetings, too lazy for baseball (though Vernon Parrington pitched a mean curve on the Emporia Browns), too sophisticated for the local poker game, and too young and full of visions to let the world go by without trying to understand it. Though certainly we were as blind as anyone. How could we know that the syncopated puff-puff of the gasoline engine in Kincaid's cabinet shop . . . was the machine gun of an impending revolution?"[7]

In the year of White's return Parrington with some sadness left his home town to join the English faculty of the University of Oklahoma. The university in the Sooner State offered him more money than his old college gave him.

Parrington's role in the bookstore gang of Commerical Street must have been that of aesthete.[8] His poems appeared from time to time in the college paper. At Commencement in 1895, when Emporia awarded him an unearned M.A., he addressed the assembled students and visitors on the subject "Poetry and the Mission of Poetry." "It was full of beautiful and poetical thoughts," reported the *Emporia Gazette* just being acquired by William Allen White, "and was an appeal to the students to see the beautiful in life and the concealed poetry in it."[9] Probably Parrington at this time was reading John Ruskin and William Morris. Certainly within a few years after the M.A. he was deeply immersed in Morris.

During Parrington's teaching years at Emporia and the eleven which followed at Norman, the nineteenth-century English-Gothic Revival led by Carlyle, Ruskin, and Morris spread to the United States. At the beginning of the twentieth century the faculty of Yale College fixed Carlyle and Ruskin in what became a famous freshman English course. In the 1890's Elbert Hubbard, after a sojourn with Morris, established the Roycrofters at West Aurora near Buffalo, New York. Morris—poet, printer, proponent of natural decoration and pure color produced by handwork and inspired by a passion for beauty, antagonist of commercialism, critic of industrialism, utopian socialist—captivated the young instructor in literature. In 1897 Parrington published in *College Life* of Emporia College a series entitled "Some Political Sketches," in which he leaned heavily on Ruskin and Morris in the authors' criticism of American faith in government by businessmen.[10]

Main Currents carries the stamp of Morris in particular. The imprint illuminates Parrington's thought processes. Emerson reminded him of the craftsman of Kelmscott. "There is more than a suggestion of William Morris," wrote Parrington,

in the doctrine elaborated in *Man the Reformer;* that the industrial revolution with its factory system, must be judged in the light of its effect upon the workmen, that the true function of work must be explored and every man ply his tool to his own good. The suggestion that "a man should have a farm or mechanical craft for his culture," was an implicit denial of industrialism in the days of its first triumphs—a denial that Morris would have endorsed.[11]

Concerning Thoreau, Parrington commented:

In other bits Walden is curiously like *Hopes and Fears for Art,* and the drift of the whole is one with the revolutionary teachings of Morris, that the abiding satisfactions are those which spring from free creative work. . . . Thoreau needed only to have lived in a world that honored craftsmanship to have opened fully the vein of gold that Morris dug his philosophy from; he had the instinct of a craftsman but not his training."[12]

This is an odd comment on a young man trained to the craft of pencil making. For Parrington's appraisal of Henry Adams, Morris again provided perspective. "Even in his rebellion against his past," wrote the author of *Main Currents,*

[Adams] could not get away from it, but like Ruskin and John Henry Newman came to affirm . . . that the singular glory of the Middle Ages was the *élan* that came to expression in the adoration of the Virgin. As a child of generations of Puritans he came back finally in the twilight of his studies to the great ideal of faith. Yet it is not without suggestion that William Morris, who more nearly than any other modern expressed in his life the spirit of the Middle Ages, never concerned himself much with the medieval church—neither its cathedrals nor its scholasticism nor its miracles—never talked about an age of faith, would scarcely have understood, indeed, what was meant by a mystical *élan*; but discovered the secret of the earlier civilization in the gild rather than the church, and traced the source of the haunting beauty that clings to all its works to the psychology of craftsmanship that had found delight in shaping the raw material to the craftsman's dreams.[13]

For Adams, Morris provided a suggestive foil. In his discussion of Bellamy, Parrington disclosed that, if he had ever joined with Morris in his rejection of the machine, the American had changed his mind:

"A horrible cockney dream," William Morris called *Looking Backward* and by way of answer sketched his *News from Nowhere*, loveliest of utopias with its anarchistic freedom set in country fields. Morris was an artist with an ample share of Ruskinian prejudice against the machinery that Bellamy so greatly developed; nevertheless Bellamy was far more realistic in his understanding of the part the machine will play in the society of the future—to put upon it the slave-work of society, surely means much for human freedom.[14]

Parrington in 1927 had obviously learned the prophetic significance of the gasoline engine in Kincaid's cabinet shop.

The highways which radiated from Emporia and from Norman traversed the farmlands of the Plains. The tumultuous industrialism of the distant Northeast, of the Great Lakes, and of the Ohio Valley touched these centers of commerce primarily through the railroad. Yet no intelligent citizen in these communities could fail to note the march of economic events. The English medievalists of the nineteenth century seem first to have turned the thought of the young professor of literature in Kansas and Oklahoma to criticism of the emerging industrialism and to have suggested a philosophy on which to found an appraisal. They prepared the way for later influences that were to prevail and to determine Parrington's approach to industrialism especially as manifested in big business.

In one particular Parrington took to heart the message of the gospel which inspired William Morris's *Kelmscott Chaucer*, the message that craftsmanship is the foundation of art. Parrington made writing his craft. He gave to that craft that loving care Morris demanded of all craftsmen. In the planning of *Main Currents* he gave thought to form and proportion. In the writing he took infinite pains in the choice of words and the creation of phrases. He was particularly proud of one phrase, "the great barbecue." It continued to echo beyond the middle of the century. In the matter of style Parrington achieved a success. For Charles Beard his prose stood out like a well-cut agate in a bushel of dull academic pebbles. Stark Young, himself a practiced stylist, acknowledged in his criticism the skill of the author of *Main Currents*. But Young saw Parrington as a polisher of bright surfaces that flashed a seeming profundity of thought which analysis of underlying content failed to discover.

Parrington's intellectual road from Lyon County, Kansas, to *Main Currents* had detoured little from that followed by the hopeful liberals of his generation. It began amidst the individualism and the social informalities of an agricultural community some of whose members could still remember the frontier fights of the 1850's, which brought about the emergence of John Brown in Pottawatomie County not far to the north. After Kansas had come Harvard, where Charles W. Eliot's elective system made it possible for the somewhat arty young man from Emporia to avoid both natural science and philosophy—and, for good measure, history. Parrington's artistic and literary interests drew the young professor of literature in Emporia and Norman to the English medievalists, who gave him perspective and inspiration. Then in 1908, on the campus of the University of Washington, he met James Allen Smith.

Perhaps similar experiences first drew the two men together. Marietta College in Ohio had dismissed Smith in 1896 because he published in the previous year a book suggesting theories of the gold standard at variance with those of the Establishment of the day. Parrington had lost his post at the University of Oklahoma when a new Democratic administration in the state summarily replaced the president with a party hack and about a third of the faculty were fired or resigned in protest. Twenty-one years after coming to Washington Parrington wrote, in what turned out to be his valedictory, an introduction to a posthumous publication of a book by Smith.

Parrington made it a testimony of friendship. "I have written these few pages of comment," he said in 1929, "on the life-work of a courageous and self-sacrificing scholar with a deep sense of personal loss. For nearly twenty years Professor Smith was my colleague and friend, and our intellectual interests and political sympathies traveled congenially the same paths."[15] Smith added a dynamic political philosophy to the mental furnishings of one who had come west across the mountains from Norman.

Certain experiences in his previous career had prepared Parrington for the absorption of Smith's Progressivism. Parrington's colleague at the University of Washington E. H. Eby has described the impact made by Hippolyte Taine's *Histoire de la littérature anglaise* on the professor who was teaching American literature. Taine emphasized the importance of environmental factors—racial peculiarities and epoch—in the shaping of works of letters. Taine's determinism had much in common with the economic determinism of Smith in his interpretation of the realities behind the writing of the Constitution. More important than Taine, however, the bent of Parrington's developing thought pointed toward the democratic philosophy of Smith. As early as 1897 young Parrington published "Political Sketches" in *College Life* just before leaving Emporia. In these his rejection of "The Business Ideal" was avowedly in the mood of Ruskin and Morris. He urged "The Humanitarian Ideal" for the educated man who, Parrington insisted, had the obligation, because he was educated, to participate in politics. A generous humanism, affirmed eleven years before he came to the Northwest, prepared Parrington to adopt Smith's fighting philosophy.[16]

Smith, writing six years before Charles A. Beard's *Economic Interpretation of the Constitution*, for the first time in the literature of political science described the Constitution as a "reactionary" document. "Democracy," he said, —"government by the people, directly responsible to them—was not the object which the framers of the American Constitution had in view, but the very thing the framers wished to avoid." The framers, thought Smith, with Machiavellian skill, set up a mechanism intended to make majority rule impossible while preserving its external forms. The men of the Constitutional Convention subverted majority rule by three devices: checks and balances, judicial veto, and a rigid amending process.

Smith thought the judiciary especially important. "It is easy to see in the exaltation of the judiciary," he commented,

a survival of the old medieval doctrine that the king can do no wrong. . . . The exclusive right claimed by this branch of the government to guard and interpret the Constitution is the same prerogative originally claimed by the king. The judiciary, too, is a branch of our government farthest removed from the influence of public opinion and consequently the one in which the monarchical principle most largely survives.[17]

Senator Robert M. LaFollette, reading Smith's *The Spirit of American Government*, discovered that the man from the far Northwest had provided the incipient Progressive revolt with a philosophy. Beard's *Economic Interpretation of the Constitution* in 1913 reinforced Smith's account of what went on in the Constitutional Convention. The Progressive movement began as a crusade to re-establish the power of the people—the direct primary, initiative, referendum, and recall.

Twenty years and a World War passed before Parrington published *Main Currents*. The Progressive movement had passed into history. Yet in 1927 he repeated the doctrine of Smith concerning the Constitution:

It was the first response to the current liberal demand for written constitutions as a safeguard against tyranny, but it was aimed at the encroachments of agrarian majorities rather than at Tory minorities . . . although the new Constitution professed to rest on the sovereignty of the people, the men who framed it refused to interpret the term, sovereignty of the people, in an equalitarian sense. They did not profess to be, in the words of John Quincy Adams, "slavish adorers of our sovereign lords the people."[18]

Parrington returned to his colleague's theme when he dealt with the confrontation of President Jefferson, protagonist of the principle of majority rule, and John Marshall after *Marbury* v. *Madison*. "As Jefferson watched Chief Justice John Marshall, gathering all things within the purview of the Federal judiciary," wrote the author of *Main Currents*,

preparing future strongholds by the skillful use of *obiter dicta*, legislating by means of judicial interpretation, nullifying the will of the majority, and with the power of repeal made nugatory by the complexity of the process, he saw clearly what the outcome would be. Surely that was no democracy where judge-made laws were enforced by bench warrants, and where the sovereign power lay beyond the immediate reach of popular will. The government that he desired would not rest on the legal fiction of an abstract justice above statutes and constitutions, whereof a group of judicial gentlemen were the repositories and guardians. It would be, like Paine's, "a plain thing, and fitted to the capacity of many heads"; for "where the law of the majority ceases to be acknowledged, there government ends; the law of the strongest takes its place."[19]

Progressivism had supplanted Parrington's earlier preoccupation with artistic and aesthetic matters. He undertook to broaden a history of American literature into a narrative of American thought. The liberalism whose origin he found in Jefferson and which came to flower in Progressivism provided him with his theme.

Parrington published *Main Currents* in the year in which Charles Lindbergh flew solo across the Atlantic. Parrington's was also a solo flight from oblivion. The book zoomed like a Fourth of July rocket across the American sky. In time, however, the trail of incandescence faded. The completed episode threw a light of its own on a period of history.

In 1913 when he began work on his *opus*, Parrington was a modern. In the academic world of the time professors of literature, English and European, had shouldered aside the classicists from their long-held pre-eminence in the humanities. In 1913 an ambitious young literary scholar normally looked across the Atlantic for material with which to test and display his talents. He chose Chaucer or Shakespeare or Goethe or Dante, to mention only a few of the giants. When put beside this gallery, American writers seemed diminutive. The atmosphere in the departments of English had not changed appreciably in 1927 when *Main Currents* appeared. "Professors of the subject [American literature]," wrote Howard Mumford Jones in the following year, "seem to be suffering from an inferiority complex; conscious that they have to present no Shakespeare or Goethe or Dante, they have adopted a morbid fear that comparisons prove them odious."[20] In 1913 Parrington, undertaking the study of the literature of the Republic, pioneered with the small company that defied the dominant trend. At least he taught courses in American literature at a young university on the Coast.

But when, with the care of an architect at his drawing board,

Parrington sketched out plans for his book, he decided against literary history. Perhaps he accepted the prevailing judgment concerning the inferiority of American writing. Whether or not he did, he undertook a maneuver that would enable him to avoid being accused of spending his time with second rate art. Reading Cooper, Hawthorne, Emerson, and even Charles Brockden Brown, he discovered that their writings reflected facets of American thought. He took pains to make a disclaimer at the very outset of his book. "With aesthetic judgments I have not been greatly concerned," he wrote in the foreword of Volume II. "I have not wished to evaluate reputations or weigh literary merits, but rather to understand what our fathers thought, and why they wrote as they did." What he meant by the last phrase is suggested by the ideas of economic determinism he had gotten from Taine and from Beard's *Economic Interpretation of the Constitution.*

In Volume II Parrington gave short shrift to Poe and to Longfellow. They belonged, he thought, with writers of belles-lettres. They could contribute little to his more robust story of American thought. Parrington's treatment of the two poets evoked bellows of rage. Harry Hayden Clark pointed out that the author of *Main Currents* had produced nine hundred pages in the first two volumes of which "two and a quarter pages are devoted to Poe and two and a half to Longfellow." "It is an obvious fallacy," Clark added, "and a dangerous sign, to favor economic determinism and then omit—or nearly omit—whatever disproves the theory." Parrington replied that he had not undertaken a history of American literature. "I have been concerned in the present study with the total pattern of American thought."[21] The slighting of Poe and Longfellow called forth a shrewder criticism from Yvor Winters. "The text," said Winters in 1940,

is wholly dependent upon two serious errors; namely that one can write a history of a culture with reference only to one intellectual tradition, in this case a tradition of extremely small influence in the first hundred and fifty years, that is, during the formative period, and that one can determine the ideas governing a work of art without making an attempt to understand the art as art.[22]

The significance of the Winters comment lies in the fact that Parrington allotted considerably more than half the space in *Main*

Currents to discussion of literary figures. Subsequent scholarship in this field, which had included the examination of literary art as art, has achieved extraordinary new insights into the thought expressed by many American men of letters.

Winters' remark about one intellectual tradition referred, of course, to Jeffersonian liberalism. Readers of the book could scarcely miss the emphasis. Twenty years later Merrill D. Peterson expressed a commonly held opinion. "*Main Currents*," he said, "is best understood as a history of American thought and expression within the limited ideological framework of Jeffersonian 'liberalism.' "[23] Parrington's rejoinder to the criticism of Harry Hayden Clark suggests that the author of *Main Currents in American Thought* believed that Jeffersonian liberalism and its opposite, Hamiltonian conservatism, constituted the totality of American thought. Parrington had, in fact, implied as much when he said in the foreword of Volume I: "The point of view from which I have endeavored to evaluate the materials, is liberal rather than conservative, Jeffersonian rather than Federalistic. . . ."

Parrington's statement in 1923 that he had attempted to find out what the Fathers thought, and his discovery of what might be called a protoliberalism at the very beginning of the seventeenth-century American story, attracted the almost immediate attention of Esther E. Burch of Reed College, to the south of the University of Washington. She worked through the bibliography which Parrington had listed for the thought of the early New Englanders, and in 1929 she published an essay entitled "The Sources of New England Democracy: A Controversial Statement in Parrington's *Main Currents in American Thought*." She discovered that the sources noted did not warrant the conclusions Parrington drew from them. She undoubtedly considered her essay a footnote to the statement which Parrington made in the foreword of Volume I: ". . . and very likely in my search I have found what I went forth to find, as others have discovered what they were seeking." Later scholarship concerning Puritan thought in early New England has supplanted the Parrington account. Esther Burch published her analysis in the spring of the year 1929, whose autumn saw the collapse of the stock market in October and the subsequent slalom of the economy into disaster.

Yvor Winters wrote in 1940 after the nation had climbed painfully out of depression. A sense of urgency filled the Winters commentary.

Main Currents had scored in the 1930's a remarkable success. In the opinion of Winters the use of the book as a text in the majority of the courses in American literature had magnified the evil influence of its bad scholarship. Actually one of its two chief defects, namely the preoccupation with a single tradition which Winters excoriated, provided the foundation for the sales appeal of the book. The story told in *Main Currents* fitted the mood of depression years. The prestige of the businessman, especially the banker, had plummeted. Millions of unemployed shuffled along the sidewalks or sat at home without purpose and with little hope. Some found momentary forgetfulness in Walt Disney's pioneer animated cartoon, "The Three Little Pigs" with its song for the times, "Who's Afraid of the Big, Bad Wolf?" Chaos in the economy shouted for reform—some thought for revolution. Concerned liberals who journeyed to Moscow came home to describe "the Soviet challenge to America" as the challenge of the idea and the fact of social planning. Among other liberals a fair number of men of letters began to look to Communism as the humanitarianism to end an age of suffering. Some joined the Communist party.

One of these, Granville Hicks, delivered in 1939 an extended critique of Parrington in *Science and Society, A Marxian Quarterly*. Hicks was at the time an established critic. In 1933 Macmillan had published his *The Great Tradition: An Interpretation of American Literature Since the Civil War* and had brought out a revision in 1935. In this book the keen quality of the literary criticism was blunted at times by the hopeful Marxism of the recent convert. "Parrington," said Hicks,

belonged to and was interested in a group of Jeffersonians who saw more or less clearly that, with the closing of the frontier, they must abandon the hope of establishing democracy on a basis of agrarian individualism. They turned their attention, though somewhat skittishly, to the proletariat, which Jefferson had feared, and they urged collective action of a circumscribed sort. Parrington might try to defend himself, Charles Beard, and others from the charge of going to school to Karl Marx, but he did not deceive their critics. If he was primarily and most of the time Jeffersonian, he was also, on occasion and to a certain extent, a Marxist. If that is a paradox, the fault is Mr. Parrington's.[24]

What Hicks had in mind was economic determinism, which Hicks found useful to explain the villains of Parrington's narrative but of no pertinence for the understanding of the heroes. These heroes were, in Parrington's words, "cultural sports of variations from the cultural type."[25] Of course Hicks intended his characterization of Parrington as a sometime Marxist as a compliment. It is clear that Hicks wrote the piece before the Hitler-Stalin pact of friendship in 1939 swept away his rosy illusions and caused him to quit the party. But Hicks made clear the fact that *Main Currents* attempted to trace the history of liberalism in the American scene for citizens who were caught in a desperate predicament. It was an age in which American liberalism set the United States, through the New Deal, on a democratic middle-of-the-road course between the contemporary extremisms of Europe, that of Communism on the one hand and of Fascism on the other. *Main Currents* fell on fortunate years.

The success of the book in the 1930's, however, did not blind some commentators to defects. Winters in 1940 pointed out that Parrington's treatment of men of letters was inadequate because he failed to analyze their art as a vital aspect of their thought. Hicks, writing the year before, noted that Parrington's treatment of writers after the Civil War was "more often than not superficial."[26] The defects were disturbing because of the intellectual setting of the writing of the second and the uncompleted third volume of Parrington's.

In the 1920's, in the words of Robert E. Spiller, "the literary movement of the century had become stabilized, its shape and scope definable."[27] Between the two world wars American literature manifested one of its greatest periods. For the first time in our literary history, moreover, criticism gave important aid to the artists in poetry and fiction—so important, in fact, that criticism became a part of literature. Joel Elias Spingarn, Van Wyck Brooks, and H. L. Mencken, each after his own fashion, discussed the issues and problems, the writers and the writing of the dynamic third decade of the twentieth century. Irving Babbitt and Paul Elmer More, harking back to standards of the ancient classical world, set forth a philosophy of humanism to give guidance to moderns. Other essayists included Edmund Wilson, Malcolm Cowley, Allen Tate, Kenneth Burke, and R. P. Blackmur. The function and importance of criticism in a great literary age received an extraordinary demonstration in 1946 when Malcolm Cowley's *The Portable Faulkner* (New York) focused attention upon a little-understood and neglected artist and brought his work to the attention of a wide public.

Writing in the early decades of such a period Parrington specifically dissociated himself from literary criticism. Making his field the
history of ideas he chose to emphasize a deterministic environmentalism, applying the philosophy of environmentalism to those ideas he
disliked. He saw ideas with which he had sympathy as creative and
original.[28] Such inconsistency, such dependence on emotion within a
very limited philosophy exposed him to dangers.

Parrington suffered disaster on one occasion when, abandoning
history, he turned to a writer of his own period. In a time of the
rising importance of criticism, Parrington ventured into the field not
hesitantly but confidently. Granville Hicks read Parrington's essay on
James Branch Cabell, published in the posthumous third volume of
Main Currents, with bewilderment. Parrington had let himself go,
when he came to Cabell, in an outburst equal in emotional intensity
to that caused by Cotton Mather but at the opposite extreme. "Mr.
Cabell," wrote the scarcely believing Hicks of Parrington's essay,

"is as whimsical as Bernard Shaw, as provocative as Chesterton." His
Cords of Vanity is "Congreve at his best . . . and is Marlowe also."
Indeed, Cabell, who in addition to all other virtues, has "something of
the intellectual austerity of Matthew Arnold," is "one of the great
masters of English prose, the supreme comic spirit thus far granted us,"
and "he stands apart from the throng of lesser American novelists, as
Mark Twain stood apart, individual and incomparable."[29]

"The essay on Lewis," Hicks added, "is by no means so absurd, but it
does not encourage us to feel that Parrington had the clearest possible insight into his contemporaries."

Such a failure as that with respect to Cabell seems more surprising
when one remembers Parrington's early and long preoccupation with
art. As a young man he painted pictures. Throughout his life he
wrote poems. In the writing of *Main Currents* he emphasized form
and style. The logical development of his thought would seem to
have inclined him toward literary criticism. But the professor of
literature seems to have made a sudden change of direction when he
came to the University of Washington and became an intimate of
J. Allen Smith. Caught up emotionally and intellectually in the crusade of Progressivism, Parrington avowedly at the beginning of his
book devoted himself to political and social thought, especially as
that thought was expressed in the long-continued Hamiltonian-Jeffer-

sonian debate. Perhaps the popular success of the two published volumes persuaded him, as he worked at the third, to depart in the two essays on Cabell and Lewis from the position he had taken in dealing with Poe and Longfellow. These pieces represent a digression from the pattern of the whole work which is primarily history—intellectual history.

Parrington commented on the postwar reaction against Progressivism in an essay in the completed third volume called "A Chapter in American Liberalism." "It is a discouraging essay," he wrote sadly. He wondered if a later generation would be as amused at the sophisticates of the 1920's as they were at the faith in the people which had been the central tenet of the Progressive creed. He did not know.

Among the disillusionments of the 1920's was disenchantment in some quarters with democracy. A simplistic philosophy of elitism challenged the old Progressive doctrine. Ralph Adams Cram, architect and philosopher, as early as 1917 equated democracy with the triumph of mediocrity: ". . . the people are incompetent to govern," he asserted. "Through democracy they have satisfied that desire, but only at great price; for the mediocrity of the rulers conjoined with the mediocrity of the people have destroyed leadership and established 'the reign of mediocrity.' "[30] In the 1920's hopeful young literary expatriates fled the American scene to Paris. Mencken stayed at home, uninhibited prophet of the young men and young women who thought of themselves as sophisticated. Mencken divided American society into the few and the many, the latter the "booboisie." "The vast majority of men," he wrote in 1926, "cannot take in new ideas, and they cannot get rid of old fears . . . they are unable to reason from a set of facts before them, free from emotional distraction. But they also lack something even more fundamental: they are incompetent to take in the bald facts themselves."[31]

Parrington dealt with the philosophy of elitism indirectly in a remarkable affirmation of faith, in one of the last pieces he wrote. The editor of the new *American Literature* asked him to review Albert Beveridge's *Abraham Lincoln, 1809–1858* for the first number. The Lincoln Memorial had risen beside the Potomac in the national capital. The Lincoln symbol had become important in American discourse. Parrington wrote a careful review containing both adverse criticism and praise. Then, having made his appraisal of the book, he launched into an extraordinary paragraph. Ignoring the fact that throughout his public life Lincoln had faced a barrage of criticism from all manner of men, Parrington wrote about the leader and the people. He wrote about democracy. "But Lincoln," he said,

remained part and parcel of the mass from whom he sprung and he thought and said what the mass was thinking and saying. His mind and heart were at one with theirs and by reason of sympathetic understanding he came to be a sort of projection and embodiment of the unphrased ideals and latent sense of justice of the nameless multitudes with whom life deals harshly. When he talked with them they discovered responsive impulses stirring vaguely in their souls and they accepted his conclusions because they trusted him. The outside might be crude, the expression homely, but through his speech shone an honest kindly spirit that plain men understood. If Lincoln came to be more than a small-town lawyer politician, it was due to the simple integrity of his nature that trusted the simple integrity of other men.[32]

Whether or not he intended to in this paragraph, Parrington replied to Cram and to Mencken. But it was more. It was secular, humanistic mysticism—an expression of homage that ranks with the best in the large body of quasi-religious literature that has come into being about the Lincoln image. In an age of disillusionment Parrington's democratic faith did not falter.

The mid-twentieth century, too, owes a debt to the lone explorer who appeared suddenly over the western horizon in 1927. He, first among American scholars, undertook to survey a line through the entire chronological extent of American thought. True, as John Higham has pointed out, "he showed slight interest or competence in metaphysics and theology; he scarcely touched scientific thought and development, or the rise of the social sciences; he ignored legal thought, intellectual institutions, and the nonliterary arts."[33] True also that in emphasizing the theme of Jeffersonian liberalism he chose political thought, in which historians from the time of George Bancroft had been interested and could give him aid. Even so Parrington's gigantic undertaking, which included so much material unfamiliar to historians, lightened the task of later students as any preliminary reconnaissance must do.

Parrington pointed out to a generation inclined to doubt it that American literature was of a quality to warrant intensive study and that the writing of American men of letters carried a freight of ideas.

He demonstrated values to be achieved by combining the study of literature and history in the exploration of a national culture. An impressive body of scholarship since 1927 dealing with the literature of the Republic has, however, not only outdated Parrington's account but has discovered quality and artistic achievements unguessed when *Main Currents* went to press. Parrington might have been an early contributor to the study of American literature as art had he not in 1913 put behind him his own interest in aesthetics and given himself to the cause of Thomas Jefferson. Yet he made his contribution. It is impossible not to assume that his *Main Currents*—which contained a *history* of literature and which dominated survey courses in American literature for more than a decade—did not give an impetus to the literary scholarship which bloomed in later years.

Subsequent scholarship has displaced most of Parrington's conclusions concerning the mind of early Puritan New England. The march of events and the investigations of historians and political scientists has broadened and deepened our understanding of the history of liberalism which Parrington made his central interest. Looking back across the decades at Parrington's narrative of the fortunes of liberalism, his greatest achievement, we see a period piece done in the intellectual style and thought patterns of the Progressive era. It has value for anyone who wishes to sense the mood and grasp the preoccupations of that exuberant age with which the twentieth century opened in the United States.

This survey of achievements, defects, and failures provides a background for John Higham's appraisal of *Main Currents* in the middle of the twentieth century. "Today," he wrote in 1952, "the book appears as a noble ruin in the landscape of our scholarship." But *Main Currents* was a literary achievement. In 1962 Robert A. Skotheim and Kermit Vanderbilt subjected the book to a literary analysis of a thoroughness rarely devoted to a historical work. They set forth the character of the art within its covers—the rhetoric of high sentiment and biting sarcasm, the metaphors as sharp and varied as the patterns of an oriental rug, the grand design of the whole all the more impressive because left uncompleted at the death of the author.[34] They might have added that the style of *Main Currents* was powered by Parrington's dedication to the cause of humane liberalism, by his ultimate humanistic, democratic faith. He saw the democratic dreams of the romantic first half of the nineteenth century as the climax of an epic story toward which earlier Americans moved and from which later Americans fell away. He thought of himself as a realist, particularly when he described the retreat from the summit after the Civil War. No one but a romantic, however, could have written the sentences on Lincoln in the Beveridge review. If it is true that *Main Currents* is a ruin in the landscape of scholarship, then it is the Melrose Abbey of American historiography. It will long be visited. On balance Alfred Harcourt did well when he sent his promise to publish a book not yet written to a discouraged professor on the Pacific coast.

Let us turn now to the academic environment in which Parrington's work emerged. American universities in the first third of the twentieth century underwent rapid and significant growth. The major disciplines had become professionalized by 1900. The American Economics Association, the American Historical Association, and the Modern Language Association had all come into being in the 1880's. These organizations assisted in the development of a sense of community, which reinforced in each discipline a drive to achieve excellence. The success of the natural sciences gave prestige to scientific method, a prestige magnified around the turn of the century by discoveries which led to the exploration of the atom. Henry Adams wrote to the teachers of history that they must take the laws of physics into account in their thinking about the march of human events. As the century opened scholars in the humanities and the social sciences strove to approximate in their own disciplines the rigorous methods which had brought triumph to the natural sciences. Economists before World War I refined and extended the theory, which had come down from early-nineteenth-century England, some introducing mathematics into their formulations. Scholars in literature tried to achieve fact and exactitude through philology and made the study of Old English a requirement in graduate study. Historians ignored the admonition of Adams but labored to perfect "method" in the gathering and use of evidence. Anthropologists, working in a younger discipline, abandoned the use of haphazard travelers' accounts of behaviors in nonliterate societies and sought exactitude through systematic observation by scientists in the field.

A by-product of this drive for excellence was a heightened sense of the separateness and particularity of each of the disciplines. This growth of specialization in the intellectual world reflected a major trend in American civilization as a whole as technology made spectacular advances and industrialism swept forward to the rationalization of the assembly line and of mass production. By the end of the first third of the century the vigorous life within the various disciplines had brought the leading universities of the United States to such a level of maturity as to give them rank with their European contemporaries.

A lesser and counter trend in the first third of the century opposed the trend toward departmental particularity. Robert Frost opened a poem destined to become famous with the line

> Something there is that doesn't love a wall . . .

A small company of scholars in various fields shared Frost's dislike of unnecessary fences. Thorstein Veblen of the University of Chicago and the New School for Social Research took his students beyond economics into anthropology, sociology, and psychology. Frederick Jackson Turner of Wisconsin and Harvard thought in terms of geography, sociology, and economics as well as history. The "New History" of James Harvey Robinson urged the members of the guild to transcend boundaries. In 1906 Harvard College established a general concentration in history and literature under the chairmanship at first of the poet-philosopher, George Santayana. For more than a decade this enterprise emphasized only non-American materials but, by the end of the 1920's, it included a combination of American history and American literature. In 1919 the faculty at Columbia adapted to peacetime uses the "war issues" course, which had been a standard item throughout the nation in the curriculum of the Student Army Training Corps. The resulting course, called Contemporary Civilization, brought together teachers and material from several disciplines. It had influence beyond the borders of the university and had a long and fruitful career. Contemporary Civilization and courses in other institutions of a similar nature and purpose demonstrated a sense of responsibility on the part of the universities for the training of generalists as well as specialists.

A development in anthropology paralleled in the 1920's enlargement of outlook on the part of some historians. Early in the century William Graham Sumner of Yale had isolated the concept of *mores* and had advanced the thesis that the *mores* provide the basic controls in society. By the third decade anthropologists, moving beyond Sumner, had formulated the concept of culture to encompass the over-all behavior patterns of a particular society. Culture included in their view, among other things, institutions to satisfy basic human drives and needs, material artifacts on which man depends together with the knowledge (science) of how to make them, religious and social beliefs, and ethical codes. It included also the varied expressions and creations of the human mind and spirit in the field of art. The anthropologists saw culture as a whole in which changes in one aspect, and conspicuously the growth of science, affected all other aspects. They explored many different cultures and undertook to organize and systematize a mounting body of information. In the same decade historians became increasingly dissatisfied with a definition, ascendant at the end of the nineteenth century, which described history as past politics and past wars. In the 1920's some scholars began venturing into the unmapped country of social history. By the end of the decade others undertook to explore social theory, religious beliefs, ethical codes, science itself, the subject matter of intellectual history. In economics as well as in history and anthropology horizons widened vastly in the two decades which followed the end of World War I. Literary criticism, borrowing from many fields of knowledge, became a powerful and constructive force.

Yale established near the beginning of the 1930's in its Graduate School a Department of History, the Arts and Letters. The men who organized it sought advice at Cambridge and profited by the experience of the earlier concentration in history and literature at Harvard. The new interest in intellectual history provided a powerful impetus. Another arose from the desire to achieve insights and understandings which could only come by bringing together into a single undertaking the study of three areas of societal life. The present writer, participating in the American subdivision, had been conditioned by association with men in the field, by the Sumnerian thesis, and later by the concept of culture as it evolved in the 1920's. In addition to a subdivision in American Studies, the new department had one dealing with English civilization and another concerned with the French Middle Ages. In 1933 Yale awarded the first Ph.D. in History, the Arts and Letters to A. Whitney Griswold, later, after a brilliant career as scholar and teacher, to become president of the university. Griswold worked in the American field and his degree was probably the first doctorate in American Studies in the nation. After World War II the Department of History, the Arts and Letters disappeared and American Studies became an independent program in Yale College and in the Graduate School which, possessed of a budget, functioned separately. The more limited threefold approach of History, the Arts and Letters broadened into a wide-ranging effort to explore the culture of the American people and its evolution in time.

The latter 1930's and early 1940's saw American Studies spread widely in varied patterns among American universities. A professor of American literature at George Washington University initiated a program in American Studies in 1936–37 and pioneered in the establishment of a proseminar for seniors. The faculty and student involved in this course attempted to interpret American civilization through the factors of geography, immigration, government, political-social-economic history, religion, philosophy, education, literature, other forms of communication of ideas, and the arts and crafts. The conspectus suggests the spreading influence of the new concepts of anthropology in particular. At Princeton in the early 1940's the undergraduate interested in American Studies could major in any one of six departments while focusing his primary attention upon American civilization and its backgrounds in Europe. In his last year he joined a senior conference which considered in depth a subject involving more than one discipline. Out of this enterprise came some useful publications. In later years these and other programs in American Studies appeared as an early manifestation of a movement toward interdisciplinary programs with other and varied objectives. And these, in turn, pointed toward the idea and the programs of general studies, as well as toward the notion of Comparative Studies.

The first third of the twentieth century had marked an extraordinary period in the intellectual life of the nation. It was a time in the academic disciplines of increasingly sophisticated efforts to achieve professional excellence. Vigorous criticism of works of scholarship in multiplying scholarly journals furthered professional progress in the older disciplines such as economics and history and in younger social sciences forging rapidly ahead. The intellectual climate of an age which opened with Charles Saunders Peirce's insistence on the importance of uncertainty and William James's "radical empiricism" reinforced the trend to question old certitudes and absolutisms in the law, in economic theory, and in the late-nineteenth-century formulations of historical "method." The period saw American men of letters moving away from the Genteel Tradition and abandoning older conventions in poetry, bringing into being between the two wars a second great age in American literature. The first third of the century encompassed the *élan* of the Progressive era and the disenchantments of the prosperous 1920's and of the years when the nation plunged into the Depression. To this dynamic period Vernon Parrington contributed his *Main Currents of American Thought,* caught the attention of the generation of the 1920's and 1930's, and reinforced the tendency in the academic world to venture into new and unconventional explorations. It was one of the "books that changed our minds"—at least in the 1930's. To be listed in that category with Beard, Adams, Turner, Freud, Lenin, Spengler, and John Dewey was no small recognition for a scholar from the American hinterland.[35]

Perry Miller

ROBERT MIDDLEKAUFF

6)

THE OLD SAW "actions speak louder than words" must have annoyed
Perry Miller. It seems to have been tossed at him several times in his
life by Yankees who insisted that their forefathers had founded New
England only in the interest of taking fish from the sea; his contention that the Founders had come on a religious mission was so much
flapdoodle repeated by one who took public professions too seriously.
Whatever the Founders may have said, they made their living by
catching cod, didn't they? The study of the actions of men of the
world was also recommended to Miller after he published *From
Colony to Province,* in which—in a note at the end of the book—he
wrote that at least until the end of the nineteenth century "the
history of New England's mind was written as much, if not more, by
the actions of merchants and men of business as in the publications
of theologians and politicians."[1] This comment exonerated reviewers
from thinking through Miller's analysis, which was largely based on
the writings of theologians and politicians and which in fact reconstructed the entire drift of a century's cultural change from those
writings. It also seemed to invite them to ask why Miller had not
chronicled the activities of businessmen and to imply that, because of
this neglect, what he had done was not altogether relevant to New
England's history after the founding. Such reproaches did not lure
Miller into one of those academic squabbles which disfigure the back
pages of scholarly journals; rather, ignoring his critics until 1961,
when the paperback edition of the book was issued, he insisted that
the Puritan utterances contained the most revealing evidence of the

motives and direction of social development in seventeenth-century New England. And he emphasized that the histories of merchants and their activities, however important, could not provide a theme around which the history of grand alterations in a mind of a society might be woven.[2]

Miller's insistence that historians of New England should study *thought* did not arise from a disdain for *action*, or from a lack of experience in what is commonly taken to be the real world: where battles are fought and men work with their hands and worry about bills, business, and the market. He sought to know that world at a fairly early age and remained interested in it all his life. His writings reflect this interest and in some ways bear its impress.

Miller was born February 25, 1905, on the West Side of Chicago. He was reared in the city, a fact he always considered especially important in the making of his mentality: "I realize that I was peculiarly fortunate in thus having had borne in upon me the full impact of the twentieth century, in which I was to live."[3] He attended the Tilton School and the Austin High School there and in 1922 entered the University of Chicago, only to give up his studies in the next year in favor first of "bumming around," as young men still put it, and of trying his hand on the stage and the sea. These early travels, first to Colorado and then to New York, were in search of adventure. No adolescent in this frame of mind ever knows what he wants; the idea of adventure is to do different things in the hope that perhaps he will find out. The stage was calculated to satisfy some of his inner urgings, and Miller played in stock companies around New York—including a Shakespeare troupe—and then went to sea. He ended up in the Belgian Congo, an adventurous setting, doing the unadventurous work of unloading drums of case oil from the United States. Three years of this life as a wanderer served Miller well; he came back to the University of Chicago fixed in purpose and commenced his studies. Graduate school at Harvard followed and then a career of teaching and scholarship broken only by the Second World War, in which he served in the Army and the OSS. Miller died at Harvard in his fifty-ninth year while at work on an intellectual history of the United States.

Although university scholars today are not the cloistered creatures described in popular myths, they usually do not have the variety of experience that Miller had. The armed forces have claimed many in time of war, of course; and many have worked in nonacademic occupations. But few have gone to sea; not many have acted in the professional theater; and almost none has taken up the life of the hobo. Any experience affects the scholar's work in undetectable ways, and the account he gives of its effects is not necessarily to be trusted. At times, to be sure, historians are able to use their experience in observable ways; Francis Parkman, for example, employed the knowledge gained while living with the Western Indians in his great studies of France and England in the New World. More commonly historians tend to believe that their contacts outside the scholarly world increase their sensitivity to certain problems: for instance, that a career in the diplomatic service gives insight into the realities of statecraft. Miller had no such career. One suspects that he acquired his sense of modernity less from immediate contact with the everyday world than from profound immersion in his studies—even though those studies only occasionally touched the contemporary period. Certain it is that he pondered long over his own time; and though his references to it in his work—ranging from the internal combustion engine to existentialism—seem casual and unconnected, there is a perspective in his work that suggests he had penetrated as far into its secrets as into those of the seventeenth century. In *Jonathan Edwards*, he weighed the effects of Lockian psychology and Newtonian physics on a mind escaping from scholastic theory; and in "The End of the World,' the atomic bomb, the modern contribution to eschatological horror, preoccupied him. This perspective probably helped him to diagram the shifts in the mind and society of seventeenth-century New England. For what evidently impressed him about his own day was also characteristic of the seventeenth century: the intensity with which men pursued flux and instability, and the complexity that resulted from the shattering of an old order.[4]

It was Miller's preoccupation with the modern world that sent him into the past. Sitting along the Congo surrounded by drums of oil, he says he received a sudden epiphany that his mission was to expound America to the world. His peculiar situation—isolated in a wilderness bursting with potential power engaged in transporting actual power from the most industrialized nation in the world—may have contributed to his inspiration. He discovered in Africa the necessity of beginning at the beginning and hence his absorbing concern with the Puritans in New England. He tells this story of his early resolve without apology and without arrogance. He seems to have thought that there was something faintly ridiculous in it: he compares his vision with Edward Gibbon's—"To bring into conjunction a minute event in the history of historiography with a great one"—but the dedication with which he pursued the vision, and the results of the pursuit, hardly permit one to dismiss it as ridiculous.[5]

Elsewhere in commenting on his work, Miller sometimes strikes a humble note, but such expressions of humility usually seem false because following them come jibes at other—lesser—kinds of history, carrying more than a whiff of arrogance. But one suspects that for all his posturing and his abrasiveness Miller's arrogance did not go very deep; it was largely verbal and perhaps was intended in some crude fashion, as Edmund S. Morgan has suggested, to protect his intellectual virility.[6] There is in his writing a sense of his own fallibility; and there remains in his egotism an openness to ideas, and to fresh ways of looking at them, which reveal the intellectual humility within the personal arrogance.

Miller came to the study of Puritanism just as it was being reclaimed by serious historians from the latest of a long line of social commentators who persisted in blaming the Puritans for what they found most repellent in the American character, its supposed incapacity for aesthetic satisfaction, its prudery, and its prohibitionism. These critics included the acerbic wit Henry Mencken, the literary historian Van Wyck Brooks, and the historian of New England, James Truslow Adams. Different as they were, all condemned the Puritans in a fashion reminiscent of the seventeenth century, when the view that the Puritans were the enemies of nature, especially anything in nature that gave pleasure, was first sounded. The most sardonic expression of this idea had appeared in the book *New England Canaan*, by Thomas Morton, who had some reason to be unhappy with Puritans in Massachusetts and Plymouth.[7] A party of these Puritans, led by Miles Standish, "Captain Shrimp" in Morton's account, had toppled a maypole he and other English gentlemen erected at Merrymount and while they were at it had confiscated Morton's liquor supply and scattered the Indian lasses he had recruited for frolics around the pole. When they finished this grim work, the Puritans dispatched Morton back to England, where he nursed his outrage until he could vent it in print.

H. L. Mencken did Morton's hatchet work for the twentieth century. In his most pungent denunciation Mencken described Puritanism as "the haunting fear that somewhere, someone might be happy."[8] Through comments of this order Mencken gave us the modern version of what might be called the stereotype of the Puritan as killjoy. The Puritans, the old story goes, opposed bear baiting not because they found the torment of an animal cruel, but because they feared the onlooker would get some pleasure out of the spectacle. The stereotype also instructed us on the Puritan's appearance: he dressed the part, wearing nothing but black suits and black steeple-crown hats. This dark figure lived in a dreary log cabin, despised beauty, relished hell-fire sermons, and spent most of his time worrying about the state of his soul, spying on his neighbors, and burning witches.

At the time the stereotype enjoyed its greatest vogue, historians began to smash it. Kenneth Murdock and Samuel Eliot Morison began the demolition, Murdock in a warmly sympathetic biography of Increase Mather, and Morison in *Builders of the Bay Colony* and his studies of Harvard College. Had they chosen they might have drawn on scattered short stories, novels, and an old biography in which the Puritans were at least taken seriously. Most of these works—the fiction by Nathaniel Hawthorne and Esther Forbes and the biography *Cotton Mather* by Barrett Wendell—did not make the Puritans very attractive, but they rendered them faithfully and always succeeded in making them interesting. Morison and Murdock, soon to be joined by Clifford K. Shipton, as scholars, had to work from the sources. To some extent these historians may have been reacting to popular diatribes; Morison in particular seemed to feel the barbs of the Puritans' critics. In his zeal to correct the old distortions, he may have very nearly created new ones, for he proceeded on the assumption that the Puritan was a contemporary. Morison enjoyed pointing out that the Puritan, far from being a prohibitionist, enjoyed beer and wine—taken in moderation, of course. To prove the point Morison quoted Increase Mather's dictum that wine is from the Lord and drunkenness from the devil. Nor were the Puritans prudes: they recognized the human need for sexual intercourse and pronounced it good, provided it occurred in the beds of married couples. Morison and other social historians also took great satisfaction in showing that Puritans wore bright clothing and painted their houses in cheerful

colors, and that they eschewed hell-fire sermons in favor of efforts
which today would rank as systematic theology. Except for their
fondness for theology, Puritans in these accounts could pass muster
in the twentieth century. Morison's work suggests that it is possible
to study them almost as one's neighbors—they had warm blood in
their veins and they enjoyed tilting a glass occasionally.[9]

Perry Miller's work departed from this pattern especially in its
method and its concern with ideas. Murdock, Morison, and Shipton
worked largely through biography, which served their purposes admirably because it permitted painting the brighter sides of Puritan
character. Miller never employed the biographical form, though he
wrote a brilliant intellectual biography of Jonathan Edwards, and
though in *From Colony to Province* he paused lovingly over John
Wise, and not so lovingly over Cotton Mather. Nor were his studies
in any way apologetics: he never concealed his distaste for the
Mathers and almost delighted in describing the irony of faithful
adherence to creed—he did not call it fanaticism—leading to corruption. The way to an understanding of Puritans and of America,
Miller believed, lay through ideas, and it was a way he traveled
exuberantly. Yet if he began as an intellectual historian, his interests
broadened as the problems he worked with increased in complexity;
and he ended as the historian of a culture.

In a retrospective moment Miller once wrote that he began his
story at the wrong place, with an explication of the intricacies of
nonseparating Congregationalism. This beginning appeared as his
first book, *Orthodoxy in Massachusetts, 1630–1650*, published in
1933. In its insistence that the pronouncements of men must be
taken seriously—though not necessarily at face value—the book
anticipates a part of Miller's later method. The problem it considers
had been dismissed by other historians as not worth the trouble, the
elaborate rationale of a group of Puritans who espoused a form of
Congregational polity while they insisted that they had not separated
from the Church of England, which was of course episcopalian in
organization. These Puritans' claims had bewildered their contemporaries, who persisted in pointing out that it was impossible to be one
thing while claiming to be another. Sharing this confusion, historians
accepted the logic and dismissed the Puritans' assertions as meriting
study only for what they revealed about sophistry and perhaps
hypocrisy.

Miller was inclined to agree that nonseparating Congregationalism, as he baptized this persuasion, displayed sophistry, but he deemed it worth study for other reasons. What it revealed under Milller's dissection was that—contrary to the legend of their going to school at Plymouth Colony—the Puritans of the Bay developed their ecclesiastical polity before they came to New England. This shocked the admirers of simplicity beguiled by the story that had Deacon Samuel Fuller of Plymouth journey to Salem where he presumably instructed the Puritans of Massachusetts in the intricacies of Congregationalism—long since invented by the Pilgrims. To the believers of this folk tale, Miller's contention appeared as a betrayal of an ancient truth. Some, like Samuel Eliot Morison, who as late as 1958 accused Miller of trying "to rob the Pilgrim Fathers of credit for turning the First Church of Salem into Congregational channels," refused to believe it.[10]

Miller's argument about the origin of these ideas was startling, but the great achievement of the book was its demonstration that, though the rationale these Puritans offered of their polity was aberrant, in their insistence that they had not separated they were proclaiming their allegiance to one of the great ideas of the age, the idea of uniformity. No more than Catholics or Anglicans could they escape the regnant, and unexamined, commitment of the age to the notion of the church as a seamless unity extending from the beginnings of Christianity to the end of the world. If they were unaware that this notion was nothing more than an articulation of a profound organic mood stemming from the medieval heritage, no matter; the fact was that separatism led to disorders in politics and society. Puritans had witnessed anarchic upheavals on the continent and in England itself. Hence their insistence that despite differences they were snugly within the Church of England. What Miller showed, then, was that the inconsistencies of these nonseparatists occurred within a larger consistency.

If, in protesting their devotion to the Church of England, the Puritans revealed their sensitivity to one of the impulses of the age, they could not know that their children would see it die. In the next century multiplicity in religion, as in most things, soon overpowered uniformity. After publishing *Orthodoxy in Massachusetts* Miller turned to the melancholy story of the children suffering the strains of the new order of things. In telling this history, he faced the problem of accounting for changes in ideas far more complicated than any he had dealt with in his first book.

Orthodoxy in Massachusetts hinted that the Puritans believed certain propositions, those surrounding uniformity for example, without quite knowing why. Perhaps they were more fully aware of their assumptions than men of most ages, but still lacked a full comprehension of their own motives. In the case of their dedication to nonseparation, they were inspired as much by a dread of chaos as they were by a set of ideas about the nature of church and society. What was true of the founders and their forebears was also true of their children. They and other men in Miller's work rarely understand why they hold their store of ideas. This may be said of all men in all times, but Miller applies it strenuously to the seventeenth century.

Miller assumed that within the peculiar psychological limitations of men, ideas take on a life of their own. They are not simply constructs devised by men trying to cope with the world or to penetrate its mysteries. They seem almost to have some inner force impelling men to take up unanticipated positions; certainly the consequences of thought are never predictable. Though Miller suggested these propositions only casually in a phrase here and there, they color all of his work on the Puritans.

The assumption that ideas are autonomous seems to allow their treatment apart from experience. This has been a technique of many historians, and it was one Miller resorted to gratefully in *The New England Mind: The Seventeenth Century*.[11] In this volume Miller not only ignores experience, he deals with the Puritan mind as if it were static, reconstructing its basic formulations as if they were unchanging. The history of the changes is taken up in a second book, *The New England Mind: From Colony to Province*.[12]

What Miller found distinguishing the Puritan mind was not simply its terms of thought or its ideas, which he shows were largely inherited and borrowed, but at its center a tension between piety and intellect. Piety, an enormous hunger and longing for union with God, Miller contended, gave Puritanism its thrust; it was the life spirit of the movement. The intellectual side of the mind, usually characterized as reason in Miller's work, affected other levels of Puritan being. It expressed the piety; it was in various forms, the piety intellectualized. But reason also opposed religious emotion, pressing its claims as a means of expressing the human spirit against claims of passion. The tension between the two in the mind came most directly out of the unconscious thrust of the reason in search of ways to confine the sovereignty of God and to carve out a guarantee of rational order within it. Piety implied the exaltation of the divine; it connoted unending worship of God's power and mercy and justice; it involved the surrendering of the self to the most high. Intellect urged the claims of man, who was after all created in the image of the divine; it enjoined recognition of human powers and capacities; it counseled control of the spirit lest inner promptings lead men to an ecstatic anarchy. In every area of their thought—and especially in theology, psychology, logic, political theory—Puritan divines sought to achieve a balance between the claims of reason and the spirit.

Emotion largely defies analysis by the tools of intellectual history, and Miller, of necessity, chose to explicate Puritan ideas, all the while insisting that the ideas in some complicated ways expressed, when they did not oppose, religious zeal. Miller's technique of explication is unvarying. First he offers an elaborate description of the ideas; and then he relays contemporary versions of them, usually with quotations which impart the tone of their authors. Their relevance for Puritan thought is discussed and their place within the total scheme is located. After this meticulous description, he exposes the implications of the ideas which were often unsuspected by their holders and, faithful to his leading theme, shows their relationship to the tension between piety and intellect.

This technique is especially clear in Miller's treatment of Ramist logic, which Puritans employed so assiduously as to make their sermons appear a dialectician's dream. On first sight no more unpromising method for a divine seeking to nourish faith can be imagined than the pedantry of Ramist logic. Miller carefully explains the use of its "arguments," its dichotomies, its "artificial" and "inartificial" distinctions, and its classifications. He asserts that it molded theology and provides evidence of its influence by citations from sermons. But its greatest utility, he argues in his discussion of its unsuspected implications, lay in its unarticulated premises. Unlike the dialectic of Aristotle, which held that logic was a mental construct, that of Ramus insisted that true method corresponded to things. It eased the still nagging uncertainty of the realist-nominalist debate by assuming that universals were real and thereby permitted Puritans to indulge in an unreserved acceptance of scriptural assertions. Because it did not admit that any gap existed between the observer and the external world, no unsettling epistomological difficulties disturbed its serene service to truth. Its total effects then were to provide enormous reassurance.

Miller's account of the Puritan preoccupation with method makes it the history of men striving for the reassurance that men can discover eternal truth. He presents Puritan metaphysics in the same light, arguing that it provided the most crucial connections between piety and intellect. Technologia, as Puritans designated their metaphysics, offered a suprasensuous version of truth: reality, it held, was an emanation of the divine mind, for God held the idea of the world in his mind when he created it.

Miller's devotion to his theme is great but not single-minded; indeed, in his explication of Puritan ideas it disappears from the text for many pages, only to be resurrected at crucial points to give meaning to his account. But if Miller's intention in these long and apparently descriptive passages is to prepare the reader for revelations about the relationship of the two halves of the mind, it is also to make the mind comment upon Puritan character. His detailed descriptions of ideas pile abstraction upon abstraction until the reader begins to despair of discovering their connections to human concerns. This is part of Miller's technique; he is never content to rely on mere assertion, but accompanies it with an elaborate demonstration. But at the right moment the connection is made: there is, for example, more to technologia than neat distinctions between archetypal and entypal art. Technologia, this simple metaphysic which attained complexity only in Puritan explications, helped mold a way of conceiving action and in itself encouraged action. Miller shows that Puritan metaphysics did not simply enjoin action; it assumed the existence of an organic connection between the way the world was comprehended and the enterprises of men. Crudely phrased, thought imposed the obligation to act; as a Puritan sermon put it, "Our eupraxis [purpose] begins from Analysis, is finished in Genesis."[13] What Miller achieves in this reconstruction is more than a demonstration of the intellectual basis of action: he shows the remarkable congruity of theology and the structure of the mind.

In *The New England Mind: The Seventeenth Century,* Miller exhibits a body of thought coloring Puritan character and culture.

The impulses for action in this culture are apparent, but for purposes of study Miller does not show them operating in a specific social context. So unless one ponders the hints dropped along the way, especially in the final chapter, "God's Controversy with New England," the directions Puritan experience took remain obscure. Though these casual suggestions in *The New England Mind* remain undeveloped, they betray the doubt that any cast of thought so freighted with intensity could long survive. This view becomes explicit in such statements as "When the belief and the temper which the first settlers brought to America is examined, when the piety is estimated on the emotional and non-theological level, it seems obvious that the reason later generations ceased marching to the Puritan beat was simply that they could no longer stand the pace."[14] At other places in this account Miller seizes upon inconsistencies in the structure of Puritan philosophy and suggests that in the history of New England they will provide the basis for change. For example, the Puritan inability to decide whether reason was a faculty or a repository of ideas, and the failure of technologia and dialectic to supply a workable metaphysics and epistemology, seemed to invite new intellectual efforts. The very imperfections of the system, Miller implies, impelled a grand alteration. And the thrust of the intellect to confine the piety, makes the impulses for change comprehensible. In one way or another all are related to this central tension; and their resolution would bring unanticipated shifts of thought.

Although this grand theme supplies a major premise of *From Colony to Province*, the second volume of Miller's major account of the New England mind, it is not the most important one. Had Miller chosen to follow the paths of conventional wisdom, he might have organized this book around the accommodations to social change of the ideas he treated in the first volume. He could have culled scattered quotations from the sources about man, nature, logic, technologia—all the topics he had initially taken up. Or, had he anticipated his critics, he might have studied the actions of men of the world in order to describe social change. One critic, in fact, has credited Miller with astuteness in extemporizing social change from the body of evidence which, in his ignorance, he unwittingly used.

Miller dismissed both ways. The first, judging from his comments on Frederick Jackson Turner, he believed to err in assuming that ideas were inert; it implied that the landscape gave its color to them and they left it untouched. This was a proposition he thought the evidence itself refuted. And the second method misread his intentions as to the purposes of intellectual history. He did not conceive of his function as the deduction of the history of a society—or even of social changes—from the sources. What concerned him were the Puritans' perceptions of social change and their responses to their altered circumstances. Their notions of what was happening to themselves struck him as infinitely more revealing of a culture, its underlying impulses, and its conception of itself, than any "objective" social history.

From his study of Puritan attempts to cope with their experience, Miller came to see that the formal propositions of thought changed very little before 1730. The theology, including such disparate elements as the covenant theory and the doctrine of predestination, remained substantially what it had been at the founding in 1630. No conscious repudiation of the intellectual heritage occurred in the course of the seventeenth century and no deliberate adaptation of new ideas began. But the mind changed: throughout one hundred years of experience the way it held ideas, the emphasis it unwittingly gave them, saw the whole altered until, in tone and pattern, it differed greatly from its beginnings in 1630.

The subtlety of Miller's understanding of this change in the styles, or psychology, of thought and his technique of detecting it are apparent in his ruminations on covenant theory. In its inception covenant theory was nothing more than a way of speaking, a language which described the relationships of God to man. But in time, because how man approached God was so urgent, this language gradually assumed the proportions of a doctrine, of a statement of the way things actually were. No one quite knew how this happened, or even that it was happening. In 1630 when the Massachusetts Bay was settled, the covenant of grace and the church covenant had accumulated elaborate statements of theory. The notion of a national covenant, the idea of a people contracting to serve the Lord's purposes, had been broadened but its formulation was primitive even after John Winthrop cast upon a striking metaphor which likened New England to a city upon a hill, a holy place in the Lord's service drawing the attention of the world. But this figure did not begin to control experience (as the other covenants did) until Puritan ministers perceived that the children of the founders, unable to share their fathers' religious intensity, were not becoming full members of the churches who received the Lord's Supper. This situation raised frightful problems, which year by year became worse until the specter of churches without members seemed unavoidable. The solution was to change qualifications for membership, which was done in the Half-Way Covenant, and recall the people to the terms of their covenant as the Lord's chosen nation.

These solutions had concealed implications, which gradually revealed themselves: given the new and easier standards of membership, ministers found themselves actually conniving at external performance in place of inner faith. Without recognizing the importance of what they were saying, they cajoled their congregations with promises that the Lord would be satisfied with attempts at faith, and then with professions. Finally they were reduced to urging that even hypocrites had their uses in support of the national covenant. This process, telescoped in this brief account, is lavishly portrayed by Miller, who at appropriate moments reminds his readers that the covenant idea, which had implied a condition of bargaining and even equality between contracting parties, had always contained these possibilities.

By itself the process of the alteration of the theory of the national covenant would have great interest for what it tells of Puritan character. Miller makes it a chapter in the history of cultural transformation: in revising this theory Puritans in New England, he explains, had insensibly recast their identity. During most of the seventeenth century, they had striven to think of themselves in terms imposed by the covenant. But by the end of the century, in seeking for means to defend the national covenant, they had resorted to ideas inherently incompatible with it. And in their desperation, careless of implications, they began to use a language of politics, which was not at first to their liking and not even framed by themselves. The leading examples, "English liberties" and "religious toleration," were the legacies of the Glorious Revolution. The Revolution removed the threatening Governor Andros, but brought new, more subtle dangers in this inheritance. The Puritans failed to recognize the hazards of their new course; and before long, without knowing what they were doing, they had transformed the old to a new way.

In his analysis of this transformation of the covenant and the fashioning of the new identity Miller's interest broadens until he is telling the history of a culture as well as of a mind. He recaptures the beginnings of the shifts in New England by his extraordinary sensitivity to the ways Puritans conceived of their problems and their manner of discussing them. His technique here involves taking a curious collection of evidence of such disparate matters as choices of words, indirection in speech, the organization of a literary work (John Wise's *Vindication*), and the omission of venerable assumptions of the first generation in the writings of the third, in order to demonstrate the appearance of a culture that departed profoundly from that of the founders. The phrasing of political discourse in terms of English liberty rather than of the covenant, for example, reveals a more realistic apprehension of actuality after 1690. Or to take another case, the use of words such as "affable" in funeral sermons indicates the penetration of the old culture by prevailing English fashions. What is left unsaid is also important in Miller's reconstruction: the group of Puritan divines around Benjamin Colman reveal their estrangement from the Mathers in their sermons, which simply drop the language and the premises of the covenant theology. By themselves most of these bits and pieces may seem trivial; generations of historians of New England have ignored them. In Miller's re-creation they become evocative of the passing of an old order and the birth of a new one.

Miller's achievement in his study of the Puritans surely owes more to some indefinable quality of his imagination than to his method. Yet his method should be made as explicit as possible if only to reveal how much of his technique cannot be recaptured. In its ruthless concentration upon ideas, the method is as much an angle of vision, or a focus of study, as it is anything else.

Miller did not grant all ideas equal analytical worth: some not only revealed more than others about a society, they defined the ground of social experience itself. Thus the idea of the covenant, Miller believed, provided a dramatic example of the control that form exerted over cultural experience. This was not a suprahistorical insight but one extracted from the study of the past. It also apparently justified for Miller other leading assumptions of his technique: that Puritan thinking, whether as creation or as response to change, was more important, and more revealing, than the "objective" changes in society themselves.

One may wonder whether Miller himself was aware of all the

implications of this proposition. Implicit in it seems to be the notion that all important experience will find some expression in words and, perhaps, even that no significant experience will defy verbalization. From Miller's account it is clear that he believed that sooner or later Puritan experience would obtain recognition in sermons and tracts. His studies document unstintedly Puritan attempts to disguise, where they did not conceal, unpalatable social changes—in church membership and in the locus of political power, for example. But the question remains of how sensitive to change Puritan ideas were, not how accurate they were; and, if indeed, Puritan ideology, as it became less innovative and more conservative, failed to detect the inner springs of social workings. Ideology that seeks to conserve, as theorists as different as Marx and Weber have shown, sometimes divorces itself from reality. To be sure, Miller has commented on this point in his declaration that whatever the reality, Puritans' perceptions remain the most revealing indicators of the character of a culture. And yet, even if he is correct, one may suppose that a fuller understanding of these perceptions might be obtained by observing what the nature of the relationships between perception and reality was. And certainly appreciation of how social reality actually imposes limits on thought and action would be increased.

To some extent these criticisms can be tested by examining the inferences about society that Miller draws from the lamentations of such third-generation Puritans as Cotton Mather. In the writings of Mather and his contemporaries, Miller detects a culture tortured by anxieties and fragmented by competing social groups. His evocation of the mood of social unease which beset New England is imaginative and sensitive. Though the main emphasis of his research is into the thought of a body of intellectuals who were losing their nerve, he is able to discover the existence of competing groups which held values in contradiction to the the assumptions inherited from the founders. In the towns there were "pragmaticals" and in the cities there were merchants, both groups complacent in their materialism, hostile to clerical leadership, and bent on taking their purposes from business and in some cases from business in London.

As brilliant as Miller's account is, by its peculiar adherence to the technique of working through the perceptions of Puritan divines who were cut off from social leadership, perhaps it does not succeed as fully as it might in assessing the alterations in the culture. Consider how Miller proceeds: first, from the intensity with which ideas were held, and reluctantly yielded up, he detects a profound social tension. Then he offers the feeling of distress as a measure of cultural shifts—and rightly so. But one suspects that these feelings would emerge with even greater starkness and even subtlety were they set more directly against the values of the apostates from Puritanism.

There may be still another difficulty in the way Miller uses the perceptions of Puritan divines. Perceptions are a reading of experience, not a passive recording; they bear the peculiar imprint of prevailing ideas, especially ideas which Miller considers to be forms. Form for Perry Miller may be thought of as having existence outside of experience; form indeed may be outside of history. When idea as form enters history, it acts to shape and control experience: the covenant idea provides the classic model of form controlling substance. Miller believed that men's perceptions permit an understanding of the connections of ideas and experience; these connections go a long way toward the creation of the historical process. What has to be asked at this point is how revealing those perceptions are which have to be mediated through traditional ideas fast losing their authority as forces controlling experience. How revealing are they in the late seventeenth century, when covenant ideas, for example, are dying, and new forms, many of them repugnant to Puritan intellectuals, are taking their place? Miller never resolved these questions adequately.

Although Miller's major work dealt with seventeenth-century Puritanism, at the time of his death he was working on an intellectual history of the United States from the Revolution to the Civil War. He had taught the American literature of this period in his courses at Harvard for years and he had published articles, anthologies, and a book, *The Raven and the Whale*, all treating in some way problems of intellectual life in ante-bellum America. Almost all this work is suggestive, and one part of it has great distinction: *Consciousness in Concord: The Text of Thoreau's Hitherto "Lost Journal"* (1840–1841). In it Miller wrote a long Introduction, which, through the examination of all Thoreau's work, shows that Thoreau's surface life in Concord concealed a relentless concern with self and a cultivation of his consciousness. The journal, Miller argues, was not the product of spontaneous jottings; indeed there seems to have been nothing spontaneous in Thoreau's life. The journal arose from what Miller calls the ur-journal, containing notes made as thoughts and sensations intruded into Thoreau's consciousness, which were then reworded and polished for final entry. This process was carefully contrived, as in fact was every part of Thoreau's life: his interest in nature extended no further than his responses to it; his ruminations on friendship masked an incapacity for it and a disinclination to become involved with another human being (Miller shows that the "love" of Ellen Sewall is a fancy of later sentimentalists); and death, with the loss of his brother John, posed problems which evoked elaborate self-deceptions. What fascinated Henry Thoreau was "Me" and its peculiar relationships to the "Not-Me," as he phrased it. The fascination led, as Miller demonstrates in a superb reconstruction, to a taut innerness that structured a consciousness and all its responses to the external world.[15]

The second of Miller's large-scale nineteenth-century studies, *The Life of the Mind in America*, posthumously published by his widow, who wrote a brief foreword to it, was incomplete at his death.[16] Although this volume is unfinished in style and substance, it possesses interest both for what it says and for what can be seen of Miller's method of attack. Three parts are included, the first on nineteenth-century evangelicalism, the second on the legal mentality, and the third, a fragment of one chapter, on science. The first two offer a theme that is reminiscent of the *New England Mind: The Seventeenth Century*, the theme of the head versus the heart. In evangelicalism Miller discovers the heart and in the law, the head; each in its own way has, or implies, a conception of America. They seem to be juxtaposed in the book to demonstrate the existence of a profound cleavage in the culture, a cleavage that extends far deeper than groups and interests to a sense of American national identity. All this is suggested by Miller, and much more, but it remains unfinished—provocative but not fully realized.

With the exception of his first book, and a few articles, Miller's work is written in a style that puzzles and even angers some readers. Much of the bewilderment and anger arise from a feeling that he is making history too difficult for understanding or that he is revealing more of himself than he is of his subject; and interesting as he is, he has promised the reader something besides himself under such titles as *The New England Mind*. Listening to these complaints, one is inclined to offer sympathy, but not too much. The difficulty of Miller's style is real, but it has been exaggerated. Miller wrote a complex prose and he rarely turned out anything which, in the popular phrase, could be termed "readable." Neither his sentence structure nor his choice of words make for quick comprehension, yet his writing is almost always clear and often graceful. And he possessed a sense of literary structure that lent his books coherence and power.

Miller's is a romantic style with none of the metaphysical imprecision and vagueness of romanticism. On first reading, what is especially impressive is its range of sounds and its success in transmitting a sense of the moods of men and eras. At the same time it manages to express Miller's own imagination, and his understanding of meaning and implication.

Miller achieved these effects through the unconventional employment of conventional literary devices. Every historian quotes his sources either to pass on information or more commonly to give a sense of flavor or tone. Miller quoted for these reasons, but he also used quotations as miniature texts revealing the essence of a body of thought. Thus he shows that a passage from Samuel Mather's notebook which begins "All the Arts are nothing but the beams and rays of the Wisdom of the *first Being* in the Creatures, shining, and reflecting thence, upon the glass of man's understanding; and as from Him they come, so to him they tend: the circle of Arts is *a Deo ad Deum*"[17] summarizes the heart of the doctrine of technologia.

He also plays on quotations, especially metaphors and other figures, extending them in his gloss and enriching his language with the vocabulary of the sources. In discussing the Puritan conception of grace as a force recreating decaying capacities, he consciously makes use of a favorite Puritan comparison of conversion to construction: "As in the ruins of a palace, so runs one of their favorite metaphors, the materials still exist, but the 'order' is taken away; grace reestablishes the order by rebuilding with the same materials." In discussing the Puritans' use of the idea of a covenant, Miller clarified the nature of the contractual arrangement between God and man and remained faithful to the Puritan manner of phrasing. A representative passage runs: "For by conceiving the relationship between man and God as a contract, the sin of Adam appeared in a new light. Adam in his disobedience had broken a bond, had violated a lease. The punishment he received as a consequence was not deterioration so much as it was the infliction of a judicial sentence; it was expulsion for non-payment, it was not inherent pollution."[18]

The restraint in Miller's use of the metaphors of his source in this passage characterizes his work in the explication of ideas. In books and articles given to analysis, he mutes his romantic disposition. His customary mode in such work is to turn an idea over and over, explaining it in several ways, setting it forth in passages dense with quotations. The restraint largely disappears when his story is one of change. Here the extraordinary quality of his prose style arises from his appeal to the senses of his readers as well as to their intellects. The history of the transformation of Puritanism in the seventeenth century obviously moved him deeply and he expressed his feeling in choosing the adjectives "immense," "momentous," "tremendous," and "enormous." His verbs favor the strongly active: in his history Puritans do not ponder or reflect on a book, they "ransack" it for meanings. Ideas "assail" minds; and men "reel" and "stagger" under the assault. As readers of Cotton Mather's *Diary* know, that worthy spent many a night on the floor of his study in prayer; Miller pictures him in other more active roles, as, for example, when he "trounced New England with the gory threat of Indian atrocities." Mather also shrieks, screams, rages, and pants in the pages of *From Colony to Province*. Others act vigorously too; one Rusticus, for example, "thumbed his nose at Mather's erudition."[19]

One of the most passionately eloquent passages in Miller's writings and his most successful play on sound occurs in his cashiering of Samuel E. Morison for his attempt to whitewash Cotton Mather for his part in the Salem witchcraft episode. Miller begins with the charge: "Samuel Eliot Morison says that Robert Calef tied a tin can to Cotton Mather which has rattled and banged through the pages of superficial and popular historians." He then, in a tone of mock mildness, takes up the excuse: "My account is not popular, and I strive to make it not superficial; assuredly, if by tin can is meant the charge that Mather worked up the Salem tragedy, it does not belong to him; but what Calef was actually to charge was that he prostituted a magnificent conception of New England's destiny to saving the face of a bigoted court." Then comes the triumphant din of the clattering can: "In that sense, the right can was tied to the proper tail, and through the pages of this volume it shall rattle and bang."[20]

The wit displayed in this passage lightens many others in Miller's work. In contrast to his passion, which burst through in violent spurts, Miller's humor flows evenly, even lazily, when he permits it to appear. At times it is ironical and approaches deadpan—surely only a writer who believes that the grotesque speaks for itself would conceal "bras and girdles" in a list of examples of "technological transformation." Miller's glee at this sort of joke is unmistakable.[21]

There are ironical passages in Miller's books, but most are not humorous. Miller seems deliberately to have avoided treating some men and events with irony; he exposes, for example, the irony of Solomon Stoddard, whose authoritarianism earned him the title of "Pope," reforming the sacraments in order that the democracy might enter the church. But he did not treat Stoddard with irony. Nor was he ironic at the expense of the Puritans, though he presents them as a people who failed in part because they succeeded beyond their wildest dreams. He saw the incongruities in their ideals and conduct and he described them with relish, but he also felt the Puritans' joy and agony so deeply that he could not detach himself from them. Nor could he reject the Puritans, or their experience. The complexity of his attitude prevented either light or savage irony, and the depth of his feeling found other kinds of expression: admiration for their courage, anger at their self-righteousness, and an undecipherable passion at the glory of their attempt to know God and live according to His wishes. This complex feeling shaped his prose and gave it enormous vitality.

If in the twentieth century in America the most important attempts at understanding the Puritans began with a rejection of popular stereotypes, from that point on the popular culture supplied fewer of the questions to be asked about the Puritans and the private culture of historians more. Once freed of the necessity to provide champions of religious liberty, such as Roger Williams, or to explain the sterility of American culture, historians turned to such apparently narrow matters as church polity and covenant theology. Perry Miller's part in this process was more important than any other historian's.

Yet it has been suggested by Edmund S. Morgan in a powerful tribute that Miller's "influence was incommensurate with his genius." Morgan explains this curious fact by urging that at the level Miller worked on, "thought will not bear leading." What seems to be implied in this statement is that Miller did not think in terms of easily managed arguments which could be converted into simplistic formulas. But certainly he left an abundance of insights that have stimulated other scholars.[22]

Although the scholarship of any field has its own peculiar history, in fields in which highly creative men have worked scholarship seems to follow a depressingly familiar process. If the great man of the field has offered a formulation that can be reduced to a "thesis," a mass of journeymen will undertake to amplify it—usually along lines suggested by the master. Soon a more critical lot, sensing the flaws of this, will begin to attack it. A portion of Max Weber's work has suffered this fate, and so has Frederick Jackson Turner's. As yet Perry Miller's has not.

If the complexities and the level of Miller's work help explain his lack of influence and the happy absence of vulgarization of his thought, so also does the sophistication of the field in which he worked. Puritan studies have attracted other giants and a large number of only slightly less gifted scholars. They have given the study of Puritanism a subtlety and a ripeness that few areas of scholarship possess. They have also established a tradition of independent judgment that breeds a critical attitude. The result has been that neither a single point of view nor a single mode of study dominates Puritan scholarship; and it has enjoyed the inspiration of such different talents as Max Weber, Richard Tawney, William Haller, and Perry Miller.

To stimulate another is the most admirable influence any scholar can desire. Miller has had this effect upon Edmund S. Morgan, who is today the ablest scholar of New England Puritanism. Morgan accepts Miller's assumptions about Puritans and his assumptions about how they should be studied. Yet Morgan is neither a slavish adherent nor an imitator. He has thus far chosen to work on a smaller scale, studying in depth the relations of Puritan ideas to society. His work includes books on the family, John Winthrop's influence on the early political development in Massachusetts, Roger Williams' ideas about church and state, the conception of visible sainthood; and a biography of Ezra Stiles, an eighteenth-century President of Yale College, in which he examines a figure who reconciled Puritan and Enlightenment ideas. Morgan's studies indicate that he believes the Puritans applied their ideas rationally (in

Weber's sense, systematically), paying particular attention to the harmony of the ideas within themselves. He does not find their application bloodless or schematic, however, and he is extraordinarily sensitive to the irrational results of the Puritans' application of their ideas, contending in *The Puritan Dilemma* that a rigid fidelity to one set of ideas yielded Anne Hutchinson's antinomianism and Roger Williams' separatism. And in *Visible Saints* Morgan shows that literal devotion to an idea of purity in the church led the Puritans to devise a test for membership which carried them farther away from the world than they expected and inevitably produced a situation in which continued adherence to purity threatened to deprive their churches of members.[23]

Morgan tells all his history in a simple and graceful style which conveys a sense of the way men remained flesh-and-blood creatures while working out theological abstractions. Miller renders most kinds of personalities well, but he is especially effective in dealing with those he dislikes—the Mathers in their bitterness and fear—or those he warmly admires—John Wise in his lusty earthiness. Just as Miller does, Morgan eschews fancy and formal psychological techniques but he recreates personality even more skillfully, in part because his range of sympathy is greater.

Morgan's work testifies to the power of Miller's inspiration and to the continuing relevance of the study of Puritan ideas. Other approaches, which have yielded important knowledge of Puritanism, help locate the limits of Miller's influence but in no way compromise the value of what he has done. Perhaps they also suggest the need for some even larger synthetic study than has yet appeared.

Since the Second World War the most important of such different techniques has been an application of the sociological analysis of Weber and Tawney. The leading exponent recently of such an approach is Christopher Hill, whose work owes more to Tawney than to anyone else. Indeed Hill's major work, *Society and Puritanism*, is in certain ways an extended comment on "The Puritan Movement," which makes up Chapter 4 in *Religion and the Rise of Capitalism*. Hill sees Puritanism in England as rooted in a social class, the "industrious sort," made up of entrepreneurs, tradesmen, all men on the make. For them Puritan doctrine became an ideology of social discipline and industrial development. What Hill's analysis reveals is that the appeals of Puritanism lay in its social utility, which contributed to industrial change. If Hill's study does not account for the origins of ideas, it does, perhaps, indicate the emphasis those ideas received in England and even why they developed as they did.[24]

Hill's work adds depth and specificity to the views of Tawney and Weber, and the detail he provides increases our understanding of the process by which the medieval order was smashed in England. But what is lacking in all of his work is a full recognition of the persistence of medieval values within Puritanism. Tawney saw this persistence but at the same time was especially sensitive to the enormous social energy released by Puritanism. And Tawney, better than Hill, describes the historical reconciliation of Puritan ethics and modern acquisitiveness.

By their very differences in technique and imagination and interests, the work of Morgan and Hill indicates the growing vitality of Puritan scholarship. In the years since the Second World War, there have been books and articles by other scholars on Massachusetts law, church organization, economic activity, literature and aesthetics, politics and revolution. Miller's explorations penetrated deeply into some of these subjects and touched them all. None of the recent books simply amplifies his insights but almost all owe something directly to his studies.[25]

Miller wrote several times of his pleasure at the development of interest in Puritanism and of his delight in students who went beyond his own work. There may have been moments when he felt himself to be the intellectual father of Puritan studies in the United States. He was a self-conscious man, very much aware of his own great talents and obsessed with the desire to use them to their fullest.[26]

But for all Miller's interest in his field and in other students in it, he did not crave disciples. His model, if he had one, was not the master scholar with apprentices; it was the lone wolf, the scholar who recognized the modern world for what it was—a "civilization of machines"—and who, accepting its indifference to humanistic scholarship, followed his studies wherever they took him. The valuation modernity placed on what was dear to him did not make him weep for the good old days. Rather, it confirmed his belief that the scholar, as lone wolf, had a responsibility both to insist upon the relevance of intellectual life in machine civilization and to preserve its integrity.

There may be something romantic in a scene he liked to conjure up of the lonely scholar shutting the door of his study on the world; but there is something noble in the assumption underlying it: the lonely scholar has great responsibilities, especially when he closes his study door. Miller once praised Vernon Louis Parrington's noble prejudices but said that Parrington should be read only for inspiration. Perry Miller, one suspects, had his own kind of nobility, and he will long be read for his inspiration. But he will be read for another reason, too, a quality of mind that informs as it inspires.

Samuel Flagg Bemis

H. C. ALLEN

7)

MODERN HISTORIOGRAPHY is perhaps two hundred years old, about as old as the independent United States of America. Certainly the writing of history as we understand it had come into existence by the time of the publication of the first volume of Gibbon's *Decline and Fall of the Roman Empire* in 1776, that *annus mirabilis* which saw not only the Declaration of Independence but also the appearance of two other harbingers of the modern world, Jeremy Bentham's *Fragment on Government* and Adam Smith's *Wealth of Nations*.

For a century after this date historical writing tended to be dominated by historians of Gibbon's type, producing great panoramic works, such as the fifty-one published volumes of Leopold von Ranke. Before long, however, even during this period, the persistent trend, exemplified in Adam Smith, toward increased specialization, which has been inherent in the growth of all modern knowledge and especially that of the natural sciences (which had already in a different way had a profound effect on Ranke), began to show itself. In Britain, for example, the popular Lord Macaulay of the *Essays* was also the author who wrote five volumes on less than twenty years of English history, while Bishop Stubbs gained his deservedly great reputation almost exclusively as a constitutional historian. In France, the concentration of Albert Sorel on the history of his country's foreign relations made him one of the fathers of modern international history.

In the English-speaking world as a whole in the nineteenth century, there was in most historians, for economic and also for social and cultural reasons, a strain of leisureliness if not amateurism, which, it has often been claimed, placed undue emphasis on the literary aspect of historical writing. But in the works of the first American historian to write on the grand scale, George Bancroft, elegance of literary style was not sufficient to compensate for what many critics regarded as the tendentious character of the conclusion, that in some sense the triumph of American democracy was divinely predestined. This was even more extreme than the analogous interpretation of the Whig school of historians in Britain. Such excessive teleology was for the most part absent from the writings of his successors in America, but they remained in some respects historians by avocation rather than vocation. John Fiske, for example, was part philosopher and part sociologist, J. B. McMaster was an engineer by training, James Ford Rhodes was an ironmaster, and Francis Parkman led the life of a semi-invalid. Even Henry Adams, perhaps the first great academic American historian, who was in his way a true specialist in the early history of the Republic, always showed (as, for example, in his work on the Middle Ages) his sense that he was more than this—more indeed than a historian.

Not until the twentieth century, largely as a result of the powerful mid-nineteenth-century influence of the German academic tradition on institutions of learning in the United States and the consequent establishment of modern methods of graduate training, especially in history and the sciences, did fully trained professional historians, specializing in particular fields, begin to dominate American historical writing. Even Frederick Jackson Turner, the great historian of the frontier, taught ancient history in his early years. One of the first and most important of these specializations was in modern diplomatic history.

Although it owed much in origin to Sorel, and had an early European exponent in the Dutchman H. T. Colenbrander, as well, in some ways, as the Englishman J. R. Seeley (to whose *Expansion of England* the subject of this essay acknowledges his debt), it could be argued that the study of the history of national foreign policies probably first reached its highest and most specialized development to date in twentieth-century Britain and America. In Britain, its leading exponents were men like J. Holland Rose, G. P. Gooch, H. W. V. Temperley and, above all, C. K. Webster, specifically acknowledged by our subject as "a towering figure." The developing British and American schools of diplomatic history in the twentieth century were so closely intertwined as to constitute a kind of symbiosis. This was partly the result of the common language, partly the result of the common subject (with Anglo-American relations as the necessarily dominant, if at times unhappy, theme of early American history), and partly the result of the continuous, and ever-increasing, intellectual and academic intercourse between Britain and the United States. Historians like Webster not only worked in American archives but also taught in American universities (in his case Harvard), and almost every American diplomatic historian of distinction must have sojourned long in the Public Record Office in London. We might note in passing that these men had a by no means inconsiderable influence (for the most part highly beneficial) on the actual development of Anglo-American relations in recent times.

Their expertise was not confined to American and British records: far from it. The essence of the new international history was that it was multiarchival and sought to avoid the distortions resulting from national viewpoints by going back, like all good modern historical research, to the basic, primary materials in each country. Languages were its essential tools, and its practitioners had to be familiar with the official records of many states, as well as many individuals and government departments. One of the leading American representatives of the school brings this out clearly in a famous and amusing passage, analyzing the part that Theodore Roosevelt later claimed he had played toward Germany in the Venezuela crisis of 1902:

There are the strongest reasons for believing that the idea that an ultimatum was addressed to Germany was the product of the Rough Rider's exuberant imagination rather than of his memory. In the archives of the Wilhelmstrasse is not a word that confirms the story; there is not a word in the despatches of Sir Michael Herbert, the British Ambassador at Washington; there is not a word in the State Department; there is not a word about any special orders to the American fleet in the Navy Department; there is not, in short, one single scrap of contemporary evidence that substantiates the Roosevelt narrative.[1]

The first generation of this twentieth-century American school of multiarchival international history is in many respects best represented by Samuel Flagg Bemis.[2] If he is not actually its *doyen*, his work is the weightiest and most comprehensive and by no means the least penetrating and perceptive. He has not, perhaps, the unique mastery of one great subject which Dexter Perkins has shown in his history of the Monroe Doctrine. He has not, certainly, had the particular revisionist fervor and hence the special impact of Julius W. Pratt on nineteenth-century historiography. He has not concentrated his energies as much as has Thomas A. Bailey on relatively modern events of great contemporary interest to Americans. He has not made the intense study of a single crisis and even of a single man that Charles Seymour (although he began his career in British domestic history) made of World War I and of Colonel Edward Mandell House. He has not written any single work as strikingly seminal as John Bartlet Brebner's *North Atlantic Triangle*. He has not the specialized expertise in recent and contemporary international history of Herbert Feis, or the experimental approach of Richard W. Van Alstyne. But in the scope, combined with depth, of his research and writing, especially on the first century of American history, Bemis has no equal among American diplomatic historians.

The names cited above in no sense constitute a complete list of the eminent names in the first generation of American diplomatic historians: for example, that of W. L. Langer (combined with those of his collaborators) might be included, as well as those of George F. Kennan and A. P. Whitaker, and there are others whose contributions were on a lesser scale, such as, for example, Frederick Merk and Tyler Dennett. The history of the United States, including its foreign policy, is already by far the most intensively studied of all national histories, and, though the river of research and writing has been in spate for a number of years, the flow increases rather than diminishes.

Now comes a younger generation, containing many already distinguished names, among them Charles S. Campbell, Jr., Alexander De Conde, Robert H. Ferrell, Norman A. Graebner, Walter La Feber, Richard W. Leopold, Ernest R. May, Robert R. Osgood, Bradford Perkins, and William A. Williams. On some of this younger generation of American diplomatic historians Bemis has had an important influence, not merely as a practicing writer of history, but as a teacher; for he has successfully driven in tandem those two unruly steeds, without whose joint efforts the finest accomplishments of modern historians are intensely difficult, if not impossible: teaching and research. This direct influence has extended beyond America, to such a rising

British international historian, for example, as J. A. S. Grenville, who was a member of Bemis's influential seminar at Yale.

This seminar, indeed, was an excellent instance of the classic American pattern of graduate training, which in the teaching of history (and that of other disciplines as well) is an unsurpassed instrument for the professional instruction of substantial numbers of would-be writers and teachers, especially when combined, as in Bemis's case, with a large and successful undergraduate lecture course, which can provide a steady flow of recruits for graduate work, though most of these in due time probably come from other universities. It gives the widest possible scope for the development of those spiritual successions, sometimes familylike, sometimes almost dynastic, of teachers and pupils, with which in every culture scholars, but perhaps especially historians, are familiar. Bemis, who graduated from Clark College in his native Massachusetts in 1912, with a B.A. in History and English, and took his M.A. in History in 1913, under George H. Blakeslee, an eminent teacher of international relations, would have gone on to the Law School at Harvard if he had been able to afford it, but applied instead for a history fellowship there. He joined Edward Channing's seminar at the time that the professor was working on the fourth volume of his massive *History of the United States*. The work of the seminar kept pace with the writing of the book, and Bemis (whom Channing regarded as one of his most outstanding students) was assigned Jay's Treaty of 1794 as his thesis subject for the Ph.D. In due course it became his first book, finally published after World War I, in 1923, though his first article, on "The Settlement of the Yazoo Boundary Dispute: The First Step in Southern Expansion" (on which he does not now look back with approval), had been published ten years earlier in the new *Magazine of History* of October–November, 1913.

At Harvard Bemis also worked under Frederick Jackson Turner, and wrote a paper for him based partly on the Canadian archives, at a time when (as his Canadian-born contemporary, A. L. Burt, the distinguished historian of Britain, Canada and the United States, once remarked) these were virtually unknown to scholars. From this time on Bemis was never long absent from one or another of the great national archival collections, but the experience of sitting at the feet of the great master of the history of the West left an almost equally important mark on him. Henceforward there seems to become increasingly apparent in him not merely the fondness of this New Englander for (and his understanding of) the majestic nature of the continental historical role of the United States, but also the perhaps not unconnected strain of vigorous American patriotism which was always to characterize his work. Though he himself ascribes the first suggestion that he should do so to his friend Samuel Eliot Morison, it seems typical of the man that (anonymously as was the rule) he submitted his *Jay's Treaty* under the pseudonym "Christopher Columbus" for the prize offered in 1923 by a patriotic fraternal society, the Knights of Columbus, for the best book of that year on United States history by an American college teacher—and that he won it.

At this time such a success must have been most gratifying, for he had just emerged from a period of great physical and psychological difficulty—one of those periods which must exist in the life of every intelligent and sensitive person and which cannot but have profound effects upon their character and career. In this case, the private difficulty was precipitated by a public experience, one of extraordinary irony in the case of a distinguished diplomatic historian. A traveling fellowship from Harvard enabled him to seek, in the midst of the Great War, more material on Jay's Treaty in the British and French archives, and he went to Europe and spent his first period in the British Museum and the Public Record Office. In March 1916, en route to Paris, the Channel steamer *Sussex* in which he was traveling from Folkestone was torpedoed; the time he spent in the cold water before he was rescued damaged his health. On his return to the United States he was awarded his Ph.D., but was advised, on account of the tuberculosis which had been diagnosed, to go west to mountain country for his health. He went, understandably enough, in a deeply depressed state of mind, and for a brief period was associated with the organization of the Los Alamos Ranch School for Boys in New Mexico.

After a year he took up his first university teaching post, in Colorado College, and three years later moved on to Whitman College in Walla Walla, Washington. Before long the tonic of life in the Rocky Mountains did its work, reinforcing in practice the intellectual influence of Turner; the mature Bemis never had any doubt that the benefits of the experience of living in the West far outweighed the disadvantage of remoteness from the great libraries and the then dominant academic centers of the East. His substantial publications while in the West (ten articles between 1918 and 1923) and his activities in the historical associations made their mark, and in 1923, when the editor of *The American Historical Review*, J. Franklin Jameson (who had accepted a number of Bemis's articles), was appointed Director of the Division of Historical Research for the Carnegie Institution of Washington in 1923, he made Bemis an Associate Research Fellow in his office. While he was in the West Bemis had married the late Ruth M. Steele, from his home town of Worcester, Massachusetts, who was to be a devoted yet independent companion and helpmate throughout his life. He was now thirty-two years old and fully prepared and ready for his subsequent career.

Yet he was still willing to accept and acknowledge the help and guidance of an older scholar such as Jameson, with whom his close association lasted for ten years. (Bemis was affiliated during this period with George Washington University.) Of Jameson, Bemis says:

The greatest man I ever knew personally, a man of immense erudition and disciplined imagination. He knew pure scholarship, was enormously helpful and sympathetic to scholars, and became, in effect, a teacher to historians rather than a writer of great history. He probably did more than any other one person to serve the profession of American historians in this way.[3]

It was during these years in Washington that Bemis laid the foundations of his massive record of publication in American diplomatic history, with his editorship of (and contributions to) the ten-volume *The American Secretaries of State and their Diplomacy* (1927–29). He also paid his first visit to Spain and began to acquire that interest in Spanish history which was not only to make possible his second monograph, *Pinckney's Treaty: A Study of America's Advantage from Europe's Distress, 1783–1800* (1926), but also to be so invaluable in his later work on Latin America.

In 1931 he moved back into the Revolutionary period with the publication of *The Hussey-Cumberland Mission and American Independence: An Essay in the Diplomacy of the American Revolution*, and followed it in 1935 with *The Diplomacy of the American Revolution*. It was this year and the year after, 1936, which saw the culmination of this decade of intense research in the Washington archives and elsewhere. In the first year appeared a fundamental work of historiography and bibliography, the *Guide to the Diplomatic History of the United States, 1775–1921*, compiled jointly with Grace Gardner Griffin, which remains to this day (granted the limitation of its date of publication, 1935) the basic, indispensable tool for any historian of American foreign policy. In the second year, at the age of forty-five, came what was in a sense the distillation of his now wide and deep knowledge of American foreign policy—his *Diplomatic History of the United States.*

This weighty and meticulous, lucid and powerful one-volume narrative history of American foreign policy was to go through four revised and extended editions in the next twenty years and must have been the most generally employed work of its kind in this period, and is still in wide use today. But it was much more than a college textbook. It was a pioneer work, ahead of all its nearest counterparts; and it was, to a greater extent than is usual with such works, based directly on original materials. The result is a majestic book, synthesizing all the rapidly accumulating knowledge of American diplomatic history.

It appeared during his initial year in a new post at Yale, where he was to remain until his retirement in 1960, and where he still resides. For the first ten years he was Farnam Professor of Diplomatic History, and for the last fifteen Sterling Professor of Diplomatic History and Inter-American Relations. In 1937–38 he had visited Latin America and delivered a series of lectures which were published two years later under the title *La Politica Internacional de los Estados Unidos: Interpretaciones.* His attention now turned more and more to the history of America's relations with Central and South America, and, building on the foundation of his Spanish knowledge, he produced in 1943 another major study, *The Latin American Policy of the United States*, which, as well as breaking new ground, drew together with great skill the existing threads of knowledge.

He was to publish two shorter general diplomatic histories, adaptations and abbreviations of his existing work, in 1950 and 1959 (*The United States as a World Power: A Diplomatic History, 1900–1950* and *A Short History of American Foreign Policy and Diplomacy*). He still had within him two more volumes, published when he was fifty-eight and sixty-five respectively, which many scholars believe to be his finest works—*John Quincy Adams and the Foundations of*

American Foreign Policy and *John Quincy Adams and the Union.*
Together they constitute (for perhaps all good historians feel the
need to attempt a "life") a striking political biography—the first
being what Bemis himself called "a diplomatic biography,"[4] the
second covering the "second career"[5] of its subject and chiefly concerned with affairs at home in the decades of mounting tension
before the Civil War. It is interesting that this pre-eminently diplomatic historian should make his last substantial monograph a life in
which he tries, as he says, "to look behind the statesman to see more
of the man himself, his compulsive psychology, his social and family
relations, his religious feeling and attitude toward life on this earth
and hereafter."[6]

This attempt at biography in some psychological depth is fascinating evidence of the extent of the development which had taken place,
during his working lifetime, in the criteria by which good biography
is judged. In that period men's understanding of the human mind
and emotions had grown and deepened very rapidly, and the purely
political biography had ceased to satisfy. (Compare, for example,
John Morley's life of Burke, published in 1867, with Philip Magnus's
published three-quarters of a century later. There is possibly something of this kind of difference even between Bemis's two volumes on
Adams.) It is also evidence of the responsiveness of Bemis to
changing patterns of events and currents of opinion in his later years.
In this, as in a number of other characteristics, he has perhaps some
affinity with the fellow New Englander about whose life he was
writing. (The first of the two volumes, as he himself says, was
brought out "as an independent book standing by itself,"[7] because of
his uncertainty as to whether he might be able to complete the other.
This in my view does to some extent mar the unity of the whole
work, but it is by any standard a remarkable biography.)

This life of Adams constituted a fitting culmination to a life of
historical writing, in which Bemis was sole author of nine substantial
and original volumes, editor of ten others, and part author of yet
another. Most of these went through numbers of revisions and editions. In addition between 1913 and his Presidential Address to the
1961 meeting of the American Historical Association, he published
more than seventy-five serious articles on subjects ranging from
"Talleyrand and Jaudenes, 1795" (1925) to what he calls a "foreboding review," "First Gun of a Revisionist Historiography for the

Second World War" (1947). This corpus of historical writing, while not perhaps "great" history in the fullest sense of the word, made up a scholarly output which, in quantity combined with quality, has never been surpassed by any historian of the United States, and not often surpassed by any historian of any country. Through his whole career he has shown that infinite capacity for taking pains without which modern historical writing of the first order is not possible.

In this he was truly representative of his generation of multi-archival diplomatic historians, who were as a "school" at special pains, by thorough, prolonged, and intensive research in the records, not merely to establish the "real facts," but also to avoid those passions which are almost always so apparent (and frequently so destructive) in the subject of their study, the relations of states and peoples with one another. This effort at impartiality has laid the diplomatic historians open to charges of aridity and dullness, and it is, indeed, of the nature of professional diplomacy itself to be monotonous except in times of crisis, which does not help historians, even though they may in fact very often be concerned with the critical moments of their story. Bemis is no exception to this rule. Necessarily, in the vast tracts of historical ground which he has covered, there are areas which lack excitement, even troughs of tedium, as there are in the work of every historian who has written at great length. The overriding general impression, however, is one of clarity and vigor, incisiveness and penetration.

Furthermore, there are occasional sparkles of vivid and pawky Yankee humor and irony, which break through the surface of his New England phlegm, in writing as in speech. These are often of a semantic character: he loves words as well as jokes. I well remember, when, many years ago, I had brought home his *Diplomatic History* to read, how an old friend staying in the house—not an academic, an R.A.F. officer, in fact—was picking about in it, and was almost literally convulsed by the sentence with which Bemis introduced perhaps the least-stimulating subject in the history of Anglo-American relations, the late-nineteenth-century controversy about pelagic sealing in the Bering Sea: "Amphibious is the fur seal, ubiquitous and carnivorous, uniparous, gregarious and withal polygamous."[8]

Bemis has, however, avoided the worst risk of total detachment in the historian—that of becoming Carlyle's Dry-as-Dust—because he has been much involved in the contemporary foreign-policy controversies of his day. This entails the opposite risk, which all truly living historians, and particularly perhaps historians of foreign policy, run, that of being influenced in their historical judgments by their personal opinions of the world in which they live. To the school of "scientific" historians, founded and exemplified by Ranke, this was more than the great professional risk: it was the temptation to sin against the Holy Ghost. The historian, like the scientist, had to be "completely objective," to exclude rigidly from his historical writing all his personal life and feelings.

Yet, what an extraordinary illusion this belief in the possibility of totally objective history is. For the historian there is no test tube in which to conduct controlled experiments, while for the scientist (or at least the natural scientist), there is seldom much cause for the human passions which the study of mankind's past must tend to arouse, though if we look, for example, at the biological sciences, to say nothing of psychology, we find them frequently and ferociously rent in twain over a Darwin, a Pasteur, and a Lysenko, and perhaps above all a Freud. The search for total detachment in the historian is the pursuit of a will-o'-the-wisp, as Carl L. Becker, one of "objective" history's earliest and most powerful critics, long ago pointed out: for him it was "a set of artificially induced and cultivated repressions such as would enable a careful historian to write . . . an account of the Battle of Cold Harbor without revealing that his father was an ardent admirer of Grant."[9]

As George H. Sabine put it in his memoir of Becker:

The idea that facts could be made "to speak for themselves," that history could be made scientific by techniques for criticizing documents or by the mere suppression of the historian's more obvious social interests and judgments of value . . . neglected the psychological relation of emotion to thought, and also the fact that every historian, even the most scientific, is bound to have some kind of preferences which must manifest themselves in his selection and explanation of facts.[10]

For this direct attempt at objectivity a far more complex and difficult psychological operation must be substituted, one "intellectually sophisticated in a high degree":

Becker believed that real historical detachment is produced not by a vain effort to have no interests or prepossessions but by becoming as fully aware as possible of the prepossessions one has. . . . In a report which he once wrote for the Historical Association on the reviewing of historical books, Becker said: "In seeking to avoid having a philosophy of history, the historian does not succeed in not having one: perhaps after all he succeeds only in having a bad one."[11]

Historians of foreign policy, Bemis among them, naturally and on the whole properly, tend to reflect the interests of their own country in their own day; they usually turn their attention first to the history of their own nations and governments and only later to that of others; they tend also to concentrate on those aspects which are of greatest contemporary influence. Thus as H. Hale Bellot has written,

before 1914, except that some pioneer work had been done upon the history of the relations of the United States with the Far East, mono-graphic studies that were to be of permanent value were . . . excepting works relating to the early period, virtually limited to the field of Latin American policy. This . . . had its origin in the preoccupations of American statesmanship. . . . The treatment of the history of diplo-matic relations with the European powers in respect to European prob-lems has been by comparison jejune and fragmentary. . . .[12]

Full American historiographical interest in the Far East did not reawaken till after Pearl Harbor, but it is notable that Bemis's two great fields of concentration were indeed the early history of the foreign policy of the Republic and the whole history of her Latin American policy, though his broad sweep inevitably involved him in the consideration of the later history of America's relations with Europe.[13]

In his treatment of America's relations with the outside world, especially Europe, it cannot be doubted that Bemis has shown the powerful influence of his own age and his own experience and beliefs. (It is at this point that the difficulty of the historian of historians in treating a living subject becomes clearly apparent. If we are to speak only good of the dead, how much more difficult to be critical of the living, especially those seniors whom we know and respect! But he is after all a historian, and one may cite the words of Burke: "I speak with the freedom of history and I hope without offence.") Bemis for many years profoundly believed in the benefits which America had derived from her isolation, especially during the nineteenth century—which he talks of as being, under British imperialism, one of "un-precedented happiness for mankind."[14] He was deeply convinced of the wisdom of Washington when, in his Farewell Address, the latter said of America's "detached and distant" position, "Why forego the advantage of so peculiar a situation?" He actually gave to his second work, published in 1926 in the full onset of American isolationism, a subtitle which encapsulated his view: A *Study of America's Advantage from Europe's Distress.* He also repudiated the late-nineteenth-century phase of American imperialism by which the United States acquired a modest colonial empire in the Orient, calling it "a great aberration," although understandably he approved of, or at least accepted, the earlier phase of continental expansion which was known as Manifest Destiny, on the ground that "American expansion across a practically empty continent despoiled no nation unjustly, and that there is no American today who would want to see that expansion undone"[15] (whatever—the critics may say—the dead might feel). With this opinion went a heartfelt nationalism, an intense faith—sometimes amounting in the opinion of those critics almost to chauvinism—in the past achievements and future prospects of the United States polity and the American people.[16]

In these views he was at one with many, indeed most, Americans of his generation, and after the not entirely unjustified, if dangerously overweening, national euphoria of the Republican-dominated 1920's it took both the Great Depression and the Second World War to alter the hope of those Americans that, as Anne Morrow Lindbergh put it in 1940, "in America, if nowhere else in the world, it should be possible to meet the wave of the future in comparative harmony and peace. It should be possible to change an old life to a new without such terrible bloodshed as we see today in the process in Europe."[17]

This point of view is implicit, if not fully explicit, in the marked difference of emphasis and interpretation between the original 1936 edition of Bemis's *Diplomatic History* written on the high tide of isolationism and the most recent, fifth edition, completed in 1964 after the experience of the Second World War and its aftermath. The opening words of the new Preface to the latter embody this fact: "The world into which we were born is gone. . . ."

Yet Europeans, with their own overwhelming interests in the matter, are in no position to criticize loftily the isolationism of the prewar United States, especially those who like myself were as young men (at least for a time) supporters of appeasement—the British counterpart of American isolationism. Modern war must still be adjudged, in itself, a failure of civilization; and the American dream, drawing upon the deep aspirations of men who sought either a new heaven or a new earth, a Zion or a Utopia, and sought them in the end for all men equally, was a far from ignoble vision; it gave America "birth and happiness and the peace which she has treasured."[18]

It is a failure of imagination for the historian of the United States not to understand, and not to sympathize with, the hope of Tom Paine expressed in 1776: "Not a place upon earth might be so happy as America. Her situation is remote from all the wrangling world, and she has nothing to do but to trade with them."

It would be equally a failure of perception not to see how powerful the feeling could be in the case of this Massachusetts "farm boy," "plebeian not Brahmin," who "would be called underprivileged today." The words are, characteristically (especially perhaps "plebeian"), those he himself has used of his origins; this New Englander, who recalls with particular affection his five years (the highly impressionable ones from nine to fourteen) on his grandfather's farm at Sturbridge, with the "bucolic" attractiveness of its Walden-like pond—that evocative New England word. If, in the case of this son of a newspaper man (to whom his literary debt was great, as he says), it was scarcely a case of rags to riches, it was close enough to the archetypal (if sometimes mythical) pattern of an American's individual and enterprising development for him to regard himself as "an example of the American dream."

And when he first left American shores to visit the Old World, in the midst of perhaps the worst of those "agonizing spasms of infuriated man" of which Jefferson had warned, the youth who was to spend his life in the study of international affairs was torpedoed on the high seas and his health seriously affected. As a result of his testimony and that of "other American survivors, President Wilson sent a sharp diplomatic protest to Berlin stating that if the Germans again attacked an unarmed passenger liner without warning, the United States would break relations. . . . For Bemis, the submarine in American diplomacy has been more than an academic matter. . . ."[19] From this experience of the maelstrom of war in Europe the young man went to meet the distant mountains of Colorado, and there, in the land of a still-living Western frontier, he got well and did great things. After that he moved to the streets of the national capital, at the heady height of the boom of the twenties, and there he remained for eleven years, a deeply patriotic American, who might well have cried with Turner's citizen of Seattle,

"Why should I not love the West! It . . . spread before my eyes a vision of snow-capped peaks and smiling fields; it brought abundance and a new life to me and my children and I love it, I love it! If I were a multi-millionaire I would charter freight cars and carry away from the crowded tenements and noisome alleys of the eastern cities and the Old World the toiling masses . . . and let them . . . learn what life really is!"[20]

This intense belief in traditional Americanism did sometimes arouse the ire of those who stood farther to the left than he did in the political spectrum or who in other ways disagreed with his views, particularly on intervention in Europe. Nor was he ever afraid to embroil himself in controversy, although he had tender sensibilities. (He confesses that he would have been unhappy, had he become a lawyer as he originally intended, amidst the "clash of the law.") Toward the end of his public career, his vigorous Presidential Address to the American Historical Association in December, 1961, had the unusual distinction of eliciting a mildly dissenting reply (what Bemis has called in conversation "a righteous riposte") from the Secretary of State, Dean Rusk. Though by now wholeheartedly committed to the support of states and peoples whose independence might be threatened by "Communist revolution and slavery,"[21] in other words to intervention "in defense of the Blessings of Liberty," Bemis had lost none of his belief in the necessity for the American people to remain especially, if no longer uniquely and aloofly (the words which he quotes are from John F. Kennedy), "committed in every fiber of our being [to] . . . the struggle for the cause of freedom. . . . "[22] This struggle is in his view now world-wide.

Surely [he said], the history of our foreign policy in relation to the successive postures of power in the world shows that during the eighteenth and nineteenth centuries the United States profited adventitiously from the highly favorable circumstances of a secure and prosperous isolation. Surely this fortunate age cannot recur. America no longer enjoys a detached and distant position—on the contrary. Europe's distresses and those of Asia and Africa are no longer America's advantage; they are now America's distresses, too.[23]

But the struggle is not only more extensive but also more trying and more testing than ever before, and here Bemis, a member of the older generation, intrudes his doubt, the doubt to which Secretary of State

Rusk took exception—how fit for this task are the Americans of today?

A great and virile people, Theodore Roosevelt's characterization of the American people, can also waste itself away when it turns to massive self-indulgence. In self-study and self-indulgence we have been losing sight of our national purpose rather than failing to have one. During the letdown of the last fifteen years we have been experiencing the world crisis from soft seats of comfort, debauched by mass media of sight and sound, pandering for selfish profit to the lowest level of our easy appetites, fed full of toys and gewgaws, our military preparedness held back by insidious strikes for less work and more pay, our manpower softened in will and body in a climate of amusement. Massive self-indulgence and massive responsibility do not go together. A great nation cannot work less and get more, with fun for all, in today's stern posture of power. How can our lazy social dalliance and crooning softness compete with the stern discipline and tyrannical compulsion of subject peoples that strengthen the aggressive sinews of our malignant antagonists? Only if we freely sacrifice for the Blessings of Liberty what they are forced to sacrifice for the compulsions of tyranny.[24]

In his comment on Bemis's "excellent presidential address"[25] the Secretary of State (himself by origin a teacher of history) said:

What of the American base? Is ours a society really given to "loose [sic] social dalliance and crooning softness"? There is enough dalliance to merit our genuine concern, but my view of our condition is less somber than your president's.

Democracies have always given an appearance of some disarray and self-indulgence. As a student I well knew interwar Britain. It was a costly conclusion that Hitler and Mussolini—and perhaps Stalin—deduced from surface phenomena that Britain of those years had lost its fiber. . . . I am confident that we still have the will and the dedication required for the great tasks ahead.[26]

Right or wrong, nothing shows better than this verbal passage of arms the ardent Americanism which is so important a feature of Bemis's work.

It also shows a virtue (not too common in historians, and indeed in men of all callings)—a readiness to change his opinions in the light of new evidence or of reconsideration of old. Emerson wrote that "A foolish consistency is the hobgoblin of little minds, adored by little statesmen and philosophers and divines"; but not by this historian, who, when asked whether his views had changed in the fifty years during which he had studied the role of the United States in the world, replied forthrightly, "Of course my views have changed. F.D.R. was right and I was wrong." This willingness to change his mind entitles him to be considered, overall, what he himself claims he is, "a pretty objective American"—if always a vigorous and outspoken one, who has at various times in his life, as he points out, been accused of being pro-British and pro-German as well as excessively pro-American.

In his career he was certainly a very American, in many ways quintessentially American, figure, whose overriding concern was to study and to learn from the history of America's place in the world. In so doing he was far from insensitive to the movements of opinion and the changes in ideas which were going on around him. This was true not only in the substance of his studies but in their method. His last work, on John Quincy Adams, certainly pointed the way forward for diplomatic historians, or at least pointed in the direction which the writing of international history was taking, and must take, in its emphasis on the psychological factors which have so vital an effect on human relationships. This was more than the increasing introspection which men advancing in years may show, one in this case who had written for his family and deposited in the Yale library a personal autobiography, which the strict professional historian in him causes him to describe warningly as "highly subjective." That it was more is demonstrated by his further wry and characteristic comment on the autobiography—that it displays "no Freudian depths or Adlerian shallows."[27]

The older history, and especially the studiously impartial history of diplomacy, in its anxiety to avoid the personal involvement of the historian and to maintain a neutrality which was necessarily in part illusory, ran the serious risk of ignoring, and hence failing to understand—let alone explain—the irrational in human, individual and (even more) group, behavior. In part this arose from a peculiarly (and understandably) intense effort by historians of foreign policy, for methodological reasons, to eschew all emotion which might disturb the processes of pure historical reason; it also acquired additional intensity, by a sort of osmosis, from its subject of study. Something of the rigid effort of professional diplomacy to preserve the public face, to recognize overtly only the official, impersonal facts and arguments, rubbed off onto the diplomatic historians, rendering their work on occasion not merely arid, but also shallow. It is hard for us to comprehend today that the great Sir Charles Webster's two-volume study of the foreign policy of Castlereagh contained scarcely a reference to the facts of his suicide, let alone to the long series of circumstances which must have led up to it.[28]

The fundamental danger of this approach was that it could lead to a perilous assumption of rationality in human decisions, political as well as historical, which it perhaps needed the career of Adolf Hitler finally to overturn. It was this tradition of assuming human reasonableness (common to both diplomacy and diplomatic history) which perhaps made it so hard for a man like Lord Halifax, the British Foreign Secretary before World War II, to comprehend at all the full depths of Hitler's desperate designs. For the historian, the intellectual problem is even more difficult and subtle than for the statesman, though the results of failure are less catastrophic. The historian has to take account not merely of the real passions of the individual politician he is studying, however well concealed, and of the emotional preconceptions of the society in which that politician moves, however complex, but also of those of the witnesses on whose evidence he relies and of the historians who may have predigested his raw material—as well as of his own, often deeply and urgently felt, opinions and inclinations.

The attitude of the historian, in other words, must be—the description, once more, is that by George H. Sabine of the view of Carl L. Becker—one of great complexity and sophistication. It implies

in the historian an extreme form of self-consciousness. The thing that the historian describes is a state of mind induced by a set of conditions which has itself supervened upon an older state of mind. . . . But this is in fact only half the complication, for the historian is himself caught in his own climate of opinion, from which he can no more escape than could the characters in his description. His own writing is part of the process by which his own climate of opinion rewrites the past for a present purpose of which he is the instrument. History seen from Becker's point of view is like a hall of mirrors in which image reflects image until the reality imaged vanishes in a never ending series of images. No point is absolutely fixed, not even that of the historian's own present from which he views the shifting points in his past.[29]

Bemis would have agreed, and unlike Webster on Castlereagh, Bemis on Adams captures the entire hall of mirrors. This effort to interpret events at what amounts to more than one level necessitates important changes in the methods of writing international history, of which there have been signs for some time, as for example in the concentration of historians like Frederick Merk and J. W. Pratt on public mood and opinion. Bemis became aware of the need for these changes, even though he fully belonged to that first generation of professional diplomatic historians, whose particular task it was to lay, by indispensable, impeccable scholarship, the groundwork for future advance. This stage of solid historiographical development could not have been omitted. The bricks, the building materials, constituted by the so-called facts of history must be tested and counted and assessed before the historian in one era can build his particular house and before, at a later stage again, other historians can understand why he has built it in such and such a way, and thus prepare to rebuild theirs in their own fashion.

The bulk of the work of Samuel Flagg Bemis must be judged by the standards of his contemporaries. By these standards he accomplished admirably the design he set for himself through half a century of professional life, to write "American diplomatic history from the international point of view." This he did on a large and multiarchival scale, in a vigorous and expressive style, and as a result of meticulous and profound research. In the process he not only taught and deeply influenced many students, both undergraduate and graduate, but also, by a unique bibliographical contribution to diplomatic history as well as by his scholarly example, had a lasting and beneficial influence on the works of more than one generation of American diplomatic historians.

Daniel J. Boorstin

J . R . POLE

8)

The rediscovery of America, which takes place with each attempt to comprehend the American experience as a whole, has always involved Europe. Even so nationally centered a historian as Turner got his bearings by repudiating the theory that attributed American institutions to a long line of European descent. Professor Daniel J. Boorstin, whose work has grown to be one of the most ambitious and persuasive of all attempts to impose on American history the vision of a unified interpretation, has never lost sight of the necessity to plot his course by taking his bearings from Europe and particularly from England.

The America that comes to life under Boorstin's hand is, in its early periods, itself a country of contrasts and of varied cultures. The main unifying effects of growing up on the American continent came from the fact that the experience differed so completely from that of Europe. But eventually a national quality was formed, partly out of a direct experience of settlement and recent tradition, partly out of shared hopes, partly out of myth. A powerful, persuasive sense of homogeneity takes precedence over those divisions of time, of region and of theory which are common to Europe. The contrast enables Boorstin to bring forward this theme of homogeneity, a theme that develops as he traces the shaping influences that rose from the problem presented by the creation and survival of society in an unsettled land.

Professor Boorstin draws on more than one tradition, the earliest being Frederick Jackson Turner's. The emphasis is on what was new, unexpected, and what Americans owed and still owe to the land. The older the settlement, the less part it plays in Boorstin's story; the eastern seaboard, once left behind by the movement of civilization, lies at a lengthening distance from his center of attention and his central themes. But these themes are far more varied and complex than Turner's. Where Turner's primary emphasis was on democracy and public institutions, Boorstin's is on the whole experience of a growing community, on the style and quality of the life it lived. Boorstin's method also makes him a partial exponent of comparative history; Turner merely revolted from an older tradition and then became absorbed in America, but Boorstin, without dwelling on Europe as a developing civilization, seldom loses sight of the alternatives it could propose. All this gives Boorstin a place of his own among the modern proponents of American consensus.

The view that America owed more—and particularly more of its successes—to a tradition of consensus about fundamental principles than to a tradition of internal conflict was advanced by Richard Hofstadter in 1948[1] and was reinforced from the point of view of comparative political science by Professor Louis Hartz.[2] Hartz, having created a large and receptive space by pointing out the fact that America lacked a feudal heritage, filled it by explaining the importance of the "liberal" philosophy imported from Europe. Other scholars, both in early American history and in early and recent political science, have emphasized in recent years the immense amount of common ground shared by Americans in political practice and belief.[3] Boorstin's mature work on America has the density of a vast fund of carefully sifted facts, which contrasts with Hartz's and Hofstadter's interest in ideas, theories, and ideals; but Boorstin is concerned with the manner of the life based on those facts, and the definition of "experience" includes imagination and sensibility. Each of his books is different, and his work continues to grow. The justification for reviewing his achievement at this stage is that it would continue to exert a profound influence over American historical thought even if he were now to make an entirely new departure. It may be said of Boorstin as perhaps of any major historian that his thought is both mature and incomplete.

Boorstin's strong sense of the comparative nature of his work has a biographical as well as a purely intellectual source; after graduating, *summa cum laude,* from Harvard in 1934, Boorstin went to Oxford as a Rhodes Scholar. His record there was remarkable; he took two degrees—those of B.A. and B.C.L.—getting first-class honors in both; contemplating a career in the law, he also ate the prescribed number of dinners at the Inner Temple, passed the examinations, and was called to the bar. At Balliol, the most distinct influence was perhaps that of A. D. Lindsay, who was Master, and under whom Boorstin read philosophy, and it was during his years at Balliol that he laid—or deepened—the foundation of a twofold interest that has had enduring significance. One of these is in this comparative method—the identification of America by comparison and contrast with Europe. The other is in law. Boorstin, having qualified as a barrister in England, took a J.D.S. degree at Yale Law School and also became a member of the Massachusetts bar; his double armament has been a source of strength, but he is not likely to need the qualifications of the lawyer, in the manner of many American politicians, to sustain him during intervals between tenures of office.

Boorstin began his work as a historian in a distinctively legal context. His first book, which he wrote as a law student at Yale and an instructor at Harvard, was a study of Blackstone (1941).[4] Even then Boorstin was not a historian of law; rather he used the view of social order and of political priorities implied in the legal system as an instrument for uncovering social history. In his Blackstone his method is explicit. In his later work, it is sometimes subdued, sometimes not required. But as an influence on his intellectual development it has never disappeared, and it is present in the shaping of his approach to some of the central questions that he has tackled. When he says of the American Revolution that it was "a prudential decision taken by men of principle rather than the affirmation of a theory"—a remark to which it will be necessary to return—he seems to imply that the leaders had the attitude of lawyers acting in the true interests of their clients rather than in the heat, and risk, of anger or enthusiasm; it is perhaps the scholar of law, both as history and procedure, who inclines to see in this cool light the acts of the revolutionary leaders.

The study of law appears to have contributed to Boorstin's controlling sense of the distinction between theory and practice. In later works he develops the distinction with great care and an amplitude of illustration, reaching to a point at which theory seems not so much to support and explain practice as to stand over against it, as an alternative or even an obstruction to doing what needs to be done. It is as well to remind ourselves that in an amusing but by no means unserious remark made in a much later essay, he alluded to the American view of the law as being "the ethical minimum."[5]

Boorstin's first book was about England, his second, *The Lost World of Thomas Jefferson* (1948), was about America. Despite these obvious differences, these two books belong to the same phase of his thought. Both are eighteenth-century studies; and they are concerned with historical problems of similar genre though dissimilar in subject matter. The problem is the reconstruction of a complete mode of thought—of the social and intellectual assumptions of an influential group of contemporaries who, in certain ways, gave laws or gave a style of their generation. Boorstin's analysis of Blackstone is little less than an analysis of the idea of law in eighteenth-century England. By contrast, though *The Lost World of Thomas Jefferson* is clearly consistent with the earlier study, the interests that dictated it were no longer so distinctly those of the student of law.

It is to the lawyer, as well as to "the student of history and the student of method in the social sciences" that the study of Blackstone is addressed.[6] Blackstone's *Commentaries on the Laws of England*, which were delivered in his capacity as the first Vinerean Professor of English Law at Oxford and were published between 1765 and 1769, form for Boorstin a microcosm of the prevailing rules and values of English society. The explicit lesson is that "the ostensibly impartial processes of reason are employed by the student of society to support whatever social values he accepts."[7] What emerges, as the substance to support this conclusion, is an interpretation of the mind of Blackstone and his contemporaries accompanied by a subtle critique of Blackstone's reasoning. This critique is essential to Boorstin's purpose. Probably every system of law involves the acceptance of certain legal fictions, some tautology or circular reasoning; it is by the penetration of these points that we can see what the system means to its upholders, what they are most heavily committed, through its agency, to defending.

For Blackstone, as Boorstin shows, the discussion of every section of the law becomes the exposition of "rational principles."[8] The laws of England might have been a disordered mass, their practices piled on several centuries of precedents, statutes, and customs, but Blackstone found everywhere that the rule of reason prevailed, and he satisfied himself that the reasons to be discovered in English law were always the best reasons. The laws of England, in fact, were little other than the working application of the laws of God, and it was, perhaps, for this reason among others that although they were rational they were unfathomable. And in one of those observations with which Boorstin can epitomize a complex reflection he concludes, "The conflict between Blackstone's science of Law and his Mystery of Law was never to be entirely resolved. For this was nothing less than the conflict between man's desire to understand and his fear that he might discover too much."[9]

The laws of England protected three great values, Humanity, Liberty, and Property. Boorstin's analysis of them shows that, as all the principal requirements of natural law were already covered, no improvement was to be expected from tampering with institutions. As for Liberty, for which England was particularly admired, Blackstone showed that it represented first the free expression of the will of the individual and secondly the full assertion of his rights. Civil society itself sprang from the free exercise of the wills of individuals. But the rights that society protected marked the limits of those proclaimed in the name of Liberty; thus property restrictions on the suffrage were justified because they assured unfettered expression to the wills that were truly free; it was not to be desired that liberty should spread to those without property; liberty protected rights and the protection of rights was the primary end of government. In fact, Boorstin points out, the whole structure of the *Commentaries* is built on the concept of rights, the first and second books being on "Rights" and the third and fourth on "Wrongs."[10] But the most important right and highest value was that of Property. Property was absolute. Blackstone's cry, as Boorstin says, would not have been "Liberty and Property" but "Liberty *of* Property."[11]

Property was created by nature, and civil society recognized and protected it; yet the definition of property was to be found only in the laws of England: the protection of the law became the only test of the existence of a right of property. The circularity of this definition provides a clue to Blackstone's method; and Boorstin is at his best in explaining, without lack of sympathy, what values Blackstone meant to uphold, while exposing the flaws in his arguments. The circularity of much of Blackstone's reasoning, which treated law as an isolated and self-consistent system of logic and often assumed what it purported to prove, and in which "tautology was often concealed by the copiousness of legal vocabulary"[12]—these are the intellectual methods by which he organized his immense mass of learning and reduced the laws of England to a system. The method is extensive. In principle, it governs Blackstone's use of the "maxim" as the rule of common law. The authority of the maxim rests on general reception and usage, but Blackstone could give a maxim as the "reason" for a specific rule. Blackstone, a recipient of Locke's psychology, attached importance to the doctrine that both ideas and knowledge were rooted in experience; he had no use for metaphysics but shared the prevailing belief in the utility of universal rules and principles. Experience, moreover, meant the experience of mankind; the principles that governed past civilizations would also be found in the present. Everywhere, he found a reason behind the received legal practice and related that reason to those values of eighteenth-century England which he regarded as sacred, as given by authority—in this case that of the Glorious Revolution—and therefore protected by law. If the method was circular the circle at least had a long circumference.

Boorstin, however, does not expose in order to destroy but rather to reconstruct. The rights of property at the heart of Blackstone's legal system were held in cohesion by the needs of a complex and largely customary society. Throughout, the reader appreciates that Blackstone was a part of a living world, and Boorstin criticizes those lawyers and social scientists who think institutions can be analyzed "scientifically" without regard to the fact that the agent is guided by what he believes to be good and is limited by the values of society. Blackstone, he observes, did insist that society had a moral purpose and that man should not let science lead him by the nose; he does not think that philosophical consistency is the only virtue to be praised, even in a work on law, and points out that Blackstone had a sort of *social* consistency; and he concludes by offering a defense of Blackstone's attempt to give a reason for defending a social and moral framework.[13]

The strength of this study does not rest on sympathy with Blackstone's ideas but rather on appreciation of his integrity of purpose. Boorstin already possessed the comparative insight essential to the historian. He knew that the first thing to grasp about the eighteenth century is that it was different from our own and did not hold itself responsible for twentieth-century values. Yet, as he shrewdly remarks, subsequent history has been written in the eighteenth century's own terms, so that trying to reconstruct its intellectual history is like trying to see the color red through red-colored spectacles;[14] and this remark reveals an insight into the intellectual problem of relating past to present and a preoccupation with the need to do so that continue to pervade Boorstin's work.

He was still engaged primarily in intellectual history when he turned to the reconstruction of the philosophical and scientific world-picture of Thomas Jefferson.[15] But now both the scene and the sources were different. For the earlier work, the *Commentaries* of Blackstone provided a solid, already organized foundation, but the picture of the world, as seen through Jefferson's eyes, had to be put together from the numerous and scattered writings of Jefferson and his philosophical contemporaries. The scene itself, of course, had shifted to North America—to be more exact, mostly to Philadelphia, where the American Philosophical Society held its sessions—and Boorstin constantly keeps before the reader the importance of the local experience.

This theme opens the book; and here begins the published record of Boorstin's lasting preoccupation with the influence of the specifically American experience of life on the making of a specifically American mind.[16] Jefferson's intellectual circle formed a remarkably interesting group, and Boorstin is able to recreate the frame of their shared ideas about nature and nature's God, about the equality of the human species deriving from its descent from an original creation, about the essential materialism of their psychological, moral, and religious beliefs, and about society and politics. The beliefs held in common by these men, without being highly systematic, were closely related, and their inquiries into the natural world were intended to supply information to prove what they already believed.

Their interests were extremely wide, and in a sense it was the seriousness of their commitment to certain preconceived ideas that determined their incessant search for facts. They believed in original creation and human equality and hence, for example, sought to explain the Negro's color as a medical abnormality; they believed in the economy of nature and hence that no natural creation could be either duplicated or extinct; and since they rejected the idea of development, they believed in the sovereignty of the present generation and had little interest in history. Like Blackstone, they had no use for metaphysics, and Jefferson maintained that the problems of moral perception could be reduced to those of a rarefied but essentially practical form of anatomy. A keynote to their outlook is given by Benjamin Barton's claim that "the strong democracy of facts should exert its wholesome sway," and Boorstin adds that "by a 'fact' the American philosopher meant anything recordable by man's physical senses."[17] It was wholly in keeping with their beliefs that even thought should have been reduced to a branch of physiology—"the mode of action called thinking." But by rejecting the value of metaphysical speculation, the Jeffersonians isolated themselves within their own system and deprived themselves of the possibility of perceiving that it *was* a system, with gaps which they lacked the means to close. This comment contains an irony which later turns on its author. For Boorstin was soon to embark on a full-scale interpretation of American history that owes much to the Jeffersonian viewpoint; Boorstin sees American society as a product of American geography, denigrates the value of theoretical speculation, isolates himself within his own system, and exposes himself to the criticism he makes of the Jeffersonians.

When Professor Boorstin turns to the political science of the Jeffersonians we begin to perceive connections between the forgotten world of their vision and the continuing traditions that have been kept alive in American thought and institutions.

Rejecting the study of history, and any formal interest in institutions, Jeffersonians centered their political science on the relationship of man to nature. "Jefferson's often quoted aphorism that the people were governed best who were governed least," remarks Boorstin, "was simply another way of insisting on [the] distinction between imperfect human institutions and the Creator's perfect rule."[18] The dismissal of theoretical presuppositions, in a political philosophy based on natural rights, made successful action the final test of human institutions; and Boorstin insists that Jefferson took his cue from political science, not from any preconceived purpose "but from the struggle already going on among men."[19] But in what sense and how far may a philosophy of natural rights be said to involve metaphysical conceptions? It is here that Boorstin is more critical, perhaps, than anywhere else in his analysis of the Jeffersonian mind. "All the Jeffersonians," he says, were great believers in "Bills of Rights," and the word "rights" is the most familiar and significant word in their political idiom. Contrary to general belief, this emphasis did not express a conscious reliance on metaphysical foundations, nor a "rationalistic" or abstract basis of the state. It revealed, rather, the unsystematic and inarticulate character of Jeffersonian political theory. A list of "rights" substituted for a systematic theory of government. "Rights" are indefinitely enumerable, and (in the absence of a comprehensive theory of "right") the addition or subtraction of any one does not necessarily require the subtraction or addition of others.[20]

We shall not often find Boorstin so strongly implying the advantages of a systematic theory of government. It was, he explains, faith in the perfection of the Creator's design for mankind (within which human conflicts seem to have canceled each other out to the attainment of an ultimate good), that "saved the persistent iteration of 'rights' from seeming an anarchic individualism."[21] And he does not fail to point out that the insistence on rights is accompanied by a marked indifference to any complementary idea of duties.

Despite these reservations, Boorstin's conclusions are affirmative. The American continent, awaiting settlement and the filling out of the Jeffersonian expectations for society, provided a favorable setting for the confirmation of their dreams. "The Jeffersonian philosophy was futuristic without being utopian or apocalyptic," he observes; "its vision of the future was foreshadowed not in any sacred document nor in any private revelation, but in the American continent itself, and in the very shape of man." The naturalistic theme, which played so large a part in the Jeffersonian view of the American future, was not to be fully played out until the end of the nineteenth century.

One of the characteristic difficulties encountered by Americans, when reviewing their history, is that of establishing, with what a European might be forgiven for considering a normal degree of clarity, the distinction between the past and the present. The problem is compounded by the innocence as to the possibility that such a problem might exist. But no one is more keenly aware of this difficulty than Professor Boorstin. His work shows a constant respect for the past, in its integrity, as the past. Yet he has also shown an equally constant and frequently anxious concern about the present; and an important feature—perhaps at times a motive—of his work has been the recognition of a need to establish that peculiarly subtle dialogue in which past can speak to present in a voice that it would recognize as its own. The need to do this by understanding history for its own sake is expressed in his penchant for quoting a remark of Charles H. McIlwain's that trying to teach the lessons of history without teaching history is like trying to plant cut flowers.

It is clear that Boorstin had these problems very much in mind soon after he returned from Oxford. The appreciation of the fact that the past was not engaged in attempting to answer present questions, which marked his study of Blackstone, caused him to recoil from the profoundly unhistorical attitudes which prevailed in American law schools and dominated much of the writing of legal history in Britain. As early as 1941 he criticized in the *Harvard Law Review* the prevailing practice in the writing and teaching of the history of legal doctrines; the history of contract, for example, was treated as though medieval arrangements which had a touch of contract about them were to be considered as imperfectly realized attempts to achieve the modern law of contract.[22] Boorstin regretted "the subservience of legal historian to practising lawyer" and attacked the use of "present legal categories as the framework of legal history," as a result of which "the classifications found in legal textbooks and treatises have become the classifications for the material of legal history." Seven years later he addressed to the Association of American Law Schools a powerful and eloquent plea for the recognition of historical values in the teaching of legal history.[23]

Among the strong continuities marking the development of Boorstin's thought nothing is more consistent than his interest in the problem of the "lessons" or "moral" of history, a moral that can be extracted only by absorbing oneself in the substance of history. "Our past" he wrote in the preface to *The Lost World of Thomas Jefferson,* "must serve not as an anthology from which to cull apt phrases for current needs, but as a stage for observing in all their tantalizing complexity the actual ways in which men in America have faced the ancient problems of the human race." In his introduction to *An American Primer,*[24] which is an anthology, not of "apt phrases" but of carefully selected and edited documents, he juxtaposes the questions of the historian with those of the citizen: "Historians reading the words of John Winthrop usually ask 'What did they mean to him?' Citizens ask 'What do they mean to us?' Historians are trained to seek the original meaning; all of us want to know the present meaning. These are two quite different quests which often get in each other's way." He adds the hope that the book will "remind us how to keep our traditions alive," a hope that perhaps reveals more confidence than American traditions can be relied on to bear. It depends which tradition one chooses. Racial discrimination is an American tradition; so is civic corruption, so is violence; so also are equality, morality and the rule of law. There is at least a hint of patriotic history in this expression of purpose and a satisfaction with the way things have turned out that not all Americans, past or present, appear to share. Americans have yielded to the general temptation, as Boorstin has elsewhere remarked, to homogenize experience, "to empty each age of its vintage flavor in order to provide ever larger receptacles into which we can pour an insipid liquor of our own making. By homogenizing I mean the tendency to make ideas or things seem more alike in order to serve some current purpose."[25] But he has, at this point, just issued a cogent reminder of what the true historian does: "Our greatest historians—whatever else they may have done—have somehow added to our understanding of what it meant to be alive at a particular time and place in the past."[26]

Boorstin clearly thinks that, as the American past differs from Europe's, so the American conception of the past differs from that which is commonly found in Europe. The great difficulty is to convince Americans that they have a past. They must discover that what they have in the space reserved for history is something other than a backward extension of the present.

The idea that the past and present exist in a sort of continuum which virtually permits them to talk to each other without raising their voices is supplemented, and the related intellectual difficulties are complicated, by the feeling Boorstin discerns that American ideals and institutions all derive from an experience that was "given" rather than being historically accumulated. These views are developed in a book that stands as a landmark in his thought and influence. *The Genius of American Politics*, published in Chicago in 1953, owes some of its formulations to ideas that can be traced in his earlier work; nevertheless, it seems to be the product of some profound reflection that began with the work on the intellectual world of the Jeffersonians. This work has the concreteness and simplicity of exposition of a publication intended at least in part to be didactic; he wrote it during the period when the international crisis of the Cold War was compounded by the domestic crisis of McCarthyism, and part of the purpose was to give his countrymen some historical bearings by which they could help to steady themselves.

The thesis is that the special character of American democracy and institutions is due to the special, and unrepeatable, circumstances of American development; that the concrete experience of that development, in all its ramifications, and not fixed ideology or preconceived political theory, has given America both its values and its characteristic methods of political action; and that as these experiences were unique both in place and time, they cannot be exported or made a basis for imitation by other countries. Boorstin is at pains to repudiate the idea that American development—particularly the successful side of it—has been due to the successful application of theory; his argument supposes the existence of an almost schematic opposition between theory and practical experience. It is not perfectly clear whether his principal assertion is that Americans have repudiated political theory, or rather that they have shared a common theory presented to them as part of the deed of gift that went with the continent, a gift that rendered all further speculation needless. "For the belief that an explicit political theory is superfluous precisely because we already possess a satisfactory equivalent, I propose the name of 'givenness,' " he says. " 'Givenness' is the belief that values in America are in some way or other automatically defined: *given* by certain facts of geography or history peculiar to us."[27] At this point, then, what is given is not a theory but an equally satisfactory substitute. He proceeds to explain the sources by which this belief is given. The first is "the notion that we have received our values as a gift from the *past*"—from the explicit ideals of the Founding Fathers; he calls this the "preformation ideal." The second, which seems at first sight to conflict with the first, is that American values are a gift from the *present*, "that our theory is always implicit in our institutions." This view depends heavily on geography, and in its full extension, which significantly takes the title, "Values Given by the Landscape: The Land of the Free,"[28] it is more reminiscent of Turner than any other side of Boorstin's work. The city does not seem to play much part in this picture. "We have been told again and again, with the metaphorical precision of poetry, that the United States is the *land* of the free."[29] The meaning of the land itself plays a dominant part here, and is emphasized in later works, where the vagueness of the land, its vast promise and lack of definition, are held to have determined the American imagination.[30] It is in this connection that Boorstin invokes Turner, pointing out that much of his work and that of his followers constitute "a theory to justify that absence of an American political theory."[31] "If American ideals are not in books or in the blood but in the air, then they are readily acquired; actually, it is impossible for the immigrant to avoid acquiring them. He is not required to learn a philosophy so much as to rid his lungs of the air of Europe,"[32] Boorstin comments, leaving us, however, in some doubt as to whether the "if" at the beginning of the sentence has closed the argument, or opened it.

The third element in the idea of "givenness" links the other two, which are described as axioms. It is the homogeneity, the continuity of American history in a steady stream, free from violent oscillations of regime and void of violent ideological challenges. "Because our road has been relatively smooth," he concludes this chapter, "we have easily believed that we have trod no historical road at all. We seem the direct beneficiaries of our climate, our soil, and our mineral wealth."[33]

From these premises, or maxims, the historian goes further, to maintain that the United States has been built up without theoretical foundations, owing its very success to its peoples' readiness to embrace experience and to reject or ignore the teachings of theory. This view—this theory, for it is that—becomes one of the organizing principles of his later work, *The Americans*, where it plays not an exclusive part but certainly a part without which the more positive elements would tend to fall away from each other.

The historical evidence in *The Genius of American Politics* is chosen in support of each phase of the argument with a precise sense of relevance; the book stands as a cogent warning to Americans, badly needed at that phase of the Cold War, to avoid trying to superimpose their political habits of mind on other peoples with other histories and other ideals. Moreover, the central observations of the book are so significant and so far-reaching that they are likely to have lasting influence even after they have been separated from the didactic theories which they were intended to sustain.

Near the end of the book, Boorstin, having built a case that seems irresistible by virtue of having covered all relevant ground and encircled such opponents as might have been inclined to resist, proposes the course by which Americans should try to reconcile themselves to their history and formulate attitudes to it. He rejects any attempt to build a democratic philosophy. "When people already agree," he comments, "the effort to define what they agree on is more likely to produce conflict than accord."[34] This remark, even if not too seriously intended, does not strengthen the presumption of real agreement; but that presumption in fact controls much of the argument by defining outlines of relevance beyond which disagreements are merely factious or trivial. It was a remarkably buoyant and optimistic assumption to make about the political health of the United States in an age which witnessed the rages of an anti-Communist hysteria potent enough to close the gates of reason in many of the highest offices of the land and most of the smaller ones, which was cowed and dominated by the contemptuous triumphs of the late Senator Joseph R. McCarthy, and was only to be slightly muted by the presence in the State Department of John Foster Dulles.

What Professor Boorstin asked Americans to do, instead of building an artificial democratic philosophy, was "to bring to the surface those attitudes which have been latent in the notion of 'givenness' itself, to discover the general truths about institutions by which we have actually lived."[35] But this program, whatever might be its merits as a counterblast against either McCarthy or Soviet Communism, is weakened by a defect in its logical foundations. The Boorstinian description of the maxims of "givenness" creates a reasonable expectation that he will explain the origins and reception of a mystique, perhaps an illusion, certainly a partly fantastical view of American life. The doctrine of "preformation" contains an obvious bedrock of truth: we knew that the principles of the Founders, including the principle of compromise, had been handed down and resorted to by generation after generation of Americans, though often pursuing opposed ends with devious arguments; yet it was precisely in the interstices between the agreements of the Founders that the infection grew that would later burst into sectional conflict. Thus although "preformation" provides a valuable concept and a useful clue, it does not close the argument about what kind of country was being built. When we come to the qualities given by the land itself, the argument is even more elusive.

Does Boorstin really believe that the encounter with the land gave

Americans concrete values to live by, and does he himself proclaim
these values, or is he only telling us that Americans were hallucinated
into a kind of rapture, not unlike the mystique about the desert
entertained by the British contemporaries of T. E. Lawrence, and
that this rapture acted as a substitute for systematic or connected
thought? Such an explanation could in itself be valid; the sources of
our beliefs, or ideals, are not necessarily rational; the trouble is that
Boorstin fails, in his own analysis, to make the relevant distinctions.
The title of his opening chapter is: "How Belief in the Existence of a
Theory Has Made a Theory Superfluous"; and the shortened version
of this, as page headings, reads, "Why a Theory Seems Needless."
These formulations are not accidental. What he is describing is not
the existence of a theory but only the *belief* in the existence of a
theory; but either the belief is correct, and a theory did exist, or the
belief is incorrect, and no such theory existed. What he is giving an
account of here is not represented as a fact, but as a belief about a
fact. "For the *belief* that an explicit political theory is superfluous
precisely because we already possess a satisfactory equivalent, I propose the name of 'givenness,' "[36] as he explains. When we go on to
consider the issues in American history which he maintains can be
reconciled with an emphasis on persistent shared experience of
"givenness," we expect that a moment of revelation is coming;
Professor Boorstin has so shrewdly discerned some of the ideas, some
even of the sense perceptions, which have contributed to shaping
American minds that he seems to have prepared himself for the task
of separating illusion from reality; is he not about to warn Americans
against the dangers—for surely there are dangers!—of absorbing
uncritically the images and ideals that have seeped into them from
such vague and contradictory sources and confusing them with the
substance of history? Boorstin's own earlier comment has raised this
expectation; "Because our road has been relatively smooth," he has
said, "we have easily believed that we have trod no historical road at
all. We seem [not "we are"] the direct beneficiaries of our climate,
our soil, and our mineral wealth." But the moment of exposure never
comes. In the end it turns out that Boorstin is himself encircled, that
the illusion was the fact.

Boorstin's concept of "givenness" makes it possible to extract a
more historical theme from his own work. Passages in *The Genius of
American Politics* show that he thinks the sense of "givenness" began

to appear with the decline of the first generation of Puritans (at least in New England), prevailed throughout the settlement of the continent, and began to fade at the end of that period, when the land and its values began to be displaced from the American imagination by the city and the automobile. But he continues to speak of a "belief" in "givenness" rather than in the fact, and he never comes to the point of saying how much was valid, how much was illusory, what might have been valuable, what might have been pernicious, in either the illusion or the fact.

This ambiguity can be understood in the light of another logical difficulty which, like the first, follows from one of his deepest shafts of insight. A clue is dropped very early, when in his book on Blackstone he notes that Blackstone's use of the "maxim" repeated a confusion already present in the idea of the law of nature—on which Blackstone heavily relied. "The law of nature confused the world as it was with the world as it ought to be"—and the maxims stating those rules showed a similar confusion.[37] The same point is picked up again, briefly, when Boorstin explains the "apotheosis of nature" in Jeffersonian thought. "All facts," he observes, "were endowed with an ambiguous quality: they became normative as well as descriptive. . . . By describing a work of art as successful, we mean that it is hard to separate description from judgment, the "is" from the "ought," the facts about the work from the standards against which those facts are to be judged."[38] In an absorbing chapter on the rise of sociology in America, and the incorporation of sociological data into the sectional argument, Boorstin adds a significant development to this theme, for statistical details became clues to a way of life. " 'Givenness' was here expressed in the assumption that life as it was in America—whether in the North or in the South—gave the outlines of life as it ought to be, that values were implicit in experience."[39] Boorstin has repeated the point recently—again discussing statistics, but in more general terms—observing that "more and more Americans, in more and more departments of their lives, look to statistics not merely for facts but for norms. By making the fact the norm, we all make it somehow the law, the measure, and the external deposit of our moral life. We make the 'is' the substance and not merely the shadow of the 'ought.' "[40]

In these remarks, Professor Boorstin has touched on a critical problem in the interpretation of American history. Men and women in America have achieved so much of what they have aspired to, so many simple dreams have come true (if at the cost of acquiring a rather greater degree of complexity), that the historian, relying largely on material that is in fact evidence of these successes, has difficulty in writing as though the history of facts were not also and necessarily the history of norms. This is, in a sense, the prevailing American extension of the old "Whig" interpretation of history; and the strength of this standpoint can be seen from the difficulty of constructing an alternative; for whatever one's sympathies, the history of failure, or defeat, can hardly become that of a *continuing* norm, even though it may recognize the existence of a conflict of values at some time in the past.

Boorstin's respect for the integrity of the past might have led us to expect a fuller recognition than he is willing to accord, not only to the passionate intensity of the major conflicts in American history, but also to the intellectual depth and seriousness of the opposed positions. "Success" he shrewdly observes, "has made us unphilosophical";[41] but it might be added that a preoccupation with the conditions of success has induced him to minimize the element of conflict; major issues of principle are treated rather as though, within the total context of "givenness," they ought to have been seen to be irrelevant. His chilly dismissal of the abolitionists is accompanied by the accurate observation that much of the politically effective northern opposition to slavery was based "less on love for the Negro than on concern for the white working man;" but it was the abolitionists who succeeded in infusing into the northern conscience a concern with the totality of the problem of slavery, which merged into a conviction that the conflict was not, as Boorstin insists, merely sectional, but was a conflict about what the United States, as a country, was to become in the future. That is the burden of Lincoln's "house divided" speech at Springfield, Illinois, but it is a burden which Boorstin declines to assume, leaving it on Lincoln's shoulders while quoting him on the virtues of compromise and the importance of preserving the West for free white labor.[42]

Professor Boorstin evinces a revulsion against Reconstruction even more intense than his contempt for the abolitionists. The "crimes" and "senseless bitterness" that were visited on the South were "vindictive" and "narrowly provincial."[43] It is doubtful whether this explanation does full justice to Thaddeus Stevens, who did appreciate that the distribution of power in the South was an economic problem requiring an economic solution; and it leaves a considerable vacancy in the place that might reasonably have been assigned for discussion of the Thirteenth, Fourteenth, and Fifteenth Amendments.

The burden of *The Genius of American Politics* is a deeply committed argument that the experiences which Americans share as members of one community are vastly more important than those which have divided them. But it might have been possible to propound this argument without going so far as to deny that Americans have ever been seriously divided on fundamental principles. Thus, after the Civil War "both sides were still thinking on similar constitutional assumptions." True; but on the other hand Alexander H. Stephens has just been quoted as saying that the war was over "different and opposing ideas as to the nature of what was known as the General Government."[44] If this is true, these ideas (not the facts of experience, but ideas) could neither both prevail nor live side by side, and whether the differences are theoretical and speculative or not is beside the point. At the most pragmatic reckoning, the absence of any tendency to philosophical speculation failed to avert the bloodiest civil war of the nineteenth century.

It is on the same basis that Professor Boorstin makes his celebrated statement that the American Revolution was "a prudential decision taken by men of principle rather than the affirmation of a theory."[45] Insofar as the decision was vindicated by events, and the Americans were subsequently happier under their own rule than they would have been under British rule, the decision was certainly prudent, though the word "prudential," with its tone of the board meeting or the insurance policy, effectively conceals the frantic activity, passionate agitation, and background of military operations that brought the leadership up to, and past, the point of independence. And assuredly they were men of principle. But what principle? The answer, which Boorstin does not give, is that these men were Whigs; their unifying principle was Whiggery; and despite their many and serious differences, it was enough to enable them to speak a common political language and to declare a common purpose. Why then, is it important, or even significant, that they did not affirm a theory? What theory, other than that of their Whig principles, could anyone have expected them to affirm?

Here Boorstin's didactic purpose seems to have led him astray from his history. The kind of total theories of society, the desire to use revolutionary means to impose a schematic new order, that have caused such indescribable pain and suffering in our own twentieth century were almost unknown in the eighteenth. Even the French *philosophes*, though holding physiocratic theories about political economy, wanted to achieve their aims not by revolution but by strengthening the monarchy. It was a consequence of the French Revolution, not a motive for it, that social and political theory began to remodel the state (a process, incidentally, that brought a great deal of permanent improvement to France). Boorstin's carefully poised antithesis therefore becomes historically irrelevant and gives rise to the suspicion that he is using the weapons that belong to the eighteenth century to fight the battle of his own generation.

This brings us to a point of some importance. If, as Boorstin says, the American leaders were men of principle (in a political sense; it would be trivial to say merely that they were "upright" or "men of honor"), then in fundamental matters they did possess a theory, and thus in a very significant sense Professor Boorstin has been right. His "performance" theory describes a fact, after all, not simply a belief held by generations of half-bemused Americans; and it provides later generations with a common political language and does much to explain the modern strength of the theory of consensus. But it is one thing to look on the theory of the state as a plan of action, as socialists, fascists and communists, among others, have done; it is quite another to attempt to reduce to a system, to codify (as Blackstone did) the accumulated principles, institutions and customs given by history. In his major work, *The Americans*, Boorstin continues to write of Europe as though, in contrast to America, its institutions represented the deliberate enactment of preconceived theories of the state. His identification of America involves an antithesis with Europe in which the contrast between systematic theory on the European side and pragmatic experiment on the American side plays a part as basic as—and interdependent with—the contrast between "aristocracy" and "democracy" in social life, education, and politics.

This contrast involves a good deal of oversimplification—and rather too often disparaging oversimplification—of European culture and institutions. Even when discussing modern European political parties, which, as he knows, often define themselves by adherence to theoretical principles, he fails to observe how much European gov-

ernment is in fact coalition government.[46] European education and
social thought become, under this treatment, aristocratic education
and thought limited by dogma and authority. The Enlightenment is
said to have "acquired much of the rigidity and authoritarianism
which it set out to combat." It was, he adds, "in fact little more than
a confinement of the mind in a prison of 17th- and 18th-century
design. . . . The best European minds of that age labored to build
the new-model walls in which they were to be confined."[47] By the
eighteenth century, we further learn, "many European thinkers had
arrived at the idea of progress by devious and painful intellectual
paths. . . . But in America . . . progress seemed confirmed by daily
experience."[48] English culture also takes some painful blows. "It was
an age which chose David Hume for its arbiter of Truth, Dr. Samuel
Johnson for its arbiter of Beauty, and *Pamela* and *Tom Jones* for its
epics."[49] While pausing only momentarily to reflect that if these
dicta be true, the age could have done worse, it seems desirable in the
interests of distributive justice to notice that most of the leading
influences in the intellectual and scientific life of Europe were not
products of aristocracy and many owed little or nothing to the aristocratic patronage of education. Such careers as those of Pope, of
Johnson, of Voltaire, Rousseau, Diderot, of Hume or Priestley, not
to enumerate most of the luminaries of German literature and music,
suggest an extraordinary flexibility and receptiveness to talent in these
prisons of the mind. Even in such eminently nonmetaphysical matters as scientific agriculture and technology, the basic advances, both
theoretical and experimental, began in Europe and were often picked
up slowly in America.

However, Professor Boorstin is not writing European history.
Europe stands in contrast, a backcloth against which America is
staged, and it is because of this backcloth function that Europe
appears more static, more tradition-bound than it really was or is.
Even without these somewhat artificial contrasts American society
comes vividly to life. And this remains the most important thing to
say about *The Americans*, because there is probably no living historian of America who is quite Boorstin's equal in the essential historian's power of bringing the past to life. The expert economy of his
literary style is an instrument of this power, and his ability to turn a
phrase is used not for decorative purposes but to sum up and give
point to an explanation. But with Boorstin the historian as with an

artist it is really the eye that controls: the hand is merely an agent; and the eye sees the past in its own terms of reference. He is always willing to explain his meaning by illustration—a method that he employs more freely in *The National Experience*—and his keen eye for the revealing incident gives his mature writing an anecdotal vitality without detracting from its seriousness of purpose.

The Americans is planned as a trilogy, of which *The Colonial Experience* reaches the Revolution, and *The National Experience* describes the growth and character of American society during the settlement of the interior and the formation of a separate Southern consciousness; the third volume is yet to appear.

The Americans is general history, but not in the comprehensive style of a William Lecky or Channing, or Osgood or Rhodes. It is neither social history without politics nor political history without society nor economic history without either; it is the history of a society in the widest sense. Boorstin is therefore a historian concerned not to establish sequences of events but rather to establish their context. American events arose from a social texture that might have given rise to different sequences, but could never have given rise to the events that belong to European history; and this applies to such differing contingencies as a common law judgment by Justice Lemuel Shaw, the presidential election of Jackson, or the explosion of a steamboat on the Mississippi. Above all, Boorstin is the historian of the character and consciousness of the American community. His themes are rich, varied, and textually subtle; and they are interwoven with a certain deliberate looseness. He is too sophisticated to be interested in being "definitive," and the somewhat loose and open framework hints at the open character of American life. Style and method are part of the interpretation. The artistry is, perhaps, unobtrusive, but it is conscious and even elaborate.

In this view, the history of society is conceived as that of certain broad types of experience, some of which are shared by the vast majority but some of which are the result of special circumstances. It is essential to appreciate this implicit theme in Boorstin's work, that of the experience of the community, which continues whatever defeats some sections may suffer, whatever changes the rest may undergo. What is retained through change, what has been absorbed into the bones of American life, is constantly implied as he moves over the varied ground both of the society and of the geography on which it stands. It is, in the view he takes, the task of the historian of America to meet the people's need to understand the history they are made of—the myth as well as the reality.

Political history is displaced from the central position conventionally accorded to it. Politics becomes a function of the community; political activities emerge as manifestations of the energies, interests, and rival ambitions of sectors of the society whose character and style of life is under review. It is a view of politics peculiarly appropriate to the American past; and it enables Boorstin to show with complete authority that government was one of the most potent agencies of economic growth and also in many cases the principal source of capital.[50] These points, which dispose of a great deal of weighty and still-active political mythology, are not made in a polemical spirit; the historian is not arguing a thesis with a view to present politics but is collecting the evidence from the past and arranging it, for the benefit of present readers, in a manner which compels one to feel that it would have been acceptable to contemporaries.

The method, or rather the concept which employs this method, is open to the criticism that the historian's principle of selection is liable to result in the dismissal, as incidental or even irrelevant to the "mainstream" of American history, of whatever past conflicts either obstruct the passage of his implied argument or more simply do not interest him. According to the American norm many events ought not to have happened; admittedly such events often did happen, but they need not have done, and so can be treated as of secondary importance. The concept of "givenness" controls the historian's selections and weakens his critical apparatus. It is in this that Boorstin's earlier criticism of the Jeffersonians seems to anticipate the flaw in his own method. While it would be impossible to write any general history that was not at some point susceptible to this kind of criticism, Professor Boorstin shows, both by implication in the structure of *The Americans*, and expressly elsewhere, that he does believe in a mainstream of American history—more so, in all probability, than in the history of many other countries. His emphasis on the "homogeneity" of American history is a statement of this approach; "We view our national history," he elsewhere remarks, "—and the facts support us—as a single broad stream, the unbroken living current of the American Way of Life, not as a miscellaneous series of great epochs."[51]

But which facts support us? Epochs are generally the creation of historians trying to reduce to intelligible order the mass and continuity of their materials; but it would be a little strained, in the interests of homogeneity, to deny any epoch-making significance to the American Revolution, to the Civil War, or to the closing of the frontier. A more serious difficulty, however, arises because the same method insists, *ex hypothesi*, that the major conflicts of interest and opinion were due to prejudice, ignorance, or intellectual error rather than to genuine convictions about the fundamental principles. Thus Professor Boorstin gives very slight attention to the divisions of American opinion on Independence, or the Constitution; the bitter disputes of the Confederation period do not concern him, and although in *The National Experience* he treats the rivalries of Whig and Democratic parties as facts of politics, he gives very little indication of why political parties should ever have come into existence in the United States. Alexander Hamilton appears in the index only three times, and never with reference to his major economic policies; the Second Bank of the United States appears only incidentally in one passing reference to Nicholas Biddle.

Yet it is arguable that if Hamilton had not been Secretary of the Treasury, if Jackson had not vetoed the Bank recharter or if it had been carried over his veto, the lives of the masses, the development of the society which primarily interests Boorstin, would have been different. Conflicts of opinion on these issues, it may be argued, were on matters of vital importance, and the way they were resolved determined the course of events. At the center of Boorstin's reconstruction of American history lies the belief in the consensus of aims. The divisions which he regards as legitimate have been divisions over method; and the relative absence of ideological division between the leading political parties becomes a source of comfort and strength.[52] To this whole theme it might be possible to oppose an alternative. The differences between the Robert Morris–Alexander Hamilton school and the John Taylor–Thomas Jefferson school; between the pro- and antislavery camps; and between the Populists and the new industrial order—to name only three major issues—arose because of conflicts of ideals about the future of America as a whole. In reply, the consensus school argues that the United States possesses in its Constitution, supplemented by its party system, a mechanism for resolving major conflicts of principle; even the Civil War appears not to have been a conflict over Constitutional principles, though obviously the Constitution, as a mechanism for resolving conflict, broke down. Behind this view of the Constitution there does lie a theory, either implicit as in Boorstin's argument, or explicit as with Louis Hartz, and this theory affirms the constancy of a unifying agreement on aims. Thus for Hartz, much as for Boorstin, the conflicts were in principle avoidable. Hartz argues for the omnipresence of the Whig-liberal stream of political theory; Boorstin amasses the evidence, not from the rarefied sources of speculative debate, but from the records of life as it was lived and known, for a community of shared experience.

Hartz introduced into the modern discussion a negative concept which has helped us to understand American development. American history knew no feudalism: the commercial, liberal strand was extracted from England and planted in American soil, where it grew into the commercial, liberal, and modern state. To this concept Boorstin has added another negative. He insists that America flourished in the absence of dogma, in the absence of preconceived theory, and even in the absence of too much formal knowledge. This theme is made to bear a greater burden of explanation than is usually required of absences, of spaces reserved but not filled.[53]

Boorstin has little difficulty in showing that highly schematic plans, which omitted to take account of local conditions, met failure. The Puritan settlements survived because of the willingness of the second and subsequent generations to modify their dogma and adapt themselves to conditions; the Virginians flourished because they transplanted working institutions that were easily adapted. The Quaker experiment in government failed, in the last resort, because it could not satisfy the needs of the people of Pennsylvania for defense in a nonpacifist world. The philanthropic experiment in Georgia failed because its planners ignored local economic conditions. Boorstin himself notes that Puritan dogma began to decline in England in the second half of the seventeenth century, so that its decline in America is not a peculiarly local phenomenon, though it may well have been a necessary one. The Quaker attempt to set up a pacifist government would, of course, have failed anywhere in the world when violent enemies appeared; and it seems equally remarkable that in Pennsylvania it should have lasted a lifetime. As for Georgia, one would not have to be an enemy of economic theory to agree that a theory that takes no account of local economic conditions, or of the motives of those participating in the settlement, would be likely to fail. America proved these points, but it would hardly have been necessary to call the New World into existence to do so. The argument insists that success was achieved almost exclusively in the absence of preconceived theory. It makes room for a great deal of instruction, particularly where Boorstin discusses the professions, which in England were clogged by tradition and a jealous and cautious monopolism. But it could be rejoined that the principal point to emerge is that the problems Americans were confronted with in the process of settlement tended, for the most part, to be of the limited type that could be handled with drive and ingenuity. When fundamental advance was in question, it had to take place where the speculative faculties were more highly respected and had full play. The whole course of this overextended argument shows that Boorstin has lost sight of one of the points he emphasized in his Blackstone; for then he insisted on the transference of law and ideas across the Atlantic and showed the prolonged influence of Blackstone on American legal training. That most acute of critics, Miss Cecelia Kenyon, asked Professor Boorstin to take to heart his own remark at the end of his chapter on Pennsylvania: "Finally, the Quakers made a dogma of the absence of dogma."[54]

Positive themes, however, are everywhere implicit—though they are often less openly stated—in Boorstin's argument. The ambition of Americans surges forward to open up a continent of boundless possibilities; and the very lack of definition is here an implied theme: the vagueness of America's physical limits and the myths about its fantastic West—which Boorstin rediscovers with such brilliance that we see why they were believed and almost wish to share those impossible dreams—imply that an open, classless society was in the making and begin to take over the role of historical explanation.

With these, Boorstin links the more specific sectors of legal, educational, and technical history, to which he brings a depth that would be worthy of an expert in each separate field. The common-law tradition in America is seen to be one of adaptability rather than strict precedent and so is enabled to serve the needs of a society in which change tends to be both rapid and normal; it is interesting to contrast the fact that in Massachusetts, trade unions were freed from the threat of charges of conspiracy by a common-law decision in 1842, while in Britain they were legalized by statute (twelve years earlier, incidentally). Education, because of its social range and distinctive practical bent, tends to serve immediate needs, and in doing so helps to sustain the democratic character of society and politics. Boorstin is particularly fascinating when he turns to language and its adaptation in a mobile, expanding, and, it should be added, irreverent society. Not all Americans liked what was happening to language on their continent, and Noah Webster himself was a pillar of linguistic conservation. But once again, the collecting and distilling of vast funds of information serve the irresistible purpose of describing the quality of life in America as though we had been there ourselves.

Although his approach seems to attach more importance to "scene" than to development, the idea of development is in fact implicit throughout Boorstin's work. Thus the conservative press that served the colonies and was restricted by colonial governments becomes the free intensely partisan press of the early nation; the culture of the colonies, which was defined by its lack of a capital, becomes "culture with many capitals" in *The National Experience*. The growth of the city begins to change the face of the land; like the growth of transport, it is a product, as has been noted, of much public enterprise, and this brings us back to the central theme of community. Boorstin insists on it. In the process of settlement, the community precedes formal government, and calls government into being just as settlement itself so often in fact preceded the formalities of survey.

As the innumerable facts and flashes of connecting insight gather strength, the whole work mounts a tremendous power: even to disagree with some of its thematic implications is to be instructed not only in the history of American society, but in how to think about it. Yet much of this instruction will be in dissent rather than agreement. Although movement and change are implicit as the subject of Boorstin's themes, his interests seldom call for intense analysis of specific processes; a vague determinism, mainly geographic in bias, underlies both events and social forms. The missing dimension would conventionally be called that of historical explanation. Why, we may ask, did political parties come into being? Why did community precede forms of government, and still more significant, why did Americans adopt these rather than other forms? The encounter with the land obviously presented hard necessities, but the land did not itself put into American heads the ideas of government and social organization on which they chose to act. Why did they choose as they did rather than otherwise? By ignoring the realm of preconceived ideas, the substratum of institutional thought, he has weakened his power of explanation.

Yet behind the institutions, the inventions, the ways of life, lies a deeper implication still. Boorstin brings to light the texture of life in which the American imagination came into being. Henry Nash Smith's reconstruction of the vision of the nineteenth century,[55] in which "the myth of the desert" is transformed into "the myth of the garden," here flows into Boorstin's stream, and he describes the subject matter of those numerous naturalistic paintings which delighted Americans with the sheer spectacle of the interior of their vast and various continent. This leads to one of his most fascinating themes; for much of what Boorstin says implies that wherever Americans overcame their obstacles, the experience gave them—in part their success arose from—a new vision. A new way of looking is implied. The pragmatic mind, the open land, the open society—all are fused in a new and distinctively American imagination and mode of thought. Yet it is worth recalling that it was Locke whose psychological theories introduced an experimental epistemology and that empirical method is fundamental to English science from Bacon; and as a note on the theoretical possibilities that remain to be discussed it may also be remarked that, while nineteenth-century American painters were using thoroughly conventional techniques of representation to portray new scenes, in France painters were experimenting with new ways of seeing.

Boorstin is not alone among recent historians in his preoccupation with the collecting of facts which then speak for themselves and in his deliberate extrusion of ideology from the substance of history, or rather from what he holds to be the best and most worthy to endure. In spite of differences, there is a comparison with Sir Lewis Namier; and he resembles Namier in his keen, humane eye for incident. Not, however, for character; little in Boorstin's writing suggests Namier's interest in character or his penetrating psychological insight into the minds of the dead. Neither should the comparison be stretched: Namier believed the past should have undergone crystallization before the historian touched it; Boorstin believes the past does speak to the present and that the historian has a social duty to transmit what it says.

All is not as it has been. The sense of "givenness" that Boorstin has discovered in the creation of American values has declined since the completion of settlement; and the decline has been accompanied by the rise of a mass media, the artificial stimulation of responses and cooking of events. It is wholly in keeping with Boorstin's sense of social duty that he has concerned himself with these changes. His witty but serious book *The Image*[56] is a work of social criticism, to which we already owe the concept of the "pseudo-event," that event which is called into existence solely for its value as news or propaganda, and which provides a large amount of the materials used by newspapers and television. He is commenting here not only on the invention of "news"—as in press conferences and the numerous sessions of the sort that Professor J. K. Galbraith has called "no-business meetings"[57]—but on an underlying phenomenon in the nature of experience; for what disturbs him is the decline of the immediacy of experience. Increasingly we see, hear, and know things at second hand, and increasingly, he suggests, our experience comes preselected, arranged by various sorts of advertiser, editor, or impresario, prepackaged and predigested. The fact that a wider range of information is thus available would not satisfy Professor Boorstin that the quality of our experience is unimpaired. It used to be the Americans' peculiar advantage that they were in direct touch with facts; but now images have displaced facts: "we have used our wealth, our literacy, our technology, and our progress, to create a thicket of unreality which stands between us and the facts of life."[58] Americans have lost their power to delight in natural things.

The Image is thus an attack on the degeneration, under the conditions of modern technology, of all that was best because it was most natural in the American heritage. It thus represents a grave departure from the confidence that marked Boorstin's earlier thought. As another critic has observed,[59] the corruption and the threat are now within the community itself and cannot be ascribed to the temptations of alien ideology.

Yet much of the story he has so far recounted is of success. In fact his method has placed a premium on success, for what fails by definition misses or drops from the "mainstream" of American history. It might be objected that there is a defective sense of cost and loss in all this. Yet Boorstin is not unaware of these dimensions, as he has shown in a sensitive essay on the possibilities of a dialogue between the American and the Jewish traditions.[60] "To see history *sub speci*

Americani is to be encouraged in an excessive (if well substantiated) optimism,"[61] he remarks; but Jews, whatever their Zionist utopianism, are not historically inclined to exuberant optimism and, until the founding of Israel as a state, were not given to the conquest of nature so much as to speculation and introspection. There are marked signs that the "well-substantiated optimism" for which he finds grounds in earlier American history is giving way, that he discerns the disintegration of the values he has ascribed to "givenness," that the fabric that joined the "Is" and the "Ought" is splitting at the seam. Boorstin has never been committed to a single theme or a single mood. As his vision of American triumphs has not been wanting in a tinge of irony, so it seems likely that his account of recent America, with its immense material gains and its pathetic atrophy of vital experience, will not be untinged by a sense of comedy.

Oscar Handlin

MALDWYN A. JONES

9)

OSCAR HANDLIN is one of the most prolific of contemporary American historians. He is also one of the most versatile. His writings range from learned monographs to popular works, from biography to collections of original documents, from specialized essays to wide-ranging surveys. A similar diversity is apparent in his choice of subjects. Though many of his works are concerned with aspects of immigration, he has written on such contrasting topics as the origins of American Negro slavery, John Dewey's educational theories, the social and economic thought of pre–Civil War Massachusetts, and the development of American historiography.

The significance of Handlin's work does not, however, stem from its volume or its variety, impressive though these are. It arises rather from its ambitious attempt to remedy two widespread defects of modern historical writing in America—though not, it should be added, in America alone. One of these weaknesses is the almost universal tendency to slight the historical role of ordinary men and women; the other is the way in which historians ignore the lay public and write merely for each other.

Complaints that historians show little interest in the mass of mankind go back a long way. As early as 1856 Frederick Law Olmsted observed that men of literary taste were "always apt to overlook the working classes," with the result that posterity found it difficult "to discern the very real influence their character and condition [have] had on the fortune and fate of the nation."[1] Today, more than a century later, despite the increased emphasis on social, economic, and cultural, as opposed to political, history, the complaint is hardly less valid. What Thomas C. Cochran has called the "presidential synthesis"—the preoccupation with great men and outstanding events—is still predominant in American historical writing. Calls for a reversal of perspective, for a history "written from the bottom up,"[2] have won only a limited response, even from those who are prepared to concede the inadequacy of the traditional approach.

The lack of contact between historians and the American reading public is, by contrast, a comparatively recent phenomenon. The classic American historians of the nineteenth century, especially Bancroft and Parkman, wrote not for a specialized audience but for a wide public. But they have had few successors. As history grew more professionalized, it became correspondingly esoteric. As scientific precision replaced readability as the historian's cardinal virtue, historical works declined in popular appeal, and even the best were read by few people outside the profession.

Handlin's dissatisfaction with these and other trends in American historiography was expressed in a paper he delivered to a meeting of the International Congress of the Historical Sciences in Rome in 1955. He did not at that time specifically criticize the historian's neglect of the common man, but he did remark that "the radical shifts in economic, sociological and psychological theory in recent decades [had] not led to a corresponding alteration of emphasis in the work of historians."[3] While historians paid lip service to the need for an interdisciplinary approach, only rarely had they used the social sciences to alter the traditional view of the past. Furthermore, while Handlin believed that historians were still conscious of an obligation to write for as broad a group of readers as possible, he felt that the training they received in graduate schools made it difficult for them to do so.

Though Handlin claimed no special virtue for himself, his work does in fact show a determination to avoid what he diagnosed as the characteristic failings of American historiography. He has consistently tried, not merely to draw upon the social sciences, but to do so in such a way as to demonstrate the connection between social, cultural, economic, and political events. At the same time he has sought to call attention to the "dumb masses" who left few written monuments, but whose lives were, in his view, no less significant a part of the national story than those of America's conventional heroes. In the

Foreword to his first book he quoted some lines from a poem by the
Irish immigrant Thomas D'Arcy McGee.[4]

> Not of the mighty! not of the world's friends
> Have I aspired to speak within these leaves;
> These best befit their joyful kindred pens—
> My path lies where a broken people grieves. . . .

This description of *Boston's Immigrants* could well be applied to all
his work. It reflects Handlin's conviction that history is about people;
all of the people, not just the prominent few.

It was only with time, however, that Handlin became sensitive to
the historian's obligation to reach a wide audience. His earliest books
were addressed primarily to his fellow historians. But *The Uprooted*,
published in 1951, displayed a greater awareness of the needs of the
nonacademic reader, and since then his writings have, with some
exceptions, been directed as much to the general reader as to the
scholar. In a twofold sense, therefore, Handlin can be regarded as a
historian of the American people. While seeking to bring out the
common man of earlier times from the shadows where most historians have been content to leave him, he has also attempted to
convey to the mass of his fellow citizens a deeper understanding of
the American past.

Oscar Handlin, the son of Russian Jewish immigrants, was born in
New York City in 1915. He was educated in the public schools of
that city, graduated from Brooklyn College in 1934, and then went to
Harvard to do graduate work in history. Among the courses he took
at Harvard were those taught by Arthur Meier Schlesinger, Sr., on
American social history. Schlesinger, like Handlin the son of immi-
grant parents, had long been interested in immigration as a factor in
American social development. His lectures and writings reflected this
interest, and it was at his suggestion that Handlin chose as the subject of his doctoral dissertation the history of immigration into
Boston from the date of the first federal census to the end of the
Civil War. Completed in 1940, the dissertation was published in
revised form the following year as *Boston's Immigrants, 1790–1865: A
Study in Acculturation.*

In turning his attention to immigration Handlin was entering a
field which, until a short time before, historians had not studied

seriously. The scientific historians of the nineteenth century, with their institutional approach and their preoccupation with politics, had not felt it necessary to treat the subject in detail. Believing that American institutions had Teutonic antecedents, such representatives of the scientific school as John Fiske and Henry Cabot Lodge had contented themselves with drawing sharp distinctions between "old" immigrants from northern and western Europe and "new" immigrants from southern and eastern Europe, and with expressing doubts as to the wisdom of admitting newcomers who were not of Teutonic origin. Similar prejudices colored the writings of social historians. Scholars like John B. McMaster and Ellis P. Oberholtzer did at least recognize that immigration was an important factor in American development, but their accounts, besides displaying a racist bias, were sketchy.[5]

The reaction against institutionalism, symbolized by Turner and by James Harvey Robinson's "New History," led after 1900 to an extension of the traditional boundaries of history but did not immediately bring to an end the neglect of immigration by professional historians. As late as 1922 Arthur M. Schlesinger could remark that historians had "given little or no attention to immigration as a dynamic factor in American development."[6]

To be sure, the history of immigration had been much written about by the immigrants themselves and their descendants. Reacting to the attacks of the restrictionists and anxious to disprove the notion that American culture was exclusively Anglo-Saxon, representatives of the different immigrant groups assumed the task of recounting the contributions of their ancestors. These filiopietistic writers did their work painstakingly and unearthed a good deal of information. But their histories were uncritical and ill-balanced. Ignoring the role of the great mass of the immigrants, they showered extravagant praise on a few exceptional, and hence unrepresentative, individuals; their favorite practice was to draw up long lists of personages who had achieved distinction in one sphere or another—especially politics and war. Moreover the filiopietists paid a disproportionate amount of attention to the Colonial and Revolutionary periods, though immigration had then been comparatively slight. They were less interested in the millions who took part in the mass movements of the nineteenth century than in the small groups of Germans or Irishmen or Jews who were among the earliest colonists or who had served in Washington's army.

The failure of historians, both professional and amateur, to deal adequately with immigration meant that the subject had been left largely to the social scientists. To early twentieth-century economists and sociologists immigration was one of the most pressing of contemporary social problems, and they played a leading part in the long debate on immigration restriction. Some of their writings were polemical, and many exhibited a racist bias against the newer immigrant groups. On the other hand there were a number of sympathetic studies, and some of the best—like Thomas and Znaniecki's classic work, *The Polish Peasant in Europe and America*, and several of the volumes of the Americanization Studies series financed by the Carnegie Corporation of New York—had given a new dimension to the subject by revealing what immigration had involved both for the individual immigrant and for community life. But whether favorable to the immigrant or not, the writings of economists and sociologists were lacking in historical perspective. They took it for granted that there was something novel and distinctive about the influx of recent decades, and they failed to grasp that immigration was a social process which stretched back to the very beginning of American history.

In the 1920's, however, scholars at last began to show some awareness of the possibilities of immigration as a field of historical study. This development in part reflected the growing strength of the movement to broaden the scope of history. It also owed something to the Immigration Quota Acts of 1921 and 1924 which brought to a close both the era of mass immigration and the long public debate on restriction. Accordingly in the 1920's and 1930's the first serious historical studies of the subject began to appear. They were the work of second-generation immigrants like George M. Stephenson, Theodore C. Blegen, and Carl Wittke, who were also trained historians. Though most of them confined their attention to their own ethnic groups, their natural sympathies did not lead them to eulogize their ancestors as the filiopietists had done. Their objective approach shed new light both on the Old World background and on the American transition.

But the outstanding figure among the new historians of immigration was to be Marcus Lee Hansen.[7] Born in Wisconsin of Scandinavian parents, Hansen began his work on immigration at Harvard under Frederick Jackson Turner. From Turner Hansen learned to look on immigration as "the complement of the westward movement" and on America as the frontier of Europe. It was in Europe, therefore, that the study of American immigration had to begin, and Hansen accordingly devoted much of his life to collecting material from European archives. In Europe he came to realize the inadequacy of a country-by-country approach.

The significance of the transatlantic migration [he wrote], is broader than the experience of detached groups; and its full meaning will not be revealed until the natural emigration areas of Europe, at present obscured by statistics, laws and conventional treatments, are delineated and until the mysterious forces that, disregarding political boundaries, operated to set mankind in motion, are understood.[8]

Hansen planned a three-volume history of immigration from Jamestown to the twentieth century, but when he died in 1938 he had completed the manuscript only of the first volume, which carried the story up to the Civil War. After revision by Schlesinger this was published in 1940 as *The Atlantic Migration, 1607–1860*. It was a masterly account of the expulsive forces which affected one European neighborhood after another and of the factors which determined the destination of the emigrants. The breadth of Hansen's analysis enabled him to challenge many of the old orthodoxies. By beginning his story in 1607 rather than in 1776 he stressed the unity of the process of migration throughout American history, and demonstrated the fictitious nature of the distinction between "colonists" and "immigrants" which restrictionist historians had been accustomed to make. He showed also that the forces underlying the exodus were not primarily political or religious but social and economic, and furthermore that these forces were common to Europe as a whole. Finally his account was concerned not with the exceptional few whose doings had obsessed earlier writers but with the ordinary men and women who made up the vast majority of the immigrants.

In aggregate these changes of emphasis amounted to a radical recasting of the history of immigration. But *The Atlantic Migration* has certain limitations. It was, in the first place, a history written largely from official and upper-class sources; the point of view of the immigrants themselves rarely emerged, and they remained a shadowy, undifferentiated mass. And while Hansen wonderfully illuminated the European background to immigration, he did not attempt the same detailed treatment of the American aspects of the story. It is true that in *The Immigrant in American History*, published in 1941, he considered aspects of the immigrants' American experiences. But these suggestive essays fell a long way short of a full-scale treatment of the impact of immigration on American society.

Thus while a good deal of valuable work had already been done when Oscar Handlin embarked on the study of immigration, the full complexity of the subject had still to be revealed. The investigations of the previous twenty years had been concerned largely with the older groups of immigrants, and more particularly with those who had settled in rural areas of the Middle West. No one had yet studied intensively the more numerous groups that had flocked to the great industrial cities. Still less had there been an attempt to make use of sociological concepts to illuminate the way in which a particular urban community reacted to the stress of mass immigration.

These were the tasks that Handlin assumed in *Boston's Immigrants*. In describing how Boston was transformed from a cozy commercial center with a culturally homogeneous population into a bustling industrial metropolis torn apart by group conflict, Handlin took as his model the community studies produced by sociologists in the 1920's and 1930's. Some of the most notable of these had been the studies of urbanization made by Robert E. Park and his students—that celebrated Chicago group who were to be such a formative influence on American sociology.[9] Building on Park's theory of natural areas, these scholars embarked upon minute studies of Chicago neighborhoods and described the cycle of social disorganization, social control, and social reorganization that followed the coming together of a large heterogeneous population in relatively small areas. These studies had an obvious relevance for the historian of urban immigration, and a particular significance attached to Harvey Zorbaugh's *The Gold Coast and the Slum* and Louis Wirth's *The Ghetto*, which explored the effects of urbanization on the social organization of specific subcommunities, and to Everett Stonequist's *The Marginal Man*, which examined the cultural and psychological implications of exposure to diverse subcultures. No less important had been the Lynds' *Middletown* volumes, which examined the social dislocation produced by industrialization in Muncie, Indiana. These and similar studies had demonstrated the value of studying a community as an organic whole—an approach which Handlin believed to be particularly necessary when investigating the contact of dissimilar cultures. Handlin recognized that community studies presented greater difficulties for historians than for sociologists, since direct access to the subject by means of questionnaires and observation was impossible. Thus the only way to reconstruct "the intimate lives and deepest feelings of humble men and women who [had left] behind few formal records" would be to piece the story together from widely diversified sources.

The sources from which Handlin wrote *Boston's Immigrants* were indeed varied, but he relied especially on two types of material—the immigrant press and public documents. Immigrant newspapers, he contended, expressed the impulses of the immigrant community in a number of ways: they chronicled immigrant activities, reflected and influenced the views of the immigrants on the problems they faced and on the society they had entered, and, "most important of all . . . were the most comprehensive repositories of immigrant literature." Public documents, though unimaginatively compiled, he found to be equally enlightening. The federal, state, and municipal censuses yielded a vast amount of social data which earlier historians had not fully exploited, and other public records provided information on numerous aspects of Boston life—public health, education, housing, manufactures, and charitable institutions.

Out of such materials Handlin constructed a lucid and comprehensive account of the ways in which Boston changed under the impact of its first large-scale immigration. The nature of the changes, he showed, was determined by the fact that the poverty-stricken Irish peasants who flocked to the city were not only the most numerous of Boston's immigrants but also the most divergent from Boston's economic, social, and cultural norms.

Lacking both skills and capital, and rudely transplanted to a city which initially offered few industrial opportunities, the vast majority of the Irish became an indigestible proletariat, though ultimately the existence of a large pool of cheap Irish labor created a new industrialism in Boston. The character of the immigrants' physical adjustment had equally striking effects. Forced to live near their work by the fact that Boston was waterlocked, the Irish clustered together in and around the city's old commercial center, thereby turning the North End and Fort Hill into slums. "By their immobility," Handlin wrote, "the Irish crammed the city, recasting its boundaries and disfiguring its physical appearance; by their poverty they introduced new problems of disease, vice and crime, with which neither they nor the community was ready to cope."

But what made the Irish still more "a discordant element in a closely-knit society" was their distinctive habits of mind. Handlin argued that in contrast to the buoyant, optimistic outlook of the native Bostonian, the Irish brought with them "an immense sadness, a deep-rooted pessimism about the world and man's role in it." Fostered by conditions in Ireland, this attitude was reaffirmed by the difficulties of their new environment. The characteristic Yankee faith in progress, the confident notion that man could manipulate his environment to make life better—these were repugnant to Irish patterns of thought. Hence the immigrants remained opposed to the Bostonian reform ethos, whether expressed in movements for abolition, women's rights, penal reform, or public education.

Handlin went on to describe how the divergent socioeconomic situation of the Irish and the persistence of their inherited mental attitudes stimulated group consciousness and led to the growth of autonomous social institutions. Unable or unwilling to participate in the normal associational life of the community, immigrants created their own institutions—churches, schools, newspapers, fraternal societies, and militia companies. These social instruments reflected a complex of overlapping aspirations—an anxiety to preserve a distinctive cultural heritage, the desire to care for material needs, a simple yearning to be with one's own kind.

The development of immigrant group consciousness and of distinctive immigrant institutions testified, in Handlin's view, to the disruption of what had formerly been a culturally homogeneous community. For now, he remarked, "two distinct cultures flourished in Boston with no more contact than if 3,000 miles of ocean rather than a wall of ideas stood between them." Yet mere pluralism, he insisted, was not enough to produce conflict. So long as the Irish remained a politically impotent minority, differences could be tolerated because the newcomers presented no threat to the stability of the old society. But once the Irish became sufficiently numerous and well-organized to acquire a position of political importance, group conflict erupted. The frustration of native-born reformers at finding their wishes thwarted by the Irish led to the violent nativist movement of the 1850's. And even though the Civil War softened group antagonisms by providing an issue on which the Irish supported, instead of menaced, the existing social order and its values, group conflict had left a permanent scar on Boston's social life.

Boston's Immigrants bears the stamp of an acute and original mind. Working in a field which had been not merely neglected but unformulated, Handlin displayed great skill and restraint in applying sociological concepts to a complex historical problem. For this reason his book is a landmark in American historiography.

This is not to say that there is no room for disagreement with some of Handlin's conclusions. It may fairly be doubted, for example, whether the Irish were quite as pessimistic as they are made to appear in *Boston's Immigrants*; the mere presence of so many of them in Boston would seem to suggest that their attitude was not one of "complete acceptance toward mundane problems so long as salvation was unthreatened." Nor were Irish immigrants always the passive victim of Yankee prejudice that Handlin assumes them to be. The vituperative newspaper attacks on "Puritan bigotry" launched by George Pepper, Thomas D'Arcy McGee, and their successors make it plain that the Irish were capable of giving as good as they got.

It is also necessary to enter a reservation about Handlin's use of immigrant newspapers generally. The heavy reliance he placed on this source was due to his belief that "the newspapers furnished the foreigners' only reading matter and the fiction, the poetry and the history that attracted their readers are the most sensitive mirrors of what went on in immigrant minds." But these journals cannot have had an extensive circulation, for, as Handlin himself pointed out when discussing the immigrants' educational attainments, "the ability to read was by no means commonplace." Furthermore, Handlin did not always look closely enough at the source of the writings on which he based some of his generalizations about Irish social attitudes. Thus among the evidence he cited to illustrate Irish attitudes to such matters as religion, social class, and race relations were the novels of Mrs. Anna H. Dorsey, which were serialized in the Boston *Pilot*. But Mrs. Dorsey, despite her name, was not Irish and appears to have had no contact with immigrants in Boston or elsewhere. A member of an old Maryland family who became a Catholic convert, she wrote novels permeated by a religious devotion well calculated to appeal to editors of hierarchy-dominated journals like the *Pilot*. She was not, perhaps, the most reliable guide to "what went on in immigrant minds."[10]

These reservations apart, Handlin's analysis was remarkably authentic. It was immediately seen to be a new kind of venture for a historian, and in the quarter of a century since its publication it has become a classic. Besides being indispensable to an understanding of the Boston community, it remains the best specialized study of immigration. There have, indeed, been very few comparable studies, and most of them follow fairly closely the lines Handlin laid down.[11] What historians know of the social relationship between immigration and urban growth is still largely what was revealed to them in Handlin's pioneer work.

At this point Handlin turned aside from immigration to write, in collaboration with his wife, Mary Flug Handlin, a work which, though very different in subject matter, bore certain methodological resemblances to *Boston's Immigrants*. This was *Commonwealth, A Study of the Role of Government in the American Economy: Massachusetts 1774–1861*, which appeared in 1947 as one of a series of studies of state economic policy commissioned by the Social Science Research Council's Committee on Research in Economic History.

The abundance of materials available for the study of Massachusetts history—greater, perhaps, than that existing for any other state—would have made the Handlins' task in any case a formidable one. But what was to tax their industry and imagination further was the ambitious conceptual framework they employed. The obvious approach to an inquiry into state economic policy was an analysis of the interaction of politics and the economy in strictly institutional terms. But the Handlins rejected the institutional mode of analysis in favor of a cultural approach. It was their aim, they announced, "to find in the life of the people of Massachusetts a key to the role they expected government to play in their economy." In an effort to grasp those "unformalized preconceptions" which determined men's views of the world, they would treat "the sword and the plow, the scales of justice and of trade as aspects of men's needs and desires, of their struggles for betterment and advantage."

The Handlins accepted that such an approach would entail the comparative slighting of certain aspects of the story. They thus made little attempt either to judge the efficiency of administration or to assess the effect on economic trends of the various governmental actions they discussed. This had the effect of leaving unexamined

topics which some would regard as an integral part of the inquiry.
But it had the virtue of enabling the authors to concentrate more
effectively on their central theme, the nature of the ideas men held
about the role of government in the economy in the period between
the Revolution and the Civil War.

For the Handlins the period was one of gradual transition from
mercantilism to liberalism, one in which the concept of the commonwealth gave way to that of the regulatory police state. Aware that this
transformation was peculiar neither to Massachusetts nor to the
United States, the authors argued that this at least was not a case of
the rise of *laissez faire*. The shifts they detected in men's thinking
resulted rather from internal developments within the community.

One of these was the proliferation of corporations. The initial
notion that the government should in the common interest take an
active part in productive enterprise was hampered in practice by a
lack of funds and by the fear of debt which was the legacy of the
Revolutionary years. Consequently in the post-Revolutionary period
the characteristic method of encouraging capitalistic development
was the indirect one of granting charters to those private corporations—banks, insurance companies, bridge companies, factories,
canals, and railroads—which passed the test of public usefulness. But
because of a feeling that it would be undemocratic to restrict such
advantages to a favored few, corporation privileges came to be more
and more freely dispensed until eventually they were accessible to any
competent petitioner, without much regard .to whether the grant in
question would promote the common good. The effect of this diffusion of privilege, the Handlins demonstrated, was to transform the
character of the corporation from that of a government agency to
that of a business form. Moreover diffusion took place on such a scale
as to emasculate the state's capacity to direct production and to
"obfuscate the old justification in terms of the Commonwealth idea."

Equally effective in eroding traditional modes of thought were the
rapid economic and social changes which Massachusetts experienced
in these years. The Handlins showed that the growth of factory
production, the competition of Western agriculture, and the influx
of immigrants produced far-reaching changes in the social structure
of the state. A series of related developments drove deep fissures into
what had hitherto been a homogeneous society.

In describing this process the Handlins stressed the themes of social disorganization and mobility which had been prominent in *Boston's Immigrants* and which were to receive still greater emphasis in Handlin's later books. The picture they painted of Massachusetts society was one of a formerly stable, integrated community fragmenting under the impact of "precipitous social change." The consequences were the snapping of communal ties and the decay of the old proprieties. This situation, in which "the conventions of trade, of commercial negotiations, of family behavior, of simple neighborliness grew less binding" seemed to the Handlins to be the source of men's increasing readiness to look to the state to provide equitable conditions for all. The state was now to have a twofold function. It was "to enable men to compete with each other on an equal footing by leveling all artificial barriers erected by government." Special favors, the social justification for which had disappeared with the collapse of social unity, were now to be withheld and those already granted withdrawn. At the same time the state would have the more positive role of bringing about social progress through improvement of the individual. In order to ensure to each the chance for the fullest development of his capacities the state should employ its energies "to save men from the consequences of poverty, to fit them by education for the problems of citizenship and the economy, and to guard them against the temptations of dissipation, gambling, liquor and crime." Thus it was that after 1840 the democratic reform state emerged, one which no longer sought to direct productive enterprise by the granting of special privilege, but which, inspired by liberal humanitarianism, concerned itself instead with such problems as public education, poor relief, and the insane.

Commonwealth was the product of massive and imaginative research. In an effort to dig beneath the surface and reach the lives and thoughts of the people who were the subjects of government activity the Handlins exploited an unusually wide range of sources—controversial tracts, town histories, legislative and judicial records, personal and business papers, the writings of economic theorists, periodical literature, and even election sermons. Somewhat surprisingly in view of the basic conception underlying their study, they did not make use of workingmen's newspapers. The consequence was that they gave disproportionate weight to the ideas of merchants and manufacturers and did not deal adequately with the labor attitude to economic affairs. A certain lack of balance resulted also from their reliance upon polemical literature and upon petitions to the legislature. Such materials expressed the views only of the aggrieved elements of society.[12]

Nor was the Handlins' picture of sudden social fragmentation an entirely convincing one. They assumed that Massachusetts before the Revolution had been a stable, closely integrated society whose members were sustained by communal ties and responsibilities. But this assumption was nowhere examined, still less substantiated, and even if one accepts that historians have in the past exaggerated the internal tensions within colonial society, class divisions seem to have antedated the economic changes the Handlins described.

These flaws did nothing, however, to detract from the book's significance. *Commonwealth* was at the same time an original synthesis of economic thought and a penetrating analysis of social change. It was also a remarkably effective attempt to weave social, economic, and intellectual history into one, coherent whole.

Boston's Immigrants and *Commonwealth* were both specialized studies, admirably broad in their approach and their mode of analysis, but nevertheless confining their attention to one particular state during a relatively limited period of time. But in *The Uprooted* (1951), Handlin employed a larger canvas. In this book he attempted to distill the experience of the 35 million immigrants who left Europe in the century after 1820 to find homes in the United States.

In contrast to the many earlier studies which had examined the effects of immigration upon American political, economic, and social development, *The Uprooted* sought to analyze the impact of immigration on the newcomers themselves. This reversal of perspective was not a complete novelty, for a number of sociologists like William Carlson Smith and Hannibal G. Duncan had adopted just such an approach.[13] In fact one earlier study, *Old World Traits Transplanted*, by Robert E. Park and Herbert A. Miller,[14] had anticipated the viewpoint of *The Uprooted* by portraying the state of mind of simple peasants thrown into chaos by the stress of life under changed standards. But all such attempts by sociologists to look at immigration from the point of view of the human beings involved in it had lacked an historical dimension. No one had yet attempted to reconstruct the lives of the millions who had taken part in history's greatest migration. Thus in trying to discover what immigration had entailed for them, Handlin was rightly conscious of breaking new ground.

Viewed from this unfamiliar perspective the history of immigration took on a harsher appearance. Instead of being a simple success story it became "a history of alienation and its consequences." Those who left one world for another went through a shattering ordeal; their experience was one of "broken homes, interruptions of a familiar life, separation from known surroundings, the becoming a foreigner and ceasing to belong." Nor were the traumatic effects of transplantation soon to be shaken off. "The shock, and the effects of the shock, persisted for many years, and their influence reached down to generations which themselves never paid the cost of the crossing." The sundering of old roots before new ones were established constituted in Handlin's eyes a trial more complex, and for that reason more testing, than the much publicized sufferings of those who had colonized New England and Virginia in the seventeenth century.

The Uprooted begins with an account of European peasant society and of the forces which disrupted it. The peasant masses who were to become America's immigrants came, according to Handlin, from stable, self-sufficient village communities where men were bound to one another by ties of neighborliness and mutual obligation. Deriving their identity from having a fixed place in a harmonious social unit, and drawing strength from their intimate connection with the soil, the peasants were content with their lot. But the far-reaching changes in agriculture and industry which spread across Europe in the eighteenth and nineteenth centuries, coupled with an unprecedented rise in population, brought about the collapse of the old social order. Those displaced by these changes had to leave in order to escape an inevitable loss of status, and it was now, according to Handlin, that the process of social disorganization began. Ceasing to be members of the integrated community they had been born into, they lost the security it had conferred, and for the first time in their lives they were cast on their own individual resources.

Handlin argued that the harsh consequences of separation had begun to make themselves felt even before the immigrant set foot in America. He saw the journey to the New World as "a nightmare of hostile encounters," each stage bristling with its own peculiar hazards —fraud, ill treatment, disease, the relentless scrutiny of officialdom. These unnerving experiences, Handlin suggested, left a deep mark on

the immigrants. For one thing they reached their new homes in a
state of physical and mental exhaustion. For another the necessity of
fending for themselves had led to a questioning of the validity of
village standards of conduct.

In Handlin's pages, however, the crossing was only a prelude to
still greater tribulations. It was not merely that the physical environment of the New World was uncongenial; nor was it primarily a
matter of harsh industrial conditions. In his view the greatness of the
ordeal through which the immigrants passed stemmed rather from
the fact that the entire American universe—its economy, its politics,
its ways of thought—was fundamentally different from the one the
immigrants had known; and because of the way they had been conditioned by life in a peasant society, they lacked the mental and
moral equipment to adjust successfully to their new surroundings.

A prime source of immigrant disorganization, Handlin contended,
was the severing of life-giving contact with the soil. Enmeshed in an
"unnatural" productive system in which he no longer played a recognizable role, the immigrant felt himself to be degraded, to be less of a
man than he had been when he drew his bread from the land.
Moreover, in his new role of hired laborer the preconceptions which
had hitherto guided his conduct became irrelevant. The values
appropriate to a community regulated by a sustaining network of
reciprocal obligations were simply a source of confusion in an individualistic, competitive society dedicated to ideals of progress and
success.

More baffling still to Handlin's immigrants were the forms and
underlying assumptions of American politics. It was difficult for those
who in Europe had been excluded from the exercise of political
power to comprehend that in democratic America all men were expected to vote. Equally alien to their thinking was the notion that
the state might extend its protecting arm around them. It had been
to a local lord rather than to a remote government that they had
been accustomed to look for protection in Europe, and in the course
of their adjustment to America, they found it natural to turn for help
to a local political boss. Voting for machine-nominated candidates
was regarded by them simply as a proper return for favors received.
Thus, between the thinking of the immigrant, who looked on politics as an instrument for safeguarding his own personal welfare, and

that of the reformer, who campaigned for efficiency and good government, there stretched an unbridgeable chasm.

The disorder and confusion which Handlin saw as the characteristic experience of immigrants reached down, he believed, into the most intimate aspects of their lives. The family, which in Europe had formed a closely knit entity, with the role of each member clearly defined, crumbled under the pressure of new conditions. Ceasing to be the sole or even the main breadwinner, the man lost his place as head of the family and with it his authority over wife and children. Differences of experience, too, created divisions among those who had earlier shared a common life. Husbands, continuously rubbing shoulders with the American world in factory or mine, became alienated from wives confined to an immigrant ghetto. Children, Americanized in the public schools, rejected the old ways and the parents who symbolized them.

Handlin went on to show how the sense of alienation which pervaded the immigrants' lives led to the growth of autonomous social organizations whose aim was to rebuild their shattered communities. Conscious of having become detached from their moorings, they not only clung together in ethnic ghettos but made persistent efforts to reinstitute the forms and preserve the values of the old way of life. In these attempts at reconstruction Handlin believed religion to have played a crucial role. The church was the only bulwark of the former existence that had survived the transfer to the New World, and upon it the immigrants concentrated their efforts to maintain a connection with the past. Yet all such endeavors were doomed to failure for it proved impossible to transplant unaltered an institution which in Europe had constituted an integral part of everyday life. The strangeness and looseness of the American environment necessitated other forms. Each group continued to insist upon its own church, but the edifice built "out of the scrimped savings of poor laborers" was not, Handlin insisted, the Old Country church; "what they had recaptured was more the form, and that out of context, and not so much the way of life." In this, as in all aspects of the immigrant experience, the disruption was irreparable.

The Uprooted is a fascinating and a moving book. Written in a style that matches the nobility of its theme, it has a simple eloquence that at times reaches the heights of poetry. Handlin's emotional involvement in his subject and his capacity for capturing the texture and mood of the immigrant's world combine to make the book extremely persuasive. As one reads it, one cannot fail to grasp something of what it was like to have been one of the millions who stepped hopefully ashore at Castle Garden or Ellis Island.

It was this quality which accounted for the book's great popular appeal. *The Uprooted* has the ability to arouse the interest and fire the imagination even of those who are not historically minded. But it is no mere work of popularization. It is a work of serious scholarship, and it should be judged as such.

As a work which put forward a challenging interpretation of one of the major themes of American history, *The Uprooted* could hardly fail to provoke dissent. And in fact it has been heavily and persistently criticized. Many critics have felt that the book paints an exaggeratedly gloomy picture.[15] They have argued that by reciting the woes and frustrations of immigrants, while omitting any mention of their joys and triumphs, Handlin had told only one side of the story. How could one explain America's continued attraction to Europe's downtrodden masses if all they found in the promised land was misery and sadness? Other commentators have asserted that Handlin's generalizations were too sweeping. They have charged that *The Uprooted*, though in form a book about immigrants generally, is in fact only about a certain type of immigrant—the village dweller from southern and eastern Europe who got bogged down in the slums of American cities. Doubting whether Handlin's generalizations apply fully even to this group, such critics have denied that they apply at all to the immigrants who settled in rural areas.[16]

The sharpest dissent has come from Rudolph J. Vecoli, whose study of Italian immigrants in Chicago led him to challenge Handlin's entire approach.[17] Vecoli claimed that the Italians exhibited few of the characteristics of Handlin's peasants. They were not village dwellers, they had no reverence for the soil, and the basis for their solidarity was not the community but the family. Moreover, religion was not the focal point of their lives; on the contrary, Italian indifference to the Church was a continuing source of worry to the American Catholic hierarchy. And contrary to Handlin's dictum that immigrants were unable to transplant the social patterns and institutions of the Old Country, the Italians of Chicago were extraordinarily successful in reconstructing the old life. To Vecoli it seemed that in *The Uprooted* Handlin had "subordinated historical complexity to

the symmetrical pattern of a sociological theory." Instead of constructing ideal types of "peasants" and "immigrants" and ascribing to
them a common life style and a single set of values, it would have
been more profitable to have studied "the distinctive cultural character of each ethnic group and the manner in which this influenced
its adjustments to the New World."

Vecoli has suffered the usual fate of the revisionist of being himself
revised,[18] and some of the evidence he adduced about Chicago's
Italians is susceptible of an interpretation which would support,
rather than refute, Handlin's views. All the same he was right to draw
attention to the fact that the 35 million immigrants about whom
Handlin generalized were not the undifferentiated mass they are
made to appear in *The Uprooted*. There was a good deal of substance, too, in his complaint that Handlin overstated the disorganiz-
ing effects of immigration. Moreover, it was true that Handlin left
out the more cheering aspects of the story and exaggerated the immigrants' sufferings—for example, in asserting that, during the Atlantic crossing, "the normal mortality was about 10%"[19]

Another of *The Uprooted*'s weaknesses—to which Vecoli, among
others, drew attention—was its failure to portray accurately what
things had been like in Europe. Handlin's view of European peasant
society is a highly romanticized one, reminiscent in many ways of the
plantation myth associated with the Old South. And like the South
in which happy darkies lived under the benevolent sway of tender-
hearted planters, Handlin's Arcadia of contented peasants, "just
masters," and respected lords was a largely imaginary society. It bore
little resemblance to those parts of Europe from which immigrants
came. There was little social unity, for example, in the villages of
Austria-Hungary, where the landowners—usually German and Mag-
yar—were hated by the submerged nationalities who formed the bulk
of the peasant class. Nor could Ireland be described as a harmonious
social entity when evictions and outbreaks of peasant violence alter-
nated with each other in a seemingly unending cycle. In situations
such as these the "peasant" was hardly the deferential, passive
creature of *The Uprooted*.

It should be recognized also that substantial numbers of immigrants did not come from a peasant background and, for that matter,
knew nothing of agriculture. Nearly all East European Jews had lived
in towns; they had been mainly tradesmen, artisans, and factory

workers. Many members of other groups, too, notably the British and the Germans, had lived in cities before they came to America. For such people immigration did not entail a fundamental change of environment.

It was incorrect also to suppose that all immigrants came to the United States fresh from their European villages. The tidal currents of migration, as Frank Thistlethwaite has shown, were extremely complex.[20] The westward movement across the Atlantic represented only one aspect of the story, for there was a continuous and extensive migration inside Europe itself, both within national boundaries and across them. Moreover, those who went overseas did not always choose the United States. Consequently, many of America's immigrants had earlier been immigrants elsewhere—Poles in Germany, Irishmen in England, Italians in France or even in South America. Such men were not exactly innocents abroad when they reached the United States. They were practiced travelers for whom the native village had long ceased to constitute the world, and whose peasant attitudes had been significantly modified long before they set foot in America.

The exaggerated contrasts Handlin drew between the security of peasant life in Europe and the shattering nature of the American experience thus betokened a failure to comprehend the realities of the European background. In writing about European peasant society Handlin apparently relied less upon historical fact than upon the celebrated distinction of German sociology between *Gemeinschaft* and *Gesellschaft*, a distinction which postulated on the one hand a small, cohesive, rural society and, on the other, a large, dehumanized, urban society. But if the somber tone of the book reflected the influence of sociological theory, it stemmed no less obviously from the fact that *The Uprooted* was based upon materials which gave undue prominence to the debit side of transplantation.

The Uprooted had no footnotes and only the briefest of bibliographies, for Handlin felt that the nature of the work made it possible to dispense with the usual historical documentation. But he nevertheless indicated broadly the kind of sources upon which he had drawn. These were of three main kinds—the newspapers produced by and for the different immigrant groups; published collections of immigrant letters, life histories, and miscellaneous historical documents; and finally, novels.

The extensive use Handlin made of immigrant newspapers arose from his belief that they, more than any other single source, reflected the inner lives of those who read them. "These journals," he remarked, "chronicled the affairs of the immigrants, gave voice to their points of view, and provided media for the record of their thoughts in literature."[21] Which newspapers Handlin had in mind he did not make clear, but of the varied papers that made up the foreign-language press, only a few merited this description. Perhaps only the Yiddish dailies of New York City do so fully. They are an invaluable historical source, illuminating as they do every aspect of the lives of Lower East Side Jews.[22]

But no other ethnic group could match the Jews, either in journalistic talent or in having so literate and articulate a reading public. Unlike the Yiddish press, moreover, the papers serving some other ethnic groups—particularly those belonging to the "old" immigration—did not exist to facilitate their readers' adjustment to America. Their function was simply to maintain contact between people who shared a common religious faith or came from the same part of Europe. Typical of such journals were the predominantly religious weeklies circulating among Germans and Scandinavians in rural areas. Characterized more by nostalgia for the past than by concern for the present, these papers tell us comparatively little about the intimate lives of their readers. They are certainly revealing, but they do not always afford an adequate basis for generalizing about immigrant social attitudes.

For that matter, even the Yiddish dailies have certain limitations as a historical source. Their editors, like newspaper editors generally, attempted to attract and retain the interest of their readers by stressing the colorful and the dramatic to the exclusion of the commonplace, and thus gave undue prominence to crime.[23] Moreover the letters which, to the historian of immigration, are probably the most rewarding feature of the Yiddish press, need to be interpreted cautiously. Thus the *bintl brief*, that uniquely illuminating series of letters which appeared in the *Jewish Daily Forward*, were not by any means representative, as Marvin Bressler made clear in his analysis of them. Bressler concluded:

The *Bintl* letters were limited in their detail by their "trouble letter" form which tended to confine them to representations concerning a relatively narrow segment of experience from a point of view which was necessarily partisan and distorted. . . . It is clear that there is a selective process involving both the type of people who write and the nature of their revelations. Correspondents to the *Bintl Brief* do not include those persons who have achieved a reasonably satisfactory adjustment, who are not sufficiently motivated to write . . . or who simply bear their tribulations in silence. In addition the editor's selection of a specific letter for publication is subject to a policy which is sensitive to considerations of journalism. . . .[24]

A similar bias can be detected in the published documents Handlin used. Of the three collections he cited, two consisted largely of material such as official reports and social case records.[25] Designed "for the use of classes in graduate schools of social service," these compilations deal with the casualties of immigrant life, not with immigrants generally. Handlin's third printed source, Thomas and Znaniecki's *The Polish Peasant in Europe and America*, was in a separate category. In this pioneer sociological study Thomas, the main author, established the personal document and the life history as basic tools of social science. He based his findings on a series of immigrant letters which covered a long period of time and whose comprehensiveness enabled him to identify the status and point of view of the writers.[26] To this seminal work *The Uprooted* clearly owed a good deal. Thomas's approach to the study of the Poles provided a model for Handlin to follow. He had defined his purpose in *The Polish Peasant* as being to determine as far as possible what relation home mores and norms bore to adjustment and maladjustment to America. Moreover the theory Thomas propounded in that book—namely, that the process of social change was a continuous one involving adaptation as well as disruption—influenced fairly clearly the form of *The Uprooted*.

The Polish Peasant constitutes a unique source for the study of the psychological adjustment of one particular immigrant group. But one cannot generalize from a single study about the adjustments of European immigrants as a whole—least of all from this study. Thomas once admitted that one of the reasons that led him to choose the Poles as a subject of study was that "they were one of the most incomprehensible and perhaps the most disorganized of all the immigrant groups."[27] Knowing this, he hoped subsequently to extend his analysis to include the Jews, a group that was at the opposite extreme to the Poles, having a low incidence of crime, family strife, and other indices of social disorganization. But the Jewish study was never completed, and *The Polish Peasant* must thus be regarded as an incomplete and in one sense a biased source for the study of immigration generally.[28]

Similar criticism can be made of Oscar Handlin's use of novels. Fictional works can, of course, be a stimulus to the imaginative and critical faculties of the historian; they can enlarge his sympathies by compelling him to see abstract generalizations in terms of individual human beings. But the historian must be extremely cautious when seeking to apply the novelist's insights to a specific historical situation. Thus while Faulkner's novels display great insight into the psychology of the South, it would be wrong to take him for a realist. Moreover, the historian should not assume the point of view of a particular novel without taking fully into account its author's background and purposes.

Whether Handlin observed these precautions in writing *The Uprooted* may be doubted. Of the four novels of immigrant life to which he acknowledged a particular debt the most obvious progenitor of *The Uprooted* in style and tone was Ole E. Rölvaag's *Giants in the Earth*. The theme of this novel, a somber, brooding account of Norwegian immigrants on the South Dakota prairie, is the human cost of transplantation as revealed in the life of its central character Beret, the wife of the pioneer Per Hansa. Her nostalgia and mental anguish on being separated from her homeland are the novel's dominant motifs, as they were to be of Handlin's book.

Like many novels, *Giants in the Earth* represented an attempt to give fictional form to the author's own experiences and feelings. Rölvaag, the son of a Norwegian fisherman, emigrated to the United States as a youth and subsequently became a university professor in Minnesota. But despite his success he was a melancholy man with more than a normal share of Scandinavian fatalism. His diary and letters are full of nostalgia, and the notion came easily to him that immigration involved a loss of many of life's intangibles. As an intellectual of an introspective turn of mind he felt this loss deeply. But that his fellow immigrants did not share his feelings he was fully aware, for in a Fourth of July address to Norwegian immigrants in 1911, he admitted that most of his hearers believed that in coming to America they had gained more than they had lost.[29] Rölvaag's novel should not, therefore, be taken as evidence that Norwegian immigrants, still less immigrants generally, lived sad and frustrated lives. It is a revealing book but, like the other novels Handlin relied on, it was unduly pessimistic.

At some of its salient points, therefore, *The Uprooted* can legitimately be criticized. Yet this does not by any means invalidate Handlin's main thesis. To demonstrate that his conclusions are not applicable to immigrants generally is simply to reiterate the familiar and pointless charge that broad generalizations—which are the only ones worth making—cannot stand up to close scrutiny. This is a criticism *The Uprooted* shares with every work inspired by the notion that the historian should be an eagle rather than a mole. Nor is it fatal to Handlin's interpretation to show that, like all innovators, he exaggerated and overemphasized a single theme. For, as G. M. Trevelyan once remarked, "No one historian can possibly see more than a fraction of the truth; if he sees all sides he will probably not see very deeply into any one of them."[30] And the particular aspect of the truth that Handlin illuminated was one to which less imaginative, more materialistically minded historians had been blind—namely, that while the promise of plenty was not altogether a delusion, there was a price to be paid for its fulfillment. Exactly what that price was and whether it was paid equally by all are matters on which there is room for disagreement. But however much Handlin's interpretation may be modified in emphasis or detail, his central argument will be difficult to refute and impossible to ignore. This argument, stated with such splendid simplicity in *The Uprooted*, was that the material gain that immigration brought to the individual was balanced by a spiritual and intellectual loss that impoverished not only the immigrants but the society they entered.

One of the central themes of *The Uprooted*, the story of group consciousness, was carried a stage further in the volume Handlin contributed in 1954 to the Library of Congress Series in American Civilization. Despite its title, *The American People in the Twentieth Century* did not deal with American society as a whole but rather with its racial and ethnic minorities. The characteristic feature of American society, Handlin insisted, was not its uniformity—as Europeans were wont to assume from the absence of class divisions—but its diversity. In the most important aspects of their social life Americans fell into a wide range of groups which reflected the variety of their ethnic antecedents. Furthermore, the freedom and mobility which brought such groups into being usually prevented them from becoming rigid. Completely voluntary in their membership, without any status in law, they could not maintain themselves once they had ceased to serve the functions for which they had been formed. The constant expansion of the nation, socially as well as territorially, was a continual source of instability that not only shifted individuals from one group to another, but often altered the very structure of the groups themselves.

Handlin admitted there were exceptions to this generalization. Negroes, Orientals, and Indians did not share fully in the mobility and expansiveness of American society; their identities were not self-created but were thrust upon them by the color line. But all white men could adjust freely to the opportunities of American life; their ethnic ties developed and were modified spontaneously and in accordance with their own desires.

This situation Handlin assumed to have existed at the beginning of the twentieth century. But in the following half century the radical transformations through which the United States successively passed brought severe pressures to bear upon voluntary group action. The growth of racism, the Americanization movement, the demand for complete conformity bred by World War I and the Red Scare—these, Handlin showed, represented a challenge to ethnic loyalties. Moreover, the ending of free immigration, the rise of the mass media, and the onset of the Depression all helped to undermine ethnic institutions. Only in the 1940's was the trend toward conformity halted. World War II discredited racism and demonstrated that the era of economic and social expansion was not yet over for America, while the longing for stability produced by the Cold War gave roots a new significance. In these circumstances group life recovered some of its old fluidity.

In tracing the changing meaning of the ethnic bond during these decades Handlin had suggestive things to say about immigrant nationalisms, the problem of Americanization, and, most of all, the process of differentiation. He showed how local European loyalties gave way in America to wider spheres of action. The experience of being strangers brought an increased awareness of identity, while the need to unite to achieve common objectives made necessary wider affiliations, the basis of which was a common tongue or a common faith, or the closest available approximation to them. In such fashion the immigrant masses drew together into tentative groups, and on the success of their efforts at group identification was to depend the character of their adjustment to America.

This attempt to analyze twentieth-century American society in the light of the immigrant experience was widely praised for its insight but equally widely criticized for its general approach. To William E. Leuchtenburg, Handlin's point of view seemed ambivalent and indecisive. Handlin, he charged, did "not appear to have resolved in his own mind whether to write of the experience of the immigrant in terms of alienation or of a new birth of freedom."[31] There was no reason why he could not have done both, but in fact he had oscillated from extremes of anguish over uprooting to extremes of rejoicing over America's richness and diversity. But to make such a criticism was merely to acknowledge that Handlin had now succeeded—as he had not in *The Uprooted*—in capturing the ambivalent character of the immigrant experience. Nor was Leuchtenburg entirely justified in complaining that Handlin had depicted a culture more fragmented than it actually was. "It is rewarding," he wrote, "to treat America as an amalgamation of ethnic groups, but America [is] much more than that; in part because the immigrant has been so swiftly assimilated, in part because the white Protestant middle class has always held a disproportionate amount of power."[32] It was true that Handlin's analysis gave to minorities a prominence that in many respects belonged more appropriately to the dominant cultural group. But such an emphasis could be justified in the light of Handlin's conviction—admittedly not sufficiently emphasized in this book—that alienation and freedom were the characteristic experiences not of immigrants alone but of all Americans.

Equally severe criticism came from John Higham.[33] In questioning the validity of "the partly nostalgic contrast" Handlin drew between the tolerant nineteenth century and its increasingly intolerant successor, Higham put his finger on what had become a recurrent fault in Handlin's writings, namely, a tendency to romanticize the past. From *Boston's Immigrants* onward his books had begun with a nostalgic glance at an idyllic, or at least a more harmonious, past, against which the ensuing disorganization could be contrasted with greater effect. The use of this literary device could only distort history, and Higham thought it had done so in this case. It was only half-true, he asserted, that nineteenth-century Americans had generally accepted the principle of ethnic diversity; their acceptance of a heterogeneous present had "always rested on sublime confidence in a homogeneous future."

But Higham's most telling criticism was one which called into question the view of ethnic relations held not only by Handlin but by liberals generally. The liberal approach, he asserted, was essentially that of the sociologists and social psychologists for whom the study of prejudice had become in recent years a major preoccupation. These social scientists, reacting against the crudities of 100 per cent Americanism, had, according to Higham, treated group differences "as having tremendous subjective significance but little objective reality"; they had assumed that ethnic antipathies were "largely prejudices referable to subjective, irrational processes." The liberal historian, in endorsing these views, had overlooked some of the realities of the case. By emphasizing the psychological value of the ethnic tie for immigrants, Handlin had neglected their countervailing urge toward assimilation; he had also conveyed the impression that separate ethnic groupings did not differentiate people in any very fundamental way. Yet in fact, Higham insisted, the history of the several immigrant groups had been deeply affected by their contrasting cultures and it was only by recognizing these objective realities that historians could do justice to the diversity which characterized the American population.[34]

This criticism was to be elaborated some years later when Higham challenged Handlin's views on anti-Semitism. This was a topic which had attracted Handlin's attention as early as 1948, when he had felt moved to dispute the notion that group prejudice was the product of capitalist exploitation.[35] Handlin was unconvinced by the argument, set forth by Carey McWilliams in *A Mask for Privilege*, that anti-Semitism arose in the United States after the Civil War because capitalists needed an issue to divert the attention of the masses from their own grievances. Such a thesis, he felt, assumed wrongly that all anti-Semitic forces developed indigenously; it also disregarded the part played in anti-Semitic movements by liberal reformers and by organized farmers and laborers. An economic interpretation, he concluded, must give way to one based on psychological and ideological factors.

Three years later Handlin put forward his own revisionist interpretation.[36] In this he argued that the prevailing American attitude toward Jews in the nineteenth century had been overwhelmingly tolerant, but in the 1890's a new and unfavorable conception of the Jew emerged, from which openly hostile attitudes would later develop. This new stereotype—of a mysterious, international financial power—Handlin traced partly to the increased prominence of Jewish banking houses in Europe, especially the Rothschilds, but even more to the growing preoccupation of many Americans in the 1890's with the money question. Frustrated and baffled by their inability to secure a change in the currency, reformers looked for an external scapegoat, and with increasing frequency found one in the Jews. The Christian imagery of Bryan's "Cross of Gold" speech and the anti-Semitic strain in Ignatius Donnelly's utopian novel *Caesar's Column* reflected the discontents of the disadvantaged elements in American society. Mostly rural and small-town folk, these people looked with fear and suspicion upon the city and upon trade, and hence upon the Jew, who was the symbol of both. It was out of such feelings, Handlin argued, that anti-Semitism was enabled to grow in the twentieth-century atmosphere of racism and xenophobia.

Handlin's interpretation—which in its references to Populism anticipated views which Richard Hofstadter would later express—came under fire from more than one quarter. Norman Pollack flatly denied that the Populists were anti-Semitic and questioned Handlin's use of his sources.[37] To this Handlin retorted that his article had not been about Populists or Populism as such, but about the attitudes of Americans generally.[38] This was true, but in view of the prominence given in the argument to Donnelly's novel, it was not surprising that Handlin should have been misinterpreted. Accordingly, in his later writings he somewhat softened his references to Populism, though still maintaining that it embodied unsavory tendencies.

But it was once again from John Higham that the weightiest contribution to the debate was to come.[39] Higham agreed that Handlin had been right in assigning to the late nineteenth century a crucial place in the development of American anti-Semitism, but denied that there had been a sudden shift from tolerance to intolerance. American attitudes toward Jews, he declared, had always been ambivalent, and many Americans, not least the rural radicals whom Handlin had singled out, were both pro- and anti-Jewish at the same time. Higham also reiterated and expanded his earlier view that it was important to recognize the role that the minority group itself plays in a conflict situation. "Though prejudices distort reality," he remarked, "they also reflect it." In analyzing ethnic hostilities one should not, therefore, stress irrational forces to the exclusion of objective realities. Applied to the question of late nineteenth-century anti-Semitism, this principle required a recognition that social discrimination against Jews was due partly to the exceptional speed with which they rose up the social ladder and partly to the mass influx from eastern Europe, which complicated the entire Jewish problem. And finally, a comparative approach was essential. The status of American Jewry had to be compared not only with that of other ethnic groups in America but also with that of Jews elsewhere. Such an approach, Higham believed, would reveal that anti-Semitism was part, firstly, of a larger American nativism and, secondly, of international anti-Semitism. Noting that the periods of anti-Semitic ferment in both America and western Europe were also those of economic depression, he felt that the economic interpretation still had a certain validity. And since they were also periods of nationalist fervor, it was from the jingoism of the Populists rather than from their radicalism that their anti-Semitic rhetoric stemmed. Not that Higham believed the Populists to be alone in their anti-Semitism; for him the most virulent anti-Semites were, on the one hand, patrician intellectuals like Henry Adams and, on the other, the urban immigrants for whom the Jews were rivals for living space, jobs, and status.

Higham's analysis was certainly more comprehensive than the one Handlin had offered in his pioneer essay, and in some respects it differed sharply from the Handlin view. But the differences between their viewpoints should not be exaggerated, especially as Handlin, in his popular account of Jewish immigration, *Adventure in Freedom*, had qualified and expanded his earlier views in such a way as to anticipate a number of Higham's key points. While still giving the Populists a prominent place in the development of anti-Semitic feeling, Handlin had pointed out in that book that American anti-Semitism was not wholly indigenous, that Jews were not the sole targets for racist attacks, and that their special difficulties arose from the fact that they climbed up the social ladder much faster than other groups of recent foreign origin.[40]

Handlin's concern with anti-Semitism developed in the 1950's into a preoccupation with the wider aspects of prejudice. Several of his articles on this subject, most of them written originally for popular consumption, were gathered together in book form in 1957 under the title *Race and Nationality in American Life*. These essays covered a wide range; they included an account of the racist strain in scientific thought from the eighteenth century onward, an analysis of the divided loyalties of American Jews, and an attack on the racist bias of the Dillingham Commission which reported on immigration in 1911. But most of the essays were variations on a single theme—namely, the growth of racist ideas and the changing intellectual and emotional milieu within which they took hold.

The weightiest of these essays—and, as it ultimately turned out, the most controversial—was one which examined the condition and status of labor in the seventeenth-century colonies. Entitled "The Origins of Negro Slavery," this essay, written jointly with Mary F. Handlin, had first appeared in a scholarly journal in 1950.[41] In it the Handlins had challenged the notion—earlier discredited but recently revived—that from the time of their first importation into the colonies Negroes had been treated as a distinct and inferior caste. Reiterating that slavery had not existed from the start of the colonial period, the Handlins had denied also that it was simply imitated from elsewhere or that it was a response to any unique qualities in the Negro. Rather it was the case that slavery emerged gradually from the adjustment to American conditions of traditional European institutions and that, for several decades, the status of the Negro was indistinguishable from that of servants generally. Only in the 1660's did Negro and white servants assume a different status; while the condition of the latter improved, color became the badge of a perpetual and heritable servitude.

The Handlins did not in this essay tackle overtly or directly the complex question of the relationship between chattel slavery and race prejudice. But implicit in their argument was the view that racism was the result and not the cause of American Negro slavery. It was some time before historians began to react to the wider implications of this thesis but, in the course of the 1950's, as awareness grew of the dimensions of America's racial problems, the question of whether or not racial prejudice antedated the enslavement of the Negro took on a new relevance. The

Handlins' article was now seen to have raised an issue charged with both moral and practical significance, and not merely for historians but for Americans generally.

In the ensuing debate the Handlins' conclusions were sharply attacked. Carl N. Degler, though agreeing that the legal status of the Negro had been indeterminate for several decades, asserted that Negroes had had a special and inferior status almost from the start and that slavery, far from being the source of racial discrimination, was itself molded by the prejudices of the early colonists.[42] Another critic, Winthrop D. Jordan, has found the views of the Handlins and of Degler equally unconvincing. Noting that there is too little evidence for the crucial years after 1619 to say with certainty whether Negroes were treated like white servants or not, and that the first evidences of enslavement and of other forms of debasement appeared at about the same time, Jordan has suggested that slavery and prejudice may have been equally cause and effect, "constantly reacting upon each other, dynamically joining hands to hustle the Negro down the road to complete degradation."[43]

It may well be that the debate on this topic has only just begun[44] and that before the issues the Handlins raised can be resolved it will be necessary to consider the origins of racial prejudice not merely in the United States but in Western culture generally. In such a context the Handlins' view that slavery was the source of racial prejudice may turn out to have been an oversimplification for, as David Brion Davis has noted, "there is evidence of such prejudice in eighteenth-century Europe, where slavery could not have been a direct cause."[45]

The essays comprised in *Race and Nationality in American Life* reflected a fundamental shift in Handlin's view of the function of history. That they were written for the general reader was important, but less so than the fact that they had been called forth by contemporary controversies, such as those over desegregation and the amendment of immigration quotas. Handlin went out of his way, in fact, to draw attention to this feature of his writings on racism; "they were all composed," he remarked, "by an historian who searched the record of the past for clues to the problems of the present."[46]

Such an avowal represented nothing less than a return to the present-mindedness of the relativist historians of the 1930's. It was all the more remarkable for having been made by a historian who had earlier been one of relativism's severest critics. In a 1946 review of *Theory and Practice in Historical Study*, a document inspired by the conviction that written history should serve as a guide to present problems, Handlin had been skeptical about the relevance of the "connection between the intellectual interests of historians and the social milieu." Rather he had felt at that time that one of the strengths of the historian was that he possessed "attributes which somehow stand apart from time and place."[47] A decade later, however, he was led by his concern for contemporary social issues to echo Carl Becker's view that historians ought to subordinate the past to the present.

Nor was this present-mindedness a passing phase. On the contrary it was to give form to most of what Handlin wrote from 1954 onward. His survey of Jewish immigration, *Adventure in Freedom* (1954), was avowedly an attempt "to interpret the main lines of development in the past as they have a bearing upon the present and upon the problems of the future." Identical considerations inspired *The Newcomers* (1959), which dealt with Negroes and Puerto Ricans in present-day New York in the perspective of the city's earlier experience with immigrants. On occasion, Handlin's present-mindedness gave to his books a slightly polemical flavor. Thus *Firebell in the Night* (1964), which questioned whether integration was the only road to equality for Negroes, was not so much an account of race relations in the decade since 1954 as a contribution to the continuing debate on civil rights. There were occasions, however, when the connection between Handlin's writings and current controversy was purely fortuitous. It could have been assumed that *Al Smith and His America* (1958), which asked whether a Catholic could be elected President of the United States, had been planned with an eye on the 1960 election in general and on the presidential candidacy of Senator John F. Kennedy in particular. But the book had in fact been planned and undertaken several years earlier, when there had been no immediate prospect of a second Catholic presidential candidate. All the same there could be no doubt of Handlin's overriding preoccupation with the historical roots of present problems and even when he was not addressing himself to a current social problem, his concern was with a prevailing social mood. Thus in *Chance or Destiny* (1955) he sought to offset the deadening effect on his contemporaries of what Roy F. Nichols called "an historical determinism which, like other forms of totalitarianism, is destroying belief in the individual and his endeavors."[48]

These works were always readable and often suggestive, but few of them displayed the originality and the depth of understanding that had characterized Handlin's earlier writings. Occasionally, too, his anxiety to reach a mass public led him into oversimplification and distortion. This was the case, for example, in *Chance or Destiny*, in which he attempted to demonstrate the role of chance in history by studying eight critical episodes from the American past. Not all the episodes he chose supported his thesis, and in some of them—notably that on the effect of the battle of Gettysburg on the danger of European intervention in the Civil War—the narrative was too telescoped for men and events to remain in focus. There was, moreover, a marked lack of cohesion between the eight stories and the two analytical chapters tacked on at the end of the book; and though these were perceptive, they were tantalizingly short.

Handlin's biography of Al Smith was in some ways a more successful attempt at *haute vulgarisation*. It was a skillfully constructed and well-written book which, in less than two hundred pages, captured the essence of Smith's personality and shed much light on the character of Tammany politics. And while Handlin's sympathy for his subject may have led him to be a little harsh on Franklin D. Roosevelt, he did not gloss over Smith's intellectual limitations or the extent of his decline after 1933.

But the book labored under the handicap of an untenable thesis. This was that Smith's defeat in the 1928 presidential election was due mainly to religious bigotry. Handlin in fact displayed here the same preference shown in his earlier books for explanations which stressed subjective factors. He was reluctant to admit that Smith was disliked as much for his Tammany associations as for his religion or his immigrant origins; prohibition, which in many areas was the paramount issue in 1928, he dismissed as a cloak for prejudice. Nor did the book give sufficient weight to "Republican prosperity," which would almost certainly have ensured a Republican victory no matter who ran on either ticket. In any case Smith lost only four of the states the Democrats had won in 1920 and 1924, and if these losses were in fact attributable to bigotry, it would have been logical to apply the same ugly name to the forces that deprived Hoover of the predominantly Catholic but normally Republican states of Massachusetts and Rhode Island.[49]

Handlin's attempts to reach a popular audience have, however, occupied only part of his energies in recent years. Among other things he has found time to add to his scholarly writings on immigration and social mobility, to produce a number of valuable teaching aids and to edit a collection of documents concerning the Massachusetts Constitution of 1780.[50] And he broke still more new ground in 1961, when, in collaboration with his wife, he wrote *The Dimensions of Liberty*. This arose out of Handlin's appointment three years earlier as Director of the Harvard Center for the Study of the History of Liberty in America; the book's purpose was to provide a frame of reference for the more detailed studies that other scholars would undertake. But though conceived only as a prospectus, it was a stimulating and erudite volume. In defining the scope of the inquiry Handlin challenged the traditional notion that liberty implied simply the absence of external restraints; such a negative concept circumscribed the subject, he believed, in a way that excluded some of its most crucial aspects. Nor did it seem to him likely that the development of American liberty could be linked to a single cause; neither to the wide diffusion of private property nor to the frontier, neither to Puritanism nor to institutions transplanted from the German forests. Where a truer interpretation might be found he did not attempt to spell out in detail, for his purpose was to ask questions rather than answer them. But he performed his task so illuminatingly and with such a wealth of documentation that the book attained an importance belied by its modest proportions.

But the most ambitious of Handlin's recent works—in some ways, perhaps, the most ambitious of all his writings—was *The Americans: A New History of the People of the United States* (1963). In technique and style this book resembled *The Uprooted*, to which it was intended to be complementary, having as its theme the influence of migration upon the American people from colonial times to the present. This was a formidable undertaking for, given Handlin's conviction that the settlement of the continent had been the central experience of Americans, it entailed a survey of the whole of the American past.

It was thus a book which retold a familiar story. But it had nothing in common with the college textbook, with its conventional periodization and its well-worn milestones. The presidential synthesis got short shrift. Handlin merely sketched in the political background and had little to say about wars except in their social contexts. Nor was his a story merely of great men. His characters were "the men and women, exceptional and ordinary, whose lives responded to the presence of the great social forces of the times." His focus was upon "the developments common to the whole people rather than upon the exceptional individual," and in analyzing these developments he again made skillful use of the methods and hypotheses of the social sciences as well as of the insights of imaginative literature. But *The Americans* was by no means the "social science synthesis" that some historians had called for ten years before;[51] it made use of social-science abstractions but was careful never to subordinate historical complexity to them.

In this book Handlin's concern was with the subtle, unexpected and often contradictory ways in which the empty land had reshaped men's characters and compelled them to recast the ideas and institutions they had brought from Europe. It was not, he insisted, mere love of innovation that had brought about deviations from European models. Rather was it the case that space, climate, and isolation had combined to create a fluid, mobile society and to give distinctive forms to law, religion, methods of production, political institutions, and habits of mind.

But while mobility had enlarged freedom, Handlin believed that it had also fostered disorder, and it was the continuous dialectic between these two forces that he took to be the distinguishing feature of the American experience. It had also shaped the American character—the product, he declared, "of a situation that compelled men who cherished security constantly to seek out and to take risks."

This insistence upon the ambivalent nature of the American experience and upon its effect on the American character was striking evidence of the book's debt to sociology. Handlin's antinomies of freedom and disorder echoed the sociological theories of Park and, at a further remove, those of Durkheim. Park's analysis of mobility had suggested that "freedom from group constraints could also entail freedom from group supports," and that it was this kind of situation which often led to personal disorganization.[52] But this theory could be traced back to Durkheim's study of suicide. The process of social differentiation, Durkheim had shown, freed men from group ties but in doing so left them isolated and deprived them of meaningful values—a condition to which Durkheim had applied the name of "anomie" or normlessness.[53] It was this condition, according to Handlin, which characterized the history of the American people.

Handlin's pages were full of such imaginative applications of sociological theory to the fabric of history. He was also notably successful in *The Americans* in re-creating the atmosphere, not alone of the physical world of past ages, but also of vanished worlds of ideas. This was particularly true of a remarkable chapter on twentieth-century individualism, in which he employed a literary style reminiscent of Dos Passos' Newsreel and Camera Eye. And not least effective were Handlin's sharp dissections of American society at crucial stages in its history.

The book was not, however, well suited to the nonscholarly audience to which it was addressed. Handlin's allusiveness, his fondness for paradox, his frequent changes of mood, and his occasional lapses into obscurity were calculated to bewilder the general reader, especially in the absence of a conventional narrative framework. Indeed, the disappearance of familiar landmarks made the American past seem not only formless but meaningless. Notwithstanding the absence of sound and fury Handlin's account may have persuaded the nonspecialist that the history of the United States signified nothing.

For the scholar, too, the book was in some respects unsatisfactory. Interspersed with illuminating insights were trite or misleading statements, the consequence of compressing those aspects of the story of little relevance to Handlin's main theme. Moreover, his failure to document or even to argue his theses left the scholar with the alternative of accepting his often oracular pronouncements or of summarily rejecting them. But in spite of these limitations, *The Americans* was a wise and valuable book. It was also a considerable work of scholarship—if that term means not the cluttering of the text with scholarly paraphernalia in such a way as to suggest the flaunting of borrowed plumes, but the ability to mold diverse sources into new shapes by the exercise of historical imagination and the application of new as well as of traditional techniques. Handlin's dedication to this truer scholarly ideal gave to his survey of the American past a freshly minted look. It was refreshingly different from the first page to the last, and its best passages had the authority and the dimension of life.

Handlin's efforts to write serious history in a language the common man could understand have been only partially successful. His skill in exposition and analysis and his capacity for writing lucid prose have given his popular writings a wide circulation, and the best of them have been very effective in revealing to the general reader the histori-cal roots of current controversies. But Handlin has found it difficult to avoid the pitfalls of oversimplification and distortion into which the popularizer is always apt to fall, and when he has sought to make clear to a lay audience the complexity of the past, the effect has often been to rob it of much of its meaning. Thus he has not so far become a great popular historian in the tradition of Bancroft and Parkman.

But in the sense of having reconstructed the lives of the masses, whose collective biography forms the history of the United States, Handlin must be considered one of the foremost historians of the common man. "To recover some of our ancestors' real thoughts and feelings," wrote G. M. Trevelyan, "is the hardest, subtlest and most educative function that the historian can perform."[54] And when the ancestors in question left behind them few written records, as was the case with those whose lives Handlin has chosen to study, the diffi-culty and complexity of the task are immeasurably increased. Such a task demands a degree of insight, sympathy, and imagination—not to speak of industry—comparable to that required of an archaeologist seeking, through the study of potsherds and ruined temples, to recapture the essence of everyday life in a vanished civilization. These qualities Handlin has displayed in abundance and, where he has not succeeded, the fault can largely be attributed to the difficulties inherent in the problem.

One ought not, however, to minimize the extent to which Handlin has overcome many of those difficulties and, in the process, has re-vealed the potentialities of history "written from the bottom up." He has sought out and subjected to critical examination whatever mate-rials might provide the social historian with a substitute for the social survey that students of modern communities can obtain by means of personal observation and questionnaires. At the same time he has pressed into service a variety of social-science techniques and theories without, however, becoming a social scientist. As a scholar sensitive to the obligation to go only so far as the historical record would take him and as one, moreover, who has recognized both the complexity of human behavior and the role of chance in history, Handlin has felt little temptation to make history over in a social-science image or to order his view of the past so as to conform to hypotheses or "laws."

At the same time his historical writings reveal an unusual readiness to utilize the thinking of scholars in other fields and this receptiveness, combined with his interest in the common citizen, has given a distinctive cast to his map of the American past. It is one in which, as Daniel J. Boorstin has remarked, "the mountain peaks of clichés" are smoothed away;[55] and even if, as Boorstin believed, the flat landscape that remained was drab and unexciting, it at least had been swept bare of the stage props that had long obscured the natural topographical features.

Not that Handlin's achievements ought to be expressed in negative fashion. His studies of immigration, initiated at the local level and broadened subsequently to embrace its national and international contexts, were the first to reveal the full dimensions of the subject. Handlin has succeeded, as perhaps no other historian has done, in breathing life into Emma Lazarus' "huddled masses"; he has revealed how the characteristic immigrant institutions served to reconcile Old World heritages with New World standards; and he has demonstrated that the great accomplishments of the immigrants were rooted in tragic origins. That he has sometimes overemphasized the elements of tragedy may be counted a fault but, if so, it is a pardonable one in an historian of a country whose past has all too often been written about in naïvely optimistic terms.

For Handlin, however, immigration has been more than a major theme in American history; it is also the key to an understanding of American civilization. This view, implicit in the steadily broadening scope of his inquiries, was explicitly stated in a 1961 essay.[56] It was wrong, Handlin insisted, to draw too sharp a line between immigrants and other Americans, for "the immigrants experienced in an extreme form what other modern men have felt—the consequences of the breakdown of traditional communal life." It was not merely that Americans were an unusually mobile people, though those who moved from one part of the country to another duplicated much of the immigrants' experience. The real point was that even those who stayed in their birthplaces were "often themselves made aliens in the world about them." Accordingly, "insights derived from the extreme experiences of the immigrants have significant implications also for men who never made a move."

This was not the first time that the American character had been analyzed in such terms. Almost half a century before the young Walter Lippmann had written in *Drift and Mastery:*

All of us are immigrants spiritually. . . . We are an uprooted people, newly arrived and *nouveau riche.* As a nation we have all the vulgarity that goes with that, all the scattering of soul. The modern man is not yet settled in his world.[57]

But Handlin was not merely echoing Lippmann. What Lippmann described simply as the decay of authority, Handlin saw as the disruption of community. And whereas Lippmann's was an impressionistic judgment applicable only to the society of his own day, Handlin's was a carefully worked out interpretation intended to apply to each successive generation of Americans from Jamestown onward.

What substance there may be in Handlin's interpretation only time can tell, for as yet little is known of the social experiences of those whose communities were continually dissolving. But it was a characteristically stimulating contribution from a historian whose whole work has exhibited a capacity for basic thinking all too rare among those who study the past. It is this quality of Handlin's which has forced historians in each of the fields he has entered to re-examine their fundamental assumptions. Often his writings have provoked controversy, but Handlin shares with Turner and Beard the distinction, not merely of having initiated fruitful debates about the American past, but of determining the lines they would follow.

Richard Hofstadter

ARTHUR M. SCHLESINGER, JR.

10)

RICHARD HOFSTADTER was one of the first major American historians to come out of the cultural life of New York City; and this fact no doubt accounts in part for the character and direction of his work. The leading historians of the preceding generation came typically from small towns. Indeed, if American historians had come from cities at all, it was usually from Boston, or from a cultural colony of Boston, like James Ford Rhodes' Cleveland. Though Hofstadter was born in Buffalo, New York, and took his bachelor's degree at the University of Buffalo, he began his graduate work in New York City at Columbia University in 1937 at the age of twenty-one and has lived there most of the time ever since.

At Buffalo Hofstadter majored in philosophy and history. "I think philosophy interested me a bit more," he told an interviewer in 1960, "but I was astute enough to see (a) I had no gifts in the field and (b) jobs for philosophers were still harder to come by." The diplomatic historian Julius Pratt was a strong influence in leading him to history. "He is a thoroughly professional historian," Hofstadter recalled, "which I think I'll never be, and a wonderful teacher. He always kept bringing me back to the problems of history and the facts of life. He left the theoretical problems of history to the philosophers and I've tried to do the same."[1]

New York City in the late Depression was a place of ferment, and young Hofstadter entered rapidly into the passionate intellectual life so vividly described by Alfred Kazin in his memoir *Starting Out in the Thirties*. But he appears to have been in rather than of this life.

Kazin remembers him as "a natural conservative in a radical period, with a melancholy knowledge of the shoals and traps of human nature," but not melancholy himself and expressing his detachment through wit and mimicry; he was also "the most charming man I had ever met."[2] Kazin's reference to Hofstadter's conservatism applied to his temperament rather than his politics. Hofstadter shared, if more quietly and skeptically, the radical mood of the times; and this evidently crystallized his sense of vocation. "What started me off as an historian," he later said, "was . . . engagement with contemporary problems. As one who matured in the 1930's, my interest has centered mainly in politics."[3]

In the thirties, and especially in New York City, politics meant economics. "My generation," as Hofstadter wrote in 1962, "was raised in the conviction that the basic motive power in political behavior is the economic interest of groups."[4] This, of course, was the view so compellingly argued by Charles A. Beard, and for Hofstadter Beard was "really *the* exciting influence. . . . He was for me what Turner has been for so many others. . . . It was Beard who got me excited about American history. Turner never did. I'm too much of an Easterner."[5]

The political concerns of young New York intellectuals extended, of course, beyond domestic affairs. New York was, as Hofstadter later said, the center of "a battle of ideologies roughly similar to that which took place in a world-wide theatre. . . . Not since the era of the French Revolution has America felt itself to be as much involved in the ideological battles of the Western World as it did in the mid-thirties." This exposed him to Marxism; but, while he became thoroughly conversant with the Marxist approach to historical problems, he was too explicitly a Beardian (and too implicitly a pluralist) to capitulate for very long to the Marxist system. Still, the ideological battle did influence his historical interests; for curiosity about the formation and development of ideologies became "a natural response to the conflict raging around us." He thus found himself attracted by intellectual as well as by political history. The two, however, seemed to him "parallel rather than convergent," and he did not have a very clear idea how they could be put together.[6] This was doubtless one reason why he found sustenance not only in the Beards' *Rise of American Civilization* but in Parrington's *Main Currents in American Thought*. The "generous sweep and literary grace" of Parrington's writings as well as his use of intellectual history as a means of illuminating politics deeply impressed him.[7]

Beard and Parrington thus set the parameters with which Hofstadter began his own historical work. "That early American politics centered about a struggle between agrarian and capitalist interests," he wrote in 1941, "is not likely to be questioned."[8] But he was already displaying qualities of his own—qualities of subtlety, detachment, and intellectual restlessness—which prevented his resting comfortably in the conception of the American past as a conflict between agrarianism and capitalism. From the start Hofstadter approached history with a duality of vision which kept his mind simultaneously on the events which took place in the past and on the historians' renditions of these events. One feels, indeed, that he almost needed the stimulus of the subsequent interpretations to incite him to look at the antecedent facts—that he reacted more keenly to historians than to history. "He was strikingly passive," Kazin wrote of him as a young man, "he took things in, he thought them over and waited them out; he let other people take the initiative, but was always more penetrating."[9] Hofstadter himself has said, "One always has to reckon with the generation that has gone before. I think where one gets one's real intellectual impetus is reacting against ideas one has felt strongly."[10]

The next stage in his development was consequently a fairly sustained critique of—and by that process a liberation from—leading historians of the previous generation, above all Beard and Parrington but also U. B. Phillips and Frederick Jackson Turner. (Other historians he abandoned without symbolic acts of parricide. Thus he had once read and liked Carl Becker, but, as he said in 1960, "I haven't reread him for years and don't think as much of his work now.")[11] The critique began mildly enough with his first scholarly article, published in the *American Historical Review* in 1938 when he was hardly twenty-two years old. In a sober and detailed argument, Hofstadter sought to correct what he convincingly showed to be the Beards' overemphasis in *The Rise of American Civilization* on the tariff as a causal factor of the Civil War.[12] This was, however, more a revision than a rejection; and the depth of Hofstadter's involvement in Beard was suggested by the tortuousness of his disengagement over the next three decades.

Thus when he wrote *The American Political Tradition* in 1948, he was still considerably protective of Beard. He spoke of the "anti-democratic position of the Constitution-makers" and declared that "modern critical scholarship" had reached "a high point in Charles A. Beard's *An Economic Interpretation of the Constitution*"; it was a "great study."[13] Half a dozen years later, writing on "Charles Beard and the Constitution," Hofstadter lavished special praise on Beard's technique. It was, he said,

one of the work's greatest achievements. Methodologically it is a triumph of systematic intelligence. . . . Had his technique been seized upon by his own generation and refined and applied systematically to the major events and movements in American history, the resulting contribution to historical understanding would have been immense. . . . Historical writing today . . . is still wanting in method, in no small part because of a curious failure to explore the vision opened up by Beard forty years ago.

As for Beard's substantive thesis, it had been, Hofstadter judged, "absorbed into the main body of American historical writing. . . . It has entered calmly into history. It has become less and less a book to argue over."[14]

At just that moment the argument resumed, and it concentrated particularly on Beard's technique. Reviewing R. E. Brown's *Charles A. Beard and the Constitution* two years later, Hofstadter, while objecting (quite rightly) to the "often unnecessarily polemical and censorious" tone of Brown's book, conceded that "the historiography of the future will be much closer" to Brown than to Beard. He also offered a fine statement of his own sense of indebtedness to Beard:

As one of the generation that began to read American history during the 1930s and who has since had to unlearn a good deal of what he learned from Beard, I still feel that tribute is due him for the sense of passion and urgency with which he pursued his craft. . . . Many of the mistakes Beard made are of the sort that are likely to be made in the course of any ground-breaking inquiry into a complex subject. Minds like Beard—and Turner, who also misled us at critical points—perform services even when they are wrong.[15]

He disposed of Parrington more summarily. By 1941 he had reached the point where, "without questioning the fundamentals" of Parrington's analysis, he had to "criticize the neatness of its schematism." The work as a whole, he thought, suffered from "the inevitable lapses of a synthesis, however masterly, which is undertaken long before analysis reaches its proper depth."[16] He then proceeded to destroy Parrington's contention that Jefferson had been a disciple of the physiocrats. "That helped me get Parrington out of my system," he said in 1960. ". . . I suspect that to some degree Parrington influenced me. I don't think much of him now."[17]

He had to get others of the older generation out of his system. In an oddly uncharacteristic essay—uncharacteristic both in its subject matter and in its gestures toward the quantitative method—he dealt in 1944 with U. B. Phillips. His purpose was to demonstrate through statistical analysis of Phillips's data that his samples had been atypical and had resulted in an excessively genial picture of Southern slavery. Hofstadter's critique does not seem to have had much specific influence on historians' attitudes toward slavery or toward Phillips.[18] None the less, Hofstadter's historical insight enabled him at a relatively early time—in the same year as the publication of Myrdal's *An American Dilemma*—to set forth with marked prescience the agenda for the next generation of historians of slavery:

Let the study of the Old South be undertaken by other scholars who have absorbed the viewpoint of modern cultural anthropology, who have a feeling for social psychology (a matter of particular importance in the study of a regime in which status was so vital), who will concentrate upon the neglected rural elements . . . who will not rule out the testimony of more critical observers, and who will realize that any history of slavery must be written in large part from the standpoint of the slave—and then the possibilities of the Old South and the slave system as a field of research and historical experience will loom larger than ever.[19]

Turner was next to fall. Turner's frontier interpretation, Hofstadter wrote in 1949, stood along with Beard's economic interpretation as the "two major theories or models of understanding" produced by American historical writing in the past century. Of the two, if Beard's meant more to a city boy like Hofstadter, it was the frontier thesis, Hofstadter freely conceded, "that has embodied the predominant American view of the American past." Still, as he reexamined the thesis, he found it so compact with vagueness and ambiguity that, in the hands of Turner's disciples, it became "less a working hypothesis than an incantation." Its strength, he suggested, rested on "the appeal of the frontier to the American imagination" and on the desire, common in the progressive age, "to have a 'materialistic' interpretation of history that did not risk the ideological pitfalls of the class struggle idea." In recent years, he wrote, the frontier thesis had been seriously damaged by the rising view that the great nineteenth-century upsurges of democracy, the Jeffersonian and the Jacksonian, were "more intelligible in terms of social classes than of the East or the West," as well as by the growth of intellectual history, which made it impossible to "hold very long to the notion that the main stream of American ideas and habits of behavior moved from West to East." Hofstadter concluded by saying of Turner that "his historical writing was better than his frontier thesis, and not least because he regularly made use in practice of historical factors which were not accounted for in his theory."[20]

Hofstadter made his final—or at least his most recent—[21] reckoning with Turner, Beard, and Parrington in *The Progressive Historians* (1968). Here he confronted what he had come to regard as an uncomfortable question: why did these historians, whom he had once found so exciting, now seem so inadequate and even irrelevant? He conceded that the "progressive historians" took the "writing of American history out of the hands of the Brahmins and the satisfied classes, where it had too exclusively rested, and made it responsive to the intellectual needs of new types of Americans who were beginning to constitute a productive, insurgent intelligentsia." In so doing, these men "above all others" explained "the American liberal mind to itself in historical terms"; they "gave us the pivotal ideas of the first half of the twentieth century."[22] But why did they have so little to say to the second half of the century?

There followed three long, subtle, searching essays, skillfully interweaving biography and analysis. Hofstadter's personal engagement seemed greatest with Beard; his assessment of Parrington contained the most fresh information and insight; the essay on Turner was cool and astute. In each case Hofstadter saw his subjects in relation not only to their historical ideas but to their families, their education, their jobs, their professional colleagues, their politics, and their temperaments. The evident sympathy with which he wrote about the fathers of us all made his "parricidal forays" the more convincing. In the end, none emerged as a very serious figure. Turner demanded respect less for his highly ambiguous thesis than for the controversy it created; Beard was "our supreme tragic example of the activist mind in history"; the "abrupt decline" of Parrington's reputation could not be contested.[23]

The progressive doctrine, as Hofstadter saw it, was that political and economic conflict was the key to American history; and its effect, he contended, was to oversimplify and overdramatize the complex and shifting actuality of the national experience. The progressive historians, he concluded, relied too heavily on geographic or economic determinism. They took past conflicts as direct analogues of present conflict. They tended to impute discreditable motives to historical figures on the "wrong" side. They drifted on occasion toward conspiratorial interpretations.

Hofstadter's historiographical preoccupations have always somewhat stood between himself and historical research. Still, while he was engaged in his early settling of accounts with the progressive historians, he was nonetheless proceeding with his own primary work. His first book, written between 1940 and 1942 and published in 1944, was *Social Darwinism in American Thought*. "Although it was meant to be a reflective study rather than a tract for the times," Hofstadter said in an Author's Note for a revised edition, "it was naturally influenced by the political and moral controversy of the New Deal era."[24] This was doubtless so. Yet the book stands on its merits as a thoughtful and penetrating essay in intellectual history.

It has been noted that in the late thirties Hofstadter felt simultaneous pulls toward political and intellectual history but could not see clearly how the two could be fused. As a result, *Social Darwinism*, for all its political implications, registered predominantly a concern with ideas. It was a relatively straightforward account of the effect of Darwin's work on social thinking in America, admirable in its lucidity, in the conciseness of its summaries and the incisiveness of its judgments. "There was nothing in Darwinism," Hofstadter concluded,

that inevitably made it an apology for competition or force. Kropotkin's interpretation of Darwinism was as logical as Sumner's. Ward's rejection of biology as a source of social principles was no more unnatural than Spencer's assumption of a universal dynamic common to biology and society alike. . . . Darwinism had from the first this dual potentiality; intrinsically it was a neutral instrument, capable of supporting opposite ideologies.

If this were so, how then to account for the initial ascendancy in the United States of the rugged individualist's version of Darwinism? The answer, in Hofstadter's view, lay in the nature of the American environment. "American society saw its own image in the tooth-and-claw version of natural selection and . . . its dominant groups were therefore able to dramatize this vision of competition as a thing good in itself." Ideas, he noted, had effects as well as causes; but the history of Darwinian individualism seemed to him "a clear example of the rule that changes in the structure of social ideas wait on general changes in economic and political life. In determining whether such ideas are accepted, truth and logic are less important criteria than suitability to the intellectual needs and preconceptions of social interests."[25]

This was plain enough, but Hofstadter confined this argument pretty much to his concluding chapter. The bulk of the book made little attempt to display the interaction between ideas and the changing social structure. Indeed, the author later ruefully thought that the effect of *Social Darwinism* had been perhaps to encourage what he called the "intellectualist fallacy"—the assumption "that we are ruled by ideas and by little else." This led, he feared, to an exaggeration of the influence of ideas "by stripping them out of the social context in which they were formed and interpreted."[26]

Hofstadter, in short, had not yet worked out his sense of the relationship between ideas and society. But there were already in *Social Darwinism* hints of deeper preoccupations which might in time form parts of an integrated approach. Thus the book declared a marked sympathy for pragmatism—the "philosophy of possibility" as against Spencer's "philosophy of inevitability." One notes also, as in the peroration that same year of the Phillips essay, a concern with the problem of social status and an interest in the dilemma of a "middle class worried about survival." And again, as in the Phillips essay, this led Hofstadter to urge on historians the value of cultural anthropology and social psychology. The life of man in society, he wrote in his conclusion, "must be explained in the distinctive terms of a cultural analysis."[27]

He had not yet clarified in his own mind, however, the form such a "cultural analysis" might take. And soon he was busy on a book expressing the other side of his historical concern—his interest in political history. *The American Political Tradition and the Men Who Made It* was published in 1948. It marked an enlargement in Hofstadter's conception both of his own expertise and of his audience, implying a rejection of the prevalent view within the historical guild that a serious historian should confine himself to a single period and write only for fellow scholars. Where *Social Darwinism* was addressed to other historians, *The American Political Tradition* was addressed to the adult reading public. With its impressive breadth, confidence, and learning, it had immediate impact.

It consisted of a dozen biographical portraits, all of decisive political leaders (except for Wendell Phillips), all drawn with brilliant freshness and economy, all adorned with an enviable felicity of quotation. But its impact came only in part from the sparkling charm and penetration of the individual essays. For the essays carried, or half-carried, a thesis. They were, as their author saw them, "studies in the ideology of American statesmanship," and they were designed, he wrote in his Introduction, to meet the need "for a reinterpretation of our political traditions which emphasizes the common climate of American opinion." The tendency to place political conflict in the foreground of history, Hofstadter continued, had obscured the fact that the struggles, however fierce, were "always bounded by the horizons of property and enterprise."

However much at odds on specific issues, the major political traditions have shared a belief in the rights of property, the philosophy of economic individualism, the value of competition; they have accepted the economic virtues of capitalist culture as necessary qualities of man. . . . The sanctity of private property, the right of the individual to dispose of and invest it, the value of opportunity, and the natural evolution of self-interest and self-assertion, within broad legal limits, into a beneficent social order have been staple tenets of the central faith in American political ideologies.[28]

I suggested a moment ago that the book only "half carried" this thesis. For the thesis is not often mentioned in the body of the text; when mentioned, it is mostly asserted rather than argued, and, when argued, it is done in an almost desultory way. This is so much the case that, on rereading the book, one wonders whether Hofstadter appended the Introduction as an afterthought, or perhaps as a last-minute recognition and articulation of what had unconsciously rather than consciously controlled the narrative.

He plainly had not thought the thesis through with his usual rigor. Thus the quotation inset above talks of "traditions" and "ideologies" in the plural, while the title of the book, and most of the argument, refer to a single tradition and a single ideology. His notion of the life cycle of the tradition, moreover, remained obscure. He seemed to feel that the original American political tradition had been for some time in decline. In consequence—and here he introduced an idea which was natural enough for a city-bred historian and which would play a growing role in his thought—nostalgia for an agrarian past was an increasingly incongruous factor in American politics. "Beginning with the time of Bryan," he wrote, "the dominant American ideal has been steadily fixed on bygone institutions and conditions. In early twentieth-century progressivism this backward-looking vision reached the dimensions of a major paradox." He concluded by suggesting, without ever quite saying so, that the old tradition substantially perished with Hoover. The ideas Hoover represented, Hofstadter wrote,

were precisely the same ideas that in the remoter past of the nineteenth century . . . had had an almost irresistible lure for the majority of Americans. In the language of Jefferson, Jackson, and Lincoln these ideas had been fresh and invigorating; in the language of Herbert Hoover they seemed stale and oppressive. . . . Hoover was the last presidential spokesman of the hallowed doctrines of laissez-faire liberalism, and his departure from Washington marked the decline of a great tradition.[29]

With Roosevelt and the New Deal, one is led to believe, this dominant American tradition came to an end, even though Roosevelt himself, with his excessive reliance on personal leadership, failed to achieve a fundamental redefinition of the national political faith.

This formulation raised several questions. Could it not be said, for example, that Roosevelt's politics were also bounded by "the horizons of property and enterprise"? Yet thus to identify Hoover and Roosevelt would be to drain meaning from American political conflict. After all, Hoover and Roosevelt saw themselves as mortal antagonists, and Hofstadter as a politically engaged man knew in his own lifetime the serious differences between them; neither they nor he could have been all that self-deceived. Still, if this were so, how could he be so certain that political conflicts he had not personally experienced were all that meaningless? More particularly, in what sense could it be claimed that Hoover's ideas were "precisely the same ideas" as those of Jefferson, Jackson, and Lincoln? Certainly not in the sense of the pragmatism for which Hofstadter expressed such sympathy in *Social*

Darwinism: James contended that the meaning of an idea lay in its practical consequences.

To attain perfect clearness in our thoughts of an object . . . we need only consider what conceivable effects of a practical kind the object may involve—what sensations we are to expect from it, and what reactions we must prepare. Our conception of these effects, whether immediate or remote, is then for us the whole of our conception of the object.[30]

By the pragmatic criterion, the ideas of Hoover and, say, Jefferson, far from being "precisely the same," were very likely considerably different in operational content—or at least operational identity could not be proved simply by a similarity in language.

In the main, Hofstadter ignored such questions. Only in one part of the book did he move systematically beyond his vivid biographical portraits to incorporate his thesis into the analysis, and that was the section which had the greatest influence on historical scholarship— his treatment of Jacksonian democracy. The Jackson period had evidently interested Hofstadter for some years. In his Parrington essay in 1941, he had written that in the Jackson era Jeffersonian economic ideas, "in urban garb, were now paraded by the new working-class element in the democracy." Citing William Leggett and William M. Gouge, he noted that neither "had any quarrel with the fundamental premises of a capitalist economy either from an agrarian or a socialist point of view. . . . They did not propose to abolish capitalism or even to restrain it; they merely wished to give it a democratic bias." The Jacksonian dilemma, Hofstadter suggested, lay in the fact that "it accepted the capitalist order, without desire or ability to propose an alternative society, and restricted itself to reforms which interfered with its smooth functioning." The Jacksonian program "might impede the advance of capitalism, but never prevent it."[31] He developed these views two years later in a piece on Leggett. While acknowledging "the newly won political power of the unpropertied classes" and the new political consciousness of labor, and conceding that Leggett saw his political philosophy "as a rationale for the working class," Hofstadter concluded that his aim was "not to abolish or even to limit private property but simply to democratize the country's economic life" and that his agitation "probably did far more to develop the corporate institution in the United States than to destroy property rights."[32]

The American Political Tradition expanded these insights to produce an intelligent and searching criticism of the viewpoint set forth by this writer in *The Age of Jackson* (1945). Hofstadter agreed with *The Age of Jackson* that Jacksonian democracy was more intelligible in terms of classes than of sections. But he disagreed as to which classes were primarily involved and what their objectives were. The typical American of the day, he suggested, was "an expectant capitalist," and the Jacksonian movement "grew out of expanding opportunities and a common desire to enlarge these opportunities still further by removing restrictions and privileges that had their origin in acts of government; thus, with some qualifications, it was essentially a movement of laissez-faire." If it was a phase in the expansion of democracy, "it was also a phase in the expansion of liberated capitalism." The Jacksonian upsurge was "closely linked to the ambitions of the small capitalist."[33]

Hofstadter's entrepreneurial thesis of Jacksonian democracy, reinforced by the impressive work of Bray Hammond and by subsequent studies by Walter Hugins, Lee Benson, Edward Pessen, and others, soon swept the field. Indeed, it was eventually carried to the point where it almost obliterated any difference between the Jacksonians and the Whigs and made the bitter political conflict of the age of Jackson a mystery.[34] This was doubtless further than Hofstadter intended to go; and I think I am not wrong in detecting a reaction today against exaggerated statements of the entrepreneurial view. But it succeeded at the time because it fitted so exactly into the social mood of the 1950's—the mood which, in the service of contemporary conservatism, began to see the American past as one happy homogeneous continuity.[35]

In a sense, Hofstadter's *The American Political Tradition* can be said to have foreshadowed the consensus history of the fifties.[36] No doubt Hofstadter's emphasis on the "common climate of American opinion" and his absorption of everyone from Jefferson to Hoover into a single tradition helped both stimulate and legitimatize the impulse of historians in the fifties to minimize the role of conflict in the national past. Nonetheless, there is an important difference between *The American Political Tradition* and a work like Daniel Boorstin's *The Genius of American Politics* (1953). For Hofstadter perceived the consensus from a radical perspective, from the outside, and deplored it; while Boorstin perceived it from the inside and celebrated it.[37] The political assumptions of *The American Political Tradition* were not aggressive, but they were unmistakable.

Radical notes sounded quietly throughout the book. Hofstadter seemed to feel about reform movements in general, as he wrote about Jefferson's reform movement in Virginia, that the accomplishments "have been subject to fantastic exaggeration by historians."[38] The Founding Fathers failed because of their belief in

unchanging human nature. Modern humanistic thinkers who seek for a means by which society may transcend eternal conflict and rigid adherence to property rights as its integrating principles can expect no answer in the philosophy of balanced government as it was set down by the Constitution-makers of 1787.[39]

Bryan failed because he lacked "a sense of alienation. He never felt the excitement of intellectual discovery that comes with the rejection of one's intimate environment";[40] this last was almost the same phrase Hofstadter later used about himself when he traced his intellectual impetus to reaction against ideas one has felt strongly. The Progressive mind failed because it was too "easy to please."[41] Franklin Roosevelt failed because he rested content

with his belief in personal benevolence, personal arrangements, the sufficiency of good intentions and month-to-month improvisation, without trying to achieve a more inclusive and systematic conception of what is happening in the world.

A "corporate and consolidated society," Hofstadter wrote in his introduction, demanded "cohesion, centralization, and planning." Roosevelt, by rejecting the American political tradition without reconstructing it, was responsible for "the rudderless and demoralized state of American liberalism."[42] The one figure singled out for portraiture who was not a man of power was Wendell Phillips, "the patrician as agitator." The agitator, Hofstadter wrote with sympathy,

thinks in terms of the *ultimate potentialities* of social conflicts rather than the immediate compromises by which they are softened. His moral judgments are made from the standpoint of absolute values, with which the mass of men cannot comfortably live. But when a social crisis or revolutionary period at last matures, the sharp distinctions that govern the logical and doctrinaire mind of the agitator become at one with the realities. . . . Often mistaken, [Phillips] had often been utterly right when others were terribly wrong.[43]

It was doubtless this sense of his own perspective which led Hofstadter in the fifties to protest against the assumption that *The American Political Tradition* was a contribution to consensus history. When another historian cited him as the ablest representative of a school of intellectual history which denied "any distinction" between the principles of liberal and conservative statesmen and in whose writings "all alike are made to seem reactionary," Hofstadter responded vigorously that this was "a view which I not only do not hold but consider utterly untenable." He declared his "hearty agreement" with his critic over the importance of distinguishing "reactionary conservatives from progressive ones" and contended that his own book had only argued that "our politicians, liberal and conservative, have had more in common with each other than the agitated rhetoric of political controversy usually suggests."[44] One can understand Hofstadter's concern over the misunderstanding of his thesis in the age of Eisenhower; but it may be said that he encouraged that misunderstanding by writing with a different emphasis in the twilight of the New Deal.

Oddly enough, Hofstadter three years later wrote not unfavorably that "the same mood which has recently brought upon us what we so loosely call the 'New' Conservatism has also brought a new note into historical writing." He cited Boorstin and Louis Hartz as rejecting the Beard-Turner notion of conflict in favor of the view that American politics "has been built socially upon a middle-class basis and ideologically upon a liberal consensus." On this occasion he did not insist on preserving a role for conflict. Hofstadter returned to the problem of consensus history in the *Progressive Historians*. His own attitude toward it, he wrote in 1968, had become "essentially ambivalent. . . . I trust it will be clear that while I still find use for insights derived from consensus history, it no longer seems as satisfactory to me as it did ten or twenty years ago." He credited consensus history with "the rediscovery of complexity" in the American past—with producing a new focus on the religious, ethnic, and racial complex of American life, on immigration, acculturation, nativism, race, slavery, mobility, status tensions.[45] (This would seem a considerable overstatement: social history brought many of these issues into the historical domain forty years earlier with the *History of American Life* series. Still Hofstadter was surely right in suggesting that consensus history offered fruitful new perspectives on the past, that its methods were more sophisticated than those of the social historians of the previous generation and that the monographic fallout has greatly enriched American historical writing.)

On balance, though, he now saw consensus history primarily as an "indispensable corrective," its merits "distinct" but "transitional." In the end, it seemed "an essentially negative proposition. . . . As a positive principle, it does not go very far." Consensus history, he felt, could not explain the American Revolution or the Civil War or the racial, ethnic, and religious violence of American life. He concluded: "In one form or another conflict finally does remain, and ought to remain, somewhere near the center of our focus of attention." As a result, however, of the consensus fling, we could better understand the variety and ambiguity of conflict and should therefore be able to "return to the assessment of conflict in American life and thought without going straight back to the arms of the Progressives."[46] Some critics will say that, as consensus history reflected the alleged domestic tranquillity of the Eisenhower years, so the revival of history-as-conflict reflected the savage turbulence of the late 1960's. I have no doubt that Hofstadter would agree.

Social Darwinism had concluded with an appeal for social explanation in "the distinctive terms of a cultural analysis." *The American Political Tradition*, though it represented movement in the direction of putting intellectual and political history together, did so in a fairly conventional way. Its quality lay in novelties of insight rather than of method. There were occasional gestures toward a sociocultural approach:

Democratic ideas are likely to take root among discontented and oppressed classes, rising middle classes, or perhaps some sections of an old, alienated, and partially disinherited aristocracy. . . .

The frantic growth and rapid industrial expansion that filled America in [Theodore Roosevelt's] lifetime had heightened social tensions and left a legacy of bewilderment, anger, and fright, which had been suddenly precipitated by the depression of the nineties. His psychological function was to relieve these anxieties with a burst of hectic action and to discharge these fears by scolding authoritatively the demons that aroused them. Hardened and trained by a long fight with his own insecurity, he was the master therapist of the middle classes.[47]

But these were somewhat metaphorical and, in any case, well within the tradition. Only in the Jacksonian case did they seriously inform the interpretation.

He was still seeking some framework which, in a more ordered and systematic manner, would fuse political and intellectual history with cultural anthropology and social psychology. *The American Political Tradition* confirmed his rejection of Beard and Parrington. Nor did technical analysis of unit-ideas in what he called the "severe tradition" of A. O. Lovejoy meet his needs. Indeed, he clearly located his concern as less in abstract propositions themselves than in the circumstances of their acceptance; ideas were "far more interesting for their extraordinary appeal to various types of individuals than they were for their rational or philosophic content." His interest increasingly concentrated "in individual and social character types, in social mythologies and styles of thought as they reveal and affect character, and in politics as a sphere of behavior into which personal and private motives are projected."[48] By 1963 he defined his concern as "with widespread social attitudes, with political behavior, and with middle-brow and low-brow responses, only incidentally with articulate theories."[49]

As such language suggests, the writings of Karl Mannheim were playing a significant role in shaping Hofstadter's historical strategy. Hofstadter later testified that they "provided the link I had been seeking between ideas and social situations."[50] First of all, he welcomed the self-consciousness about intellectual processes required by the doctrine of the sociology of knowledge. "Skill in dealing with the human context of ideas," Hofstadter wrote in 1954,

is in large part a by-product of self-evaluation, in which alone the full personal urgency and the psychological dialectic of ideas can be felt. The highest pitch of understanding of the formation of ideas is not likely to emerge in a climate of opinion where intense self-examination has not yet begun.[51]

In addition, Mannheim's concept of styles of thought evidently supplied Hofstadter with a valuable integrating device—a means of defining clusters not just of ideas but of attitudes, values, and preconceptions and of identifying their function in social equilibrium and change. He amplified this approach by taking from the cultural anthropologists the idea of cultural configurations, of styles of life. From the social psychologists, he gained a more explicit sense of the significance for history of such notions as frustration and anxiety. He sought further illumination in Freud, whose influence on the historian, he thought, "though even more far-reaching, must of necessity be more indirect than that of a thinker like Mannheim."[52] In all of this, it is perhaps not too fanciful to suppose, he reflected the special preoccupations and opportunities of an historian living in so varied, intense, and contemporary a city as New York.

It is important to define Hofstadter's idea of the relationship between history and the social sciences with more precision. "The historian's contact with the social sciences," he wrote in 1956, "is clearly of more importance to the present generation of historians than it has been at any time in the past." He himself had found that "my interest and gratification in my own discipline have been enormously intensified by what I have been able to take for it from the other disciplines." None the less "that I am unable to systematize or formalize what it is that I owe, as a historian, to the social sciences I find puzzling." But, he concluded, the social sciences in a general way had suggested a new resolution to "the problems created by the duality of the historian's role," poised as he was between his function as a writer of narratives, in which capacity he must often retell old stories, and as an author of monographs, in which capacity he must add new, if often minute, information or analysis. The social sciences now offered the historian "a host of new insights and creative possibilities."[53]

It is clear that Hofstadter picked up a good deal more from the concepts than from the methods of the social sciences. He did not show much interest in what the social scientists call "empirical research"—to such an extent that one historian recently wrote of him a little disdainfully, "May I respectfully suggest that Professor Hofstadter—who has given us a host of brilliant *interpretive* works—may be somewhat out of contact with the new breed of younger historians, those who for the past ten years or so have been doing the grubby, tedious work of digging up data."[54] It was rather the substantive findings of the social sciences, "their intellectual concerns, and their professional perspectives . . . their ability to open up new problems which the historian has usually ignored"—it was these things which engaged him. The social sciences led him to a concern not with computers, sampling, content analysis, panel studies, and quantitative techniques but with social status, social stratification and mobility, generational differences, the sociology of knowledge and of the professions, the forms of mass culture, and other such theoretical issues. The social sciences, as Hofstadter used them, added not to the rigor and certitude of history but to its "speculative richness."[55]

The historian, Hofstadter insisted, could benefit greatly from the social sciences but was not himself a social scientist. The essential difference was that the historian had abandoned the scientific ideal which still inspired the social scientist. "I consider the search for absolutely universal principles, or rules, or terms," he wrote,

by which our knowledge of nature and our theories of society can be wrought into some kind of comprehensive interlocking unity, fruitless. To achieve the unity of knowledge is not merely a chimerical goal in itself but one which, if taken seriously, may impede the pursuit of that partial knowledge in which it is always possible for us to engage fruitfully.[56]

The historian regarded events as "essentially unique"; "he may not disparage science, but he despairs of it."[57]

Moreover, the historian had in the literary ideal a "powerful alternative" to the scientific ideal. Hofstadter would even argue, despite the dismal patois of social scientists, that the social sciences "should be able to help quicken history as a literary art" by offering a fresh store of ideas and better means for the understanding of character and behavior, and thereby "a fuller consummation of the mind and spirit of the historian." His interest in the social sciences, in short, did not diminish Hofstadter's own commitment to "the imaginative as well as the cognitive side" of the historian's work nor dilute his feeling of "how much history is indeed akin to literature."[58]

This was very much his practice as well as his principle. In his forays into the domain of the social sciences, Hofstadter always took care to civilize his captives and teach them English. He conceived the writing of history as a conscious literary act; and one of his triumphs was his own style—cool, graceful, ironic, subtle, adapted not so much to narrative in the grand manner as to controlled and fastidious analysis—a style derived not at all from social scientists and not even from other historians ("I don't think any historian has deeply influenced my own style," Hofstadter said in 1960) but as much as anything from literary criticism—from Edmund Wilson, from Lionel Trilling, from H. L. Mencken.[59]

Hofstadter's immersion in the social sciences became intense in the years after 1948. In an essay on "Manifest Destiny and the Philippines," published in 1952, he enlarged the idea, briefly sketched in

The American Political Tradition, of a "psychic crisis" in the 1890's. Earlier he had portrayed Theodore Roosevelt as the master therapist; now he analyzed the elements of the crisis itself. The depression which began in 1893 was, as he saw it, central in the background; and the effect of the depression was heightened by other events—the Populist agitation, raising the specter of drastic social convulsion; the spread of economic concentration, threatening the old order of competitive opportunity; the apparent filling up of the continent and the exhaustion of the frontier. "To many historically conscious writers, the nation seemed overripe, like an empire ready for collapse." The consequence, Hofstadter argued, was the rise of two new moods: on the one hand, the intensification of protest and social reform; on the other, the assertion of nationalism, expansion, jingoism. "The events of the nineties had brought frustration and anxiety to civically conscious Americans"; they had also created "a restless aggressiveness, a desire to be assured that the power and vitality of the nation were not waning." This, he felt, was especially the case among the underdog classes whose restlessness had been exacerbated by Bryan's defeat in 1896. It was this underlying psychological crisis, Hofstadter contended, which made it possible for the yellow press to whip up the war against Cuba.

I suspect that the readiness of the public to overreact to the Cuban situation can be understood in part through the displacement of feelings of sympathy or social protest generated in domestic affairs; these impulses found a safe and satisfactory discharge in foreign conflict.[60]

This inquiry had led him, Hofstadter conceded, "onto the high and dangerous ground of social psychology." Historians were inexpert psychologists; they could not get for this period the data which would verify their psychological hypotheses; "however, we have little other choice than to move into this terrain wherever simple rationalistic explanations of national behavior leave us dissatisfied."[61] The essay was an illuminating attempt to uncover the springs of expansionism and a bold demonstration, if literary rather than "scientific" in its mode, of the usefulness to historians of insights borrowed from the social sciences.

In 1954 a faculty seminar on political behavior at Columbia considered the phenomenon, then in its waning stages, of McCarthyism. Here Hofstadter, talking with a group of sociologists and social psychologists, further developed his cultural analysis. The seminar soon decided that conventional explanations of political behavior, especially in terms of the conflict of economic interests, did not go very far in dealing with McCarthyism; and the converging views of Hofstadter and the sociologist S. M. Lipset focused the group's attention on the conception of "status politics." Hofstadter and Lipset distinguished status politics from what the first called "interest politics" and the second "class politics." Status politics, as Hofstadter put it, expressed "the clash of various projective rationalizations arising from status aspirations and other personal motives," interest politics, "the clash of material aims and needs among various groups and blocs." Status politics flourished in prosperity; interest politics in depression. And, where interest politics advanced programs and panaceas, status politics fulfilled itself "in vindictiveness, in sour memories, in the search for scapegoats."[62]

The idea of status politics now gave Hofstadter's cultural analysis its basic pattern, providing a framework within which he could merge his interests in political and intellectual history. Status politics made room for the variety of noneconomic factors in political history—party habits and loyalties, ethnic and religious affiliations, moral and intellectual traditions, social aspirations and frustrations, and so on. It preserved political history, Hofstadter wrote, from "the excessive rationalism that infused the work of the two preceding generations of historians and political scientists" under the influence of such men as Beard, Turner, and Parrington. It enabled Hofstadter himself through the analysis of styles of thought to deal with "the symbolic aspects of politics" and thereby offset the concern of conventional historical discourse with political institutions and structure at the expense of the milieu in which political action took place.[63] It might be added that preoccupation with status was for America primarily an urban problem, and thus a natural category for a New York City historian. In any case, it became the organizing principle of his historical analysis.

In the years after 1954 Hofstadter somewhat modified and refined his conception of status politics. In the original formulation, for example, he relied considerably on the clinical work of T. W. Adorno and his associates in *The Authoritarian Personality*. Later he came to feel this emphasis on individual psychological explanation "excessive" and preferred to rest his case more on "purely behavioral and historical grounds."[64] As time went on, too, he gave more importance to the role of religious fundamentalism in shaping American habits of thought; indeed, by 1962 he was writing that those who would understand the right-wing mind "will do well to supplement their acquaintance with Rorschach techniques or the construction of the F-scale with a rereading of the Book of Revelations."[65] On occasion he even questioned the term "status politics" as "somewhat too specific" and wondered whether a more general term—"cultural politics" or "symbolic politics"—might not better suggest that there were noneconomic issues in addition to social status which fed the stream of American politics.[66] But, with whatever amendment, "the distinction . . . between status politics and interest politics," Hofstadter wrote in 1965, "seems to me to be of fundamental significance, and to have a general usability in understanding our political history that goes far beyond the issues of the 1950's which it was invoked to explain."[67]

Status politics, in short, provided him with a new perspective on American history. He used this principle in the next decade to discuss McCarthyism ("The Pseudo-Conservative Revolt," 1955); Populism, Progressivism, and the New Deal (*The Age of Reform*, 1955); anti-intellectualism (*Anti-intellectualism in American Life*, 1963); and Goldwaterism ("Goldwater and Pseudo-Conservative Politics," 1965). It may be most convenient, however, to consider his application of this perspective according to the chronological order of the events he has analyzed rather than that of the books he has published. The relationship between American society and the intellectual in the age of McCarthy had given him his first clue to the role of status anxiety; and he now resolved to pursue this relationship through the course of American history. *Anti-Intellectualism in American History* thus became a sort of sequel to *The American Political Tradition*. Hofstadter wandered once again through the tangled forests of the American past; but his new torch picked out quite different configurations in the surrounding darkness.

Anti-Intellectualism in American History is a great grab bag of a book, deeply personal, confusingly organized and sometimes obscurely argued, but overflowing with a breadth of knowledge, a subtlety of insight, and a richness of interpretation that make it a work of great vitality and distinction. The key to anti-intellectualism, in Hofstadter's view, lay in the continuing clash between "the elite upon which culture depended for its transmission" and "the vulgarization of culture which [democratic] society constantly produces." Anti-intellectualism, in other words, was "founded in the democratic institutions and the egalitarian sentiments of this country." Its primary sources were the movements which succeeded in dethroning the patrician elite: the fundamentalism of the evangelical churches; the egalitarian or, as he often prefers to call it, "populistic" character of politics; the practical obsessions of a commercial and technological culture; and the philistinism of a school system committed to mass education under "progressive" doctrine. As a consequence of the debasement of the elite by democracy, "throughout most of our political history, the intellectual has been for the most part either an outsider, a servant, or a scapegoat."[68]

Hofstadter conceded in passing that the elite itself has on occasion contributed to its own discomfiture,[69] but he did not permit this point to distract him from his central thesis. While one can understand his desire to expose the sentimental progressive view of the "people" as faithful guardians of all virtue, there is, one thinks, a good deal more than Hofstadter's book admits to Hawthorne's contention that "the influential classes, and those who take upon themselves to be leaders of the people, are fully liable to all the passionate error that has ever characterized the maddest mob." Status politics would admit this, however, only in the cases of threatened or dispossessed elites, and in *Anti-intellectualism* Hofstadter clearly arraigned democratic forces as the abiding enemies of the free and cultivated mind.

This view placed Jacksonian democracy, for example, in somewhat different light from the entrepreneurial illumination offered in *The American Political Tradition* fifteen years earlier. Jacksonian America no longer appeared a society unified by a common lust for the acquisitive scramble. The Meyers amendment, which portrayed the Jacksonians as politicians of nostalgia, fell too. In *Anti-intellectualism* the age of Jackson was seen in terms which would have appealed to William Graham Sumner (and, indeed, to John Quincy Adams) as the era of "the decline of the gentleman" before the ignorant and vengeful self-assertion of the rabble. "The first truly powerful and widespread impulse to anti-intellectualism in American politics," Hofstadter wrote, was, in fact, given by the Jacksonian movement. Its distrust of expertise, its dislike for centralization, its desire to uproot the entrenched classes, and its doctrine that important functions were simple enough to be performed by anyone, amounted to a repudiation not only of the system of government by gentlemen which the nation had inherited from the eighteenth century, but also of the special value of the educated classes in civic life. . . . The estrangement of training and intellect from the power to decide and to manage had been completed.[70]

One sees in a broad way what Hofstadter meant. Yet it would seem hard, for example, to convict the first President who used a brain trust of a distrust of experts; or, for that matter, to convict the man who vastly enlarged presidential authority of a dislike for centralization. Or, to take another example, Hofstadter cited as an instance of Jacksonian anti-intellectualism Davy Crockett's opposition to a bill authorizing the federal government to transfer to Tennessee some public lands as an endowment for education; yet the bill had been introduced by James K. Polk, a loyal Jacksonian, and Crockett, of course, ended up as a violent anti-Jacksonian and a Whig. Hofstadter conceded that many intellectuals and writers supported the Jacksonians and were rewarded by them; and to say that "the record of Jacksonian democracy in achieving a *rapprochement* between the intellectual or man of letters and the popular mind was inferior to that later achieved by Progressivism and the New Deal,"[71] while this may be true, hardly justified the proposition that the Jacksonian movement created anti-intellectualism in American politics.

Anti-intellectualism conveyed Hofstadter's growing sense of the fatal ambiguity of democratic reform; the mistrust of the intellect had become "a broadly diffused quality in our culture," he concluded, ". . . because it has often been linked to good, or at least defensible, causes."[72] This point applied not only to Jacksonianism but equally to Populism, which he described as "a larger trend of thought stemming from the time of Andrew Jackson" and expressing "the discontent of a great many farmers and businessmen with the economic changes of the late nineteenth century," to be best understood "not as a product of the frontier inheritance, but as another episode in the well-established tradition of American entrepreneurial radicalism." Nor did this trend of thought stop in the 1890's. As he added in the introduction to *The Age of Reform,* "Populist thinking has survived in our own time, partly as an undercurrent of provincial resentments, popular and 'democratic' rebelliousness and suspiciousness, and nativism."[73]

Since Hofstadter's interpretation of Populism has provoked such lively discussion, it is important to understand precisely what he wrote. He began with an expert account in terms of interest politics of the circumstances leading to the agrarian revolt of the nineties. He showed how prices had steadily fallen in the world agricultural market during the two decades after the early 1870's. He showed how each of the three centers of Populism in the United States was dominated "by a product whose price had catastrophically declined" —cotton, wheat, silver—and how "the American staple-growing regions showing the highest discontent" were committed to "the products most dependent upon exports."[74] Having solidly established the material grievances which lay behind Populism, he then had favorable things to say about the proposed Populist remedies. "Populism," he wrote,

was the first modern political movement of practical importance in the United States to insist that the federal government has some responsibility for the common weal; indeed, it was the first such movement to attack seriously the problems created by industrialism. . . .

Most of the "radical" reforms in the Populist program proved in later years to be either harmless or useful. . . . It was in their concrete programs that they added most constructively to our political life.

The Populist movement, despite its defeat, activated a stream of agrarian organization and protest that subsequently carried point after point. . . . While it reasserted for the last time some old ways of thought, it was also a harbinger of the new.

The Progressives did not, as a rule, have the daring or the originative force of the Populists of the 1890's, and . . . a great deal of Progressive political effort was spent enacting proposals that the Populists had outlined fifteen or even twenty years earlier.[75]

All this was essentially what historians had been saying for a generation about the origin and impact of Populism. But on balance these passages in *The Age of Reform* were rather like the eulogy of the bourgeoisie in the *Communist Manifesto*; they were there all right, but they were somehow outweighed by the rest. For, having begun this astute analysis of Populism in terms of interest politics, Hofstadter suddenly shifted over to status politics as the basis for his larger interpretation. "Rank in society! That was close to the heart of the matter, for the farmer was beginning to realize acutely not merely that the best of the world's goods were to be had in the cities . . . but also that he was losing in status and respect."[76] In this way—or so at least it seemed to many readers—the economic motives behind Populism were suddenly swallowed up by the psychological; the world of economic reality gave way to a world of mental fantasy. The resulting portrait was very different from the idea of a rather practical, forward-looking movement responding to real problems; it was even different from the idea of a new manifestation of entrepreneurial radicalism.

Hofstadter appeared to suggest that the "reality" of Populism lay not in its program but in its rhetoric; in, moreover, precisely that side of its rhetoric which expressed the politics of nostalgia and con-spiracy. "The utopia of the Populists was in the past, not the future." They "looked backward with longing to the lost agrarian Eden." They wanted to "restore the conditions prevailing before the development of industrialism and the commercialization of agriculture."[77] Locked into a world of chimeras, they saw plots everywhere, pursued scapegoats, especially Jews and foreigners, and were a retrogressive force in American life. The longer Populism lasted, moreover, the worse it became. In our day the Populist tradition "has turned sour, become illiberal and ill-tempered." The process of "deconversion from reform to reaction" presumably led straight to McCarthyism.[78]

This view of Populism found considerable resonance in the 1950's. Edward A. Shils expounded it with skill and authority the next year in *The Torment of Secrecy*; other influential writers—Daniel Bell, Peter Viereck, David Riesman, Will Herberg, Talcott Parsons— offered variations on the theme. It quickly passed into fashionable lay discourse, where it still intermittently flickers. Within the historical profession, however, it soon fell under attack—by C. Vann Woodward in a measured 1959 article "The Populist Heritage and the Intellectual"; by Norman Pollack in two useful books and a number of unduly polemical and *ad hominem* articles; by W. T. K. Nugent in a monograph of 1963; and by M. P. Rogin in a study of 1967.[79]

The criticisms varied in tone and relevance. But, in general, they argued that the Populists, far from rejecting industrial society, accepted it and were, indeed, in advance of many of their Eastern contemporaries in their perception of social, economic, and even financial problems; that the Populist program aimed not at a rural utopia but at a mixed economy; that, as for status politics, "The Populist may have been bitten by status anxieties, but if so, they were certainly not bred of upward social mobility, and probably few by downward mobility either—for the simple reason that there was not much further downward for most Populists to go. . . . Whatever concern the farmers might have had for their status was overwhelmed by desperate and immediate economic anxieties" (Woodward);[80] that they were no more liable to conspiratorial theories of history or to anti-Semitism than nonagrarian groups in the America of their time; that, far from being racists, Southern Populists opposed racism and defended the political rights of the Negro.

Many of these points were sustained, or at least persuasively documented, in monographic research; and my impression is that the counterrevisionists went far to rescue Populism from extreme anti-Populist interpretations. On the other hand, the Hofstadter view certainly discouraged whatever tendency there may have been to regard the Populists as splendidly reasonable and far-sighted reformers. On this point Woodward well summed up the present state of professional reaction:

It is undoubtedly true that liberal intellectuals have in the past constructed a flattering image of Populism. They have permitted their sympathy with oppressed groups to blind them to the delusions, myths, and foibles of the people with whom they sympathized. Sharing certain political and economic doctrines and certain indignations with the Populists, they have attributed to them other values, tastes, principles, and morals which the Populists did not actually share. It was understandably distasteful to dwell upon the irrational or retrograde traits of people who deserved one's sympathy and shared some of one's views.[81]

Thus Hofstadter's partial assimilation of Populism to the "paranoid style" in American politics will probably stick, though his critics will successfully insist that Populism existed more in the realm of interest politics than of status politics and that it represented an attempt more to solve problems of the economy than problems of the bruised psyche.

His attempt to apply the status interpretation to Populism showed how deeply this insight had captured Hofstadter's imagination. For he himself had previously argued that, "during depressions, the dominant motif in dissent . . . tends to be highly programmatic . . . future-oriented and forward looking"; it was "in prosperity . . . when status politics becomes relatively more important" and the tendency prevailed "to embody discontent not so much in legislative proposals as in grousing."[82] By Hofstadter's own criteria, in short, Populism should have been a movement for interest analysis, and the Progressive movement, arising in good times, would offer a surer test of the validity of the status thesis.

The account of Progressivism constituted the second part of *The Age of Reform*. Hofstadter's thesis was that the Progressive leaders became Progressives

not because of economic deprivations but primarily because they were victims of an upheaval in status. . . . Progressivism, in short, was to a very considerable extent led by men who suffered from the events of their time not through a shrinkage in their means but through the changed pattern in the distribution of deference and power. . . . They were expropriated, not so much economically as morally.[83]

Progressivism, like Populism, thus became, if not quite so completely, an exercise in nostalgia—"a brave attempt to recapture that bright past in which there had been a future." The "general theme" of Progressivism "was the effort to restore a type of economic individualism and political democracy that was widely believed to have existed earlier in America." Like the Populists, the Progressives tried "to hold on to some of the values of agrarian life, to save personal entrepreneurship and individual opportunity and the character type they engendered, and to maintain a homogeneous Yankee civilization." The Progressives too dreamed the Jeffersonian dream.

Progressivism, at its heart, was an effort to realize familiar and traditional ideals under novel circumstances. . . . The ideas of this Progressive tradition, as one might expect, were founded not merely upon acceptance but even upon glorification of the competitive order. The Jeffersonians, the Jacksonians, and after them most of the Progressives . . . preferred to keep the positive functions of government minimal, and, where these were necessary, to keep them on the state rather than put them on the national level.

The Progressives were consequently characterized by a "persistent individualism." Their "central fear was fear of power."[84]

Hofstadter's elaboration of this theme was a very remarkable piece of historical writing. Unfolding his argument in a series of brilliant analytical vignettes—on, for example, such subjects as the alienation of the professionals, the decline of the clergy, the rise of the professors, the shift from Mugwumpery to Progressivism, the Progressive idea of reality, the Progressive conception of the economy as a means of building individual character, the difference in political ethos between Yankees and immigrants—he showed superbly how insights derived from the social sciences and from literary criticism could illuminate without interrupting a historical narrative. In general, the concept of status revolution appeared to work a good deal better with the Progressives than with the Populists.

Still, Hofstadter's interpretation of Progressivism raised problems and provoked criticism. Some criticism was directed at the terms of the status interpretation. Thus R. B. Sherman, comparing the leaders of the Progressive party of Massachusetts with those of the Republican party, found that they had "essentially similar class characteristics"; they all tended to be Anglo-Saxon, Protestant, college-educated, urban, native-born, well-off, and so on; indeed, "the Massachusetts Progressive leadership was actually less well educated than the Republican, and its ethnic composition was more diverse." Even the leadership of the Massachusetts Democratic party was "remarkably well-placed in many ways." In short, the characteristics which Hofstadter, George Mowry, and A. D. Chandler, Jr., had ascribed peculiarly to the status-displaced Progressives were, in Massachusetts at least, typical of nearly all the political leadership. "If there was a status revolution," Sherman asked, "how do we explain the difference in reaction to it?" In Massachusetts certainly "status was not an independent variable."[85]

Where Sherman questioned the notion of a deep difference in social origin between Progressives and others, J. J. Huthmacher questioned the notion of a deep difference in political ethos between Progressives and immigrants. "If this were the case," he asked, "how does one explain the drive and success of Progressive Era reform movements in places like New York and Massachusetts?" In the New York and Massachusetts legislatures, he pointed out, Progressive measures "received more uniform and consistent support from representatives of the urban lower class than they received from urban middle-class or rural representatives." Indeed, Huthmacher contended, the very character of their political ethos predisposed the immigrants to accept and applaud paternalistic government. The real difference lay in the interest of urban middle-class Progressives in "cultural" reforms like prohibition and immigration restriction.[86]

Other criticism suggested that, if interest politics exaggerated the role of issues in political life, status politics, by understating the role of issues, ended in reductionism and misunderstanding. Thus Hofstadter's own preoccupation with psychology at the expense of ideology led him to ignore, or to dismiss as cryptoconservatism, that strain of Progressivism represented by such men as Theodore Roosevelt, Herbert Croly, Charles A. Beard, and Walter Lippmann. It can hardly be said of Roosevelt, for example, that his "central fear was fear of power," that he preferred to keep the positive role of government minimal and on the state rather than the federal level, or that his purpose was to recapture a bright Jeffersonian past. To portray Progressivism as part of the politics of nostalgia, Hofstadter had to construe Progressivism as meaning LaFollette, Wilson, and Brandeis and gloss over that powerful and original side of Progressive thought which insisted on the inevitability of economic concentration, the need for national control, and the obsolescence of Jeffersonianism— the side which believed not in drift but in mastery.

Where Hofstadter minimized the significance of this ideological split, John Braeman, for example, argued that "this division within the progressive ranks" was "a fundamental one." Similarly A. M. Scott suggested that the Progressives were agitating not just because of frustrations produced by the decline in deference and power but because "they were genuinely troubled by such problems as child labor, exploitation of women and children in industry, the absence of security for old-age and illness, sanitation in the food industry, and municipal corruption."[87] If these things were so, might it not be that the Progressive era had to be interpreted in terms of interest politics as well as of status politics?

This view was urged both by those, like Scott, who considered the Progressive era genuinely progressive, and those, like Gabriel Kolko, who considered it essentially conservative. Where one school argued that Progressivism was a serious and honorable attempt to humanize an emerging industrial society, the other saw Progressivism, in Kolko's words, as the manipulation of the national government by business "to attain conditions of stability, predictability, and security

—to attain rationalization—in the economy";[88] but both agreed in seeing the Progressives as concerned less with their own status than with social reality Oddly enough Hofstadter himself in his 1963 introduction to a series of readings on *The Progressive Movement, 1900–1915* discussed Progressivism less in terms of the status revolution than as an exercise in interest politics. The Progressive movement, he then said, "may be looked upon as an attempt to develop the moral will, the intellectual insight and the political and administrative agencies to remedy the accumulated evils and negligences of a period of industrial growth."[89] This suggests his own later judgment that the status interpretation, while offering valuable and fascinating sidelights on Progressivism, might be a supplement to rather than a substitute for interpretation in terms of the problems and issues themselves.

The Age of Reform concluded with a discussion of the New Deal. Hofstadter had long perceived the New Deal as representing the great discontinuity in the history of American reform—"a drastic new departure . . . different from anything that had yet happened in the United States." It differed, first of all, in its problems; alone among American reform movements it had to meet the problems of economic collapse. It differed in its constituencies and its objectives: it was concerned less with restoring opportunity to old-American entrepreneurs than with offering security to urban workers and ethnic minorities; the later New Deal had "a social-democratic tinge that had never before been present in American reform movements." And it differed sharply from the Progressive era in its intellectual temper and moral tone. As against the traditional moral indignation of American reform, the New Deal was skeptical of moralism as of ideology; its "relentless emphasis" was upon results; Hofstadter called it "the new opportunism."[90]

The New Deal thus rejected the politics of nostalgia. For the first time, he said in his introduction to the revised edition of *Social Darwinism*, "the 'liberal' or 'progressive' side in American politics was also the side that was wholeheartedly identified with social and economic innovation and experiment."[91] Franklin Roosevelt, he had already written in *The American Political Tradition*, stood out among all American statesmen since Hamilton "for his sense of the failure of tradition, his recognition of the need for novelty and daring." Alas, his striking capacity for "innovation in practical measures" was not accompanied by a comparable capacity for "innovation in ideas." Consequently he provided "no clearly articulated break with the inherited faith," employing "dynamic personal leadership" as a substitute for "a coherent and plausible body of belief."[92]

It is possible to contend—as A. M. Scott and others have contended—that Hofstadter exaggerated the differences between the New Deal and earlier reform movements. If, for example, instead of equating Progressivism with the New Freedom, he had given more weight to the program and philosophy of the New Nationalism, then the big-government, welfare-state aspects of the New Deal would hardly have come to his reader with great impact of novelty. Nor, for that matter, did the New Deal lack those who looked back to a golden age of competitive opportunity. In many respects, the New Deal recapitulated the old debate between Roosevelt and Wilson, Croly, and Brandeis. Indeed, Roosevelt's antimonopoly message of 1938—which Hofstadter had called in 1948 "one of the most remarkable economic documents that have ever come from the White House"[93]—could be considered a reversion from twentieth-century realism (at least as viewed by J. K. Galbraith, A. A. Berle, Jr., the later David Lilienthal, and other New Dealers) to Jeffersonian nostalgia. Without accepting Scott's judgment—that "the Progressive Era was more original than the New Deal and more daring as well"[94]—many historians today would feel that Hofstadter overdid the case for a "drastic" difference between the two reform movements.

But what is more relevant to a discussion of Hofstadter as a historian—and what made it possible for the difference to seem drastic indeed in the pages of *The Age of Reform*—was his failure to apply the status interpretation to the New Deal. For the New Deal, too, was preceded by a status revolution.[95] Many leading New Dealers were from the same social classes and presumably from the same psychological predicaments which produced Progressivism—by-passed patricians, declining professional men, rising academics and intellectuals, and so on. Yet a persevering effort to place the New Deal in the perspective of status politics would inevitably have drained its issues of their sharpness and thereby have weakened the case for its break with tradition. The discontinuity proclaimed in *The Age of Reform* perhaps resulted from the shift in Hofstadter's historical approach as much as from the shift in problems and constituencies created by economic crisis and social change.

There remains the question of McCarthyism—the problem which provoked Hofstadter's first experiments in the status interpretation. McCarthy's pseudo conservatism, Hofstadter suggested, was "in good part a product of the rootlessness and heterogeneity of American life, and above all, of its peculiar scramble for status and its peculiar search for secure identity." Social, geographical, and occupational mobilities combined to give "personal status problems . . . an unusual intensity." McCarthyism became for people of a certain psychological predisposition the means by which they could assert their Americanness and protect or improve their social status. "A populistic culture like ours, which seems to lack a responsible elite with political and moral autonomy" became, in Hofstadter's view, peculiarly vulnerable to McCarthyite movements.[96]

The most striking thing about this explanation was that it should have come from a historian, for it so largely lacked the historical dimension. Presumably status tensions did not suddenly become unbearably acute in the years 1950–53. If status tensions were always with us, why then the explosion of McCarthyism at this particular time? The natural historical answer would be to suggest the Korean War as the detonating factor. Surely it was the frustrations generated by Korea which transformed McCarthy's anti-Communist crusade from an eccentric sideshow, like that carried on by Martin Dies in the thirties, into a dangerous popular movement. When Communists were killing American boys in Korea, people began to wonder why suspected Communists should be given the benefit of doubt in the United States. Yet Hofstadter did not mention the Korean War (indeed, Korea went almost unmentioned throughout *The New American Right*; Lipset actually wrote, "On the national scene, McCarthy's attacks are probably more important in terms of their appeal to status frustrations than to resentful isolationism)."[97] Replying to this criticism in 1962, Hofstadter argued that it was based on "a fundamental misconception of what these essays were trying to do"; they were trying to account not for McCarthyism but for "the whole complex of forces that underlay the responses of the public to the frustrations of the 1950s."[98] If this were the case, it was left lamentably unclear in the original publication.

The New American Right, in addition to launching the general concept of status politics, expounded a particular theory of the origins of McCarthyism. McCarthyism, it was suggested, had its roots in the agrarian radicalism of the late nineteenth century. Like Populism, McCarthyism challenged the established political and intellectual elites; it espoused a conspiratorial view of history; it encouraged nativism, xenophobia, and anti-Semitism; it stood for mass plebiscitarian democracy against the carefully wrought representative institutions of a free society. Peter Viereck, who gave this case its most explicit statement, wrote:

What all these groups are at heart is the same old isolationist, Anglophobe, Germanophile revolt of radical Populist lunatic-fringers against the eastern, educated, Anglicized elite. Only this time it is a Populism gone sour. . . . What figure represents the transition, the missing link, between the often noble, idealistic Populist-Progressives . . . and the degeneration of that movement into something so different, so bigoted as McCarthy. . . . That missing link is Father Charles Coughlin.[99]

This interpretation of McCarthyism received close examination in 1967 by M. P. Rogin in his trenchant book *The Intellectuals and McCarthy: The Radical Specter*. With effective use of voting statistics, Rogin was able to show that McCarthyism grew not out of radical but out of conservative rural politics. McCarthy's popular following, Rogin contended, came not from " 'mass,' 'populist,' or 'status' concerns" but from the "traditional right wing of the midwestern Republican Party" and from "those citizens mobilized because of communism and the Korean War."[100] Moreover, he suggested, McCarthy operated within, not beyond, the conventional boundaries of American politics.

Having mortally damaged the notion of McCarthyism as a latter-day Populism, Rogin raised searching questions about the status approach in general. He noted, for example, that it had been generally used only against reform politics. "How," he asked, "does conservative ideology fare by the standards applied to Populist thought?" If this were done, he continued, it would be "possible to argue that the Populist movement was less anti-Semitic than late-nineteenth century America as a whole." Moral indignation, he suggested, was "not a peculiar feature of pre–New Deal reform movements but rather an essential element both of American politics in general and traditional conservatism in particular."[101] Moreover, status analysis was at least a two-edged weapon; it could be used, for example, to explain opposition to agrarian radicalism as easily as support for it. Indeed, to treat mass movements in status terms "was to make them a priori irrational. When they are viewed as responses to social crises, a different picture emerges." The status interpretation underestimated the role of issues and "the extent to which ideological commitments and the requirements of political alliance amalgamate discrete interests and discrete groups. Positions on political issues decisively influence who will ally with whom. In the real political world alternatives are structured; some issues are tied to others."[102]

The defenders of the status interpretation have not yet subjected Rogin to the same sort of analysis to which he subjected them; and there is no reason to suppose that the question is settled. Yet the Rogin attack may well have helped crystallize accumulating doubts about the usability of the status concept. For, on close examination, the status approach appeared to adapt itself to every situation. Hofstadter, with characteristic candor, noted this fact without drawing the methodological consequences.

Modern students of social psychology have suggested that certain social-psychological tensions are heightened both in social groups that are rising in the social scale and those that are falling. . . .

[The Progressive political public] was recruited in large measure from people who had either risen upwards or moved sideways in the social scale. . . .

Persons moving downward, and even upward under many circumstances, in the social scale tend to show greater prejudice.[103]

In a mobile society, then, who was not a member of the status revolution? People moving up the social ladder, people moving down, people moving sideways and people staying in the same place—all evidently suffered from status anxiety. In the same way old Yankees had status anxiety because their position was threatened, and new immigrants had it because their position was insecure. Protestants were anxious, and so were Catholics, and so were Jews; and so were the old, and so were the young. Every view everyone held, no matter how incompatible particular views might have been, could be traced to origins in some form of status insecurity.

But a theory that explains a reaction and its opposite with equal facility does not greatly help in making clear why individuals choose one rather than the other. As Schumpeter has observed, "*All* functions that can be distinguished in the case of a given people and in a given historical situation are 'socially necessary.' This criterion, alone, therefore, cannot decide their relative evaluation."[104] The status interpretation verges on becoming a heads-I-win-tails-you-lose proposition. It begins by explaining too much and ends by explaining all too little. It offers the historian marginal illumination, but it does not really work as the backbone of historical analysis.[105] As Dorothy Parker says, there is perhaps less there than meets the eye.

While it was true that Hofstadter pronounced the status interpretation "of fundamental significance" in understanding American political history, it would be wholly wrong—and wholly against the grain of his approach to historical problems—to suppose that he became a crusader on its behalf. "If the essays in *The Radical Right* dwelled on status resentment," he wrote in 1965, "it was not because the authors thought they had found a final, single explanation . . . but because we had come upon a hitherto neglected and unexplained side of the movement."[106] Hofstadter's cast of mind, it has been noted, was almost more historiographical than historical. Where most historians tried to grapple directly with the facts and to arrange them into some solid and unassailable pattern, Hofstadter, the sociologist of knowledge, saw the past, not face to face, but darkly, through receding glasses of interpretation. His emphasis on the status interpretation thus appears to have sprung in part from his perennial desire to restore the historiographic balance.

But this desire was intimately associated with his continuing sense of contemporary involvement. Knowledge of the past was explicitly for him (as it is implicitly for everyone) a backward extension of the consciousness of the present. "I still write history," he said in 1960, "out of my engagement with the present"; and he went on to quote Mannheim: "that our social thinking is determined by our social position is not necessarily a source of error. On the contrary, it is often the path to political insight." So Hofstadter had written in *The Age of Reform*: "my own interest has been drawn to that side of Populism and Progressivism—particularly of Populism—which seems very strongly to foreshadow some aspects of the cranky pseudo-conservatism of our time." What counted for him was "that the sense of engagement with current issues is used legitimately to re-understand the past. I know there are traps. That is one reason I try to avoid a dogmatic stand in my work."[107]

His motive in *The Age of Reform*, for example, would seem to have been not only to illuminate conservatism but to admonish liberalism—above all, to discourage liberal intellectuals from any tendency to idealize and sentimentalize the masses. Liberals, Hofstadter commented,

> periodically exaggerate the measure of agreement that exists between movements of popular reform and the considered principles of political liberalism. They remake the image of popular rebellion closer to their heart's desire. They choose to ignore not only the elements of illiberalism that frequently seem to be an indissoluble part of popular movements but also the very complexity of the historical process itself.[108]

This stress on the ambiguity of democratic reform expresses Hofstadter's own growing sense of the complexity of historical movements—or perhaps it was the flowering of the natural conservatism which Alfred Kazin detected thirty years ago. In *The American Political Tradition* he was still critical of Franklin Roosevelt for his dependence on personal arrangements and improvisation rather than centralization and planning; but a dozen years later he observed that his opinion of F.D.R. had gone up "as my understanding of what can and cannot be done in the political processes has increased. I have more respect now for the 'broker function' of the politician that FDR represents so well."[109] His defense of "the political intelligence" in *Anti-intellectualism* is revealing:

> It accepts conflict as a central and enduring reality and understands human society as a form of equipoise based upon the continuing process of compromise. It shuns ultimate showdowns and looks upon the ideal of total partisan victory as unattainable, as merely another variety of threat to the kind of balance with which it is familiar. It is sensitive to nuances and sees things in degrees. It is essentially relativist and skeptical, but at the same time circumspect and humane. . . . Whereas the distinctively political intelligence begins with the political world, and attempts to make an assessment of how far a given set of goals can in fact be realized in the face of a certain balance of opposing forces, the secularized fundamentalist mind begins with a definition of that which is absolutely right, and looks upon politics as an arena in which that right must be realized.[110]

With this view of politics, Hofstadter rejected the notion—prevalent in some American intellectual circles in the 1960's—that "an intellectual is one 'whose most essential job rests on resistance to his society.'" To this Hofstadter replied that the job of the intellectual was the disinterested pursuit of truth and then asked, "By what authority do we then decide in advance that the intellectual is always more right when he arrives at a judgment hostile to his society than when he finds he can approve of it?" A "commitment to hostility," Hofstadter suggested, could be just as distorting as any other a priori commitment. To suppose that the intellectual life became impossible "where there is a taint of concern with practice or with power would be to deny the significance of a large part of our heritage of political and social speculation." He sharply questioned the modish "fetishism of alienation": "to identify the maximum degree of alienation with the optimum exercise of intellect, and to prescribe it as a kind of moral obligation for intellectuals, is in effect to prescribe a single intellectual style for the entire community of thinkers." For himself, he preferred a plurality of intellectual styles, arguing that the intellectual community should have within it

types of minds capable of mediating between the world of power and the world of criticism. . . . It would be tragic if all intellectuals aimed to serve power; but it would be equally tragic if all intellectuals who become associated with power were driven to believe they no longer had any connection with the intellectual community: their conclusion would almost inevitably be that their responsibilities are to power alone.[111]

His intense self-awareness, his conviction of the relativity of historical judgment, accounted for what Hofstadter himself described as "a certain tentativeness" in his work. "People take you in absolutely dead earnest," he has complained, "as though the ideas you advance are your final thoughts on the subject."[112] His work was marked by an unceasing process of revision and reformulation, after publication as well as before. "I hope," he wrote in *The Age of Reform*, "that my observations will be taken as a prelude and a spur to further studies . . . not as an attempt to render a final judgment."[113] He was not given to final judgments. What he wrote of *Anti-intellectualism in American Life* was more or less true of all his books since *Social Darwinism* (and may be why he declined to describe himself as "a thoroughly professional historian")—that it was "by no means a formal history but largely a personal book" developed in a manner "that is by choice rather impulsive and by necessity only fragmentary."[114]

This "tentativeness" was obviously one of Hofstadter's strengths. It kept his mind constantly open to the possibility of new perspective and fresh insight. It enabled him to absorb relevant perceptions from literary criticism and social science into his historical method. It preserved his receptivity to the preoccupations and anxieties of the younger generation. These qualities by themselves might have led only to an amiable ecumenicism. But in Hofstadter's case they were controlled by his own lucid sense of identity—his knowledge that, for better or worse, some things interested him more than others and that, for better or worse, he could do some things better than he could do others.

The other factor which could never be underestimated in his work was his belief that history is a part of literature and therefore should be as much a conscious art as fiction or poetry. In the long run, as the social milieu changes, historians will move on to new insights and new patterns of interpretation: one feels that this would not surprise or disappoint Hofstadter. The permanence of his own historical writing will rest rather in the grace, subtlety, and elegance of his literary style. He has, in particular, shown that it is possible to use the techniques of literary criticism and social science without succumbing to their vocabularies; he has shown that it is possible to fuse traditional historical narrative and modern cultural analysis in a single homogeneous text. He has, in short, helped solve for the historian the difficult problems of artistic technique and organization created by the increasing relevance of social science and literary criticism to historical method. His artistic achievement will survive when his own substantive contributions may be transformed or superseded.

David M. Potter

SIR DENIS BROGAN

11)

In 1942 there was published an expanded Yale thesis by a young doctor of philosophy, David M. Potter, under the title *Lincoln and His Party in the Secession Crisis*. At once this was seen as a very remarkable performance, although remarkable and original Ph.D. theses are a good deal commoner in the United States than they are in Britain. To one reviewer, myself, the excellence of this dissertation recalled what is perhaps the most remarkable Ph.D. dissertation in modern American historiography, Arthur M. Schlesinger, Sr.'s, *Colonial Merchants and the American Revolution*. Formally, young Dr. Potter's thesis was not as original as young Dr. Schlesinger's. It may well have seemed that the Civil War and its origins and the role of Lincoln before and during the war had been written almost to death. Since then a great deal of valuable scholarship has been devoted to reconsidering the numerous problems that the war raises. We have had the opening of the Lincoln papers. We have had R. P. Basler's edition of Lincoln's *Works*. We have had admirable sociological and historical books on the "peculiar institution." We have had some new and valuable biographies of leading figures like Charles Sumner, Charles Francis Adams, and Edwin M. Stanton, all of them people closely connected with Lincoln in the period covered by Potter's dissertation. But the fact that the dissertation has been continually reprinted and was issued in 1962 in a new paperback edition with an important revisionary preface shows that the impression made by Potter's first work was durable.

In the period between the publication of *Lincoln and His Party* and the writing of a detailed work on the origins of the Civil War or, more strictly speaking, on the political history of that period in American history out of which the Civil War emerged, Professor Potter published a set of original essays under the title *People of Plenty: Economic Abundance and the American Character* (1954). He had also contributed essays, papers, and review articles to a variety of journals. Most of them were on problems arising out of the most disputed question in American historiography, the origin and character of the Civil War.

It must not be thought, however, that Potter has cast himself in the role of Civil War historian, still less in the role of Southern historian. He *is*, in the ordinary sense of the word, a Southerner; but to Georgia, Mississippi, and Texas, he added experience in Yale, Oxford, and now Stanford. He is an *American* historian who has concentrated mainly on the problems of the middle period of American nineteenth-century history, and that of course involves concentration, but not an exclusive concentration, on the history of "the South." But many of his essays and, above all, *People of Plenty* provide a much wider conspectus of American history than even his first impressive work and the equally impressive work in progress which has not yet been published.[1]

People of Plenty shows how deeply Potter has reflected on the problems of American history, on the character of American society, and on the problems presented by the alliance or shotgun marriage between history and the new "social sciences." He has also written not only on the bibliography of the historiography of the war, but on historical method in general, and he has shown both in *People of Plenty* and in some of his articles a mastery of the modern literature on historiography and of the relevant disciplines of sociology, economics, and anthropology. He is in no way swamped by this knowledge. No American historian better deserves the compliment that Tennyson paid to Lushington, the great Greek scholar, on "his load of learning lightly borne." Indeed, the lightness with which Potter bears his load of learning may deceive some orthodox readers who expect great themes to be treated in a solemn, pontifical, almost parsonical way. For Professor Potter as a literary artist—and he is a literary artist—cultivates, to more than a British degree, the art of understatement. At the end of *People of Plenty* he, in a sense, turns the tables on the sociologists and anthropologists; but he does it so deftly that some of them will not feel the wound or realize that many of their simplicist theories of American social practice are quietly bleeding to death.

Thus, in the course of an apparently neutral and, if one likes, rather narrow and technical discussion of the historical development of Eastern-Southern freight relationships,[2] he advances a definition of the South. This definition does not draw upon the excessively romantic or Southern "patriot" view:

> In the matter of railway rates, then, as in almost no other regional matters, the sectional tendency took a tangible institutional form. Since Appomattox "the South" has had no boundaries, no capital, no political authority. But the Southern Classification Bureau and the Southern Freight Association have more tangible boundaries than the Confederacy ever achieved.

Equally successfully, he dismisses one of the great American historical legends when he writes, "In fact the status of the frontiersman as an independent thinker is questionable indeed."[3] He attacks some of the most sacred cows of the American legend when he writes in his lecture on "American Women and the American Character" (p. 6),

> As symbol, the typewriter evokes fewer emotions than the plow, but like the plow, it played a vital part in the fulfillment of the American promise of opportunity and independence.

He attacks some deep psychological theorizing when he insists that "what woman envies still is not male maleness but that men can have the best of both worlds socially and economically and so sexually."[4]

These gibes at the American traditional wisdom would not escape notice; but the deliberately *sotto voce* way in which Potter approaches historical questions may deceive the reader accustomed to rhetoric and to ostentatious moral judgment. Of course, there are few American historians today (apart from one or two in the South) who fall back on eloquence in the manner of George Bancroft, and even a most successful rhetorical historian (whose work is of great value apart from his style), Bruce Catton, has been castigated for his style in his recent volumes. But few historians have so carefully avoided the usual rhetorical tricks or powerful verbal appeals as has Potter. The beautifully organized style that Potter uses is, itself, a rhetorical trick of great effectiveness, however. In some ways it resembles the almost

Benthamite prose of Richard Hildreth—prose which is so superior, it seems to me, to the style of his more famous contemporary, Bancroft. But, again, to warn against misunderstanding, no historian is more conscious than Potter of the fact that the neutral history of certain academic aspirations is neither possible nor desirable. It is impossible, with all the will in the world, to escape "evaluative criteria" of what is beneficial for society. Potter clearly believes that those evaluative criteria involve deciding for the historian—and if possible for his readers—what is good and what is bad and not merely "what happened."

But Potter, although he keeps his strong ethical passions and his beliefs in what is good and what is bad under control, is not in the least disposed to ignore that the beliefs of the people who were actors on a particular historical scene at a particular epoch are part of the story, however foolish, irrelevant, or actively dangerous these beliefs may have been. For in many ways Potter's historical aim, if not his literary method, recalls the work of the late Perry Miller. Like Miller, he wishes to know what people said and what people asserted they were doing, and he is willing, in most instances, to believe that what they asserted that they were doing was what they thought they were doing, although they were often mistaken as to their motives and as to the value of what they were doing. On the other hand, there is nowhere in Potter's works a formal dogmatic assertion of rightness and of error. Perhaps Potter's unemphatic method is more effective than the more aggressive methods of Miller. But this suggests another comparison and resemblance. When Perry Miller undertook to study New England in the terms of the New Englanders, not in the terms of modern "liberal" political or theological thought, he announced more than once that he himself was an atheist, but that made it all the easier to assess, to find out what John Cotton, the two Mathers, and Jonathan Edwards had actually said, since Miller was not committed to showing that they were enemies of the Enlightenment, or of modern civilization, or that they were slightly misunderstood ancestors of Bancroft or Theodore Parker. Potter, although never denying his Southern origins or his Southern interests, and writing about them with great penetration, is not, it seems to me, so burdened with the *damnosa hereditas* of the South as is the historian with whom one most naturally compares him, C. Vann Woodward.

It is therefore quite natural for Potter to express skepticism of the attempted establishment, by people like the late William E. Dodd, of a Southern "normative" history. In that normative history as written by a "liberal" in the American sense of the term—and by a New Deal ambassador—Jefferson is the normal Southern statesman. His ideal commonwealth of independent farms is what the South almost was and what, but for various accidents, it would have become.

Potter avoids the easy method of counterattack, of pointing out that neither Jefferson, Madison, nor Monroe was a "dirt farmer." He does not stress the fact that their economic status was based on a slave economy, however much they disliked an economy which had this basis. He hints that Calhoun's Greek polity—with its aristocracy, its perpetual slaves, and its obedient whites whom we call "poor whites"—was possibly just as much a Southern norm as the Jeffersonian small farmers' republic. Indeed, Calhoun's republic, it may be suggested, with his South Carolina plantation gentry as the Spartiates, with the poor whites as the Perioeci, and with the slaves as Helots, was at least as true a symbol of the realities of the South as was Jefferson's somewhat Utopian vision and, it may be, was what the South was really fighting for—a way of life very remote from the simplistic, Populistic democracy of Dodd or even of the early Tom Watson.

Potter is not as shocked or as surprised, therefore, as C. Vann Woodward at the fact that Tom Watson "went wrong," because he does not quite believe in the liberal values of Southern society which have been so often and so successfully argued. In this sense, Potter *does* attempt to do what Leopold von Ranke recommends, to describe the past as it really happened, but to do it without any passionate commitment to discovering that what really happened was what led to those things you appreciate or disapprove of in modern society. Moral lessons, lessons in wisdom, *can* be learned from history, but they can be learned only if one starts with the aim of discovering "history" (with all the ambiguities that such a name suggests) rather than starting to find weapons for use in current controversy. In the somewhat heated controversial atmosphere of modern American historiography, especially in the still bitterly disputed questions on and about the Civil War, the voice of David Potter is not merely refreshing, it is extremely educative.

This initial bias against teleological explanations of historical phenomena leads Potter to carry on a continuous campaign against what he seems to think the greatest of historical sins, the sin of hindsight. This dislike of hindsight is apparent in his first book. To borrow an example from a field of history on which, as far as I know, Potter has not written—the history of Scotland—many historians have committed the crime of applying to history the motto of Mary Queen of Scots, "In my end is my beginning." If one approaches history that way, so Potter argues, both specifically and by implication, one does not know what the beginning really was. But there is more than a mere methodological trick in the dislike of hindsight. For unless one is a complete determinist, and Potter is not, and one is searching for causes, which (here agreeing, as he repeats more than once, with E. H. Carr) is what historians must do: one must consider the possibilities that did not materialize before one can understand what did happen.

This is perhaps the main theme of this first book. An immense amount of literature on the origins of the Civil War, even in the narrow sense of "war guilt," assumes and investigates what went on, say, between the Kansas and Nebraska Act of 1854 and the firing on Fort Sumter in 1861, as if "what happened" was the only thing that could have happened, and as though people knew that it was about to happen. It may be, in the deepest sense, that "the South" was on a collision course with the North, and that nothing that could have been done could have avoided the collision, the war, and the results of the war. Thus, perhaps, it did not matter whether Fort Sumter was fired on or not, because somewhere or other a clash was sure to come, at Fort Pickens if not at Sumter, on the Mississippi if not on the Potomac. Because we know that the clash came at Sumter and the war was fought on both the Mississippi and the Potomac, we find it very hard to conceive of any other beginning of the crisis—what for Potter, in his new book, will begin with the Kansas and Nebraska Act. Having this conviction in our minds, we tend to dismiss as a mere waste of time the desperate attempts to avoid the inevitable, including hopeful efforts toward conciliation such as the Crittenden amendment.

It can, of course, be argued—and it has been argued very recently with great ingenuity by Eugene Genovese in The Political Economy of Slavery (1966)—that Southern society was so constructed that it could only surrender or fight, and that it preferred to fight. Indeed, given the character of Southern society and its rule by the planter aristocracy, with the absence of countervailing forces such as a more advanced capitalist civilization would have given it, it could do no other. There is no doubt a good deal of plausibility and possibly truth in this thesis.[5] Potter argues, with even greater plausibility, that people did not think themselves to be in quite such a bind as modern ex post facto wisdom suggests they were in. That is to say, we can understand the crisis beginning with the formal triumph of the Republicans in 1860 and the outbreak of the war only if we realize that the outcome was only one of the things that could have happened.

In the same way, in his analysis of the beginning of the crisis in 1854, Professor Potter points out that we assume that the heir of the dying Whig party was bound to be the infant Republican party. The Republican party turned out to be the heir of the Whig party (and of course of a great part of the Democratic party, too), but a case could have been made between 1854 and 1856 for saying that the true heir of the Whigs was the Know-Nothing party, and that "nativism" was a far more powerful force than antislavery feeling, or even than the objections to the expansion of slavery into the territories. If we think that the way things did turn out was the only way things could turn out, we will not be able to understand why they did turn out the way they did. An historian must "keep his options open" as much as the statesman and the politician. Unless he looks over all the hands of the poker game, he cannot understand the run of the play.

Closely connected with the dangerous temptations of hindsight is the unwillingness to believe that people meant what they said or even that they said what we know they said, simply because we find it very hard to accept the fact that the actors of the time did not know how the play was going to end. Therefore, many of their actions seem irrational or indeed incredible. One result of this attitude is to disregard testimony which suggests (this is one of the chief themes of *Lincoln and His Party*) that people thought they could get their own way, or most of their own way, without fighting for it. Thus the South could believe in peaceful secession, and the North could believe in peaceable "reconstruction." We must bear in mind that we must study a great deal of apparently waste motion simply because the people who were making the motion did not know it was waste but thought, to use a modern American phrase, that "it was a piece of the action." This in general seems to me the great historical novelty of *Lincoln and His Party*, and it results, as I shall try to show later, in a very important rewriting of American history in this period.

There are other examples of this bias of hindsight which Potter thinks are dangerous. Perhaps especially dangerous is the belief that the South and the North represented two cultures politically linked, but in almost all other ways as separate as though they were completely foreign countries. Potter's skepticism about this inevitable separation or, if you like, accidental separation covered up by an increasingly inadequate constitutional garment is linked with his skepticism about the more naïve versions of the frontier theory, even or perhaps especially the frontier theory as expressed in variant forms by Frederick Jackson Turner. Because, if the frontier theory explains as much as, until recently, it was thought to explain, American history has been until very recent times—more recent than the official "closing of the frontier" in the census of 1890—above all an agrarian history. Against this superstition, for such he believes it to be, Professor Potter argues in a great many different articles as well as in his books. The clash between the increasingly industrial North and the still agrarian South could make the Civil War seem inevitable because the two societies, on a naïve economic interpretation of history, would be very much opposed indeed.

But of course the frontier was not merely agrarian, which in many cases meant the farmers' frontier; it was a mineral frontier; it was a cattle frontier; it was a business frontier. The "abundance" of American society, to which Potter devoted his second book, was not based merely on the exploitation of great resources of unused arable land; it was based on a good many other types of resources, and based too on social structures not purely agrarian, which made the exploitation extremely profitable. Horace Greeley might say, "Go West, young man, and grow up with the country," but he himself went East, to New York, which is where he grew up politically, economically, and—as far as he did—intellectually.

Concentration on the agrarian side of American history makes the Civil War easier to explain in its origins and character, but it disguises the character of American society in the period in which, on a fatalistic theory, the sections of the United States were set on their collision course. So it was more than "the mystic chords of memory," words which Seward got Lincoln to insert in the first inaugural, that bound all the United States together: it was an industrial and social structure which all sections of the United States shared. Potter does not, of course, deny that "the South," however interpreted, is a section and perhaps a section of an especially definite character. He not only notices the evaporation of the idea of an independent Southern culture (as preached, for example, by the "Nashville agrarians" in 1930), he asks what kind of agrarian South the authors of *I'll Take My Stand* were describing and prescribing. Were they seeking to save special values in the South of Thomas Jefferson, or in that of John C. Calhoun?

In any event, neither remedy was relevant to the problems on the eve of the Depression. It was not only Turner, but even some of his most intelligent disciples like Carl L. Becker, who clung to a purely agricultural explanation of "the South":

The ordinary restrictiveness of this agrarian preoccupation is shown very clearly, it seems to me, in a statement by Carl Becker. . . . Becker said, "The United States has always had, until very recently, more land than it could use and fewer people than it needed." Certainly this premise would be difficult to refute. Then he continues: "This is not only the fundamental economic difference between the United States and European countries, but it is a condition which has more influence than any other in determining the course of American history." Today the United States has, perhaps, as large an industrial capacity as the rest of the world, and yet it was well on the way to such leadership when Becker wrote; yet the factor which he offers as the key to the fundamental difference between America and the Old World turns its back upon this major development of our economic life. Clearly, it is not merely the greater endowment of land which has differentiated America's growth from Europe's. It is the great supply, also, of timber, of iron, of copper, of petroleum, of coal, of hydroelectric power. By some mystic process these may be subsumed under the term "land," but if we should speak of land in this sense, as meaning everything except sea and air, we ought at least to recognize that it is in this form too broad for the agrarians to claim a franchise on it. Indeed, it then becomes more nearly equivalent to physical abundance, or at least potential physical abundance, than to soil.[6]

This same insistence on precision and on looking at things as they were and are without trying to find them more desirable than they were or are is again one of Potter's most original and more carefully used historical methods. Here he is not the child who sees that the emperor has no clothes; he is the acute historian and social observer who sees that the emperor has a great many different suits which he may wear all at the same time or alternately. This covers all aspects of American history, although this approach is especially valuable from Potter's point of view in discussing Southern history, or rather the history of the crisis in the relations between the Southern states and the rest of the states of the Union between 1854 and 1861.

It could be said that however valuable these habits of work are, they do not add up to a general historiography. This of course is true, and Potter would not pretend that he has answered all the questions which the social sciences of today and, indeed, the habit of what one may call philosophical reflection would put to the practical historian if he would stay for an answer. In a remarkable essay, Potter points out how little connection there often is between historical practice and even rhetorical historical theory. The difficulties of this union of theory and practice are very great, especially as the technical side of historical research can go a long way without asking or answering any very subtle questions. If these questions are put to historians, they often answer in a fashion which suggests that the question has no real point or no pragmatic value:

Such historians, when asked why they have not concerned themselves with such questions, will reply with a double-barreled answer. They do not need to become entangled in theory, they will first assert, because they are not engaged in interpretation; they confine themselves to facts. And then they will add that theirs is a pragmatic approach—that is, one free from a priori generalizations—rather than a theoretical one. In a battle between pragmatists and theoreticians they will fight to the end, they announce, against the warping of facts to fit ideological formulas. They intend to keep on chopping away at the facts and to let the chips fall where they may. They make these assertions with great sincerity and in a way that sounds most convincing.[7]

As Potter points out, some historians *do* ask this kind of question and provide certain answers. For example, J. H. Hexter and E. H. Carr ask and try to answer questions which Avery O. Craven, for example, thinks should not be put and need not be answered. Potter is obviously sympathetic with the attempts to discover causes, and he sets up as a standard to which all good men can try to repair an attempt to discover what are the working assumptions of the practical historian:

Can their common, working assumptions be systematized and refined to some degree and raised above the threshold of the subconscious? If there is to be a method for the practices which historians actually engage in and not merely for those which they imagine that they engage in, such an ordering of the historian's interpretative procedures would seem to be of the essence.

When I state this problem as a question, I intend it as a question—one to which the answer is really in doubt, for there are immense difficulties in the way of reducing the almost infinite range of operative historical assumptions to a system.

Historical writing, in all its various forms, deals with people, as individuals, or as aggregates, acting in relation to other individuals or aggregates, responding, with more or less freedom of response, to forces in the primary or secondary environment and motivated to follow a course of thought or action, often in preference to alternative courses of thought or action—with the result that certain developments become manifest. These manifestations, taking place in a context of specific culture and institutions, modify and are modified by the context, and historical change occurs. Historical writing also frequently offers conclusions, if not on the virtue and wisdom, at least on the effectiveness and suitability of given courses of thought and action.[8]

Potter is, like Carr, deeply involved with what is meant by motivation. He gives as an example the various theories as to the conduct of Woodrow Wilson, psychologically, educationally, and merely politically—the explanations of Alexander George, William Allen White, and H. C. F. Bell. (He has not, fortunately, had to deal with the Bullitt-Freud explanation of Wilson, which is a parody of historical and psychological investigation.) Let him speak again:

Until historians recognize their own generalizations they will frequently not even understand what it is intrinsically that they are discussing. This would be even worse than not being aware of the assumptions which they have employed.

In sum, what all this amounts to is that generalization in history is inescapable and that the historian cannot avoid it by making limited statements about limited data. For a microcosm is just as cosmic as a macrocosm. Moreover, relationships between the factors in a microcosm are just as subtle and the generalizations involved in stating these relationships are just as broad as the generalizations concerning the relation between factors in a situation of larger scale.[9]

Historians should have to

analyze their practice of generalization, to define the principal kinds of generalization which they engage in, to subject these to critical study, and to seek an organized, conscious view of elements which have remained unorganized though ubiquitous in historical writing.[10]

But—and this is perhaps the proper point to turn to an examination of Potter's specific historical contribution—he does not believe that history can be reduced to a science, even to a social science:

If the historian has a responsibility not only to work in a context of infinite items of data but also of an infinity of attendant circumstances for each item of data, his only criterion of selection, as Carr observes, must be the significance of the points which he choses to emphasize. But we have no yardsticks for measuring significance. The evaluation of significance may be a matter of sagacity and applied experience which cannot be taught as method. When we encounter this sagacity in politics, we call it statesmanship, and we do not for a moment suppose that students can be trained in school to be statesmen. When we encounter it in historical studies, we are likely to call it "an awareness of the historical process" (akin to what Finley calls "professionalism"), and we are justified in a skepticism about whether this awareness can be reduced to a science merely by shifting the spotlight of method away from the questions of the validity of data, with which historians are only occasionally concerned, to an analysis of the nature of historical relationships, with which they are constantly concerned.

Whether a systematic analysis and a systematic approach to this problem can ever be developed or not, it would seem that the mere effort to develop them might have therapeutic value. Surely it would temper the recklessness of many historians who are scrupulously objective about their data but subjective about the relationships within the data. It would help to define what is really at issue in many historical controversies where the ostensible point of dispute is only the hook on which the real disagreements are hung. And it would serve the purpose which is served by many other unattainable goals, such as the goal to "know thyself." For even a failing attempt to get there would take the historian far along a road which he needs to travel.[11]

It is time to turn to David Potter's two most important books, and to examine them not merely as examples of historiographical theories and practice, but as helping to provide that wisdom which history cannot teach. *Lincoln and His Party* is an extremely acute specimen of the first-class dissertation, an exemplification in a narrow sense of what one means by professionalism, and a model for aspiring doctoral candidates. But of course these are very minor aspects and very minor claims on our attention compared with the basic merits of the book. This writer had better admit his tepidity when he approaches subjects of diplomatic history. He does not deny the importance of specialized and accurate study of diplomatic crises. He has read a great many of such works and has learned something from them. But much diplomatic history seems to him an isolation of comparatively narrow technical problems from the general movement of life in the period with which the diplomatic historian is concerned. There are, of course, diplomatic crises which can be almost confined to diplomatic problems and to the themes developed by a series of learned diplomatic historians. For example, the Venezuelan crisis in the administration of President Cleveland can be narrowed in a way which leaves out nearly everything but the activities of the State Department and the Foreign Office. This leaves out too much, but it is not totally disastrous. In the same way, certain crises in Latin American affairs can be isolated and told without demanding much knowledge of either the United States or the Latin American country concerned: e.g., the odd behavior of the United States Navy toward Brazil during the Civil War. Even so great a crisis as the *Alabama* affair can be cut out of the main history of the American Civil War without producing totally meaningless or misleading results. Again, in some types of modern European diplomatic history timetables are almost as important as in the old-fashioned detective story. Narrow questions of the authenticity of documents or the precise meaning of diplomatic language can be raised and settled.

The first thing to say about *Lincoln and His Party* is that Professor Potter does all the things the traditional diplomatic historian does, and very well, but he does a great deal more. He investigates the ideas and passions of the total American society in the period which led to the firing on Fort Sumter, dealing with such questions as the reasons *why* Fort Sumter became a symbol. He studies the way in which "the South" was trapped into attacking it or, alternatively, chose to attack it as the only way to hold together the very shaky confederation set up at Montgomery, Alabama, a few weeks before. On all the technicalities of this much-debated problem, he is lucid and calm. Because of his lucidity and calmness, Potter was rewarded—as few historians are—by the passage of time. In the first edition of his book, he assumed that the repeated statements that Major Robert Anderson had sent a confidential message revealing a shortage of supplies, which made much harder the holding of Sumter than he had hitherto asserted, were true. But the original message had never been found in any of the ordinary archival depositories. It was therefore possible for such a violent advocate for the Southern view in general as John S. Tilley, in his *Lincoln Takes Command* (1941), to assert that Lincoln had provoked the attack on Fort Sumter without any necessity, to force the war on the South on a ground of his own choosing, by denying that any messagè had been sent out. Potter gave good reasons for believing that, although it could not be found, some such message *had* been sent. He had the gratification, due to his pertinacity, of being able to report in the 1954 edition of his book that the missing dispatch had in fact been sent, but had merely been misplaced. Still more revealing as an example of the advantages of rigorous scholarship is the fact that although Potter used the famous *Diary of a Public Man* as a source, and later learned after the publication of Frank Molloy Anderson's book that this was a bogus source, a forgery or at any rate an ingenious pastiche that could not be used, his argument did not suffer except in a merely formal sense.

But the importance of Potter's first book, which makes it possible to link it with his "work in progress," is, of course, not merely a matter of the excellences of his scholar's techniques. He is concerned with a more important issue than the narrow question of "war guilt" discussed around the responsibility for firing on Fort Sumter on April 12, 1861. For Potter used this crucial period in American history to exemplify his own ideas of what, in a deep sense, history is about, to illustrate his idea of what happened at this time, and to raise the question of political responsibility for the War—for the fact, as he quoted Lincoln, that "the war came." Potter's argument and exemplification are so tightly organized that it is possible here to study his thesis only in general and give one or two examples of it.

He attacks the legends which clustered around the opening of the greatest catastrophe in American history, and yet he accepts the mass of these legends. Thus, he downgrades the political sagacity which Lincoln showed between his election and inauguration, without lessening in the least degree the importance of Lincoln's action (although I do not think he shows quite enough sympathy for Lincoln's basic position). In his inaugural lecture as Harmsworth Professor of American History at Oxford, given in 1948—a brilliant exposition of what Lincoln essentially was—he said that Lincoln was a great man and was soon thought to be such. But he would stress the importance of the *mythology* about the man. This mythology is not merely a question of the stories that were created almost at once about Lincoln's birth, life, and death or the use of political legend to support party interests.

"Myths after Lincoln" is interpreted in a very special sense, for the fame of Lincoln is, historically speaking, anomalous. In the middle of the nineteenth century, in the age of the steam engine, of the electric telegraph, of the railroad, of the McCormick reaper, the new printing presses, and virtually universal literacy (excepting among the immigrants and the poor whites and Negroes of the South), Lincoln was a historical figure to whose life there were hundreds of witnesses, to whose actions there were hundreds of thousands of authentic documents; he was also, in the moment of his death, a mythical figure. Had he not saved the Union, and freed the slaves, plucking up —as an English man of letters, Gilbert Keith Chesterton, put it—"the Upas Tree of Slavery as old as the World"? It was the tears of the Negroes in Washington over the death of the President that Gideon Welles most noticed in his diary. It was of Lincoln that the highly unsentimental and, as Potter suggests elsewhere, highly "unethical" politician, Secretary of War Edwin Stanton, said, "Now he belongs to the ages." But this is not all. It is not more, in a way, than was done after the death of Napoleon. It was not more than was done, and is being done, since the death of John F. Kennedy. But Lincoln was also a Promethean figure, a King Alfred figure out of remote legend, and some of the legends about him have an archaic sound. Some of the things said about Lincoln, as Potter points out, in fact recall legends going back for many, many hundreds of years. Old traditional English legends were revived for the new legend of the saint and hero who had come from Illinois to save "the last, best hope of Earth." The coincidence of death on Good Friday was not ignored. There was even a parody of the New Testament, for there were stories that his body had been taken away from its appointed grave. Some of this is a kind of historical common form, and some of the stories told about Lincoln (slightly altered) are told about Kennedy. All the prefigurations of the catastrophe and the ghost that walked after it have an easy if undemocratic explanation in *Julius Caesar:*

> When beggars die, there are no comets seen;
> The heavens themselves blaze forth the death of princes.

Against a double legend—of the great statesman who not only won the war and saved the Union, but also gave to the Union cause its literary consecration in the only two works of American political prose that can compete for rhetorical perfection with the Declaration of Independence (the Gettysburg Address and the Second Inaugural)—historical scholarship long fought a losing battle.

Of course, Lincoln had become a great historical asset of the still uncertain, unstable, threatened Republican party. His death was used, quite consciously, to identify the Republican party with a martyr—and it can also be held, I think, that the presidency itself, and not merely the Republican party, gained immensely in sacredness and prestige by this joint consecration by victory and violent death. As Potter says in his Oxford lecture, any unkind truth about Lincoln, any attack on the popular legends that grew up so fast, was either ignored or denounced. (Indeed, Potter himself, innocently, is a victim of this hagiographical attitude. For although he notes the importance of the "lives of the saints" biographies of Lincoln, he attributes to the Lincoln legend what was in fact an imitation of the Lincoln legend for that much less impressive martyr, President James A. Garfield. It was to a life of Garfield by W. M. Thayer, not to a life of Lincoln, that the title *From Log Cabin to White House* was given.) Even when we get the first beginnings of serious historical study of Lincoln with the works of J. G. Nicolay and John Hay, whose real merits he stresses, there is a constant defense of all that Lincoln did, a defense which it would be an understatement to call "apologetic."

Of course, this hagiography was not universal even in the North and was very far from universal in the South. But the victorious North wrote most of the history and provided most of the market for historians. With a scholar like James Ford Rhodes, it was not a matter of repeating some of the more fantastic accretions of legend, those accretions which are more interesting, perhaps, to the anthropologist and the student of comparative religion than to the old-fashioned political historian. Still, it was very hard for Rhodes and for his numerous imitators not to fall for the temptations of hindsight and make of the Lincoln of 1865 simply the Lincoln of 1860 five years older. Most historians attributed to Lincoln many admirable characteristics (which he had) without discussing whether he showed them or used them adequately in the period between his nomination in May of 1860 and the firing on Sumter. There was a curious unwillingness to think that Lincoln might have changed a great deal, especially for the better, as he underwent his terrible ordeal of power. (From an allusion, I suspect that Potter regrets that one of the pioneering revisions of the Civil War, Albert Beveridge's *Abraham Lincoln*, was stopped by its author's death when he had reached only 1858.)

So the first novelty of *Lincoln and His Party* is the firm resolution not to look forward to what Lincoln became, to what he did or said at Gettysburg or in the Capitol, but to look at what the record tells us of what he did as a candidate, as President-elect, and in his first weeks as President. With this rule very rigorously imposed on himself, Potter was able to approach the whole problem of Lincoln's role in the origins of the war without being led astray. To turn for a moment to his still unfinished book, the same rigorous self-control and the same hostility to hindsight is displayed in his discussion of "The Background of the Civil War." Just as Potter refuses to see the later and greater Lincoln as visible in the Lincoln of 1860–61, he refuses to see Lincoln in terms of "the Ordeal of the Union." He greatly admires Allan Nevins's book on this period, but he suggests that calling it *The Ordeal of the Union* when there was, in the strict sense, no ordeal until the author reaches his own fifth volume, is prejudging the historical issue.

Potter stresses, as before, the suspect and insidious nature of hindsight. Thus, when we say Lincoln was elected in 1860, we too easily move on, in explanation of this, to assert that his election was a deliberate choice by the American people of a course of action based upon political principles that involved a very serious and accepted risk of civil war. Potter asks us to remember that no pre-1960's President has ever been elected with so small a proportion of the popular vote cast for him as Lincoln received in 1860. That is to say, the congressional elections show that Lincoln and his party did not get a clear mandate to push their own principles and enforce their own platform at the risk of civil war. Indeed, it could be argued, but is not argued in detail by Potter (although he alludes to the possibility), that we may be mistaken in stressing so much the opposition to slavery rather than the expansion of the Republican platform to include other items of policy offered to a voting public which more sagacious Republican leaders knew would never buy the more doctrinaire platform of 1856. If Lincoln got a mandate, it was an ambiguous and limited mandate.

Elsewhere Potter points out the confusion caused by the way in which the slavery issue was presented to the American people. For many people in the North, but nowhere for a majority, slavery was an evil thing either to be extirpated or to be abandoned to its own sinfulness. Garrison had a very different set of priorities from Lincoln, since his object was to wash his own and the North's hands of this sin and not to preserve the Union or, in terms of practical politics, to end slavery in the South. There were, of course, people in the North who, from a distance, admired that ambiguous and not really edifying character John Brown, and who put their first hopes in a servile insurrection. And there were Southerners who saw, or professed to see, in Brown's criminal enterprise at Harpers Ferry justification for exaggerating the peril in which that insurrection placed the "peculiar institution."

Then—and here I think Potter's demonstration is quite conclusive—a great many people not only voted for Lincoln for other reasons than hostility to the extension of slavery into the territories, but were not willing to run the risk of disunion or civil war even to carry out the narrow promise of the Republican platform of 1860. As he points out, the confusion in the American mind was compounded by the fact that the issues were never put to the American people: Is slavery a bad thing? Ought the United States to be set on its extinction? Is it moral questions on which all politics should be centered? Never put, that is, in any politically effective form. Too much attention devoted to abolitionist propaganda ignores the fact that the American people were never asked how far they would go to extinguish slavery and the cost they would incur, monetary and sanguinary. The whole issue was discussed in a narrow, legalistic, and historical way that perhaps was more disastrous to the prospects of peace than a straightforward confrontation of two views of society would have been. Potter thus has no difficulty in showing how alarmed many of Lincoln's supporters were by the prospect suddenly presented by the Republican victory of November, 1860—a victory discounted, of course, months before. Unless something were hastily done it would be too late to do anything inside the existing Constitutional framework.

In discussing this problem, which of course he was not the first person to stress, Potter's hostility to hindsight serves him very well indeed. He assesses the alarm that was felt by business, which had no desire (*pace* the Beards) to crusade against the agrarian society of the South for the very doubtful profit of the recently industrialized society of the North. But the alarm was also felt by many Republicans. The anxiety and fear that the Party was breaking up on the question of what we would now call—and what was then called—"appeasement" are reflected in the correspondence of such determined defenders of the Republican position as Salmon P. Chase and Ben Wade. The victory of 1860 had been something like a miracle, a miracle largely made possible by the political incompetence of the Buchanan administration. If the miracle was to be snatched away, it might never recur in the lifetime of such party chiefs as Lincoln, and certainly might not occur soon enough to hold together the very unstable coalition which had adopted the Jeffersonian name of "Republican."

For this writer it is impossible to disagree with this diagnosis of the American situation in November and December of 1860. The Republican party was pressed between the need to keep the support of its *militants*, without whom the Party would not have existed, and also to keep the support of the numerous individuals and groups who had joined the Party because they had nowhere else to go. It would be unjust to say that Lincoln was one of these; but he had been near enough to them in the period between 1854 and 1856 to understand them. The Republican party might split either because it meant to carry out the platform of 1860 no matter what the cost; or it might split because it made no serious attempt to do so. There was, too, the question of how to win over to a new party, whose gristle had not yet hardened into bone, the people who had voted for John Bell and Stephen A. Douglas, if not for John C. Breckinridge. There was the problem of effective control of Congress, and how difficult that would be, of course, depended on how complete the secession of the slave states might be. The more successful the policy of keeping the border slave states in the Union with the Northern states, the narrower the margin of Republican congressional supremacy. Perhaps this side of the situation is not emphasized enough.

But there was no doubt that as it became evident that secession was not a mere bluff, the tide began to flow against the nominal victors of November, 1860. In the last months of the campaign one of the main arguments against the Republicans was the one that had been used effectively in 1856, as Potter points out, against John C. Frémont. So, whether he wanted it or not, the instrument of destruction of the Union would be Lincoln, if no concessions were made to the South in general and, above all, to the majority of the slave states which had not left the Union. And we are reminded that when Lincoln was inaugurated, a majority of the slave states had not yet left the Union. It is against this background of popular alarm expressed in all parties and in all sections of society in the North, and in the border states, that Lincoln's attitude is examined. Potter argues that a compromise was wanted by the majority of the Americans who were still inside the Union, and he plausibly maintains that it was likely that a compromise was wanted by a majority of the American people formally outside the Union as well. That is to say, all attempts at compromise were not equally sensible or practical, but the idea of compromise was popular and was not a mere expedient but an adequate solution to the immediate crisis. In discussing this part of his problem, Potter undertakes a penetrating, if too brief, analysis in the introduction to the 1962 edition of his work. For he is perfectly conscious that the climate of opinion had changed since 1942, and that "appeasement" was even more a dirty word than it had been then. Potter's handling of this question is bold and original and, in a sense, unanswerable, involving a problem in political arithmetic to which there is no absolutely certain answer.

We turn to the traditional Northern view of the Civil War, the theory that the war was bound to have come as a natural result of the "Aggressive Slavocracy" and of the follies, ambitions, mendacity, and timidity of many politicians, North and South, above all of the Northern "doughfaces." Potter gives close attention in his latest book to this thesis. He condemns Buchanan with more openly hostile judgment, based on moral issues, than he uses on any other of the dramatis personae of this time. (John Brown is treated as a paranoiac madman not subject to the ordinary criteria of ethical judgment.) Buchanan is condemned not only for incompetence and for misjudging his duties, but for not carrying out his duties even in the light of his own limited awareness. Stephen Douglas, if not made a hero in the manner of Beveridge or of George Fort Milton, is not condemned as one of the guilty makers of the war, even though the Kansas-Nebraska Bill is treated as one of the indubitable causes of the war.

Indeed, it is one of the paradoxes of *Lincoln and His Party* that, as far as any one politician is regarded as the immediate human cause of the war, it is Lincoln himself. This is not merely a matter of showing how inert Lincoln was after his nomination and even after his election. It is not merely pointing out the unfortunate impression he made on his journey east to Washington. It is something much more definite: there was a chance of compromise before the war; that chance was killed by the deliberate decision of Lincoln. In one of the most ingenious parts of his book, Potter shows how Lincoln took over command, not openly, and bound to his will and purpose the originally torpid William H. Seward and used him to impose, in the period between the election and the inauguration, a veto on the only possible compromise which could have worked. Potter's succinct, conclusive accumulation of evidence shows that the Crittenden compromise would, at any rate, have held all the border states in the Union. More than this, much of the period before the firing on Sumter is made more intelligible by an analysis of the illusions of the North, above all the illusion that secession was bluff, an illusion dangerous in 1856 and fatal in 1860; and also a briefer analysis of the illusion of the South, that Northern bluster about the Union meant nothing.

The illusions of the North about the South were more important because it was Northern failure to see in time that the South was not "loyal" in the sense that was attributed to the word in the North, which allowed the attempt at compromise to come so late. It also gave rise to a great deal of later historical confusion, for it led to the taking of remarks made by people who did not believe that secession was a real danger in November of 1860 as if they were serious statements of policy to be acted on in 1861. So Horace Greeley was not quite such a weathercock as mere quotation of his statements might make him appear. He was simply a man of ready rhetoric who changed his tune as he belatedly began to realize the truth about the Southern attitude.

Even more important, Potter points out how deep was the belief in "reconstruction." Reconstruction did not mean what the word meant in 1865, or in the last years of the war. It meant a possible reconstruction of the Union when the cotton states and the Gulf states discovered that they were a small fraction of the nation and that they had seceded from what remained an important—and rich—going concern. The belief that the Deep South would come back into the Union, if tempers and heads were kept, was not merely a comforting illusion: some leaders of the Deep South feared that unless the Border states could be induced to leave the Union, or some dramatic breach with the past could be organized or would come about by Northern action, the whole experiment of Southern secession would turn out to have been simply a somewhat more serious version of the nullification crisis of 1832. We now think we know that the whole of the fears and hopes which "reconstruction" aroused were beside the point because the clash *had* to come. When it came all the hopes and fears turned out to be baseless. But this is merely to say that we know what did happen, not to say that we know that it had to happen if other things had not happened at the same time. And the most important things that happened were Lincoln's decision to make no basic compromise and the possibly inevitable confusion which arose from an attempt to fight off a showdown at Sumter while not openly abandoning the terms of Lincoln's first inaugural address.

Lincoln's decision—conveyed to Seward and by him to the congressional Republican party—not to accept the Crittenden compromise was the more important of the two immediate causes of the war. It was the more important because the crisis at Sumter was a consequence of the evaporation of hopes of compromise and because it was the decision, as far as Potter can judge, of one man. Of course, a great many people shared Lincoln's dislike of the Crittenden compromise or of any compromise, but their dislike would have had no consequences if it had not been for the decision of the President-elect.

It is on this point that I feel that Potter does not fully do justice to Lincoln's attitude. In a sense, it is true that Lincoln was head of a "faction." "Faction" since Madison's day had been a pejorative word. It was the reverse side of "party" and was never used in any laudatory sense. If it is true that Lincoln was head of a faction—i.e., the Republican party—it is also true that he was head of a faction within that faction, the faction of the Republican party that would say "no" to many of the proposals for compromise made in 1860–61. Above all, he would not accept any compromise that gave a chance for the further extension of slavery into any new territory of the United States.

Potter uses the word faction innocently, and from one point of view it is a legitimate usage. But is it quite legitimate when the head of the faction has another function, that of being President-elect of the United States? All through the war, we can see that Lincoln acted on a principle, and sometimes declared it, which recalls the "high prerogative" attitude of certain rulers and statesmen of the seventeenth and eighteenth centuries in England. He had some duties and some rights as the new head of the Republican party. He had far greater duties—and far more important rights—as President-elect of the United States. So I think it is unjust to assess Lincoln's action, from either a moral or a practical point of view, without allowing for the fact on which he always insisted for the rest of his life, that he had special responsibilities and duties that fell on no other American, senator, congressman, governor, or plain citizen.

It is necessary to bear this in mind in any discussion of Lincoln. He was very much underestimated when nominated—and when elected—and he continued to be underestimated in the first few weeks of his presidency. Perhaps on the performance of this period, he deserved to be underestimated. There is some justice in the famous picture of Seward bringing Charles Francis Adams to the White House to thank the President for nominating Adams as Minister to London. But as Potter makes plain, Seward quickly discovered, and Adams discovered a good deal later, who was the real ruler. Indeed, some of the confusion caused in the minds of some Southern and of a great many Northern leaders by the ambiguous conduct of the Lincoln administration in its first weeks, was due to the overweening confidence of Seward, to his excessive belief in the possibilities of "wheeling and dealing," and to his underestimation of his President. The confusion was because of Seward's promises to Southern representatives, and because of his inability to settle the case when the crisis over Fort Sumter was exacerbated by charges of bad faith on the side of the South, charges justified as against Seward but probably not as against Lincoln.

Potter's ingenuity is again admirably demonstrated in his explanation of the apparently reckless foreign policy of Seward which represented not an extreme example of American aggressiveness (as many Europeans thought) so much as a sudden realization that the whole fabric of compromise that Seward had created had been rent in twain. The expedition to Sumter and the reaction to the firing on the fort revealed at once where the real authority lay—with Lincoln.

Although no one has developed this theme so convincingly as Potter, it was not a totally new one when he wrote in 1942. The theme had led, naturally enough, to a further application of the *cui bono* principle: Lincoln's policy was at a dead end when Sumter was fired on. He had not kept the promises of his first inaugural. He had not been able to give enough guarantees to Virginia to be sure of keeping the Old Dominion in the Union. The firing on Sumter and the patriotic reaction of the North "got him off the hook." Following J. G. Randall, Potter points out that the *cui bono* principle is not an adequate working tool. It is one thing to say that Lincoln planned an opening of the war in which the moral advantages would be on his side and another to say that he realized the importance of having the moral advantage of being attacked if the war came. The old Indian hunting maxim, "the blood of the goat excites the tiger," may be true, but on the charge that Lincoln deliberately provoked an attack on Sumter, Potter gives a clear verdict of "not guilty."[12]

In the preface to the 1962 edition of *Lincoln and His Party*, Potter takes up a deeper problem. It is possible to hold that the only way slavery could have been abolished was by a victorious Northern war. Therefore, given the intrinsic sinfulness of slavery, the end justified nearly any means, so that if Lincoln did provoke war, he was innocent of any deep moral guilt. Potter had answered this in 1942 by asserting that Lincoln did not provoke war except in the sense that he created a situation in which war became more and more likely. But in his preface of twenty years later, he takes up a more fundamental moral problem and gives it an answer which is and must be ambiguous.

Potter's argument is really a reply to those who believe that great social evils are hardly ever cured except by "blood and iron." We do not think the unification of Germany under Bismarck was such a desirable thing that "blood and iron" were justified. But we can think, as Potter obviously does, that the abolition of slavery was a necessary good if the United States was to become a healthy nation, and yet think "the price of revolution" excessively high. In a sense Potter is replying to a principle laid down by one of the most acute American social thinkers, Barrington Moore of Harvard. In his *Social Origins of Dictatorship and Democracy*,[13] Moore writes, "The costs of moderation have been at least as atrocious as those of revolution, perhaps a great deal more." I presume Potter would agree that this may sometimes be true, but that it is not a universal law on which to rely. (Since I myself have made the same argument with less acuteness in *The Price of Revolution,* I ought to declare that I am naturally biased in Potter's favor.) Potter's refutation of the general application of what one may call Moore's Law is, like all his arguments, deliberately couched in the low tone which adds to its effectiveness:

I am very reluctant to dismiss Crittenden's plan as a stopgap so long as we maintain a double standard on the subject of stopgaps. For our evaluation of them depends very much upon whose gaps are being stopped. Thus no *modus vivendi* with the Soviet Union can be much more than a stopgap today, given our basic disagreements with that country. But we would be prone to regard it as most praiseworthy to defer a showdown, even for as much as five years. Our attitude is not unrelated to the fact that this would assure us of five years of immunity from being killed by the Russians. It is quite true, no doubt, that if war had been averted in 1861, it would not have meant a settlement of issues. It would only have meant an indeterminate interval of immunity from being killed by the Rebs or the Yanks, as the case may be—immunity specifically for those who were killed between 1861 and 1865. Since all of these individuals would be dead by now even if the Rebs or the Yanks had not killed them, we can afford to be very bland about how right it was that the issue was met in 1861, and was not put off. All I suggest is that historians who believe so zealously in the virtue of facing up to issues in the past ought not to believe in the expedients of peace in the present. If an interval of peace, without any fundamental solution of issues, is worth something today, it was worth something in 1861. In 1861, as today, it would be worth a great deal less than a real peace—a real settlement of the basic issues.

Those who despise the advantages of a stopgap peace will point out, of course, that the Civil War did settle the basic issues. It saved the Union, and it freed 4,000,000 slaves. Certainly this is true, and it is important. But it can hardly be said that these immense values were gained at a bargain. For every six slaves who were freed, approximately one soldier was killed; for every ten white Southerners who were held in the Union, one Yank or one Reb died. A person is entitled to wonder whether the Southerners could not have been held and the slaves could not have been freed at a smaller per-capita cost. Certainly few would have purchased these gains at the time if they had known the price, and the mere fact that it has already been paid is not a reason for historians to let it go without questioning now.[14]

"Appeasement" was perhaps even more a dirty word in 1962 than it would have been in 1942. After all, Senator Barry Goldwater was to be nominated by Lincoln's party on a nonappeasement ticket in 1964. But under the shadow of the atomic bomb, Potter's lowering of the temperature was, if one may use such a word, immediately useful in a country in which historical precedents play such a part in present-day politics. Potter asserted and, I think, proved "that Lincoln wanted peace and believed until the last moment that he might be able to preserve it"; and he showed that a great deal of the confusion in which the Civil War started arose from the genuineness of Lincoln's devotion to the cause of peace. In this sense he was an appeaser.[15]

Professor Potter's next important book, *People of Plenty: Economic Abundance and the American Character*, was a set of Walgreen Foundation lectures given at the University of Chicago and first published in 1954, but it is far more than the usual volume of collected lectures. In this comparatively short book of just over two hundred pages, all Potter's merits are fully demonstrated. There is the same bland and occasionally humorous dismissal of theories which he thinks unimportant, irrelevant or nonsensical. Thus, he spends no time (apart from mentioning it) on Geoffrey Gorer's theory on the origins of the Russian character. He argues, forcibly, for making historians take notice of and use the new social sciences. He shows that they should not go on using terms like "motives" without some investigation of what such words mean when inspected by the new sciences at our disposal. He quotes Professor Hugh Trevor-Roper on the necessity for political theory to have "a theory of man." The historian deals with man and so he must also have a theory of what he is dealing with.

So far that theory has not been supplied or even seriously looked for. "In a sense," Potter writes, "this is equivalent to saying that historical method has not included any means for analysis of the chief factor with which history deals."[16] The deficiency of historical theory, it is asserted, has shown itself most acutely "in the historian's failure to take an analytical view of the one factor which is present in all history—namely, the human factor, both in its singular manifestation, where it involved the individual man, or in its group manifestation, where it involves society." Few historians have more successfully "sent up" the naïve practice of their colleagues. Yet it is always dangerous to take Potter *au pied de la lettre,* for he carries with him a double burden, or a double asset, of fundamental skepticism. This is illustrated in his extremely penetrating examination of what is meant by the frontier theory, an examination to which I have already referred.

More important and more interesting is the way in which he turns the tables on the more naïve of the social scientists. For he shows the shallowness of the view that social structures, social practices, and even applied social techniques can be understood without any reference to the historical framework inside which they have come into being. He does this by a most ingenious analysis of what is meant by "abundance." The idea that the settlers in English North America were enriched by moving into a great empty treasure house is not novel. The history of North America might have been very different if the French had settled in the valley of the Hudson instead of the far less rewarding valley of the Saint Lawrence. The economic attractiveness of North America, even in its raw state, was insisted on again and again in the promotional literature of the seventeenth-century colony founders. The importance of the economic development of the British colonies and the absence of what he called "dearth" was insisted on by Adam Smith in *The Wealth of Nations,* and a naïve frontier theory seemed to explain almost everything that was admirable in American life by the impact of the settlers on the great empty and fertile land. What Pastorius, the leader of the German settlers in Pennsylvania at the end of the seventeenth century, called the *antiqua silva,* was an astonishing sight and treasure house for Europeans.

But not only does Potter argue against this naïve agrarian theory of settlement, he also argues against the simple view that the resources were there and were sure to be developed. This raises the question of why the Indians had not developed them and involves some discussion of the character of the settlers in what is now the United States. But the best example of Potter's application of historical method to certain nontechnical discourses on an explanation of "the American way of life" is in his demonstration of how "plenty" accounts for a great deal, perhaps for most things in the modern American way of bringing up children. Diet is involved, as are interior heating, absence of nannies, and of servants in general, and the flight of American women from mere chores. One could go on. All of this analysis of the special position of the American woman, an aspect of the economy of plenty, does not debunk but does explain in historical terms even such sacred figures as Dr. Benjamin Spock. Only in an economy of abundance could a phenomenon like Dr. Spock appear and become a prophet. And Potter suggests with great delicacy that a mere social science approach to the problems of American society will often fail in the somewhat individual art of history.

In the same way, the concept of plenty is called on to explain and assess a very important American phenomenon that historians have not taken seriously enough and have left mainly to public relations men and to novelists: advertising. The history of advertising explains a great deal about the United States as well as about advertising. And even love—that is, romantic love—can be reduced to or explained by an aspect of abundance. Perhaps in the Middle Ages only great ladies could afford troubadours and those who would advertise them. Everybody in the United States, or nearly everybody, can afford the pleasures and perils of romantic love.

Abundance does not explain everything, and abundance, possibly, does not cure more problems than it brings. But in approaching and explaining the importance of abundance in the history of the American community of communities, Potter has given a lesson to historians as well as to social scientists, to avoid as far as possible vague and ambiguous and bogus scientific terms and to search, in no naïve economic sense, for a clue to what for generations the people of Europe have seen as the main character of American life. The great European legend of the "Uncle from America" is as illuminating for the historian and sociologist of American life as are the ancient legends that were revived after the death of Lincoln.

In a remarkable review article published in 1950, "An Appraisal of Fifteen Years of the Journal of Southern History, 1935–1949," Professor Potter rejoiced in the turning away of Southern historiography from the mere question of war guilt and, indeed, from an excessive concentration on the war. There is something of the same transformation in his own work. From the brilliant but narrow examination of one particular problem in the origins of the war, first published in 1942, he moved to a far broader examination of the history of the American people during that period, to an interpretation of what is peculiarly American in American society, and to the problem of the American character, and in a way far more subtle and far more intelligent than Turner's famous frontier theory, making Potter one of the truly great interpreters of American history. This has been done not only by extremely exact and ingenious scholarship, but by a literary method approaching that recommended by the French poet nearly a century ago: "Take eloquence and wring its neck."

Arthur M. Schlesinger, Jr.

MARCUS CUNLIFFE

12)

DURING HIS early career Arthur M. Schlesinger, Jr., was sometimes referred to by other historians as "Young Arthur." This was a way of distinguishing him from his father, Arthur M. Schlesinger, Sr. It was also a tribute, not always free from disapproval, to the precocity of Arthur Junior. The academic life cycle used to entail several years of postgraduate apprenticeship; periods of teaching at sundry institutions (in ascending order of prestige), initially overshadowed by the baleful presence of the still-to-be-completed doctoral thesis; and the authorship at decent intervals of suitably weighty articles and books. All being well, the scholar would at length be rewarded by a full professorship at one of the better universities or colleges. In fact this had been more or less the route taken by Arthur Schlesinger, Sr.: undergraduate years at Ohio State, graduate training at Columbia, an instructorship back at Ohio State (thirteen hours a week of teaching), completion of his Ph.D. thesis in 1917, when Schlesinger Senior was then twenty-nine years old, publication by Columbia University Press in an edition of one thousand copies (with a $250 subsidy from the author), a move to the University of Iowa in 1919, and a further final move to a Harvard chair in 1924. Such a professional progress was also often an orientation, in the old sense of the word. Schlesinger Senior was a Middle Westerner, drawn east like those other Middle Westerners Frederick Jackson Turner and Frederick Merk who had preceded him to Cambridge, Massachusetts.

Arthur Junior operated on an accelerated time scale. Born in October, 1917, he entered Harvard as a freshman at the age of sixteen. He graduated *summa cum laude* in 1938 (two years ahead of his exact contemporary John F. Kennedy). He fitted in an English year at Peterhouse, Cambridge, during which his Harvard honors thesis, *Orestes A. Brownson: A Pilgrim's Progress*, was published and drew cordial reviews. Returning to Harvard in 1939, he was the beneficiary of a handsome experiment in academic emancipation. The Society of Fellows liberated its members from postgraduate courses and examinations. Instead of passing through the initiation rites of the doctoral candidate, they were free to go their own way. The conception might have been designed expressly for young Schlesinger, brimming with confidence and eager to apply himself to some ambitious venture. In 1940 the *New England Quarterly* printed an offshoot of his inquiries—an essay on the historian-intellectual Richard Hildreth. After two years he was far enough along with his main task to present his provisional findings as a lecture series, "A Reinterpretation of Jacksonian Democracy," in the venerable atmosphere of Boston's Lowell Institute.

World War II supervened. In June, 1942, Schlesinger Junior, ending his three years with the Society of Fellows, left Harvard to work for the OWI (Office of War Information) in Washington. Eventually he was transferred to the OSS (Office of Strategic Services). In his father's words:

The OSS, desiring early in 1944 to send him abroad, sought a navy commission for him, but the Navy Bureau of Personnel refused, alleging that he failed to meet the "overall requirements." This vague phrase covered the fact . . . that he was deemed untrustworthy for having favored intervention in the war at too early a stage (for example, while connected with the Harvard Defense Group) and . . . because of the suspicion that his father was a Communist. This latter notion derived from the fact that I had signed a petition to Roosevelt back in 1937 to lift the arms embargo against the Spanish Republicans . . . Arthur eventually served overseas for the OSS in an army private's uniform, being variously stationed in London and Paris and then, after the German collapse, in Wiesbaden.[1]

Before he went abroad he had managed to complete the manuscript of *The Age of Jackson*. The foreword is dated May, 1944; the book was published in September, 1945, shortly before the author's twenty-eighth birthday. It aroused a remarkable response, among the general public and within the historical profession. Some sixty thousand copies were sold and it secured a Pulitzer Prize. Next year Schlesinger gained the compliment of promotion to an associate professorship at Harvard (a full professorship came his way in 1954). Though he remained on the Harvard faculty for another fifteen years, he was thenceforward in the public eye—a contributor to periodicals as eclectic in scope as *Partisan Review* and *Life, The Nation* and the *Atlantic Monthly*. He had arrived, swiftly yet undeniably.

Or to change the figure, he was in orbit. The foreword to *The Age of Jackson* acknowledged a profound indebtedness to "my father . . . for his wise counsel and keen criticism." Arthur Senior could be regarded as the first stage of the rocket; Arthur Junior's success was a second-stage development. The influence of *père* upon *fils*, while far from producing a carbon-copy brand of historical writing, was manifold. The boy had been named Arthur Bancroft Schlesinger; Bancroft was the maiden name of his mother, who was a remote relative of the historian George Bancroft. At fifteen, when he was acquiring a passport, he "asked that his middle name appear as Meier instead of Bancroft, so as thereafter to be known as Junior." This, Schlesinger Senior dryly added, "we acceded to without foreseeing the confusion that would arise when . . . he adopted his father's profession and taught at the same university." In 1934 Schlesinger Senior gave the Commonwealth Fund lectures on American history at University College, London. He recorded with pride in his autobiography: "Arthur Jr., then a Harvard professor, delivered a group of addresses . . . at the University College in the very same series, exactly twenty-five years after listening as a lad of sixteen to his father."[2] The elder Schlesinger instituted a famous Harvard course on the social and intellectual history of the United States. Subsequently his son, who had audited Schlesinger Senior's lectures, offered a course entitled Intellectual History of the United States.

This was a field pioneered by Schlesinger Senior. His *New Viewpoints in American History* (1922) was designed to direct attention to neglected aspects of the nation's growth. These agreeably brisk, deceptively modest essays covered such then-unfamiliar topics as immigration, the role of women, the decline of aristocracy, and cycles of reform. There was also an analysis of "The Significance of Jacksonian Democracy." Arthur Junior said in 1968 that he was not consciously aware of the essay when he wrote *The Age of Jackson*. But "I remember reading it some years later and being surprised at the extent to which I was developing insights he had already set forth. However, I have no doubt that he had communicated to me the substance of these insights in the incessant (and fascinating) conversations we held through the years on all manner of historical topics."[3]

At the University of Iowa in 1922–23 Schlesinger Senior had launched a course in American social and cultural history which, he subsequently realized, was probably "the first instruction ever offered in any college or university on that phase of our past." He soon discovered the lack of adequate texts on which to base teaching. In conjunction with Dixon Ryan Fox (and, for a while, Carl L. Becker) he therefore undertook the editing of the multivolume *History of American Life*, to which he himself contributed *The Rise of the City, 1878–1898* (1933). He and Fox, he said in retrospect, "aimed to free American history from its traditional servitude to party struggles, war and diplomacy and to show that it properly included all the various interests of the people." We may discern here the provenance of a later, lighthearted definition by Schlesinger Junior of the American national character as embracing "a belief in the universal obligation to work . . . and certain miscellaneous traits such as overheated houses and a passion for rocking chairs and ice water": exhibits out of social history.[4]

Schlesinger Senior had a far more direct impact upon the historical profession. In thirty years at Harvard he supervised a quantity of remarkable dissertations in the "growth" areas of urban history, immigration, the history of science, the history of religion, and so on. Among his graduate students were Merle Curti, Carl Bridenbaugh, Paul H. Buck, Oscar Handlin, and Donald Fleming. Harvard colleagues such as Samuel Eliot Morison, Kenneth Murdock, Howard Mumford Jones, and Perry Miller added their own impressive strengths to the study of the ideas of the past.

It was a congenial milieu for a youthful scholar. Arthur Junior absorbed knowledge from his mother as well as his father, from the parental library, from the graduate students who came calling on Sunday afternoons, and from the friends and visitors who sat at table in the cheerfully erudite Schlesinger home. As an undergraduate, Schlesinger Junior said in 1968, he had derived from Morison "a tremendous sense of the role of *style* both in writing history and in being an historian," and from Frederick Merk a no less powerful "sense of what meticulous, scrupulous, passionate scholarship was all about." Perry Miller, his tutor in his second and fourth years, "helped develop my interest in intellectual history and taught me highly useful techniques of clarity, astringency and indictment." Bernard De Voto, from whom he took a course in English composition and who later became an intimate friend,

helped redress my eastern/urban orientation, taught me about the west (particularly in a trip we took together along the Santa Fe trail in the summer of 1940, preparatory to his writing *The Year of Decision*), made me understand the complexity of the frontier and the importance of things like conservation and also encouraged my instinct toward polemics and participation.

Another exceptional figure was F. O. Matthiessen, Schlesinger's tutor in his junior year. In after years the two were separated by political differences ("for a time after the war he stopped speaking to me because of my anti-communism"). But as a student Schlesinger learned a great deal from Matthiessen about modern poetry—"which I began reading with him and have read ever since"—and "more generally, about the relationships between literature and society."

The academic environment thus by no means excluded an awareness of contemporary issues. Schlesinger Senior had always "in a quiet way," his son recollected, "been something of a political activist." As a possible inheritance from his mother—"one I prize"—Schlesinger Junior felt he was invariably "less detached and judicious than my father, more eager for commitment and combat. I think this from time to time disconcerted him, but . . . he always backed me . . . no matter how misguided he may privately have thought my activities to be."[5] Schlesinger's parents set him an example in responsible liberalism. Nurtured in the Progressivism of the Middle West, Schlesinger Senior had cast a vote for Woodrow Wilson in 1912. He observed in *New Viewpoints* that on the surface there was little to choose between Democrats and Republicans. However he did believe that "the Republicans tend to cling to the concrete benefits and positive achievements of the past, whereas the Democrats are likely to respond more quickly to demands for social and economic reform. . . ."[6] So, somewhat against the grain of the communities in which he was living, Schlesinger Senior remained a Democrat through the 1920's and became an enthusiastic supporter of F.D.R.

in the 1930's. His liberal sympathies, stimulated by close friendship with Felix Frankfurter of the Harvard Law School, led him to take up the cause of the doomed Massachusetts anarchists, Sacco and Vanzetti. Frankfurter's involvement as adviser to Franklin D. Roosevelt opened a window for the Schlesingers onto New Deal Washington. At the age of fifteen Arthur Junior gained a synoptic view of the world beyond the United States by accompanying his parents on an eleven-month global journey. It closed with two months in a continental Europe gripped by economic crisis, and torn between Fascism and Communism. When war broke out in Europe in 1939, the Schlesingers were prompt to join others at Harvard in insisting that the United States must discard its old isolationist illusions.

The honors thesis on Orestes Brownson, prepared under the guidance of Perry Miller, was a natural early product of a bookish yet sophisticated upbringing. It was a fluent and perceptive venture in intellectual biography—the biography of a man who for young Schlesinger

symbolized the intellectual restlessness and vitality of the period before specialization made it impossible for one man to work with equal facility in a dozen fields. . . . In the diversity of his interests he typified the generation. The rejection of Calvinism, the concern with workingmen's reform, the *Church of the Future*, Transcendentalism, the Democratic party of Jackson and Van Buren, Brook Farm, Catholicism, Calhoun and state rights, spiritualism, feminism, emancipation—there was hardly a question, large or small, that agitated the country from 1830 to 1870, on which Brownson did not make comments. To many of them he made contributions.[7]

Arthur Junior had begun to define for himself a place in the broad realm of Schlesingerian inquiry. It was the place at which ideas and society intersected. If Brownson, he implied, had been merely an eccentric, whose opinions had no direct bearing upon the problems of nineteenth-century America, such an investigation would have been only an academic exercise. True, Brownson abandoned radicalism midway in his career. Thereafter he made vehement sallies against liberal America from the fortress of the Roman Catholic Church. The essential fact for Schlesinger Junior, however, was that Brownson kept faith with himself. He *cared*, and cared about fundamentals. In his own eyes he was not inconsistent. His seemingly erratic life was a pilgrim's progress: he did not so much *change* as *advance*. *Orestes Brownson* in its published form was not definitively comprehensive. That was not to be expected of an undergraduate even as mature as young Schlesinger. Still, it revealed an unusual capacity to handle a various mass of ideas within a narrative framework. In the light of the author's subsequent development, *Brownson* is notable, too, for its fairness. Though he might be an ardent young liberal, Schlesinger displayed a sympathetic appreciation of the doctrines of American conservatism as expounded by Brownson and John C. Calhoun.

The Age of Jackson was conceived on an ampler scale and argued more emphatic lessons. Schlesinger explained in the foreword that the book attempted to link the politics of Jacksonianism to the ideas of the time. Jacksonian democracy, he believed, was "shaped much more by reasoned and systematic notions about society than has been generally recognized"; and "many of its controlling beliefs and motives came rather from the East and South than from the West." In *American Renaissance* (1941) F. O. Matthiessen had brilliantly and spaciously evoked the imaginative climate of the United States in the age of Emerson and Whitman. There is no evidence that Schlesinger took Matthiessen for a model. Nevertheless his *Age of Jackson* was a comparable act of intellectual discovery and recovery. Schlesinger constructed a sort of collective biography of the men of good will of Jackson's day—novelists, essayists, pamphleteers, economists, orators, politicians—with incisive contrasting portraits of men of ill will, or at any rate restricted sensibility, who like Nicholas Biddle, Henry Clay, and Daniel Webster opposed the Jacksonian Democrats.

Other historians were quick to disagree with what they took to be the main contentions of the book. Few directly challenged its minimizing of the importance of the West. By 1945 the Turnerian vision of Jacksonianism as mainly a frontier upsurge was out of favor. The criticism of Schlesinger was rather that he had replaced Frederick Jackson Turner's myth of spontaneous, sturdy Western Jacksonianism with a new myth of an articulate, class-conscious Eastern radical movement championed by the Democrats. One of the most eloquent challenges appeared in a review by Bray Hammond. Schlesinger, he complained, "represents the age of Jackson as one of triumphant liberalism when it was as much or more an age of triumphant exploitation; it fosters a simplistic view of continuing problems of human welfare; and it thickens the myths around a political leader who had more capacity for action than for accomplishment."[8]

Several scholars known to tidy historiographers as the Columbia School addressed themselves to the Schlesinger picture of the urban workingman. In sum they denied the coherence of the workingmen's movement, or that laborers were markedly anticapitalist, or that Jackson either saw himself or was seen as a friend of the American working class—insofar as there was such a class at all. Bray Hammond's *Banks and Politics in America* (1957) extended his previous contention that Jacksonians who had anything better than the haziest grasp of banking were not hostile to capitalist enterprise, but simply determined to assert their own entrepreneurial claims. He argued that the Jacksonian attack on the second Bank of the United States, depicted by Schlesinger as a blow struck for the underprivileged, was actually a blow struck by rival banking promoters. To Hammond the destruction of the Bank was a piece of folly whose consequences the nation would suffer far into the future.

Not all of these controversies were provoked by Schlesinger, or aimed at him.[9] He did not write in a narrowly academic context in order to demolish the theories of other historians. Nor did he later cling adamantly to every proposition put forward in *The Age of Jackson*. It was, he confessed to the British journalist Henry Brandon in 1966, "very much a young man's work," partisan in tone. "I knew almost nothing about economics, and it was possible in the 1940s to write a book about the Jackson Administration without knowing very much about economics." Such a deficiency was no longer acceptable. He envisaged another book, "The Age of Jackson Revisited"—"a series of essays and reflections twenty-five years later, on issues raised in the earlier book." It might, he speculated, examine the United States as a developing country, "approaching the stage that Walt Rostow has instructed us to call 'take-off.'" Presumably, then, Schlesinger would wish to revise his 1945 interpretation in 1970, so as to make it less politically partisan and more open to the idea of a nation of expectant capitalists, Whig *and* Democrat, reacting to what George R. Taylor has termed the "Transportation Revolution."[10]

The Age of Jackson both embodied early formative influences upon Schlesinger, and staked out a position he was to maintain, despite modifications, in the next quarter-century. For our purposes it has a triple importance: it disclosed, first, additional aspects of his father's influence; second, the problem of "presentism"—namely, the coloration of the past by the assumptions of the historian's own time; and third, the analysis of a tradition of American liberalism.

On the first point, we must beware of exaggeration. Schlesinger Junior was to be much less committed to academe than was Schlesinger Senior. He would probably in any case have been attracted, along with such contemporaries as Oscar Handlin and Richard Hofstadter, to the exploration of ideas in history. In common with his generation, and somewhat in contrast to his father's, he was less fascinated by social history. Possibly this was because social history tended—as in some of the *History of American Life* volumes—to be descriptively miscellaneous, and to lack either the rigor of intellectual history or the sustaining momentum of a narrative treatment. *The Age of Jackson* does nevertheless testify to the parental legacy. The extent and limits of this influence may be estimated from the 1922 essay on Jacksonian Democracy in Arthur M. Schlesinger Senior's *New Viewpoints* which, it will be recalled, his son had not consciously studied. To the father, the rise of the West was a Turnerian factor ("The democracy of the frontier was not derived from the reading of philosophical disquisitions but grew out of the hardy experiences of the pioneers . . ."). Here father and son were at variance. On the other hand, Schlesinger Senior attributed Jacksonian democracy not only to "the rise of a new society west of the Alleghenies," but to the emergence of "a dynamic labor movement in the East," to the "literary, social and religious aspirations of the people," and to "profound changes in political organization and governmental practice"—an enumeration that could almost serve as a prospectus for *The Age of Jackson*. We notice a kinship in the stress laid on the effects of industrialism ("The revolt of labor against these hard conditions . . . formed an integral part of the democratic upheaval of Jackson's time"), and in the effort to synthesize the spirit of the period ("Andrew Jackson, James Fenimore Cooper, Ralph Waldo Emerson and William Lloyd Garrison, however differing in external qualities and interests, were essentially products of the same era"). There is a similarity in the conception of Andrew Jackson. To Schlesinger Senior, Jackson was "a product, rather than the creator, of the new democratic spirit, for he rode into power on a tide of

forces that had been gathering strength for more than a decade.
. . ." To Schlesinger Junior, Jackson was a figure of considerable
stature, whose symbolic leadership was of undoubted significance; but
Jackson is only one figure in a book which presents the biography of a
whole age, not merely that of the person who lent his name to it.[11]

There is also a specific use in the book of Schlesinger Senior's
theory of "Tides of American Politics"—a notion that he had first
hinted at in *New Viewpoints*, explained in a 1924 lecture, and
expanded in a 1939 article. The theory, as paraphrased by Schlesinger
Junior in *The Age of Jackson*, was that

American history has been marked by recurrent swings of conservatism
and of liberalism. During the periods of inaction, unsolved social problems pile up till the demand for reform becomes overwhelming. Then a
liberal government comes to power, the dam breaks and a flood of change
sweeps away a great deal in a short time. After fifteen or twenty years the
liberal impulse is exhausted, the day of "consolidation" and inaction
arrives, and conservatism once again expresses the mood of the country,
but generally in the terms of the liberalism it displaces.

Schlesinger later remarked that there was nothing predetermined in
the precise duration of the cycle. But he continued to believe in the
general validity of the theory, and employed it in 1960 to encourage a
swing away from Republican conservatism to a reforming, Democratic administration.[12]

This application brings us to the second point: the charge that he
had infused propaganda into historical analysis. Bearing in mind that
his next major work, *The Age of Roosevelt*, bore a related title, one
can certainly trace the preoccupations of the twentieth century in
what he said of the nineteenth. Inevitably he perceived similarities
between the two eras, and in particular between the two presidents.
To some extent, one feels, he visualized Jackson as a desirably strong
executive who, like F.D.R., took office at a time of confusion. Jackson, like Roosevelt, headed the party that was both Democratic and
democratic—its moral and intellectual vitality being provided largely
by Eastern intellectuals. The resemblance to F.D.R.'s death ("The
funeral [of Jackson] was a great mass meeting, white and black
jostling together in an agony of grief") is fortuitous, since the passage
was written while Roosevelt was still alive. Other parallels seem
deliberate. The chapter on the 1836 election, for example, is entitled
"The Third Term." It treats the Democratic candidate, Martin Van

Buren, as Jackson's natural successor, ideologically almost identical with him. After reporting Van Buren's victory Schlesinger comments: "The Jacksonian revolution was going into its third term."[13]

Consciously or not, Schlesinger appeared in places to force the Jacksonian story into a straitjacket. There is surprisingly little detail on what Jackson himself thought or did about things, except for the Bank issue. The defection of former Jackson men is passed lightly over. There is no direct discussion of the Senate censure motion. Jackson's defiance of the Supreme Court is cursorily dealt with. The tussle between the Cherokee Indians (with their missionary protectors) and the state of Georgia is cited mainly to indicate the anti-Jackson sentiments of clerical groups. Jackson's tacit support of Georgia, against the Supreme Court, is chronicled without noting that his sympathy for state rights on this occasion led South Carolina to expect indulgence from him over the nullification dispute. Schlesinger comes back to Jackson's defiance of the Court in a later chapter on the Dred Scott case, telescoping the two together: "The Jacksonian tradition had always been vigorously against aggression by the judiciary; and the political antislavery movement, in the general process of fortifying itself behind the main Jacksonian positions, had taken over the case against judicial usurpation."[14] Here, we may suppose, Schlesinger's interpretation was affected by a reaction to Roosevelt's troubles with his own "nine old men" of the federal judiciary.

In the same way, to a latter-day reader he perhaps insists unduly on the parallel between Jackson's opponents and those of F.D.R. There is a tendency to portray the Whigs as malefactors of great wealth. Whig complaints are brushed aside as disingenuous or hysterical, as though such opposition spokesmen constituted an early version of the Liberty League of the 1930's. Whig intellectuals get short shrift. Magnanimous toward Orestes Brownson for his changeableness, Schlesinger mocks the idiosyncratic Horace Greeley. No credit is allowed to John Quincy Adams' vision of a federally sustained program of national works, or to Clay's "American system."[15] Whig doctrine is considered mere self-interest. Whig opposition to the Mexican War is almost ignored; indeed the war is alluded to chiefly as an instance of democracy flexing its national muscles. In *The Age of Jackson* it could be said that Schlesinger voted for Roosevelt, much as that earlier American historian George Bancroft is said to have voted in his works for Andrew Jackson.

Other disputable features may be left aside for the moment. But to condemn *The Age of Jackson* for bias would be unjust. All historians are biased, unless their work is too safely antiquarian to make much difference to anyone. The reputation of Andrew Jackson (along with those of Jefferson, Hamilton, and almost every other man who counted in American history) has fluctuated wildly on the historiographical stock market. A poll of historians conducted by Arthur Schlesinger, Sr., in 1948, to establish the standing of American presidents, rated Jackson among the "great." By 1962, when the experiment was repeated, Jackson had dropped to "near-great." *The Age of Jackson* came out just before what was to prove the temporary eclipse of a whole generation of liberally conceived historical writing. The attachment to progressive ideals, and to the idea of the nation's history as a conflict between sections or between haves and have-nots, was to yield to a period of "consensus" scholarship. At the time when Schlesinger wrote, the conception of "Jacksonian Democracy" was dominant.[16] Few historians seriously questioned its soundness. He had perforce to leave to his immediate successors, in an altered intellectual climate, the casting into doubt of the class-conflict thesis, and the blurring of the previous sharp differentiation between Democrat and Whig.

In certain respects Schlesinger was abreast if not ahead of his time. Until his book was published no one had attempted so far-reaching or so intellectually alert an assessment of Jacksonian America and its aftermath. The verve, the scale, the dexterity of his survey were enough to guarantee the book a long life. Moreover, his judgments were less doctrinaire than the above paragraphs may have conveyed. His broad generalizations might be contested: at close quarters his narrative turns out to provide hospitality for alternative viewpoints.

Above all, *The Age of Jackson* is held together by its basic theme. The book is really about American liberalism—Schlesinger's overriding concern in nearly everything he has written. The last fifth of this book ranges on beyond Jackson, into the twentieth century. An epigraph from George Bancroft, placed at the beginning, offers a key to Schlesinger's inner intention:

The feud between the capitalist and laborer, the house of Have and the house of Want, is as old as social union, and can never be entirely quieted; but he who will act with moderation, prefer fact to theory, and remember that every thing in the world is relative and not absolute, will see that the violence of the contest may be stilled.

The first part of this utterance is more frequently quoted than the second. It is true that Schlesinger depicts American history as an "enduring struggle between the business community and the rest of society." He rams home the lesson throughout *The Age of Jackson*: when he speaks of the "fury of the business community" against Lincoln in 1860 we again perhaps catch a whiff of the 1930's in the phraseology. But the struggle *is itself* "the guarantee of freedom in a liberal capitalist state." In short, Schlesinger accepts capitalism as a permanent and on the whole beneficial element in American life. The question then is how to harness the forces that the system generates. Capitalism, he assumes, enlarges the pie: the task of the liberal is to ensure that the pie is cut more equitably than would be done if entrepreneurs followed their selfish inclinations. The object of liberalism, he declares in the final chapter, "has never been to destroy capitalism, as conservatism invariably claims—only to keep the capitalists from destroying it."[17] In other words, the American business community in its shortsighted fashion has historically been hostile to liberalism, but not vice versa. Liberalism has been a corrective, not a destructive, agent.

Hostility to liberalism has also come from "the theory of socialism, which in the Fourierite form excited so many intellectuals in the 1840's. This theory would say that capitalism is hopelessly wrong in principle, and salvation can lie only in its abolition and the formation of new collectivisms." According to Schlesinger, the Jacksonians believed that there was a deep-rooted conflict between the "producing" and the "nonproducing" classes. His search for a middle ground is indicated in a footnote dissociating the Jacksonian analysis from Marxism. The Communist Manifesto of 1848 was antedated by the independent views of Jacksonians like Amos Kendall and Brownson. Schlesinger quotes a letter by Marx of 1852 to underline his contention. "The honour does not belong to me," said Marx, "for having discovered the existence either of classes in modern society or of the struggle between the classes." What Marx added was a determinist assertion that the struggle must lead to the dictatorship of the proletariat and the ultimate abolition of all classes.

To Schlesinger, however, the lesson of American history was dual.

There was an "enduring struggle," in fact an "irrepressible conflict" between the underprivileged and the overprivileged. There was also a pattern of alternation. America's hope lay in the very legitimacy of the conflict, the refusal to be bound to any extreme solution: "Democracy shuns codification. It suspends in solution logical antinomies which work out more or less harmoniously in practice. Thereby it gains in flexibility and expands the range of political possibilities, whatever it may lose (to the sorrow of the dogmatist) in philosophical chastity."[18]

In *The Age of Jackson* he began to deploy a characteristic vocabulary, adapted in part from the philosopher William James, who was among his heroes. The American liberal needed to be "tough-minded" and "pragmatic," to "wrestle with new problems as they come, without being enslaved by a theory of the past, or a theory of the future." It followed that the intellectual must be prepared to engage in day-to-day contests. The glory of many Jacksonian intellectuals, such as the scholarly Bancroft and even the shy novelist Hawthorne, had consisted in commitment. By contrast, Schlesinger condemned the "pure transcendentalists" of the Bronson Alcott stamp—"incapable of effective human relations, terrified of responsibility, given to transforming evasion into a moral triumph." Emerson, the profoundest man of his day, set the worst example: "He would not succumb to verbal panaceas, neither would he make the ultimate moral effort of Thoreau and cast off all obligation to society. Instead he lingered indecisively, accepting without enthusiasm certain relations to government but never confronting directly the implications of acceptance."[19]

The main purpose of *The Age of Jackson* was, to recapitulate, not to refute Frederick Jackson Turner, or to substitute a class-conflict interpretation. It was rather to construct a history of American liberalism, and the enemies of liberalism, in a book that stretched from the Jacksonian era down to modern times. A subsidiary aim was to consider the role of the American intellectual.

During the next few years, of the Truman era, Schlesinger lived out the injunctions of his book. He was a founder-member of ADA (Americans for Democratic Action), a group of politically minded liberals most of whom were not politicians. In collaboration with the political journalist Richard H. Rovere he produced *The General and the President* (1951), a witty and trenchant account of the high-handedness of General Douglas MacArthur and his clash with President Harry S. Truman. Schlesinger had written another book, *The Vital Center: The Politics of Freedom* (1949), and was hard at work on the first volume of his forthcoming *Age of Roosevelt*. In a letter to Felix Frankfurter (August, 1949) he described *The Vital Center* as "a political tract, designed to get my private political views out of my system so they won't get in my way when I write the New Deal book." His comment is perhaps not to be taken entirely at face value, though in later years he spoke a little deprecatingly of having been at this stage a "crusading anti-communist." He also in retrospect felt that *The Vital Center* had been too hard on American businessmen. Some were more flexible than he had been ready to admit; he had been "beguiled to extreme conclusions by Joseph A. Schumpeter's brilliant but exaggerated argument [in *Capitalism, Socialism and Democracy*, 1947] that the processes of capitalism were inevitably destroying entrepreneurial initiative."[20]

Much of the material on the shortcomings of American conservatism—for instance, the view that it was plutocratic rather than aristocratic—was a gloss on positions already held in *The Age of Jackson*.[21] The novel feature of *The Vital Center* was its attack on forms of totalitarianism, whether of the right or left, not so much for their economic errors as for their denial of the basic freedoms of liberal society: denials that would leave no room for an intelligentsia. He was kinder to the Supreme Court, presumably because it had recently blossomed as a defender of civil rights. Anxious to find a reasonable compromise between tolerance and the risks of subversion, he was scornful of "doughface progressives," identifying the Henry Wallace movement of 1948 with those "democratic men with totalitarian principles" of a century earlier who had pretended that Negro slavery was indistinguishable from the "wage slavery" of white Northerners. He was sharply critical of American fellow travelers for their blend (as he saw it) of deceit and self-deceit.[22]

In his vocabulary at this stage "radicalism" was good, "progressivism" bad. Schlesinger did not mean to indict the Progressivism of Theodore Roosevelt and Woodrow Wilson, which (then and later) he described approvingly. His objection to the "progressive" mentality was its irresponsibility and sentimentality. Unlike the sensible, empirical, pragmatic, "radical" tradition, the "progressive" tradition in this sense was "utopian." Thanks to the harsh lesson of twentieth-century totalitarianism, the "bubble of the false optimism" of the nineteenth century had been broken. History was no straightforward onward march toward a better world, with the United States in the van.

One particular problem, that of slavery and the "inevitability" of the American Civil War, engaged Schlesinger's attention. No doubt its relevance was heightened for him by the nation's involvement in World War II. At any rate he tackled the question in "The Causes of the Civil War" (1949), an article which has been frequently reprinted as a critique of revisionism. It is so: Schlesinger incisively answers the contentions of such scholars as J. G. Randall and Avery O. Craven, who attributed the Civil War to "fanaticism" and to the blunders of political leaders. The war, they suggested, was needless and fruitless: slavery was a dying institution, and forcible emancipation poisoned race relations in the South. When Schlesinger goes on to discuss why revisionism should ever have become fashionable among historians, he resorts to a slightly odd argument. The obvious explanation would seem to be that Randall and Craven wrote in the aftermath of World War I. Revisionist interpretations of the origins of that catastrophe suggested a parallel with the earlier contest. The appalling costs in men and material of 1914–18 appeared in retrospect to have been futile: could not the same be said of the six hundred thousand lives lost in 1861–65? How could future wars be averted? American historians in the 1970's and 1980's, influenced by the Vietnam imbroglio, may possibly come to similar conclusions when they look back on the nation's past. (Indeed Schlesinger's own analysis, *The Bitter Heritage: Vietnam and American Democracy, 1941–1966*, could be taken as an anticipatory example of such neo-revisionism.) A generation ago, however, the approach of World War II raised different queries for youths like Schlesinger. Was the struggle against totalitarianism not a moral issue? Was this not a just war?[23]

He therefore associated the vogue of Civil War revisionism with "the modern tendency to seek in optimistic sentimentalism an escape from the severe demands of moral decision." It was a somewhat surprising verdict on a group of historians who probably were guilty, as he claimed, of dodging the deeper meanings of sectional controversy. They displayed a rather repellent indifference to slavery as an institution, but they had surely arrived at their thesis as the result of disillusionment instead of rosy optimism.

Believing as he did that the United States had been right to go to war against the Axis powers, and that Soviet Communism might prove an equally dangerous enemy, Schlesinger pursued the analogy with his own day. Seemingly influenced by the spectacle of Stalinist Russia, he said of the American South:

A society closed in the defense of evil institutions thus creates moral differences far too profound to be solved by compromise. Such a society forces upon everyone, both those living at the time and those writing about it later, the necessity for a moral judgment; and the moral judgment . . . becomes an indispensable factor in the historical understanding.[24]

The old South was not merely iniquitous in itself, but morally reprehensible because, following the logic of repression, it sought to seal itself off from the competition of other ideas.

The charge of sentimentalism may be indicative of Schlesinger's endeavor to work out a satisfactory general interpretation of the course of American history. He was searching for key explanations and grappling with awkward elements in the pattern. In *The Vital Center*, trying to draw a distinction between healthy and unhealthy class conflict, he even speculates that it is "perhaps fortunate for the continuity of the American development that the Civil War came along to heal the social wounds opened up in the age of Jackson; that one world war closed the rifts created by the New Freedom and another those of the New Deal." An almost brutally casual remark, this, and not followed up. It harks back, though, to the passages in *The Age of Jackson* that seek to account for the demise of Jacksonian reform. The short answer, for Schlesinger, is that "the antislavery crusade . . . drained off the energies" and indeed destroyed "the party of Jacksonian democracy." This leads him into some interpretative difficulties. The Jacksonian picture of the Civil War, as expounded, for instance, by Frank Blair, Jr., was, he says, fallacious. What Blair took still to be a conflict of "caste and privilege" versus democracy was in fact principally a sectional conflict. Does this mean that class-conflict was mitigated by genuine social and economic improvements, or merely that it needed to be given a lower priority, in face of the national emergency, than the struggles to end slavery, and to preserve the Union? It is not clear whether Schlesinger is arguing that a different analysis would have been more *accurate*, or more *politically effective*. In either case, he implies, it could not have been a class-conflict analysis. Schlesinger, apparently thinking of World War II, is inclined to scold the latter-day Jacksonians for their lack of tough realism ("Ever since liberalism 'emancipated' itself from nationalism, it has found it hard to cope with the facts of war"). The reasoning here is opaque. However, it would seem that the sectional theory of the Civil War at length too thoroughly supplanted the old class-conflict theory of a basic American social polarity. The "continuities of reform" were disrupted; liberalism was "disarmed" for the postwar problems. The "business community" then captured the Republican party, which had briefly become the repository of liberal principles, and acquired "the prestige of representing freedom and democracy."[25]

In *The Vital Center* Schlesinger examines another thorny problem raised in *The Age of Jackson*: namely, the role of the federal government in promoting the national welfare. As a matter of recent history, there were good grounds for maintaining that Roosevelt's New Deal had saved America. But the Democratic party of Jefferson and Jackson was decidedly averse to enlarging the powers of the state. The Federalists and Whigs, Schlesinger's parties of the "business community," were much more favorable to "statism." Could it be that Hamilton was a better guide to the future than Jefferson, or that John Quincy Adams and Clay were better guides than Jackson? In *The Age of Jackson* Schlesinger's replies are possibly more ingenious than sound. The desire to extol Jacksonianism and castigate the Whigs induces him to play down the apparent inconsistency in the first half of the book, and to conjure it away in the broad assertions of the concluding chapters. *The Vital Center* is more convincing. He concedes that, since "American radicalism . . . was born in a specific revolt against arbitrary government," the experience had "a traumatic effect on the early radicals. The state had given them, so to speak, a prenatal fright, and they never quite recovered." Or rather, they did not start to recover until the beginning of the twentieth century, and even then remained unsure whether to opt for the economic radicalism of Theodore Roosevelt's New Nationalism or the political radicalism of Wilson's New Freedom. Schlesinger implies that such uncertainty was the unavoidable price to be paid for a liberal-capitalist society—not an ideal society, but simply the best attainable in an imperfect world.[26]

Among the writers cited with special approval in *The Vital Center* was the theologian Reinhold Niebuhr. ("Man's capacity for justice makes democracy possible; but man's inclination to injustice makes democracy necessary.") The two men first became acquainted during the winter of 1946–47, when they were associated in the founding of ADA. At one time a socialist, Niebuhr had gradually modified his opinions. Dissatisfied alike with the complacent absolutes of the Social Gospel and the hollow relativism of the Dewey style of social thought, and disdainful in the New Deal years of what he took for intellectual flabbiness in the approach to reform, Niebuhr had come to believe that America's possible salvation lay in an open, undoctrinaire politics of piecemeal reform. His intelligence, his integrity, and his abiding concern to relate morality to public issues made him a figure of great importance to certain liberal intellectuals. Schlesinger was one of them. Initially "impressed and charmed," Schlesinger recollected, "I then began reading his books. I suppose that *The Nature and Destiny of Man* [1941–43] had more influence on me (and my attitudes toward history) than any other single book." He was also deeply affected by Niebuhr's *The Children of Light and the Children of Darkness* (1944):

Niebuhr's rendition of the Christian interpretation of human nature, his sense of the frailty of human striving along with the duty none the less to strive, his sense of the tension between history and the absolute—all these things gave form to my own gropings about human nature and history and showed me how skepticism about man, far from leading to a rejection of democracy, established democracy on its firmest possible intellectual basis. . . . Niebuhr also . . . confirmed my sense that irony was the best human and historical stance—an irony which does not sever the nerve of action. The line leads straight from Niebuhr to the Kennedys. Also, through the years, Niebuhr more than anyone else I have known has served as the model of a really great man.

Little by little Niebuhr had evolved a devastating yet not despairing conception of the "irony of American history" (the title of a book he published in 1952). He postulated a nation committed to improvement but purged of its old superficialities. His revised outlook accorded closely with Schlesinger's evolving scheme of an American liberal tradition.[27]

Perhaps, too, Schlesinger derived support from Niebuhr's skepticism as to the pretensions of the social sciences. Though historians of Schlesinger's generation were willing to learn from sociology and psychology, he was less receptive than some of his contemporaries. In a lively, somewhat Menckenesque review written in 1949, he poked fun at social psychologists for their "remorseless jargon," their ponderous scholarly apparatus, and their laboring of the obvious. Their "whole system of interpretation" was, he suspected, "inherently deficient" in two crucial respects: "a sense of individual psychology" and "a sense of history." He was more polite in a few subsequent comments, but there was no sign of a real change of heart.[28]

There are many references to Niebuhr in Schlesinger's writings. The journalist Walter Lippmann, sometimes negatively, furnished another kind of lesson in life styles. Lippmann's career, Schlesinger said in a genial but not uncritical essay, had been a constant "search to define the role of the intellectual in the polity of a free society"—a search of much interest to Schlesinger. After graduating from Harvard Lippmann had, in championing Theodore Roosevelt, experimented with a "partnership between the intellectual . . . and the statesman." He had worked for the Wilson administration, in Washington and in Europe. But then Lippmann installed himself as a commentator—one who preferred to stand away from and above the hurly-burly of public life, who in rather wayward fashion proposed a succession of creeds to govern the conduct of affairs. He was not only reluctant to embroil himself; he apparently felt that detachment was a necessity if the thinking man were to think straight. "It is impossible to mix the pursuit of knowledge and the exercise of political power," he announced in 1936, "and those who have tried it turn out to be very bad politicians or they cease to be scholars." Cautionary words.[29]

By the end of the 1940's Schlesinger was thus an academic historian who had more than an academic affiliation with the politics of democracy. It was natural for him to devote his chief efforts to recent history. *The Age of Jackson* was a sort of prologue to *The Age of Roosevelt*, whose first volume, *The Crisis of the Old Order, 1919–1933*, was published in 1957. (Two more volumes, *The Coming of the New Deal* and *The Politics of Upheaval*, appeared in 1958 and 1960; they took the story to the end of 1936.) The theme was outlined in the foreword to *Crisis of the Old Order*:

The age of Roosevelt is a watershed in the history of the United States, the great dividing line in the nation's life between innocence and responsibility. During his years, America emerged from nineteenth-century simplicity, encountered world war and depression and world war again, and began to bear both the grandeur and the guilt of international power. Before the age of Roosevelt, Americans lived under a cheerful illusion of security. Afterwards, the world could never be the same for them again.

F.D.R. was not himself cut off entirely from the past. Schlesinger saw him as the heir both of his "kinsman" Theodore Roosevelt and his "hero" Woodrow Wilson, and more broadly as the inheritor of a "robust and resolute tradition of liberal pragmatism." But F.D.R.'s presidency "showed the limitations as well as the strengths of pragmatism." It worked well in a responsive atmosphere. It "could lead to confusion and tragedy when it refused to recognize impassable differences in purposes"—especially in foreign affairs, at least during the later years of the Roosevelt administration.[30] Such criticisms of F.D.R. had been emphatically voiced in Edgar E. Robinson's *The Roosevelt Leadership* (1955), and implied in cool assessments by Richard Hofstadter, Eric Goldman, and others. By comparison, Schlesinger seemed a champion of F.D.R., and of the Democrats.

The approach of *The Age of Roosevelt* resembled that of *The Age of Jackson*. Though the two presidents provide a focus, each is in a way only *primus inter pares*, the most prominent figure in a crowded scene. Except for scattered references Roosevelt hardly appears until the second half of *Crisis of the Old Order*. Before then the reader is regaled with a sparklingly assured sketch of the United States in a period of economic ease and moral sloth. Throughout *The Age of Roosevelt* there is a skillful intermingling of people, events, and ideas—a technique explained by Schlesinger in 1966:

It has always seemed to me that the trick of writing history is to fuse narrative and analysis in a consistent literary texture. The history which is purely narrative . . . I find . . . ultimately unsatisfactory. It's not enough to describe the events . . . without giving some indication why they were happening. . . . Purely analytical history . . . by leaving out the emotions and the color and the atmosphere . . . is dehydrated history . . . it doesn't recreate the mood in which choices were made at the time. . . . [What] one must try to do . . . is to write a combination of narrative and analytical history, in which you describe as vividly as seems appropriate what happened; at the same time you try to indicate what the problems were . . . and what the social or political or intellectual forces were that were operating upon the actors and the events.[31]

The Age of Roosevelt demonstrated Schlesinger's exceptional talent for marshaling the raw stuff of history like an impresario directing a cast of thousands. Cutting deftly from one vignette to another, from popular sentiment to political calculation to economic theory, he imposes a clear shape on his material, and does so by various devices. He returns again and again to the idea of pragmatic liberalism. For him it is truly the vital center, the middle ground amid all the despondencies and polemics of a nation perilously close to losing its nerve. Liberalism is the great source of Roosevelt's magic, whether or not he is fully aware of the nature of his armory. It is the creed that vitalizes the Democratic party, and whose lack makes the Republicans sound so sour and narrow as a party. Hence, no doubt, the contrast in *Crisis of the Old Order* between the derisive account of the intellectual poverty of the Republican party platform in 1932, and the indulgent description of the not much more impressive Democratic platform of the same year.

A further shape is provided by Schlesinger's distinction, in *The Politics of Upheaval*, between the "first" New Deal of 1933–35 and a "second" New Deal, which he sees as beginning in 1935. "In this year," he says, "the strategy and tactics of the New Deal experienced a subtle but pervasive change." The early New Deal had striven to "reshape American institutions according to the philosophy of an organic economy and a coordinated society." The second phase, something of a retreat from these vast aspirations, witnessed the effort "to restore a competitive society within a framework of strict social ground rules and on the foundation of basic economic standards." There was a corresponding shift in personnel, from the "social evangelists" whose spiritual and often actual headquarters was Columbia University (Raymond Moley, Rexford Guy Tugwell) to the more restrained and legalistic products of the Harvard Law School (Felix Frankfurter, Thomas G. Corcoran, Benjamin V. Cohen). The changed, possibly diminished, New Deal meant the eventual victory of a viewpoint whose most formidable exponent was Justice Louis D. Brandeis—a viewpoint tempered by the influence of Keynesian economics. In several works Schlesinger discusses the difference between Theodore Roosevelt's New Nationalism and Woodrow Wilson's New Freedom. Brandeis, an old Wilsonian, could be regarded as upholding to a later generation the liberalism of decentralized, relatively unregimented government, while the first

New Deal smacked more of governmental control.[32] Schlesinger clearly preferred the energetic, humanitarian pragmatism of F.D.R., Justice Stone, and Harry Hopkins to what he regarded as the less generous, more temporizing pragmatism of, say, Chief Justice Hughes and Brandeis. But he vastly preferred either brand of pragmatism to the theories of what he called the "Platonists"—the doctrinaires, whether of the left wing or the right wing, of American politics.

The Age of Roosevelt, so far an unfinished work, ought not to be judged with finality. So far, for example, it has excluded foreign policy. But its three existing substantial volumes supply a solid enough basis for at least some comment. The reaction of reviewers was almost uniformly favorable, and rightly so. No historian had (with the exception of Frank Freidel's multivolume biography of F.D.R.) told the story of New Deal America in such copious detail. None excelled Schlesinger in literary ability, in breadth of knowledge, or in warmth of understanding. Here and there the account was perhaps unduly partisan; an inveterate Republican might well gasp and groan at Schlesinger's arraignment of his party's behavior. But, as with *The Age of Jackson,* one finds on close reading that the author, while withering in his treatment of those he takes for fools and knaves, is careful not to overpraise his heroes, including F.D.R. Though he compiles a harsh dossier on Herbert Hoover, he is distinctly kind to Governor Alfred M. Landon, the Republican presidential candidate in 1936.

Some of the men actually engaged in Roosevelt's administration have felt that Schlesinger overstates the difference between the New Deal of 1933–35 and that of subsequent years. Felix Frankfurter, for instance, told Schlesinger in a letter of June, 1963, that the historian had placed too much credence on interviews with Tommy Corcoran, "a romantic and uncritical spinner of yarns." (There is no doubt that oral history has its pitfalls.) Frankfurter would not accept that there had been any real clash between the first New Dealers and the next wave. "This assumes," he said, "that the respective parties had coherent and systematic views on some of the problems that are involved in Roosevelt's policies." He felt, and so does his biographer Max Freedman, that Brandeis was a less dominant and dogmatic personage than the one depicted in *The Politics of Upheaval.* This may be so. Schlesinger was, however, building upon a distinction that some men felt at the time, and that was used by the historian Basil

Rauch (*History of the New Deal*, 1944) before him. The viability of the distinction is candidly weighed in a note to *The Politics of Upheaval*, which includes a long excerpt from a "powerful *caveat*" sent to Schlesinger by an old New Dealer, Leon Keyserling. If an overstatement, it was not an arbitrary invention of the author's, nor an interpretation obstinately maintained.[33]

Through the 1950's Schlesinger continued to blend scholarship with political activity. He had the uncomfortable honor of being accused of un-American proclivities by Senator Joseph McCarthy. He served on Adlai Stevenson's staff during the presidential campaigns of 1952 and 1956. He joined other liberals, such as his Harvard friend John Kenneth Galbraith, on an *ad hoc* body known as the Democratic Advisory Council. Like Galbraith, after painful deliberation, he transferred his allegiance in 1960 to John F. Kennedy, in the conviction that Kennedy was the strongest candidate the Democratic party could put forward. In this he was, incidentally, associated with the Columbia historians Allan Nevins and Henry Steele Commager. One of his contributions to the 1960 campaign was a short book entitled *Kennedy or Nixon: Does It Make Any Difference?* Schlesinger made his own answer abundantly clear.

A few months after the Democratic victory of November, 1960, he accepted an invitation, on the initiative of Robert Kennedy, to come and work as a special assistant to the President. At the outset he was on leave from Harvard, with several other "New Frontier" professors. When the leave period expired in 1962 Schlesinger decided to resign his professorship and remain in Washington. His part in government affairs included liaison with Ambassador Stevenson and the U.S. Mission to the United Nations, Latin American affairs, informal liaison with the liberal and intellectual communities, some cultural activities, and fewer activities in civil rights. His involvement, however, was much less direct than that of, say, his former Harvard colleague McGeorge Bundy. On the other hand, being an intimate of the Kennedy "clan," he was automatically a Washington celebrity—a theme and sometimes a target for gossip writers and cartoonists. All at once the horror of the Dallas assassination brought an end to the White House interlude. His connection with John F. Kennedy, easy and intuitive, could not be renewed under Lyndon B. Johnson. In the ensuing years he eventually took up a new appointment to an Albert Schweitzer chair in the humanities at the City University of

New York. Though back in academic life he was still in the public eye, and still in rapport with New York's Senator Robert Kennedy.

While in the White House Schlesinger had disavowed any intention of taking advantage of his post to write an *Age of Kennedy*. The murder of the president changed everything. Before long Schlesinger and John F. Kennedy's old associate, Theodore Sorensen, were both rumored to be at work on books about the former president. Some of the more sensational columnists described these labors as if they were a *grand prix* race, the winner to take all in royalties on sales. So far as the authors were concerned there was in fact no neck-and-neck rivalry. Sorensen's *Kennedy* was published several months before Schlesinger's *A Thousand Days: John F. Kennedy in the White House* (1965). But there was a new flurry of excitement when excerpts from Schlesinger's forthcoming book were printed in *Life* magazine. These passages revealed that the President had not been enthusiastic about his Secretary of State, Dean Rusk, and had contemplated replacing him at some future date. Schlesinger was accused of betraying governmental confidences, of damaging the reputation of the Secretary of State (whom President Johnson had retained in office), of being a "White House tattler" and a "peephole historian."[34]

Although *A Thousand Days* was highly praised by the great majority of reviewers on both sides of the Atlantic, and eventually received both the Pulitzer Prize and National Book Award, Schlesinger's professional standing seemed for a while to be damaged. Or rather the controversy supplied ammunition to a variety of people who in one way or another objected to what they thought his career symbolized. His critics echoed the comment once made by the historian William H. Prescott on the career of George Bancroft—that he had exchanged the "muse of history" for the "strumpet of faction." Disappointment with the Kennedy administration, and lingering attachments to Adlai Stevenson, accounted for the disapproval of Schlesinger expressed by certain intellectuals. They suggested he had become a publicist. There was also, of course, the traditional belief, as expressed by Walter Lippmann, that scholar-intellectuals ought to stay out of the kitchen because the heat would damage them and their manuscripts. Such suspicion was intensified by the revival of radicalism in the 1960's. In part it represented a generation conflict: the desire of younger scholars to repudiate the (to them) insufficiently radical ideas of their middle-aged seniors. One of the younger historians, Christopher Lasch, singled out Schlesinger as the "most representative spokesman" of the "liberal orthodoxy." According to Lasch, liberals of the Schlesinger stripe were seduced by the idea of power; impatient with utopian and dissenting ideas, they persuaded themselves that there was a meaningful difference between the two major political parties and so, in vain pursuit of the chimera of "qualitative liberalism," they pretended that Kennedy's New Frontier was a noble enterprise.[35] Against the fading memory of the New Frontier, radicals began to set up the image of the New Left. A number of New-Leftish historians assembled their views in *Towards a New History: Dissenting Essays in American History* (1968), under the editorship of Barton J. Bernstein. One of the more polemical contributions, by Lasch, again characterized Schlesinger as a "Cold War intellectual."[36]

Schlesinger was distressed by the reaction to the excerpted sections of *A Thousand Days.* He had discussed some of the problems of eyewitness history in an article of 1963. "Participation," he had remarked, "spins a web of commitments which may imprison the chronicler in invisible fetters." He admitted that the bias of partisanship might be dangerous. Thus, a sense of loyalty may induce a historian to act the part of an advocate for a President and his administration so that he exaggerates its virtues and minimizes its defects. On the other hand, Schlesinger suggested that firsthand experience gave a man an awareness of the complex ways in which government is actually conducted—an experience that might save the historian from arrogance, excessive addiction to theory, and oversimplification. He had ruefully quoted Sir Walter Raleigh's observation, from the preface of Raleigh's *History of the World,* that "whosoever in writing a modern history, shall follow truth near the heels, it may haply strike out his teeth." Quoting the observation again to an interviewer, Schlesinger defended what he had done in *A Thousand Days:* "The people in a democracy have a right to know these things. And . . . from the point of view of the historian, it's much better that accounts of this sort be published when the participants are alive so that they have a chance to set forth their own version. . . . The notion that it would be much better to write these things and then lock them in a safe until everyone is dead means that there is no opportunity for correction and amendment."

This justification was not entirely sound. Mr. Rusk might have retorted that serving officials are not free to issue their own version of what took place. Moreover, it depends whose ox is gored. Supposing—to take a hypothetical case—Schlesinger had become aware of some personal or other scandal reflecting adversely upon the dead President Kennedy. Might not all sorts of considerations—concern for Mrs. Kennedy, or for the good name of the Kennedy administration—have induced him not to reveal it? Might not the contemporary historian be distinctly selective in his revelations?

A subsequent essay, "On the Writing of Contemporary History," showed Schlesinger had given much thought to these dilemmas. The acceleration of the rate of change in the modern world had inevitably produced a greater interest in the recent past, and a corresponding stimulus to supplement its abundant yet tantalizingly incomplete record by means of "oral history" and other projects. In this article Schlesinger draws a distinction between the right of a democracy to know the truth about the *public* acts of its public men, and the right of such men (and their families) to be protected in their *private* lives. He had himself, he conceded, departed once from this rule in the serialized version of A *Thousand Days*—"and belatedly realizing my breach of the historian's principle, dropped it from the book."

The rule might be contested. If, for example, a high public official were a secret drinker, or a compulsive womanizer, or fond of the company of persons of doubtful honor, it might arguably be the duty of a scholar-commentator to say so. The rule would nevertheless seem to be a sensible guide for contemporary historians, as to the desirable and relevant material upon which they should focus. The deeper issue is perhaps not whether a contemporary historian is liable to tell too much but whether, having joined forces with a particular persuasion, he may not be inhibited from telling enough. In Schlesinger's career the alignment was at least open, candid, and of long standing. There is no indication that he would have written very differently of the Kennedy administration if he had stayed behind at Harvard during the Kennedy years instead of joining the White House staff.[37]

Schlesinger would certainly not withdraw from other, long-held beliefs that America's best hope lay in the tradition of democratic liberalism; that the tradition was—however inadequately—more of a Democratic than a Republican concern, at least over the previous half century; and that an intellectual should feel pride rather than shame in entering actively into political debate. These were, as we have seen, recurrent themes in his work. Schlesinger returned to them in *A Thousand Days,* partly in order to answer the charges that John F. Kennedy had been too much of an intellectual to be an effective leader, and also that he had not been enough of an intellectual to be a leader of genuine stature. As for the problem of bias Schlesinger, in conversation with Henry Brandon in 1966, suggested there was a difference between the mistaken quest for "neutrality" and the essential virtue of "objectivity":

The attempt to be neutral, say, as between those who believe slavery is a great thing and those who are against slavery, seems to me ridiculous; or as between Hitler and the antifascists. I don't see how history can be written if one declines the judgment as to whether Roosevelt or Hoover was more intelligent in his attitude toward the problems of the Depression. Once you make such a judgment, which seems to me inevitable, then those who disagree are going to raise questions of injecting politics and so on, but that's one of the hazards of the game.[38]

A *Thousand Days* measures up to these tests. It is not "neutral" in that Schlesinger clearly admires Kennedy and gladly gives him the benefit of the doubt over such issues as Kennedy's early indifference to McCarthyism. He believes that the New Frontier was a genuine step forward, not a promotional gimmick. He recognizes that matters so recent are bound to be matters of opinion. As he told Brandon, he was necessarily writing another type of book from those on Jackson and Roosevelt: "a personal memoir by a participant—testimony hopefully for some future historian." But, he also said, *any* important historical issue, ancient or modern, could not help but be controversial: that was an index of its importance and permanent relevance. A *Thousand Days* covers a thousand pages, with the same large sweep as his previous works.[39] It is certainly not "instant history" in a pejorative sense, though some readers disagree with its estimate of Kennedy's qualities. Moreover, for a historian sometimes accused of arrogance it is a remarkably modest account; Schlesinger did not pretend to be privy to every aspect of the Kennedy administration.

Nor, it should be noted, was Christopher Lasch challenging Schlesinger's competence as a historian, but only his wisdom as a spokesman for contemporary liberalism. Liberalism of the Schlesinger kind is easy to attack. It can be construed as a timid, straddling philosophy. The word "compromise" has a number of associations, most of them uncomplimentary, some of them equated with "appease-ment." The liberal rhetoric is apt to sound evasive and bland—full of "on the one hand . . . on the other" qualifications. Liberalism was not a position that had much appeal for the newly awakened radical-ism of the late 1960's. But in other respects Schlesinger's career seemed to fit most of the radical prescription. He had in *The Age of Jackson* argued along class-conflict lines. He had incurred the wrath and suspicion of right-wing groups in the United States. He had been an activist. He had insisted that history must deal with significant issues, and in this way must serve the present day. He had kept himself well informed on contemporary opinion of all shades, while remaining able to distinguish matters of moment from matters of the moment. It is therefore interesting but not surprising to discover that the allusions to his historical work in *Towards a New History* are either neutral or favorable. The "consensus" historians were the ones liable to be challenged and perhaps overthrown by the younger generation. Schlesinger, it was apparent, had never really belonged to that persuasion.[40]

In 1968 Schlesinger was once more drawn back toward the storms of politics when his friend Robert Kennedy decided to seek the Democratic nomination for the presidency. Again with the rest of the nation he saw high aspirations struck down by an act of violence. He was moved to write an eloquent pamphlet, based upon a commence-ment address delivered the day after Robert Kennedy's murder, on *The Politics of Violence: America in the Sixties*.[41] In understandable grief and anger, he contended that the nation had nurtured a tradi-tion of violence whose roots ran deep, and that in recent years the habit of violence had proliferated to an ominously novel extent. Further reflection would possibly lead him to modify the view that something unprecedented was now loose in the American psyche. There was historical evidence, for example, in his own *Age of Jack-son*, that the United States had long ago grown accustomed—too accustomed—to the highest crime and homicide rates in the civilized world. Yet though he wrote in grief, his liberal faith was not shaken beyond recovery. He had, as his admiration for Niebuhr shows, never indulged in the millennial hopes, the fatuous optimism that helped to give liberalism a bad name. At the end of *The Age of Jackson* Schlesinger quoted Pascal's sobering reflection on mankind, that "he who would act the angel acts the brute." In *The Politics of Violence*, discussing the theories of the New Left on the suppression of undesirable ideas, he repeated Pascal's words. Over a period of a quarter of a century he has sought to apply the tenets of a disabused but not hopeless liberalism to the study of American society, past and present.

C. Vann Woodward

DAVID M. POTTER

13)

In 1938, the Macmillan Company published a biography, *Tom Watson, Agrarian Rebel,* by a twenty-nine-year-old assistant professor of Social Science at the University of Florida, Comer Vann Woodward. At the time the book appeared, Woodward had lived for all but one year in the South. The son of Hugh Allison and Bess (Vann) Woodward, he was born in 1908 in the tiny village of Vanndale, Arkansas, some fifty miles from the Mississippi River. Later, he attended high school at Morrilton, a town of 4,000 population at that time, near the center of the state. After two years at a small college in Arkansas, he went to Emory University in Atlanta, where he took his bachelor's degree in 1930. During the next three years he taught English for a year at Georgia Tech, spent a year getting an M.A. at Columbia (1932), went back for another year of teaching at Georgia Tech, and then, in 1934, enrolled at the University of North Carolina at Chapel Hill, where he wrote his study of Watson as a doctoral dissertation. Receiving his Ph.D. in 1937, he married Glenn Boyd McLeod and went to the University of Florida that same year.

Atlanta and Chapel Hill were lively places for a young Southerner in the years between 1926 and 1937, for they were two of the strategic points where the post-bellum South, running about thirty years behind the calendar, began to move into the twentieth century. For two generations after Appomattox, the compulsive memories of the Lost Cause had held the Southern mind in thrall; myth had grown like ivy

over the brick and mortar of Southern historical experience; sentimentality and veneration had inhibited realism.

But by the late twenties the ancient post-Confederate monolith
was breaking up. Voices from the outside were coming in. Students
at Emory and North Carolina could read in the *American Mercury*
H. L. Mencken's monthly excoriations of the South as a Bible Belt
and a Sahara of the Bozart (Beaux Arts). Atlanta was the headquarters of the Commission on Interracial Cooperation, founded in
1919, through which Will W. Alexander was working tirelessly to
make white Southerners aware of the injustice with which Southern
Negroes were obliged to live. Emory had as a debate coach a young
but influential graduate student, Glenn Rainey, whose probing questions led a good many Southern youths to reflect for the first time
that segregation was perhaps not a necessary part of the order of
nature, like sunrise and sunset.[1] Rainey showed the tenor of his social
thought by writing an M.A. thesis on the riots in Atlanta in 1906,
which exposed racism at its worst. About 1930, Rainey went to an
appointment in English at Georgia Tech, where he was so outspoken
that at one time, the Georgia legislature, which could not fire him,
could at least reduce the annual appropriation of the institution
where he taught, by the exact amount of his salary, with his name
specified in the bill. Both Rainey and Alexander were, significantly,
friends of Woodward's.

Alexander, who was very active in securing foundation support for
Southern schools and scholars, both white and Negro, was more or
less in charge of a program of Southern fellowships offered by the
Social Science Research Council, and he spotted Woodward as a
suitable recipient for one of these fellowships. After holding the
Fellowship, Woodward was a frequent visitor at the offices of the
Interracial Commission. Similarly, Rainey was responsible for the fact
that Woodward was twice appointed to teach English at Georgia
Tech. Woodward later warmly acknowledged his intellectual appreciation of Rainey in the introduction to his study of Watson.[2]

The changing temper of the times in Atlanta was also suggested by
the fact that it was there that Angelo Herndon, a young Negro
Communist who had organized demonstrations by unemployed Negroes, was arrested in 1932 and prosecuted under a statute dating
from the Civil War which made it a capital offense to incite "insurrection."

The Herndon case was like the more famous Scottsboro case, which occurred at about the same time, in the sense that the Communist Party attempted to exploit it to propagate Communism rather than to save the accused. Woodward was active in efforts to save Herndon—too active, in fact, to suit Alexander's taste. He became a temporary chairman of a local committee for Herndon's defense and was later left in an awkward position by the party's cynical take-over of the case as a propaganda device.[3]

If Atlanta offered a number of new outlooks upon the South, Chapel Hill offered others still. In fact, the University of North Carolina, in the years when Woodward was there, was experiencing a remarkable period of creative activity. Within the South, it was excelled in the field of literature by Vanderbilt, where John Crowe Ransom, Allen Tate, Robert Penn Warren, Andrew Lytle, Donald Davidson, and others were joining in an "agrarian" protest against modern industrialism, and were proclaiming, for the first time since the Civil War, that the South, as an agrarian stronghold, had a significant message to offer to the nation. But agrarianism was nostalgic and devoid of a realistic or even a recognizable program. By contrast, North Carolina was the headquarters of a pragmatic school of regionalism, headed by two master sociologists, Rupert B. Vance and Howard W. Odum. Vance and Odum conceived of the South in terms of a regionalism which would no longer isolate Dixie from the national scene, but would enable it to share in the prosperity and the constructive activities of the nation, while preserving its own distinctive qualities and values. Woodward, whose father had become head of the Emory Junior College at Oxford, Georgia, met Odum, whose family also lived in Oxford, and Odum helped arrange a General Education Board fellowship, on which Woodward went to Chapel Hill. It was in 1936, while Woodward was there, that Odum completed the work on his great milestone, *Southern Regions of the United States*. Although Woodward was in history, working under the direction of Howard K. Beale, he was much influenced by Odum and Vance. Also, during these years, on a visit to Nashville, he formed a lasting friendship with Robert Penn Warren.[4]

There are certain similarities and certain differences in the point of view of Beale and in the later point of view of Woodward, and it is instructive to compare the two, for Woodward avoided a certain basic fallacy from which Beale did not escape. Though Beale was not

a Southerner, this was a fallacy to which scholars who combined an
intellectual commitment to liberalism with a personal loyalty to the
South were peculiarly liable.

Essentially, this fallacy was to regard the South as dominantly
"agrarian," as opposed to the "North," which was dominantly industrial. This simple dualism had been put forward even by Charles
A. Beard, a notably hardheaded and "realistic" historian. It incorpo-
rated, of course, a large measure of truth, but in a falsely simplified
form it provided Southerners with a remarkably effective device for
sweeping the awkward questions of slavery and the Negro under the
rug. In a sense, this was an old piece of Southern legerdemain. The
Southern acceptance of Jefferson and Lee (two critics of slavery)
rather than Calhoun and Davis (two apologists of slavery) as patron
saints of the South gave evidence of the South's psychological need
for a self-image which would divert focus from the subordination of
the Negro, either as a slave or as a sharecropper. The work of such
Southern historians as William E. Dodd and Frank L. Owsley reinforced this self-image at a more intellectual level by treating the
South of Jefferson as normative and the South of Calhoun as an
aberration, and by picturing the ante-bellum South as a yeoman
society in which slaveholders were not dominant and slaves were
somehow just not a central part of the picture. The curious effects
which could be attained by the employment of this concept became
particularly evident when it was applied to the Reconstruction
period. Treated in this way, the struggles of Reconstruction could be
made to appear not as a contest between defenders and opponents of
Negro rights, but as a battle between the landed ("agrarian") cause
and the cause of industrial capitalism, defended by the Radical Republican hirelings of the new postwar robber barons. Did not the
Radicals conspire to frame a Fourteenth Amendment which, under
the pretense of protecting the freedmen, would in fact protect
corporations from control by the states? So strong was the psychological impulse to identify with the opponents of the robber barons
that it lured more than one defender of civil rights as a twentieth-
century issue into the anomalous position of defending the Southern
whites of the 1860's who enacted the Black Codes and resisted every
measure in support of Negro citizenship, Negro enfranchisement,
distribution of land to Negroes, and all other measures to improve
the lot of freedmen. A supreme bit of irony lay in the fact that

Andrew Johnson was rehabilitated as the protagonist who held the Radicals at bay, and Lloyd Paul Stryker, soon to become a dedicated civil-rights zealot, published in 1936 a long and adoring biography of the President who vetoed every piece of civil-rights legislation for Negro welfare between 1866 and 1869.[5]

Howard Beale, a devoted liberal and active member of the American Civil Liberties Union and of an organization for conscientious objectors, accepted this simplified agrarian-industrial dualism, and in 1930 he set the theme for his book *The Critical Year* by picturing the situation after the defeat of the Confederacy in 1865: "an industrialized Northeast, dominated by business principles that were to create the machine-made American of today, faced an agrarian South and West contending for those time honored principles of frontier individualism and plantation aristocracy which had dominated an America that was passing."[6] Beale's sympathies were all with the South.

Woodward's sympathies were with the South also, and he too was a devoted liberal, but he was too shrewd and too realistic to accept the old dualism. Where previous students had seen only what may be called an "external" fight between victorious Northern industrialists and defeated Southern agrarians, Woodward, far more subtly, perceived that there had always been Whiggish forces in the South, ready to embrace industrial goals, and that the defeat of the Confederacy had set the stage for these forces to take over. Therefore the real struggle was internal—within the South—rather than external. It began at Appomattox and continued so steadily for the remainder of the century that the traditional historical emphasis upon the end of Reconstruction as a major breaking point between two eras was largely illusory. In his first published article, Woodward laid his doctrine on the line: "The class that seized power in Georgia after the overthrow of the Reconstruction regime was neither the old planter oligarchy nor the small farmer. It was the rising class of industrial capitalists."[7] For purposes of protective coloration, these industrial capitalists—notably Joseph E. Brown, John B. Gordon, and Alfred Colquitt—wrapped themselves in the Confederate flag and offered prayers at the shrine of the Old Order. But Woodward was not to be deceived. He recognized that when the agrarian cause discovered a leader in the person of Tom Watson, that leader found all the forces of the orthodox Southern establishment arrayed against him.

This point of view had been partially foreshadowed in previous works—notably in Benjamin B. Kendrick and Alex M. Arnett, *The South Looks at Its Past* (1935), but most earlier writers had blurred the point by picturing the struggle as a conflict between an Old South party of agrarianism and a New South party of industrialism. But Woodward saw that the agrarian view had not really been dominant in either the Old South or the New, and that the conflict was far more than a rivalry between those who looked to the past and those who looked to the future.

Woodward's vision of the so-called Redeemer period between 1877 and the end of the century was a startling one. Previous writers had pictured it as an era of solidarity in the fullest sense. Southern whites were portrayed as standing united in a single party to prevent the recurrence of Negro rule and the other traumas of Reconstruction. Concurrently, all worked together to fulfill the gospel of a New South, in which industry would restore the vigor of a region prostrated by military defeat. But to Woodward it was a period of profound division, with the "wool hat" boys conducting the political equivalent of an unsuccessful guerrilla warfare against the Confederate brigadiers.

Woodward's basic recasting of post-bellum Southern history was accomplished primarily in three books published over a period of thirteen years. First, there was the biography of Watson (1938), second, a study of the Hayes-Tilden election contest of 1876–77, entitled *Reunion and Reaction* (1951), and later in the same year, *Origins of the New South, 1877–1913*. During these years, Woodward had moved from Florida (1937–39), to a visiting appointment at the University of Virginia (1939–40), from Virginia to an Associate Professorship at Scripps (1940–43), from Scripps to three years of service (1943–46) as a lieutenant in the Navy (Office of Naval Intelligence and Naval Office of Public Information), and from there to The Johns Hopkins University. He was to remain at Hopkins for fourteen years and then to move once more to a Sterling Professorship at Yale in 1961.

The historical structure which Woodward erected in these three books has won such wide acceptance today that it will be difficult for many readers to grasp how sweepingly his revision altered the prevailing version of Southern history. Before his life of Watson was published, there was no mature treatment available on the history of the

South since Reconstruction. Historically, the whole subject remained in a relatively primitive stage. A number of good monographs existed on limited topics such as, for instance, the history of Populism in a particular state, but the subject as a whole had been only superficially treated in a literature ridden with clichés about the "New South," the "Redeemer governments," the restoration of honest politics through the elimination of the corrupt Negro vote between 1890 and 1908, etc. Woodward detected these banalities with unerring accuracy, demonstrated their flimsiness with trenchant evidence, and put in their place a mature and comprehensive history of the period from 1877 to 1913, based for the first time on extensive research in the primary sources.

Building upon his basic concept of the internal struggle between agrarian and industrial forces, and the defeat of the agrarians, Woodward was able to revise many important features of the then-accepted version of post-bellum Southern history.

First of all, he recognized that the Civil War had not solved the problems of Southern Negroes by emancipation, and that the end of Reconstruction had not solved them by leaving it to Southern whites to set the pattern of race relations in the South. In the New South the rigors of tenancy and of agricultural exploitation had their most brutal impact upon the Negro. Moreover, Woodward avoided the practice of using emphasis upon the agrarian tradition, as it had so often been used, to divert attention from the unlovely realities of the biracial system. Indeed, an agrarian emphasis, instead of diverting attention from the Negro, required an especial focus upon the Negro, for the man who had his roots most firmly in the soil was not the landowner, who might even be an absentee, but the cultivator, who, more likely than not, was a ragged Negro, owning perhaps a mule and a plow but not owning any land whatever. The biography of Watson showed in full detail not only Watson's own ideals of a neo-Jeffersonian agrarian society, but also the complex of legal disabilities, self-perpetuating debt, economic handicaps, and social discriminations which prevented Negro farmers, as well as most whites, from attaining anything like true agrarian status as independent, landowning, diversified farmers who produced for their own use rather than for market.

When this basic approach was applied to specific developments, it exposed an overlay of myth which had completely encrusted many familiar themes, and it led to a remarkable transformation in many images of the past.

To begin with, Woodward's studies demolished the traditional Reconstruction melodrama which depicted all Republicans as spoils-men and looters, while the Redeemers were separated from them by an impassable gulf and were the saviors of honesty and probity. Others had made this point before, but none quite so effectively as Woodward. He showed clearly that political opportunists like Joseph E. Brown moved readily back and forth across party lines, and that after the carpetbaggers had been driven out, orthodox Democrats used the "New South Gospel" as a cover for lucrative alliances with prominent robber barons. For instance John B. Gordon was not only the most eloquent eulogist of the Confederacy but also one of the most valuable allies of Collis P. Huntington.

A second ironical feature of the post-Reconstruction South which Woodward brought into clear focus was the relationship between the "Bourbons" (though Woodward avoids this ambiguous term) and the Negro vote. Post-Reconstruction myth-makers had created the impression that the Democratic party became the party of white supremacy during the contest with the carpetbaggers in the seventies and that it remained the inveterate foe of Negro participation in politics thereafter. But again Woodward clearly demonstrated that in 1877 leaders of the Southern whites pledged themselves to protect Negro suffrage, and that, after Reconstruction, the Democrats of the Black Belt counties, who were the most rock-ribbed Democrats of all, not only countenanced a continuation of Negro voting, but even controlled a captive Negro vote and employed it flagrantly to defeat the white voters of the hill counties, who were more numerous than those in the Black Belt. This practice became a characteristic phe-nomenon in the nineties and was used with deadly effect against the Populists. More than once, as Woodward shows, it was the Negro vote which "saved the party of White Supremacy."[8]

Transcending all such points as these, however, is the skill and subtlety with which Woodward has handled the interplay of race and class in the half century after Reconstruction. Very often the truly significant political issues involved interest groups—for instance, the desire of Southern promoters to secure a vast federal grant for a railroad across Texas to California, or the desire of property interests to neutralize the power of agricultural protest organizations—both

Negro and white—during the nineties. But these issues between interest groups or social classes were made to appear as race issues, partly in order to conceal the conflict of interest among whites, partly to capitalize on racial antipathies, and partly to divide the white and Negro tenant farmers from one another. For instance, the decision of Southern congressmen not to obstruct the counting of the electoral vote in favor of Hayes was explained to their constituents in terms of a sacrifice made for the sake of inducing Hayes to withdraw federal troops, thus ensuring the overthrow of carpetbag governments in South Carolina, Louisiana, and Florida. But in fact the apparent willingness of Hayes to countenance the Texas and Pacific legislation, and the unwillingness of Tilden, were decisive in determining the course of many Southern congressmen. Similarly, the disfranchisement of the period 1890–1908 was made to appear simply as a device to eliminate voting by Negroes, on the ground that these votes were ignorant, controllable, and corruptible, and that their elimination was necessary to achieve honest elections. But in fact, the disfranchisement of illiterate voters by a literacy test or of impoverished voters by a poll tax had the effect of eliminating many low-income whites as well as virtually all Negroes. In many Southern states, the franchise was confined, for practical purposes, to less than half of the male citizenry, and to that part in which property ownership was concentrated.

Significant and revealing insights such as these were set by Woodward in a context of skillful and expert historical exposition. This is a quality not easy to explain, or to illustrate by examples, and yet it has been a vital factor in gaining for Woodward the commanding position which he occupies among American historians. The biography of Watson, although his first book, is the best and most revealing biography that has been written of any Southerner living in the period since the Civil War. Moreover, it is one of the foremost psychological studies in American historical literature, even though Woodward abstains completely from offering psychological hypotheses or from applying formal psychological theory. In terms of technique, Woodward is an expert and remarkably versatile historian. For instance, in his *Reunion and Reaction* he has unraveled, from the sources, the story of a secret negotiation between Southern Democrats, interested in the Texas and Pacific railroad project, and Northern Republicans, interested in the election of Hayes to the Presidency. This negotiation had been hidden for more than seven decades, and the parties to it had taken care to avoid leaving any explicit record. Yet by the kind of detective work which historians dream about, but are seldom challenged to employ, Woodward reconstructed virtually every step in the cryptic process by which the participating parties, highly distrustful of one another and acutely apprehensive of disclosure, made indirect approaches to one another, arrived at a scarcely spoken understanding, and ultimately threw dust in the eyes of the spectator public so that the real basis of cooperation was hardly suspected.[9]

In all of this work, Woodward combined a solid command of freshly mined data with a singular talent for interpretation and a capacity for perceiving the meaningful item and for construing his material in broad terms. In fact, it may be said that very few historians have combined his closeness in research with his flair for interpretation, and this combination has been a source of great strength to him. The rare quality of the combination becomes evident when one tries to think of other historians who possess the same dual strength. Often, the man who compares with him in one respect falls short in the other. Richard Hofstadter, for instance, may be his peer in interpreting the Populists, but Hofstadter's data seem sketchy and insubstantial compared with Woodward's. On the other hand, John D. Hicks probably researched the Populists quite as thoroughly as Woodward has done, but the thoroughness of his investigation did not give him the insights upon society as a whole which Woodward was able to derive from delving into the Southern Populist sources.

From the outset, it was evident that Woodward had exceptional versatility as well as interpretive power. This versatility is perhaps best illustrated by his second book, *The Battle for Leyte Gulf*, which preceded *Reunion and Reaction* and *Origins of the New South* by four years. As a result of his naval service, mentioned above, he had been drawn into an intensive study of the operations which took place in the Philippine seas in October, 1944. Abrupt retooling was demanded of many scholars in the years between 1942 and 1945, but few such conversions were more drastic—or more effective—than this one, which required an historian who had previously dealt only with the South, the Negro, the cotton economy, and the politics of agrarian frustration and discontent, to write expertly of Japanese admirals, naval strategy, the fire power of fighting ships, and the complexities of navigation amid the islands of the Philippine archipelago. The history of naval operations is among the more technical branches of historical study, but Woodward mastered it so thoroughly that he was able to make a clear and vivid narrative of a particularly complex series of naval engagements. Not many books have come out of the Second World War possessing both the narrative and dramatic qualities which appeal to a wide public and the technical virtuosity which wins the respect of professional warriors, but *The Battle for Leyte Gulf* is one of the few which does both.[10]

The Battle for Leyte Gulf is a tour de force which showed what a wide range of things Woodward could do when he put his hand to them. But it is almost purely narrative, and reveals little of his historical philosophy. This philosophy is concerned primarily with the relation of history to society's understanding of itself, and it is most clearly evident in a number of brooding, deeply reflective essays which have very far-ranging implications.

It is perhaps natural that his concern with this broader problem grew out of his preoccupation with Southern history, especially since Southern history, more than most branches of historical study, seems to point up the anomalous relationships between the past, or our image or legend of the past, and the present, or our image of the present. He first came to grips with this question in a presidential address to the Southern Historical Association in 1953 entitled "The Irony of Southern History." Woodward's title was doubtless suggested by Reinhold Niebuhr's *The Irony of American History* (1952), and it shared Niebuhr's skepticism concerning the American idea of progress as an antidote against evil. But its especial focus was to suggest parallels between the moral dogmatisms of the 1860's and those of the 1950's. In brief, this paper began by arguing that a sense of history involves an awareness of the tragic aspects of life which lie beyond human control. History is incomplete without the dimension of human error and disaster following from error. Human history began, as one might paraphrase it, not with the Garden of Eden and Adamic innocence, but with the loss of innocence and the expulsion from the Garden. But the American experience has lacked this basic historical component, because the American record has been one of uninterrupted and invariable "success." Americans were invincible; there was nothing they could not accomplish; they assumed "that American ideals, values and principles invariably prevail in the end

. . . the assumption exposes us to the temptation of believing that we are somehow immune from the forces of history." Hence we have viewed our past in moralistic rather than in historical terms—that is, in terms of categorical choice between right and wrong, rather than in terms of the ambiguities and moral compromises inherent in the human condition. Hence we are especially prone to take dogmatic or absolutist positions—positions which are untempered by a sense of the magnitude of the gap between human aspiration and human attainment. In developing this theme, Woodward drew a parallel between the Southern defense of slavery in the 1840's and 1850's and the American defense of capitalism in the 1940's. The South in the 1840's needed intersectional friends, especially in the West; the United States in the 1940's needed international friends, especially in Western Europe. Both sought to win these friends. Yet the South made the mistake of insisting that the West accept "a system totally unadapted to the conditions and needs of the territories and often offensive to their moral sensibilities." The South also "abandoned its tradition of tolerance" and imposed a rigid demand for orthodoxy on the subject of slavery. The United States might now profit from this experience, Woodward suggested, first, to avoid alienating its potential Western European friends by demanding that they embrace a species of capitalism which many of them regarded with disapproval, and second, to avoid reducing its own vigor by imposing internal controls upon the free discussion of alternatives to the sacrosanct system of capitalism.

But it was not only the South which offered a warning example. There was also a lesson to be learned from the position of the North in the Civil War crisis. For the North had been "overwhelmingly moralistic in its approach." People who subscribe to the moralistic view tend "to appeal to a higher law to justify bloody and revolting means in the name of a noble end." This had happened in the Civil War, and to clinch his argument Woodward quoted Kenneth Stampp: "Yankees went to war animated by the highest ideals of the nineteenth-century middle classes. . . . But what the Yankees achieved—for their generation at least—was a triumph not of middle-class ideals but of middle-class vices. The most striking products of their crusade were the shoddy aristocracy of the North and the ragged children of the South. Among the masses of Americans, there were no victors, only the vanquished."[11]

"The Irony of Southern History" appeared at the height of the McCarthy Era and an early phase of the Cold War. It was, of course, written with reference to these circumstances. In it, Woodward showed more clearly than in any of his previous writings his unusually strong conviction that history should speak to the present. With his subtlety of mind and his disciplined awareness that our image of the past is the product of historians rather than of history, he of course avoided the simplistic ideas that "history repeats itself" or that analogues are ever complete. The context of "The Irony" reminded the reader that slavery was not capitalism, the Western states and territories were not the nations of Europe, and the moral validity of a crusade against slavery was not interchangeable with the moral validity of a crusade against Communism. But if the lessons were not read too literally, he believed that the past had a relevance not only in shaping the present, but in guiding our response to the present. In the case under discussion, the past might serve to remind us that ideological dogmatism could separate a society from its friends and could impair the realism of the society itself; that there was no direct ratio between the degree of moral purpose which went into a crusade and the degree of moral gain which came out, even when the crusade proved "successful"; and that war can have victors without necessarily having winners.

In 1958, Woodward returned to his efforts to relate the unique experience of the South in the past to the generalized experience of American society in the present. In "The Search for Southern Identity," he observed that economically the South, so long a distinctive region, was becoming more and more homogeneous with the rest of the country; the "Bulldozer Revolution" was making it so. With the traditional doctrines of white supremacy discredited, the distinctive Southern feature of segregation was also about to disappear. But when these tangible differentials were obliterated, would there be any distinctive feature left to keep the South from being "submerged under a national steamroller" and rendered "virtually indistinguishable from the other urban-industrial areas of the nation?" Yes, said Woodward, the South would still have its distinctive past experience: this experience included military defeat and subjugation and economic poverty and frustration in a nation which had known only victory and affluence; it included the psychological, subconscious awareness of the guilt of slavery and of discrimination against the

Negro in a nation which has known only a complacent and two-dimensional "innocence"; it included the life of an organic society, with strong communal ties and a coherent social order, in a nation which has been structured by rational abstractions operating upon isolated individuals outside of any nexus of concrete personal ties such as one found in the kinship systems of the South.

In this essay, the discourse of the past with the present was brief, but it was pungent. Why did it matter at all whether the Southerner preserved any distinctive identity? And if he did preserve it, why did it matter for him to recognize it? It mattered because "The South . . . remains more American by far than anything else, and has all along. After all, it fell to the lot of one Southerner from Virginia to define America. The definition he wrote in 1776 voiced aspirations that were rooted in his native region before the nation was born. The modern Southerner should be secure enough in his national identity to escape the compulsions of less secure minorities to embrace uncritically all the myths of nationalism. He should be secure enough also not to deny a regional heritage because it is at variance with national myth. It is a heritage that should prove of enduring worth to him as well as to his country."[12]

"The Search for Southern Identity," like "The Irony of Southern History," dealt with the relation of past and present, especially in terms of the South and the Southerner. But in "The Age of Reinterpretation," a paper delivered at the meeting of the American Historical Association in 1959, Woodward turned in far more general terms to the problem of the role of the historian as an intermediary between the experience of men of the past and the understanding of men of the future. In this essay, which is widely regarded as his most significant single piece of work and as one of the major contributions to the interpretation of American history, he pointed out, first, the rapidity of change in modern society, and the perspective which this change gives us upon the past. Since 1945, we have entered an age of thermonuclear weapons and of intercontinental missiles, and we have seen the end of the world hegemony of the nations of Western Europe. As these epochal changes occur, they throw much of our past experience into a new light. To begin with they give us a focus, for the first time, upon the fact that for a century and a half the United States enjoyed a unique condition of "free security." During this era of immunity from military or naval threats from other countries, we did not have to use our resources for the maintenance of armament nor the energies of our young men for military service. In terms of economic growth alone, this freedom to direct all our strength into economically productive activities, without diverting it into military preparation, was an inestimable boon, and contributed significantly to the rapid rate of American economic growth in the nineteenth century. Because of its pervasive nature, this security also had some far-reaching side effects. For instance, it got us into the careless practice, in rare occasions of crisis, of going to war first and preparing for it afterward. Another, more important consequence was that it enabled us to get along without real concentrations of political power. Distrustful of power as we had been ever since the time of George III, we happily accepted this opportunity to dispense with it, and set up a governmental system which, through the separation of powers and checks and balances, was subject to long intervals of governmental paralysis, deadlock, or inertia. But our free security enabled us to afford the luxury of a political system that operated only intermittently.

Second, our passage into the nuclear age now enables us to see the history of war in a new light. When war occurs today, we try to keep it a limited war, meaning a nonnuclear war, but all wars before 1945 were nonnuclear wars. As such, they had relevance for one another. The warriors of World War II might still learn from the operations of the Civil War, just as the generals who fought between the Potomac and the James might profit by studying Napoleon's maxims or the military doctrine of Jomini. But changes in man's powers of destruction since 1945 have rendered most of our past military experience obsolete: "We can already see that the vast fleets that concentrated off the Normandy beaches and at Leyte Gulf, or the massed armies that grappled in the Battle of the Bulge or across the Russian Steppes, or for that matter the old-fashioned bomber squadrons that droned back and forth across the English Channel year after year dropping what the air force now contemptuously calls 'iron bombs' were more closely related to a remote past than to a foreseeable future."

Here, as I read it, Woodward is saying that devotees of history frequently seek to justify their study on the ground that there is always a continuity between the past and the present. The study of

the past, it is assumed, will reveal the continuity and thus will offer
guidance for the present. But, he implies further, this assumption is
sometimes wrong. In times of very rapid and fundamental change,
the continuity between the past and the present is broken. The task
of the historian is not simply to trace the continuity, even when it is
tenuous, but to examine the relationship between past and present
for the purpose of exposing the discontinuity as much as for emphasizing the continuity. For we could be as dangerously misled by an
apparition of continuity which does not really exist as by a failure to
recognize continuities which are genuine.

Much of the existing historical literature was written when "free
security" was taken for granted and when wars were fought with
limited weapons, and that was taken for granted also. It will be a
large task to rewrite this history in a way that takes account of our
new awareness that these factors were peculiar to a given place and
time, and were neither universal or immutable. But an even greater
body of the existing literature was Europe-centered. This literature,
also, was most pervasive. Non-Europeans as well as Europeans shared
the orientation which saw Europe as the center of the world. "The
. . . assumptions of Europocentric history have very largely shaped
the interpretation of Asiatic, African, and other non-European history . . . for Europe successfully marketed its historiography abroad,
along with its other cultural products, in remote and exotic climates."
The recognition, at last, of the restrictiveness of this view creates a
need for the rewriting of a very substantial proportion of all of
modern history from a new standpoint.

From these three new challenges to the historian Woodward
turned back, near the end of his essay, to an evocative and statesman-
like affirmation, again, of the role of the historian. The historians of
this generation, he asserted, have a peculiar responsibility as inter-
mediaries between a past that could not foresee the future and a
future which may not be able to understand the past. For these
historians carry with them into the new order a personal experience
of the old.

Americans among them will remember a time when security was
assumed to be a natural right, free and unchallengeable. Among them
also will be men of many nations who manned the ships and fought the
battles of another age of warfare. And nearly all of this generation of
historians will have been educated to believe that European culture was

Civilization and that non-European races, if not natively inferior, were properly under perpetual tutelage. They will be the only generation of historians in history who will be able to interpret the old order to the new order with the advantage and authority derived from firsthand knowledge of the two ages and participation in both.

Here Woodward again affirmed his faith that it is not enough for the historian to understand the past; he must also interpret it to those who live in the present. In the final paragraph of "The Age of Reinterpretation," he made this affirmation even more explicit. The accelerated process of historical change, he said, gives a peculiar urgency to the public demand for answers to questions about the past and its relation to the present and the future.

If historians evade such questions, people will turn elsewhere for the answers, and modern historians will qualify for the definition that Tolstoi once formulated for academic historians of his own day. He called them deaf men replying to the questions that nobody puts to them. If, on the other hand, they do address themselves seriously to the historical questions for which the new age demands answers, the period might justly come to be known in historiography as the age of reinterpretation.[13]

In this statement, renouncing a traditional concept of restrictions upon the academic historian, Woodward formally enunciated a position which, in operative terms, he had occupied from the beginning of his career. Consistently, his writing had reflected a purpose to identify the true values of the past and to make them meaningful to his contemporaries. In his quest for values, he held to two especially.

One of these was from his own birth and rearing—the value of the Southern heritage. In "The Search for Southern Identity," he had said, "After Faulkner, Wolfe, Warren, and Welty, no literate Southerner could remain unaware of his heritage or doubt its enduring value."[14] This belief in the enduring values of the South is deepseated, and when Woodward totally rejects the traditional Southern attitudes on race, he regards it not as a rejection of Southernism but a rejection of a spurious value which has discredited the true Southern position. But he is still capable of resenting even attacks on biracialism when they run over into disparagement of the South as a whole. This fact was evident in his courteous but nonetheless devastating review of Dwight Dumond's indiscriminately worshipful treatment of the abolitionists in a work entitled *Antislavery*.[15] It was evident also in some pointed comments in his essay "From the First Reconstruction to the Second" (1965):

> The South has lately had its "Epitaph" written and its "Mystique" debunked. The implication would seem to be that the South's disputed "distinctiveness" and Southern identity inhere essentially in retrograde racial policies and prejudices. With the gradual disappearance of these, Southerners are expected to lose their identity in a happily homogenized nation. Quite apart from the South's preferences, there are other reasons for skepticism in this matter. The South has long served the nation in ways still in great demand. It has been a moral lightning rod, a deflector of national guilt, a scapegoat for stricken conscience. It has served the country much as the Negro has served the white supremacist—as a floor under self-esteem. This historic role, if nothing else, would spare the region total homogenization, for the national demand for it is greater than ever.[16]

To say that the Southern heritage had enduring value meant that it must not be defined in terms of things that lacked value—such as segregation and the doctrine of white supremacy. Hence Woodward rejected Ulrich Phillips's formulation of "The Central Theme of Southern History," which identified the South in terms of the region's conviction that the South "shall be and remain a white man's country." There is, of course, copious and unedifying evidence that this conviction has been an enduring element in the quality of Southernism, and people who do not like the South are quite ready to make racism a prominent factor in their analysis of Southernism. But precisely because Woodward attached enduring value to some aspects of the Southern tradition, he could not accept their view. The South might have, in one side of its character, a quality of racism, discrimination, and repression, but it also had on the other side, a record of Jeffersonian liberalism. It must be saved from its worse side by an appeal to its better side. Once before the South had made the mistake of giving "priority to the worse side by choosing to identify its whole cause with the one institution [slavery] that was most vulnerable," and it had paid dearly for this folly. This must not happen again:

> . . . if Southernism is allowed to become identified with a last ditch defense of segregation, it will increasingly lose its appeal among the younger generation. Many will be tempted to reject their entire regional

identification, even the name "Southern," in order to disassociate themselves from the one discredited aspect.[17]

As a comment on the consequences of identification with a discredited cause, this observation was, no doubt, pragmatic and sagacious, but in terms of historical method, it possessed startling implications. For it clearly implied that the degree of the historian's emphasis upon the identification of the South with slavery and later with segregation should be determined not by the actual extent of the South's commitment to these practices, but by the effect which such an identification would have upon the loyalties of Southerners to the better values of Southernism. The use of history to sanction meritorious values would take a priority over the use of it to portray realistically some of the evils of the past.

To leave the statement at this point would do an injustice to Woodward by picking out one strand of his thought and separating it from the broader fabric of which this strand was a part. This broader context was one of scrupulous adherence to rigorous historical criteria. As much as almost any contemporary American historian, Woodward has approached his material with a dedicated purpose to take the whole record into account, to see all sides of a topic, to qualify and hedge his generalizations, and to avoid the ease of simplification. These traits are strikingly evident, for instance, if one compares his treatment of slavery with the treatments by William E. Dodd and Frank L. Owsley. All three of these men were Southerners; all were committed to a liberal's sympathy with the dirt farmer; and all were embarrassed by the Southern treatment of the Negro. Dodd and Owsley expressed this embarrassment by avoiding the issue—Dodd by arguing that the South would, on its own initiative, have gotten rid of slavery but for the distorting effect of extraneous forces; Owsley by constructing an image of a South populated by "plain folk" (white) or yeomen—a land in which slaveholders were not important and slaves were, somehow, not quite visible.[18] Woodward, by contrast, faced up to the problems of racism, and the latter half of his biography of Watson is a grim record of Negrophobia, blatant discrimination, and lynch law, just as the first half is a record of Watson's effort, in the first phase of his life, to achieve an accord between Negroes and whites in the Populist movement. ("The People's Party," declared Watson, "says to these two men [the Negro farmer and the White farmer], 'You are made to hate each other because upon that hatred is rested . . . the financial despotism which enslaves you both.' ")[19]

Woodward found an ideal topic in Watson because the early part of Watson's career brought Woodward's second major value, liberalism, into conjunction with his first, the value of the Southern tradition properly understood. The early Watson hated economic exploitation, hated racial antagonism, denounced lynch law, and demanded recognition of the legal rights of Negroes. Woodward, looking for such experience in the past as would be meaningful to the present, found it, almost to perfection, in the career of Watson. That career did not conceal the grim and realistic actuality that segregation and injustice to the Negro dominated the Southern scene in the first two decades of this century, but it did show that *there had been an alternative*. Watson had seen the alternative, though his vision later failed and he lost sight of it. To Woodward, with his conviction that the historian must reconstruct the past accurately and at the same time make it speak to the present, the accuracy of the reconstruction lay in the recognition of Watson's failure and in the ultimate ascendancy of the worst features of his nature. But the message for the present lay in the fact that Watson had for a time seen a vision of a better way. The better way was not illusory; it had been a viable alternative. It failed not because inevitable forces caused it to fail, but because men who might have grasped it did not do so. Other men, in the present, might do so. No deterministic force, in Woodward's belief, foredoomed their effort, for as he has declared, "I am not a determinist of any sort."[20] The first lesson of the past to the present is that men have choices and that no iron law of the operation of blind forces prevents men from exercising these choices.

This viewpoint was peculiarly pertinent to Southern attitudes toward segregation, for white Southerners showed a marked tendency to believe that the sharp separation of Negroes and whites was as old as the world, a reflex of basic human nature, and quite beyond the reach of any social policy. Many developments in the 1930's and 1940's led liberals to believe, with increasing conviction, that segregation must be done away with, and that social attitudes toward questions of race must be changed in order that racial relations might change. This conviction was already strong when the decision of the Supreme Court in the case of *Brown* vs. *The Board of Education* was handed down by the Supreme Court in May, 1954. When the Court spoke, the first reaction throughout the country was to ask how the South would respond? Would it show the old fierce resistance to "outside" attempts to change the harsh taboos of racial separation, or would it comply with the decision of the Court? Here was a time, indeed, for the past to speak to the present in other than purely traditional terms.

During the following autumn, Woodward delivered the James W. Richard lectures at the University of Virginia. In 1955, while Woodward was Harmsworth Professor of American History at Oxford, they were published under the title of *The Strange Career of Jim Crow*, and they quickly became and have remained his most famous book. These lectures really do not compare with his *Watson* or his *Origins of the New South* as major works of history, but they will nevertheless require almost as extensive discussion here because of the misunderstandings and controversy which they engendered and because of the fundamental questions which they raised.

In the first chapter of the *Strange Career*, significantly entitled "Forgotten Alternatives," Woodward sought to develop a point which he had stated clearly, in more condensed form in *Origins of the New South* (pp. 209–212): namely, that the formal structure of legal segregation which the South believed had existed forever had, in fact, not existed in full form until some years after the end of Reconstruction. True, he recognized, separation began soon after the Civil War in the churches, and it began in the schools as soon as former slaves began to go to school. But there was, he believed, scarcely any "evidence of a movement to make segregation universal. . . . More than a decade was to pass after Redemption [the end of Reconstruction] before the first Jim Crow law was to appear upon the law books of a Southern state, and more than two decades before the older states of Virginia, North Carolina, and South Carolina were to adopt such laws." In elaboration of this statement, Woodward proceeded to quote two Northern travelers, one British traveler, two Southern editorials, one Southern white, and one Negro, all seven of whom testified that Negroes and whites in the South mingled, with very little tension and with considerable spontaneity and ease, in public saloons, dining rooms, trains, street cars, theaters, and soda fountains. If this evidence was limited, it was explicit and seemingly quite reliable. With scrupulous care, Woodward also pointed out that there had never been a "golden age of race relations" in the South, and that "the evidence of race conflict and violence, brutality and exploitation in this very period is overwhelming." But the over-all impression, formed by many readers, was that this was a subsidiary point.

Having made this qualification, he then moved on to say that, "before the South capitulated completely to the doctrines of the extreme racists, three alternative philosophies of race relations were put forward": one a conservative or aristocratic philosophy which accepted a responsibility for the paternal care of the Negroes and regarded all lower-class people, either Negro or white, with very much the same condescension; another, a radical philosophy which sought to form a political combination of Negro and white dirt farmers against those who were exploiting them economically; and third, a liberal philosophy which, on principle, advocated equal rights and protection for all citizens. He traced each of these three briefly, and then again entered a disclaimer: he did not wish to exaggerate the degree of interracial harmony. There were Negrophobes and hypocrites in all of these camps. Indeed he concluded:

My only purpose has been to indicate that things have not always been the same in the South. In a time when the Negroes formed a much larger proportion of the population than they did later, when slavery was a live memory in the minds of both races, and when the memory of the hardships and bitterness of Reconstruction was still fresh, the race policies accepted and pursued in the South were sometimes milder than they became later. The policies of proscription, segregation, and disfranchisement that are often described as the immutable "folkways" of the South, impervious alike to legislative reform and armed intervention, are of a more recent origin. The effort to justify them as a consequence of Reconstruction and a necessity of the times is embarrassed by the fact that they did not originate in those times. And the belief that they are immutable and unchangeable is not supported by history.[21]

Despite all Woodward's care to insert caveats, qualifiers, and disclaimers, the *Strange Career* ran into two difficulties. First was the problem that when the past speaks to the present, it cannot speak to everyone alive in the present, but must speak to particular groups. When Woodward delivered the Richard lectures at Charlottesville, he was speaking to such a group—to Southern whites who needed to learn that segregation had not been included among the Ten Commandments. If he had been able to limit his message to the audience for whom it was intended, there would never have been any confusion. The audience knew that segregation and discrimination had been the dominant patterns of the South, and what Woodward told them was that these patterns had not been either absolute or universal or immutable. This was a useful fact for them to learn. But as soon as the lectures were published, they reached a vast audience. Ironically, Woodward's least substantial book was the one that made his public, as distinguished from his professional, reputation. More than any modest man could possibly have anticipated, he found himself addressing a vast, amorphous audience of people, many of whom had formed their impressions of the South from *Gone With the Wind* or *Tobacco Road*, who regarded the region as a never-never land, and who, unlike the people of Charlottesville, were prepared to believe anything. Many of these avid readers wishfully read into Woodward's lectures an idyllic image of a South in which race antagonism did not rear its unlovely head until the twentieth century.

To state this in another way, the historian who seeks to interpret the life of the past to the men of the present usually winds up by giving less of his attention to reconstructing what the past was "really" like, than to identifying the misconceptions of men in the present, and devising ways to correct these misconceptions. But since all sorts of various people entertain all sorts of various misconceptions, the labor of correcting the misconceptions impels the historian to address himself to a focus which is neither unitary nor fixed. What he writes will be relative in any case, but instead of being relative to what happened to a determinate group of people in the past, it becomes relative to what misconceptions are held, at a given moment, by indeterminate groups of people in the present. His task becomes a labor of Hercules. Perhaps the labor it most closely resembles is that of cleaning the Augean stables.

The second difficulty encountered by the *Strange Career* arose from the fact that when an historian has a strong ideological commitment, a tension may be set up between his devotion to the commitment and his devotion to realism for its own sake. In Woodward's own terms, it is ironically conceivable that when a deaf man gives answers to questions which no one is asking he may be worth listening to precisely because he is more concerned with what he himself sees than with what other people, at the moment, want to know. In any case, Woodward had undertaken the arduous task of finding answers in the Southern past to questions which people were asking in 1954. This undertaking never led him to the obvious fallacies of simpler minds engaged in the same task—the fallacy, for instance, of believing that the South seriously considered abolishing slavery as late as 1830. But it did lead him to an inner struggle in which his historical realism was pitted against his liberal urge to find constructive meanings in the past for the affairs of the present. His realism never lost hold, but his liberal urge constantly impelled him to emphasize viewpoints which his realism constantly impelled him to qualify and dilute.

This inner struggle was, I believe, especially evident in the *Strange Career*. It was evident in the sense that the array of evidence presented, though by no means all on one side, would lead a reader to minimize the importance of segregation in the South in the 1870's, 1880's, and 1890's, far more than the general bulk of other evidence would do.[22] This fact became apparent subsequently, from a series of intensive analyses of Negro-white relations in the late nineteenth century by a number of investigators working state by state: Charles E. Wynes for Virginia (1961), Frenise A. Logan for North Carolina (1964), and Joel Williamson for South Carolina (1965).

Of these "revisionists," only Wynes discussed Woodward by name, and Wynes was the least disposed of the three to take issue with him. The picture of segregation in Virginia between 1870 and 1900, as Wynes saw it, was mixed. Often the Negro who sought to frequent places of public resort met with rebuffs, but "Occasionally the Negro met no segregation when he entered restaurants, bars, waiting rooms, and other places of public amusement." "The Woodward thesis," he thought, "is essentially sound," but "most of the time, however, he [the Negro] did meet segregation, opposition, or eviction."[23] For North Carolina, Logan emphasized the dominance of segregation somewhat more: "The most effective limitations . . . on the relationship between white and Negro were the unwritten agreements among the whites that any approach to 'social equality' should be resisted at all costs. The matter of social equality was most sharply focused upon when it revolved around the segregation of Negroes on public carriers, in waiting rooms, and in hotels and restaurants."[24] But it was Williamson's conclusions that were most at variance with Woodward's. His evidence seemed to show that "the physical separation of the races was the most revolutionary change in relations between whites and Negroes in South Carolina during Reconstruction." "The pattern of separation was fixed in the minds of the whites almost simultaneously with the emancipation of the Negro. By 1868, the physical color line had, for the most part, already crystallized." But the real separation, he continued, was "mental separation. . . . The rigidity of the physical situation, set as it was like a mosaic in black and white, itself suggested the intransigence of spirit which lay behind it . . . the heartland of racial exclusiveness remained inviolate; and South Carolina had become, in reality, two communities—one white and the other Negro."[25]

More telling, perhaps than any of these analyses of the post-bellum period was Richard C. Wade's study in 1964, *Slavery in the Cities*. Woodward had regarded it as almost axiomatic that "segregation would have been impractical under slavery"—that where slavery existed, the circumstances giving rise to segregation did not exist. But Wade presented evidence to show that in the towns of the South long before the Civil War, where the surveillance of the Negroes, characteristic of the slave system, could no longer be maintained, "the distinction between slave and free Negro was erased; race became more important than legal status; and a pattern of segregation emerged inside the broader framework of the peculiar institution."[26]

In later editions of the *Strange Career* Woodward scrupulously took note of these studies, and in fact he anticipated them as early as 1957 in a foreword to the first paperback edition, in which he recognized that segregation was initially foreshadowed in the cities, even before the end of slavery, and in which he called attention to a number of early segregation laws (Mississippi and Florida, 1865; Texas, 1866; Tennessee, 1881),[27] which were inconsistent with his earlier statement that it was more than a decade after Redemption "before the first Jim Crow law was to appear upon the law books of a Southern state."

If Woodward's dislike of segregation influenced him to minimize its prevalence, some critics have also felt that his desire to demonstrate the historical possibility of close and harmonious working relationships between Negroes and whites led him to overemphasize the importance of the cooperation between Negro and white farmers' alliances in the Populist contests of 1892. Again, this is very much a matter of emphasis. But in any case Woodward had not failed to point out that Watson himself, the chief architect of the cooperation, had recognized that race antagonisms were extremely real, and that the race issue was a great handicap to Southern Populism ("Bryan had *no everlasting and overshadowing Negro question to hamper and handicap his progress.* I HAD," said Watson).[28]

But there was one other case in which his impulse to find sanction in the past for ideas that he approves in the present may have led him to take a position from which he later felt impelled to withdraw. In 1958, in the *American Scholar* he published an essay, "Equality, the Deferred Commitment." In this paper he discussed the war aims of the Civil War: first, simply the preservation of the Union; later, freedom for the slaves; and finally, near the end, equality for the freedmen. The commitment to this third aim, he recognized, was never as clear-cut as the first two commitments—there was never an equality proclamation. But though "made piece-meal . . . and with full implications not spelled out until after the war . . . it [the commitment] was made." Challenged by Southern aggression against Negro rights after the war, the radical Republicans "proceeded to make equality as much the law of the land as freedom." Citing the Fourteenth and Fifteenth Amendments and the Civil Rights Acts of 1866 and 1875, Woodward concluded that

by every device of emphasis, repetition, reenactment, and reiteration, the radical lawmakers and Constitution-amenders would seem to have nailed down all loose ends, banished all ambiguity, and left no doubt whatever about their intention to extend Federal protection to Negro equality. So far as it was humanly possible to do so by statute and constitutional amendment, America would seem to have been fully committed to the principle of equality.[29]

Here again, Woodward was seeking to make the past speak to the present. The past had made a promise to American Negroes and then defaulted on it. It was the obligation of the present to honor and fulfill the promise. But some other scholars hesitated to read the promise of the past in this way or to agree that the United States had made a firm commitment a century ago to racial equality in the full sense. For instance, W. R. Brock, in his influential study *An American Crisis* in 1963 wrote: "racial equality was a hypothesis which was generally rejected. It was not accepted in the North any more than it was in the South and even abolitionists were anxious to disclaim any intention of forcing social contacts between the races and all shied away from the dread subject of racial amalgamation."

Brock did not go into much detail about the enactment of the specific measures which were regarded as embodying the principle of equality, but also in 1963, in a doctoral dissertation on radical Republican policy toward the Negro, written at Yale just before Woodward went there, Selden Henry presented a full and close analysis of the many complexities, parliamentary and otherwise, attending the enactment of the principal "equalitarian" measures. Henry made a strong, detailed demonstration that none of these measures involved a clear-cut showdown between the advocates and the opponents of equality for Negroes, and his evidence indicated that opposition to full equality remained in the ascendant throughout Reconstruction.

Woodward, it should be said, had always recognized, even in his "deferred commitment" essay, that there were many crosscurrents in the public attitude toward the freedmen and many mental reservations in the acceptance of equality, but as he considered the problem further, he began to stress the qualifications more than the thesis. By 1965, he was writing, "Even in . . . [the Civil Rights acts, the Reconstruction acts, and the Fourteenth and Fifteenth Amendments]—the very legal foundation for the new order of freedom and equality—can be found the compromises, half-measures, and ambivalences that are in essence concessions to racism." In another year, he made his reversal explicit in an essay in which he cited Henry and declared, "On the issue of Negro equality, the party remained divided, hesitant, and unsure of its purpose. The historic commitment to equality it eventually made was lacking in clarity, ambivalent in purpose, and capable of numerous interpretations." A footnote adds the laconic comment that, "This admittedly represents a change from views earlier expressed on the subject by the author."[30]

The urgency of Woodward's desire to find answers in the past which would aid in the quest for solution of the problems of the present must have had some effect upon these views of the past. If it could be shown historically that legalized segregation was relatively a new phenomenon, and that promises of equality were a century old, it might be easier to induce people to abandon segregation and to accord equality to Negroes. Since Woodward himself later modified or even changed his position on both of these matters, it seems reasonable to suppose that the tension between his devotion to liberal goals and his devotion to historical realism distorted his image of the past, at least for a time and to a limited degree.

But, as has already been suggested, Woodward never ignored the complexities. He never failed to point out that he was engaged in weighing conflicting bodies of evidence and that important evidence existed which ran counter to the view he was presenting. Always committed to the historian's task of translating the past to make it intelligible to the present, he was also always scrupulous not to translate too freely. But what he did not reckon with was that many of his readers, with far less disciplined ideological commitments than his, and with painfully limited appreciation of the historical context in which he was writing, did some translating on their own of his translation. The result was that many such readers came away from his writings with the totally fallacious notion that the American people had accepted Negroes as equals a hundred years ago and that a utopia of interracial harmony and good will had prevailed until the 1890's.

Woodward has commented unhappily on the strange career which the *Strange Career of Jim Crow* has experienced. In the Preface to the second revised edition (1966) he said: "Books that deal with subjects over which current political controversy rages are prone to uses and interpretations beyond the author's intentions or control. The present work has proved no exception and the author has been embarrassed by finding it cited—and misinterpreted—for purposes with which he sympathizes as well as for purposes he deplores." More recently, in *Harper's Magazine*, speaking of himself in the third person, he wrote:

One historian suggested that the full blown system of legally enforced segregation was not an immediate sequel of Appomattox, only to find himself cited as authority for the doctrine that Jim Crow was superficially rooted and easily eradicated. And when he called attention to the union of Negroes and whites in Southern Populism, he was interpreted as prophesying millennial developments in politics. It is no news to teachers, of course, that the lessons taught are not always the lessons learned.[31]

If Woodward has been troubled to find his words read in a way which he did not intend, he has clearly been much more troubled to have his hopes for the steady advancement and peaceful success of the Civil Rights movement frustrated. With a liberal's conviction that truth about the past can contribute with certainty to win public backing for voluntary, broadly based social progress, Woodward always intended for history to serve the cause of civil rights without sacrificing its integrity, and for the civil-rights cause to prevail without destroying the more vital values of the Southern tradition. In the first edition of the *Strange Career* he spoke of "the need of the times for whatever light the historian has to shed upon a perplexing and urgent problem." He also asserted that the changes in "the old system of disfranchisement and segregation" were so extensive that they could be termed a "New Reconstruction." His tone, as he himself expressed it, was one of "restrained optimism," and in the 1957 edition he said, "In spite of resistance and recent setbacks, therefore, the preponderant evidence points to the eventual doom of segregation in American life and the triumph of the Second Reconstruction *in the long run*."[32]

One feature which accentuated the optimistic tenor of the *Strange Career* was that, in it, Woodward did not, in fact, attempt to treat the whole biracial system, in all its historical, economic, and cultural complexities. Instead he dealt quite explicitly with only one feature—namely, the structure of formal, institutional arrangements—mostly in the form of statutes or ordinances—by which the separation of whites and Negroes had been enforced. Indeed it was this structure, strictly speaking, which constituted the "Jim Crow" phenomenon. The Jim Crow structure, of course, did much to maintain the whole system of biracialism, and was so interwoven with the whole system that some optimists mistakenly believed that biracialism could not exist without it. Woodward did not make this error, but he did restrict his focus to one aspect of the system, and to the most vulnerable aspect of all. Once the Brown decision had been made, it was relatively easy to sweep away all the accumulation of public regulations which had imposed legal disabilities and *de jure* segregation upon Negroes. After the court decisions were reinforced by a series of civil-rights acts by Congress in 1957, 1960, and 1964, and by a voting-rights act in 1965, it was possible to say, as Woodward did in the 1966 edition of the *Strange Career*, that "Jim Crow as a legal entity was dead."[33]

But written statutes in books are far easier to change than educational differentials, employment differentials, residential differentials, and other disparities that have already molded the society and irrevocably shaped the lives of millions. Also formal enactments are easier to get at than covert attitudes and unspoken feelings of apartness. Therefore, even at a time when Jim Crow was dying, racial tensions were becoming in some ways more acute. Because of this, the reader of the 1966 edition of the *Strange Career* was brought abruptly at the end of the book to the disconcerting realization that while his attention had been focused upon the slow demise of formal segregation, the principal issues of interracial antagonism had been shifting elsewhere as the Negro revolution changed course. Only five days after Lyndon Johnson signed the Voting Rights Act, which might be regarded as the final step in the elimination of Jim Crow, the Watts riot broke out in Los Angeles.

Just as the abolition of slavery had ended one stage of the relationship of Negroes and whites in America without solving the problem of that relationship, the abolition of Jim Crow ended another stage, but again without solving the problem of the relationship. Woodward recognized this in three final paragraphs in the 1966 edition, in which he asserted vaguely that "civil rights laws were not enough," and that "broader and more drastic remedies" were needed.[34]

Woodward's impulse to think of the handicaps of American Negroes in terms of formal segregation was, of course, in line with most of the thinking on the subject during the first decade after the Brown decision. Most of the reform activity of that decade was directed toward destroying the barriers of legal separation in schools, buses, waiting rooms, restaurants, etc. So long as this was so, the decline of Jim Crow gave the deceptive appearance of being equivalent to the ending of racial tensions. For a long time no one asked about the cultural, occupational, economic, and other disparities that would be left when formal segregation was swept away, and about the antagonisms that might develop when discrimination and Negro disadvantages were found to remain after all legal inequality had been abolished. Woodward's view was no more restrictive than anyone else's, but his hope, as a Southerner, for a new order, voluntarily instituted, and his faith, as a liberal, in rational, peaceful reform through mediated changes in public policy—these things had given him a perfect affinity for the civil-rights movement, but found him far less compatible with the impulses toward Negro revolution. It is, of course, not yet clear how much of a revolutionary component the Negro movement holds, nor is it clear just how Woodward will respond to some aspects of it. His difficulty in responding showed up rather clearly in 1966 in the brief, hasty, tacked-on passages about the Watts riot. These seemed far less thoughtful than most of his writing, which has consistently been distinguished for its contemplative quality and its interpretive power.

But in January, 1967, in an essay in *Harper's Magazine* entitled "What Happened to the Civil Rights Movement?" he gave a more considered evaluation to the confused status of current Negro-white relationships. This statement offered some striking perspectives, if few answers, and it showed one more phase in Woodward's own quest for the use of history as a means of enabling the past to speak to the present.

From his viewpoint as a liberal,[35] he found the situation discouraging. The article was as pessimistic as any that he has published. Beginning with a foreboding reminder of the way in which the First Reconstruction (1865–1877) had lost its idealistic momentum, he sketched the peak of high idealism which the Second Reconstruction (since 1954) had reached in the sit-in movement, the marches on Washington and other cities, and all the singing and the dedication. From this peak, there had been a swift descent with "the triumph of tokenism," the divisions among Negroes, the ghetto riots, and the falling away of white participants in the movement as they shifted their attention to Vietnam, reacted negatively to Negro militancy, or simply became bored with long-sustained idealism, as people so often do. "If we are realists," he said, "we will no longer pretend that the movement for racial justice and Negro rights is sustained by the same foundation of moral assurance, or that it is supported today by the same political coalitions, the same inter-racial accommodations, and such harmony of purpose, commitment and dedication as recently prevailed." Noting "numerous white defections from the commitment to racial justice, the sudden silence in many quarters recently vocal with protest, the mounting appeal to bigotry and the scurry of retreat in Congress," he warned that "it would be the better part of realism to expect things to get worse before they get better." He suggested no specific measures that could make things better.[36]

But even as he discounted the social hopes that have shone implicitly through all of his writing from *Tom Watson* on, even as he recognized the fact that the present, at least at the moment, is not prepared to hear from the past the things which he has spent thirty years trying to show that the past has to say, he reaffirmed the two personal commitments, to historical realism and to liberalism, which he has sometimes had difficulty driving in tandem, but which he has used in conjunction as purposefully, as successfully, and with as evenhanded respect for the integrity of both commitments as any American historian.

His basic historical philosophy from the outset has been that the multiplicity of elements in any situation always offers diverse potentialities, and these diverse potentialities always offer society a choice of alternatives. History can help to show these alternatives. When society sees them, it can escape determinism and exercise choice. In the situation in 1967, Woodward saw many factors reducing the force of the civil-rights movement, but he also saw the presence of the largest body of independent Negro voters in history, and the existence of "a corps of Negro leaders that has not been surpassed in dedication, astuteness, and moral force by the leadership of any other great social movement of the century." The presence of these factors offered an alternative to the threatened deterioration of the civil-rights movement. So long as such elements exist, "there is no realism in accepting the current reaction as irreversible, and no rationality in despair."[37]

This statement was not only a seasoned evaluation, at a crucial transition point in its history, of a movement with which Woodward has been concerned from the beginning. It was also an affirmation, in a new context, of his conception of history as a key which the past gives us for guidance in confronting the problems of the present. But the difficulty with this concept lies in the dilemma: can history retain its integrity as a rigorous and disciplined form of scholarly inquiry even while partaking of public and functional uses in our encounters with current issues? The ideological assertion that it can is not a new conception and does nothing to resolve the dilemma. The resolution can only be meaningful at the operative level, and it is here that Woodward has made one of his most distinctive contributions to historiography. Despite what may have been his errors in regard to the absence of formal segregation in the generation after Reconstruction, and the nature of the commitment to equality in the decade after Appomattox, he has been remarkably successful in demonstrating that history can retain its basic scholarly validity even in a context of active presentism. It is not by theoretical logic that he has done this, but by his own treatment of the history of race relations in America.

His greatest significance to historical studies may lie in the fact that he has made himself the foremost practitioner of a concept of history which holds that the experience of the past can find its highest relevance in the guidance which it offers in living with the problems of the present. His work has shown that history can be used in this way, but only in the hands of a scholar of extraordinary maturity, humane understanding, breadth of mind, and capacity to combine tolerance with idealism. And his vicissitudes have shown that, even for a man with these qualities, this may be the most difficult as well as the most rewarding use of history.

Appendix

A Word About the Selected Publications

We feel that these essays are enhanced by the bibliographies which accompany them. These listings of titles are not meant to be definitive, however, for most scholars—and certainly those who feel a commitment to a general public as well as to their guild—write numerous articles for popular journals, most of which are distillations or by-products of their more serious work, and all review extensively. To list all such titles would be not only to double the size of our volume, for our historians were prolific, but to conceal the chief purpose of the bibliographies: to show, by a chronological listing, the development of a man's work. Titles are therefore restricted to books, written wholly or in part, or edited, by the scholar under review, and to articles published in the scholarly journals or for avowedly scholarly purposes.

Introduction

NOTES

1. An example of this approach is *The American Historian: A Social-Intellectual History of the Writing of the American Past* (New York, 1960) by Harvey Wish. While extremely useful in many ways, the book—as well as the approach—is rather like trying to recognize many old friends peering out upon us from a rapidly moving railway car as we stand on the platform of our own environment.
2. Too often this has been the case with the pamphlet publications of the

Service Center for Teachers of History (American Historical Association, Washington). Of the first 71 of these to appear, 35 deal with American history. The most recent of these, *The United States Since 1945* (1968) by Dewey W. Grantham, Jr., is very good of its kind, but its kind forces the author to deal with 160 books in 38 pages of prose.

3. *History* (Englewood Cliffs, N.J., 1965).

4. Bellot, *American History and American Historians* (Norman, Okla., 1952); Kraus, *The Writing of American History* (Norman, Okla., 1953); Wish is cited in note 1, above.

5. Those interested in the professionalization of history in the United States and elsewhere should consult Michel François, Boyd C. Shafer, et al., *Historical Study in the West* (New York, 1968), and John Snell, Dexter Perkins, et al., *The Education of Historians in the United States* (New York, 1962).

6. The most recent, and on the whole most successful, attempt to analyze the development of the historiographical position that speaks from this point of view is "The 'New Left' and American History: Some Recent Trends in the United States Historiography," by Irwin Unger, in *The American Historical Review* 77 (July, 1967): 1237–63. Often perceptive and usually friendly, this article nonetheless suffers from attempting to include too many historians who would not recognize themselves under the "New Left" rubric. Interested readers should, however, familiarize themselves with the work of William Appleman Williams, Eugene Genovese, or Staughton Lynd, and consult Barton J. Bernstein's collection of original essays by a variety of exponents of the still undefined position, *Towards a New Past: Dissenting Essays in American History* (New York, 1968).

7. The essays stand much as they were written, reflecting the individual approaches of the several contributors. We have exercised our editorial prerogative to bring a certain consistency into the essays, especially in mechanical matters, but since all historians know that a man is reflected through his style, we have not thought to insist upon a uniform approach. Some therefore write at greater length than others on the early, and personal, life of their subjects, and some prefer a present-tense approach to the past. We provided guidelines, including the suggestion that the essays on those historians still at mid-passage might be shorter than the others, but we did not tell anyone how to write his essay. A uniformity of tone, edited in, would merely be a foolish consistency, false to the variety of historical approaches. We did, however, supply a few connective phrases and reference points between the essays, editing them with the assumption that, while each could be read separately, the reader would gain most from reading the book as a whole, taking the essays in the order in which we have presented them.

1. Francis Parkman BY WILLIAM R. TAYLOR

NOTES

1. Parts of this essay appeared in my "A Journey into the Human Mind," *William and Mary Quarterly*, 3d ser. 19 (1962): 220–37, and in my "That Way Madness Lies: Nature and Human Nature in Parkman's La Salle," in Reuben A. Brower and Richard Poirier, eds., *In Defense of Reading* (New York, 1962), pp. 256–81.
2. Howard Doughty, *Francis Parkman* (New York, 1962); Wilbur R. Jacobs, ed., *Letters of Francis Parkman*, 2 vols. (Norman, Okla., 1960); Mason Wade, ed., *The Journals of Francis Parkman*, 2 vols. (New York, 1947). All of Parkman's histories are now in print.
3. For a selective bibliography of Parkman's published writings, see pp. 413–14.
4. See, for example, W. J. Eccles, "The History of New France According to Francis Parkman," *William and Mary Quarterly*, 3d ser. 18 (1961): 163–75; Sigmund Diamond, "An Experiment in Feudalism: French Canada in the Seventeenth Century," ibid., pp. 3–34; Howard H. Peckham, *Pontiac and the Indian Uprising* (Princeton, 1947); Wilbur R. Jacobs, "Was the Pontiac Uprising a Conspiracy?", *The Ohio Archaeological and Historical Society Quarterly* 50 (1950): 26–37.
5. See both Diamond, "Experiment," and Peckham, *Pontiac*.
6. Ibid.
7. The best biographical source for Parkman, apart from his own letters, is Howard Doughty's *Francis Parkman*. Doughty also provides the most careful and discriminating examination of Parkman as a literary stylist. Wilbur R. Jacobs has provided an informative and useful introduction to his edition of Parkman's letters. Parkman's papers are at the Massachusetts Historical Society.
8. Gabriel Kolko has argued very persuasively against the going thesis that Proper Boston as a whole was alienated from American economic development at the close of the century. See his "Brahmins and Business, 1870–1914: A Hypothesis on the Social Basis of Success in American History," in *The Critical Spirit*, ed. Kurt H. Wolff and Barrington Moore, Jr. (Boston, 1967), pp. 343–63. I would simply remind Professor Kolko that the term Brahmin was intended to refer to Proper Boston's secular priesthood, not to the class as a whole. He himself concedes that "among the nineteenth-century Brahmins could be found alienated, culturally accomplished, and pretentious elements, probably more than in any other city in the United States at the time" (p. 347).
9. Cited by Doughty, pp. 49–50.
10. Ibid.

11. An intelligent and balanced summary of recent attempts to analyze the nature of Parkman's ailments is to be found in the Introduction of Jacobs, ed., *Letters*, 1, xlv–xlvi, n. As Jacobs points out, several careful students of Parkman's symptoms have attributed his problems to specific physiological ailments, among them astigmatism and arthritis. The most interesting, and to me convincing analysis, however, is that of Dr. Louis Casamajor, "The Illness of Francis Parkman," *American Journal of Psychiatry* 17 (1951): 749–52, also cited by Jacobs. Casamajor emphasizes the neurotic pattern which appears to have underlain his other more obvious physical difficulties. All of these studies, perhaps necessarily, are excessively cautious and leave the situation far from clear. Most cautious of all is Doughty, who nonetheless provides the most convincing account of the consequences of Parkman's illness for his work. See especially pp. 221–26.

12. Jacobs, *Letters*, 1:178.
13. Ibid.
14. Doughty, p. 224.
15. Jacobs, *Letters*, 1:141–74.
16. Ibid., p. 184.
17. Ibid., p. 153.
18. Ibid., pp. 151–52.
19. Ibid., p. 143.
20. *Book of Roses* (Boston), pp. 95–96.
21. Jacobs, *Letters*, 1:143.
22. Ibid., p. 146.
23. Ibid., p. 162.
24. Ibid., p. 167.
25. Ibid., p. 185.
26. Ibid., pp. 165, 163.
27. Doughty, p. 315.
28. Parkman, Introduction to *Pioneers* (1905), p. xx.
29. Ibid., p. xxii.
30. *Montcalm and Wolfe* (1886), 2:282ff.
31. Ibid., p. 414.
32. The point is made by Doughty, p. 380.
33. Ibid., p. 358. See Howard R. Lamar's essay on Turner in the present volume.
34. *Pioneers*, p. 331.
35. Ibid., p. 332.
36. *La Salle and the Discovery of the Great West* (1886), p. 155.
37. Ibid., p. 155.
38. Ibid., p. 248.
39. Ibid., p. 280.
40. Ibid., p. 288. The succeeding paragraphs draw heavily on my "That Way Madness Lies."

41. Ibid., p. 54.
42. Ibid., p. 60.
43. Ibid., p. 139.
44. Ibid., p. 37.
45. Ibid., p. 37.
46. Ibid., p. 192.
47. Ibid., p. 165.
48. Ibid., pp. 196–97.
49. Ibid., pp. 396–97.
50. Ibid., p. 230.
51. Ibid., p. 184 n.
52. Ibid., pp. 406–08.
53. Ibid., p. 2.
54. Ibid.
55. Ibid., p. 199.
56. Ibid., p. 406.
57. Ibid., p. 3.
58. Ibid., p. 328.
59. Ibid., p. 329.
60. Ibid., p. 319.
61. Ibid.
62. Ibid., p. 320.
63. Ibid., p. 408.

SELECTED PUBLICATIONS

Books

The Oregon Trail. New York, 1849.

The Conspiracy of Pontiac and the Indian War After the Conquest of Canada, Boston, 1851.

Vassall Morton: A Novel. Boston, 1856.

Pioneers of France in the New World. Boston, 1865.

The Book of Roses. Boston, 1866.

The Jesuits in North America in the Seventeenth Century. Boston, 1867.

The Discovery of the Great West. Boston, 1869. A revised edition, including new materials, was published as *La Salle and the Discovery of the Great West* (Boston, 1879).

The Old Regime in Canada. Boston, 1874.

Count Frontenac and New France Under Louis XIV. Boston, 1877.

Montcalm and Wolfe. Boston, 1884.

Some of the Reasons Against Woman Suffrage. No date. Printed in 1887 at the request of a private group and containing a restatement of his arguments in two articles on the subject. See below.

Our Common Schools. Boston, 1890.

A Half-Century of Conflict. Boston, 1892.

Articles

"Exploring the Magalloway." *Harper's Magazine* 29 (1864).
"Manners and Customs of Primitive Indian Tribes." *North American Review* 101 (1866).
Articles in the *American Journal of Horticulture, and Florist's Companion:* "Cherokee Rose," "Spring Flowers," "Flowers of May," 1 (1867); "Aquilegia famosa," "Aquilegia durandii," "Large-flowered Campanula," "Durand's Columbine," "Magnolia Seedlings," "New Weigelias," 2 (1867); "Manure and the Flower-Garden," "The Phlox" (as F. P.), "A Plant for the Millions" (as F. P.), 3 (1868); "New Dwarf Perpetual Flowering Carnations," "Forest Pyrethrums," "Lilium auratum," "A New System of Rose-Culture," "Thujopsis dolabrata," "Tritoma uvaria," 4 (1868); "Comtesse de Chabrilland Rose," "Letter from Paris," 5 (1869); "A Distinction Without a Difference," "Variation of Flowers from Seed," "Hybrids of Lilium aurutum," "Tree-Weigelias," now *Tilton's Journal of Horticulture and Floral Companion* 6 (1869); "How to Propagate Shrubs," "The Japan Lilies," "Rose Victor Verdier," 7 (1870); "Clematis jackmani," "Spanish Iris," "Lilium pomonium," "The Pyrethrums," "How to Propagate Shrubs," 8 (1870); "Duetzia crenata flore pleno," "Hardy Spring Flowers," "Lilium tenuifolium," "Hybrid Perpetual Rose Mr. Charles Wood," "Stuartia pentagynia," "What Shall I Plant?" 9 (1871), the last issue of the journal.
"Cavalier de La Salle." *North American Review* 125 (1877).
"The Failure of Universal Suffrage." *North American Review* 126 (1878).
"Mr. Parkman and His Canadian Critics." *Nation* 27 (1878).
"The Woman Question." *North American Review* 129 (1879).
"The Woman Question Again." *North American Review* 130 (1880).
"The Acadian Tragedy." *Harper's Magazine* 69 (1884).
"Revocation of the Edict of Nantes." *Critic* 7 (1885).
"A Convent at Rome." *Harper's Magazine* 81 (1890).

Stories, Essays, Reviews, Letters, and Journals

"The Ranger's Adventure." *Knickerbocker Magazine* 25 (1845).
"The Scalp Hunter." *Knickerbocker Magazine* 25 (1845).
"A Fragment of Family History." *Knickerbocker Magazine* 25 (1845).
"The New Hampshire Ranger" (by Captain Jonathan Carver, Jr.). *Knickerbocker Magazine* 25 (1845).
"Satan and Dr. Carver" (by Captain Jonathan Carver, Jr.). *Knickerbocker Magazine* 25 (1845).
Review of James Fenimore Cooper's "Works." *North American Review* 74 (1852).
Review of H. H. Bancroft's "The Native Races of the Pacific States of North America." *North American Review* 120 (1875).

Review of Pierre Margry's "Découvertes et établissements des Français dans l'ouest." *Nation* 23 (1876).
Review of C. S. Sargent's "The Forests and the Census." *Atlantic Monthly* 55 (1885).
The Journals of Francis Parkman. Edited by Mason Wade. 2 vols. New York, 1947.
The Letters of Francis Parkman. Edited by Wilbur R. Jacobs. 2 vols. Norman, Okla., 1960.

2. Henry Adams BY J. C. LEVENSON

NOTES

1. *The Education of Henry Adams* (Boston, 1918), p. 16.
2. Adams to Charles Milnes Gaskell, Washington, November 25, 1877, in Worthington Chauncey Ford, ed., *Letters of Henry Adams,* 2 vols. (Boston, 1930, 1938), 1: 302.
3. Adams to Francis Parkman, Washington, December 21, 1884, Harold Dean Cater, ed., *Henry Adams and His Friends* (Boston, 1947), p. 134.
4. Adams to Charles William Eliot, Boston, March 2, 1877, in Cater, ed., pp. 80–81.
5. Adams to Gaskell, Beverly Farms, Mass., September 24, 1882, in Ford, ed., *Adams,* 1: 339.
6. "Von Holst's History of the United States," *North American Review* 23 (1876): 355–56.
7. Adams to Henry Cabot Lodge, Beverly Farms, Mass., August 23, 1876, in Ford, ed., 1: 296.
8. Adams to Lodge, Paris, October 6, 1879, in Ford, ed., 1: 314.
9. *The Life of Albert Gallatin* (Philadelphia, 1879), p. 273.
10. Ibid., p. 561.
11. Ibid., pp. 272–73.
12. Ibid., p. 559.
13. Ibid., p. 560.
14. Ibid., p. 432.
15. Adams to Lowell, Paris, September 24, 1879, in Cater, ed., p. 92.
16. Henry Adams, *History of the United States During the Second Administration of Thomas Jefferson: 1805–1809.* (Privately printed, John Wilson and Son, University Press, Cambridge, Mass., 1885), p. 227. One of six copies printed from the draft text of the *History,* this volume was sent to Charles Francis Adams, Jr., for critical comment and returned to the author with marginal annotations (Massachusetts Historical Society).
17. *History of the United States,* 9 vols. (New York, 1889–1891), 1: 182–83.
18. Ibid., 1: 172.

19. Ibid., 1: 174.
20. Ibid., 1: 60.
21. Ibid., 1:242.
22. Ibid., 3: 114.
23. Ibid., 3: 387.
24. Ibid., 3: 124.
25. Ibid., 4: 135.
26. Ibid., 1: 214, 217.
27. Ibid., 4: 273.
28. Ibid., 4: 277.
29. Ibid., 4: 272.
30. Ibid., 4: 289.
31. Ibid., 7: 70.
32. Ibid., 3: 45.
33. Adams to Samuel Jones Tilden, Washington, January 24, 1883, in Cater, ed., p. 126.
34. *History of the United States*, 9: 52.
35. Adams to William James, Beverly Farms, Mass., July 27, 1882, in Cater, ed., pp. 121–22.
36. *History of the United States*, 8: 20.
37. "The Tendency of History," in Brooks Adams, ed., *The Degradation of the Democratic Dogma* (New York, 1919), pp. 126 ff.
38. *American Historical Review* 1 (1895): 51.
39. *Mont-Saint-Michel and Chartres* (Boston, 1933), p. 224.
40. *Education*, p. x.
41. Ibid., p. 4.

SELECTED PUBLICATIONS

Books

Chapters of Erie and Other Essays. Charles F. Adams and Henry Adams. Boston, 1871. Includes "The New York Gold Conspiracy" (1870), "Captain John Smith" (1867), "The Bank of England Restriction" (1867), "British Finance in 1816" (1867), "The Legal Tender Act" (1870).

Essays in Anglo-Saxon Law. Henry Adams, ed. Boston, 1876. Includes "Anglo-Saxon Courts of Law" by Henry Adams.

Documents Relating to New England Federalism, 1800–1815. Henry Adams, ed. Boston, 1877.

The Life of Albert Gallatin. Philadelphia, 1879.

The Writings of Albert Gallatin, Henry Adams, ed. 3 vols. Philadelphia, 1879.

Democracy: An American Novel. New York, 1880.

John Randolph. American Statesmen Series. Boston, 1882.

Esther: A Novel. [Frances Snow Compton]. New York, 1884.

History of the United States of America During the First Administration of Thomas Jefferson. Cambridge, Mass., 1884. Privately printed. Six copies. No copies of this private edition have been found so far.

History of the United States of America During the Second Administration of Thomas Jefferson. Cambridge, Mass., 1885. Privately printed. Six copies.

History of the United States of America During the First Administration of James Madison: 1809–1893. Cambridge, Mass., 1888. Privately printed. Six copies.

History of the United States of America During the First Administration of Thomas Jefferson. 2 vols. New York, 1889. Corrected and revised from the privately printed volume.

History of the United States of America During the Second Administration of Thomas Jefferson. 2 vols. New York, 1890. Corrected and revised from the privately printed volume.

History of the United States of America During the First Administration of James Madison. 2 vols. New York, 1890. Corrected and revised from the privately printed volume.

History of the United States of America During the Second Administration of James Madison. 3 vols. New York, 1891.

Historical Essays. New York, 1891. Contains "Primitive Rights of Women" (revision of Lowell Institute lecture of December 9, 1876), "The Declaration of Paris," "Harvard College, 1786–1787" (1872), "The Session, 1869–70" (1870), "Napoleon at St. Domingo" (French version, 1884), and four essays from *Chapters of Erie.*

Memoirs of Marau Taaroa, Last Queen of Tahiti. Washington, 1893. Privately printed. Revised and enlarged as *Memoirs of Arii Taimai E Marama of Eimeo Teriirere of Tooraai Teriinui of Tahiti.* Privately printed. Paris, 1901.

Mont-Saint-Michel and Chartres. Washington, 1904. Privately printed.

The Education of Henry Adams. Washington, 1907. Privately printed.

Letters of John Hay and Extracts from Diary. 3 vols. Washington, 1908. Privately printed by Clara Hay. "The major work of selecting and transcribing the materials was done by Adams as the initial editor. He also wrote the unsigned introduction, vol. I, pp. i–xxii"— Ernest Samuels.

A Letter to American Teachers of History. Baltimore, 1910. Privately printed.

The Life of George Cabot Lodge. Boston, 1911.

Mont-Saint-Michel and Chartres. Boston, 1913.

The Education of Henry Adams. Boston, 1918. "Editor's Preface" signed "Henry Cabot Lodge" was written by Adams; subtitle "An Autobiography" was not authorized by Adams.

The Degradation of the Democratic Dogma. With an introduction by Brooks Adams. New York, 1919. Title was given by Brooks Adams.

Includes "The Tendency of History" (1894), *A Letter to American Teachers of History* (1910), and "The Rule of Phase Applied to History" (first written in 1908).

Letters to a Niece and Prayer to the Virgin of Chartres. Mabel La Farge, ed. Boston, 1920.

A Cycle of Adams Letters, 1861–1865, Worthington Chauncey Ford, ed. 2 vols. Boston, 1920.

Letters of Henry Adams, 1858–1891, Worthington Chauncey Ford, ed. Boston, 1930.

Letters of Henry Adams: 1892–1918, Worthington Chauncey Ford, ed. Boston, 1938.

Henry Adams and His Friends. Letters edited (with a Biographical Introduction) by Harold Dean Cater. Boston, 1947.

The Great Secession Winter of 1860–1861 and Other Essays. George Hochfield, ed. New York, 1958. Includes fourteen essays and reviews: "The Great Secession Winter of 1860–61" (1910, written in 1861), "The Session" (1869), "Civil Service Reform" (1869), "Von Holst's *History* of the United States" (1876), "The Independents in the Canvass" (1876), "Count Edward de Crillon" (1895), and essays from collections listed above.

Articles

Articles in collections listed above are the principal ones.
In addition,

"American Finance, 1865–1869." *Edinburgh Review* 129 (1869). Unsigned.

"Albert Gallatin," in *Memorial Biographies of the New England Historic Genealogical Society,* vol. 1. Boston, 1880.

"King," in *Clarence King Memoirs.* New York, 1904.

With Sigourney W. Fay. "The Genesis of the Super-German," *Dublin Review,* April, 1918. Signed by Fay.

Other

The letters in collections listed above are of primary importance. Newspaper letters, book reviews, etc., are listed in the definitive biography, Ernest Samuels, *The Young Henry Adams, Henry Adams: The Middle Years,* and *Henry Adams: The Major Phase.* 3 vols. Cambridge, Mass., 1948–64. The principal collection of manuscripts and a major part of Adams' library are at the Massachusetts Historical Society. William Jordy, *Henry Adams: Scientific Historian.* New Haven, 1952; Arthur J. Beringause, *Brooks Adams.* New York, 1955; J. C. Levenson, *The Mind and Art of Henry Adams.* Boston, 1957; and George Hochfield, *Henry Adams: An Interpretation and Introduction.* New York, 1962, cover several aspects of Adams' historiography.

3. Frederick Jackson Turner   BY HOWARD R. LAMAR

NOTES

1. Phillips, "The Traits and Contributions of Frederick Jackson Turner," *Agricultural History* (1945), pp. 21–23. Accounts of Turner as teacher, scholar, and friend are numerous. A brilliant evaluation is to be found in Howard W. Odum, ed., *American Masters of Social Science* (1931), pp. 353–67, by Carl L. Becker. See also Avery O. Craven's tribute in William T. Hutchinson, ed., *Marcus W. Jernegan Essays in American Historiography* (Chicago, 1937), pp. 252–70. More personal are: Edgar E. Robinson, *North Dakota Historical Quarterly* 6 (1932): 259–61; Frederick Merk, *American Historical Review* 37 (1932): 823–24; Grace Lee Nute, *Minnesota History* 13 (1932): 159–161; and Max Farrand, Massachusetts Historical Society, *Proceedings* 65 (1935): 432–40. Still others may be found in O. L. Burnette, Jr., comp., *Wisconsin Witness to Frederick Jackson Turner* (Madison, 1961), p. 201 n.
2. Turner, "The Significance of the Frontier in American History," American Historical Association *Annual Report*, 1893 (Washington, 1894).
3. Quoted in Wilbur R. Jacobs, ed., *Frederick Jackson Turner's Legacy* (San Marino, Cal., 1965), pp. 36–37.
4. Fulmer Mood et al., *The Early Writings of Frederick Jackson Turner* (Madison, Wis., 1938), pp. 30–31; also Curti in Burnette, *Wisconsin Witness*, p. 185.
5. Curtis P. Nettels, "Frederick Jackson Turner and the New Deal," *Wisconsin Magazine of History* 17 (1934): 257–65.
6. For the best, see Gene M. Gressley, "The Turner Thesis: A Problem in Historiography," *Agricultural History* 32 (1958): 227–49; and Ray A. Billington, *America's Frontier Heritage* (New York, 1966), pp. 1–22 and 237–45.
7. Turner to Becker, February 13, 1926, in *Letters of F. J. Turner to Carl L. Becker, 1896–1932* (microfilm of materials from the Carl L. Becker Papers, Cornell University), State Historical Society of Wisconsin, Madison.
8. Mood, *Early Writings of Turner*, pp. 43–68.
9. Ray Allen Billington, "Young Fred Turner," *Wisconsin Magazine of History* 46 (1962–63): 38–48.
10. "Genesis of the Republican Party," March, 1898 (n.d.), Wisconsin *State Register*. Clipping in the Andrew Jackson Turner Papers, State Historical Society of Wisconsin, Madison.
11. "Turner's Autobiographic Letter of Constance Lindsay Skinner," in Burnette, *Wisconsin Witness*, pp. 55–67. See also Nute, in *Minnesota History*, in which she says: "Flowers, birds, music, art, a Maine trout at the end of his line, ducks settling on a reedy

lake and his friend Benson's etchings of them, dogs, the sea, and young minds entered largely into the pattern of his life." See also Billington, "Young Fred Turner," p. 42.

12. Ward actually grew up on an Iowa farm, and the Veblen family moved to Minnesota soon after Thorstein's birth.

13. Henry George, *Progress and Poverty* (New York, 1904), bk. 7, chap. 5, "Property in Land in the United States." The first edition of *Progress and Poverty* appeared in 1879.

14. Richard T. Ely, *Ground Under Our Feet* (New York, 1938), p. 198.

15. William Francis Allen in *Dictionary of American Biography* [hereafter, *DAB*] (New York, 1943), 1:211; also David B. Frankenburger, et al., eds., *Essay and Monographs by William Francis Allen: Memorial Volume* (Boston, 1890), but especially Allen's course notes "Medieval Institutions" and "History of Civilization" in Frederick Jackson Turner Papers, State Historical Society of Wisconsin, Madison; Mood, pp. 6–10; and Jacobs, *Legacy*, pp. 10–11.

16. Ely, *Ground Under Our Feet*, p. 182.

17. Billington, "Young Fred Turner," pp. 46–48.

18. Mood, pp. 11–15. Turner by this time had met and married Caroline Mae Sherwood. They had three children, only one of whom survived Turner.

19. Ray Allen Billington, *America's Frontier Heritage* (New York, 1966), p. 7.

20. Adams had been a founder of the American Historical Association; Small founded the *American Journal of Sociology*; Ely helped found the American Economic Association; and Wilson was a leading political scientist as well as historian.

21. Jacobs, p. 19; Billington, *America's Frontier Heritage*, p. 6.

22. Paxson, *When the West Is Gone* (New York, 1930), pp. 65–80. This book represents one of the most militant defenses of the frontier thesis in existence, and it is possible that many of the criticisms directed at Turner should have been pointed at Paxson.

23. Jacobs, pp. 85–104.

24. Turner to Becker, October 3, 1925, *Becker Papers* (microfilm), State Historical Society of Wisconsin.

25. *Herbert B. Adams: Tributes of Friends* (Baltimore, 1902), p. 38, 45, 67, 79, 109; Burleigh T. Wilkins, *Carl Becker: A Biographical Study in American Intellectual History* (Cambridge, Mass., 1961), pp. 50–51. "Turner and Burgess had in common a belief that if any reconciliation was to take place between the community and the citizen, it will be because we have learned to think historically," pp. 52–53.

26. "The Character and Influence of the Indian Trade in Wisconsin" (1891) is conveniently reproduced in Mood, pp. 84 ff.

27. "Thomas Chrowder Chamberlin" in *DAB*, 3:600–01.

28. *Bulletin of the University of Wisconsin, Economics, Political Science and History Series* 1 (1894).

29. W. L. Williamson, "A Sidelight on the Frontier Thesis: A New Turner Letter," The Newberry Library *Bulletin* 3 (1953); 46–49.

30. *Adams: Tributes of Friends*, pp. 21 ff. Turner recommended Shinn to Walter Hines Page in 1896 as the best man to write about the "spirit" of the Pacific states. Merrill Jensen, ed., *Regionalism in America* (Madison, 1951), pp. 92–93.

31. "Charles Richard Van Hise" in *DAB*, 19:194–95.

32. Billington, *America's Frontier Heritage*, pp. 9–11.

33. Lee Benson, *Turner and Beard, American Historical Writing Reconsidered* (Glencoe, Ill., 1960), pp. 42–91.

34. Ibid., p. 7, and also Turner quoting Loria, p. 27.

35. Wilkins, *Becker*, p. 36.

36. John T. Juricek, "American Usage of the Word 'Frontier' from Colonial Times to Frederick Jackson Turner," *Proceedings* of the American Philosophical Society 110 (1966): 10–34.

37. See Herman C. Nixon, "Precursors of Turner in the Interpretation of the American Frontier," *South Atlantic Quarterly* 28 (1939): 83–89.

38. Curti in Burnette, p. 193.

39. Benson, *Turner and Beard*, p. 87 n.

40. John W. Caughey, "The American West: Frontier and Region," *Arizona and the West* 1 (1959): 7–12.

41. Dale, "Memories of Frederick Jackson Turner," *Mississippi Valley Historical Review* 30 (1943): 339.

42. George Edward White, *The Eastern Establishment and the Western Experience: The West of Frederic Remington, Theodore Roosevelt, and Owen Wister* (New Haven, 1968).

43. Ely, p. 62.

44. A convenient bibliography of Turner's writings has been compiled by Everett E. Edwards, in Mood, pp. 231–72.

45. Turner, "The Problem of the West," *Atlantic Monthly* 78 (1896): 289–97. See also chap. 7 in Turner, *The Frontier in American History* (New York, 1920), pp. 205–06.

46. Turner, *The Frontier in American History*, p. 221.

47. "Dominant Forces in Western Life" is reprinted as chap. 8 in ibid.

48. "The Middle West" (1901) and "Contributions of the West to American Democracy" (1903) are reprinted as chaps. 4 and 9 in ibid.

49. See his "Pioneer Ideals and the State University" (1910), and "Middle Western Pioneer Democracy" (1918), chaps. 10 and 13 in ibid.

50. New York, 1906.

51. Jacobs, p. 28.

52. Turner to Becker, November 17, 1899, Becker Papers (microfilm), State Historical Society of Wisconsin; Jacobs, p. 29.

53. Dale, "Memories of Turner," pp. 339–57.
54. Turner to Becker, July 3, 1896, November 7, 1898, and April 13, 1907, Becker Papers (microfilm), State Historical Society of Wisconsin.
55. A. C. Krey, "My Reminiscences of Frederick Jackson Turner, April 18, 1960," typescript in the Turner Papers, Wisconsin State Historical Society; also "Notes on Turner's Harvard Lectures (1911–12)" by George P. Ettenheim, ms. in ibid. For a convenient summary see Wilbur R. Jacobs, "Frederick Jackson Turner—Master Teacher," *Pacific Historical Review* 23 (1954): 49–58.
56. Turner to Becker, December 16, 1925, *Becker Papers* (microfilm), State Historical Society of Wisconsin.
57. Turner to Becker, ibid. A convenient list of Turner's prominent students is to be found in Jacobs, "Frederick Jackson Turner—Master Teacher."
58. Jacobs, *Legacy*, pp. 31–33. Turner was also deeply involved in the role sports and particularly football—which he greatly enjoyed—were to play in college and university life. See Turner Papers, Box 2, State Historical Society of Wisconsin.
59. Jacobs, *Legacy*, pp. 33–34.
60. "Social Forces in American History" is reprinted as chap. 12 in Turner, *The Frontier in American History*.
61. Ibid., pp. 320, 279.
62. Benson, *Turner and Beard*, pp. 72–78, 83–89.
63. Jacobs, *Legacy*, p. 78.
64. Turner to Joseph Jastrow, October 5, 1910, Turner Papers, State Historical Society of Wisconsin.
65. "Sections and Nation," *Yale Review* 12 (1922): 1–21.
66. See Ralph H. Gabriel, *The Course of American Democratic Thought* (New York, 1940), pp. 269–79, as well as Josiah Royce, *Race Questions and Other American Problems* (1908).
67. "The Significance of the Section in American History" (1925) is to be found in Turner, *The Significance of Sections in American History* (New York, 1932).
68. Wilbur R. Jacobs, ed., "Frederick Jackson Turner's Notes on the Westward Movement, California and the Far West," *Southern California Quarterly* 46 (1964): 161–68; see also Earl S. Pomeroy, "Old Lamps for New: The Cultural Lag in Pacific Coast Historiography," *Arizona and the West* 2 (1960): 107–26, which points up the validity of Turner's observations about Bolton.
69. Turner, *The United States, 1830–1850: The Nation and Its Sections* (New York, 1935).
70. Benjamin F. Wright, "American Democracy and the Frontier," *Yale Review* 20 (1930): 349–65; and his "Political Institutions and the Frontier," in Dixon Ryan Fox, ed., *Sources of Culture in the Middle West* (New York, 1934), pp. 15–38; Louis B. Wright, *Culture on the Moving Frontier* (Bloomington, Ind., 1955).

71. Pierson, "The Frontier and Frontiersmen of Turner's Essays," *Pennsylvania Magazine of History and Biography* 64 (1940): 454–78; see also his "American Historians and the Frontier Thesis in 1941," *Wisconsin Magazine of History* 26 (1942): 36–60, 170–85; and finally his "The Frontier and American Institutions— A Criticism of the Turner Theory," *New England Quarterly* 15 (1942): pp. 224–55.

72. Pomeroy, "Toward a Reorientation of Western History: Continuity and Environment," *Mississippi Valley Historical Review* 41 (1955): 579–600.

73. Shannon, "A Post-Mortem on the Labor-Safety Valve Theory," *Agricultural History* 19 (1945): pp. 31–38.

74. Potter, *People of Plenty* (Chicago, 1954), p. 158.

75. Kesselman, "The Frontier Thesis of the Great Depression," *Journal of the History of Ideas* 29 (1968): 253–68. See also Warren I. Susman, "The Useless Past: American Intellectuals and the Frontier Thesis, 1910–1930," *Bucknell Review* 11 (1963): 1–20.

76. Discussion of the frontier "myth" now threatens to dominate Turner historiography. Especially useful are: Richard Hofstadter, "Turner and the Frontier Myth," *The American Scholar* 18 (1949): 433–43; Smith, *Virgin Land* (Cambridge, Mass., 1950); Ekirch, *Man and Nature in America* (New York, 1963), and his *The Idea of Progress in America, 1815–1860* (New York, 1944); Pearce, *The Savages of America: A Study of the Indians and the Idea of Civilization* (Baltimore, 1953); Ward, *Andrew Jackson, Symbol for an Age* (New York, 1955); Sanford, *The Quest for Europe and the American Moral Imagination* (Urbana, Ill., 1961); Moore, *The Frontier Mind: A Cultural Analysis of the Kentucky Frontiersman* (Lexington, Ky., 1957); Richard Hofstadter, *The Progressive Historians: Turner, Beard, Parrington* (New York, 1968); and Richard Hofstadter and Seymour Lipset, *Turner and the Sociology of the Frontier* (New York, 1968).

77. Becker in Odum, *American Masters of Social Science*, p. 13.

78. "The First Official Frontier of the Massachusetts Bay," chap. 2 in Turner, *The Frontier in American History*. For a challenge both to Turner's thesis and Becker's approach to the Revolution, see Robert E. Brown, *Middle Class Democracy and the Revolution in Massachusetts, 1691–1780* (Ithaca, N.Y., 1955).

79. "The Old West," chap. 3 in Turner, *The Frontier in American History*.

80. Thomas P. Abernethy, *Three Virginia Frontiers* (University, La., 1940); see also Francis S. Philbrick, *The Rise of the West, 1754–1830* (New York, 1965).

81. John D. Barnhart, *Valley of Democracy: The Frontier Versus the Plantation, 1775–1818* (Bloomington, Ind., 1953); Stanley Elkins and Eric McKitrick, "A Meaning for Turner's Frontier," *Political Science Quarterly* 69 (1954): 321–53, 562–602; Merle

Curti, *The Making of an American Community: A Case Study of Democracy in the Frontier County* (Stanford, Cal., 1959).

82. Lamar, *Dakota Territory, 1861–1889: A Study of Frontier Politics* (New Haven, 1956).

83. For examples of human and technological adjustments see Walter Prescott Webb, *The Great Plains* (New York, 1934); Gilbert Fite, *The Farmers' Frontier, 1865–1900*; Allen Bogue, *From Prairie to Cornbelt* (Chicago, 1963); and William N. Parker, "The Social Process of Agricultural Improvement: Sources, Mechanism and Effectiveness in the U.S. in the Nineteenth Century," Ms. paper presented to the Third International Congress of Economic History (Munich, 1965).

84. See, for example, Earl S. Pomeroy, *The Territories and the United States, 1861–1890* (Philadelphia, 1947), his "Toward a Reorientation of Western History," and his *The Pacific Slope: A History* (New York, 1965). See also William H. Goetzmann, *Exploration and Empire* (New York, 1966).

85. Pomeroy, "Toward a Reorientation of Western History," pp. 581–83.

86. Lamar, *The Far Southwest, 1846–1912: A Territorial History* (New Haven, 1966), and Rex W. Strickland, "The Turner Thesis and the Dry World," a paper read before the Southwestern Social Science Association (Texas Western Press, El Paso, 1960).

87. For a larger view of the Desert Frontier see Leonard Arrington, *Great Basin Kingdom* (Cambridge, Mass., 1958), and Eugene Hollon, *The Great American Desert* (New York, 1966).

88. Huntington, "Political Modernization: America *vs.* Europe," *World Politics* 18 (1966): 378–414.

SELECTED PUBLICATIONS

Books and Pamphlets

Outline Studies in the History of the Northwest. Chicago, 1888.

The Character and Influence of the Indian Trade in Wisconsin: A Study of the Trading Post as an Institution. Baltimore, 1891.

Suggestive Outlines for the Study of the History of the Middle West, Kentucky, and Tennessee. Madison, Wis., 1901.

Rise of the New West, 1819–1829. New York, 1906.

Guide to the Study and Reading of American History. With Edward Channing and A. B. Hart. Boston, 1912.

Reuben Gold Thwaites: A Memorial Address. Madison, Wis., 1913.

The Frontier in American History. New York, 1920.

The Significance of Sections in American History. New York, 1932.

The United States, 1830–1850: The Nation and Its Sections. New York, 1935.

Articles

"The Character and Influence of the Fur Trade in Wisconsin." Wisconsin State Historical Society, *Proceedings* 36 (1889).

"The Significance of History." *Wisconsin Journal of Education*, no. 21 (1891).

"The Extension Work of the University of Wisconsin." *University Extension* 1 (1892).

"The Significance of the Frontier in American History." American Historical Association, *Annual Report*, 1893. Washington, 1894. Also in State Historical Society of Wisconsin, *Proceedings* 41 (1894).

"Western State-Making in the Revolutionary Era." *American Historical Review* 1 (1895).

(Ed.) "Selections from the Draper Collection in the Possession of the State Historical Society of Wisconsin, to Elucidate the Proposed French Expedition under George Rogers Clark against Louisiana in the Years 1793–94." American Historical Association, *Annual Report*, 1896. Washington, 1897.

"The West as a Field for Historical Study." American Historical Association, *Annual Report*, 1896. Washington, 1897.

(Ed.) "Carondelet on the Defence of Louisiana, 1784." *American Historical Review* 2 (1897).

With others. "The Mangourit Correspondence in Respect to Genet's Projected Attack upon the Floridas, 1793–94." American Historical Association, *Annual Report*, 1897. Washington, 1898.

(Ed.) "Documents on the Relations of France to Louisiana, 1792–1795." *American Historical Review* 3 (1898).

(Ed.) "Jefferson to George Rogers Clark, 1783." *American Historical Review* 3 (1898).

(Ed.) "English Policy Toward America in 1790–1791." *American Historical Review* 7 (1902).

(Ed.) "Correspondence of the French Ministers to the United States, 1791–1797." American Historical Association, *Annual Report*, 1903. Washington, 1904.

"George Rogers Clark and the Kaskaskia Campaign, 1777–1778." *American Historical Review* 8 (1903).

(Ed.) "Documents on the Blount Conspiracy, 1795–1797." *American Historical Review* 10 (1905).

"The Policy of France Toward the Mississippi Valley in the Period of Washington and Adams." *American Historical Review* 10 (1905).

"The Colonization of the West, 1820–1830." *American Historical Review* 11 (1906).

"The South, 1820–1830." *American Historical Review* 11 (1906).

"Problems in American History." In Howard J. Rogers, ed., *International Congress of Arts and Science, Universal Exposition, St. Louis, 1904*. Boston, 1906.

"Is Sectionalism in America Dying Away?" *American Journal of Sociology* 13 (1908).

"The Old West." Wisconsin State Historical Society, *Proceedings* 56 (1908).

"Pioneer Ideals and the State University." *Indiana University Bulletin* 8 (1910).

"The Significance of the Mississippi Valley in American History." Mississippi Valley Historical Association, *Proceedings*, 1909–10.

"The Place of the Ohio Valley in American History." *Ohio Archaeological and Historical Quarterly* 20 (1911).

"Social Forces in American History." *American Historical Review* 16 (1911).

"The Harvard Commission on Western History." *Harvard Graduates' Magazine* 20 (1912).

"The Territorial Development of the United States." in *The Harvard Classics University Extension Court* 1. Cambridge, Mass., 1913.

"The First Official Frontier of the Massachusetts Bay." Colonial Society of Massachusetts, *Publications* 17 (1914).

"Frontier in American Development." In Andrew C. McLaughlin and A. B. Hart, eds., *Cyclopedia of American Government*, vol. 2. New York, 1914.

"Sectionalism in the United States." In *Cyclopedia of American Government*, vol. 3. New York, 1914.

"West as a Factor in American Politics." In *Cyclopedia of American Government*, vol. 3. New York, 1914.

"The West and American Ideals." *Washington Historical Quarterly* 5 (1914).

"Middle Western Pioneer Democracy." *Minnesota History Bulletin* 3 (1920).

"Greater New England in the Middle of the Nineteenth Century." American Antiquarian Society, *Proceedings*, n.s. 29 (1919).

A definitive bibliography, including book reviews, appears as "A Bibliography of the Writings of Frederick Jackson Turner and References on His Life and Work," compiled by Everett E. Edwards, in Fulmer Mood et al., *The Early Writings of Frederick Jackson Turner* (Madison, 1938), which also brings together fugitive pieces. Some of Turner's collected letters and related material are cited in the footnotes to my essay. The Turner papers are deposited in the Henry E. Huntington Library, San Marino, California.

4. Charles A. Beard BY FORREST MCDONALD

NOTES

1. Charles A. Beard, "Written History as an Act of Faith," *American Historical Review* 39 (1934): 226.

2. Howard K. Beale, "Beard's Historical Writings," in Beale, ed., *Charles A. Beard: An Appraisal* (Lexington, Ky., 1954), pp. 262–63.

3. In this matter I am in agreement with William Appleton Williams, "A Note on Charles Austin Beard's Search for a General Theory of Causation," *American Historical Review* 62 (1956): 59.

4. Eric F. Goldman, "Charles A. Beard: An Impression," in Beale, *Charles A. Beard*, p. 2; Cushing Strout, *The Pragmatic Revolt in American History: Carl Becker and Charles Beard* (New Haven, 1958), p. 88.

5. Williams, "Beard's Search for a General Theory of Causation," p. 63; Strout, *Pragmatic Revolt*, pp. 88, 109; Mary R. Beard, *The Making of Charles A. Beard* (New York, 1955), pp. 14–20; Max Lerner, "Charles Beard's Political Theory," in Beale, *Charles A. Beard*, pp. 26–41. To mention Ruskin and Marx is not to overlook the fact that Beard read and was influenced by other great European writers in related veins, notably Maitland, Sombart, Loria, Jhering, and Lassalle.

6. Beard acknowledged his debt to Seligman, Simons, Turner, and Libby in *An Economic Interpretation of the Constitution* (New York, 1913), pp. xix, 5–6. On the remainder of this paragraph, see Strout, pp. 13–29; Morton G. White, *Social Thought in America: The Revolt Against Formalism* (New York, 1949), pp. 11–31.

7. On this point I am again in general agreement with Williams, pp. 62–69, though he misreads Madison on one point. Williams says (p. 66) that Madison began his categorization of interest-based factions with "the broadest split," that between debtors and creditors, whereas actually Madison begins with the division between the propertied and the unpropertied, and then goes on to enumerate lesser divisions, the first of these being debtors and creditors; *The Federalist* (Modern Library edition), no. 10, p. 56. See also Beard's explicit statements regarding Madison in the *Economic Interpretation of the Constitution*, pp. 14–15, and in the Introduction to the 1935 ed. of the same, p. vi. For charges that Beard misread Madison, see Douglass Adair, "The Tenth Federalist Revisited," *William and Mary Quarterly*, 3d rev. 8 (1951): 60–61; White, *Social Thought in America*, pp. 119, 123–24; and Robert E. Brown, *Charles Beard and the Constitution: A Critical Analysis of "An Economic Interpretation of the Constitution"* (Princeton, 1956).

8. The original quotations are from Madison in *The Federalist*, pp. 54, 56; Beard's citation and analysis of them are in *Economic Interpretation of the Constitution*, pp. 14–15, 152 ff.

9. Ibid., p. 14; Beard, *Economic Origins of Jeffersonian Democracy* (New York, 1915); Beard, *The Economic Basis of Politics* (New York, 1922, but originally delivered as a lecture series at Amherst in 1916).

10. These and the quotations in the following paragraphs are from Beard's *Economic Interpretation of the Constitution*, pp. 63, 151, 154–79, 290, 291, 324–25. The language of the summaries given here follows closely that of the summaries I gave in *We the People: The Economic Origins of the Constitution* (Chicago, 1958), pp. 4–7.

11. Crowl, *Maryland During and After the Revolution* (Baltimore, 1943), and "Anti-Federalism in Maryland," *William and Mary Quarterly*, 3d rev. 4 (1947): 446. McCormick, *Experiment in Independence* (New Brunswick, N.J., 1950); Pool, "An Economic Interpretation of the Ratification of the Federal Constitution in North Carolina," *North Carolina Historical Review* 27 (1950): 119–41, 289–313, 437–61; Thomas, "A Reappraisal of Charles A. Beard's 'An Economic Interpretation of the Constitution,' " *American Historical Review* 57 (1952): 370, and his unpublished dissertation at Columbia University on Beard's interpretation regarding Virginia; Brown, *Beard and the Constitution*. The summaries of my own research are from *We the People*, pp. 349–57.

12. See Lee Benson, *Turner and Beard: American Historical Writing Reconsidered* (Glencoe, Ill., 1960); Jackson Turner Main, *The Social Structure of Revolutionary America* (Princeton, 1965), and *The Antifederalists: Critics of the Constitution, 1781–1788* (Chapel Hill, 1961).

13. It should be pointed out that I have concluded, after several years of research, that two important aspects of Beard's interpretation are totally compatible with the facts as I know them. One is his estimate of the popular vote on the ratification, and the other is his analysis of the attitude of the Founding Fathers toward the sanctity of private property. On the latter point, see my *E Pluribus Unum: The Formation of the American Republic, 1776–1790* (New York, 1965).

14. Beard, *Economic Origins of Jeffersonian Democracy*, passim; Bassett, *The Federalist System* (New York, 1906); Libby, "A Sketch of the Early Political Parties in the United States," *The Quarterly Journal of the University of North Dakota* 2 (1912): 205–42.

15. Charles, *The Origins of the American Party System* (Williamsburg, Va., 1956); Cunningham, *The Jeffersonian Republicans: The Formation of Party Organization, 1789–1801* (Chapel Hill, 1957); Chambers, *Political Parties in a New Nation: The American Experience, 1776–1809* (New York, 1963); Kurtz, *The Presidency of John Adams: The Collapse of Federalism, 1795–1800* (Philadelphia, 1957); Dauer, *The Adams Federalists* (Baltimore, 1953); Goodman, *The Democratic-Republicans of Massachusetts: Politics in a Young Republic* (Cambridge, Mass., 1964); Young, "The Mechanics and the Jeffersonians: New York, 1789–1801," *Labor History* 5 (1964): 247–76, and his "The Demo-

cratic Republican Movement in New York State, 1788–1797,"
Ph.D. dissertation, Northwestern University, 1958.

16. Charles and Mary R. Beard, *The Rise of American Civilization* (New
York, 1930) II, pp. 54, 106, 166.

17. Cochran, "Did the Civil War Retard Industrialization?," *Mississippi Valley Historical Review* 42 (1961): 197–210. For the
sharpest challenge to Cochran's proposition about the long-range
effects of the war, see Stephen Salsbury, "The Effect of the Civil
War on American Industrial Development," in Ralph Andreano,
ed., *The Economic Impact of the American Civil War* (Cambridge, Mass., 1962), pp. 161–68. Cochran is most vulnerable in
the areas of finance and credit. For one thing, he underrates the
importance of the National Banking Act in facilitating the expansion of credit. More important, he omits the fact that the Civil
War (like the nation's three earlier wars) created two enormous
pools of capital, one in the form of public debt and other public
paper, the other by removing political barriers to the development
of vast areas of public lands. It was these great accumulations of
capital that made possible the subsequent development of finance
capitalism. In this broad sense Beard's interpretation of the war is
sound; but, curiously, he omitted these two vital factors from his
own account.

18. Coben, "Northeastern Business and Radical Reconstruction: A Re-
examination," *Mississippi Valley Historical Review* 46 (1959):
67–90.

19. Unger, *The Greenback Era: A Social and Political History of American Finance, 1865–1879* (Princeton, 1964), pp. 118, 162.

20. Ibid., p. 9.

21. It has, in fact, often been suggested that Beard's *Economic Interpretation of the Constitution* was not only a product of the
milieu of the Progressive era, but that he wrote it for an immediate
political purpose—namely, to break down excessive respect for the
Constitution as a barrier to progressive social legislation. But to
suppose that Beard wrote the book for a political purpose—which
he expressly denied—is to suppose that he so little understood the
workings of the Supreme Court as to fail to realize that his book
could have little if any influence on it for a decade or two; to
forget that when Beard became enthusiastic about a political
cause, he was a man of direct action, not long-range persuasion; to
overlook the fact that Beard had enormous respect for the process
of judicial review; and to disregard the fact (of which he was
aware) that the book could be just as well used as a justification
for opposing progressive legislation as it could for upholding it.
(As a matter of fact, the first United States Supreme Court justice
who cited the book used it as an argument for striking down a
social-welfare law.) Finally, it seems hardly likely that Beard
anticipated that the book would have anything like the great in-

fluence that it did have. The very fact that he overstated his case and polarized his data to prove it, as I shall attempt in a moment to demonstrate, would, it seems to me, indicate that he felt it necessary to exaggerate and build a spectacular argument, lest he not be heard at all.

22. To say that Beard's work was unchallenged is not to say that it was no longer denounced; for example, at the 1934 meeting of the American Historical Association Professor Theodore Clarke Smith vigorously attacked Beard for being a Marxist, but he did not get down to specifics and cope directly with any of Beard's major interpretations.

23. The changes wrought by the factual explosion were epitomized by an incident at the Southern Historical Association meeting in 1960, after I had delivered, as a paper, a portion of the present essay. One of the critics prefaced his comments by saying, rather whimsically, that "It's kind of sad. It's getting so that so much is known by the specialists in this field [the making of the Constitution] that not just everybody can argue about it any more."

24. One characteristic of Beard's work, often pointed out, was generally regarded as a weakness, but I do not consider it as such. That is, Beard never seemed to make up his mind as to just what he meant by "economic interpretation": whether he was saying that men acted out of an individual or group profit motive, or that their associations with members of their "class" conditioned and shaped the attitudes they had on public questions, or that the logic of class conflict delimited and determined men's actions, is never consistently clear. Various scholars have argued that Beard "really" meant one or another of these, and others have argued that he did not but should have made clear his choice. See the works of Lerner, Benson, and Brown, previously cited. The fact is that Beard used each of them and more than all three, and refused either to commit himself to one meaning or to assign an order of preference. Indeed, sometimes he used "economic interpretation" in two or three different ways at once. This resulted occasionally in contradictions and more often in ambiguity; but these characteristics can reflect as well as distort the reality of history, for contradiction and ambiguity are persistent attributes of human action. Thus by refusing to be bound by a single, rigid, schematic system Beard remained free to see American history in "hard" or "tough-minded" terms without becoming entrapped in a mechanistic, logically closed determinism. I do not therefore believe this characteristic of his work was necessarily a weakness.

25. I emphasize "open society"; it seems to me likely that in some societies—say, in pre-Revolutionary France—an even simpler class system might be a valid interpretive device. Likewise, in a society in which social mobility is not prohibited but relatively frozen—say, as in nineteenth-century Austria—a fairly simple scheme

might also be valid. But in a society as fluid as America has been since the Revolution, such is not the case.

26. *Economic Interpretation of the Constitution*, pp. 19–51.

27. *We the People*, pp. 398–99.

28. In addition, two or three minor examples might not be superfluous. As Alfred D. Young and Staughton Lynd have pointed out, "So uncertain was Beard as to the derivation of Jeffersonian support among 'the poorer orders' of New York City that at one point he offered the suggestion that it came from the 'truck gardeners, laborers and farmers of the outlying districts'—the city agrarians, as it were." Lynd and Young, "After Carl Becker: The Mechanics and New York City Politics, 1774–1801," *Labor History* 5 (1964): 217, citing Beard, *Economic Origins of Jeffersonian Democracy*, pp. 246, 387, 466. In the *Economic Interpretation of the Constitution* (pp. 255–56) Beard used 1793 tax returns to estimate the amounts of the various kinds of personalty that existed in New Hampshire in 1787; part of his problem, he indicated, was that since 1787 Vermont had been "cut off" from New Hampshire. Where he got the notion that Vermont had been a part of New Hampshire in 1787 is a mystery. Again, in the same volume (pp. 110–11) Beard analyzed the question of whether Hamilton mixed politics and business for personal gain, and concluded that Hamilton was personally "clean." But in that context he casually mentioned that Hamilton was a shareholder in the Ohio Company. Beard somehow managed to avoid knowing that the Ohio Company was an extremely highhanded employer of political influence in behalf of a vast land speculation; he identified the company innocuously as "proprietors of land on the Muskingum River."

29. Holmes to Sir Frederick Pollock, June 20, 1928, in Max Lerner, ed., *The Mind and Faith of Justice Holmes* (Boston, 1943), p. 448.

30. Beard, *Economic Interpretation of the Constitution*, p. 75 n.; *Economic Origins of Jeffersonian Democracy*, p. 106 n.; Strout, pp. 97–98.

31. Beard was, in fact, at least vaguely aware that it was possible to determine who the original holders were; in dealing with William Few, a delegate from Georgia to the Philadelphia Convention, he remarks that Few funded a certificate "which he had secured from one Spears" (*Economic Interpretation of the Constitution*, p. 91). Apparently, however, Beard did not have the patience to make such a determination for all the delegates he dealt with.

32. Herbert Baxter Adams, "History and the Philosophy of History," *American Historical Review* 14 (1909): 236; Strout, pp. 18–20.

33. For an eloquent statement of this proposition, see Kenneth S. Templeton's combined review of my *We the People* and Strout's *Pragmatic Revolt*, "Clio's Tattered Robes," in *National Review*, January 17, 1959. The thesis refining was done mainly in regard

to the Turner frontier thesis. The detail filling was done mainly in the shadow of Beard's interpretations. In regard to the *Economic Interpretation of the Constitution* alone, it is staggering how many young scholars uncritically repeated his thesis while digging up data that, if approached inductively, would have resulted in sharply different interpretations. For example, see E. Wilder Spaulding, *New York in the Critical Period, 1783–1789* (New York, 1932); Richard F. Upton, *Revolutionary New Hampshire* (Hanover, N.H., 1936); Charles G. Singer, *South Carolina in the Confederation* (Philadelphia, 1941); and Robert L. Brunhouse, *The Counter-Revolution in Pennsylvania, 1776–1790* (Harrisburg, Pa., 1942). Spaulding, for instance, unearthed a large amount of valuable new information, but he so slavishly followed Beard that he even repeated (pp. 200–203) Beard's errors of addition.

34. *Economic Origins of Jeffersonian Democracy*, pp. 353–414. Incidentally, in this account Beard has another embarrassing factual error (p. 404): as evidence that Federalist leaders negotiated with Burr in 1801, Beard cites a letter to Hamilton saying that "Genl. Smith had an interview with Burr at Philadelphia last Saturday"; Smith was Samuel Smith, an ardent Jeffersonian—as Beard himself indicates a few pages later.

35. *Rise of American Civilization*, 1: 377, 380, 382–83.

36. See Goldman, "Charles A. Beard: An Impression," in Beale, ed., *Charles A. Beard*, p. 7 ("When I come to the end," Goldman quotes Beard as saying late in life, "my mind will still be beating its wings against thought's prison"); and, in the same volume, Max Lerner, "Beard's Political Theory," pp. 25 ff.

37. Arthur W. MacMahon's "Charles Beard, the Teacher," in Beale, *Charles A. Beard*, pp. 213–30, is disappointing, but his comments on p. 224 catch some of the spirit of the particular tactic discussed here. I have had the benefit of hearing the late Professor Beale and Professor William T. Hutchinson describe Beard's teaching techniques; the most vivid description, however, came from my own teacher at the University of Texas, Professor C. Perry Patterson, who studied under Beard as a graduate student for several years before World War I.

38. *Economic Interpretation of the Constitution*, p. xix.

39. See note 24, above; *Economic Interpretation of the Constitution*, Introduction to the 1935 edition, pp. v–vi; William T. Hutchinson to Merle E. Curti, cited in Beale, *Charles A. Beard*, p. 299.

40. Beard, *Economic Interpretation of the Constitution*, pp. 77, 93–94, 116–18, 138–39; William Pierce's sketches of the delegates, in Max Farrand, ed., *The Records of the Federal Convention of 1787*, 3 vols. (New Haven, 1911), 3: 93; *National Cyclopoedia of Biography*, 9: 530; "Ledger C, Treasury 6%," vol. 42, fol. 368 of the Records of the Loan of 1790, in the National Archives,

and, in the same collection, Ledger B, N.Y. Office, Deferred 6%, 1790, fols. 10, 152, 457, and vol. 1, 258, fol. 221.

41. *Economic Interpretation of the Constitution*, pp. 90–92; "Autobiography of Col. William Few of Georgia, *Magazine of American History* 7 (1881): 352; Register of Certificates of Public Debt Presented to the Auditor of the Treasury, Book A, in the Records of the Loan of 1790, National Archives.

42. See Lerner, "Beard's Political Theory," in Beale, *Charles A. Beard*, pp. 28–32.

43. See note 33 above.

44. The literature on this episode in British and American history is far from satisfactory, but see the following: James D. Squires, *British Propaganda at Home and in the United States from 1914 to 1917* (Cambridge, Mass., 1935); H. C. Peterson, *Propaganda for War: The Campaign Against American Neutrality, 1914–1917* (Norman, Okla. 1939); George S. Viereck, *Spreading Germs of Hate* (London, 1931); *Final Report of State Council of Defense of Illinois, 1917–1918–1919* (Springfield, Ill., n.d., ca. 1919); Harold D. Lasswell, *Propaganda Techniques in the World War* (New York, 1927); and George Creel, *How We Advertised America* (New York, 1920).

45. The names of several active members of the History Subcommittee are contained in the last two works just cited, and also in the pamphlets of the Committee itself. See, for example, Andrew C. McLaughlin, *The Great War: From Spectator to Participant*, pamphlet 4 of the War Information Series, published by the Committee on Public Information, Washington, August, 1917.

46. Beard and William C. Bagley, *The History of the American People*, special edition for Army Educational Commission, American Expeditionary Forces, 1918.

47. For a complete bibliography of Beard's writings, see Beale, *Charles A. Beard*, pp. 265–86.

48. "Written History as an Act of Faith," *American Historical Review* 39 (1934): 219–29.

49. Strout, p. 144.

50. *American Foreign Policy in the Making, 1932–1940: A Study in Responsibilities* (New Haven, 1946); *President Roosevelt and the Coming of the War, 1941: A Study in Appearances and Realities* (New Haven, 1948). For a good brief account of the reaction to these works by a writer sympathetic to Beard, see George R. Leighton, "Beard and Foreign Policy," in Beale, *Charles A. Beard*, pp. 180–81. As Leighton pointed out, the works have not been thoroughly tested or rebutted; instead, they were simply dismissed without a hearing. My own inexpert opinion is that Roosevelt did at least engage in a great deal of deception and was determined to lead the United States into the war, one way or another; and that it would have been unspeakably immoral for him not to

have intervened in the war. Whether Beard was right or wrong, however, is beside the point. The point is that Beard overwhelmingly and obviously twisted the facts to make his case. For the most thoroughly documented charge that he did so, see Basil Rauch, *Roosevelt from Munich to Pearl Harbor: A Study in the Creation of a Foreign Policy* (New York, 1950).

51. *Rise of American Civilization*, 2: 800; Beard, "National Politics and War," *Scribner's* 97 (1935): 70; Strout, pp. 141–56. One of the major elements in Beard's disenchantment with Roosevelt was the president's movement away from the concept of the planned economy, even before the NRA was declared unconstitutional.

52. Strout, p. 153. It may be, of course, that the story does not end there. No small number of critics of President Lyndon B. Johnson's foreign policy might have agreed with Beard's plea, written in 1940, for "a recognition of the limited nature of American power to relieve, restore, and maintain life beyond its own sphere of interest and control—a recognition of the hard fact that the United States, either alone or in any coalition, did not possess the power to force peace on Europe and Asia, to assure the establishment of democratic and pacific governments there, or to provide the social and economic underwriting necessary to the perdurance of such governments." A few months later he argued that America should "stay out to the last ditch, and preserve one stronghold of order and sanity even against the gates of hell." Perhaps he was a prophet, after all.

SELECTED PUBLICATIONS

A complete bibliography of Charles A. Beard's writings appears in Howard K. Beale, ed., *Charles A. Beard: An Appraisal by Eric F. Goldman, Harold J. Laski, Howard K. Beale, Walter Hamilton, George Soule, Merle Curti, George R. Leighton, Richard Hofstadter, Max Lerner, Luther Gulick, George S. Counts, Arthur W. MacMahon* (Lexington, Ky., 1954), pp. 265–84, and a list of the major articles about Beard appears on pp. 284–86 of the same work. Various other and more recent articles about Beard are cited in the notes to this essay.

Because Beard's writings were so voluminous—they include 285 articles, 18 essays by Beard that appeared in cooperative works, 214 book reviews, 23 prefaces, forewords, and introductions, and 36 letters to editors, in addition to his books—the editors of the present volume have decided to list here only Beard's books. For the complete bibliography, the reader is referred to Beale's *Charles A. Beard.*

Books and Pamphlets by Beard Alone

The Industrial Revolution. London, 1901.
The Office of Justice of the Peace in England, in Its Origin and Development. New York, 1904.

An Introduction to the English Historians. New York, 1906.
European Sobriety in the Presence of the Balkan Crisis. New York, 1908.
Politics: A Lecture Delivered at Columbia University in the Series on Science, Philosophy, and Art, February 12, 1908. New York, 1908.
American Government and Politics. New York, 1910. Subsequently revised through the ten editions, 1914–1949.
American City Government: A Survey of Newer Tendencies. New York, 1912.
The Supreme Court and the Constitution. New York, 1912.
An Economic Interpretation of the Constitution of the United States. New York, 1913. Reprinted with a new introduction, 1935.
Contemporary American History, 1877–1913. New York, 1914.
Economic Origins of Jeffersonian Democracy. New York, 1915.
Six Years' Experience with the Direct Primary in New Jersey. New York, 1917.
How American Citizens Govern Themselves. New York, 1919.
Public Service in America. Philadelphia, 1919.
The Traction Crisis in New York. New York, 1919.
Cross Currents in Europe Today. Boston, 1922.
The Economic Basis of Politics. New York, 1922. New Edition 1934; revised edition, 1945, with a new chapter 5 entitled "Economics and Politics in Our Revolutionary Age."
The Administration and Politics of Tokyo: A Survey and Opinions. New York, 1923.
A Collection of Lectures (in Japanese). Tokyo, 1923.
My Views Regarding the Reconstruction of Tokyo (in Japanese). Tokyo, 1924.
Government Research, Past, Present, and Future. New York, 1926.
The American Party Battle. New York, 1928.
A Charter for the Social Sciences in the Schools. New York, 1932.
Issues of Domestic Policy. Chicago, 1932.
The Myth of Rugged American Individualism. New York, 1932.
The Navy: Defense or Portent? New York, 1932.
Hitlerism and Our Liberties: Text of Address Given at the New School for Social Research, Tuesday, April 10, 1934. New York, 1934.
The Nature of the Social Sciences in Relation to Objectives of Instruction. New York, 1934.
The Presidents in American History. New York, 1935.
Cumulative Annual Guide to American Government and Politics. New York, 1935–1938.
The Devil Theory of War: An Inquiry into the Nature of History and the Possibility of Keeping out of War. New York, 1936.
The Discussion of Human Affairs: An Inquiry into the Nature of the Statements, Assertions, Allegations, Claims, Heats, Tempers, Distempers, Dogmas, and Contentions Which Appear When Human Affairs Are Discussed and into the Possibility of Putting Some Rhyme and Reason into Processes of Discussion. New York, 1936.

Jefferson, Corporations, and the Constitution. Washington, 1936.
The Unique Function of Education in American Democracy. Washington, 1937.
Giddy Minds and Foreign Quarrels: An Estimate of American Foreign Policy. New York, 1939.
Philosophy, Science and Art of Public Administration: Address Delivered before the Annual Conference of the Governmental Research Association, Princeton, New Jersey, September Eighth, 1939. Princeton, 1939.
A Foreign Policy for America. New York, 1940.
Public Policy and the General Welfare. New York, 1941.
The Republic: Conversations on Fundamentals. New York, 1943.
American Foreign Policy in the Making, 1932–1940: A Study in Responsibilities. New Haven, 1946.
President Roosevelt and the Coming of the War, 1941: A Study in Appearances and Realities. New Haven, 1948.

Books in Collaboration with Others

A. With William C. Bagley

The History of the American People. Special edition for Army Educational Commission, American Expeditionary Forces. New York, 1918. Five subsequent editions, 1920–1932.
The History of the American People, for Grammar Grades and Junior High Schools. New York, 1918.
A Manual to Accompany "The History of the American People." New York, 1919.
A First Book in American History. New York, 1920. Subsequent editions in 1924 and 1934. Braille edition in 1934.
Our Old World Background. New York, 1922. Revised edition 1925.
Elementary World History: A Revised and Simplified Edition of Our Old World Background. New York, 1932.

B. With William C. Bagley and Roy F. Nichols

America Today. New York, 1938.
America Yesterday. New York, 1938.
America Yesterday and Today. New York, 1938 (Braille edition).

C. With Mary Ritter Beard

American Citizenship. New York, 1914.
History of the United States. New York, 1921. Later editions have subtitle *A Study in American Civilization.* Three subsequent editions, 1929–1934.
The Rise of American Civilization. 2 vols. New York, 1927.
The Making of American Civilization. New York, 1937.

America in Midpassage. 2 vols. New York, 1939.

The American Spirit: A Study of the Idea of Civilization in the United States. New York, 1942 (Braille edition).

A *Basic History of the United States.* New York, 1944. Braille and talking book editions, and Austrian, Japanese, and Swiss editions.

D. With William Beard

The American Leviathan: The Republic in the Machine Age. New York, 1930.

E. With William G. Carr

Schools in the Story of Culture. Washington, 1935.

F. With the Commission on Social Studies in the Schools

Conclusions and Recommendations of the Commission. New York, 1934.

G. With the Educational Policies Commission of the National Education Association

The Unique Function of Education in Democracy. Washington, 1937.

H. With Robert Moses and Others

Report of Reconstruction Commission to Governor Alfred E. Smith on Retrenchment and Reorganization in the State Government, October 10, 1919. Albany, 1919.

I. With Frederic A. Ogg

National Governments and the World War. New York, 1919.

J. With George Radin

The Balkan Pivot: Yugoslavia: A Study in Government and Administration. New York, 1929.

K. With James Harvey Robinson

The Development of Modern Europe: An Introduction to the Study of Current History. 2 vols. Boston, 1907–1908. Revised and enlarged edition, 1929–1930.

Readings in Modern European History: A Collection of Extracts from the Sources Chosen with the Purpose of Illustrating Some of the Chief Phases of the Development of Europe During the Last Two Hundred Years. Boston, 1908–1909.

History of Europe, Our Own Times: The Eighteenth and Nineteenth Centuries, the Opening of the Twentieth Century, and the World War. Boston, 1921. Later editions have altered subtitle: *The Opening of the Twentieth Century, the World War, and Recent Events.* Revised editions 1927 and 1932.

L. With James Harvey Robinson and James Henry Breasted

Outlines of European History. 2 vols. Boston, 1912–1914. Subsequent
    editions 1918, 1927.

M. With James Harvey Robinson, Donnal V. Smith, and Emma Peters
    Smith

Our Own Age (vol. 2 of *A History Of Civilization*). Boston, 1937.

N. With Birl E. Shultz

Documents on the State-Wide Initiative, Referendum, and Recall. New
    York, 1912.

O. With George H. E. Smith

The Future Comes: A Study of the New Deal. New York, 1933.
*The Idea of National Interest: An Analytical Study in American Foreign
    Policy.* New York, 1934.
The Open Door at Home: A Trial Philosophy of National Interest. New
    York, 1934.
The Recovery Program (1933–1934): *A Study of the Depression and the
    Fight to Overcome It.* New York, 1934.
Current Problems of Public Policy: A Collection of Materials. New York,
    1936.
The Old Deal and the New. New York, 1940.

Books Edited by Beard

Readings in American Government and Politics. New York, 1909.
*Loose Leaf Digest of Short Ballot Charters: A Documentary History of
    the Commission Form of Municipal Government.* New York,
    1911.
Whither Mankind: A Panorama of Modern Civilization. New York, 1928.
Toward Civilization. New York, 1930.
America Faces the Future. Boston, 1932.
A Century of Progress. Chicago, 1932.
The Enduring Federalist. Garden City, N.Y., 1948.

5. Vernon Louis Parrington BY RALPH H. GABRIEL

NOTES

1. Alfred Harcourt, *Some Experiences* (privately printed, 1951), p. 108.
2. Parrington, *Main Currents in American Thought*, 3 vols. (New York,
   1927–30), 1: 30.
3. Ibid., p. 109.
4. Ibid., pp. 355–56.
5. Young, "More Encaustics for Southerners," *Virginia Quarterly Review* 13 (1937): 42, 44.

6. Colwell, "The Populist Image of Vernon Louis Parrington," *Mississippi Valley Historical Review* 69 (1962): 52–66. I have depended heavily on Colwell's painstaking and judicious research for the early life of Parrington.
7. *The Autobiography of William Allen White* (New York, 1946, p. 302.
8. See Robert A. Skotheim and Kermit Vanderbilt, "Vernon Louis Parrington: The Mind and Art of a Historian of Ideas," *Pacific Northwest Quarterly* 53 (1962): 101.
9. Colwell, "Populist Image," p. 61.
10. Ibid., p. 64.
11. Parrington, *Main Currents*, 2: 396.
12. Ibid., pp. 407–08.
13. Ibid., 3: 224.
14. Ibid., 3: 312.
15. Smith, *The Growth and Decadence of Constitutional Government* (New York, 1930), p. xvi.
16. For an extended discussion on these pieces, which are omitted from my bibliography, in that they are not works of scholarship, see Colwell, pp. 64–65.
17. Smith, *The Spirit of American Government* (New York, 1907), pp. 29–30, 104–05.
18. Parrington, *Main Currents*, 1: 279, 283.
19. Ibid., p. 353.
20. Norman Foerster, ed., *The Reinterpretation of American Literature* (New York, 1928), pp. 64–65.
21. Quoted in Granville Hicks, "The Critical Principles of V. L. Parrington," *Science and Society, A Marxian Quarterly* 3 (1939): 458.
22. *American Literature* 12 (1940): 297–98.
23. Peterson, *The Jefferson Image in the American Mind* (New York, 1960), pp. 321–22.
24. Hicks, "Critical Principles," pp. 446–47.
25. Ibid., p. 458.
26. Ibid., p. 454.
27. Spiller, *The Cycle of American Literature* (New York, 1956), p. 243.
28. Robert A. Skotheim, in his *Intellectual Histories and Historians* (Princeton, 1966), gives us an extended discussion of this aspect of Parrington's method.
29. Hicks, pp. 454–55.
30. Cram, *The Nemesis of Mediocrity* (Boston, 1917), p. 55.
31. Mencken, *Notes on Democracy* (New York, 1926), p. 21.
32. *American Literature*, 1 (1929): 101.
33. Higham, "The Rise of American Intellectual History," *American Historical Review* 56 (1952): 461.
34. Skotheim and Vanderbilt, "Vernon Louis Parrington," pp. 100–13.
35. Malcolm Cowley and Bernard Smith, eds., *Books That Changed Our Minds* (New York, 1938).

SELECTED PUBLICATIONS

The Connecticut Wits. Edited with an introduction. New York, 1926.

Main Currents in American Thought: An Interpretation of American Literature, vol. 1, 1620–1800, *The Colonial Mind*; vol. 2, 1800–1860, *The Romantic Revolution in America*. New York, 1927.

Main Currents in American Thought: An Interpretation of American Literature from the Beginning to 1920, vol. 1, *The Colonial Mind*; vol. 2, *The Romantic Revolution in America*; vol. 3, *The Beginnings of Critical Realism in America*. New York, 1927–1930. Reprinted edition, 2 vols., 1954.

El Desarrollo de las Ideas en los Estados Unidos. Translated by Antonio Llano. Lancaster, 1941.

Sinclair Lewis, Our Own Diogenes. Seattle, Wash., n.d.

6. Perry Miller BY ROBERT MIDDLEKAUFF

NOTES

* I wish to thank Alan Heimert and Henry F. May for their perceptive readings of this essay.

1. *The New England Mind: From Colony to Province* (Cambridge, Mass., 1953), p. 489.

2. The paperback was published by the Beacon Press (Boston, 1961); see the "Preface" to this edition.

3. Perry Miller, "The Plight of the Lone Wolf," *American Scholar* 25 (Autumn, 1956): 445. For biographical information about Miller, I have relied upon this article; the *Harvard Review* 2 (Winter-Spring 1964), a memorial issue; the autobiographical comments throughout *Errand into the Wilderness* (Cambridge, Mass., 1956); and conversations with friends and students of Miller.

4. "The End of the World," chap. 10 in *Errand into the Wilderness*; *Jonathan Edwards* (New York, 1949).

5. *Errand*, p. viii.

6. Edmund S. Morgan, "Perry Miller and the Historians," *Harvard Review* 2 (Winter-Spring, 1964), 52. This is a moving and perceptive tribute.

7. Thomas Morton, *New England Canaan* (Amsterdam, 1637).

8. For an elaborate expression of Mencken's views see his essay "Puritanism as a Literary Force," in *A Book of Prefaces* (New York, 1924).

9. Murdock, *Increase Mather: The Foremost American Puritan* (Cambridge, Mass., 1926); Morison, *Builders of the Bay Colony* (Cambridge, Mass., 1930); *The Founding of Harvard College* (Cambridge, Mass., 1935); *Harvard College in the Seventeenth Century* (Cambridge, Mass., 1936); see also Morison's *The Intellectual Life of Colonial New England* (New York, 1956), first published as *The Puritan Pronaos* (New York, 1936). Hawthorne's great

works, of course, are well known; Esther Forbes' novel is *A Mirror For Witches;* Wendell's *Cotton Mather: The Puritan Priest,* first published in 1891, has been reissued by Harbinger Books (1963). Shipton has written important articles on Puritanism, among them, "The New England Clergy in the Glacial Age," *Colonial Society of Massachusetts, Publications* 32 (1938): 24–54; "A Plea for Puritanism," *American Historical Review* 40 (1935); 460–67; and *Roger Conant: A Founder of Massachusetts* (Cambridge, Mass., 1944).

10. Morison, "New Light Wanted on the Old Colony," *William and Mary Quarterly,* 3d ser. 15 (1958), 364.

11. (New York, 1939), reissued by the Harvard University Press, Cambridge, Mass., 1954.

12. (Cambridge, Mass., 1953.)

13. *The New England Mind: The Seventeenth Century,* p. 174.

14. Ibid., p. 59.

15. *The Raven and the Whale: The War of Words and Wits in the Era of Poe and Melville* (New York, 1956); *Consciousness in Concord: The Text of Thoreau's Hitherto "Lost Journal"* (1840–1841) *Together With Notes and a Commentary* (Boston, 1958).

16. *The Life of the Mind in America from the Revolution to the Civil War* (New York, 1965).

17. *New England Mind: The Seventeenth Century,* p. 180.

18. The quotations in this paragraph are from *Errand into the Wilderness,* pp. 79, 80–81.

19. *From Colony to Province,* pp. 206, 361.

20. Ibid., p. 204.

21. "The Responsibility of Mind In a Civilization of Machines," *American Scholar* 31 (Winter, 1961–62): 54.

22. Morgan, "Perry Miller," *Harvard Review,* p. 59.

23. The full titles of Morgan's books are *The Puritan Family: Essays on Religion and Domestic Relations in Seventeenth Century New England,* new ed. (New York, 1966); *The Puritan Dilemma: The Story of John Winthrop* (Boston, 1958); *Visible Saints: The History of a Puritan Idea* (New York, 1963); *The Gentle Puritan: A Life of Ezra Stiles, 1727–1795* (New Haven, 1962).

24. *Society and Puritanism in Pre-Revolutionary England* (New York, 1964); see also *Puritanism and Revolution* (London, 1958).

25. Examples of these studies are George Lee Haskins, *Law and Authority in Early Massachusetts* (New York, 1960); Geoffrey F. Nuttall, *Visible Saints: The Congregational Way, 1640–1660* (Oxford, 1960); Ola Winslow, *Meetinghouse Hill, 1630–1783* (New York, 1952); Larzer Ziff, *The Career of John Cotton* (Princeton, 1962); Norman S. Grabo, *Edward Taylor* (New Haven, 1961); Richard S. Dunn, *Puritans and Yankees: The Winthrop Dynasty of New England, 1630–1717* (Princeton, 1962); Alan Simpson, *Puritanism in Old and New England* (Chicago,

1955); and Bernard Bailyn, *The New England Merchants in the Seventeenth Century* (Cambridge, Mass., 1955). Important studies which have appeared since this essay was written are Alan Heimert, *Religion and the American Mind* (Cambridge, Mass., 1966); Norman Pettit, *The Heart Prepared: Grace and Conversation in Puritan Spiritual Life* (New Haven, 1966); and Conrad Cherry, *The Theology of Jonathan Edwards: A Reappraisal* (New York, 1966).

26. Although this essay cannot take up Miller's influence on literary studies, it should at least note that his discussions of typology in *Roger Williams* (1953) and in *Images or Shadows of Divine Things* (New Haven, 1948) have contributed to an understanding of American symbolism.

SELECTED PUBLICATIONS

Books

Orthodoxy in Massachusetts. Cambridge, Mass., 1933.

With Thomas H. Johnson. *The Puritans*. 2 vols. New York, 1938 and 1963.

The New England Mind: The Seventeenth Century. New York, 1939.

(Ed.) Jonathan Edwards. *Images or Shadows of Divine Things*. New Haven, 1948.

Jonathan Edwards. New York, 1949.

The Transcendentalists: An Anthology. Cambridge, Mass., 1950.

From Colony to Province. Cambridge, Mass., 1953.

Roger Williams: His Contribution to the American Tradition. New York, 1953.

Errand into the Wilderness. Cambridge, Mass., 1956.

The Raven and the Whale: The War of Words and Wits in The Era of Poe and Melville. New York, 1956.

The American Puritans, Their Prose and Poetry. New York, 1956.

The New England Courant, with Essays by Benjamin Franklin. Boston, 1956.

The American Transcendentalists: Their Prose and Poetry. New York, 1957.

Consciousness in Concord: The Text of Thoreau's Hitherto "Lost Journal" (1840–41), Together with Notes and a Commentary. Boston, 1958.

(Ed.) John Wise. *A Vindication of the Government of New England Churches*. Gainesville, Fla., 1958.

(Ed.) Phillip Schaff, *America, A Sketch of its Political, Social, and Religious Character*. Cambridge, Mass., 1961.

The Legal Mind in America: From Independence to the Civil War. New York, 1962.

Margaret Fuller, American Romantic: A Selection from Her Writings and Correspondence. New York, 1963.

(Ed.) Roger Williams. *Complete Writings*, vol. 7. New York, 1963.
The Life of the Mind in America: From the Revolution To the Civil War. New York, 1965.
Nature's Nation. Cambridge, Mass., 1967.

Articles

"The Half-Way Covenant." *The New England Quarterly* 6 (1933).
"The Puritan Theory of the Sacraments in Seventeenth-Century New England." *The Catholic Historical Review* 22 (1937).
"Solomon Stoddard, 1643–1729." *The Harvard Theological Review* 34 (1941).
"The Social Context of the Covenant." *Bulletin of the Congregational Library* 6 (1955).
"The Plight of the Lone Wolf." *The American Scholar* 25 (1956).
"The New England Conscience." *The American Scholar* 27 (1958–59).
"The Common Law and Codification in Jacksonian America." *Proceedings of the American Philosophical Society* 103 (1959).
"The Responsibility of the Mind in a Civilization of Machines." *The American Scholar* 31 (1961–62).

Other Publications

"A Note on the *Manuductio ad Ministerium*." In Thomas J. Holmes. *Cotton Mather: A Bibliography of His Works*. Cambridge, Mass., 1940.
(Ed.) Daniel Drake. *Discourse on the History, Character, and Prospects of the West*. Gainsville, Fla., 1955.
(Ed.) Brooks Adams. *The Emancipation of Massachusetts*. Boston, 1962.

7. Samuel Flagg Bemis BY H. C. ALLEN

NOTES

1. Dexter Perkins, A *History of the Monroe Doctrine* (Boston, 1955), p. 219.
2. I am indebted for some of the material in this essay to the introductory chapter of a *Festschrift*, which should shortly be published, in honor of Professor Bemis by a number of his former students, *Diplomatic Gallery: Essays in Honor of Samuel Flagg Bemis*, edited by John A. De Novo and Russell H. Bastert. I am even more indebted to Professor Bemis himself for talking to me at length and allowing me to draw on that conversation.
3. Quoted in *Diplomatic Gallery*, cited above.
4. *John Quincy Adams and the Foundations of American Foreign Policy* (New York, 1949), p. ix.
5. *John Quincy Adams and the Union* (New York, 1956), p. ix.
6. Ibid.
7. Ibid.

8. Bemis, A *Diplomatic History of the United States*, 5th ed. (New York, 1964), p. 413.
9. Becker, *Freedom and Responsibility in the American Way of Life* (New York, 1945), p. xxv.
10. Ibid.
11. Ibid., pp. xv, xxvi.
12. *American History and American Historians: A Review of Recent Contributions to the Interpretation of the History of the United States* (London, 1952), p. 257.
13. This comprehensiveness also cleared Bemis himself of Bellot's charge that American diplomatic history "has suffered perhaps more than most historical subjects from the facility with which dissertations to be submitted for higher degrees can be compiled by the almost mechanical juxtaposition of the papers of a couple of chancelleries, so that the literature of the subject is peculiarly unequal in quality." Ibid.
14. This verbal comment he has expressed more formally in *The Latin American Policy of the United States* (New York, 1943), p. 386: "After Waterloo, during the happiest century mankind has known on this planet, the British Navy ruled the seas, and Great Britain held the balance of power in the world."
15. Bemis, *Diplomatic History*, p. 216.
16. In 1943 even his criticism of late-nineteenth-century imperialism was fairly muted: "A careful and conscientious appraisal of United States Imperialism shows, I am convinced, that it was never deep-rooted in the character of the people, that it was essentially a protective imperialism, designed to protect, first the security of the Continental Republic, next the security of the entire New World, against intervention by the imperialistic powers of the Old World. It was, if you will, an imperialism against imperialism. It did not last long and it was not really bad" (*Latin American Policy of the United States*, pp. 385–86).
17. *The Wave of the Future*, quoted in Clarke A. Chambers, ed., *The New Deal at Home and Abroad, 1929–45* (New York, 1965), p. 163.
18. Woodrow Wilson, April 2, 1917, in Henry Steele Commager, ed., *Documents of American History*, 4th ed. (New York, 1948) 2: 312.
19. Quoted in *Diplomatic Gallery*.
20. Turner, *The Frontier in American History*, reprint ed. (New York, 1950), p. 299.
21. Bemis, *American Foreign Policy and the Blessings of Liberty and Other Essays* (New Haven, 1962), p. 15.
22. Ibid.
23. Ibid., p. 13.
24. Ibid., pp. 14–15.

25. Rusk, "Some Issues of Contemporary History," *Department of State Bulletin*, January 15, 1962, p. 83.
26. Ibid., pp. 87–88.
27. I was unable to take advantage of Professor Bemis's generous offer that I should use this manuscript, since it could only be read in the Yale library and could not be photocopied, but on reflection I think that, advantageous as it would have been in some ways, it might have made the writing of this essay for publication in his lifetime impossibly difficult.
28. Webster demonstrated this aspect of the matter when he remarked in later years to a rising young diplomatic historian, seeking an introduction to the custodian of some of the personal papers of a certain statesman, "Why do you want to see them? Everything you need is in the Public Record Office."
29. Becker, *Freedom and Responsibility*, p. xv.

SELECTED PUBLICATIONS

Books

Jay's Treaty: A Study in Commerce and Diplomacy. New York, 1923. Rev. ed., New Haven, 1962.

Pinckney's Treaty: A Study of America's Advantage from Europe's Distress, 1783–1800. Baltimore, 1926. Rev. ed., New Haven, 1960.

(Ed. and contributor) *The American Secretaries of State and Their Diplomacy*. 10 vols. New York, 1927–29. Reprinted in 5 vols., New York, 1958.

The Hussey-Cumberland Mission and American Independence: An Essay in the Diplomacy of the American Revolution. Princeton, 1931.

With Grace Gardner Griffin, *Guide to the Diplomatic History of the United States, 1775–1921*. Washington, 1935. Reprinted, Gloucester, Mass., 1959.

The Diplomacy of the American Revolution. New York, 1935. 3d ed., Bloomington, Ind., 1957.

A Diplomatic History of the United States. New York, 1936. 5 editions, revised.

La Politica internacional de los Estados Unidos: interpretaciones. Lancaster, Pa., 1939. Lectures delivered in Latin American countries, 1937–38.

The Latin American Policy of the United States, New York, 1943. Spanish translation.

John Quincy Adams and the Foundations of American Foreign Policy. New York, 1949.

The United States as a World Power: A Diplomatic History, 1900–1950. New York, 1950. Reprinted with adaptations, as pt. 3 of 3d ed. of *Diplomatic History of the United States*.

John Quincy Adams and the Union. New York, 1956.

A Short History of American Foreign Policy and Diplomacy. New York, 1959.

American Foreign Policy and the Blessings of Liberty and Other Essays. New Haven, 1962.

Articles

"The Settlement of the Yazoo Boundary Dispute: The First Step in Southern Expansion." *Magazine of History* 17 (1913).

"Relations between Vermont Separatists and Great Britain, 1789–1791." *American Historical Review* 21 (1916).

"The United States and the Abortive Armed Neutrality of 1794." *American Historical Review* 24 (1918).

"A Proposed Solution of the American Industrial Problem." *Pacific Review* 1 (1921).

"The Yap Island Controversy." *Pacific Review* 2 (1921).

"Alexander Hamilton and the Limitation of Armaments." *Pacific Review* 5 (1922).

"Jay's Treaty and the Northwest Boundary Gap." *American Historical Review* 27 (1922).

"Shall We Forget the Lusitania?" *The Outlook* 131 (1922).

"The London Mission of Thomas Pinckney." *American Historical Review* 26 (1923).

"Professor Channing and the West." *Washington Historical Quarterly* 14 (1923).

"Captain John Mullan and the Engineers' Problem." *Washington Historical Quarterly* 14 (1923).

"British Secret Service and the French-American Alliance." *American Historical Review* 29 (1924).

"The United States and Lafayette." *Daughters of the American Revolution Magazine* 58 (1924).

"Talleyrand and Jaudenes, 1795." *American Historical Review* 30 (1925).

"Payment of the French Loans to the United States, 1777–1795." *Current History* 23 (1926).

"The Background of Washington's Foreign Policy." *Yale Review* 16 (1927).

"Acquisition of Source Material for American History." *Report of the Librarian of Congress for the Fiscal Year Ending June 30, 1929.* Washington, 1929.

"Fields for Research in the Diplomatic History of the United States to 1900." *American Historical Review* 36 (1930).

"Canada and the Peace Settlement of 1782–3." *Canadian Historical Review* 14 (1933).

"John Jay." *Dictionary of American Biography*, vol. 10. New York, 1933.

"Washington's Farewell Address: A Foreign Policy of Independence." *American Historical Review* 39 (1934).

"A Clarifying Foreign Policy." *Yale Review* 25 (1936).

With Lawrence Martin, "Franklin's Red-Line Map Was a Mitchell."
    New England Quarterly 10 (1937).
"The Rayneval Memoranda of 1782, and Some Comments on the French
    Historian Doniol." *Proceedings* of the American Antiquarian So-
    ciety 47 (1937).
"Main Trends of American Foreign Policy." In Frank P. Davison and
    George S. Viereck, eds., *Before America Decides*. Cambridge,
    Mass., 1938.
"Observaciones y sugestiones acerca de la historia diplomatica." *Boletin
    de la Academia Nacional de la Historia* 12 (1939).
"The New Holy Alliance Crosses the Ocean." *Quarterly Journal of Inter-
    American Relations* 1 (1939).
"Early Diplomatic Missions from Buenos Aires to the United States,
    1811–1824." *Proceedings* of the American Antiquarian Society 49
    (1939).
"The Training of Archivists in the United States." *American Archivist* 2
    (1939).
"Papers of David Curtis DeForest and J. W. DeForest." *The Yale Uni-
    versity Library Gazette* 14 (1940).
"America Faces Her Greatest Crisis." *Social Science* 16 (1941).
"John Quincy Adams and George Washington." *Massachusetts Historical
    Society Proceedings* 67 (1941–44).
"Walter Lippmann on U.S. Foreign Policy." *Hispanic American Histori-
    cal Review* 23 (1943).
"Joseph Vincent Fuller." *Dictionary of American Biography*, vol. 21,
    supp. 1. New York, 1944.
"La universidad de Yale en la democracia norteamericano." *Cuadernos
    del Ateneo de la Habana* 1 (1945).
"John Quincy Adams and Russia." *Virginia Quarterly Review* 21 (1945).
"First Gun of a Revisionist Historiography for the Second World War."
    Journal of Modern History 19 (1947).
"The Shifting Strategy of American Defense and Diplomacy." *Virginia
    Quarterly Review* 24 (1948).
"The United States as a World Power." *World Political Geography*.
    New York, 1948.
"The Scuffle in the Rotunda: A Footnote to the Presidency of John
    Quincy Adams and to the History of Dueling." *Massachusetts
    Historical Society Proceedings* 71 (1953–1957).
"Woodrow Wilson and Latin America." In Edward H. Buehrig, ed.,
    Wilson's Foreign Policy in Perspective. Bloomington, Ind., 1957.
"Henry Adams, 2nd." *Massachusetts Historical Society Proceedings* 70
    (1950–1953).
"Secret Intelligence, 1777: Two Documents" (with annotation by Helen
    C. Boatfield). *Huntington Library Quarterly* 24 (1961).
"The Adams Family and Their Manuscripts." In *The Adams Papers*.
    Boston, 1962.

"American Foreign Policy and the Blessings of Liberty," presidential address to the American Historical Association at Washington, D.C., Dec. 9, 1961. *American Historical Review* 67 (1962).

"America and Americans." *Yale Review* 57 (1968).
"Alum Pond and Walden." *New England Galaxy* 10 (1968).

For a fuller bibliography, including articles in the *Encyclopaedia Americana* and *Britannica*, see Bemis, *American Foreign Policy and the Blessings of Liberty and Other Essays*, pp. 417–23.

8. Daniel J. Boorstin   BY J. R. POLE

NOTES

1. *The American Political Tradition and the Men Who Made It* (New York, 1948), Introduction.
2. Hartz, *The Liberal Tradition in America* (New York, 1955).
3. Robert E. Brown, *Middle-Class Democracy and the American Revolution in Massachusetts: 1691–1780* (Ithaca, N.Y., 1955); Benjamin F. Wright, *Consensus and Continuity* (Boston, 1958); Samuel Lubell, *The Future of American Politics* (New York, 1952); Richard P. McCormick, *The Second American Party System* (New York, 1966).
4. *The Mysterious Science of the Law* (Cambridge, Mass.).
5. "A Dialogue of Two Histories," in *America and the Image of Europe* (New York, 1960), p. 177.
6. *Mysterious Science*, p. 1.
7. Ibid.
8. Ibid., p. 20.
9. Ibid., p. 31.
10. Ibid., p. 162.
11. Ibid., p. 186.
12. Ibid., pp. 122, 124.
13. Ibid, pp. 187–190.
14. Ibid., p. 5.
15. *The Lost World of Thomas Jefferson* (New York, 1948).
16. He is not describing Americans in general, though; the leading figures of this work are David Rittenhouse, the astronomer; Benjamin Rush, the physician and professor of medicine; Benjamin Smith Barton, the botanist; Joseph Priestley, the Unitarian theologian, radical, and chemist; Charles Willson Peale, the artist; Thomas Paine, the radical publicist; and Thomas Jefferson, the Universal Man. On the other hand James Madison, one of Jefferson's closest associates, is conspicuous by his absence precisely because his attitude to history and the works of man was so different.

17. Ibid., p. 129.
18. Ibid., p. 173.
19. Ibid., pp. 190, 201.
20. Ibid., p. 194.
21. Ibid., p. 196.
22. "Tradition and Method in Legal History," *Harvard Law Review* 54 (1941), 960–75.
23. "The Humane Study of Law," *Yale Law School Journal* 57 (1948), xiii.
24. Two vols. (Chicago, 1966).
25. "The Myth of an American Enlightenment," in *America and the Image of Europe* (New York, 1960), p. 67.
26. Ibid.
27. *Genius*, pp. 8–9.
28. Ibid., p. 22.
29. Ibid., p. 25.
30. *The Americans: The National Experience* (Chicago, 1966).
31. *Genius*, p. 26.
32. Ibid., p. 28.
33. Ibid., p 35.
34. Ibid., p. 169.
35. Ibid.
36. My italics.
37. *Mysterious Science*, p. 116.
38. *Lost World*, p. 54.
39. *Genius of American Politics*, p. 106.
40. "The Rise of the Average Man," *The U.S. Book of Facts Statistics and Information* (New York, 1966).
41. *Genius of American Politics*, p. 39.
42. Ibid., pp. 111, 113–14, 130–31.
43. Ibid., p. 131.
44. Ibid., p. 129.
45. Ibid., p. 95.
46. Ibid., pp. 138–39. Elsewhere he describes European culture as "dying of poverty, monopoly, aristocracy, and ideology" (p. 182).
47. *The Americans: The Colonial Experience* (New York, 1958; London, 1965), p. 173.
48. Ibid., pp. 179–80.
49. Ibid., p. 90.
50. *The National Experience*, pp. 134–47; 249–56.
51. "An American Style in Historical Monuments," in *America and the Image of Europe*, p. 83.
52. "A pretty good rule of thumb for us in the United States is that our own national well-being is in inverse proportion to the sharpness and extent of the theoretical differences between our political parties" (*Genius of American Politics*, p. 3).

53. Support for the same general theme could be supplied from a most unexpected source: "The Revolutionist's Handbook" brandished by Tanner in G. B. Shaw's *Man and Superman*. Shaw kindly appends the handbook to the text of the play, and its key turns out to be: "The golden rule is that there is no golden rule."

54. Cecelia Kenyon, Review of "The Americans: The Colonial Experience," *William and Mary Quarterly*, 3d ser., 16 (1959): 585–89.

55. Henry Nash Smith, *Virgin Land* (Cambridge, Mass., 1950).

56. *The Image: A Guide to Pseudo-Events in America* (New York, 1962), p. 9.

57. *The Great Crash: 1929* (London, 1955), pp. 128–30.

58. *The Image*, p. 34.

59. David W. Noble, *Historians Against History* (Minneapolis, 1965), pp. 173–74.

60. "A Dialogue of Two Histories: Jewish and American," in *America and the Image of Europe*.

61. Ibid., p. 175.

SELECTED PUBLICATIONS

Books

The Mysterious Science of the Law. Cambridge, Mass., 1941.

The Lost World of Thomas Jefferson. New York, 1948.

The Genius of American Politics. Chicago, 1953.

The Americans: The Colonial Experience. New York, 1958; Harmondsworth, Eng., 1965.

America and the Image of Europe. New York, 1960.

The Image: A Guide to Pseudo-Events in America. New York, 1962; Harmondsworth, 1963.

The Americans: The National Experience. New York, 1965; Harmondsworth, 1969.

The Landmark History of the American People. New York, 1968.

(Ed.) *Delaware Cases, 1792–1830.* 3 vols. St. Paul, Minn., 1943.

(Ed.) Chicago History of American Civilization. About 30 vols. Chicago, 1956 to present.

(Ed.) *A Lady's Life in the Rocky Mountains.* Norman, Okla., 1960.

(Ed.) *An American Primer.* 2 vols. Chicago, 1966.

Articles

"Tradition and Method in Legal History." *Harvard Law Review* 54 (1941).

"The Elusiveness of Mr. Justice Holmes." *The New England Quarterly* 14 (1941).

"The Autonomy of Scholarship." *The Journal of Higher Education* 19 (1948).

"The Humane Study of Law." *The Yale Law Journal* 57 (1948).
"Self-Discovery in Puerto Rico." *The Yale Review* 45 (1956).
"The Place of Thought in American Life." *The American Scholar* 25 (1956).
"America at the Moment." *Forum* 2 (1959).
"The Rise of the Average Man." *U.S. Book of Facts, Statistics and Information for 1967*. New York.

9. Oscar Handlin BY MALDWYN A. JONES

NOTES

1. F. L. Olmsted, *A Journey in the Seaboard Slave States* (New York, 1856), pp. 214–15.
2. Caroline F. Ware, ed., *The Cultural Approach to History* (New York, 1940), pp. 273–86.
3. Handlin, "The Central Themes of American History," in *Relazione del X congresso internazionale di scienze storiche* 1 (1955): 165.
4. Handlin, *Boston's Immigrants, 1790–1865: A Study in Acculturation* (Cambridge, Mass., 1941), p. vii.
5. Edward N. Saveth, *American Historians and European Immigrants* (New York, 1948), passim.
6. Arthur M. Schlesinger, *New Viewpoints in American History* (New York, 1922), p. 21.
7. For Hansen see Allan H. Spear, "Marcus Lee Hansen and the Historiography of Immigration," *Wisconsin Magazine of History* 44 (1961): 258–68; C. Frederick Hansen, "Marcus Lee Hansen—Historian of Immigration," *Common Ground* 2 (1942): 87–94; John Bartlet Brebner, *Dictionary of American Biography*, 22: 278–79; and Handlin, Introduction to the Harper Torchbook Edition of Hansen, *The Atlantic Migration, 1607–1860* (New York, 1961).
8. Hansen in *American Historical Review* 37 (1932): 572–73.
9. Maurice R. Stein, *The Eclipse of Community* (Princeton, 1960), chap. 1.
10. For Mrs. Anna Hanson McKenney Dorsey (1815–1896) see *Dictionary of American Biography*, 5: 384.
11. See Robert Ernst, *Immigrant Life in New York City, 1825–1863* (New York, 1949), and Gerd Korman, *Industrialization, Immigrants and Americanizers: The View from Milwaukee, 1866–1921* (Madison, Wis., 1967).
12. See the review by Robert B. Morris in *Political Science Quarterly* 62 (1947): 581–87.
13. Smith, *Americans in the Making* (New York, 1939); Duncan, *Immigration and Assimilation* (Boston, 1933).

14. This book was in fact mainly written by William I. Thomas. See Morris Janowitz, ed., W. I. *Thomas on Social Organization and Social Personality* (Chicago, 1966), p. xvi.

15. See, for example, Eric Goldman in *Journal of Southern History* 18 (1952): 355–56, and Thomas T. McAvoy in *Catholic Historical Review* 38 (1952): 211–12.

16. Karen Larsen in *American Historical Review* 57 (1952) 703–704, and Vera Shlakman in *Journal of Economic History* 13 (1953): 241–44.

17. Vecoli, "*Contadini* in Chicago: A critique of *The Uprooted*," *Journal of American History* 51 (1964): 404–17.

18. See Humbert S. Nelli, "Italians in Urban America: A Study in Ethnic Adjustment," *The International Migration Review*, n.s. 1 (1967): 38–55.

19. The Annual Reports of the New York Emigration Commissioners make it clear that with the single exception of 1847 the mortality was well below 1%.

20. Frank Thistlethwaite, "Migration from Europe Overseas in the Nineteenth and Twentieth Centuries," *Rapports, XIᵉ Congrès International des Sciences Historiques* (Stockholm, 1960), 5: 32–60.

21. Handlin, *The Uprooted* (London, 1953), p. 308.

22. See, for example, Robert E. Park and Herbert A. Miller, *Old World Traits Transplanted* (New York, 1921), chap. 4; Park, *The Immigrant Press and Its Control* (New York, 1922), pp. 166 ff; and Mordecai Soltes, *The Yiddish Press* (New York, 1925).

23. Park, *The Immigrant Press*, chap. 3.

24. Marvin Bressler, "Selected Family Patterns in W. I. Thomas' Unfinished Study of the 'Bintl Brief,'" *American Sociological Review* 17 (1952): 563–71.

25. Edith Abbott, *Immigration: Select Documents and Case Records* (Chicago, 1924), and *Historical Aspects of the Immigration Problem: Select Documents* (Chicago, 1926).

26. William I. Thomas and Florian Znaniecki, *The Polish Peasant in Europe and America*, 5 vols. (Chicago and Boston, 1918–20).

27. Herbert Blumer, *An Appraisal of Thomas and Znaniecki's "The Polish Peasant in Europe and America"* (New York, 1939), p. 104.

28. Janowitz, ed., *Thomas*, p. xxviii.

29. Theodore Jorgenson and Nora O. Solum, *Ole Edvart Rölvaag: A Biography* (New York, 1939), pp. 153–56 and passim.

30. Trevelyan, *Clio, A Muse* (1913), as reprinted in Fritz Stern, *Varieties of History* (New York, 1956), p. 243.

31. William E. Leuchtenburg in *Political Science Quarterly* 70 (1955): 310.

32. Ibid., p. 309.

33. Higham in *Mississippi Valley Historical Review* 41 (1954): 544–45.
34. Ibid., and John Higham, *Strangers in the Land: Patterns of American Nativism, 1860–1925* (New Brunswick, N.J., 1955), pp. 402–03.
35. Handlin, "Prejudice and Capitalist Exploitation," in *Commentary* 6 (1948).
36. Handlin, "American Views of the Jew at the Opening of the Twentieth Century," *Publications of the American Jewish Historical Society* 40 (1951): 323.
37. Pollack, "Handlin on Anti-Semitism: A Critique of 'American Views of the Jew,'" *Journal of American History* 51 (1964): 391–403.
38. Handlin, Communication in ibid. (1965), p. 807, and Pollack's reply, pp. 807–808.
39. John Higham, "Anti-Semitism in the Gilded Age: A Reinterpretation," *Mississippi Valley Historical Review* 43 (1957): 559–78.
40. Handlin, *Adventure in Freedom: Three Hundred Years of Jewish Life in America* (New York, 1954), pp. 174–210.
41. Oscar and Mary F. Handlin, "Origins of the Southern Labor System," *William and Mary Quarterly*, 3d ser. 7 (1950): 199–222.
42. Degler, "Slavery and The Genesis of American Race Prejudice," *Comparative Studies in Society and History* 2 (1959): 49–66. See also the ensuing correspondence between the Handlins and Degler in ibid. (1960), pp. 488–95.
43. Jordan, "Modern Tensions and the Origins of American Slavery," *Journal of Southern History* 28 (1962): 18–30.
44. For further comments on the Handlins' thesis see Stanley M. Elkins, *Slavery: A Problem in American Institutional and Intellectual Life* (Chicago, 1959), pp. 37 ff. and especially pp. 38 and 39 n. David Brion Davis, *The Problem of Slavery in Western Culture* (Ithaca, N.Y., 1966), pp. 245 ff.; Herbert S. Klein, *Slavery in the Americas: A Comparative Study of Cuba and Virginia* (Chicago, 1967) pp. 40–57; and Winthrop D. Jordan, *White Over Black: American Attitudes Toward the Negro, 1550–1812* (Chapel Hill, 1968), passim.
45. Davis, *Problem of Slavery*, p. 281.
46. Handlin, *Race and Nationality in American Life* (Boston, 1957), p. xii.
47. Handlin, review in *New England Quarterly* 19 (1946): 538–40.
48. Nichols in *American Historical Review* 61 (1955): 138–39.
49. For a different view from Handlin's see Richard Hofstadter, "Could a Protestant Have Beaten Hoover?," *The Reporter* (March 17, 1960), pp. 31–33.
50. Oscar and Mary F. Handlin, *The Popular Sources of Political Authority* (Cambridge, Mass., 1966).
51. Thomas C. Cochran, "The Social Sciences and the Problems of Historical Synthesis," Social Science Research Council, *The Social Sciences in Historical Study* (New York, 1954), pp. 157–71.

52. Stein, *Eclipse of Community*, p. 18.
53. Ibid.
54. Trevelyan, *Clio*, in Stern, *Varieties*, p. 235.
55. Boorstin in *Saturday Review* (August 24, 1963), p. 42.
56. Handlin, "Immigration in American Life: A Reappraisal," in Henry Steele Commager, ed., *Immigration in American History* (Minneapolis, 1961), pp. 8–25.
57. Lippmann, *Drift and Mastery* (reprint ed., Englewood Cliffs, N.J., 1961), p. 118.

SELECTED PUBLICATIONS

Books

Boston's Immigrants, 1790–1865: A Study in Acculturation. Cambridge, Mass., 1941. Revised and enlarged ed., 1959.

With Mary F. Handlin, *Commonwealth: A Study of the Role of Government in the American Economy: Massachusetts, 1774–1861.* New York, 1947.

This Was America: True Accounts of Peoples and Places, Manners and Customs, as Recorded by European Travelers to the Western Shore in the Eighteenth, Nineteenth and Twentieth Centuries. Cambridge, Mass., 1949.

With Mary F. Handlin. *Danger in Discord: Origins of Anti-Semitism in the United States.* New York, 1948.

The Uprooted: The Epic Story of the Great Migrations That Made the American People. Boston, 1951.

With Arthur M. Schlesinger, Samuel Eliot Morison, Frederick Merk, Arthur M. Schlesinger, Jr., and Paul Herman Buck. *The Harvard Guide to American History.* Cambridge, Mass., 1954.

The American People in the Twentieth Century. Cambridge, Mass., 1954.

Adventure in Freedom: Three Hundred Years of Jewish Life in America. New York, 1954.

The Positive Contribution by Immigrants. Paris, 1955.

Chance or Destiny: Turning Points in American History. Boston, 1955.

Readings in American History. New York, 1957.

Race and Nationality in American Life. Boston, 1957.

American Jews: Their Story. New York, 1958.

Al Smith and His America. Boston, 1958.

Immigration as a Factor in American History. Englewood Cliffs, N.J., 1959.

John Dewey's Challenge to Education: Historical Perspectives on the Cultural Context. New York, 1960.

The Newcomers: Negroes and Puerto Ricans in a Changing Metropolis. Cambridge, Mass., 1960.

With John Clive. *Journey to Pennsylvania by Gottlieb Mittelberger.* Cambridge, Mass., 1960.

With Mary F. Handlin. *The Dimensions of Liberty*. Cambridge, Mass., 1961.
American Principles and Issues: The National Purpose. New York, 1961.
The Americans: A New History of the People of the United States. Boston, 1963.
A Continuing Task: the American Jewish Joint Distribution Committee, 1914–1964. New York, 1964.
Firebell in the Night: The Crisis in Civil Rights. Boston, 1964.
With Mary F. Handlin, *The Popular Sources of Political Authority: Documents on the Massachusetts Constitution of 1780*. Cambridge, Mass., 1966.
Children of the Uprooted. New York, 1966.
The History of the United States. 2 vols. New York, 1967–68.

Articles

"A Russian Archivist Visits Boston, 1861." *New England Quarterly* 15 (1942).
With Mary F. Handlin. "Laissez-faire thought in Massachusetts, 1790–1880." *Tasks of Economic History* 3 (1943).
"The Immigrant and American Politics." In David F. Bowers, ed., *Foreign Influences in American Life*. Princeton, 1944.
With Mary F. Handlin. "Radicals and Conservatives in Massachusetts after Independence." *New England Quarterly* 17 (1944).
With Mary F. Handlin. "Origins of the American Business Corporation." *Journal of Economic History* 5 (1945).
With Mary F. Handlin. "Revolutionary Economic Policy in Massachusetts." *William and Mary Quarterly* 3d ser. 4 (1947).
With Mary F. Handlin. "A Century of Jewish Immigration to the United States." *American Jewish Year Book* 50 (1949–50).
With Mary F. Handlin. "Origins of the Southern Labor System." *William and Mary Quarterly*, 3d ser. 7 (1950).
"A Note on Recent Texts in American History." *Journal of General Education* 4 (1950).
"The American Scene." In Adolf E. Zucker, ed., *The Forty-Eighters: Political Refugees of the German Revolution of 1848*. New York, 1950.
"American Views of the Jew at the Opening of the Twentieth Century." *American Jewish Historical Society Publications* 40 (1951).
"International Migration and the Acquisition of New Skills." In Berthold F. Hoselitz, ed., *The Progress of Underdeveloped Areas*. Chicago, 1952.
"American Views of the Past." *Massachusetts Historical Society Proceedings* 70 (1950–1953).
"The American Immigrant and Ideologies." *Confluence* 2 (1953).
"The History in Men's Lives." *Virginia Quarterly Review* 30 (1954).
"The Central Themes of American History." *Relazione del X congresso internazionale de scienze storiche* 1 (1955).

"Capitalism, Power and the Historians: An Essay Review." *New England Quarterly* 28 (1955).

"A Liner, a U-Boat . . . and History." *American Heritage* 6 (1955).

With Mary F. Handlin. "The Acquisition of Political and Social Rights by the Jews in the United States." *American Jewish Yearbook* 56 (1955).

With Mary F. Handlin. "Ethnic Factors in Social Mobility." *Explorations in Entrepreneurial History* 9 (1956).

"The American Jew." In Joseph B. Gittler, ed., *Understanding Minority Groups.* New York, 1956.

"College and Community in 1900." *Harvard Library Bulletin* 12 (1958).

"Changing Patterns of Group Life in America and Their Implications for the American Jewish Community." *Journal of Jewish Communal Service* 34 (1958).

"The Social System." *Daedalus: Journal of the American Academy of Arts and Sciences* 90 (1961).

"Historical Perspectives on the American Ethnic Group." *Daedalus: Journal of the American Academy of Arts and Sciences* 90 (1961).

"Immigration in American Life—A Reappraisal." In Henry Steele Commager, ed., *Immigration and American History: Essays in Honor of Theodore C. Blegen.* Minneapolis, 1961.

"Man and Magic: First Encounters with the Machine." *American Scholar* 33 (1964).

"Reconsidering the Populists." *Agricultural History* 39 (1965).

"Science and Technology in Popular Culture." *Daedalus: Journal of the American Academy of Arts and Sciences* 94 (1965).

"Goals of Integration." *Daedalus: Journal of the American Academy of Arts and Sciences* 94 (1965).

Other Publications

Intro. to Israel D. Benjamin, *Three Years in America.* Translated by Chas. Reznikoff. 2 vols. Philadelphia, 1956.

Intro. to Charles Reznikoff, ed., *Louis Marshall, Champion of Liberty: Selected Papers and Addresses.* Philadelphia, 1957.

10. Richard Hofstadter BY ARTHUR M. SCHLESINGER, JR.

NOTES

1. "Interview: Richard Hofstadter," *History* 140 (1960).
2. Hofstadter and his first wife, who died in 1945, figure in the Kazin book (like other characters) under pseudonyms. See Alfred Kazin, *Starting Out in the Thirties* (Boston, 1965), p. 100.
3. Hofstadter, "Interview," p. 136.
4. Hofstadter, "Pseudo-Conservatism Revisited," in Daniel Bell, ed., *The Radical Right* (New York, 1963), p. 98.
5. Hofstadter, "Interview," p. 141.

6. Hofstadter, "History and the Social Sciences," in Fritz Stern, ed., *The Varieties of History* (Cleveland, 1956), pp. 361, 414.
7. Hofstadter, "Parrington and the Jeffersonian Tradition," *Journal of the History of Ideas* 391 (1941).
8. Hofstadter, "Parrington," p. 392.
9. Kazin, *Starting Out*, p. 100.
10. "Interview," p. 141.
11. "Interview," p. 139.
12. Hofstadter, "The Tariff Issue on the Eve of the Civil War," *American Historical Review*, October, 1938.
13. Hofstadter, *The American Political Tradition* (New York, 1948), pp. 15, 354.
14. Hofstadter, "Charles Beard and the Constitution," in H. K. Beale, ed., *Charles A. Beard: An Appraisal* (Lexington, Ky., 1954), pp. 75, 82–83.
15. Hofstadter, "Reading the Constitution Anew," *Commentary* 273 (1956).
16. Hofstadter, "Parrington," p. 391.
17. Hofstadter, "Interview," p. 140.
18. Neither Kenneth Stampp in *The Peculiar Institution* (New York, 1956) nor E. D. Genovese in *The Political Economy of Slavery* (New York, 1965) mention the Hofstadter piece. S. M. Elkins's single reference in *Slavery* (Chicago, 1959), p. 18, is quick and glancing.
19. Hofstadter, "U. B. Phillips and the Plantation Legend," *Journal of Negro History* 29 (1944).
20. Hofstadter, "Turner and the Frontier Myth," *American Scholar* 18 (1949): 433, 435, 439, 443.
21. With characteristic candor, he writes, "At one time or another, I have changed my mind about each of these men, and it is by no means inconceivable to me that on some counts I may change it again. The historical returns are never complete." Hofstadter, *The Progressive Historians* (New York, 1968), p. xv.
22. Ibid., pp. xii, xvi.
23. Ibid., pp. xiv, 164, 349, 464.
24. Hofstadter, *Social Darwinism in American Thought*, rev. ed. (Boston, 1955), Author's Note.
25. Hofstadter, *Social Darwinism in American Thought* (Philadelphia, 1944), pp. 174, 176.
26. Hofstadter, "Darwinism and Western Thought," in H. L. Plaine, ed., *Darwin, Marx and Wagner: A Symposium* (Columbus, Ohio, 1962), pp. 60–61.
27. Hofstadter, *Social Darwinism* (1944), pp. 99, 103, 175, 176. In the 1955 edition Hofstadter replaced "survival" in the sentence about the middle class by "maintaining its status and its standard of living"; see p. 119.

28. Hofstadter, *The American Political Tradition* (New York, 1948), pp. vii–ix.
29. Hofstadter, *American Political Tradition*, vi, 286. Hofstadter's estimate of Hoover was surprisingly sympathetic; in 1960 he said he felt he had been "soft" on Hoover. "Interview," p. 139.
30. William James, *Pragmatism*, Second Lecture.
31. Hofstadter, "Parrington and the Jeffersonian Tradition," pp. 399, 400.
32. Hofstadter, "William Leggett, Spokesman of Jacksonian Democracy," *Political Science Quarterly*, December, 1943, pp. 585, 588, 594.
33. Hofstadter, *American Political Tradition*, pp. 56–57.
34. See Hammond, *Banks and Politics in America from the Revolution to the Civil War* (Princeton, 1957); Hugin, *Jacksonian Democracy and the Working Class: A Study of the New York Workingmen's Movement, 1829–1837* (Stanford, 1960); Benson, *The Concept of Jacksonian Democracy: New York as a Test Case* (Princeton, 1961); and Pessen, *Most Uncommon Jacksonians: The Radical Leaders of the Early Labor Movement* (Albany, 1967).
35. Presumably the Whigs were expectant capitalists too, just as eager to open up the competitive game; and, if this were so, what was the political shouting all about? Hofstadter did not take up this question, except to imply that the quarrel may have been between old (Whig) and new (Democratic) money. A Hofstadter protégé, Marvin Meyers, faced it, however, in *The Jacksonian Persuasion* (1957; my references are to the Vintage edition, New York, 1960). In his preface Meyers thanked Hofstadter for his "discerning critique of the manuscript" (xii); and on the back jacket Hofstadter, in an unwontedly rhapsodic mood, described the book as "one of those peak moments of insight which stand as consummations of, rather than contributions toward, historical understanding." This endorsement perhaps makes it permissible to regard *The Jacksonian Persuasion* as an amendment, accepted by the original mover, to Hofstadter's Jacksonian thesis. At any rate, it filled a significant gap in the entrepreneurial interpretation.
   Meyers, in what was indeed a thoughtful and sensitive study if hardly a peak moment of insight, took Hofstadter's rural nostalgia argument, which Hofstadter himself had localized in the age of Bryan, and carried it back to the age of Jackson. "Both parties," he argued—not altogether convincingly in the light of such studies as Paul Murray's *The Whig Party in Georgia* (Chapel Hill, 1948), H. J. Doherty's *The Whigs of Florida* (Gainesville, 1959), and the recent work of F. O. Gatell on New York and of D. B. Cole on New Hampshire—"must have reached broadly similar class constituencies," but none the less they were not "fraternal twins, devoted to the advancement of slightly varying business interests." What, then, was the difference between them, and why did the political rhetoric of the day go so far beyond practical

objects and manifest interests? Meyers's answer was that the Jacksonians, torn between the old yeoman ideal of "a chaste republican order" and the new lures of an acquisitive society, felt threatened by social and economic change. The Whigs, on the other hand, experienced "no serious tension between past and present" and rejoiced in quickening the pace of change. "The Whig party spoke to the explicit hopes of Americans as Jacksonians addressed their diffuse fears and resentments" (pp. 8–9, 12–14). Reversing Emerson, Meyers would have the Whigs the party of hope, the Jacksonians the party of memory.

It might be noted that, in the distinction which Hofstadter drew in 1955, Meyers saw Jacksonian democracy as primarily a case of "status politics" rather than of "interest politics."

36. A good account is to be found in John Higham, "The Cult of the 'American Consensus': Homogenizing our History," *Commentary*, February, 1959; reprinted in A. S. Eisenstadt, *The Craft of American History* (New York, 1966), 1: 193–205.

37. It is a fallacy to regard "consensus history" as only a right-wing phenomenon. A book like Gabriel Kolko's *The Triumph of Conservatism* (Glencoe, 1963) is a good example of consensus history from the viewpoint of the New Left.

38. Hofstadter, *American Political Tradition*, p. 20.

39. Ibid., pp. 16–17.

40. Ibid., pp. 193–94.

41. Ibid., p. 225.

42. Ibid., pp. vii, x, 352.

43. Ibid., pp. 139, 140.

44. Hofstadter, Communication, *Journal of the History of Ideas*, April, 1954, p. 328.

45. Hofstadter, *Progressive Historians*, p. xv.

46. Hofstadter, "Reading the Constitution Anew."

47. Hofstadter, *American Political Tradition*, pp. 4, 206, 231.

48. Hofstadter, "History and the Social Sciences," p. 361.

49. Hofstadter, *Anti-Intellectualism in American Life* (New York, 1963), p. 9.

50. Hofstadter, "History and the Social Sciences," p. 362.

51. Hofstadter, "Beard and the Constitution," p. 86.

52. Hofstadter, "History and the Social Sciences," p. 362.

53. Ibid., p. 360–61.

54. Communication (from Forrest McDonald), *American Historical Review* 402 (1965).

55. Hofstadter, "History and the Social Sciences," p. 364.

56. Hofstadter, "Darwinism and Western Thought," p. 69.

57. Hofstadter, "History and the Social Sciences," pp. 367, 369.

58. Ibid., pp. 363, 368, 370.

59. Hofstadter, "Interview," pp. 139–40. Hofstadter says that "people like Edmund Wilson had much more influence on my style than

any historian." As for Mencken, "no one would dream of imitating him, but he awoke me to the buffoonery and playfulness one can inject into one's style. I soaked up everything of Mencken's when I was an undergraduate at the University of Buffalo." As one who was also soaking up everything of Mencken's at the same time, I can testify to the liberating and exhilarating effect of Mencken and the way he gave a generation which disliked his political views a sense of freedom in the use of language.

60. Hofstadter, "Manifest Destiny and the Philippines," in Daniel Aaron, ed., *America in Crisis* (New York, 1952), pp. 173–75, 180–81, 198.

61. Hofstadter, "Manifest Destiny," p. 199.

62. Daniel Bell, Preface, Richard Hofstadter; "The Psuedo-Conservative Revolt," S. M. Lipset, "The Sources of the 'Radical Right,'" in Daniel Bell, ed., *The Radical Right* (New York, 1963), pp. ix, 84–85, 308–309. This volume includes the essays originally published under the title *The New American Right* (New York, 1955) along with postscripts and afterthoughts by some of the authors and two new essays. My references are to the Anchor Books edition (1964).

63. Hofstadter, *The Paranoid Style in American Politics* (New York, 1965), pp. 90, 92, vii.

64. Hofstadter, "Pseudo-Conservatism Revisited," *The Radical Right*, pp. 100–01.

65. Ibid., p. 103.

66. Hofstadter, *Paranoid Style*, pp. 86–87.

67. Ibid., p. 67.

68. Hofstadter, *Anti-intellectualism*, pp. 80, 407, 145–46.

69. Ibid., pp. 146, 165.

70. Ibid., pp. 155–56, 171.

71. Ibid., p. 157.

72. Ibid., p. 22.

73. Hofstadter, *The Age of Reform* (New York, 1955), pp. 4–5, 58.

74. Ibid., pp. 50–52.

75. Ibid., pp. 61, 95, 105, 134.

76. Ibid., p. 33.

77. Ibid., p. 62.

78. Hofstadter, *Age of Reform*, 20. It is perhaps of interest to note that some of this interpretation of Populism, including references to "religious fanaticism" and "a disquieting . . . streak of anti-semitism," was anticipated by Marvin Halverson in his article "The Religious Foundations of Populism," *Christianity and Society*, Spring, 1942.

79. C. Vann Woodward, *The Burden of Southern History* (New York, 1960), pp. 141–66; Norman Pollack, "Hofstadter on Populism," *Journal of Southern History* 26 (1960); Pollack, *The Populist Response to Industrial America* (Cambridge, Mass., 1962);

Pollack, "The Myth of Populist Anti-Semitism," *American Historical Review*, 1962; W. T. K. Nugent, *The Tolerant Populists* (Chicago, 1963); M. P. Rogin, *The Intellectuals and McCarthy: the Radical Specter* (Cambridge, Mass., 1967). See also a discussion of Populism by Pollack, Oscar Handlin, Irwin Unger, and J. Rogers Hollingsworth in *Agricultural History*, July, 1965.

80. Woodward, *Burden*, p. 153.

81. Ibid., pp. 146–47.

82. Hofstadter, "Pseudo-Conservative Revolt," p. 85.

83. Hofstadter, *Age of Reform*, pp. 135, 140. In *The American Political Tradition*, Hofstadter had noted that "the coarse, materialistic civilization that emerged in the United States during the years after the Civil War produced among cultivated middle-class young men a generation of alienated and homeless intellectuals" (p. 206). His development of this thought was undoubtedly stimulated by George Mowry's 1949 essay "The California Progressive and his Rationale: A Study in Middle-Class Politics," *Mississippi Valley Historical Review*, September, 1949.

The California progressive [Mowry wrote] reacted politically when he felt himself and his group being hemmed in and his place in society threatened by the monopolistic corporation on one side and organized labor and socialism on the other. . . . Clearly what troubled these independent progressives about both organized capital and labor was not alone a matter of economics but included questions of high politics, as well as group prestige, group morality, and group power. Involved also was the rising threat to an old American way of life which they represented. . . . On the defensive for the first time since the disappearance of the old aristocracy, this class of supreme individualists rationally enough developed a group-consciousness themselves.

He also drew on the analysis of 260 Progressive leaders through the country by A. D. Chandler, Jr., "The Origins of Progressive Leadership," in Elting Morison, ed., *Letters of Theodore Roosevelt*, vol. 8 (Cambridge, Mass., 1954), pp. 1462–65.

84. Hofstadter, *Age of Reform*, pp. 5, 12, 215, 227, 241, 260, 305.

85. R. B. Sherman, "The Status Revolution and Massachusetts Progressive Leadership," *Political Science Quarterly*, March, 1963, pp. 59–65.

86. J. J. Huthmacher, "Urban Liberalism and the Age of Reform," *Mississippi Valley Historical Review*, September, 1962, 231–41.

87. John Braeman, "Seven Progressives," *Business History Review*, Winter, 1961, pp. 581–92; A. M. Scott, "The Progressive Era in Perspective," *Journal of Politics*, November, 1959, pp. 685–701.

88. Kolko, *Triumph of Conservatism*, p. 3.

89. Hofstadter, "The Meaning of the Progressive Movement," introduc-

tion to *The Progressive Movement,* 1900–1915 (Englewood Cliffs, N.J., 1963).

90. Hofstadter, *Age of Reform,* 11–12, 303–04, 308, 316–23.
91. Hofstadter, *Social Darwinism* (1955), p. 10.
92. Hofstadter, *American Political Tradition,* pp. vii, 315.
93. Ibid., p. 341.
94. Scott, "Progressive Era in Perspective," p. 697.
95. See the discussion in Arthur Schlesinger, Jr., *The Politics of Upheaval* (*The Age of Roosevelt,* vol. 3) (Boston, 1960), chaps. 21–22.
96. Hofstadter, "Pseudo-Conservative Revolt," pp. 83–95.
97. S. M. Lipset, "The Sources of the Radical Right," Daniel Bell, ed., *The Radical Right,* p. 363.
98. Hofstadter, "Pseudo-Conservatism Revisited," p. 97.
99. Viereck, "The Revolt against the Elite," *The Radical Right,* pp. 163–64.
100. Rogin, *Intellectuals and McCarthy,* pp. 30–31, 247–48.
101. Ibid., pp. 30, 44, 174.
102. Ibid., pp. 122, 165, 281.
103. Hofstadter, *Age of Reform,* pp. 153, 218; "Pseudo-Conservative Revolt," p. 91.
104. J. A. Schumpeter, *Imperialism and Social Classes* (Meridian Books), p. 157.
105. In these two paragraphs, I have drawn on a talk I gave before the American Civilization group at Harvard soon after the publication of *The Age of Reform,* March 19, 1956.
106. Hofstadter, *Paranoid Style,* p. 82.
107. Hofstadter, "Interview," p. 130; *Age of Reform,* p. 20.
108. Hofstadter, *Age of Reform,* p. 19.
109. Hofstadter, "Interview," p. 139.
110. Hofstadter, *Anti-intellectualism,* p. 135.
111. Hofstadter, "A Note on Intellect and Power," *American Scholar,* Autumn 1961, 594, 596, 598; *Anti-intellectualism,* 430. There is recent indication that Hofstadter may have began to despair of preserving a single intellectual community; see "Two Cultures: Adversary and/or Responsible," *Public Interest,* Winter 1967.
112. Hofstadter, "Interview," p. 130.
113. Hofstadter, *Age of Reform,* p. 22.
114. Hofstadter, *Anti-intellectualism,* p. vii.

SELECTED PUBLICATIONS

General Historical Works

Social Darwinism in American Thought. Philadelphia, 1944. Reprinted by Beacon Press in a revised edition, Boston, 1955, with a new Introduction.

The American Political Tradition. New York, 1948.

With C. DeWitt Hardy. *The Development and Scope of Higher Education in the United States.* New York, 1952.
With Walter P. Metzger. *The Development of Academic Freedom in the United States.* New York, 1955.
The Age of Reform. New York, 1955.
Anti-Intellectualism in American Life. New York, 1963.
The Paranoid Style in American Politics. New York, 1965.
The Progressive Historians: Turner, Beard, Parrington. New York, 1968.

Textbooks

With William Miller and Daniel Aaron. *The American Republic.* Englewood Cliffs, N.J., 1959.
With William Miller and Daniel Aaron. *The Structure of American History.* Englewood Cliffs, N.J., 1964.
With William Miller and Daniel Aaron. *The United States.* Englewood Cliffs, N.J., 1957. Rev. ed., 1967.

Anthologies and Readers

Great Issues in American History. New York, 1958.
Intro. to W. H. ("Coin") Harvey, *Coin's Financial School.* Cambridge, Mass., 1963.
The Progressive Movement, 1900–1915. Englewood Cliffs, N.J., 1963.
With Wilson Smith. *American Higher Education: A Documentary History.* Chicago, 1961.
With Seymour Martin Lipset. *Sociology and History: Methods.* New York, 1968.
With Seymour Martin Lipset. *Turner and the Sociology of the Frontier.* New York, 1968.
The Basic Issues in American Politics. New York, 1968. This work is a reprinting of a two-volume work published in 1956 by the Fund for Adult Education and never sold on the market. The title of the original, privately published book was *The Great Issues in American Politics.*

Articles

"The Tariff Issue on the Eve of the Civil War." *American Historical Review* 44 (1938).
"William Graham Sumner, Social Darwinist." *New England Quarterly* 14 (1941).
"Parrington and the Jeffersonian Tradition." *Journal of the History of Ideas* 2 (1941).
"William Leggett, Spokesman of Jacksonian Democracy." *Political Science Quarterly* 58 (1943).
"U. B. Phillips and the Plantation Legend." *Journal of Negro History* 29 (1944).
"The Impact of Darwinism." In *Chapters in Western Civilization*, vol. 2. New York, 1948.

"From Calhoun to the Dixiecrats." *Social Research* 16 (1949).

"Turner and the Frontier Myth." *American Scholar* 19 (1949).

With Beatrice K. Hofstadter. "Winston Churchill: A Study in the Popular Novel." *American Quarterly* 2 (1950).

"Beard and the Constitution." *American Quarterly* 2 (1950). Also published in Howard K. Beale, ed., *Charles A. Beard: An Appraisal.* Lexington, Ky., 1954

"Manifest Destiny and the Philippines." In Daniel Aaron, ed., *America in Crisis.* New York, 1952. A revised version appears in *The Paranoid Style in American Politics.*

"Democracy and Anti-Intellectualism in America." *Michigan Alumnus Quarterly Review* 59 (1953).

"The Pseudo-Conservative Revolt." *American Scholar* 24 (1954–55). A revised version with further comments appears in *The Paranoid Style.*

"American Higher Education." In *College Admission: The Interaction of School and College.* New York, 1956.

"A Note on Intellect and Power." *American Scholar* 30 (1961).

"The Child and the World." *Daedalus: Journal of the American Academy of Arts and Sciences* 91 (1962).

"Darwinism and Western Thought." In H. L. Plaine, ed., *Darwin, Marx and Wagner; A Symposium.* Columbus, O., 1962.

"The Revolution in Higher Education." In Arthur M. Schlesinger, Jr., and Morton White, eds., *Paths of American Thought.* Boston, 1963.

"What Happened to the Antitrust Movement?" In Earl Cheit, ed., *The Business Establishment.* New York, 1964. Also appears in a revised version in *The Paranoid Style.*

11. David M. Potter BY SIR DENIS BROGAN

NOTES

1. Professor Potter has kindly allowed me to read in typescript the greater part of his still unfinished book, and I shall use it repeatedly, especially in comparison, and in some instances in contrast with *Lincoln and His Party.*

2. *Law and Contemporary Problems,* Duke University Law School (Durham, N.C., 1947), pp. 428 ff.

3. "Individualism in Twentieth Century America," *The Texas Quarterly* 5 (1963): 144. Of course, Professor Potter has much more to say about the frontier than this, and his views on the frontier, original as they are, will be discussed later.

4. *Stetson University Bulletin* 62 (1962): 15.

5. I once discussed with a friend of mine, a scion of a great Kentucky dynasty, why his family had not supported Lincoln's appeals for compensated emancipation. He replied, "Because we thought the

South would win the war, and if it did slavery would not be abolished in Kentucky."

6. Potter, *People of Plenty* (Chicago, 1963), pp. 148–49.
7. "Explicit Data and Implicit Assumptions in Historical Study," in Louis Gottschalk, ed., *Generalization in the Writing of History* (Chicago, 1963), pp. 181–82.
8. Ibid., p. 187.
9. Ibid., p. 191.
10. Ibid., pp. 192–93.
11. Ibid., p. 194.
12. The same charge was, of course, brought against Franklin Delano Roosevelt after Pearl Harbor with somewhat more justification, for Roosevelt was impaled on his own hook in December, 1941, while Lincoln had not impaled himself, however the situation might have impaled him, in 1861.
13. (New York, 1967), p. 505.
14. Potter, *Lincoln and His Party in the Secession Crisis*, 1962 ed. pp. xx–xxi.
15. Shortly after I read the 1942 edition of *Lincoln and His Party*, I was dining with the late Brendan Bracken, then Minister of Information in Britain, and told him of how interesting I found the book. He asked, "So you meant it shows that Lincoln was not an appeaser?" I said, "Basically it shows that he was not, although it shows that he wanted peace." He replied, "I am sure Winston would want to read that book: can I borrow it?" I lent him the book. I never saw it again and I have no reason to believe that Churchill ever read or saw it. This small anecdote shows how ambiguous the use of the term "appeasement" had become.
16. Potter, *People of Plenty*, p. xvii.

SELECTED PUBLICATIONS

Books

Lincoln and His Party in the Secession Crisis. New Haven, 1942. New preface, 1962.

Trail to California: The Overland Journal of Vincent Geiger and Wakeman Bryarly. (Ed.) New Haven, 1945.

With J. H. Croushore. *A Union Officer in the Reconstruction*, by John William De Forest. New Haven, 1948.

The Lincoln Theme and American National Historiography. Oxford, 1948.

With T. G. Manning. *Nationalism and Sectionalism in America, 1775–1877.* New York, 1949.

With T. G. Manning. *Government and the American Economy, 1870–Present.* New York, 1950.

People of Plenty: Economic Abundance and the American Character.

Chicago, 1954. In Japanese translation, 1957, and in French translation, 1966.

With Louis B. Wright, Clarence L. Von Steeg, Russel B. Nye, Holman Hamilton, Vincent P. De Santis, William H. Harbaugh, Arthur S. Link, Thomas G. Corcoran, and Carl N. Degler. *The Democratic Experience: A Short American History.* Chicago, 1963. Rev. ed., 1968.

With Curtis R. Grant. *Eight Issues in American History: Views and Counter Views.* New York, 1966.

The South and the Sectional Conflict. Baton Rouge, La., 1968.

Articles

"The Rise of the Plantation System in Georgia." *Georgia Historical Quarterly* 16 (1932).

"A Bibliography of the Printed Writings of Ulrich Bonnell Phillips." *Georgia Historical Quarterly* 18 (1934).

"Horace Greeley and Peaceable Secession." *Journal of Southern History* 7 (1941).

"The Jackson Collection of Lincolniana." *Yale Library Gazette* 19 (1944).

"Huey Pierce Long." In *Dictionary of American Biography, Supplement.*

"The Historical Development of Eastern-Southern Freight Rate Relationships." *Law and Contemporary Problems* 12 (1947).

"The Marshall Plan and American Foreign Policy." *Current Affairs* February 21, 1948.

"Sketches for the Roosevelt Portrait." *Yale Review* 39 (1949).

"An Appraisal of Fifteen Years of the Journal of Southern History." *Journal of Southern History* 16 (1950).

"John William De Forest." *Papers of the New Haven Colony Historical Society* 10 (1951).

"Democracy and Abundance." *Yale Review* 40 (1951).

"Advertising: The Institution of Abundance." *Yale Review* 43 (1953).

"Nathan Hale and the Ideal of American Union." *The Connecticut Antiquarian* 6 (1954).

"Leisure: The Economic Aftermath." *Challenge: The Magazine of Economic Affairs* 4 (1955).

Commentary on paper by J. Robert Oppenheimer, "Theory versus Practice in American Values and Performance." In Elting E. Morison, ed., *The American Style, Essays in Value and Performance.* New York, 1958.

"National and Sectional Forces in the United States." Chap. 23 in *The New Cambridge Modern History,* vol. 10: *The Zenith of European Power, 1830–1870.* Edited by J. P. T. Bury. Cambridge, 1960.

"Jefferson Davis and the Political Factors in Confederate Defeat." In David Donald, ed., *Why the North Won the Civil War.* Baton Rouge, La., 1960.

"The Six Most Fateful Weeks in American History." In Ralph G. Newman, ed., *Lincoln for the Ages*. New York, 1960.

"Interpreting the Causes of the Civil War." In T. Walter Wallbank and Alastair M. Taylor, *Civilization, Past and Present*, 4th ed. New York, 1961.

"The Background of the Civil War." In William H. Cartwright and Richard L. Watson, Jr., eds., *Interpreting and Teaching American History*. Thirty-first Yearbook of National Council for the Social Studies, 1961.

"The Enigma of the South." *Yale Review* 51 (1961).

"The Quest for a National Character." In John Higham, ed., *The Reconstruction of American History*. New York, 1962.

"American Women and the American Character." *Stetson University Bulletin* 42 (1962).

"The Historian's Use of Nationalism and Vice Versa." In Alexander Riasanovsky and Barnes Riznik, eds., *Generalizations in Historical Writing*. Philadelphia, 1963. Also, abridged, in *American Historical Review* 47 (1962).

"Explicit Data and Implicit Assumptions in Historical Study." In Louis Gottschalk, ed., *Generalization in the Writing of History*. Chicago, 1963.

"American Individualism in the Twentieth Century." *Texas Quarterly*, 6 (1963).

"On Understanding the South: A Review Article." *Journal of Southern History* 30 (1964).

"Why the Republicans Rejected Both Compromise and Secession." In George H. Knoles, ed., *The Crisis of the Union, 1860–1861*. Baton Rouge, La., 1965.

(Ed.) *An Account of Pennsylvania* (1698) by Gabriel Thomas. In Daniel J. Boorstin, ed., *An American Primer*, vol. 1. Chicago, 1966.

"Depletion and Renewal in Southern History." In Edgar T. Thompson, ed., *Perspectives on the South: Agenda for Research*. Durham, N.C., 1967.

"Television, the Broad View: The Historical Perspective." In Stanley T. Donner, ed., *The Meaning of Commercial Television: The Texas-Stanford Seminar, 1966*. Austin, Tex., 1967.

"Canadian Views of the United States as a Reflex of Canadian Values: A Commentary." In S. F. Wise and Robert Craig Brown, *Canada Views the United States: Nineteenth Century Political Attitudes*. Seattle, Wash., 1967.

Comment on "An Appraisal of the Work of Ulrich B. Phillips," by Eugene D. Genovese. *Agricultural History* 41 (1967).

"Civil War." In C. Vann Woodward, ed., *The Comparative Approach to American History*. New York, 1968.

12. Arthur M. Schlesinger, Jr. BY MARCUS CUNLIFFE

NOTES

1. Arthur M. Schlesinger, *In Retrospect: The History of a Historian* (New York, 1963), p. 141.
2. Ibid., pp. 157, 167.
3. Letter from Arthur Schlesinger, Jr., to Marcus Cunliffe, July 9, 1968.
4. *In Retrospect*, pp. 72, 112–13; Schlesinger, Jr., quoted in Cleveland Amory, ed., *International Celebrity Register* (New York, 1959), p. 671.
5. Letter to Cunliffe, July 9, 1968 (also the source of Schlesinger's comments on his Harvard teachers). There is a warm tribute to Bernard De Voto in Arthur M. Schlesinger, Jr., *The Politics of Hope* (Boston, 1963), pp. 155–82.
6. Schlesinger, *New Viewpoints in American History* (New York, 1922), p. 284.
7. Schlesinger, Jr., *Orestes A. Brownson: A Pilgrim's Progress*, reprint (New York, 1963), pp. 293–94.
8. *Journal of Economic History* 6 (1946): 79–84.
9. One of the best bibliographical essays is still that of Charles G. Sellers, Jr., "Andrew Jackson versus the Historians," *Mississippi Valley Historical Review* 44 (1958): 615–34. (The principal references to Arthur Schlesinger, Jr., are pp. 626–28, 631–32.) For a more recent discussion see Alfred A. Cave, *Jacksonian Democracy and the Historians* (University of Florida Monographs, Social Sciences, no. 22, 1964), Gainesville, Fla., pp. 54 ff. Two convenient collections of readings are James L. Bugg, Jr., ed., *Jacksonian Democracy: Myth or Reality?* (New York, 1962), and Edwin C. Rozwenc, ed., *The Meaning of Jacksonian Democracy* (Boston, 1963). For Schlesinger's own riposte to objections raised by Joseph Dorfman of Columbia, see *American Historical Review* 54 (1949): 785–86.
10. *Conversations with Henry Brandon* (London, 1966), pp. 42–43. Taylor's *The Transportation Revolution, 1815–1860* (The Economic History of the United States, vol. 4) (New York, 1951), demonstrates the importance of communications in expanding the American economy. Lee Benson, *The Concept of Jacksonian Democracy: New York as a Test Case* (Princeton, 1961), pp. 336–38, suggests that the changes in the America of 1825–50 might best be described as the "Transportation Revolution" and the "Egalitarian Revolution"—a distinction apparently between causes and consequences.
11. *New Viewpoints*, pp. 200–202, 206, 215. The parallel is pointed out in Sellers, "Andrew Jackson versus the Historians," pp. 631–32: "Actually Arthur M. Schlesinger, Jr., the leading proponent of the

labor thesis, emphasizes entrepreneurial elements in Jacksonian Democracy far more than his critics appear to realize; indeed he sees the western Jacksonians as almost wholly entrepreneurial in spirit. Basically, however, his *Age of Jackson* seems to represent a marriage of the agrarian democratic and the urban points of view. . . . Schlesinger, it should be remembered, is deeply indebted to his father, who came out of Turner's 'valley of democracy' to proclaim the city as the great new frontier for historical scholarship. The elder Schlesinger's essay on Jacksonian Democracy is even more obviously composed of equal parts of Turnerean and labor themes."

12. *The Age of Jackson* (Boston, 1945), p. 391. During his interview with Henry Brandon, Schlesinger said that "when my father first set forth this thesis, he speculated, without taking the precise number too seriously, that the period of shift was about fourteen years; by that he felt that 1918 had marked one period of shift, so he predicted there would be conservative government until 1932; and he said . . . there'd be a period of liberal government until 1946 and another period of conservative government until 1960" (*Conversations with Henry Brandon*, p. 44). In fact his father ("Tides of Power," *Yale Review*, 1939) said that the cycle averaged *sixteen* years, which would make the sequence 1932, 1948, 1964. . . . But Schlesinger Senior was himself a little hazy in recollection. He wrote of the 1960 presidential election:

> Ralph McGill of the Atlanta *Constitution* . . . believed that what he called the "Political Law of Arthur Schlesinger the Elder" had been "basic in the Democratic victory." James Reston in advance of the election had written in the New York *Times* that Kennedy, "well aware of this doctrine . . . has based his campaign on the assumption." Actually, the cycle theory timed the recession from conservatism for 1962, "with a possible margin of a year or two in one direction or the other." Had the new captain [Kennedy] taken command a little too soon to profit from the liberal swing? If this theory is valid, his difficulties with a Congress of his own party suggest as much.

A friend of Schlesinger *père*, working for F.D.R., said that Roosevelt had read the 1939 essay when it appeared, "and the prospect it held out of the existing liberal era lasting until 1947 or 1948 helped him to decide to run for a third term." (*In Retrospect*, pp. 108, 127, 190–91).

13. *The Age of Jackson*, pp. 215, 448.
14. Ibid., pp. 485–86.
15. Compare an observation made by Schlesinger twenty years later: "I agree with John Quincy Adams, when he said in his first address

to Congress, that the duty of Government is the moral and intellectual improvement of the citizens." See *Playboy* 13 (1966): 211.

16. The parallels were not lost on F.D.R. himself. Jackson's opponents, he said, "represented the same social outlook and the same element in the population that ours do." In 1936 even the newspaper proprietor William Randolph Hearst felt at times that "Mr. Roosevelt resembled Jackson": Schlesinger, Jr., *The Age of Roosevelt: The Politics of Upheaval* (Boston, 1960), pp. 637, 641, 643–44.

17. *The Age of Jackson*, pp. 307, 493, 522.

18. Ibid., pp. 306–307, 421, 514.

19. Ibid., pp. 382–84, 522. For some later remarks by Schlesinger on pragmatism, in the same vein, see Arthur M. Schlesinger, Jr., and Morton White, eds., *Paths of American Thought* (Boston, 1963), pp. 535–38.

20. Max Freedman, ed., *Roosevelt and Frankfurter: Their Correspondence, 1928–1945* (London, 1968), p. 3; *The Vital Center*, new ed. (Boston, 1962), p. 3; letter to Cunliffe, July 9, 1968.

21. Compare *The Age of Jackson*, p. 521, and *The Vital Center*, pp. 24–25.

22. Ibid., pp. 37–38, 196–201.

23. "The Causes of the Civil War," reprinted in *The Politics of Hope* (London, 1964), pp. 34–37. A crucial section of Schlesinger's book on the Vietnam problem first appeared as "The Inscrutability of History," *Encounter* 29 (1966).

24. *The Politics of Hope*, p. 43.

25. *The Vital Center*, p. 173; *The Age of Jackson*, pp. 505–507.

26. *The Vital Center*, pp. 175–76, 179.

27. Ibid., p. 170; letter to Cunliffe, July 9, 1968. Schlesinger dedicated to Niebuhr the first volume, *The Crisis of the Old Order* (1957), of his *Age of Roosevelt*. See also "Reinhold Niebuhr's Role in American Political Thought and Life," reprinted in *The Politics of Hope*, pp. 97–125; Arthur M. Schlesinger, Jr., *The Politics of Upheaval*, pp. 157–59; and Page Smith, *The Historian and History* (New York, 1964), p. 80.

28. "The Statistical Soldier," reprinted in *The Politics of Hope*, pp. 54–59.

29. "Walter Lippmann: The Intellectual vs. Politics" (1959), reprinted in ibid., pp. 130, 147.

30. *The Crisis of the Old Order* (Boston, 1957), pp. ix–x.

31. *Conversations with Henry Brandon*, p. 43. This view was also expounded in "The Historian as Artist," *Atlantic Monthly*, July, 1963, pp. 35–41. Here Schlesinger made plain a conviction, emphasized in certain other historiographical essays (e.g., "The Historian and History," *Foreign Affairs*, April, 1963, pp. 491–99),

that history was far more of an art than a science. It never arrived at ultimate truth. Its lessons, though valuable, were general and tentative. Too great a desire to emulate the natural sciences had led to the rise of "technical history," which was too narrowly professional in approach to make an impact upon the reading public. This lost audience had then unfortunately succumbed to the "prophetic" historian, "who has converted the genial visions of the romantic historian into dogmatic, comprehensive, universal, and tyrannical historical theories." Among this company of historical monists Schlesinger included Marx, Spengler, and Toynbee. His objection—a similar one to that of the Dutch historian Pieter Geyl—was that they had forced the complex, often chaotic movements of human society into single-cause, deterministic patterns. They had carried clarification too far. History was a drama, with elements of farce and of tragedy: the prophetic historians had turned it into a blackboard diagram, as stylized as the rendering of an electric circuit.

32. *The Politics of Upheaval*, pp. 385–98.
33. Freedman, *Roosevelt and Frankfurter*, pp. 25–27; *Politics of Upheaval*, pp. 690–92.
34. Interview with Schlesinger in *Playboy*, p. 75.
35. Lasch, *The New Radicalism in America, 1889–1963: The Intellectual as a Social Type* (New York, 1966), pp. 308–310; review of Lasch by Schlesinger, London *Sunday Times*, February 27, 1966; and see Harvey Swados, "Does America Deserve the New Frontier?" *New Politics*, 1963, reprinted in Swados, *A Radical at Large: American Essays* (London, 1968), p. 277: "What Mr. Schlesinger is trying to do, in the effort to conceal the truth with a slippery piece of self-serving journalism, is to create an identity between practical liberalism and the Kennedy Administration. . . ." One suspects it was the inferior quality of Schlesinger's usually admirable prose, in certain of his public pronouncements, that contributed to the annoyance expressed by intellectuals. For comments by Schlesinger on liberals in governmental employment, see *A Thousand Days: John F. Kennedy in the White House* (Boston, 1965), pp. 640–41.
36. Lasch, "The Cultural Cold War: A Short History of the Congress for Cultural Freedom," in Barton J. Bernstein, ed., *Towards a New History* (New York, 1968), pp. 341, 353–54.
37. "The Historian and History," *Foreign Affairs*, April, 1963, pp. 492–94; *Playboy* 13 (1966): 209; "On the Writing of Contemporary History," *Atlantic Monthly*, March, 1967, pp. 72–73.
38. *Conversations with Henry Brandon*, p. 50.
39. A feature of all Schlesinger's narrative works is his ear for a telling—and often extremely amusing—anecdote. One example is the account given by Schlesinger (*A Thousand Days*, p. 587 n.) of a

meeting between Kennedy and ex-Governor Landon. It brings out the character of several people in a few lines. Asked whether Kennedy reminded him of Roosevelt, Landon replied: " 'No. Kennedy is very frank and straightforward. Roosevelt was always on the stage, always giving a performance.' He then went on to describe Truman: 'For the first two years he was too humble. Thereafter he became too cocky. Kennedy is neither humble nor cocky.' (Subsequently Kennedy said about Landon, 'I liked him. Very Trumanesque.')"

40. *Towards a New History*, pp. 282, 321. There is no reference to Schlesinger in the essay on the Jacksonians by Michael A. Lebowitz.

41. New York, 1968. A revised version of this pamphlet, published in Schlesinger's *The Crisis of Confidence: Ideas, Power and Violence in America* (Boston, 1969), included a new section on the pervasiveness of violence in American history, and the peculiar failure of historians and others to recognize its existence.

SELECTED PUBLICATIONS

Books

Orestes A. Brownson: A Pilgrim's Progress. Boston, 1939.

The Age of Jackson. Boston, 1945.

The Vital Center. Boston, 1949.

With Richard H. Rovere. *The General and the President*. New York, 1951.

The Crisis of the Old Order. Boston, 1957.

The Coming of the New Deal. Boston, 1958.

The Politics of Upheaval. Boston, 1960.

Kennedy or Nixon: Does It Make Any Difference? New York, 1960.

The Politics of Hope. Boston, 1963.

With Morton White. *Paths of American Thought*. Boston, 1963.

A Thousand Days: John F. Kennedy in the White House. Boston, 1965.

The Bitter Heritage: Vietnam and American Democracy 1941–1966. Boston, 1967.

The Politics of Violence: America in the Sixties. New York, 1968.

The Crisis of Confidence: Ideas, Power, and Violence in America. Boston, 1969.

Articles

"The Problem of Richard Hildreth." *New England Quarterly* 13 (1940).

"The Causes of the American Civil War: A Note on Historical Sentimentalism." *Partisan Review* 16 (1949).

"The Historian and History." *Foreign Affairs* 41 (1963).

13. C. Vann Woodward   BY DAVID M. POTTER

NOTES

1. This comment is based in part on personal knowledge, for I was an undergraduate at Emory, 1928–1932, knew Woodward and Rainey, was coached in debate by Rainey, and was on a debate team with Woodward against the University of Florida.
2. Woodward, *Watson*, p. ix. All titles of works by Woodward are given in full in a bibliography which follows this essay.
3. Wilma Dykeman and James Stokeley, *Seeds of Southern Change: The Life of Will Alexander* (Chicago, 1962), pp. 155–56. Angelo Herndon, *Let Me Live* (New York, 1937) gives a long and full account of his imprisonment and defense, but does not mention Woodward nor the names of any persons who helped him, other than his lawyers.
4. Woodward, *Watson*, p. ix; Woodward, letter to the author, June 23, 1967.
5. Lloyd Paul Stryker, *Andrew Johnson: A Study in Courage* (New York, 1936).
6. Howard K. Beale, *The Critical Year: A Study of Andrew Johnson and Reconstruction* (New York, 1930), p. 1.
7. Woodward, "Tom Watson and the Negro in Agrarian Politics," *Journal of Southern History* 4 (1938): 14–15.
8. Almost the only previous writer who had recognized this point even partially was Paul Lewinson, in *Race, Class, and Party: A History of Negro Suffrage and White Politics in the South* (New York, 1932), and his development of the topic was not comparable to Woodward's. Also, for further analysis of the class factor in politics, see Woodward's essay, "The Populist Heritage and the Intellectual" (1959).
9. For some comments on especial points in *Reunion and Reaction*, see Harry Barnard, *Rutherford B. Hayes and His America* (Indianapolis, 1954), which argues that the factors contributing to the result were more varied than Woodward's account indicates; Joseph Frazier Wall, *Henry Watterson: Reconstructed Rebel* (New York, 1956), pp. 159–67, which denies Woodward's contention that the Southern Democrats were more instrumental than the Northern Democrats in giving up the filibuster against counting the electoral vote; and Thomas B. Alexander, "Persistent Whiggery in the Confederate South, 1860–1877," *Journal of Southern History* 27 (1961): 324- 25, which suggests that the Whiggishly inclined bloc of Southern Democrats might have acted as it did even if there had been no Texas and Pacific lobby at work.

10. Review by Captain Paul F. Dugan, U.S.N., in United States Naval Institute, *Proceedings* 73 (1947): 457–58.

11. Essay reprinted in *The Burden of Southern History*. Quoted passages are on pp. 169, 181, 182, 186, 187 (Vintage edition).

12. Essay reprinted in *The Burden of Southern History*. Quoted passages are on pp. 6, 8, 25 (Vintage edition).

13. Essay in *American Historical Review* 66 (1960). Quoted passages are on pp. 2, 11, 15, 18, 19.

14. In *The Burden of Southern History*, p. 25.

15. Woodward, "The Antislavery Myth," *The American Scholar* 31 (1962): 318–36.

16. In *Harper's*, April, 1965. Quoted passage is on p. 133.

17. "The Search for Southern Identity," reprinted in *The Burden of Southern History*. Quoted passages are on pp. 11, 12.

18. William E. Dodd, *Statesmen of the Old South* (New York, 1919); Frank L. Owsley, *Plain Folk of the Old South* (Baton Rouge, La., 1949).

19. Woodward, *Watson*, p. 220.

20. "What Happened to the Civil Rights Movement?" *Harper's*, January, 1967, p. 32.

21. The quoted passages are from pp. 16, 25, 26, 47, of *The Strange Career of Jim Crow*, 1955 edition.

22. Barton J. Bernstein calls my attention to the relevance of the Civil Rights Act of 1875 in connection with this question. Evidence concerning this act has been neglected by scholars, but it is very pertinent in two ways: (1) there is palpably a question why the act's supporters deemed it necessary unless discrimination was being practiced; (2) considerable evidence of such discrimination was presented in support of the proposed measure. Of course the discrimination may have been practiced informally, and therefore may not have involved any action by Southern state governments, but the issue of segregation was certainly involved, whether or not in the form of Jim Crow.

23. Charles E. Wynes, *Race Relations in Virginia, 1870–1902* (Charlottesville, Va., 1961), pp. 68–110, 144–50, especially pp. 149–50.

24. Frenise A. Logan, *The Negro in North Carolina, 1876–1894* (Chapel Hill, N.C., 1964), pp. 174–88, 209–219, especially p. 215.

25. Joel Williamson, *After Slavery: The Negro in South Carolina During Reconstruction, 1861–1877* (Chapel Hill, N.C., 1965), pp. 240–99, especially pp. 274, 298–99.

26. Richard C. Wade, *Slavery in the Cities: The South 1820–1860* (New York, 1964), p. 266 and passim; Woodward, *Strange Career*, 1955 edition, p. 14.

27. *Strange Career* (Galaxy edition, 1957), pp. xv–xvi. Other works treating of the degree of segregation in the post-bellum South,

and which Woodward took into account in the first edition of the *Strange Career*, include: Vernon L. Wharton, *The Negro in Mississippi, 1865–1890* (Chapel Hill, N.C., 1947), and George B. Tindall, *South Carolina Negroes, 1877–1900* (Columbia, S.C., 1952). The whole question of the origins of segregation has now assumed the dimensions of a full-scale historical controversy, and Joel Williamson has edited a brief volume of selections from Woodward and twelve other writers, including all those cited from note 21 through this note: *The Origins of Segregation*, Problems in American Civilization (Boston, 1968).

28. Quotation in *Watson*, p. 220.

29. Essay reprinted in *The Burden of Southern History*. Quoted passages are on pp. 75, 77, 78.

30. W. R. Brock, *An American Crisis: Congress and Reconstruction, 1865–1877* (New York, 1963), pp. 285–86; G. Selden [not Seldon] Henry, "Radical Republican Policy Toward the Negro During Reconstruction, 1862–1872" (Ph.D. dissertation, Yale, 1963; publication by University of Miami Press pending). It is noteworthy that even Woodward's own student James M. Mac-Pherson, *The Struggle for Equality: Abolitionists and the Negro in the Civil War and Reconstruction* (Princeton, N.J., 1964), provides copious evidence of preponderant Northern sentiment against equality for Negroes. At his conclusion, MacPherson states that when the Radical Republicans abandoned the federal enforcement of Negro rights in the South (far short of equality) "The mass of Northern people had never loved the Negro, were tired of 'the everlasting Negro question' and were glad to see the end of it" (p. 431).

Woodward, "Flight from History: the Heritage of the Negro," *Nation*, September 20, 1965, pp. 142–46; Woodward, "Seeds of Failure in Radical Race Policy," in Harold M. Hyman, ed., *New Frontiers of the American Reconstruction* (Urbana, Ill., 1966), p. 130.

31. *Strange Career*, 1966 edition, p. vii; "What Happened to the Civil Rights Movement?" (1967), p. 36.

32. The quoted passages are on pp. ix and 124 of the 1955 edition and pp. 153 and 178–79 of the 1957 edition.

33. P. 189.

34. Pp. 190–91.

35. The attribution perhaps requires no proving, but Woodward specifically classified himself as "a liberal, even more, a Southern white liberal" in a commentary at a Socialist Scholars Conference in 1966. See *Studies on the Left* 6 (1966): 35.

36. "What Happened to the Civil Rights Movement?" Pp. 32, 34, 37.

37. Ibid., p. 37.

SELECTED PUBLICATIONS

Books

Tom Watson, Agrarian Rebel. New York, 1938. Reprinted with brief
new introduction, 1955.
The Battle for Leyte Gulf. New York, 1947.
*Reunion and Reaction: The Compromise of 1877 and the End of Re-
construction.* Boston, 1951. Rev. ed., with new introduction and
concluding chapter, New York, 1956.
Origins of the New South, 1877–1913. Vol. 9 of *A History of the South.*
Baton Rouge, La., 1951.
The Strange Career of Jim Crow. New York, 1955. New and rev. ed.
with new introduction, 1957; 2d rev. ed., 1966.
American Attitudes Toward History. Oxford, 1955.
With John M. Blum, Bruce Catton, Edmund S. Morgan, Arthur M.
Schlesinger, Jr., and Kenneth M. Stampp. *The National Experi-
ence.* New York, 1963. 2d ed., 1968. Chapters by Woodward are
16–21, pp. 374–513 (2d ed., pp. 395–537).
The Burden of Southern History. Baton Rouge, La., 1960. Rev. ed.,
1968. A collection of reprinted essays.

Edited Books

With an introduction, pp. vii–xxxix, *Cannibals All! or, Slaves Without
Masters* (1857) by George Fitzhugh. Cambridge, Mass., 1960.
With an introduction, pp. xi–xlvi, *A Southern Prophecy: The Prosperity
of the South Dependent upon the Elevation of the Negro* (1889)
by Lewis H. Blair. Boston, 1964.
With an introduction, pp. ix–xxi, *After the War: A Tour of the Southern
States, 1865–1866,* (1866) by Whitelaw Reid. New York, 1965.
The Comparative Approach to American History. New York, 1968. Includes "The Comparability of American History" and "The Test
of Comparability," pp. 1–17, 346–57 by Woodward, and twenty-
two papers edited by him.

Articles

"Tom Watson and the Negro in Agrarian Politics." *Journal of Southern
History* 4 (1938).
"Bourbonism in Georgia." *North Carolina Historical Review* 16 (1939).
"Hillbilly Realism." *Southern Review* 4 (1939).
"The Fifteenth Annual Meeting of the Southern Historical Association."
Journal of Southern History 16 (1950).
"John Brown's Private War." In Daniel Aaron, ed., *America in Crisis.*
New York, 1952. Reprinted in *The Burden of Southern History.*
"The Irony of Southern History." *Journal of Southern History* 19

(1953). Reprinted in *The Burden of Southern History.*

"Can We Believe Our Own History?" In *The Johns Hopkins Magazine* 5 (1954).

"The Historical Dimension." *Virginia Quarterly Review* 32 (1956). Reprinted in *The Burden of Southern History.*

"The Lowest Ebb." *American Heritage* 8 (1957).

"The Disturbed Southerners." *Current History* 32 (1957).

"The Political Legacy of Reconstruction." *Journal of Negro Education* 26 (1957). Reprinted in *The Burden of Southern History.*

"Equality: America's Deferred Commitment." *American Scholar* 27 (1958). Reprinted in *The Burden of Southern History.*

"Toynbee and Metahistory." *American Scholar* 27 (1958).

"The Search for Southern Identity." *Virginia Quarterly Review* 34 (1958). Reprinted in *The Burden of Southern History.*

"The Populist Heritage and the Intellectual." *American Scholar* 24 (1959). Reprinted in *The Burden of Southern History.*

"The Age of Reinterpretation." *American Historical Review* 66 (1960).

"A Southern Critique for the Gilded Age." In *The Burden of Southern History.* Not printed previously.

"Reflections on a Centennial: The American Civil War." *Yale Review* 50 (1961).

"The Antislavery Myth." *American Scholar* 31 (1962).

"The Case of the Louisiana Traveler" (Plessy vs. Ferguson). In John A. Garraty, ed., *Quarrels That Have Shaped the Constitution.* New York, 1962.

"Introduction." Pp. xv–xviii, in Willie Lee Rose, *Rehearsal For Reconstruction.* Indianapolis, 1964.

"The Question of Loyalty." *American Scholar* 33 (1964).

"From the First Reconstruction to the Second." In Willie Morris, ed., *The South Today.* New York, 1965.

"The North and the South of It." *American Scholar* 35 (1966).

"Seeds of Failure in Radical Race Policy." In Harold Hyman, ed., *New Frontiers of the American Reconstruction.* Urbana, Ill., 1966.

Comment, at Socialist Scholars Conference, on paper on "The Legacy of Slavery and the Roots of Black Nationalism," by Eugene D. Genovese. In *Studies on the Left* 26 (1966).

"History and the Third Culture." *Journal of Contemporary History* 3 (1968).

"The Southern Ethic in a Puritan World." *William and Mary Quarterly,* 3rd ser., 25 (1968).

"Clio with Soul." *The Journal of American History* 56 (1969).

Index

Contributors

Harry C. Allen, Director, Institute of American Studies, University of London

Sir Denis Brogan, Professor Emeritus of Political Science and Fellow of Peterhouse College, University of Cambridge

Marcus Cunliffe, Professor and Head of American Studies, University of Sussex

Ralph Gabriel, Sterling Professor Emeritus of History, Yale University

Maldwyn Jones, Professor and Head of American Studies, University of Manchester

Howard R. Lamar, Professor and Chairman, Department of History, Yale University

J. C. Levenson, Edgar Allan Poe Professor of American Literature, University of Virginia

Forrest McDonald, Professor of History, Wayne State University

Robert Middlekauff, Associate Professor of History, University of California, Berkeley

J. R. Pole, Reader in American History and Fellow of Churchill College, University of Cambridge

David M. Potter, William Robertson Coe Professor of American History, Stanford University

Arthur M. Schlesinger, Jr., Albert Schweitzer Professor in the Humanities, The City University of New York

William R. Taylor, Professor of History, State University of New York, Stony Brook

Robin W. Winks, Professor of History, Yale University

75 76 77 10 9 8 7 6 5 4 3 2 1